Geography and Ownership as Bases for Economic Accounting

Studies in Income and Wealth
Volume 59

National Bureau of Economic Research
Conference on Research in Income and Wealth

Geography and Ownership as Bases for Economic Accounting

Edited by

Robert E. Baldwin,
Robert E. Lipsey, and
J. David Richardson

The University of Chicago Press

Chicago and London

ROBERT E. BALDWIN is professor emeritus of economics at the University of Wisconsin–Madison and a research associate of the National Bureau of Economic Research. ROBERT E. LIPSEY is professor emeritus of economics at Queens College and the Graduate Center of the City University of New York and a research associate and director of the New York office of the National Bureau of Economic Research. J. DAVID RICHARDSON is professor of economics in the Maxwell School at Syracuse University, a research associate of the National Bureau of Economic Research, and a visiting fellow at the Institute for International Economics.

The University of Chicago Press, Chicago 60637
The University of Chicago Press, Ltd., London

Printed in the United States of America
07 06 05 04 03 02 01 00 99 98 1 2 3 4 5
ISBN: 0-226-03572-7 (cloth)

Library of Congress Cataloging-in-Publication Data

Geography and ownership as bases for economic accounting / edited by Robert E. Baldwin, Robert E. Lipsey, and J. David Richardson.
p. cm. — (Studies in income and wealth ; v. 59)
Based on a conference held by the National Bureau of Economic Research in Washington, DC, on May 19–20, 1995.
Includes bibliographical references and index.
ISBN 0-226-03572-7 (cloth : alk. paper)
1. National income—Accounting—Congresses. I. Baldwin, Robert E. II. Lipsey, Robert E. III. Richardson, J. David. IV. National Bureau of Economic Research. V. Series.
HC106.3.C714 1998 vol. 59 HB522
339.3′2—dc21 98-3324
CIP

⊗ The paper used in this publication meets the minimum requirements of the American National Standard for Information Sciences—Permanence of Paper for Printed Library Materials, ANSI Z39.48-1992.

National Bureau of Economic Research

Since this volume is a record of conference proceedings, it has been exempted from the rules governing critical review of manuscripts by the Board of Directors of the National Bureau (resolution adopted 8 June 1948, as revised 21 November 1949 and 20 April 1968).

Contents

Prefatory Note

This volume contains revised versions of most papers presented at the Conference on Research in Income and Wealth entitled Geography and Ownership as Bases for Economic Accounting, held in Washington, D.C., on 19–20 May 1995.

Funds for the Conference on Research in Income and Wealth are supplied by the Bureau of Labor Statistics, the Bureau of Economic Analysis, Statistics Canada, and the Federal Reserve Board; we are indebted to them for their support. This conference was supported by the National Science Foundation under grant SBR 9409757 from the Program in Economics.

We also thank Robert E. Baldwin, Robert E. Lipsey, and J. David Richardson, who served as conference organizers and editors of the volume.

Volume Editors' Acknowledgments

This volume is the result of a conference held by the National Bureau of Economic Research in Washington, D.C., on 19–20 May 1995. We are grateful to the National Science Foundation for financial support to hold the conference. We would like to thank Kirsten Foss Davis and Rob Shannon of the NBER for the efficient manner in which they handled the conference arrangements and Deborah Kiernan of the NBER for preparing the papers and comments for publication. We also wish to acknowledge the very helpful comments of the NBER and University of Chicago Press reviewers and the patience and diligence of the authors and discussants throughout the editorial process.

Introduction

Robert E. Baldwin, Robert E. Lipsey, and
J. David Richardson

Economic accounting can be done in a variety of ways to answer different questions and serve different purposes. One of the distinctions that can be made is between measures of economic activity based on geographical location and measures based on ownership. One of the main purposes of this volume is to raise the question of the degree to which changes in the world economy may have increased the usefulness of international accounts drawn up on an ownership basis relative to those on a geographic basis. Among these changes are the growth of multinational corporations, for which many transactions across geographical borders are internal to the firm; the growth of service industries, for which the geographical location, but not the ownership of production, is ambiguous; and the seeming absence of many of the expected unfavorable consequences of persistent U.S. current account deficits, measured in geographical terms.

The United States for many years used ownership-based measures, such as national income and gross and net national product, as the central totals in its economic accounts. It joined most of the other developed countries in emphasizing geographical totals, such as gross domestic product, in the 1991 revision of the accounts. However, in the accounts for international transactions, the only strictly geographical element is commodity trade, because goods can be observed as they pass over national geographical borders. Most service transactions recorded as international take place entirely within one country and are assigned international transaction status on the basis that one of the transactors

Robert E. Baldwin is professor emeritus of economics at the University of Wisconsin–Madison and a research associate of the National Bureau of Economic Research. Robert E. Lipsey is professor emeritus of economics at Queens College and the Graduate Center of the City University of New York and a research associate and director of the New York office of the National Bureau of Economic Research. J. David Richardson is professor of economics in the Maxwell School at Syracuse University, a research associate of the National Bureau of Economic Research, and a visiting fellow at the Institute for International Economics.

is a "resident" of another country. Foreign residence is a legal characteristic rather than a geographical one. It depends on place of incorporation or legal status, rather than on the physical location of production or consumption.

The choice between geographical and ownership bases for economic accounting was discussed at the Fourth Income and Wealth Conference in 1939, not in connection with international issues, but with respect to the treatment of ownership across state lines within the United States. In the paper "Some Problems Involved in Allocating Income by States" presented at that conference, published in volume 3 of *Studies in Income and Wealth,* Robert R. Nathan concluded that the ownership-based measure was the central one. He asked, "Is there any point in determining the net value of goods and services *derived from* economic activities taking place within the physical confines of North Carolina . . . when this net product is *derived by* residents of other states?" If a choice were necessary, "it would seem more important . . . to allocate the net value of product by states on the basis of such a concept as 'the net value of product *derived by* residents of a state from their labor and from the services of their property, wherever located,' rather than on the basis of the concept of 'the net value of product *derived from* the resources of labor and wealth employed in a state.'" He went on in a way that foreshadowed the later shift in emphasis: "If a person, as a contributor of his capital to production, is the primary force rather than the capital itself, then the *derived by* concept is more significant. On the other hand, if the actual capital equipment is regarded as the primary force, the 'derived from' concept predominates." Thus there is some hint that a physical production function calls for a geographical concept (Conference on Research in Income and Wealth 1939, 401–29).

Simon Kuznets, in commenting on Nathan's paper, admitted the case for the "derived by" measure but introduced another theme, suggesting that "this inference overlooks the possibility that consciousness of a kind may extend to the productive resources to which a given group applies its labor; that inhabitants of a given state may have a sense of proprietary interest in the total output in whose production they participate." The point was intended as a justification for a geographical measure but could be applied equally to the aggregation of all the output of a firm, wherever it was produced (Conference on Research in Income and Wealth 1939, 430–34).

The merits of the two approaches appeared quite different to Richard Stone and Kurt Hansen (1953) a little more than a decade later. "The system . . . should . . . contain the distinction between 'domestic' and 'national' concepts since, to give one reason, the former is more appropriate as a basis for constructing a measure of real product." The geographical measure, with the idea of an aggregate production function in the background, had gained ascendancy.

When the U.S. Department of Commerce shifted from GNP to GDP as the "featured" total in the national accounts, one reason given was that GDP, since it referred to "production taking place in the United States," was "the appropriate measure for much of the short-term monitoring and analysis of the U.S.

economy" because it is "consistent in coverage with indicators such as employment, productivity, industry output, and investment in equipment and structures" (1991, 8). Another consideration was that GDP is the central total in the UN System of National Accounts and the use of that total simplifies comparisons with other countries. Still another point was that some of the foreign elements of GNP are not available quarterly, or are available only with considerable delay, or are not available at all. Inventory and capital consumption adjustments are mentioned in this category, and any deflation becomes much more difficult if prices are needed for foreign elements of income and production. GNP remains in the accounts. It is described as "appropriate for analyses related to sources and uses of income." It is the appropriate denominator for saving rates and "is better for analyses that focus on the availability of resources, such as the Nation's ability to finance expenditures on education."

The connection between productivity measurement and a geographical basis for economic accounting is strong if the only important inputs are land, labor, physical capital, and possibly human capital to the extent that it is attached to immobile labor. If, however, technology, organizational skills, patents, or brand names are major determinants of output and productivity, the advantage of the geographical measure disappears because these types of intangible capital reside not in locations but in organizations that may span state and national borders.

One reason for organizing the conference was that it has come to seem that, just as state borders were crossed by multiplant firms many years ago, national borders are now more porous than in the past and strictly geographical measures are in some respects increasingly artificial. With many organizations spanning national borders, many transactions that were once arm's-length transactions at market prices now take place within firms. The prices and values involved are imputed rather than market values.

Another development that makes geographically based measures less informative is the growth in importance of intangible services. It is relatively simple to know the geographical location of agricultural, mining, manufacturing, and tangible service production, but it is much harder to know the location of the production of banking, insurance, consulting, and other intangible services. For these services, the ownership of the production is clear and is known to the purchaser, even if there is no clear meaning to the location of production. Even in the tangible goods industries, there are parts of the production process, such as invention, engineering, and design, that may not have any identifiable geographical location, but for which the organizational location is clear.

An example of a comparison between geographical and ownership measures on the international level is the series of studies by Kravis and Lipsey (1985, 1987) in which they compared shares in world manufactured exports of firms located in the United States with the export shares of U.S. multinational firms, including both their domestic and overseas operations. One point of the comparison was that the factors that determined the export share of the United

States as a location, such as exchange rates, wage levels, and other prices, are quite different from those that determine the export share of U.S. firms operating in many countries. If U.S. firms had fallen behind those of other countries in technological or management capabilities, as was argued at the time, the effects should have appeared in their worldwide operations, since technology and management are assets of firms. However, although the export share of the United States as a geographical entity declined over the period of the study (1966–83), the export share of U.S. multinationals remained nearly stable.

Revived interest in ownership-based measures was signaled by the 1992 report of the National Academy of Sciences, *Behind the Numbers,* which called for supplementary international transactions accounts, drawing borders around groups of firms classified by nationality of ownership rather than around geographical entities (National Research Council 1992). One suggested accounting format provides a comparable net sales measure of both the cross-border and foreign-affiliate (U.S.-affiliate) activities of U.S. (foreign) firms in supplying goods and services to foreigners (Americans). Another format measures the value-added activities of U.S. (foreign) firms in providing goods and services to foreigners (Americans) through cross-border and affiliate transactions. Other ownership-based accounting formats that provide additional insights into the internationalization of production can also be formulated.

Two of the papers in this volume, by Baldwin and Kimura on the United States and Kimura and Baldwin on Japan, carry out the proposals in *Behind the Numbers* for the international transactions of these countries. Their findings that net sales to foreigners by foreign affiliates of U.S. firms were only 6 percent less than export sales by Americans to foreigners in 1992 and that net purchases of goods and services by Americans from U.S. affiliates of foreign firms were only 12 percent less than imports of goods and services from foreigners in 1992 bring out clearly the extent to which U.S.- and foreign-owned firms supply markets beyond their borders from foreign-based facilities, as well as by exporting domestically produced goods. By reporting only the income earned from affiliate production activities, the traditional balance-of-payments format does not adequately indicate the relative importance of these two ways of supplying foreign markets. The finding that net sales to foreigners by foreign affiliates of Japanese firms in 1992 were 38 percent greater than export sales by the Japanese to foreigners, while net purchases by the Japanese from Japanese affiliates of foreign firms were 40 percent less than Japanese imports from foreigners indicates the significant reliance of Japanese-owned firms on the marketing activities of their foreign affiliates yet the comparatively modest importance of Japanese affiliates of foreign firms as suppliers in Japan's domestic market.

The difference between a country's production measured from a geographical standpoint and a country's firms' production measured from an ownership standpoint is what is called "internationalized production" in the paper by Lipsey, Blomström, and Ramstetter. Internationalized production is production in one country by firms based in another country, or, in other words, production arising from foreign direct investment. The paper attempts to assess the extent of such production and the trend in it over time. It estimates, from very incomplete data, that such production grew from about 4.5 percent of the world's total output in 1970 to almost 7 percent in 1990, and something in the neighborhood of 15 percent of production outside the service sectors.

Ramstetter, Low, and Yeung further explore internationalized production by comparing ownership measures based on country of incorporation with measures based on country of ultimate beneficial ownership. They make the comparison for firms in Hong Kong and Singapore, countries in which a significant part of the outward foreign direct investment is from foreign-controlled firms. Their paper points out that the use solely of the ultimate beneficial ownership criterion would wipe out much of the outward direct investment and internationalized production (as defined in the paper by Lipsey, Blomström, and Ramstetter) of Hong Kong and Singapore, even though such investment has become an important policy for governments and firms in these countries.

Using China as an example, the more familiar problem of separating ownership components in cross-border trade among countries is studied by K. C. Fung. Although two-thirds of China's exports and one-third of its imports pass through Hong Kong, China did not differentiate these reexports from trade with Hong Kong until recently, thus leading to wide discrepancies between bilateral trade balances reported by China and by its trading partners. For example, according to Chinese statistics, the United States had a trade surplus with China of $0.3 billion in 1992, whereas U.S. statistics indicated a trade deficit with China of $20 billion in that year. Other sources of problems with China's trade statistics are the markups that Hong Kong middlemen add to reexports to and from China and the illegal trade between Taiwan and China. The large share of trade controlled by foreign investors is another important feature of the trade of parts of China.

Issues in accounting differences according to geography and ownership exist at disaggregate as well as aggregate levels. Using the United States as an example, the papers by William Zeile and by Mark Doms and J. Bradford Jensen investigate the extent to which domestically based firms owned by foreigners behave in economically different ways from firms that are domestically owned. In comparing the domestic content of production by foreign-owned and domestically owned firms in the United States, Zeile finds that the overall domestic content of the foreign firms is only slightly below that of the domestically owned firms, namely, 89 percent versus 93 percent. However, in five industries (his sample covers 24 industries), which include computer and office equipment, electronic components and accessories, and motor vehicles, the domestic content share of foreign-owned firms is at least 15 percent lower than that of domestically owned firms. Among his other findings are that Japanese- and German-owned firms tend to have low domestic content ratios, whereas

British- and Canadian-owned firms tend to have high ratios. Japanese firms, in contrast to British-owned affiliates, also tend to source a high proportion of their imported intermediate inputs in their home country.

Doms and Jensen compare wage, capital intensity, and productivity levels in domestic and foreign-owned manufacturing establishments in the United States. As did previous investigators, they find that, on average, foreign-owned plants pay higher wages, are more capital intensive, and are more productive than U.S. plants. However, in reclassifying the data so that they are able to compare foreign affiliates with U.S.-owned plants belonging to firms with significant assets outside of the United States, that is, U.S. multinationals, they reach the important conclusion that the key factor influencing these operating characteristics is whether the plant is owned by a multinational, domestic or foreign. Plants of both U.S. multinationals and foreign multinationals pay more, are more capital intensive, and are more productive than either large or small U.S.-owned, domestically oriented firms, with the U.S. multinationals ranking at the top with regard to these characteristics.

As foreign direct investment has become an increasingly important feature of the international economy, the effects of various tax and promotion policies on this form of investment as well as on cross-border trade has become an increasingly important research issue. The papers by John Mutti and Harry Grubert and by Deborah Swenson address particular aspects of this issue. Mutti and Grubert examine how U.S. international tax rules influence the form in which taxable income is reported and the location of economic activity. As they point out, U.S. firms can service foreign customers by supplying goods produced by affiliates abroad, by shipping goods produced domestically, or, sometimes, by exporting a service. The effects of two important provisions of U.S. tax law on the choice of these alternative delivery methods, namely, allowing a portion of export income to be regarded as foreign-source income (sales source rules) and treating royalties as from foreign sources, are analyzed by the authors. Using various assumptions about income and withholding tax rates, tariffs, and the importance of tangible and intangible capital, Mutti and Grubert show how the sales source rules stimulate exports, while the treatment of royalties as foreign-source income encourages foreign production in high-tax locations.

Swenson investigates the impact of changes in the tax and promotion policies of U.S. states on the interstate distribution of employment by foreign-owned firms. She finds that foreign firm employment in manufacturing is sensitive to tax differences—that is, states whose taxes are high appear to deter investment—but that employment in all nonbank foreign firms is not. Employment in nonmanufacturing operations appears to be directed toward sales and service functions, and thus, proximity to final markets tends to dominate the tax variable. Another important finding is that promotional policies other than reduced tax rates do not produce identifiable effects.

Issues in appropriate spatial accounting have a variety of parallels in temporal accounting. The paper by Eric Fisher extends the concept of generational accounts to open economies and illustrates these accounts using Japanese data. The aggregate generational current account measures the annual change in the expected present value of net foreign assets broadly defined and captures changes over time in the expected present value of the goods and services that a country can import from abroad. A related account presents a generational cross section of the net foreign assets of domestic residents. In calculating the country's generational account, Fisher adjusts Japanese current account data on annual inward and outward flows of long-term capital for changes in domestic and international bond and equity prices as well as for exchange rate changes in order to obtain estimates of the market value of Japan's international investment position. Year-to-year changes in this figure combined with annual estimates of the present value of net transfers from abroad yield the aggregate generational current account. Fisher shows that the present value of Japan's net foreign assets has risen markedly in the past two decades and that the market value of these assets is higher than its more familiar net international investment position measured at historical prices.

While the editors realize that no definitive prescriptions have been provided for the solution of the issues raised here, they hope that the papers will stir renewed discussion of international economic accounting measures. In particular, they hope that the adequacy of the standard measures of the net current balance can be reconsidered in the light of the spread of multinational firms, the increase in the importance of service transactions, and the apparent absence of the expected consequences of persistent U.S. current account deficits.

References

Conference on Research in Income and Wealth. 1939. *Studies in income and wealth,* vol. 3. New York: National Bureau of Economic Research.

Kravis, Irving B., and Robert E. Lipsey. 1985. The competitive position of U.S. manufacturing firms. *Banca Nazionale del Lavoro Quarterly Review,* no. 153 (June): 127–54.

———. 1987. The competitiveness and comparative advantage of U.S. multinationals, 1957–1984. *Banca Nazionale del Lavoro Quarterly Review,* no. 161 (June): 147–65.

National Research Council. Panel on Foreign Trade Statistics. 1992. *Behind the numbers: U.S. trade in the world economy,* ed. Anne Y. Kester. Washington, D.C.: National Academy Press.

Stone, Richard, and Kurt Hansen. 1953. Inter-country comparisons of the national accounts and the work of the National Accounts Research Unit of the Organization for European Economic Co-operation. In *Income and wealth,* series 3, ed. Milton Gilbert, 104–41. Cambridge: Bowes and Bowes.

U.S. Department of Commerce. 1991. Gross domestic product as a measure of U.S. production. *Survey of Current Business* 71 (8): 8.

1 Measuring U.S. International Goods and Services Transactions

Robert E. Baldwin and Fukunari Kimura

1.1 Introduction

One of the roles of economists concerned with organizing national and international economic data into meaningful accounting formats is to ask periodically whether existing sets of accounts adequately describe important economic trends and are as useful to public and private policymakers as possible. The Panel on Foreign Trade Statistics established under the auspices of the National Academy of Sciences (NAS) in 1989 (which Baldwin chaired) considered addressing this question to be an important part of its task. In particular, it focused on whether existing ways of presenting data on firms' cross-border trading activities and the sales and purchasing activities of their foreign affiliates adequately captured the close relationship between these two types of international economic transactions.

The panel concluded that the present system of economic accounting could be improved in this regard and recommended that cross-border sales (exports) and purchases (imports) of goods and services as well as net sales of foreign affiliates of U.S. firms (FAUSFs) and net sales to U.S. affiliates of foreign firms (USAFFs) be presented on an ownership basis to supplement the residency approach followed in the balance-of-payments accounts (National Research Council 1992).[1] In the net sales calculations, the selling and purchasing activities of firms are measured as those undertaken by the firms' capital own-

Robert E. Baldwin is professor emeritus of economics at the University of Wisconsin–Madison and a research associate of the National Bureau of Economic Research. Fukunari Kimura is associate professor of economics at Keio University.

The authors gratefully acknowledge financial support from the Ford Foundation and Keio University. They also thank especially Robert E. Lipsey and J. David Richardson for helpful comments.

1. It should be emphasized that the panel did not propose that the existing framework for the balance of payments be changed but rather that additional information on international transactions be presented in supplementary accounting formats.

ers and employees, that is, by the productive factors used directly to create value added by the firm. Thus, net sales of foreign affiliates are defined as sales less purchases of intermediate goods and services.[2] This suggested supplemental framework combines net cross-border sales of Americans to foreigners, net sales by FAUSFs to foreigners, and net sales of U.S. firms to USAFFs to yield a figure that shows net sales of Americans to foreigners. The panel report also estimated value added on this basis, and we believe that measuring cross-border and foreign affiliate activities on a value-added basis is also a useful accounting format for representing international transactions. However, fundamentally, the usefulness of these as well as existing or other formats depends on the purpose for which the information is utilized.

The outline of the paper is as follows. Section 1.2 discusses the need for a supplementary framework and its benefits to both private and public officials. Section 1.3 considers various conceptual and practical issues that arise in measuring cross-border and foreign affiliate activities on a net sales basis and also discusses some of the key relationships brought out in the tables measuring international transactions on an ownership basis over the period 1987–92. Measurements of cross-border and direct investment activities on a value-added basis for this period are presented in section 1.4, and important relationships based on this approach are discussed. Section 1.5 presents net sales figures on an industry basis and includes an analysis of the international structure and relative competitiveness of American industries that these figures reveal. Section 1.6 briefly summarizes the main argument of the paper.

1.2 The Need for a Supplementary Framework

A key aspect of the increasing internationalization of economic activities is that firms have found they can profitably exploit their unique technological and managerial knowledge by establishing production units in foreign countries as well as by exporting to or importing from foreign firms or permitting foreign firms to use their specialized knowledge. Thus, when supplying goods and services to foreign markets, business decision makers consider the alternatives of producing the goods and services domestically and exporting them or undertaking direct foreign investment and producing them in their facilities abroad. If they do choose to produce abroad, firms must also decide on the extent to which they will export components for further processing in their overseas facilities or purchase the needed intermediate inputs abroad. To compare the economic importance of these alternative means of serving foreign markets, it is necessary to have comparable data with respect to these different activities.

2. Consequently, purchases from foreigners by FAUSFs, e.g., include purchases by the firms of intermediate goods and services from foreign-owned firms located abroad but do not include the cost of foreign labor hired directly by the affiliates of U.S. firms.

The current set of accounts documenting the international activities of U.S. and foreign firms does not provide such comparability. The balance of payments summarizes international transactions between residents of one country and residents of other countries. Total merchandise and service exports and imports of firms residing in the United States and in other countries are recorded, but no information is provided concerning whether the exports are shipped from U.S.-owned firms to FAUSFs or USAFFs to their foreign parents. Imports also are not distinguished on an ownership basis. Furthermore, since total exports include imported inputs, one is not able to compare properly the relative importance of value added through export activities with value added through affiliate activities or with total value added (GDP).

More important, the only measure of the level of activity of FAUSFs or USAFFs in the balance of payments is the income earned on U.S. direct investment abroad and on foreign direct investment in the United States. Comparing these income receipts and cross-border merchandise and service trade leads to an apples-and-oranges adding problem. The balance-of-payments framework measures the participation of U.S.-owned firms located in the United States in cross-border activities by their sales but measures their participation in direct investment activities abroad by the income earned on these direct investment activities. Since exports and direct investment income are not comparable (the first is a sales figure, while the second represents factor income), one does not get an adequate picture of the nature of firms' international activities from the balance of payments.

Economic data on sales and purchases of foreign affiliates of domestic firms and domestic affiliates of foreign firms are available for the United States and Japan, but these are presented in other sets of accounts constructed by these governments.[3] The U.S. government, for example, annually publishes data on the operations of U.S. parent companies and their foreign affiliates and the operations of USAFFs. These reports provide information on the cross-border trade between parent firms and their foreign affiliates as well as on the foreign sales and purchases of foreign affiliates. However, prior to the work of DeAnne Julius (1990, 1991) and an earlier study by Evelyn Lederer, Walter Lederer, and Robert Sammons (1982), no effort apparently had been made to integrate information in both sets of accounts as a means of better understanding the nature of the increasing globalization of economic activities.

Not only are supplementary statistical summaries of cross-border and foreign-based transactions of firms needed to improve our understanding of the evolving international economy, but such accounting frameworks would be helpful to government officials in reaching policy decisions. As the various papers in this conference volume indicate, ownership as well as geography matters for economic behavior. For example, the domestic content of foreign-

3. Purchases by FAUSFs can only be estimated indirectly.

owned firms in the United States, though high, is substantially lower than that of domestic U.S.-owned firms. Similarly, plants owned by foreign multinational companies are more capital intensive, more technology intensive, and more productive and pay higher wages than the average U.S. plant. Moreover, the output of these firms is generally growing at a different (sometime faster, sometime slower) pace than is output of domestically owned firms. National tax rules also affect the way in which foreign-owned firms report taxable income, price their products, and locate their production activities in a manner that differs from the behavior of domestic firms. Furthermore, foreign affiliates may respond differently to domestic monetary policies than domestically owned firms do because their access to international capital markets is likely to be better. Since these various differences are important for a variety of macroeconomic and microeconomic policy decisions by governments, it is useful to have an accounting framework that facilitates the comparison and interpretation of the differences. However, quite aside from the various differences in economic behavior between domestically owned and foreign-owned firms, it seems prudent on national security grounds to measure the cross-border and affiliate activities of U.S.-owned and foreign-owned firms on a comparable basis.

Expressing cross-border and affiliate activities in comparable terms can also be helpful to trade negotiators. Increasingly, it is the objective of governments not only to reduce the restrictive effects of traditional border measures but to reduce the discriminatory effects of various rules and regulations imposed by other governments that restrict the selling and buying activities of foreign affiliates within foreign markets. To determine the extent to which a country's negotiators have achieved both objectives, it is necessary to assess the liberalization achieved in both areas in a comparable manner, a goal that is not attained by only utilizing the information available in the balance of payments. Furthermore, the proposed accounting frameworks are helpful in informing the ongoing debate on American competitiveness in the world economy. By providing data on the extent to which U.S. firms compete against foreign firms through sales and purchases from their foreign-based operations as well as through their cross-border sales and purchases, government officials can better inform the public on this issue.[4]

Of course, for most public policy and research issues, the relevant relationships are the level of domestic activity, regardless of whether it is undertaken by domestically owned or foreign-owned firms, and the income accruing to U.S.-owned firms from their foreign investment activities rather than the level of activities of their foreign affiliates. The traditional residency approach followed in the balance of payments remains the appropriate accounting framework to utilize under these circumstances.

4. However, as Guy Stevens points out in his comment on this paper, no simple accounting measure can accurately measure the many different meanings of international competitiveness.

1.3 Measuring Cross-Border and Direct Investment Activities on a Net Sales Basis

1.3.1 Some Conceptual Issues

The first issue that arises in estimating net sales of goods and services by Americans to foreigners is how to define U.S.-owned and foreign-owned firms. For balance-of-payments purposes, the Bureau of Economic Analysis (BEA) regards a business located abroad (in the United States) as representing U.S. (foreign) direct investment if one U.S. (foreign) person, in the legal sense that includes a firm, controls 10 percent or more of the voting securities of the business. Under such a practice, two or more countries can treat the same firm as a foreign affiliate. This will lead to double counting of total sales and purchases for the world if an affiliate is assigned to each country. One way of avoiding this problem would be to allocate the sales and purchases of affiliates in proportion to the ownership interests of the different countries. Another would be to include only those affiliates that are majority owned, that is, affiliates in which the combined ownership of those persons individually owning 10 percent or more of the voting stock from a particular country exceeds 50 percent. One could assign all sales and purchases of affiliates to countries with majority ownership interests or only the proportions equal to the ownership interests.

The procedure followed here is to treat only majority-owned affiliates as U.S.-owned or foreign-owned firms and assign all the sales and purchases to either the United States or foreigners, depending on who has the majority ownership interest. Unfortunately, while data on the sales and purchases of goods and services are available for majority-owned FAUSFs, data on majority-owned USAFFs, although collected, are not published. In the tables included in this paper, figures on these affiliates cover firms in which the ownership interest is only 10 percent or more.[5]

Another problem in identifying U.S.-owned and foreign-owned firms is that some FAUSFs may belong to U.S. firms that are themselves USAFFs, and some USAFFs may belong to foreign firms that are themselves FAUSFs. Unfortunately, the data for identifying such firms and properly classifying them as foreign-owned and domestically owned firms are not available. Still another issue in estimating net sales of Americans to foreigners is the lack of data on sales and purchases of U.S. citizens living abroad and households of foreign citizens living in the United States. Because of this problem, it is necessary to classify households on a country-of-residence basis, as in the balance-of-payments statistics. That is, the household of a private foreign citizen in the United States (not employed by a foreign government) is combined with house-

5. An exception is service data from DiLullo and Whichard (1990) and Sondheimer and Bargas (1992, 1993, 1994), which cover majority-owned USAFFs.

holds of U.S. citizens living in the United States and the U.S. government and regarded as an American unit. Similarly, the household of a private U.S. citizen living abroad (not employed by the U.S. government) is combined with households of foreign citizens living abroad and foreign governments and regarded as a foreign unit.

The focus is on identifying the selling and purchasing activities of FAUSFs and USAFFs. Thus, the term "Americans," as used here, refers to U.S.-owned firms in the United States and abroad, households of U.S. and private foreign citizens residing in the United States (U.S.-resident households), and U.S. government units. Similarly, the term "foreigners" refers to foreign-owned firms in the United States and abroad, households of foreign and U.S. citizens residing abroad (foreign-resident households), and foreign governments.

In comparing the net sales of Americans to foreigners over time, it is, of course, necessary to deflate the value figures by appropriate price indexes. Cross-border sales should be deflated by U.S. export and import price series, while the appropriate deflator for net sales to USAFFs is an index of U.S. producer prices. Net sales of FAUSFs should be deflated by a weighted average of foreign producer prices, where the weights reflect the relative importance of the sales of FAUSFs across the countries.[6]

1.3.2 Estimates of Net Sales of Americans to Foreigners

Estimates of the net balance of sales by Americans to foreigners for 1987–92 are presented in table 1.1. The net sales figure is the sum of three parts: (1) cross-border sales to and purchases from foreigners by Americans, (2) sales to and purchases from foreigners by FAUSFs, and (3) sales to and purchases from USAFFs by Americans. Panel I of the table indicates cross-border sales (exports) to and purchases (imports) from foreigners only. Cross-border sales to foreigners are obtained by subtracting from total exports of goods and services both U.S. exports to FAUSFs and U.S. exports shipped by USAFFs.[7] Since the first export figure represents sales by U.S.-owned firms and U.S. private residents to U.S.-owned firms located abroad and the second represents sales of foreign-owned firms to foreigners abroad, both must be excluded in estimating sales by U.S.-owned domestic firms and U.S. private residents in the United States to foreigners abroad. In 1987 exports of U.S. firms to their foreign affiliates equaled 25 percent of total exports, while exports of U.S. affiliates of foreign firms amounted to another 15 percent. In 1991 these figures

6. A problem of growing importance with regard to measuring cross-border trade is that many goods and services now pass across borders with no transactions taking place. Consequently, cross-border flows are increasingly imputations, akin to those for the services of owner-occupied housing. Moreover, for many internationally traded goods and services, there are no markets comparable to the rental market for homes from which to draw prices in imputing the value of trade.

7. These subtractions exclude both intrafirm exports and exports to FAUSFs by nonaffiliated U.S.-owned firms and by USAFFs to nonaffiliated foreigners. The BEA surveys on U.S. investment abroad collect the data needed to divide exports into these different categories, if such a breakdown is desired.

were 23 and 18 percent, respectively. The estimate of cross-border sales (exports) to foreigners by Americans in 1991 is $344,725 million. (Data for 1991 rather than 1992 are cited in the text, since the figures for 1992 are preliminary.)

The $344,725 million figure is only an approximate estimate for several reasons.[8] For example, since exports by USAFFs to FAUSFs are included in both U.S. exports to FAUSFs and in U.S. exports shipped by USAFFs, this amount is subtracted twice from total exports of goods and services. Also, data on U.S. exports of services to FAUSFs, which should be subtracted from total exports of services, are not available except for the sales of some services by U.S. parent companies to their foreign affiliates. These divergences between the desired and actual figures are not likely to be large, however.

Cross-border purchases (imports) of goods and services from foreigners are estimated in a manner similar to cross-border sales. U.S. imports from FAUSFs and U.S. imports shipped to USAFFs are both subtracted from total imports of goods and services in order to obtain just the trade between Americans and foreigners.[9] In 1987 U.S. imports from FAUSFs amounted to 15 percent of total imports, while imports shipped to USAFFs were equal to 29 percent of total imports. By 1991 the first ratio had risen to 17 percent and the second to 31 percent. As before, the $320,364 million estimate of purchases by Americans from foreigners for 1991 is only approximate because of the double subtraction of U.S. imports from FAUSFs going to USAFFs and the absence of data on service imports shipped to USAFFs, except for some services obtained by USAFFs from their foreign parent companies.

A more serious problem concerns the subtraction of merchandise imports going not just to USAFFs where the ownership interest is 50 percent or more but to USAFFs with an ownership interest of 10 percent or more. This causes the import figure of $320,364 million to be too small compared to the export figure and thus the estimate of the surplus in net cross-border sales, namely, $24,361 million, to be too large.

Estimates of sales and purchases by FAUSFs are presented in panel II of table 1.1. To obtain net sales of these firms to foreigners, it is necessary to subtract both sales among themselves and sales to the United States from their total sales. This yields sales to foreigners of $898,046 million. This figure also is only an approximation of the desired number, since it improperly excludes the sales of FAUSFs to USAFFs. But, again, this exclusion is likely to be comparatively small.

No direct data are available on the purchases of intermediate goods and services by FAUSFs, let alone their purchases of these goods and services from foreigners. A rough estimate of purchases of goods from foreigners by

8. For a detailed discussion of the differences between the estimate of net sales by Americans to foreigners and the conceptually correct measure, see National Research Council (1992, app. A).

9. The same point about intrafirm and arm's-length transactions made in n. 7 also applies here.

Table 1.1 **Net Sales of Goods and Services by Americans and Foreigners, 1987–92 (in millions of dollars)**

Transaction	1987	1988	1989	1990	1991	1992
I. *Cross-border sales to and purchases from foreigners by Americans*						
Exports to foreigners						
+ U.S. exports of merchandise and services	348,024	430,216	488,955	537,605	581,197	619,848
− U.S. exports to FAUSFs	87,647	106,036	117,218	122,631	132,352	139,587
− U.S. exports shipped by USAFFs	51,843	73,520	92,024	99,185	104,120	108,166
Total	208,534	250,660	279,713	315,789	344,725	372,095
Imports from foreigners						
+ U.S. imports of merchandise and services	500,005	545,040	579,300	615,986	609,117	659,575
− U.S. imports from FAUSFs	75,986	86,053	94,703	100,721	102,879	110,939
−U.S. imports shipped to USAFFs	146,985	159,400	176,607	188,687	185,874	189,849
Total	277,034	299,587	307,990	326,578	320,364	358,787
Net cross-border sales by Americans to foreigners	−68,500	−48,927	−28,277	−10,789	24,361	13,308
II. *Sales to and purchases from foreigners by FAUSFs*						
Sales by FAUSFs						
+ Sales by FAUSFs	815,541	927,886	999,506	1,184,823	1,213,719	1,266,717
− Sales among FAUSFs	125,107	144,401	150,392	186,427	194,133	215,797
− Sales to the United States by FAUSFs	88,923	101,444	111,106	120,437	121,540	126,378
Total	601,511	682,041	738,008	877,959	898,046	924,542
Purchases abroad from foreigners by FAUSFs	358,715	395,973	431,885	541,755	559,050	575,265
Net sales to foreigners by FAUSFs	242,796	286,068	306,123	336,204	338,996	349,277
III. *U.S. sales to and purchases from USAFFs*						
U.S. sales to USAFFs	425,915	523,318	646,596	727,988	735,018	757,244
U.S. purchases from USAFFs						
+Sales by USAFFs	723,956	860,037	1,022,163	1,139,792	1,142,903	1,181,633
− Sales among USAFFs	n.a.	n.a.	n.a.	n.a.	n.a.	n.a.

− U.S. exports shipped by USAFFs	51,843	73,520	92,024	99,185	104,120	108,166
Total	672,113	786,517	930,139	1,040,607	1,038,783	1,073,467
Net sales to USAFFs	−246,198	−263,199	−283,543	−312,619	−303,765	−316,223
IV. *Net sales by Americans to foreigners*	−71,902	−26,058	−5,697	12,796	59,592	46,362
Reference						
Cross-border merchandise trade balance	−159,557	−126,959	−115,249	−109,033	−73,802	−96,138
Cross-border trade balance of merchandise and services	−151,981	−114,824	−90,345	−78,381	−27,920	−39,727

Estimation Procedure and Data Sources: Cross-border trade data are on a calendar-year basis, while data on FAUSFs and USAFFs are on a financial-year basis. Data on FAUSFs are for majority-owned nonbank affiliates, while data on USAFFs are for nonbank affiliates with an ownership of 10 percent or more, except for data from DiLullo and Whichard (1990) and Sondheimer and Bargas (1992, 1993, 1994). In the following, figures in parentheses are for 1987, 1988, 1989, 1990, 1991, and 1992, respectively.

U.S. exports of merchandise and services: U.S. merchandise exports (250,208; 320,230; 362,116; 389,303; 416,937; 440,138) and U.S. service exports (97,816; 109,986; 126,839; 148,302; 164,260; 179,710) are from Murad (1993, 71, table 1).

U.S. exports to FAUSFs: U.S. exports of goods to FAUSFs (74,907; 90,780; 97,488; 100,232; 108,839; 114,139) are from FAUSF87, 88 (table 51), 89, 90, 91, 92 (table III.H.2). U.S. exports of services to FAUSFs are not directly available; royalties and license fees (7,400; 8,893; 10,613; 12,867; 13,819; 15,226) and other private services (5,340; 6,363; 9,117; 9,532; 9,694; 10,222) received by U.S. parent companies from their foreign affiliates, obtained from Sondheimer and Bargas (1992, tables 4.2, 4.3, 6.1, 6.2) for 1987 and 1988 data; Sondheimer and Bargas (1993, tables 4.1, 6.1) for 1989 data; and Sondheimer and Bargas (1994, tables 4.1, 4.2, 4.3, 6.1, 6.2) for 1990, 1991, and 1992 data.

U.S. exports shipped by USAFFs: U.S. exports of goods shipped by USAFFs (48,091; 69,541; 86,316; 92,308; 96,933; 100,615) are from USAFF87, 88, 89, 90, 91, 92 (table G-1). U.S. exports of services shipped by USAFFs (3,752; 3,979; 5,708; 6,877; 7,187; 7,551) are from DiLullo and Whichard (1990, table 11) for 1987 and 1988 data; Sondheimer and Bargas (1992, table 10) for 1989 data; Sondheimer and Bargas (1993, table 10) for 1990 data; and Sondheimer and Bargas (1994, table 10) for 1991 and 1992 data.

U.S. imports of merchandise and services: U.S. merchandise imports (409,765; 447,189; 477,365; 498,336; 490,739; 536,276) and U.S. service imports (90,240; 97,851; 101,935; 117,650; 118,378; 123,299) are from Murad (1993, 71, table 1).

U.S. imports from FAUSFs: U.S. merchandise imports from FAUSFs (65,542; 75,578; 84,298; 88,641; 90,512; 98,850) and U.S. service imports (10,444; 10,475; 10,405; 12,080; 12,367; 12,089) are from FAUSF87, 88 (tables 51, 42), 89, 90, 91, 92 (tables III.H.2, F.18).

U.S. imports shipped to USAFFs: U.S. merchandise imports to USAFFs (143,537; 155,533; 171,847; 182;936; 178,702; 182,152) are from USAFF87, 88, 89, 90, 91, 92 (table G-1). U.S. service imports are not directly available; royalties and license fees (1,141; 1,285; 1,632; 1,967; 2,830; 3,069) and other private services (2,307; 2,582; 3,128; 3,784; 4,342; 4,628) paid by USAFFs to their foreign parents, obtained from Sondheimer and Bargas (1992, tables 4.2, 4.3, 6.1, 6.2) for 1987 and 1988 data; Sondheimer and Bargas (1993, tables 4.1, 6.1) for 1989 data; and Sondheimer and Bargas (1994, tables 4.1, 4.2, 4.3, 6.1, 6.2) for 1990, 91, 92 data.

(*continued*)

Table 1.1 (continued)

Sales by FAUSFs: Sales of goods by FAUSFs (718,086; 816,597; 889,875; 1,051,484; 1,069,729; 1,113,043) and sales of services by FAUSFs (97,455; 111,289; 109,631; 133,339; 143,990; 153,674) are from FAUSF87, 88 (tables 40, 42), 89, 90, 91, 92 (tables III.F.14, F.18).

Sales among FAUSFs: Sales of goods by FAUSFs to other foreign affiliates (110,606; 128,425; 137,587; 173,671; 181,112; 200,761) and sales of services by FAUSFs to other foreign affiliates (14,501; 15,976; 12,805; 12,756; 13,021; 15,036) are from FAUSF87, 88 (tables 40, 42), 89, 90, 91, 92 (tables III.F.14, F.18).

Sales to the Unites States by FAUSFs: Sales of goods by FAUSFs to the United States (78,479; 90,969; 100,701; 108,357; 109,173; 114,289) and sales of services by FAUSFs to the United States (10,444; 10,475; 10,405; 12,080; 12,367; 12,089) are from FAUSF87, 88 (tables 40, 42), 89, 90, 91, 92 (tables III.F.14, F.18).

Purchases abroad from foreigners by FAUSFs: Purchases of goods abroad from foreigners by FAUSFs (309,941; 340,400; 378,908; 472,906; 483,272; 495,883) are estimated as follows: substract from cost of goods sold (629,137; 705,845; 779,024; 934,474; 970,398; 1,021,043: FAUSF87 [table 28], 88 [table 33]—see below for calculation of 1989, 1990, 1991, and 1992 figures) employee compensation (105,452; 117,418; 132,565; 151,051; 160,082; 169,623: FAUSF87, 88 [table 49], 89 [table III.G.2], 90, 91, 92 [table III.G.7]), depreciation, depletion, [and like charges] (24,847; 26,245; 29,191; 33,190; 33,542; 37,095: FAUSF87 [table 28], 88 [table 33], 89 [table III.D.2], 90, 91, 92 [table III.E.2]), production royalty payments (3,384; 2,677; 3,285; 3,424; 3,551; 3,542: FAUSF87 [table 28], 88 [table 33], 89 [table III.J.2], 90, 91, 92 [table III.E.2]), purchases from other FAUSFs (equal to sales among FAUSFs; see above for data sources), and U.S. exports shipped to FAUSF (74,907; 90,780; 97,488; 100,232; 108,839; 114,139: see above for data sources).

For 1989, 1990, 1991, and 1992, first sum up "cost of goods sold and selling, general, and administrative expenses" (913,308; 1,080,482; 1,126,092; 1,183,876: FAUSF89, 90, 91, 92 [table III.E.2]) and "other costs and expenses" (41,317; 64,634; 63,046; 67,322; FAUSF89, 90, 91, 92 [table III.E.2] and multiply it by the 1988 ratio of "cost of goods sold" (705,845; FAUSF88) to the sum of "cost of goods sold" and "other costs and expenses" (705,845 + 159,106; FAUSF88) to obtain cost of goods sold in 1989, 1990, and 1991 (779,024; 934,474; 970,398; 1,021,043). Then follow the same procedure as for 1987 and 1988.

Purchases of services abroad from foreigners by FAUSFs (48,774; 55,573; 52,977; 68,849; 75,778; 79,382) are estimated as follows: major sectors for service sales are finance, insurance, and services. Thus, estimate purchases/sales ratio of 0.78 from the sales and purchases data of these sectors of USAFFs from Lowe (1990, table 6). Then multiply total sales of services by FAUSFs (97,455; 111,289; 109,631; 133,339; 143,990; 153,674: see above for data sources) by 0.78 to obtain total purchases of services (76,015; 86,805; 85,512; 104,004; 112,312; 119,866). Subtract U.S. exports of services to FAUSF (7,400 + 5,340; 8,893 + 6,363; 10,613 + 9,117; 12,867 + 9,532; 13,819 + 9,694; 15,226 + 10,222: see above for data sources) and sales of services by FAUSFs to other foreign affiliates (14,501; 15,976; 12,805; 12,756; 13,021; 15,036: see above for data sources) from total purchases of services (76,015; 86,805; 85,512; 104,004; 112,312; 119,866).

The sum of local purchases of goods abroad by FAUSFs (309,941; 340,400; 378,908; 472,906; 483,272; 495,883) and those of services (48,774; 55,573; 52,977; 68,849; 75,778; 79,382) is local purchases abroad by FAUSFs (358,715; 395,973; 431,885; 541,755; 559,050; 575,265).

U.S. sales to USAFFs: U.S. sales of goods to USAFFs or local purchases of goods by USAFFs (356,963; 434,310; 533,167; 604,544; 602,465; 622,597) are estimated as follows: subtract from cost of goods sold (616,310; 733,908; 877,203; 984,080; 993,949; 1,024,825: USAFF87 [table E-1]—see below for 1988–91), employee compensation (96,009; 119,588; 144,158; 163,592; 175,969; 181,709: USAFF87, 88, 89, 90, 91, 92 [table F-1]), depletion and depreciation (19,801; 24,477; 28,031; 33,008; 36,813; 38,367: USAFF87, 88, 89, 90, 91, 92 [table D-8]), and U.S. merchandise imports shipped to USAFFs (143,537; 155,533; 171,847; 182,936; 178,702; 182,152: see above for data sources).

For 1988–91, first multiply "cost of goods sold and selling, general, and administrative expenses" (859,963; 1,027,871; 1,153,105; 1,164,669; 1,200,848: USAFF88, 89, 90, 91, 92 [table E-1]) by the 1987 ratio of "cost of goods sold" (616,310: USAFF87 [table E-1]) to the sum of "cost of goods sold" and "selling, general, and administrative expenses" (616,310 + 105,857: USAFF87 [table E-1]) to obtain cost of goods sold in 1988–91 (733,908; 877,203; 984,080; 993,949; 1,024,825). Then follow the same procedure as for 1987.

U.S. sales of services to USAFFs or local purchases of services by USAFFs (68,952; 89,008; 113,429; 123,444; 132,553; 134,647) are estimated as follows: major sectors for service sales are finance, insurance, and services. Thus, use again the estimate of purchases/sales ratio of 0.78 calculated above. Multiply total sales of services by USAFFs (92,820; 119,071; 151,524; 165,634; 179,135; 182,492: USAFF87, 88, 89, 90, 91, 92 [table E-12]) by 0.78 to obtain total purchases of services (72,400; 92,875; 118,189; 129,195; 139,725; 142,344). Subtract U.S. imports of services shipped to USAFFs (1,141 + 2,307; 1,285 + 2,582; 1,632 + 3,128; 1,967 + 3,784; 2,830 + 4,342; 3,069 + 4,628: see above for data sources) from total purchases of services (72,400; 92,875; 118,189; 129,195; 139,725; 142,344).

The sum of U.S. sales of goods to USAFFs (356,963; 434,310; 533,167; 604,544, 602,465; 622,597) and those of services (68,952; 89,008; 113,429; 123,444; 132,553; 134,647) is U.S. sales to USAFFs (425,915; 523,318; 646,596; 727,988; 735,018; 757,244).

Sales by USAFFs: Sales of goods by USAFFs (631,136; 740,966; 870,639; 974,158; 963,768; 999,141) and sales of services by USAFFs (92,820; 119,071; 151,524; 165,634; 179,135; 182,492) are from USAFF87, 88, 89, 90, 91, 92 (table E-12).

Sales among USAFFs: Not available.

Cross-border merchandise trade balance: From Murad (1993, 71).

Cross-border trade balance of merchandise and services: From Murad (1993, 71).

Note: FAUSFs: foreign affiliates of U.S. firms abroad; USAFFs: U.S. affiliates of foreign firms in the United States.

FAUSFs is obtained by subtracting employee compensation, depreciation, depletion, and other charges, production royalty payments, purchases from other FAUSFs, and U.S. exports shipped to FAUSFs from the cost of goods sold. Purchases of services from foreigners are estimated by applying the ratio of total purchases of USAFFs by the finance, insurance, and service sectors to the total sales of these sectors, namely, 0.78 (as calculated from Lowe 1990), to the total sales of services by FAUSFs to yield a total purchases estimate. A part of imports of services from the United States and purchases from other FAUSFs are then subtracted from the total purchases figure to yield the estimate of local purchases of services from foreigners. Adding this to the sum for goods yields a total of $559,050 million for local purchases for goods and services by FAUSFs. Since these calculations only approximate the purchases of intermediate goods and services, the figure of net sales to foreigners by FAUSFs ($338,996 million) must be interpreted carefully.

Panel III of table 1.1 presents the estimates of net sales by Americans to USAFFs. Again, the data on U.S. sales of goods and services to USAFFs, or, in other words, local purchases of intermediate goods and services by USAFFs, are not available directly. The estimate of U.S. sales of goods to USAFFs is obtained by a procedure similar to the one used in estimating local purchases by FAUSFs, except that there are no data on production royalty payments and purchases from other USAFFs. U.S. sales of services to USAFFs are also estimated in a manner similar to local purchases of services by FAUSFs. The sum of U.S. sales of goods and services is $735,018 million. U.S. purchases of goods and services from USAFFs, or, in other words, sales to Americans by USAFFs, are estimated by subtracting U.S. exports shipped by USAFFs from total sales by USAFFs. The 1991 estimate of this figure is $1,038,783 million. Data on sales among USAFFs are not available. Thus, the estimate of net U.S. sales of goods and services to USAFFs is −$303,765 million.

By summing up the three components, we obtain an estimate of net sales of goods and services by Americans to foreigners in 1991 of $59,592 million (panel IV of table 1.1). The conventional cross-border trade balance in 1991 was −$27,920 million, as shown at the bottom of the table. The estimates of net sales by Americans to foreigners for 1987, 1988, 1989, 1990, and 1992 are −$71,902, −$26,058, −$5,697, $12,796, and $46,362 million, respectively. These net sales figures have not been deflated but, instead, are expressed in current dollars.

As the table shows, in 1987 net sales to foreigners by FAUSFs were about 16 percent greater than export sales by Americans to foreigners. However, this margin gradually declined between 1987 and 1991 so that by the latter year, net sales to foreigners by FAUSFs were 2 percent less than exports by Americans to foreigners. Cross-border purchases by Americans from foreigners in 1987 were about 13 percent greater than net purchases by Americans from USAFFs. In 1991 this margin was 5 percent.

1.4 Measuring Cross-Border and Direct Investment Activities on a Value-Added Basis

Although the volume of firms' sales is widely used to compare the relative importance of their different economic activities, a comparison more closely related to national accounting procedures is based on the value added by the primary productive factors involved in these economic activities. By rearranging the data presented in table 1.1, the value added by FAUSFs and by USAFFs can easily be estimated. These estimates are presented in table 1.2. The value added by FAUSFs ($328,184 million in 1991, e.g.) is calculated by subtracting from sales of goods and services by FAUSFs the sum of local purchases abroad by FAUSFs, imported goods and services by FAUSFs, and purchases from other locally located FAUSFs.[10] The value added of USAFFs ($222,011 million in 1991) is derived in the same manner.[11]

To help readers understand the economic significance of affiliates, ratios of value added by FAUSFs to value added by all U.S.-owned firms (the latter being defined as U.S. GDP minus value added by USAFFs plus value added by FAUSFs) are also presented in table 1.2, as well as ratios of value added by USAFFs to the GDP of the United States. The former ratios indicate that in 1991 5.6 percent of the value-adding activities of U.S.-owned firms were performed by their foreign affiliates, whereas 3.9 percent of the country's GDP was contributed by USAFFs.

Another relationship brought out in the table is the lower ratio of value added to total sales for USAFFs (19 percent in 1991) than for FAUSFs (27 percent in 1991). This asymmetry could be due to several factors. One may simply be that foreign firms in the United States choose to produce products with a low value-added component. However, another may be the existence of low profits for USAFFs (see Lipsey 1993). Profits for these firms may be low because foreign firms are forced to move their production sites to the United States by the threat of formal or informal American protectionism, even if these operations are not very profitable. Or the relatively recent rapid increase in foreign direct investment in the United States may simply mean that many production plants of USAFFs are in their initial stages of activity and have not been able to earn significant profits thus far. Other possibilities are the existence of pervasive transfer pricing practices to avoid U.S. taxation and the greater concentration of USAFFs compared to FAUSFs in trading activities as opposed to manufacturing.

10. Inventory changes should be included in the calculation of value added by FAUSFs, but information on these changes is not available. However, this information is available for USAFFs in 1987 and is taken into account in estimating value added by these firms.

11. In the absence of any change in inventories, value added by USAFFs will exceed (fall short of) net sales of USAFFs to Americans by the amount by which imports of intermediate goods and services falls short of (exceeds) sales of goods and services by USAFFs to foreigners.

Table 1.2 **Value Added by FAUSFs and USAFFs, 1987–92 (in millions of dollars)**

Transaction	1987	1988	1989	1990	1991	1992
I. *Value added by FAUSFs*						
+ Sales by FAUSFs	815,541	927,886	999,506	1,184,823	1,213,719	1,266,717
− Purchases abroad from foreigners by FAUSFs	358,715	395,973	431,885	541,755	559,050	575,265
− U.S. goods and services imported by FAUSFs	87,647	106,036	117,218	122,631	132,352	139,587
− Purchases from other FAUSFS	125,107	144,401	150,392	186,427	194,133	215,797
Total	244,072	281,476	300,011	334,010	328,184	336,068
In goods and services sold to						
Americans	64,054	74,578	78,491	86,507	85,357	90,781
Foreigners	180,018	206,898	221,520	247,503	242,827	245,287
Received by						
Americans	n.a.	n.a.	n.a.	n.a.	50,820	n.a.
Foreigners	n.a.	n.a.	n.a.	n.a.	277,364	n.a.
Value added/sales ratio (%)	29.93	30.34	30.02	28.19	27.04	26.53
II. *U.S. value added in exports of U.S.-owned firms*[a]	278,410	335,294	373,115	412,115	448,452	480,981
In exports to FAUSFs	82,388	99,674	110,185	115,273	124,411	131,212
In exports to foreigners	196,022	235,620	262,930	296,842	324,042	349,769
III. *Value added by USAFFs*						
+ Sales by FAUSFs	723,956	860,037	1,022,163	1,139,792	1,142,903	1,181,633
− Purchases within the United States by USAFFs	425,915	523,318	646,596	727,988	735,018	757,244
− Imported goods and services by USAFFs	146,985	159,400	176,607	188,687	185,874	189,849
− Purchases from other USAFFs	n.a.	n.a.	n.a.	n.a.	n.a.	n.a.
+ Inventory changes by USAFFs	4,671	n.a.	n.a.	n.a.	n.a.	n.a.
Total	155,727	177,319	198,960	223,117	222,011	234,540

In goods and services sold to						
Americans	144,575	162,161	181,048	203,701	201,785	213,070
Foreigners	11,152	15,158	17,912	19,416	20,226	21,470
Received by						
Americans	n.a.	n.a.	n.a.	n.a.	223,461	n.a.
Foreigners	n.a.	n.a.	n.a.	n.a.	−1,450	n.a.
Value added/sales ratio (%)	21.51	20.62	19.46	19.58	19.43	19.85
IV. *Value added in exporting country by foreign-owned firms*[a]	398,578	431,448	455,521	484,349	475,864	515,718
In exports to Americans	260,412	281,612	289,511	306,983	301,142	337,260
In exports to USAFFs	138,166	149,836	166,011	177,366	174,722	178,458
Reference						
GDP of the United States	4,539,900	4,900,400	5,250,800	5,546,100	5,724,800	6,020,200
Ratio of value added of FAUSFs to that of U.S.-owned firms (%)	5.27	5.62	5.61	5.90	5.63	5.49
Ratio of value added of USAFFs to U.S. GDP (%)	3.43	3.62	3.79	4.02	3.88	3.90

Data Sources: Inventory changes by USAFFs, Lowe (1990, 51, table 6). GDP of the United States, ERP95 (274, table B-1). See table 1.1 for the other figures.

Note: “Gross product” of FAUSFs in *Survey of Current Business* 74 (February 1994): 42–63: 319,994 (1989), 356,033 (1990), and 356,069 (1991). “Gross product” of USAFFs in *Survey of Current Business* 72 (November, 1992): 47–54: 157,869 (1987), 191,728 (1988), 226,031 (1989), and 241,182 (1990).

[a]Figures in panels II and IV are estimated using the share of imported outputs in exports (6 percent). See the text for details.

Since value added is a more fundamental measure of economic activity than net sales, an alternative approach for measuring the international activities of a country's firms is to measure both cross-border and affiliate activities on a value-added basis.[12] This approach involves combining the value added abroad by FAUSFs ($328,184 million in 1991) and the U.S. value added by U.S.-owned firms embodied in their cross-border sales (exports) to obtain a measure of the international activities of American firms. The export figure can be calculated by subtracting exports of USAFFs from total cross-border exports and then subtracting the import component in the remaining exports. (One would also have to estimate the U.S. affiliate component in these exports to avoid double counting.) Unfortunately, good data on the use of imports as intermediate inputs do not exist, but a rough estimate can be made by utilizing information in the U.S. input-output table. A special unpublished BEA study (Planting 1990) of the use of imports as intermediate goods indicates that the share of imported inputs in U.S. exports in 1977 was about 6 percent. Using this import ratio, the estimate of the U.S. value added in exporting by U.S.-owned firms is $448,452 million for 1991, as reported in table 1.2. Thus, the estimated value added by U.S.-owned firms through their export and foreign affiliate activities is $776,636 for 1991.

In calculating the foreign value-added component in the exports of foreign-owned firms of goods and services to the United States, input-output tables of these countries should be used to net out the imported input component in these exports. Unfortunately, the lack of such tables for many countries makes it impossible to measure adequately the imported input component in the exports of foreign countries to the United States. The 6 percent share of imported inputs in U.S. exports is probably smaller than the figure for most other countries because of the large size of the United States. However, for lack of an adequate estimate for foreign countries, the U.S. figure is used to obtain an estimate of the net value added abroad through the exports of foreign-owned firms to the United States. This net value-added figure was $475,864 million in 1991. Combining this with the 1991 value added by USAFFs ($222,011 million) yields a figure of $697,875 for the 1991 total value added by foreign-owned firms in exporting to the United States and in undertaking affiliate activities in this country.

The value-added approach can also be used in focusing on transactions between Americans and foreigners, as under the net sales approach. The value added by FAUSFs can be divided into the value-added components in the goods and services sold by FAUSFs to foreigners and in the goods and services sold by these firms to Americans by assuming that the value-added share in the sales to the United States by FAUSFs is the same as in total sales. The 1991 breakdown of value added on this basis yields figures of $242,827 and $85,357

12. As Lois Stekler (1993) has pointed out, except for net changes in inventories, net sales of Americans to foreigners are equal to the trade balance plus the value added by FAUSFs minus the value added by USAFFs.

million, respectively. Similarly, the U.S. value-added component in the exports of U.S.-owned domestic firms can be divided into the value-added components in their exports to FAUSFs and in their exports to foreigners by assuming the same fraction of imported inputs in these exports. In 1991, the value-added components in these two types of exports were $124,411 and $324,042 million, respectively.

The breakdown of value added in the goods and services sold by USAFFs both to Americans and to foreigners as well as the value added in goods and services imported both by Americans and by USAFFs from foreign-owned firms located abroad can be estimated in a similar fashion. For 1991, the estimates for the first breakdown are $201,785 and $20,226 million, respectively, and for the second $301,142 and $174,722 million, respectively. The value-added component in the net sales of Americans to foreigners is the sum of the value-added components in the net cross-border trade (exports less imports) between Americans and foreigners ($22,900 million for 1991), in the net sales of FAUSFs to foreigners ($242,827 million in 1991), and in the net sales of Americans to USAFFs (−$201,785 million in 1991), or $63,942 million in 1991. As indicated in table 1.1, under the net sales approach the net sales figure for 1991 is $59,592 million.

The value-added approach indicates that in 1991 the economic activity (as measured by value added) embodied in the goods and services purchased by foreigners located abroad and produced by U.S.-owned firms in the United States ($324,042 million) exceeded the value added embodied in goods and services purchased by foreigners located abroad and produced by U.S. firms abroad ($242,827 million) by 33 percent. With regard to purchases by Americans from foreigners, the value-added approach indicates that the value added embodied in goods and services produced by foreign firms abroad ($301,142 million) exceeded the value added in goods and services produced by foreign firms in the United States ($201,785 million) by 49 percent.

The value-added data can also be arranged to show the contribution of foreign affiliates and domestic firms engaged in international trade to a nation's output and the income of its citizens. The value added in exporting by domestic U.S.-owned firms plus the value added by USAFFs ($448,452 million plus $222,011 million, or a total of $670,463 million, in 1991) measures the contribution of these activities to the GDP of the United States. Similarly, the importing and foreign affiliate activities of Americans contributed $804,048 million to the GDP of foreign countries. Furthermore, combining the portion of the value added by FAUSFs that represents the net receipts of the U.S. owners of these affiliates ($50,820 million in 1991; see Landefeld, Whichard, and Lowe 1993, table 4), the value added by USAFFs less the net receipts of the foreign owners of these firms ($222,011 million minus −$1,450 million, or $223,461, in 1991; Landefeld et al. 1993, table 4), and the value added in the United States by the export activities of U.S.-owned firms ($448,452 million in 1991) yields the income earned by Americans in these international activities, namely, $722,733 million in 1991. These relationships bring out the point that exporting activities by American firms are still twice as important as a source of income for Americans than the activities of USAFFs and that the income earned by Americans from FAUSFs is only about 11 percent of the income earned through exporting.

The sum of the income earned by foreigners from the activities of FAUSFs ($277,364 million in 1991), from the earnings of USAFFs (−$1,450 million in 1991), and from exporting to the United States ($475,864 million in 1991) amounted to $751,778 in 1991. Thus, although international activities between the United States and foreign firms contributed 20 percent more to the GDP of foreign countries than to the GDP of the United States in 1991, the division of the total value added from these activities into income shares yields a figure for foreigners only 4 percent higher than the income earned by Americans.

One argument often made in support of using only the balance-of-payments accounts to depict international economic transactions is that this accounting framework is integrated with the broader national accounts. The current account balance (exports minus imports) taken from the balance of payments (with minor adjustments) is added to the expenditures on goods and services by consumers, business, and the government, that is, $C + I + G$, to yield GDP. Exports minus imports (rather than just exports) are added to the other three components because these expenditures are measured inclusive of imports. In other words, in calculating GDP, the current account balance is used mainly to correct the other three expenditure components. The only items in the balance of payments that are direct measures of domestic or national product are the net receipts of FAUSFs and of USAFFs. In contrast, calculating trading and direct investment activities in value-added terms measures both types of international transactions in terms of standard national accounts concepts. By separating value added by firms engaged in international transactions on a nationality and geography basis, the value-added approach supplements the traditional national accounts framework under which the GDP accounts divide aggregate production activities on the basis of geography and the GNP accounts allocate value added by primary factors on the basis of nationality. The value-added approach can easily be presented in a form that yields the current account balance needed for estimating aggregate domestic and national product. Consequently, this advantage of the balance-of-payments approach could be incorporated into the value-added accounting framework.

1.5 A Sectoral Approach

1.5.1 Sectoral Net Sales

Net sales balances by nationality can be measured for individual industrial sectors as well as for the entire economy. These net sales figures provide a rough idea of the relative international performance of American and foreign firms by industry. If technological know-how and managerial ability are major determinants of firms' competitiveness in international markets, these data may be more appropriate for analyzing international activities by nationality than cross-border trade balances alone.

Nationality-adjusted sales for individual sectors are calculated by subtracting U.S. exports shipped by USAFFs, U.S. exports to FAUSFs, sales to the United States by FAUSFs, and sales to other FAUSFs by FAUSFs from the sum of U.S. cross-border exports and sales by FAUSFs. Nationality-adjusted purchases are estimated by subtracting U.S. imports from FAUSFs, U.S. imports shipped to USAFFs, U.S. exports shipped by USAFFs, and sales to other USAFFs by USAFFs from the sum of U.S. cross-border imports and sales of USAFFs. Data on sales among USAFFs or between FAUSFs and USAFFs are unfortunately not available.

A major difficulty in estimating nationality-adjusted net sales balances by industry arises in trying to estimate purchases of FAUSFs and USAFFs. Sectoral intermediate input purchases by industry origin are not available. One possible way to estimate such purchases would be to use input-output tables and assume identical input-output structures for U.S.-owned firms in the United States, FAUSFs, and USAFFs. Instead, it is assumed here that each industry purchases intermediate inputs only from its own industry. Such an assumption greatly simplifies the derivation of nationality-adjusted net sales by sector: nationality-adjusted net sales are simply cross-border net sales (net exports) plus value added by FAUSFs minus value added by USAFFs.

Another problem is that the value-added estimates for FAUSFs are classified by industry, while those for USAFFs are disaggregated on an establishment basis. As Lipsey (1993) points out, this could generate biases in the estimation procedure. In addition, the U.S. cross-border exports and imports only include merchandise trade, while value added by FAUSFs and USAFFs contains both merchandise and service transactions. However, this is unlikely to cause serious measurement errors, since the machinery industry (except electrical) is the only manufacturing sector that has large service sales (about 10 percent of total sales).

Table 1.3 shows both net cross-border sales (net exports) and estimated nationality-adjusted net cross-border plus affiliate sales for individual manufacturing sectors from 1988 through 1991. The ratios of net cross-border sales to total sales in the United States and nationality-adjusted net cross-border sales to total sales of U.S.-owned firms are also presented as indicators of firms' "revealed" international competitiveness. To discuss comparative advantage across industries, it would be necessary to adjust the net export data for macroeconomic trade balances by using some method such as the one in Bowen and Sveikauskas (1992). Table 1.3, however, presents unadjusted figures only.

Despite significant problems with the estimation process, the figures provide a number of useful insights about the competitiveness of U.S. industries. For the total manufacturing sector, the ratios of nationality-adjusted net cross-

Table 1.3 **Cross-Border and Nationality-Adjusted Sales by Manufacturing Sector**

SIC Code and Sector		Cross-Border Net Sales (Net Exports)[a]				Nationality-Adjusted Net Sales[a]			
		1988	1989	1990	1991	1988	1989	1990	1991
	Manufacturing total	−147,002	−132,163	−100,833	−69,246	−312,073	−81,733	−89,922	−68,153
22	Food and kindred products	−3,989	−3,613	−3,750	−1,754	−18,178	−9,550	−7,887	−4,311
21	Tobacco products	2,918	3,646	5,045	4,588	3,758	5,736	7,534	7,600
22+23	Textile products and apparel	−23,986	−26,446	−26,293	−26,305	−24,079	−27,094	−27,310	−27,658
24+25	Lumber and furniture	−5,570	−5,257	−4,505	−3,596	−5,369	−4,999	−4,091	−3,302
26	Paper and allied products	−4,831	−4,649	−3,896	−2,338	−5,022	−2,361	−482	−316
27	Printing and publishing	268	1,085	1,535	1,921	−6,192	−6,988	−7,469	−7,135
28	Chemicals and allied products	7,463	10,601	10,569	11,650	−28,453	−1,896	−2,454	−1,626
29	Petroleum and coal products	−10,169	−10,850	−12,318	−8,046	−67,246	36,771	−8,263	−3,764
30	Rubber and plastics products	1,326	596	2,283	4,281	2,648	−1,121	−446	1,443
32	Stone, clay, and glass products	−7,397	−7,084	−5,844	−5,364	−9,837	−14,717	−10,454	−9,865
33	Primary metal industries	−16,868	−14,203	−11,888	−8,217	−24,213	−21,163	−20,544	−16,612
34	Fabricated metal products	−5,711	−4,868	−3,488	−2,817	−2,514	−5,314	−3,758	−4,283
35	Industrial machinery and equipment	−2,158	−2,155	4,357	10,087	−16,870	18,407	29,654	31,026
36	Electronic and other electric equipment	−23,775	−21,889	−16,088	−14,847	−29,323	−25,607	−18,269	−19,032
37	Transportation equipment	−33,998	−29,156	−19,676	−11,414	−41,262	−3,143	5,661	11,993
38	Instruments and related products	744	2,765	3,224	3,617	−16,483	1,980	2,968	3,201
31+39	Other manufacturing industries	−21,268	−20,685	−20,099	−20,689	−21,385	−21,745	−20,880	−21,344

SIC Code	and Sector	Cross-Border Net Sales/Total Sales of Firms in the U.S. (%)				Nationality-Adjusted Net Sales/Total Sales of U.S.-Owned Firms (%)			
		1988	1989	1990	1991	1988	1989	1990	1991
	Manufacturing total	−5.48	−4.75	−3.51	−2.45	−10.76	−2.73	−2.88	−2.21
20	Food and kindred products	−1.13	−0.94	−0.98	−0.45	−5.00	−2.44	−1.98	−1.06
21	Tobacco products	12.24	14.13	16.86	14.32	12.71	15.85	17.90	16.60
22+23	Textile products and apparel	−18.48	−21.91	−20.17	−20.07	−18.57	−22.60	−21.14	−21.48
24+25	Lumber and furniture	−5.01	−4.55	−3.88	−3.25	−4.81	−4.30	−3.50	−2.95
26	Paper and allied products	−3.94	−3.54	−2.96	−1.81	−3.95	−1.70	−0.34	−0.23
27	Printing and publishing	0.19	0.72	0.98	1.23	−4.53	−5.05	−5.15	−4.91
28	Chemicals and allied products	2.87	3.81	3.67	3.99	−10.01	−0.64	−0.80	−0.51
29	Petroleum and coal products	−7.74	−7.55	−7.14	−5.09	−42.50	20.32	−3.96	−1.87
30	Rubber and plastics products	1.41	0.67	2.25	4.25	2.71	−1.25	−0.44	1.45
32	Stone, clay, and glass products	−11.73	−11.13	−9.21	−9.00	−17.09	−27.29	−18.62	−18.50
33	Primary metal industries	−11.31	−9.29	−8.14	−6.19	−18.36	−16.44	−17.07	−15.32
34	Fabricated metal products	−3.60	−3.20	−2.14	−1.79	−1.55	−3.44	−2.26	−2.71
35	Industrial machinery and equipment	−0.89	−0.85	1.70	4.14	−5.50	5.70	8.73	9.54
36	Electronic and other electric equipment	−12.72	−11.36	−8.26	−7.50	−15.11	−12.88	−8.87	−9.22
37	Transportation equipment	−9.60	−7.97	−5.34	−3.14	−9.27	−0.69	1.22	2.62
38	Instruments and related products	0.65	2.33	2.60	2.84	−13.38	1.57	2.23	2.34
31+39	Other manufacturing industries	−47.76	−45.27	−42.68	−44.71	−47.59	−47.84	−43.57	−45.18

Data Sources: FAUSF88 (tables 33, 40, 42, 49), 89 (tables III.D.2, E.2, F.3, F.14, F.18, G.2, J.2), 90, 91 (tables III.E.2, F.3, F.14, F.18, G.7); UN90, 92; USEST88, 89, 90, 91 (table 1.1).

Notes: Nationality-adjusted net sales = cross-border net exports + value added by FAUSFs − value added by USAFFs.

We are assuming that purchases by an industry are all from own industry since by-origin purchases data are not available.

[a]In millions of dollars.

border and affiliate sales are larger than the ratios for cross-border trade alone from 1989 through 1991.[13] This suggests that U.S. industries have a greater "revealed" comparative advantage than indicated by the cross-border trade balance alone.[14] Industries where the total ratios are larger than those for trade alone include industrial machinery and transportation equipment. Thus, considering only cross-border import penetration for these industries may be misleading in appraising their international competitiveness. Industries where the combined ratio is lower than the trade ratio are stone, clay, and glass and primary metal products. In particular, cross-border net exports indicate that the chemical industry is a leading export industry of the United States, while nationality-adjusted total net sales are negative.

1.5.2 Sectoral Significance of FAUSFs and USAFFs

Ratios of value added by FAUSFs and USAFFs relative to value added for the U.S. economy as a whole are given in table 1.2. Since the activities of FAUSFs and USAFFs are concentrated in the manufacturing industries and the wholesale trade sector, the impact of multinational enterprises on those sectors is generally more significant than at the macroeconomic level.

Table 1.4 indicates for the various manufacturing sectors the share of sales of FAUSFs in total sales of U.S.-owned firms and the share of sales by USAFFs in total sales of firms in the United States from 1988 through 1991.[15] In addition, comparable shares in employment terms are shown in the table. Note that the data for USAFFs and firms in the United States are on an establishment basis, while those for FAUSFs are on an industry basis.[16] Also note that the data for USAFFs are again for affiliates in which the foreign ownership interest is 10 percent or more. The sales, value added, and employment ratios of FAUSFs to U.S.-owned firms in the total manufacturing sector in 1991 were 22, 14, and 17 percent, respectively. Considering the size of the whole U.S. manufacturing sector, the magnitude of the activities of FAUSFs was surprisingly large. The sales, value added, and employment ratios of USAFFs to firms in the United States in total manufacturing were also significant, namely, 15, 14, and 11 percent, respectively, for 1991. Thus, more than 10 percent of manufacturing activity in the United States was accounted for by foreign companies.

It is in the chemicals, petroleum and coal, industrial machinery, electronics

13. Nationality-adjusted net sales in 1988 are much smaller than those in other years because the estimated value added earned by FAUSFs is small. In 1988, sales of FAUSFs were smaller than usual, while purchases were larger.

14. Kravis and Lipsey (1987) agree with the view that taking the activities of FAUSFs into consideration is useful in appraising the international competitiveness of U.S. firms.

15. Lipsey (1993) examines the shares of USAFFs in all U.S. firms in terms of assets, employment, and plant and equipment expenditures.

16. The definition of value added in the establishment data is also slightly different from the one used here, although the difference does not seem to cause large estimation errors. See the detailed note in U.S. Department of Commerce, Economics and Statistics Administration (1994b, M-6).

Table 1.4 Sales, Value Added, and Employment Shares of FAUSFS and USAFFS (percent)

SIC Code	Sector	Share of FAUSF in U.S.-Owned Firms				Share of USAFF in Firms in the U.S.			
		1988	1989	1990	1991	1988	1989	1990	1991
				Sales					
	Manufacturing total	17.95	19.44	21.25	22.04	11.31	13.36	14.53	14.97
20	Food and kindred products	13.42	12.91	15.36	16.66	10.44	11.17	12.20	12.29
21	Tobacco products	19.37	28.70	28.89	30.04	0.00	0.00	0.00	0.00
22+23	Textile products and apparel	3.21	4.28	4.82	4.14	3.29	4.94	5.69	5.79
24+25	Lumber and furniture	1.71	2.26	2.89	3.20	1.46	1.63	1.99	2.09
26	Paper and allied products	11.49	12.69	15.34	14.99	8.16	7.84	8.67	9.03
27	Printing and publishing	2.27	2.77	3.08	3.38	7.08	10.18	10.51	10.36
28	Chemicals and allied products	31.43	32.17	35.01	35.93	24.97	28.24	30.42	30.70
29	Petroleum and coal products	36.52	40.58	39.56	41.90	23.57	25.18	26.87	26.07
30	Rubber and plastics products	16.73	17.43	17.35	16.92	13.53	16.34	17.55	17.73
32	Stone, clay, and glass products	10.72	8.13	16.17	15.70	18.50	22.16	25.85	24.59
33	Primary metal industries	4.77	4.43	5.13	5.44	15.77	19.58	21.84	22.82
34	Fabricated metal products	9.51	9.93	10.36	10.27	7.70	8.64	8.57	9.76
35	Industrial machinery and equipment	27.34	30.88	33.64	34.65	8.46	11.93	12.10	12.69
36	Electronic and other electric equipment	17.41	19.96	22.16	23.02	14.27	17.41	17.76	19.71
37	Transportation equipment	24.55	25.02	26.73	27.82	5.16	6.35	7.84	9.09
38	Instruments and related products	16.45	17.34	18.85	19.05	10.09	11.78	12.80	12.76
31+39	Other manufacturing industries	8.61	8.13	10.41	11.10	7.79	8.62	8.84	9.24

(continued)

Table 1.4 (continued)

SIC Code and Sector		Share of FAUSF in U.S.-Owned Firms				Share of USAFF in Firms in the U.S.			
		1988	1989	1990	1991	1988	1989	1990	1991
		Value Added							
	Manufacturing total	−3.03	15.63	14.08	14.04	10.44	12.38	13.37	13.97
20	Food and kindred products	0.71	9.45	11.23	12.55	11.65	13.52	13.83	14.08
21	Tobacco products	4.67	9.95	9.94	10.95	0.00	0.00	0.00	0.00
22+23	Textile products and apparel	2.87	3.12	3.61	3.43	3.02	4.17	5.26	5.60
24+25	Lumber and furniture	1.80	1.99	2.48	2.29	1.40	1.50	1.68	1.69
26	Paper and allied products	7.35	10.54	12.85	11.29	7.66	7.19	7.87	8.22
27	Printing and publishing	−0.53	1.39	1.49	1.54	6.37	9.53	10.09	10.13
28	Chemicals and allied products	−0.98	23.53	25.58	25.85	25.32	30.08	31.91	32.21
29	Petroleum and coal products	163.73	71.27	26.10	30.35	19.84	18.74	15.09	17.94
30	Rubber and plastics products	15.65	11.25	12.78	12.89	13.26	14.44	17.55	17.80
32	Stone, clay, and glass products	11.81	−0.13	13.01	11.37	18.10	22.05	24.75	23.90
33	Primary metal industries	−0.22	3.29	3.67	3.61	12.81	15.41	19.30	20.97
34	Fabricated metal products	10.26	7.30	7.63	7.58	6.67	7.81	7.94	9.35
35	Industrial machinery and equipment	−4.03	21.98	24.68	24.12	7.80	10.04	10.26	11.33
36	Electronic and other electric equipment	7.28	12.54	13.86	14.11	12.25	15.60	15.61	17.48
37	Transportation equipment	−1.89	17.67	18.87	18.02	3.27	3.74	4.88	5.40
38	Instruments and related products	−16.87	10.02	11.63	11.40	9.59	10.92	11.90	11.85
31+39	Other manufacturing industries	7.60	4.42	6.00	6.38	8.06	8.60	8.98	8.90

Employment

	Manufacturing total	15.25	16.29	16.95	17.28	8.06	9.53	10.64	11.10
20	Food and kindred products	18.46	18.99	20.01	20.83	8.44	10.09	10.84	10.63
21	Tobacco products	44.19	48.44	51.88	52.95	0.00	0.00	0.00	0.00
22+23	Textile products and apparel	3.95	4.82	5.02	5.41	2.50	3.40	4.33	4.43
24+25	Lumber and furniture	1.48	3.04	3.82	3.74	1.08	1.21	1.44	1.51
26	Paper and allied products	15.67	18.08	19.57	18.66	7.57	7.47	7.74	7.98
27	Printing and publishing	2.07	2.25	1.97	2.00	5.08	6.22	6.76	6.76
28	Chemicals and allied products	42.68	42.81	44.50	44.94	22.58	25.27	28.41	27.49
29	Petroleum and coal products	53.73	54.14	40.37	38.86	18.83	20.69	22.91	22.51
30	Rubber and plastics products	15.29	14.93	15.59	14.90	10.22	11.32	13.90	14.09
32	Stone, clay, and glass products	12.44	13.31	13.71	13.56	15.47	18.44	20.74	20.16
33	Primary metal industries	5.19	5.08	6.78	6.69	11.16	13.44	16.73	17.83
34	Fabricated metal products	9.28	9.53	9.50	9.29	5.33	6.17	6.49	7.49
35	Industrial machinery and equipment	19.43	22.77	23.36	23.08	7.57	9.96	10.20	10.86
36	Electronic and other electric equipment	24.40	25.64	28.21	28.90	12.21	14.96	15.24	16.49
37	Transportation equipment	24.44	25.69	26.36	27.93	3.60	4.40	5.87	6.54
38	Instruments and related products	14.67	15.73	16.81	17.44	9.86	11.16	12.81	12.50
31+39	Other manufacturing industries	8.43	8.55	10.13	10.11	5.87	6.62	6.44	6.81

Data Sources: FAUSF88 (tables 33, 40, 42, 47, 49), FAUSF89 (tables III.D.2, E.2, F.3, F.14, F.18, G.2, G.7, J.2), FAUSF90, 91 (tables III.E.2, F.3, F.14, F.18, G.4, G.7); USEST88, 89, 90, 91 (table 1.1).

and electrical equipment, and transportation equipment sectors that the sales, value added, and employment shares for FAUSFs are particularly high. The presence of USAFFs is large in chemicals, petroleum and coal, rubber and plastics, stone, clay, and glass, primary metal, and electronics and electrical equipment. The chemical industry looks special in that its shares are very large for both FAUSFs and USAFFs.

1.6 Conclusions

This paper has argued that the increasing internationalization of firms' economic activities has brought about the need for supplementary accounting formats to document these activities better. In particular, because of the close relationship between firms' international trade and international investment decisions, the paper argues for sets of accounts that provide comparable data on both the cross-border trading activities of firms and the selling and purchasing activities of their foreign affiliates. In providing such comparability, the net sales and value-added approaches set forth provide information about the nature of the economic globalization process that can assist government officials in reaching decisions on a variety of international economic policy issues. Fortunately, much of the data required for constructing such accounts already exists, although certain relationships must be investigated more carefully before the figures in the accounts presented here can be regarded as more than rough estimates.[17]

References

Bowen, Harry P., and Leo Sveikauskas. 1992. Judging factor abundance. *Quarterly Journal of Economics* 107 (2): 599–620.

DiLullo, Anthony J., and Obie G. Whichard. 1990. U.S. international sales and purchases of services. *Survey of Current Business* 70 (9): 37–72.

Economic report of the president. 1995. Washington, D.C.: Government Printing Office, February. [ERP95]

Julius, DeAnne. 1990. *Global companies and public policy: The growing challenge of foreign direct investment.* New York: Council on Foreign Relations Press.

———. 1991. Foreign direct investment: The neglected twin of trade. Occasional Paper no. 33. Washington, D.C.: Group of Thirty.

Kravis, Irving, and Robert E. Lipsey. 1987. The competitiveness and comparative advantage of U.S. multinationals, 1957–1984. *Banca Nazionale del Lavoro Quarterly Review,* no. 161 (June): 147–65.

Landefeld, J. Steven, Obie G. Whichard, and Jeffrey H. Lowe. 1993. Alternative frame-

17. In particular, there is a need for sales and purchases data for FAUSFs and USAFFs on the same basis in terms of the degree of domestic ownership and for better estimates of the share of imported inputs in exports.

works for U.S. international transactions. *Survey of Current Business* 73 (December): 50–61.

Lederer, Evelyn Parrish, Walter Lederer, and Robert L. Sammons. 1982. *International services transactions of the United States: Proposals for improvement in data collection.* Paper prepared for the Departments of State and Commerce and the Office of the U.S. Trade Representative, January. Mimeograph.

Lipsey, Robert E. 1993. Foreign direct investment in the United States: Changes over three decades. In *Foreign direct investment,* ed. Kenneth A. Froot, 113–72. Chicago: University of Chicago Press.

Lowe, Jeffrey H. 1990. Gross product of U.S. affiliates of foreign companies, 1977–87. *Survey of Current Business* 70 (6): 45–53. Updated figures are reported in Gross product of U.S. affiliates of foreign direct investors, 1987–90. *Survey of Current Business* 72, no. 11 (1992): 47–54.

Murad, Howard. 1993. U.S. international transactions, first quarter 1993. *Survey of Current Business* 73 (6): 63–101.

National Research Council. Panel on Foreign Trade Statistics. 1992. *Behind the numbers: U.S. trade in the world economy,* ed. Anne Y. Kester. Washington, D.C.: National Academy Press.

Planting, Mark A. 1990. Estimating the use of imports by industries. Washington, D.C.: U.S. Department of Commerce, Bureau of Economic Analysis, March. Mimeograph.

Sondheimer, John A., and Sylvia E. Bargas. 1992. U.S. international sales and purchases of private services. *Survey of Current Business* 72 (9): 82–132.

———. 1993. U.S. international sales and purchases of private services. *Survey of Current Business* 73 (9): 120–56.

———. 1994. U.S. international sales and purchases of private services. *Survey of Current Business* 74 (9): 98–138.

Stekler, Lois E. 1993. Book review of *Behind the numbers: U.S. trade in the world economy. Journal of Economic Literature* 26 (3): 1460–62.

United Nations. 1992. *1990 International trade statistics yearbook.* Vol. 1, *Trade by country.* New York: United Nations. [UN90]

———. 1993. *1992 International trade statistics yearbook.* Vol. 1, *Trade by country.* New York: United Nations. [UN92]

U.S. Department of Commerce. Bureau of Economic Analysis. 1990a. *Foreign direct investment in the United States: 1987 Benchmark survey, final results.* Washington, D.C.: Government Printing Office. [USAFF87]

———. 1990b. *U.S. direct investment abroad: Operations of U.S. parent companies and their foreign affiliates. Revised 1987 estimates.* Washington, D.C.: Government Printing Office. [FAUSF87]

———. 1991a. *Foreign direct investment in the United States: Operations of U.S. affiliates of foreign companies. Revised 1988 estimates.* Washington, D.C.: Government Printing Office. [USAFF88]

———. 1991b. *U.S. direct investment abroad: Operations of U.S. parent companies and their foreign affiliates. Revised 1988 estimates.* Washington, D.C.: Government Printing Office. [FAUSF88]

———. 1992a. *Foreign direct investment in the United States: Operations of U.S. affiliates of foreign companies. Revised 1989 estimates.* Washington, D.C.: Government Printing Office. [USAFF89]

———. 1992b. *U.S. direct investment abroad: 1989 Benchmark survey, final results.* Washington, D.C.: Government Printing Office. [FAUSF89]

———. 1993a. *Foreign direct investment in the United States: Operations of U.S. affiliates of foreign countries Revised 1990 estimates.* Washington, D.C.: Government Printing Office. [USAFF90]

———. 1993b. *U.S. direct investment abroad: Operations of U.S. parent companies and their foreign affiliates. Revised 1990 estimates.* Washington, D.C.: Government Printing Office. [FAUSF90]

———. 1994a. *Foreign direct investment in the United States: 1992 Benchmark survey, preliminary results.* Washington, D.C.: Government Printing Office. [USAFF92]

———. 1994b. *Foreign direct investment in the United States: Operations of U.S. affiliates of foreign countries. Revised 1991 estimates.* Washington, D.C.: Government Printing Office. [USAFF91]

———. 1994c. *U.S. direct investment abroad: Operations of U.S. parent companies and their foreign affiliates. Preliminary 1992 estimates.* Washington, D.C.: Government Printing Office. [FAUSF92]

———. 1994d. *U.S. direct investment abroad: Operations of U.S. parent companies and their foreign affiliates. Revised 1991 estimates.* Washington, D.C.: Government Printing Office. [FAUSF91]

———. Economics and Statistics Administration. 1993a. *Foreign direct investment in the United States: Establishment data for manufacturing, 1989.* Washington, D.C.: Government Printing Office. [USEST89]

———. 1993b. *Foreign direct investment in the United States: Establishment data for manufacturing, 1990.* Washington, D.C.: Government Printing Office. [USEST90]

———. 1994a. *Foreign direct investment in the United States: Establishment data for manufacturing, 1988.* Washington, D.C.: Government Printing Office. [USEST88]

———. 1994b. *Foreign direct investment in the United States: Establishment data for manufacturing, 1991.* Washington, D.C.: Government Printing Office. [USEST91]

Comment Guy V. G. Stevens

Much of what appears in the present paper and in Robert Baldwin's related work in the book *Behind the Numbers* I agree with and support (National Research Council 1992). This includes agreement that balance-of-payments data are not adequate to answer many internationally oriented questions in an era when multinational firms are important; in fact, as Baldwin and Kimura make clear throughout their paper, virtually no question involving the activities of multinationals or their impact on the U.S. economy is answerable using balance-of-payments data alone. One result of this agreement has been our long-standing advocacy, along with that of numerous other researchers and public servants, of a large number of improvements in the data on multinational corporations collected by the Bureau of Economic Analysis (BEA).

In this paper the authors do many things. They refine and extend the work, begun by Baldwin in *Behind the Numbers,* on the net sales balance of Ameri-

Guy V. G. Stevens is senior economist in the division of international finance, Board of Governors of the Federal Reserve System.

The author thanks Dale Henderson, Lois Stekler, and Charles Thomas for helpful discussions and suggestions and, especially, Russell Green for programming the models, running the simulations, and preparing the tables and charts. The views expressed in this comment are the author's and should not be interpreted as reflecting those of the Board of Governors or other members of its staff.

cans to foreigners and on the measurement of trade and direct investment activity in value-added terms. They also break the net sales balance down by industrial sector. Finally, in detailing the drawbacks of balance-of-payments data for examining such policy questions as the degree of U.S. international competitiveness, they challenge and invite us to examine all the existing international data and the interrelationships among them.

In this comment, I would like to focus on two topics. The first is whether, in advocating more emphasis on the role of multinational firms in international economic activities, we should also be advocating changes in, a revamping of, or, as the authors say, a "supplementing" of the balance-of-payments accounts. The second is what the merits might be of the net sales balance, particularly as a measure of U.S. international performance or competitiveness.[1]

An Ownership-Based Balance of Payments?

Baldwin and Kimura (B&K) in this and their earlier work challenge us to reflect on the adequacy of our present *residence-based* balance-of-payments accounting system. Does the fact that much of the important data on multinational firms are not to be found in the balance of payments mean that the latter should be altered?

The authors agree that we need certain balances derived from balance-of-payments data—for example, the trade and current account balances—because of their role in national income and product calculations. Thus, they usually talk in terms of "supplementing" the balance-of-payments accounts. However, they also suggest at the end of section 1.3 in their discussion of value-added data that a value-added accounting approach that emphasizes directly the contributions of direct investment activities would also, as a by-product, contain the trade and current account balances.

In response to B&K's challenge, I have played around with the construction of an ownership-based balance of payments. By grouping transactions on the ownership principle and making use of some the direct investment identities, along with the normal balance-of-payments identity, I have convinced myself that such a beast can be constructed. As B&K indicate for the value-added approach, I agree that the trade and current account balances fall out as by-products. Moreover, all trade and service flows can be divided into those that pass through foreign subsidiaries and those that flow directly from the United States. But what of this? If one has complete and accurate data on all transactions—between affiliated and unaffiliated parties—one can group them in any way desired. However, we do not have this complete and accurate data set, as B&K's calculations make clear. Does the answer to the question of whether

1. See table 1–1 in *Behind the Numbers* (National Research Council 1992) for the use of the net sales balance as an alternative to the trade balance as a measure of "U.S. international performance." In section 1.1 of Baldwin and Kimura's present paper, this balance is called "net sales of Americans to foreigners"; in table 1.3, it is called "nationality-adjusted net sales."

we push for an altered balance-of-payments accounting system depend, then, on how such a system would promote the collection of certain data that now are either unavailable or inaccurate?

B&K's Net Sales Balance and What It Might Be Good For

Although all of us agree that some of the concepts and data developed within the U.S. balance-of-payments accounting system are crucially important, B&K argue forcefully that these concepts need to be supplemented. In this section I would like to focus on one of the major new concepts they propose, the *net sales of Americans to foreigners,* examining the purposes for which it was created and the degree to which the concept achieves these purposes (see section 1.2 in this volume; National Research Council 1992, 37–45).

The major issues the authors hope this concept will illuminate are the competitiveness of U.S. firms, the impact of U.S. international transactions on U.S. employment, and the proper measurement of the impact of policy proposals dealing with trade and other international issues. An impetus to their attempt to develop new measures to analyze these questions is their view that the change in the trade balance has been given undue weight as a measure of the severity of international problems in these three areas. It seems reasonable and compelling to argue, as they do, that a balance-of-payments measure like the trade balance, which necessarily focuses only on transactions between U.S. and foreign *residents,* cannot possibly be a relevant indicator; this seems obvious because the trade balance does not capture the effects of U.S.-owned, but nonresident foreign subsidiaries (FAUSFs in the terminology of the authors)—sales of which now amount to over 21 percent of the total sales of U.S.-owned firms in manufacturing, and as much as 35 percent for important industries such as chemicals (see table 1.4).

But what about their measure? However a measure may be constructed—and I will get to that below—I would interpret it as a good measure to the degree that (1) it moves in the same direction as the concept it purports to measure and (2), better still, it is *linearly* related to the underlying concept (at least within a relevant range). Since it may be quite difficult to determine analytically the relationship between a given measure and the underlying concept or condition, I have constructed a small simulation model, laid out in the appendix, of a country like the United States that has a multinational-based economy, featuring domestic firms with related foreign subsidiaries (but, for simplicity, no domestic U.S. firms that are owned by foreigners). The production interdependencies among the parent firms and the related foreign affiliates are developed far enough in the model, I believe, to exhibit most of the flows that B&K take pains to measure: for example, in addition to traditional exports and imports to or from unrelated parties, flows of intermediates from the United States to the foreign subsidiary, flows of intermediates and labor from the foreign economy to the foreign subsidiary, and flows of final goods from the subsidiary either to foreign consumers or to the United States.

The Baldwin and Kimura Measure

B&K make it clear that they are after, conceptually, a measure of *net sales of goods and services by Americans to foreigners.* By nearly heroic efforts, they manage to combine balance-of-payments data with BEA data on the operations of U.S. foreign affiliates and, in my opinion, get very close to an accurate measure. If this or other similar measures were eventually agreed to be of paramount value, B&K's calculations indicate some of the important flows that might be collected in the context of an ownership-based accounting system.

In my little model, because data availability is no problem, transactions may be grouped in any way that is useful, subject to the usual adding-up identities. B&K's net sales concept, what I call below the "Baldwin balance," is fairly easily defined. It can be shown to be equal to the value of foreign citizens' demand for the (single) U.S. good minus final goods imports to U.S. citizens minus intermediate purchases by U.S. foreign affiliates from foreign citizens.[2]

In passing, I might note one potential problem with the B&K definition. Their net sales balance does not subtract labor payments by U.S. foreign subsidiaries to foreign citizens, although it does subtract payments to foreign *firms* for goods and services. To me this poses a conceptual puzzle, for if what is a foreign labor payment today is turned into a payment for foreign goods and services tomorrow by a (mere) change in corporate organization, the Baldwin balance changes, but American GDP, employment, and, perhaps, competitiveness do not.[3] For this reason, I also define an alternative, Baldwin balance*, in which intermediate imports to U.S. foreign subsidiaries from foreigners are not subtracted.[4]

2. This is a somewhat simplified version of B&K's concept, but I believe that it retains the essential elements. The first element, foreign demand for the (single) U.S. good, equals the sales to foreigners from U.S. plants and U.S. foreign affiliates (FAUSFs); exports from the United States of intermediate goods to the FAUSFs cancel in this expression (although not in alternative concepts like the trade balance)—they appear in total U.S. exports but are subtracted by B&K in getting to their *net* sales concept. My version of their balance is simplified by the nonexistence of foreign-owned multinationals in the United States.

3. An example of a "mere" change in corporate organization, in my view, would be the case in which a foreign laborer employed by the foreign subsidiary became an independent contractor. Even if all production relations and productivity remained constant, the value of the Baldwin balance would fall. This seems like a contradiction to me, since all agents would be in exactly the same position before and after the change.

4. Because I did not identify separately in the models payments to foreign firms and foreign labor, to distinguish between the two Baldwin balances I have arbitrarily assumed that 50 percent of the bill for foreign labor is paid to foreign firms, which can be looked at as foreign contractors.

While ostensibly a small point, whether labor payments to foreign workers are subtracted from the various balances turns out to be important. In an analysis of an earlier, related construct by DeAnne Julius (1990), in which labor payments were subtracted, I showed in Stevens (1990) that the Julius concept could be reduced to the effect of multinational corporations on the U.S. current account, as traditionally defined. On the basis of this earlier work, I would conjecture that if labor payments to foreigners were treated symmetrically to payments to foreign firms for goods and services (some of which may be labor services), the Baldwin balance would simplify to that part of the current account that is affected by the multinational firm in question. For similar questions and reservations, see Stekler (1993).

Baldwin Balances in Performance

Employment has a straightforward definition in simple models of this kind, but competitiveness, I submit, does not. My musings on this latter concept take up part of the next (and last) section of this comment. To avoid getting bogged down, I will carry out a set of simulations that trace the effects of changes that I believe everyone would agree represent improvements in U.S. competitiveness. Each simulation begins with a shift in one or more production functions that unambiguously represents an improvement in U.S. technical capabilities. In all cases, more output of the U.S. good can be produced for any given allocation of resources; similarly, the U.S. cost function for any level of output shifts downward. I trust that, however one may want to define U.S. competitiveness, such shifts represent positive movements. Technically, I accomplish the shifts as follows: in the model, production operations in the U.S. and the foreign subsidiary are both described as the assembly, with an increasing cost technology, of intermediates supplied from outside the firm.[5] The cost of assembly is exclusively the cost of labor input. For the U.S. operation, this cost of assembly equals $W_{us}A_hO_h^2$, where W_{us} is the U.S. wage rate, A_h the intercept of the home (h) labor cost function, and O_h, the level of output produced in the home (U.S.) country; symmetrically, the cost of assembly in the FAUSF is $W_fA_fO_f^2$. Positive technical change is represented by a fall in the coefficient A_h, for U.S. assembly, or, for foreign subsidiary assembly, a fall in A_f.

Table 1C.1 shows the effects of technical change of this general type for three alternative variants of the model: (1) a model in which the firm prices competitively (price equal to marginal cost), (2) a model in which the firm prices monopolistically, and (3) a classical variant in which the foreign subsidiary is removed from the model and all sales to foreigners are exports from the United States. The last in each set of columns lists the baseline equilibrium solution for the model in question, prior to the improvement in competitiveness; thus, for example, for the competitive pricing model, the price of the U.S. good in equilibrium is \$5.71 and the exchange rate, 0.236 dollars per unit of foreign currency; output of the U.S. good is 12.027 units, 11.839 units produced in the United States and 0.188 units of the identical good produced in U.S.-owned subsidiaries abroad. Capital flows are excluded from the model, so the current account must be zero in equilibrium; because of positive direct investment profits abroad (D.I. receipts), in equilibrium there is a small trade

5. The cost functions for both the home production operation and the foreign subsidiary are of the same basic form: cost is made up of two parts, the cost of an intermediate good (a part), A_p units of which (at price P_p) are assembled by labor, and, possibly, other foreign inputs into the final product. So that we will have production in both home and foreign locations by the multinational, the labor costs of assembly are assumed to be increasing with the square of output (W_{us} is the home cost of labor, the U.S. wage rate). A typical cost function, in this case for the U.S. production operation, looks like the following:

$$C(O_h) = P_pA_pO_h + W_{us}A_hO_h^2.$$

Table 1C.1 **Effects of Improvements in U.S. Competitiveness for Alternative Models**

Variable	Competitive Pricing Model				Monopoly Pricing Model				Classical Model	
	Change in A_h	Change in A_f	Change in Both	Level Baseline	Change in A_h	Change in A_f	Change in Both	Level Baseline	Change in A_h	Level Baseline
Trade balance ($)	0.035	−0.033	0.019	−0.067	0.141	−0.218	−0.007	−0.435	0.000	0.000
Baldwin balance	−0.033	0.027	−0.020	0.063	−0.005	0.005	−0.006	0.010	0.000	0.000
Baldwin balance*	−0.035	0.033	−0.019	0.067	−0.011	0.010	−0.006	0.020	0.000	0.000
D.I. receipts	−0.035	0.033	−0.019	0.067	−0.141	0.218	0.007	0.435	0.000	0.000
Current account	0.000	0.000	0.000	0.000	0.000	0.000	0.000	0.000	0.000	0.000
Price, exports ($)	−0.229	−0.005	−0.232	5.710	−0.169	−0.002	−0.170	10.962	−0.235	5.721
Exchange rate ($/f)	−0.010	0.000	−0.010	0.236	−0.006	0.000	−0.006	0.436	−0.009	0.236
Price, imports (f)	0.000	0.000	0.000	10.000	0.000	0.000	0.000	10.000	0.000	10.000
MNC profits ($)	−1.349	−0.028	−1.363	4.272	−0.197	0.007	−0.193	50.941	−2.055	67.695
U.S. labor	−1.310	−0.055	−1.340	4.200	−0.748	−0.019	−0.752	2.359	−1.375	4.326
Total output	0.130	0.009	0.134	12.027	0.097	0.001	0.098	8.944	0.138	12.009
U.S. output	0.185	−0.085	0.123	11.839	0.121	−0.036	0.096	8.867	0.138	12.009
Foreign subsidiary output	−0.055	0.011	0.011	0.188	−0.024	0.039	0.003	0.076	0.000	0.000
Imports ($)	−0.201	−0.002	−0.202	7.827	−0.011	0.000	−0.011	10.115	−0.202	7.830
Imports (real)	0.046	0.000	0.046	3.322	0.031	0.000	0.031	2.321	0.046	3.321

deficit. The Baldwin balance, defined above, is positive at 0.063 dollars, while the alternative, the Baldwin balance*, which does not subtract off the value of goods and services purchased by the foreign subsidiary from foreigners (exclusive of direct wages), is slightly higher at 0.067 dollars.

The preceding columns in each set detail the *changes* from the baseline solution caused by three alternative combinations of technical progress in the assembly operations of U.S.-owned firms. For the column labeled "change in A_h," technical progress is limited to U.S. domestic operations; the labor requirement in assembly operations is reduced by one-third (a change in the coefficient A_h of 33 percent, from 0.03 to 0.02). The simulation reported in the column labeled "change in A_f" is based on a similar one-third reduction in needed assembly labor for the foreign subsidiary only; the third column in the first two sets presents the results for the case of a one-third reduction of labor requirements for both production locations simultaneously.

Fortunately for explanatory purposes, the results do not depend on the pricing policy of the U.S. firm; the results in the first two models are qualitatively identical. Focusing on the competitive pricing model for clarity, we note that the general pattern of price and output changes corresponds to theory: no matter where the technical change occurs within the multinational firm, either at home or in the foreign subsidiary, the price of the U.S. good falls and its overall output rises; this makes intuitive sense because the technical change in all cases implies a downward shift in the supply curve for the U.S. good, with the demand curve unchanged (all of the above assuming that the exchange rate does not change). To me the logical necessity of the observed effect on the exchange rate—an appreciation in all cases—is quite unclear, but nonetheless appealing from an intuitive point of view. For a given fall in the price of the U.S. good, there seems to be an increase in the real demand for exports that outweighs the negative effect of the fall in price, sending the ex ante balance of payments into surplus. Another way of looking at the comparative statics is to plot in price and exchange rate space, the U.S. goods market equilibrium locus along with the balance-of-payments (BOP) equilibrium; we will observe the pattern of price and exchange rate changes of table 1C.1 if, as in figure 1C.1, the BOP locus slopes upward more steeply than the goods market equilibrium locus. Although the Marshall-Lerner conditions hold for this model, they alone do not seem to necessitate these loci.

Although the changes induced in major endogenous variables—the equilibrium prices and quantities—do not seem surprising, those induced in some of the balances do. Here we will concentrate on the trade balance and the Baldwin balance. The change in neither is uniformly of the same sign. The trade balance improves in two out of the three cases of technical improvement, but in the case where technical progress is limited to the foreign subsidiary, the trade balance deteriorates. However, neither of the Baldwin balances performs better; in two of the three cases, the clear improvement in U.S. competitiveness leads to a *lower* Baldwin balance—even the clearest of the cases, where tech-

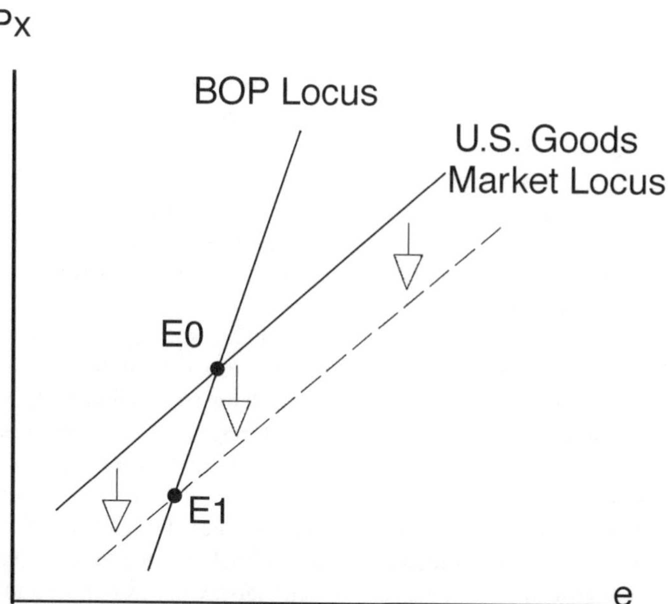

Fig. 1C.1 Shift in initial equilibrium (E0) as result of technical progress in production of U.S. good

nical progress is spread over all U.S.-owned production facilities, the balance deteriorates.

What intuitively seemed to me to be a possible key to the disappointing performance by both the trade balance and the Baldwin balance was that they are *nominal* measures, while changes in competitiveness can cause quantities and prices to change in opposite directions. The lower price of the U.S. good, certainly to be expected in this sort of case, may more than offset any increase in the real quantity of U.S. exports, thus leading to a fall in the dollar value of U.S. sales. Moreover, some of these measures, particularly those that are related to the balance of payments *and are nominal,* naturally tend to zero or some other limit; thus, in the simple model I developed above, the current account could never be used as a measure of competitiveness because it always tends to zero as a condition of equilibrium; whether the United States is technically very progressive or the exact opposite, prices and exchange rates will change in our model to leave the current account at zero.

In order to examine the truth of this intuition, I construct a real version of the Baldwin balance by dividing the nominal balance by the (endogenous) price of the U.S. export good (P_x). To my surprise, when the simulations were rerun, the results for the real Baldwin balance did not improve the situation: the signs turned out to be identical to those for the other versions of the Baldwin balance in table 1C.1.

Conclusions and Further Musings on "Competitiveness"

The previous section focused on the effects of technical progress in U.S.-owned production facilities—it is hoped a universally accepted instance of an improvement of U.S. competitiveness—on alternative quantities that might be used as indicators of changes in competitiveness. In the context of the simple models developed there, neither the trade balance nor the variants of Baldwin's net sales balance were closely correlated with this sort of change in competitiveness. These negative results invite us to reflect on what is wrong and what might be done to improve the situation.

I have come to the opinion that defining and measuring competitiveness is a very difficult, if not impossible, enterprise because the term is used as a sort of a conceptual suitcase. A good example is the definition offered by the Competitiveness Policy Council, chaired by Fred Bergsten: "Competitiveness is defined as our ability to produce goods and services that meet the test of international markets while our citizens earn a standard of living that is both rising and sustainable over the long-run" (Competitiveness Policy Council 1993, 4). The council's definition is then elaborated to include growth in per capita income, such growth to be financed by national saving, as opposed to foreign capital inflows. Such an elaborate and slippery definition has not been adopted for nothing, however: the more precise and specific measures of competitiveness that I have seen, such as those considered in the last section, seem invariably to lead to inconsistencies.

Consider, for example, the implications of adopting a definition that included only the first part of the council's definition: "our ability to produce goods and services that meet the test of international markets." A seemingly reasonable indicator of our ability to meet this goal would be the ability to produce a current account in balance; but we have seen above that, in some worlds at least, a current account balance is an equilibrium condition that *always* will be produced, whatever a country's level or rate of change of technology may be. Price changes, in particular a depreciating exchange rate, may compensate for lagging technical progress. An equilibrium current account in this latter case probably would not meet the council's supplementary competitiveness criteria of a rising and sustainable standard of living over time.

For this and the reasons discussed in the previous section, it seems that any relevant measure of competitiveness will have to be in real, not nominal, terms. But, so far, I have searched in vain for an adequate real measure—other than those that are direct measures of the underlying changes in technology that we think enhance competitiveness.[6]

6. It might be noted that even losses in competitiveness can contribute to the rising standard of living featured in the definition of the Competitiveness Policy Council. A technical innovation adopted by foreign-owned firms abroad would make foreign firms relatively more technically advanced and would generally be viewed as loss of competitiveness by U.S. firms. However, normally

If these musings are correct, we should not base our calls for a better integration of balance-of-payments and multinational firm data on searches for the best, or even better, measures of competitiveness. Rather, it would seem, such a call should be based on the demonstrated need for specific data concepts required to investigate specific international questions. Baldwin and Kimura have shown that many, and possibly most, interesting international questions require an analysis that includes the impact of multinational firms.

Appendix

Listed below are the equations for the three models on which the results in table 1C.1 are based. In table 1C.1, the models labeled "competitive pricing model" and "monopoly pricing model" feature a multinational firm that has the possibility of producing a single good at home or in a subsidiary located abroad; these two models differ only by the pricing equation for the (export) good. Both contain all of the other equations listed below. The third model, the "classical model," eliminates all equations dealing with the foreign subsidiary and also assumes competitive pricing.

The two models containing the foreign subsidiary require the firm to produce the last unit of output in the most cost-efficient way; thus, total costs for the firm as a whole are minimized—implying that, for any level of output, marginal costs are equalized in both locations. Such an equilibrium exists because marginal costs of assembly are assumed to be increasing (quadratic) in both production locations. The total cost functions for both of the models are identical, independent of the firm's pricing rule. Costs in both locations are made up of two parts: (1) the cost of components or parts, which are linearly related to both the level of output and the price of parts (e.g., $A_pP_pO_h$; see below for the definition of all symbols), and (2) the quadratic costs of labor and, possibly, other inputs into the assembly of the components (e.g., $A_hW_{us}O_h^2$). The optimality condition for cost minimization can be shown to be O_h = RATIO* O_f, where RATIO $= eW_fA_f/(W_{us}A_h)$. As noted above, the two multinational models differ only because of their different pricing rules. In the competitive pricing model, price is set equal to marginal cost. In the monopoly pricing model, marginal revenue, rather than price, is set equal to marginal cost.

Two market-clearing conditions are required to determine all the endogenous variables. The first is a market-clearing condition equating demand and supply for the U.S. good (i.e., the export good with price P_x). In addition, there

this technical advance abroad would make Americans, as well as foreigners, better off; if the U.S. terms of trade improved, U.S. consumers would share in the benefits of the innovation. The analysis in Caves and Jones (1973, sec. 25.4) suggests, I believe, this outcome.

is an ex ante balance-of-payments clearing condition, which can be justified as a linear combination of the other market-clearing conditions in the model (e.g., Stevens et al. 1984, 64–67).

Symbols

Coefficients

A_p, A_h, A_f: Technical coefficients in cost function for, respectively, parts, home labor, and foreign labor.

j, *k*, *r*, *s*, *t*, *u*: Coefficients, respectively, for demand (D_h, D_f) and import functions (*M*).

Exogenous Variables

P_p, P_m: Price of parts (for assembly) and price of imports (in foreign currency).

W_{us}, W_f: Wage rates in United States and foreign country.

CPI_{us}, CPI_f: Consumer price indexes in United States and foreign country.

Y_{us}, Y_f: Real disposable income in United States and foreign country.

Endogenous Variables

CO_h, CO_f, CO_t: Total costs in home (U.S.) plant, total costs in foreign subsidiary, and optimal total costs.

O_h, O_f, O_t: Output produced at home, output produced abroad in foreign subsidiary, and sum of the two (O_t).

D_h, D_f: Demand at home and by foreign citizens for U.S. good (whose price is P_x).

P_x, *e*: Price of U.S. final good and nominal exchange rate (dollars per unit of foreign currency).

M: Import demand (real).

$X_{final\$}$: Value in dollars of exports of U.S. good for final demand (whose price is P_x).

$X_{interm\$}$: Value in dollars of exports of U.S.-produced intermediate good (whose price is P_p).

$M_{final\$}$: Value in dollars of imports to the United States.

R_{di}: Direct investment receipts (profits of U.S.-owned foreign subsidiary).

$\mathrm{MNC}_{Revenue}$, $\mathrm{MNC}_{Profits}$: Total revenue for and total profits of U.S.-based multinational firm.

$\mathrm{BAL}_{Baldwin}$, $\mathrm{BAL}_{Baldwin^*}$, $\mathrm{BAL}_{BaldwinReal}$: Various measures of the Baldwin balance.

Equations

Goods Market

Building the total cost function:

$$CO_h = A_p P_p O_h + A_h W_{us} O_h^2,$$

$$CO_f = A_p P_p O_f + A_f W_f O_f^2,$$

$$\text{RATIO} = eW_f A_f / (W_{us} A_h),$$

$$O_h = \text{RATIO} * O_f,$$

$$O_t = O_h + O_f.$$

The total cost function for a multinational firm producing optimally in two locations:

$$CO_t = A_p P_p O_t + A_h W_{us}[\text{RATIO}/(\text{RATIO} + 1)]O_t^2 + eA_f W_f[1/(\text{RATIO} + 1)]O_t^2.$$

Home and foreign demand for U.S. good:

$$D_h = jY_{us} - kP_x/\text{CPI}_{us},$$

$$D_f = rY_f - sP_x/(e\text{CPI}_f).$$

Alternative price functions:
Competitive pricing:

$$P_x = A_p P_p + 2A_h W_{us}\left[\frac{\text{RATIO}}{(\text{RATIO} + 1)}\right]^2 O_t + 2eA_f W_f\left[\frac{1}{(\text{RATIO} + 1)}\right]^2 O_t.$$

Monopoly pricing:

$$P_x = A_p P_p + 2A_h W_{us}\left[\frac{\text{RATIO}}{(\text{RATIO} + 1)}\right]^2 O_t + 2eA_f W_f\left[\frac{1}{(\text{RATIO} + 1)}\right]^2 O_t + \frac{D_h + D_f}{k/\text{CPI}_{us} + s/(e\text{CPI}_f)}.$$

Goods market clearing condition for U.S. good:

$$O_t = D_h + D_f.$$

Balance-of-Payments Equations

Exports and imports:

$$X_{final\$} = P_x(D_f - O_f),$$

$$X_{interms\$} = P_p A_p O_f,$$

$$M = tY_{us} - u * eP_m / \text{CPI}_{us},$$

$$M_{final\$} = eP_m M,$$

$$R_{di} = P_x O_f - CO_f.$$

BOP equilibrium condition:

$$X_{final\$} + X_{interms\$} + R_{di} - M_{final\$} = 0.$$

Balances and Definitions

$$\text{BAL}_{trade} = X_{final\$} + X_{interm\$} - M_{final\$},$$

$$\text{BAL}_{Baldwin*} = P_x D_f - M_{final\$},$$

$$\text{BAL}_{Baldwin} = \text{BAL}_{Baldwin*} - 0.5 A_f W_f O_f^2,$$

$$\text{BAL}_{BaldwinReal} = \text{BAL}_{Baldwin} / P_x,$$

$$\text{MNC}_{Revenue} = P_x(D_h + D_f),$$

$$\text{MNC}_{Profits} = \text{MNC}_{Revenue} - CO_t.$$

References

Caves, Richard E., and Ronald W. Jones. 1973. *World trade and payments.* Boston: Little, Brown.

Competitiveness Policy Council. 1993. *A competitiveness strategy for the United States.* Washington, D.C.: U.S. Government Printing Office.

Julius, DeAnne. 1990. *Global companies and public policy.* New York: Council on Foreign Relations Press.

National Research Council. Panel on Foreign Trade Statistics. 1992. *Behind the numbers: U.S. trade in the world economy,* ed. Anne Y. Kester. Washington, D.C.: National Academy Press.

Stekler, Lois E. 1993. Book review of *Behind the numbers. Journal of Economic Literature* 31: 1460–62.

Stevens, Guy V. G. 1990. The "net foreign sales balance" of DeAnne Julius. Staff memorandum, 25 July. Board of Governors of the Federal Reserve System.

Stevens, Guy V. G., Richard E. Berner, Peter B. Clark, Ernesto Hernàndez-Catà, Howard J. Howe, and Sung Y. Kwack. 1984. *The U.S. economy in an interdependent world.* Washington, D.C.: Board of Governors of the Federal Reserve System.

2 Application of a Nationality-Adjusted Net Sales and Value-Added Framework: The Case of Japan

Fukunari Kimura and Robert E. Baldwin

2.1 Introduction

In the companion paper for the United States (chap. 1 in this volume), we propose a nationality-adjusted net sales and value-added framework and apply it to U.S. data in order to show its usefulness in analyzing a number of current economic issues and to specify points for statistical improvement. The framework should eventually be expanded to an internationally integrated statistical system that captures all activities of multinational enterprises in the world. As a preliminary effort, this paper applies the framework to Japan.

The proposed framework analyzes the globalization of firms' activities from a new viewpoint. Traditional balance-of-payments statistics conceptually present international transactions between economic agents in different locations, a framework consistent with GDP or national accounts statistics.[1] Since the balance-of-payments format primarily follows the residency of economic agents, the value added of foreign affiliates is conceptually decomposed into a residents' portion and a nonresidents' portion, with the latter portion being

Fukunari Kimura is associate professor of economics at Keio University. Robert E. Baldwin is professor emeritus of economics at the University of Wisconsin–Madison and a research associate of the National Bureau of Economic Research.

The authors gratefully acknowledge financial support from the Ford Foundation and Keio University. They thank Michael Plummer, Robert Lipsey, and other conference participants for constructive comments. They also thank Yoko Sazanami, Shujiro Urata, and other colleagues in a number of seminars in Japan.

1. The balance-of-payments framework determines the residency of individuals by whether or not they reside in a country for one year or more (in the International Monetary Fund [IMF] version of the balance-of-payments manual; in the Japanese version, more than two years for Japanese abroad and more than six months for foreigners in Japan) and that of firms by whether or not they are officially established and registered as local firms. This means that, e.g., a U.S. affiliate of a Japanese firm is treated as American. Hence, merchandise and service trade is basically captured as transactions between economic agents in different geographical locations rather than between economic agents with different nationalities.

captured as investment income (including retained earnings). Thus, the balance-of-payments framework is not very convenient for analyzing the behavior of globalized firms. Merchandise and service transactions between parent companies and affiliates may be qualitatively different from usual transactions between domestic firms and foreign firms. A firm may have its own resources for competitiveness, such as firm-specific technology and managerial ability, that can be used both inside and outside of the home country. Furthermore, even if a firm has multiple establishments across the world, it may make managerial decisions jointly. Our proposed framework assigns nationalities to firms and treats each firm as an individual entity. By doing so, we can analyze the competitiveness of firms in international markets, the importance of foreign-controlled affiliates in a national economy, firms' decisions on whether to export or to invest abroad, and other related issues. These features of firms' activities are particularly important in the case of Japan where firms' activities have globalized rapidly.

Although Japan is one of the few countries that collect extensive operational data on inward and outward direct foreign investment (DFI), we still encounter a number of problems in applying the framework. We try to identify explicitly various statistical deficiencies in the available data and relate them to the proposed statistical format. However, despite large possible estimation errors, we believe that the framework is very useful for analyzing the relationship of the Japanese economy to the world economy. Our analysis confirms the often-claimed asymmetry between the inward and outward DFI of Japan. We also find a rapid expansion of Japanese firms' activities abroad that exceeds the expansion of exports. In addition, we show that the activities of commercial affiliates of Japanese firms abroad, particularly those of general trading companies, play an important role in Japanese international transactions.

In section 2.2, the existing data for Japanese inward and outward DFI are briefly explained. Sections 2.3 and 2.4 present our estimation of aggregate and sectoral net sales by the Japanese to foreigners and the value added of foreign affiliates. Section 2.5 provides a preliminary overview of commercial affiliates of Japanese firms, which are specific to Japan and must be taken into consideration in developing an internationally integrated statistical format. Section 2.6 summarizes what is specific to Japan and discusses directions for the improvement of the statistical format.

2.2 Data on Sales and Purchases by Affiliates

A Ministry of International Trade and Industry (MITI) data set (hereinafter called "the old FAJF series") is the only currently available source for long time-series data on the sales and purchases of foreign affiliates of Japanese firms (FAJFs). The International Enterprises Section of MITI annually distributes questionnaires to parent Japanese companies that are identified by the Foreign Exchange and Foreign Trade Control Law as having foreign affiliates in which they own more than a 10 percent share.[2] A detailed survey was initiated in 1980 and has been conducted every three years since 1983. A shortened questionnaire is used in the other years. Among the particularly useful information collected is data on purchases by FAJFs (such data are not collected in the U.S. surveys of foreign direct investment).[3] This survey, however, is so-called *shounin toukei* ("approved statistics"), and it is not legally mandatory for firms to complete the questionnaire. Therefore, the data are much less reliable than the U.S. data. A serious problem is low coverage. For example, in 1992, only 65.5 percent of the questionnaires sent to foreign affiliates were returned to MITI. Moreover, not all firms returning the questionnaire answered all of the questions. To make matters worse, MITI does not report the number of firms that answered each question. This problem is particularly serious for purchases data. In addition, not all firms that provide total sales or purchases data report by-destination disaggregation of sales or by-origin disaggregation of purchases.

The Research and Statistics Department of the Minister's Secretariat of MITI has recently begun to publish another statistical series covering FAJFs. This survey, called the Basic Survey of Business Structure and Activity (hereinafter "the new FAJF series"), collects data on FAJFs as a part of information obtained on private firms' activities in Japan. The new series is so-called *shitei toukei* ("designated statistics"), and companies have a legal obligation to return completed questionnaires. The survey was scheduled to be conducted annually from 1994. Only figures for the 1991 and 1994 financial years have been published as of 1997. Table 2.1 presents the 1991 financial year data on the activities of FAJFs from the two sources, the old and new FAJF series. The new FAJF series provides more reliable figures than the old FAJF series, but its coverage is narrower and biased toward large companies.[4]

Data on Japanese affiliates of foreign firms (JAFFs) are also reported by the International Enterprises Section of MITI. The structure of this survey is basically the same as that of the old FAJF survey. The coverage is, however, even narrower; for the 1992 financial year, for instance, only 53.7 percent of the questionnaires were returned to MITI.[5]

2. One of the problems with this list of enterprises is that there is no systematic procedure for updating the list. It therefore may include enterprises or foreign affiliates that once existed but are not in business anymore.

3. The Bureau of Economic Analysis (BEA) of the U.S. Department of Commerce tried to collect purchases data in the past, but it deleted the question from the questionnaire because it could not collect reliable figures.

4. The new FAJF series can be used to check the accuracy of the old FAJF series. For the 1991 financial year data, e.g., one may question the quality of sales and purchases data reported by the old FAJF series, which differ widely from those in the new FAJF series. MITI is currently trying to reformat the old and new FAJF series into an integrated framework.

5. Again, one of the problems is that there is no systematic procedure to update the list of JAFFs. MITI is currently trying to integrate the JAFF series and domestic establishment surveys. The Organization for Economic Cooperation and Development (OECD) is promoting this approach with a number of countries, including the United Kingdom and France.

Table 2.1 **Comparison between the Old and New FAJF Series, 1991 Financial Year**

	No. of FAJFs covered		Number of Employees		Sales by FAJFs (million yen)		By Destination Shares in Sales by FAJFs (%)					
							Local		Japan		Third Countries	
	OLD91	NEW91	OLD91	NEW91	OLD91	NEW91	OLD91	NEW91	OLD91	NEW91	OLD91	NEW91
By Sector												
Total	8,505	2,851	1,620,829	919,294	88,737,186	67,111,539	69.8	65.5	11.8	14.2	18.4	20.3
Manufacturing	3,528	1,723	1,261,012	744,253	25,364,961	16,149,008	69.5	74.2	8.4	7.4	22.1	18.3
Food processing	157	67	33,788	9,833	493,781	214,800	53.0	62.5	25.9	23.5	21.1	13.9
Textiles	185	60	92,020	21,663	676,604	192,059	55.3	64.9	10.1	9.7	34.6	25.3
Chemicals	495	151	78,262	26,377	1,890,649	591,268	66.3	61.1	5.9	5.8	27.7	33.1
Basic metals	216	93	59,726	18,752	1,411,713	310,581	78.9	79.4	5.1	8.0	16.0	12.6
General machinery	291	162	65,687	42,072	2,367,135	1,176,577	67.2	79.5	4.4	5.7	28.4	14.9
Electrical machinery	940	530	435,796	329,712	8,107,032	5,906,542	64.0	61.2	10.9	11.2	25.0	27.6
Transport equipment	425	218	257,264	136,271	7,004,617	5,283,201	85.0	89.4	2.6	1.7	12.3	8.9
Precision machinery	139	75	28,689	25,318	405,423	361,769	48.8	54.6	19.4	24.2	31.8	21.2
Petroleum and coal products	18	3	5,644	n.a.	139,736	n.a.	61.3	n.a.	0.0	n.a.	38.7	n.a.
Other manufacturing	662	364	204,136	134,255	2,868,271	2,112,211	68.1	78.0	9.9	7.9	22.0	14.2
Commerce	2,589	1,112	238,975	171,098	58,337,017	50,811,689	69.0	62.7	14.5	16.4	16.5	20.9
Services	619	n.a.	37,588	n.a.	1,173,761	n.a.	96.1	n.a.	2.8	n.a.	1.1	n.a.
Others	1,769	17	83,254	55	3,861,447	43,620	75.4	13.8	16.9	49.7	7.7	36.5

By Location

World total	8,505	2,851	1,620,829	919,294	88,737,186	67,111,539	69.8	65.5	11.8	14.2	18.4	20.3
North America	2,399	971	444,289	272,999	40,368,155	32,957,029	84.4	77.4	10.5	12.4	5.1	10.2
United States	2,177	890	415,666	255,264	37,653,870	30,795,603	84.8	77.3	10.5	12.2	4.7	10.5
Middle and South America	584	108	105,519	52,444	2,524,748	1,218,308	59.3	47.8	24.1	28.7	16.6	23.5
Asia	3,156	949	744,520	386,110	16,702,312	11,211,411	57.5	46.9	15.2	18.7	27.3	34.4
ASEAN4	1,194	364	394,330	211,021	4,713,576	1,835,711	60.4	47.6	13.9	19.4	25.7	32.9
NIEs4	1,693	529	277,459	154,995	11,576,548	9,297,727	54.1	46.7	16.4	18.5	29.5	34.8
Middle East	51	4	9,276	n.a.	907,197	n.a.	21.5	n.a.	40.8	n.a.	37.6	n.a.
Europe	1,785	688	250,608	178,216	23,661,636	18,207,633	63.4	59.3	5.3	9.5	31.3	31.2
EC	1,615	657	240,333	175,603	22,591,507	17,952,678	66.4	59.0	5.6	9.5	28.0	31.5
Oceania	407	129	56,368	24,134	4,051,605	3,118,578	62.4	54.1	30.3	37.3	7.3	8.6
Africa	123	2	10,249	n.a.	521,533	n.a.	31.0	n.a.	31.0	n.a.	38.0	n.a.

(*continued*)

Table 2.1 (continued)

	Purchases by FAJFs (million yen)		By Origin Shares in Purchases by FAJFs (%)						Purchases/Sales Ratios (%)	
			Local		Japan		Third Countries			
	OLD91	NEW91	OLD91	NEW91	OLD91	NEW91	OLD91	NEW91	OLD91	NEW91
					By Sector					
Total	47,850,264	53,895,778	36.5	27.8	41.8	n.a.	21.7	n.a.	53.9	80.3
Manufacturing	10,380,640	10,484,599	43.6	44.6	42.4	n.a.	13.9	n.a.	40.9	64.9
Food processing	193,038	108,287	88.3	75.4	4.7	n.a.	7.0	n.a.	39.1	50.4
Textiles	173,492	105,103	44.1	50.9	20.0	n.a.	36.0	n.a.	25.6	54.7
Chemicals	482,020	266,287	62.8	52.6	23.6	n.a.	13.6	n.a.	25.5	45.0
Basic metals	725,757	201,238	51.4	60.4	17.3	n.a.	31.3	n.a.	51.4	64.8
General machinery	505,600	614,433	43.2	65.2	48.7	n.a.	8.1	n.a.	21.4	52.2
Electrical machinery	3,836,972	3,820,493	32.1	36.5	49.5	n.a.	18.5	n.a.	47.3	64.7
Transport equipment	2,910,419	3,960,656	51.2	52.2	45.4	n.a.	3.4	n.a.	41.6	75.0
Precision machinery	127.440	195,332	28.4	22.5	67.0	n.a.	4.6	n.a.	31.4	54.0
Petroleum and coal products	46,729	n.a.	58.9	n.a.	17.4	n.a.	23.7	n.a.	33.4	n.a.
Other manufacturing	1,379,173	1,212,771	61.0	31.1	21.5	n.a.	17.4	n.a.	48.1	57.4
Commerce	35,486,167	43,290,361	31.5	23.7	42.4	n.a.	26.1	n.a.	60.8	85.2
Services	441,532	n.a.	79.2	n.a.	15.6	n.a.	5.2	n.a.	37.6	n.a.
Others	1,541,928	37,282	89.0	1.3	8.7	n.a.	2.3	n.a.	39.9	85.5

					By Location					
World total	47,850,264	53,895,778	36.5	27.8	41.8	n.a.	21.7	n.a.	53.9	80.3
North America	22,215,404	27,365,443	52.7	34.4	37.2	n.a.	10.1	n.a.	55.0	83.0
United States	20,844,276	25,496,874	53.9	35.0	36.3	n.a.	9.8	n.a.	55.4	82.8
Middle and South America	1,298,949	909,132	34.6	27.2	36.3	n.a.	29.1	n.a.	51.4	74.6
Asia	9,334,981	8,665,570	33.7	24.5	39.6	n.a.	26.7	n.a.	55.9	77.3
ASEAN4	2,721,950	1,293,308	42.1	41.2	36.9	n.a.	21.0	n.a.	57.7	70.5
NIEs4	6,469,430	7,317,362	29.5	21.4	41.0	n.a.	29.5	n.a.	55.9	78.7
Middle East	605,886	n.a.	9.3	n.a.	41.2	n.a.	49.4	n.a.	66.8	n.a.
Europe	11,864,239	13,764,828	15.6	17.3	49.3	n.a.	35.1	n.a.	50.1	75.6
EC	11,039,056	13,573,922	17.0	17.3	49.3	n.a.	33.6	n.a.	48.9	75.6
Oceania	2,117,517	2,765,517	40.9	29.8	54.3	n.a.	4.8	n.a.	52.3	88.7
Africa	413,288	n.a.	78.1	n.a.	9.2	n.a.	12.8	n.a.	79.2	n.a.

Data Sources: OLD91 (57, 75, 78–101, 126); NEW91 (398–401, 450–53).

Notes: The sample set of the old FAJF series (OLD91) includes affiliates in which the Japanese have more than a 10 percent share and affiliates in which Japanese majority-owned affiliates have more than a 50 percent share, and the parent companies of which are in industries other than finance, insurance, and real estate. The new FAJF series (NEW91) covers majority-owned foreign affiliates of Japanese firms with more than U.S.$1 million of capital, in the mining, manufacturing, and commerce sectors, whose parent companies have more than 50 employees and more than 30 million yen of capital in the mining, manufacturing, and commerce sectors.

"n.a." in NEW91 means that the data are not available, which is in part the result of small sample sizes.

Sales and purchases by FAJFs obtained from NEW91 are converted from U.S. dollars to yen using IMF92 (437): U.S.$1 = 134.71 yen.

Large differences between the two series are partly due to different coverage and partly due to the data quality of the old FAJF series. One of the serious problems with the old FAJF series is that not all firms that returned the questionnaire provided figures for all questions (at least for 1991 and 1992) and MITI publicizes total figures only. What we are particularly concerned about is the quality of the calculated value-added estimates. The purchases figures are probably understated in the old FAJF series (at least for 1991 and 1992), though we could not make any adjustment because the numbers of affiliates are unknown for purchases. Lipsey, Blomström, and Ramstetter (chap. 3 in this volume) try to adjust the data for fluctuations in survey coverage using various information from other sources. We do not attempt any such adjustments.

Another difference between MITI and BEA data is that the former data set does not report sales of goods and services separately. In particular, the questionnaire by the International Enterprises Section of MITI does not explicitly specify sales and purchases as "sales and purchases of goods and services," so we are not sure if firms report service transactions. Therefore, in our estimations, we tentatively use merchandise trade (not including service trade) for cross-border trade data.

2.3 Estimation of Aggregate Net Sales

2.3.1 Defining Nationalities

MITI's old FAJF series defines "foreign affiliates of Japanese firms" as firms in which the Japanese have more than a 10 percent share and "majority-owned affiliates" as firms in which the Japanese have more than a 50 percent share. For our purposes, it is better to use data for majority-owned affiliates, but they are not available in time-series form.[6] Thus, we define FAJFs as firms in which the Japanese have more than a 10 percent share. This may cause considerable measurement error, particularly since it is a common practice for Japanese general trading companies to participate in joint ventures between Japanese and foreign companies as third parties with minor shares. For inward DFI, MITI's JAFF series defined "Japanese affiliates of foreign firms" as majority-owned affiliates until the 1990 financial year and as affiliates with more than one-third shares in the 1991 and 1992 financial years.

As in the case of the United States, we do not have data on sales and purchases by foreign citizens in Japan and those by Japanese living abroad. It is therefore necessary to classify households on a country-of-residence basis rather than on a nationality basis.

The term "Japanese" thus refers to Japanese-owned firms in Japan and abroad, households of Japanese and private foreign citizens residing in Japan (Japanese-resident households), and Japanese government units. Similarly, the term "foreigners" refers to foreign-owned firms in Japan and abroad, households of foreign and Japanese citizens residing abroad (foreign-resident households), and foreign governments.

2.3.2 Estimates of Net Sales of the Japanese to Foreigners

Table 2.2 presents estimates of the net sales of the Japanese to foreigners for 1987–92. The table consists of (I) cross-border sales to and purchases from foreigners by the Japanese, (II) sales to and purchases from foreigners by FAJFs, and (III) Japanese sales to and purchases from JAFFs.

In panel I, Japanese cross-border sales (exports) to foreigners are estimated by subtracting the sum of Japanese exports shipped to FAJFs and Japanese

6. The definition of FAJFs in the new FAJF series is "majority owned."

Table 2.2 Net Sales by Japanese to Foreigners, 1987–92 (in millions of yen)

Transaction	1987	1988	1989	1990	1991	1992
I. *Cross-border sales to and purchases from foreigners by Japanese*						
Exports to foreigners						
+ Japanese exports (merchandise only)	33,315,000	33,939,000	37,823,000	41,457,000	42,360,000	43,012,000
− Japanese exports shipped to FAJFs	20,571,156	24,271,567	25,067,600	24,644,049	19,364,991	14,653,484
− Japanese exports shipped by JAFFs	1,029,374	1,495,679	1,259,571	1,885,337	1,921,777	1,841,958
Total	11,714,470	8,171,754	11,495,829	14,927,614	21,073,232	26,516,558
Imports from foreigners						
+ Japanese imports (merchandise only)	21,737,000	24,006,000	28,979,000	33,855,000	31,900,000	29,527,000
− Japanese imports shipped by FAJFs	9,294,170	11,184,629	17,802,290	17,647,431	11,013,452	11,514,761
− Japanese imports shipped to JAFFs	2,820,984	3,198,105	4,122,046	5,714,953	5,381,077	4,724,046
Total	9,621,846	9,623,266	7,054,664	10,492,616	15,505,471	13,288,193
Net cross-border sales to foreigners	2,092,624	−1,451,512	4,441,165	4,434,998	5,567,761	13,228,365
II. *Sales to and purchases from foreigners by FAJFs*						
Sales by FAJFs						
+ Sales by FAJFs	54,808,975	68,426,994	93,177,600	99,806,407	88,737,186	79,007,218
− Sales to other FAJFs	3,354,457	4,795,450	6,228,815	7,800,237	6,570,591	8,455,537
− Japanese imports shipped by FAJFs	9,294,170	11,184,629	17,802,290	17,647,431	11,013,452	11,514,761
Total	42,160,348	52,446,915	69,146,495	74,358,739	71,153,143	59,036,921
Local purchases abroad by FAJFs						
+ Purchases by FAJFs	42,135,754	57,987,023	77,139,161	73,880,197	47,850,264	39,660,435
− Purchases from other FAJFs	3,354,457	4,795,450	6,228,815	7,800,237	6,570,591	8,455,537
− Japanese exports shipped to FAJFs	20,571,156	24,271,567	25,067,600	24,644,049	19,364,991	14,653,484
Total	18,210,141	28,920,006	45,842,746	41,435,911	21,914,682	16,551,414
Net sales to foreigners by FAJFs	23,950,207	23,526,909	23,303,749	32,922,828	49,238,461	42,485,506

(continued)

Table 2.2 (continued)

Transaction	1987	1988	1989	1990	1991	1992
III. *Japanese sales to and purchases from JAFFs*						
Japanese sales to JAFFs						
+ Purchases by JAFFs	6,284,978	7,665,564	9,247,364	12,032,837	12,060,981	11,275,793
− Sales among JAFFs	n.a.	n.a.	n.a.	n.a.	n.a.	n.a.
− Japanese imports shipped to JAFFs	2,820,984	3,198,105	4,122,046	5,714,953	5,381,077	4,724,046
Total	3,463,994	4,467,459	5,125,318	6,317,884	6,679,904	6,551,747
Japanese purchases from JAFFs						
+ Sales by JAFFs	10,420,519	12,292,986	14,003,962	16,810,563	17,792,870	16,300,170
− Sales among JAFFs	n.a.	n.a.	n.a.	n.a.	n.a.	n.a.
− Japanese exports shipped by JAFFs	1,029,374	1,495,679	1,259,571	1,885,337	1,921,777	1,841,958
Total	9,391,145	10,797,307	12,744,391	14,925,226	15,871,093	14,458,212
Net sales to JAFFs	−5,927,151	−6,329,848	−7,619,073	−8,607,342	−9,191,189	−7,906,465
IV. *Net sales by Japanese to foreigners*[a]	20,115,680	15,745,549	20,125,841	28,750,484	45,615,033	47,807,406
	(139,074)	(122,868)	(145,882)	(198,567)	(338,617)	(377,477)
Reference						
Cross-border merchandise trade balance[a]	11,578,000	9,933,000	8,844,000	7,602,000	10,460,000	13,485,000
	(80,047)	(77,511)	(64,106)	(52,504)	(77,648)	(106,475)
Exchange rates (rf; yen per dollar)	144.64	128.15	137.96	144.79	134.71	126.65

Estimation Procedure and Data Sources: In the following figures in parentheses are for 1987, 1988, 1989, 1990, 1991, and 1992, respectively; they are expressed in millions of yen (except exchange rates).

Japanese exports: Merchandise exports only. JSY90 (338), 92 (338), 95 (417): (33,315,000; 33,939,000; 37,823,000; 41,457,000; 42,360,000; 43,012,000).

Japanese exports shipped to FAJFs: One of the shortfalls of the old FAJF series is that firms in the sample report total purchases but many of them fail to report the by-origin disaggregation. E.g., out of total purchases in 1987 (42,135,754), only 38.4 percent (16,189,035) are disaggregated into local purchases (5,880,385), purchases from Japan (7,721,739), and purchases from third countries (2,586,911). We therefore estimate Japanese exports shipped to FAJFs as the sum of sectoral estimates, each of which is derived by multiplying total purchases of the sector by the share of purchases from Japan of the sector (calculated from the limited sample). OLD87/88 (94–95, 202–3), 89 (222–23), 90 (104–5), 91 (100–101), 92 (210–11): (20,571,156; 24,271,567; 25,067,600; 24,644,049; 19,364,991; 14,653,484).

Japanese exports shipped by JAFFs: AF87/88 (71, 225), 89 (73), 90 (77), 91 (75), 92 (79): (1,029,374; 1,495,679; 1,259,571; 1,885,337; 1,921,777; 1,841,958).

Japanese imports: Merchandise imports only. JSY90 (338), 92 (338), 95 (417): (21,737,000; 24,006,000; 28,979,000; 33,855,000; 31,900,000; 29,527,000).

Japanese imports shipped by FAJFs: As in Japanese exports shipped to FAJFs, firms in the sample report total sales but many of them fail to report the by-destination disaggregation. E.g., out of total sales in 1987 (54,808,975), only 42.2 percent (23,144,497) are disaggregated into local sales (15,388,102), sales to Japan (3,770,459), and sales to third countries (3,985,936). We therefore estimate Japanese imports shipped by FAJFs as the sum of sectoral estimates, each of which is derived by multiplying total sales of the sector by the share of sales to Japan of the sector (calculated from the limited sample). OLD87/88 (82–83, 190–91), 89 (210–11), 90 (88–89), 91 (88–89), 92 (198–99): (9,294,170; 11,184,629; 17,802,290; 17,647,431; 11,013,452; 11,514,761).

Japanese imports shipped to JAFFs: AF87/88 (105, 239), 89 (107), 90 (111), 91 (109), 92 (113): (2,820,984; 3,198,105; 4,122,046; 5,714,953; 5,381,077; 4,724,046).

Sales by FAJFs: OLD87/88 (83, 191), 89 (211), 90 (89), 91 (89), 92 (199): (54,808,975; 68,426,994; 93,177,600; 99,806,407; 88,737,186; 79,007,218).

Sales to other FAJFs: Although data on sales among FAJFs are not available, intrafirm transactions between affiliates can be estimated. For 1989, using the same method as in estimating Japanese imports from FAJFs, we first estimate local sales and sales to third countries of each sector. Then, by multiplying ratios of intragroup sales in local sales and sales to third countries of each sector, we can estimate the intrafirm trade of the sector. The sum of sectoral estimates provides a proxy of sales to other FAJFs. For 1987, 1988, 1990, and 1991, ratios of intragroup sales in 1989 are used. OLD87/88 (82–83, 190–91), 89 (210–11, 229), 90 (88–89), 91 (88–89), 92 (198–99, 217): (3,354,457; 4,795,450; 6,228,815; 7,800,237; 6,570,591; 8,455,537).

Purchases by FAJFs: OLD87/88 (95, 203), 89 (223), 90 (105), 91 (101), 92 (211): (42,135,754; 57,987,023; 77,139,161; 73,880,197; 47,850,264; 39,660,435).

Purchases from other FAJFs: Data on purchases among FAJFs are not available. As a proxy, we use sales to other FAJFs estimated above.

Purchases by JAFFs: AF87/88 (105, 239), 89 (107), 90 (111), 91 (109), 92 (113): (6,284,978; 7,665,564; 9,247,364; 12,032,837; 12,060,981; 11,275,793).

Sales among JAFFs: Not available.

Sales by JAFFs: AF87/88 (71,225), 89 (73), 90 (77), 91 (75), 92 (79): (10,420,519; 12,292,986; 14,003,962; 16,810,563; 17,792,870; 16,300,170).

Exchange rates: Yen per dollar (rf series). IMF92 (437), 94 (316): (144.64; 128.15; 137.96; 144.79; 134.71; 126.65).

Notes: FAJFs: Foreign affiliates of Japanese firms abroad, which include affiliates in which the Japanese have more than a 10 percent share and affiliates in which Japanese majority-owned affiliates have more than a 50 percent share. Only the parent firm with the largest share reports the figures. Only affiliates whose parent companies are in industries other than finance, insurance, and real estate are covered. Coverage of affiliate data (in terms of number of affiliates) for 1987–92 is 79.4, 78.8, 72.3, 78.2, 78.5, and 65.5 percent.

JAFFs: Majority-owned (with more than a one-third share from 1991 fiscal year) Japanese affiliates of foreign firms in Japan, which report their direct investment to MITI and have foreign participation in management. Coverage of affiliate data (in terms of number of affiliates) for 1987–92 is 50.1, 52.3, 51.8, 51.8, 51.9 and, 53.7 percent.

Years: Japanese exports and imports are on a calendar-year basis, while data for FAJFs and JAFFs are on a financial-year basis.

[a]Figures in parentheses are in millions of dollars.

exports shipped by JAFFs from cross-border exports of Japan valued on an f.o.b. basis. The estimate of such cross-border sales (exports) in 1987, for example, is 11,714 billion yen, which is much smaller than Japan's cross-border exports of 33,315 billion yen.

Quite aside from the above-mentioned coverage problem, the 11,714 billion yen figure is, for several reasons, still only an approximation. The most serious problem is that the figure for Japanese exports shipped to FAJFs (20,571 billion yen) is a very rough estimate. Among FAJFs reporting the total amount of purchases are many that do not provide figures for purchases disaggregated by origin; that is, a considerable portion of FAJFs do not report separately local purchases, purchases from Japan, and purchases from third countries. In 1987, for example, only 38.4 percent of total purchases by FAJFs can be disaggregated by origin. We, hence, first calculate the ratio of purchases from Japan to total purchases for firms in each sector reporting purchases by origin. Then we multiply that ratio by total purchases by all firms in the sector and sum up all sectors' estimates of purchases from Japan. Another potential estimation problem concerns the treatment of purchases by FAJFs from commercial FAJFs. When an FAJF in the commercial sector imports intermediate goods and sells them to a noncommercial FAJF, both the commercial and noncommercial FAJFs may treat these purchases as purchases from abroad. This means that the purchases ratios from Japan (and those from third countries) may be overstated to some extent. The estimation of purchases by FAJFs from Japan or Japanese exports shipped to FAJFs (20,571 billion yen) in 1987 may therefore differ from the true figure. In addition, exports by JAFFs to FAJFs are subtracted twice in this calculation since they are included in both Japanese exports shipped to FAJFs and Japanese exports shipped by JAFFs. This, however, probably does not affect our estimates very much.[7]

The lower half of panel I of table 2.2 shows our estimates of Japanese cross-border purchases (imports) from foreigners, namely, 9,622 billion yen in 1987. These are again much smaller than cross-border imports (21,737 billion yen). They are calculated by subtracting the sum of Japanese imports shipped by FAJFs and Japanese imports shipped to JAFFs from Japanese cross-border imports valued on a c.i.f. basis. Again, the estimates of Japanese imports shipped by FAJFs or sales to Japan by FAJFs (9,294 billion yen) may contain large errors. Since a large portion of FAJFs do not report by-destination disaggregation of their sales (to the local market, to Japan, and to third countries), sales by FAJFs to Japan are estimated by calculating the ratio of sales to Japan to total sales for each industrial sector, multiplying this ratio by total sales of the

7. Possible errors listed in this paragraph do not affect our estimation of Japanese net sales to foreigners shown in panel IV of table 2.2. As Lois Steckler of the Board of Governors points out in personal correspondence, Japanese net sales to foreigners are conceptually equivalent to cross-border net exports plus FAJF value added (sales minus purchases) minus JAFF value added (sales minus purchases). The possible error terms cancel out in the calculation of Japanese net sales to foreigners.

sector, and summing up all sectors' estimates of sales to Japan. Again, the ratios of sales to Japan to total sales may be overstated due to double counting in the transactions through commercial FAJFs. In addition, Japanese imports from FAJFs shipped to JAFFs are subtracted twice.[8]

By subtracting 9,622 billion yen from 11,714 billion yen, we obtain Japanese net cross-border sales to foreigners, 2,093 billion yen in 1987. Our estimates are considerably smaller than the cross-border trade balance, except in 1992.

Panel II of table 2.2 presents estimates of sales and purchases by FAJFs to and from foreigners. To obtain sales by FAJFs to foreigners (42,160 billion yen in 1987), we subtract from their total sales both sales among themselves and their sales to Japan. Data on sales among FAJFs are not available. However, intragroup sales of FAJFs to local markets and third countries, which are a part of sales among FAJFs, can be estimated. The old FAJF series for the years 1989 and 1992 gives shares of intragroup sales of FAJFs (to local markets, to Japan, and to third countries) to total sales of FAJFs for each sector. By multiplying each sector's total sales by these shares and adding them across sectors, we obtain proxies for sales among FAJFs. Since these shares are available only for 1989 and 1992, the 1989 shares are used for 1987–88 and 1990–91. The other term to be subtracted, Japanese imports shipped by FAJFs, may contain a large error, as discussed above.

Purchases by FAJFs from foreigners abroad (18,210 billion yen in 1987) are calculated by subtracting from their total purchases both purchases from other FAJFs and Japanese exports shipped to FAJFs. Data on purchases by FAJFs are directly available, which is an advantage the Japanese statistics have compared with U.S. BEA statistics. The next term, purchases from other FAJFs by FAJFs, is not directly available. We use intragroup sales of FAJFs to local and third countries, estimated above, as a proxy.[9] The other terms to be subtracted, Japanese exports shipped to FAJFs, may contain large estimation errors for the above-mentioned reasons. Our estimation of net sales by FAJFs to foreigners is 23,950 billion yen for 1987.

Panel III of table 2.2 presents the estimates of net sales of Japanese to JAFFs, which were −5,927 billion yen in 1987. Again, the JAFF series published by MITI directly provide data on purchases by JAFFs. Sales among JAFFs, however, are not available. We thus calculate Japanese sales to JAFFs (3,464 billion yen in 1987) by subtracting Japanese imports shipped to JAFFs from total purchases by JAFFs. Japanese purchases from JAFFs (9,391 billion yen in 1987) are obtained by subtracting Japanese exports shipped by JAFFs from total sales by JAFFs.

By summing up these three components, we obtain estimates of net sales to foreigners by the Japanese, for example, 20,116 billion yen in 1987 (panel IV).

8. These possible errors do not affect our estimation of Japanese net sales to foreigners.

9. Intragroup purchases from local and third countries can be estimated in a symmetric manner. However, the estimates differ from intragroup sales to local and third countries, though these must be equivalent in principle.

Despite the possible differences from the true figures, our nationality-based account characterizes various key feature of the Japanese economy. First, the asymmetry between FAJFs and JAFFs is apparent. As often pointed out (see, e.g., Lawrence 1993; Bergsten and Noland 1993, 79–82), the activities of JAFFs are much smaller than those of FAJFs. Second, net sales by the Japanese to foreigners are consistently larger than cross-border net sales (exports). This, of course, is due to the greater activity of FAJFs compared with JAFFs. According to our estimates, nationality-adjusted net sales grew at a considerably faster pace than cross-border net sales between 1988 and 1992.[10] The strong yen, the saving-investment balance, the "bubble economy," the competitive edge vis-à-vis the exchange rate, and fear of foreign protectionism seem to have accelerated Japanese outward DFI. Third, compared with the United States, the proportion of cross-border transactions through foreign affiliates is large. Based on our estimates for 1987, U.S. exports and imports through foreign affiliates of U.S. firms (FAUSFs) were 25.1 and 15.2 percent of total U.S. exports and imports, while Japanese exports and imports through FAJFs were 61.7 and 42.8 percent of total Japanese exports and imports. Although the ratio on the export side for Japan declined sharply to 34.1 percent in 1992, both ratios were still higher than those for the United States.[11] As we mentioned, our estimates of by-destination sales and by-origin purchases of FAJFs could contain large errors, but we can still infer that Japan depends on its foreign affiliates in export and import transactions much more extensively than the United States does. Activities by FAJFs in the commercial sector are particularly important. According to our estimates, Japanese exports and imports through commercial FAJFs amounted to 48.2 and 36.0 percent of total Japanese exports and imports in 1987. We discuss commercial FAJFs further in section 2.5.

2.3.3 Estimates of Value Added by FAJFs and JAFFs

The same data set that we used in constructing table 2.2 can also be used to estimate value added by FAJFs and JAFFs. Since the old FAJF and JAFF series published by MITI directly report total sales and purchases by FAJFs and JAFFs, value added can be calculated by simply subtracting total purchases from total sales. Strictly speaking, we need to take into consideration such factors as depreciation, indirect taxes, and changes in inventory stock, but data on these variables are not available. Table 2.3 presents our estimates. The format of the table follows that used in our companion paper for the United States.

10. The estimate of nationality-adjusted sales for 1988 is particularly small, while those for 1991 and 1992 look very large. This fluctuation is mainly due to changes in the value added by FAJFs, which may contain large estimation errors. We, however, can at least conclude that the activities of JAFFs expanded until 1990.

11. The decline in the estimated ratio on the export side for 1992 may be due to the understatement of purchases by FAJFs.

Table 2.3 also reports ratios of value added by FAJFs to value added by all Japanese-owned firms, the latter being defined as Japanese GDP plus value added by FAJFs minus value added by JAFFs, and ratios of value added by JAFFs to the GDP of Japan.[12] The ratio of value added by FAJFs to value added by all Japanese-owned firms increased during the period, but the figures of 8.33 and 7.87 percent for 1991 and 1992 may be overstated due to a purchases figure that is unusually low compared with the corresponding sales figure.[13] We can, however, conclude that Japanese firms have increased the extent of production abroad and have reached roughly the same degree of internationalization of activities as U.S. firms have. As reported in our companion paper, the ratio of value added by FAUSFs to that of U.S.-owned firms ranges from 5 to 6 percent. The ratio of value added by JAFFs to Japanese GDP, in contrast, is generally only a little larger than 1 percent. The asymmetry between the behavior of FAJFs and JAFFs is obvious.

The proportion of foreign activities by Japanese firms is often measured by the foreign production ratio, which is defined as the ratio of the value of production of FAJFs to total domestic production. The figure for the manufacturing sector in the 1993 fiscal year, for example, is estimated as 6.4 percent by MITI (1994d, 46). The value of production, however, includes the value of intermediate inputs and thus is not appropriate for measuring the size of economic activities in Japan and abroad. Our value-added method is conceptually better for indicating the proportion of foreign activities of Japanese firms, although it may contain considerable measurement error due to the quality of data.

2.3.4 Comparison of Exports and Direct Foreign Investment on a Value-Added Basis

In other empirical studies, firms' choices between exports and DFI are usually captured by comparing basically incomparable figures, namely, exports and DFI flows. Our value-added method makes it possible to compare directly two ways in which firms can sell their products to foreigners abroad: by producing domestically and exporting and by producing abroad and selling there.

Following the companion paper for the United States, we calculate Japanese value-added figures in exports of Japanese-owned firms. They are useful in comparing the proportion of Japanese firms' sales activities to foreigners through cross-border transactions and through the activities of FAJFs. To obtain the estimates, we subtract exports by JAFFs from total cross-border ex-

12. Value added by Japanese-owned firms as well as Japanese GDP includes production that takes place outside firms, such as in the government and household sectors.

13. As mentioned in the note to table 2.1, the 1991 data on sales and purchases provided by the new FAJF series suggest much smaller value added by FAJFs. The ratios of value added by FAJFs to sales under the old FAJF series in table 2.3 also look too large for 1991 and 1992. This discrepancy may be due to the small number of FAJFs providing purchases figures, though this cannot be proved from published documents.

Table 2.3 **Value Added by FAJF and JAFF, 1987–92 (in millions of yen)**

Transaction	1987	1988	1989	1990	1991	1992
I. *Value added by FAJFs*						
+ Sales by FAJFs	54,808,975	68,426,994	93,177,600	99,806,407	88,737,186	79,007,218
– Local purchases abroad by FAJFs	18,210,141	28,920,006	45,842,746	41,435,911	21,914,682	16,551,414
– Japanese exports shipped to FAJFs	20,571,156	24,271,567	25,067,600	24,644,049	19,364,991	14,653,484
– Purchases from other FAJFs	3,354,457	4,795,450	6,228,815	7,800,237	6,570,591	8,455,537
Total	12,673,221	10,439,971	16,038,439	25,926,210	40,886,922	39,346,783
In goods and services sold to						
Japanese	2,924,682	2,438,096	4,136,417	6,610,413	8,102,098	9,945,509
Foreigners	9,748,539	8,001,875	11,902,022	19,315,797	32,784,824	29,401,274
Received by						
Japanese	n.a.	n.a.	n.a.	n.a.	n.a.	n.a.
Foreigners	n.a.	n.a.	n.a.	n.a.	n.a.	n.a.
Value added/sales ratio (%)	23.12	15.26	17.21	25.98	46.08	49.80
II. *Japanese value added in exports of Japanese-owned firms*[a]	28,940,835	29,082,193	32,775,458	35,472,039	36,904,826	36,248,823
In export to FAJFs	18,439,984	21,757,033	22,470,597	22,090,926	17,672,923	12,901,895
In exports to foreigners	10,500,851	7,325,160	10,304,861	13,381,113	19,231,902	23,346,928
III. *Value added by JAFFs*						
+ Sales by JAFFs	10,420,519	12,292,986	14,003,962	16,810,563	17,792,870	16,300,170
– Purchases within Japan by JAFFs	3,463,994	4,467,459	5,125,318	6,317,884	6,679,904	6,551,747
– Japanese imports shipped to JAFFs	2,820,984	3,198,105	4,122,046	5,714,953	5,381,077	4,724,046
– Purchases from other JAFFs	n.a.	n.a.	n.a.	n.a.	n.a.	n.a.
Total	4,135,541	4,627,422	4,756,598	4,777,726	5,731,889	5,024,377

In goods and services sold to						
Japanese	3,727,018	4,064,407	5,328,771	4,241,895	5,112,798	4,456,610
Foreigners	408,523	563,015	427,827	535,831	619,091	567,767
Received by						
Japanese	n.a.	n.a.	n.a.	n.a.	n.a.	n.a.
Foreigners	n.a.	n.a.	n.a.	n.a.	n.a.	n.a.
Value added/sales ratio (%)	39.69	37.64	33.97	28.42	32.21	30.82
IV. *Value added in exporting country by foreign-owned firms*[a]	11,153,753	11,493,077	10,018,803	14,528,465	18,722,702	16,146,171
In exports to Japanese	8,625,023	8,626,296	6,323,801	9,405,581	13,899,104	11,911,536
In exports to JAFFs	2,528,730	2,866,781	3,695,002	5,122,884	4,823,597	4,234,635
Reference						
GDP of Japan	353,989,000	376,889,000	402,311,000	432,862,000	455,862,000	465,431,000
Ratio of value added of FAJFs to that of Japanese-owned firms (%)	3.50	2.73	3.88	5.71	8.33	7.87
Ratio of value added to JAFFs to Japanese GDP (%)	1.17	1.23	1.18	1.10	1.26	1.08

Data Sources: GDP of Japan: JSY92 (555), 95 (142). See estimation procedure and data source note to table 2.2 for other data.

Notes: Value added of Japanese-owned firms = GDP of Japan + value added of FAJFs − value added of JAFFs.
All data are on a financial-year (April–March) basis.

[a]Figures in panels II and IV are estimated using the import inducement coefficient of export (10.36 percent) obtained from IO90 (321, 388). See the text for details.

ports and then subtract the import component in the remaining exports.[14] In Japan, input-output tables are presented in the non-competitive-import form and hence directly provide the import inducement coefficient of exports or the direct and indirect import content of exports. This was 10.36 percent in 1990. By using this figure for 1987–92, Japanese value added in exports of Japanese-owned firms can be calculated. This amounted to 28,941 billion yen in 1987, for example. Out of the 28,941 billion yen, 10,501 billion yen was the value added in exports by Japanese firms located in Japan to foreigners abroad. This figure is directly comparable with the 9,749 billion yen of value added in the goods and services sold by FAJFs to foreigners. There are two ways for Japanese firms to sell their products to foreigners: by producing in Japan and exporting and by producing abroad and selling there. The comparison between 10,501 billion yen and 9,749 billion yen provides a clear idea of the relative importance of these two marketing methods. Compared with the same figures for the United States reported in Baldwin and Kimura (chap. 1), transactions by Japanese foreign affiliates are more important, mainly because the ratio of exports by FAJFs to total exports is large. Even after discounting the large estimates of value added by FAJFs in 1991 and 1992, transactions by FAJFs seem to be becoming more important over time.

Value added in exporting countries by foreign-owned firms is estimated in a similar way. Because input-output tables for the rest of the world are not available, the figure for Japan, 10.36 percent, is tentatively used. The estimate of value added in exporting countries by foreign-owned firms abroad is 11,154 billion yen in 1987. Out of this, value added in foreign exports to the Japanese in Japan is 8,625 billion yen. This figure can be directly compared with 3,727 billion yen, which is the value added in goods and services sold by JAFFs to the Japanese in Japan. The importance of transactions through JAFFs seems to be declining over time.

2.4 Estimation of Sectoral Net Sales

2.4.1 Sectoral Net Sales

In this section, we estimate nationality-based net sales by individual industrial sectors. We believe that they provide a better idea of firms' international competitiveness determined by technological know-how and managerial ability than cross-border net exports do.

A problem arising in sectoral matching of DFI figures and trade statistics is that affiliate data are classified by industry while cross-border trade data are classified by commodity. This difference leads to a serious problem, particu-

14. Precisely speaking, we must consider the JAFF component in these exports to avoid double counting, but the data are not available.

larly in the treatment of the commercial sector. We therefore estimate net sales only for the manufacturing sector.

Nationality-adjusted sales for individual sectors are calculated as follows:

Nationality-adjusted sales = Japan' s cross-border exports
+ sales by FAJFs + purchases by JAFFs
− Japan' s exports shipped to FAJFs
− Japan' s imports shipped by FAJFs
− sales to other FAJFs by FAJFs
− Japan' s exports shipped by JAFFs
− Japan' s imports shipped to JAFFs.

On the other hand, nationality-adjusted purchases for individual sectors are defined as follows:

Nationality-adjusted purchases = Japan' s cross-border imports
+ sales by JAFFs + purchases by FAJFs
− Japan' s exports shipped to FAJFs
− Japan' s imports shipped by FAJFs
− purchases from other FAJFs by FAJFs
− Japan' s exports shipped by JAFFs
− Japan' s imports shipped to JAFFs.

Nationality-adjusted net sales are calculated by subtracting nationality-adjusted purchases from nationality-adjusted sales. We assume that each industry purchases intermediate inputs only from its own industry, since data on sectoral purchases by industrial origin are not available. This is, of course, a strong assumption, but it should roughly hold for the manufacturing sector. Nationality-adjusted net sales of an individual industrial sector then become equivalent to cross-border net sales (exports) plus value added by FAJFs minus value added by JAFFs for the sector. By following this estimation procedure, possible estimation errors in by-destination sales and by-origin purchases by FAJFs and JAFFs cancel out in the calculation.[15]

Table 2.4 presents cross-border net sales, nationality-adjusted net sales, and their ratios to the corresponding total sales (of all firms in Japan or of all Japanese-owned firms). To be consistent with the macroeconomic figures, we

15. The sector matching list between our industry (commodity) classification and SITC Revision 2 is available upon request.

Table 2.4 **Cross-Border and Nationality-Adjusted Net Sales by Sector**

	Cross-Border Net Sales[a]						Nationality-Adjusted Net Sales[a]					
Sector	1987	1988	1989	1990	1991	1992	1987	1988	1989	1990	1991	1992
Total	11,528,693	9,939,713	8,874,690	7,550,636	10,478,920	13,504,594	20,066,373	15,752,262	20,156,531	28,699,120	45,633,953	47,827,000
Manufacturing	21,297,715	19,675,032	20,204,591	20,925,081	22,848,678	24,918,951	21,589,169	21,055,289	23,208,815	28,484,365	33,803,547	36,509,672
Food processing	−1,101,196	−1,310,955	−1,584,472	−1,707,678	−1,752,546	−1,826,175	−1,085,176	−1,269,383	−1,542,527	−1,573,097	−1,656,842	−1,647,090
Textiles	−324,978	−718,266	−1,133,064	−1,058,343	−1,017,400	−1,099,777	−214,835	−538,177	−993,237	−607,435	−541,197	−760,918
Chemicals	−296,351	−375,906	−391,840	−333,545	−336,878	−196,899	−704,518	−796,094	−941,477	−393,287	−258,662	94,310
Basic metals	905,759	455,336	281,819	62,211	115,725	637,167	1,380,705	948,252	616,772	600,633	473,811	1,365,507
General machinery	6,270,341	6,767,426	7,705,274	8,051,638	8,379,562	8,813,466	6,209,419	6,948,108	8,000,782	9,344,367	10,164,196	9,161,093
Electrical machinery	6,114,123	6,393,681	6,880,890	7,282,399	7,477,108	7,424,773	6,489,225	7,219,511	7,218,124	9,788,039	10,709,812	10,186,766
Transport equipment	8,576,168	7,640,115	8,223,757	8,784,646	9,085,143	9,731,532	9,071,394	8,349,570	9,760,246	10,850,617	13,139,792	15,183,381
Precision machinery	1,261,682	1,260,404	1,347,500	1,411,273	1,470,442	1,428,276	1,302,296	1,450,029	1,516,363	1,398,055	1,625,172	1,383,764
Petroleum and coal products	−1,059,410	−982,160	−1,228,198	−1,444,532	−1,011,156	−741,460	−2,187,322	−2,211,888	−1,717,838	−1,941,294	−1,630,928	−746,129
Other manufacturing	951,576	545,357	102,925	−122,988	438,679	748,050	1,327,980	955,361	1,291,607	1,017,767	1,778,394	2,288,990
Others	−9,769,022	−9,735,318	−11,329,901	−13,374,444	−12,369,758	−11,414,357	−1,522,796	−5,303,026	−3,052,284	214,756	11,830,403	11,317,328

Sector	Cross-Border Net Sales/Total Sales[b]						Nationality-Adjusted Net Sales/Total Sales[b]					
	1987	1988	1989	1990	1991	1992	1987	1988	1989	1990	1991	1992
Total	1.79	1.44	1.18	0.92	1.22	1.57	2.91	2.10	2.42	3.19	4.90	5.19
Manufacturing	7.75	6.63	6.27	6.01	6.24	7.09	7.70	6.88	6.92	7.83	8.88	9.96
Food processing	−3.39	−3.93	−4.61	−4.74	−4.66	−4.74	−3.33	−3.77	−4.44	−4.33	−4.39	−4.24
Textiles	−4.50	−9.66	−15.10	−14.00	−13.48	−15.15	−2.82	−6.75	−12.69	−7.37	−6.63	−9.83
Chemicals	−1.35	−1.62	−1.56	−1.25	−1.22	−0.71	−3.28	−3.51	−3.90	−1.50	−0.97	0.35
Basic metals	3.04	1.37	0.78	0.16	0.30	1.90	4.49	2.76	1.65	1.52	1.19	3.93
General machinery	22.04	20.59	20.70	19.08	18.35	20.91	21.75	20.76	21.13	20.85	21.40	21.29
Electrical machinery	15.29	14.35	14.16	13.99	13.32	14.33	15.04	14.73	13.57	17.01	17.27	17.93
Transport equipment	25.38	21.43	20.54	20.00	19.72	20.58	24.65	21.33	20.80	21.36	24.81	27.13
Precision machinery	32.17	29.81	29.44	28.40	27.64	29.80	32.55	28.41	31.23	29.81	29.96	29.35
Petroleum and coal products	−10.40	−9.90	−11.37	−11.42	−7.83	−5.99	−28.92	−29.87	−21.40	−21.24	−17.05	−7.67
Other manufacturing	1.42	0.76	0.13	−0.15	0.50	0.87	1.95	1.30	1.61	1.18	1.96	2.60
Others	−4.70	−4.37	−4.65	−5.12	−4.54	−4.11	−0.37	−1.20	−0.61	0.04	2.15	2.04

Data Sources: OLD87/88, 89, 90, 91, 92; AF87/88, 89, 90, 91, 92; EPA94; IMF92; UN90, 92.

Notes: Cross-border net sales / total sales = ratio of cross-border net exports to sales by all firms in Japan.

Nationality-adjused net sales / total sales = ratio of nationality-adjusted net sales to sales by Japanese-owned firms (all firms in Japan + FAJFs − JAFFs).

The old FAJF and JAFF series are on a financial-year basis, while the others are on a calendar-year basis.

[a]In millions of yen.

[b]Percentage.

use sectoral data on the value of output (in producer prices) obtained from the national accounts statistics as a proxy for the total sales of all firms in Japan.[16] The figures for aggregate cross-border net sales are slightly different from those for the cross-border merchandise trade balance shown in table 2.2 because the former are based on UN data reported in U.S. dollars while the latter are from the *Japan Statistical Yearbook* reported in yen. The other data are taken directly from the FAJF and JAFF series published by MITI.

For the manufacturing sector as a whole, net sales figures, both cross-border and nationality-adjusted, are positive as expected. However, whereas the ratios of nationality-adjusted net sales to total sales have increased since 1989, those of cross-border sales have not changed much. This suggests that the international competitiveness of Japanese manufacturing firms has increased, while that of firms in territorial Japan has not. We again have to note reservations about the 1991–92 figures, however. As for sectoral patterns, large positive net sales, both cross-border and nationality-adjusted, are found in general machinery, electrical machinery, transport equipment, and precision machinery, and negative net sales are shown for food processing, textiles, chemicals (except nationality-adjusted net sales in 1992), and petroleum and coal products. The ratios of nationality-adjusted net sales to total sales sometimes exhibit significant sudden changes, for example, textiles in 1989 and petroleum and coal products in 1992, even though the ratios of cross-border net sales to total sales do not change appreciably. Such jumps are mainly caused by drastic increases in sectoral value added by FAJFs.

2.4.2 Sectoral Significance of FAJFs and JAFFs

The macroeconomic significance of the activities of FAJFs and JAFFs has already been discussed. The sectoral significance of the activities of FAJFs and JAFFs can be evaluated by using sectoral data on output, value added, and employment in the Japanese national accounts statistics. Table 2.5 presents shares of FAJFs in Japanese-owned firms (firms in Japan minus JAFFs plus FAJFs) and shares of JAFFs in firms in Japan in terms of sales, value added, and employment.

Although there are some irregular up and downs partly due to the sampling problem, the figures still provide useful information for analyzing differences in the relative importance of FAJFs and JAFFs across manufacturing subsectors and across time. The value-added shares are particularly useful for comparative purposes. The major findings are as follows: first, the value-added share of FAJFs in Japanese-owned firms for the total manufacturing sector increased from 3.76 percent in 1987, to 8.57 percent in 1990, and then to 10.76 percent by 1992. The importance of the activities of foreign affiliates for

16. Alternatively, we can use sales data from "Financial Statements of Corporations by Industry" by the Ministry of Finance or value of shipments data from the "Census of Manufactures" collected by MITI, though the figures differ widely mainly due to the difference in coverage and the definition of firms or establishments.

Table 2.5 **Sales, Value Added, and Employment Shares of FAJFs and JAFFs (percent)**

	Share of FAJFs in Japanese-Owned Firms						Share of JAFFs in Firms in Japan					
	1987	1988	1989	1990	1991	1992	1987	1988	1989	1990	1991	1992
						Sales						
Total	7.39	8.52	10.47	10.40	8.91	7.99	1.50	1.65	1.73	1.92	1.92	1.76
Manufacturing	4.66	5.76	6.64	7.21	6.66	6.85	2.68	2.76	2.86	3.08	2.90	2.88
Food processing	0.84	1.35	1.49	1.37	1.31	1.43	0.64	0.61	0.56	0.57	0.81	0.56
Textiles	5.37	6.90	4.32	8.63	8.29	6.53	0.18	0.12	0.18	0.34	0.86	0.37
Chemicals	4.53	5.30	5.37	6.93	7.07	6.26	6.40	7.76	9.28	8.87	10.28	8.87
Basic metals	3.55	4.29	4.23	4.05	3.55	4.46	0.25	0.92	0.84	0.87	0.99	1.21
General machinery	3.03	3.30	2.95	7.10	4.98	2.86	2.70	1.55	1.25	1.38	1.20	0.83
Electrical machinery	10.97	13.07	12.74	13.83	13.07	12.88	3.96	4.36	4.47	4.72	4.00	4.44
Transport equipment	8.72	9.66	15.40	13.74	13.23	15.97	0.59	0.80	0.86	0.25	0.26	0.55
Precision machinery	5.22	20.78	9.23	9.05	7.47	6.42	3.31	4.37	3.68	14.15	5.65	7.93
Petroleum and coal products	0.96	0.22	0.16	0.26	1.46	6.57	26.46	25.53	25.80	27.93	27.01	26.53
Other manufacturing	1.80	2.15	3.68	3.48	3.16	2.71	0.42	0.57	0.57	0.46	0.37	0.53
Commerce	37.22	40.57	47.21	46.59	41.07	36.02	4.15	5.13	5.80	6.64	7.29	6.13
Services	0.28	0.40	0.44	0.70	0.88	0.88	0.04	0.07	0.04	0.09	0.31	0.26
Others	0.62	0.82	1.44	1.11	1.14	1.12	0.05	0.08	0.06	0.11	0.05	0.04

(*continued*)

Table 2.5 (continued)

	Share of FAJFs in Japanese-Owned Firms						Share of JAFFs in Firms in Japan					
	1987	1988	1989	1990	1991	1992	1987	1988	1989	1990	1991	1992
					Value Added							
Total	3.54	2.75	3.92	5.79	8.40	7.94	1.18	1.24	1.19	1.12	1.27	1.09
Manufacturing	3.76	4.70	5.84	8.57	10.53	10.76	3.48	3.47	3.37	2.98	3.07	2.77
Food processing	0.99	1.32	1.31	1.98	2.14	2.10	0.86	0.99	0.98	1.00	1.47	0.91
Textiles	4.30	6.61	6.06	16.54	17.54	12.08	0.07	0.04	0.31	0.60	1.12	0.47
Chemicals	3.51	4.46	5.39	9.64	13.57	11.18	8.21	8.97	10.65	10.18	12.91	8.74
Basic metals	6.33	6.44	4.63	7.55	6.63	10.47	0.44	1.24	1.31	2.38	3.28	3.37
General machinery	2.21	2.21	2.78	8.08	9.75	3.19	2.77	0.79	0.72	0.61	0.44	1.08
Electrical machinery	8.84	10.96	11.05	17.25	18.03	17.29	6.47	6.31	9.33	6.31	5.07	5.09
Transport equipment	5.30	6.92	12.21	14.60	24.30	29.66	0.74	0.76	0.40	0.28	0.31	0.69
Precision machinery	5.68	13.41	11.12	12.71	12.13	6.38	3.31	4.04	3.25	13.29	5.77	8.56
Petroleum and coal products	0.52	0.13	0.06	0.21	2.09	11.98	27.84	30.59	11.45	11.43	14.03	12.06
Other manufacturing	1.80	2.02	4.34	3.69	3.89	4.46	0.45	0.65	0.69	0.49	0.40	0.52
Commerce	15.05	8.96	13.83	17.75	28.83	26.71	1.33	1.67	1.61	1.47	2.48	2.03
Services	0.22	0.27	0.35	0.90	1.01	1.22	0.02	0.04	0.01	0.09	0.26	0.20
Others	0.55	0.34	0.58	1.36	1.20	1.04	0.04	0.06	0.05	0.13	0.04	0.04

Employment												
Total	1.84	2.05	1.76	2.30	2.36	2.03	0.25	0.27	0.27	0.28	0.30	0.28
Manufacturing	5.86	6.68	5.80	7.49	7.39	6.61	0.84	0.89	0.92	0.93	0.97	0.96
Food processing	1.56	1.91	1.81	2.03	2.03	1.84	0.27	0.18	0.19	0.22	0.28	0.22
Textiles	7.37	8.34	4.68	7.36	7.61	7.37	0.02	0.01	0.02	0.14	0.16	0.14
Chemicals	11.37	12.26	11.03	14.00	14.86	13.18	6.23	8.41	9.63	9.11	10.51	9.64
Basic metals	10.47	12.31	11.25	9.62	8.48	8.53	0.27	0.77	0.75	0.76	0.97	1.00
General machinery	3.40	3.78	3.15	4.85	3.51	2.67	1.48	0.76	0.68	0.73	0.81	0.50
Electrical machinery	12.68	13.82	11.45	14.86	14.81	13.55	1.84	2.04	2.00	2.19	1.95	2.10
Transport equipment	9.29	11.63	9.48	13.47	14.32	13.30	0.23	0.32	0.38	0.20	0.20	0.33
Precision machinery	5.91	10.63	6.39	8.55	7.82	3.66	1.22	1.34	1.12	1.50	1.98	2.35
Petroleum and coal products	4.75	12.05	0.82	13.29	13.62	2.05	22.88	21.57	20.37	20.40	18.65	19.19
Other manufacturing	2.17	2.20	3.11	3.57	3.43	2.99	0.12	0.14	0.17	0.14	0.11	0.14
Commerce	1.53	1.52	1.16	1.50	1.99	1.34	0.20	0.25	0.23	0.24	0.33	0.25
Services	0.18	0.17	0.22	0.34	0.26	0.32	0.01	0.01	0.01	0.02	0.05	0.04
Others	0.29	0.30	0.28	0.33	0.33	0.30	0.03	0.03	0.02	0.03	0.02	0.01

Data Sources: OLD87/88, 89, 90, 91, 92; AF87/88, 89, 90, 91, 92; EPA94.

Japanese-owned manufacturing firms does not appear to be as extensive as for U.S.-owned firms, but it has been increasing. We again need to discount the figures for 1991 and 1992, however. The share of JAFFs in the activities of all firms in Japan has been low and nearly constant. The asymmetry of inward and outward DFI is also apparent at the sectoral level.

Second, industries of comparative advantage for Japan, such as electrical machinery and transport equipment, have rapidly increased the ratio of value added in FAJFs to that in Japanese-owned firms. In 1992, the ratios were as high as 17.29 and 29.66 percent for electrical machinery and transport equipment. The value-added shares of JAFFs to firms in Japan, in contrast, started from a low level in 1987 and remained low in 1992—for example, 5.09 and 0.69 percent in electrical machinery and transport equipment, respectively. The value-added shares of FAJFs to Japanese-owned firms for general machinery and precision machinery show some anomalies in 1992; in that year, value added by FAJFs in these industries decreased drastically. We are not sure whether this apparent decrease is due to a small, unstable sample, to industry reclassification of firms, or to changes in firms' strategies.

Third, in industries of comparative disadvantage for Japan, such as textiles and chemicals, the shares of FAJFs in Japanese-owned firms have also increased. The share of JAFFs in firms in Japan also increased in the chemical industry up to 1991. Large outward and inward DFI characterizes the chemical industry in the case of the United States, and the Japanese chemical industry seems to behave in the same manner.

2.5 Commercial FAJFs and the Presence of General Trading Companies

A special feature of foreign affiliates of Japanese firms is the large presence of commercial FAJFs in the commercial sector, particularly in the wholesale trade sector. Table 2.6 presents a Japan-U.S. comparison of manufacturing and commercial affiliates in 1991. The table classifies industries both for parent companies and for foreign affiliates. FAJFs in the wholesale trade sector had 75 and 56 percent shares in all FAJFs in terms of sales and value added, while FAUSFs in the wholesale trade sector (excluding petroleum wholesale trade) had shares of 18 and 12 percent.[17] Although the figures for FAUSFs would be larger if the wholesale petroleum trade were included, the figures for FAJFs are still much larger than those for FAUSFs. FAJFs in the wholesale trade sector are also characterized by high value added per employee compared with FAUSFs.

17. It should be noted that FAJFs do not include affiliates (or parent companies) in the finance, insurance, and real estate sectors, while FAUSFs do include affiliates (or parent companies) in the finance (excluding banking), insurance, and real estate sectors. We should also take into account that affiliates in the service sector have a larger share in the case of FAUSFs than in the case of FAJFs.

Table 2.6 Comparison of Manufacturing and Commercial Affiliates: Japan and the United States, 1991

Industry	Affiliates		Sales		Value Added[a]		Employment		Average Number of Employees	Value-Added Ratio[b] (%)	Value-Added Productivity[c] ($)	By-Destination Shares in Sales (%)			By-Origin Shares in Purchases (%)	
	Number	%	Millions of Dollars	%	Millions of Dollars	%	Number	%				Local	Japan/US	Third Countries	Local	Imports
							Foreign Affiliates[d] of Japanese Firms (FAJFs)									
							By Parent Companies' Classification									
All industries	2,851	100.00	498,193	100.00	98,105	100.00	919,294	100.00	322	19.69	106,718	65.47	14.24	20.29	27.84	72.16
Manufacturing	2,119	74.32	240,706	48.32	67,213	68.51	741,615	80.67	350	27.92	90,631	78.10	8.36	13.54	36.85	63.15
Wholesale and retail trade	710	24.90	256,964	51.58	30,645	31.24	174,829	19.02	246	11.93	175,284	53.62	19.77	26.61	20.90	79.10
Wholesale	638	22.38	254,658	51.12	30,021	30.60	162,918	17.72	255	11.79	184,272	53.30	19.87	26.83	20.60	79.40
Retail	72	2.53	2,307	0.46	624	0.64	11,911	1.30	165	27.03	52,349	89.32	8.89	1.79	60.02	39.98
							By Affiliates' Classification									
All industries	2,851	100.00	498,193	100.00	98,105	100.00	919,294	100.00	322	19.69	106,718	65.47	14.24	20.29	27.84	72.16
Manufacturing	1,723	60.43	119,880	24.06	42,049	42.86	744,253	80.96	432	35.08	56,498	74.22	7.44	18.34	44.64	55.36
Wholesale and retail	1,112	39.00	377,193	75.71	55,833	56.91	171,098	18.61	154	14.80	326,325	62.71	16.37	20.92	23.71	76.29
Wholesale	1,012	35.50	372,534	74.78	54,795	55.85	154,294	16.78	152	14.71	355,136	62.35	16.52	21.13	23.59	76.41
Retail	100	3.51	4,659	0.94	1,038	1.06	16,804	1.83	168	22.28	61,778	90.86	4.98	4.14	34.87	65.13
							Foreign Affiliates[d] of U.S. Firms (FAUSFs)									
							By Parent Companies' Classification									
All industries	15,710	100.00	1,242,635	100.00	335,963	100.00	5,386,500	100.00	343	27.04	62,371	66.35	10.10	23.55	n.a.	n.a.
Manufacturing	10,720	68.24	982,139	79.04	n.a.	n.a.	3,945,600	73.25	368	n.a.	n.a.	65.23	10.40	24.37	n.a.	n.a.
Manufacturing (excl. petro. and coal prod.)	10,689	68.04	784,872	63.16	n.a.	n.a.	3,778,700	70.15	354	n.a.	n.a.	63.64	10.13	26.24	n.a.	n.a.
Wholesale and retail trade	1,041	6.63	127,437	10.26	n.a.	n.a.	519,000	9.64	499	n.a.	n.a.	60.21	10.31	29.48	n.a.	n.a.

(continued)

Table 2.6 (continued)

Industry	Affiliates		Sales		Value Added[a]		Employment		Average Number of Employees	Value-Added Ratio[b] (%)	Value-Added Productivity[c] ($)	By-Destination Shares in Sales (%)			By-Origin Shares in Purchases (%)	
	Number	%	Millions of Dollars	%	Millions of Dollars	%	Number	%				Local	Japan/US	Third Countries	Local	Imports
Wholesale	871	5.54	102,057	8.21	n.a.	n.a.	180,100	3.34	207	n.a.	n.a.	52.41	11.03	36.56	n.a.	n.a.
Wholesale (excl. petro. wholesale)	750	4.77	79,613	6.41	n.a.	n.a.	168,400	3.13	225	n.a.	n.a.	45.78	12.27	41.95	n.a.	n.a.
Retail	170	1.08	25,380	2.04	n.a.	n.a.	338,900	6.29	1,994	n.a.	n.a.	91.58	7.42	0.99	n.a.	n.a.
By Affiliates' Classification																
All industries	15,710	100.00	1,242,635	100.00	335,963	100.00	5,386,500	100.00	343	27.04	62,371	66.35	10.10	23.55	n.a.	n.a.
Manufacturing	6,459	41.11	680,525	54.76	n.a.	n.a.	3,355,400	62.29	519	n.a.	n.a.	62.90	10.98	26.12	n.a.	n.a.
Manufacturing (excl. petro. and coal prod.)	6,390	40.67	596,257	47.98	182,082	54.20	3,299,600	61.26	516	30.54	55,183	59.86	11.99	28.15	n.a.	n.a.
Wholesale and retail trade	4,339	27.62	367,216	29.55	n.a.	n.a.	1,040,100	19.31	240	n.a.	n.a.	70.78	6.50	22.72	n.a.	n.a.
Wholesale	4,121	26.23	327,559	26.36	n.a.	n.a.	554,800	10.30	135	n.a.	n.a.	67.55	7.27	25.18	n.a.	n.a.
Wholesale (excl. petro. wholesale)	3,807	24.23	227,069	18.27	40,832	12.15	520,500	9.66	137	17.98	78,448	70.22	4.53	25.26	n.a.	n.a.
Retail	218	1.39	39,657	3.19	n.a.	n.a.	485,300	9.01	2,226	n.a.	n.a.	97.39	0.21	2.40	n.a.	n.a.

Data Sources: NEW91; FAUSF91 (tables III.A.2, E.8, F.3, F.9, G.4, G.11); Mataloni (1994, 61).

[a]Value added: for Japan, sales minus purchases; for the United States, gross product in Mataloni (1994, 61).

[b]Value-added ratio: value added/sales.

[c]Value-added productivity: value added/employment.

[d]Foreign affiliates: for Japan, see notes to table 2.1; for the United States, see chap. 1 in this volume.

Table 2.7 **Sales and Purchases by Major Foreign Branches of Japanese General Trading Companies and Commercial FAJFs, 1987 Financial Year**

Transaction	GTC Branches[a] (a)	Commercial FAJFs[b] (b)	Total FAJFs[b] (c)	(a)/(b)*100 (d)	(b)/(c)*100 (e)
Total sales	23,482,200	39,876,831	54,808,975	58.89	72.76
To local	8,209,900	24,796,290	36,219,960	33.11	68.46
To Japan	7,631,200	7,825,381	9,294,170	97.52	84.20
To third countries	7,641,200	7,255,160	9,294,845	105.32	78.06
Total purchases	n.a.	31,914,173	42,135,754	n.a.	75.74
From local	n.a.	9,637,230	14,535,836	n.a.	66.30
From Japan	n.a.	16,063,493	20,571,156	n.a.	78.09
From third countries	n.a.	6,213,450	7,028,762	n.a.	88.40

Data Sources: GTC; OLD87/88.

Note: Cols. (a), (b), and (c) are in millions of yen; cols. (d) and (e) are in percent.

[a]Data are for major foreign branches of nine Japanese general trading companies, which include 197 affiliates in 37 countries. GTC branch data, originally in U.S. dollars, are converted by IMF92 (437): $1 = 144.64 yen.

[b]By-destination sales by commercial FAJFs and total FAJFs are estimated using sectoral by-destination ratios. See the text for details.

Table 2.6 also shows an interesting contrast between figures based on the industry classification of parent companies and those based on the classification of affiliates. In the case of FAUSFs, we see that most FAUSFs in the wholesale trade sector have parent companies in non-wholesale-trade sectors. This means that a major function of wholesale FAUSFs is undertaking foreign marketing operations for manufacturing parent companies. In contrast, in the case of FAJFs, about half of FAJFs in the wholesale trade sector have parent companies in the wholesale trade sector. This suggests that general trading companies (GTCs) play a large role in Japanese international transactions.

A special study conducted by the Japan Foreign Trade Council presents data for sales by the "major branches" of the nine largest Japanese GTCs.[18] The "major branches" are defined as foreign affiliates of GTCs that have close contacts with the Japanese headquarters and organize local activities. The sample covered 197 affiliates in 37 countries. Table 2.7 presents the sales figures. Although we have some reservations about the quality of these data, particularly because of double counting of transactions among the firms, the significance of GTC activities is apparent. Sales to Japan by GTC major branches have a 98 percent share in those by commercial FAJFs in our estimates. The same share in terms of the sales to third countries is 105 percent. These shares are, of course, subject to estimation error, but they clearly indicate that the presence of GTCs in international transactions of commercial FAJFs is large.

18. The nine largest Japanese GTCs are C. Itoh, Mitsui, Sumitomo, Marubeni, Mitsubishi, Nissho Iwai, Tomen, Nichimen, and Kanematsu Gosho. The study by the Japan Foreign Trade Council covers only the financial years 1983 and 1987.

2.6 Concluding Remarks

In this paper, we applied our nationality-based net sales and value-added framework to Japanese data. Foreign production activities of Japanese firms have become increasingly important, and the nationality-based net sales estimates proved to be useful in analyzing firms' international activities. Our value-added accounting also provides an integrated framework for analyzing both exports and activities of foreign affiliates and thereby for understanding key characteristics of the Japanese economy.

We found that Japan is special in the following four ways. First, Japanese-owned firms have become increasingly dependent on the marketing activities of their foreign affiliates, rather than depending on cross-border exports by parent firms located in Japan. Second, the asymmetry between inward and outward DFI is apparent in terms of sales, value added, and employment, at both the macroeconomic and sectoral levels. Third, Japanese net sales to foreigners are consistently larger than the cross-border net exports of Japan. Fourth, among the activities of FAJFs, the importance of commercial FAJFs is particularly large, with these commercial affiliates handling a large portion of Japanese exports and imports. Our statistical framework is useful for identifying these characteristics.

To apply our analytical framework more rigorously, a number of statistical improvements are required. First, MITI or the government of Japan must develop an enforceable data collection system for both inward and outward DFI on a proper legal basis. This statistical reform should increase the coverage of the surveys as well as improve the quality of the information requested on the questionnaires, particularly that on by-destination sales and by-origin purchases of affiliates. In this regard, the introduction of the new FAJF series has been a major step by MITI in improving data collection. We hope that more questions on foreign affiliates will be included in the survey and that the survey will be integrated with the old FAJF series. Second, the extended surveys of the old FAJF series implemented once every three years report ratios of "within the same firm group" sales and purchases to total sales and purchases, but no data on sales among FAJFs or among JAFFs are collected, as U.S. BEA surveys do. Adding questions on sales among affiliates will help us apply our method more precisely. Third, we need to develop a proper statistical framework to capture the activities of commercial FAJFs. Possible double counting in sales to or purchases from Japan or third countries by FAJFs must be corrected. In addition, possible double counting coming from the definition of FAJFs must be eliminated.

References

Bergsten, C. Fred, and Noland, Marcus. 1993. *Reconcilable differences? United States–Japan economic conflict.* Washington, D.C.: Institute for International Economics.

International Monetary Fund (IMF). 1992. *International financial statistics yearbook 1992.* Washington, D.C.: International Monetary Fund. [IMF92]

———. 1994. *International financial statistics November 1994.* Washington, D.C.: International Monetary Fund. [IMF94]

Japan. Economic Planning Agency (EPA). 1994. *Heisei 6-nen ban kokumin keizai keisan nenpou* (Annual report on national accounts, 1994). Tokyo: Economic Planning Agency. [EPA94]

———. Management and Coordination Agency. 1994. *1990 Input-output tables: Explanatory report.* Tokyo: Management and Coordination Agency. [IO90]

———. Management and Coordination Agency. Statistical Bureau. 1990. *Japan statistical yearbook 1990.* Tokyo: Ministry of Finance Printing Office. [JSY90]

———. 1992. *Japan statistical yearbook 1992.* Tokyo: Ministry of Finance Printing Office. [JSY92]

———. 1995. *Japan statistical yearbook 1995.* Tokyo: Ministry of Finance Printing Office. [JSY95]

———. Ministry of International Trade and Industry (MITI). 1990a. *Dai 18, 19 kai wagakuni kigyou no kaigai jigyou katsudou* (The 18th and 19th survey of foreign affiliates of Japanese firms). Tokyo: Ministry of Finance Printing Office. [OLD87/88]

———. 1990b. *Dai 22, 23 kai gaishi-kei kigyou no doukou* (The 22nd and 23rd survey of Japanese affiliates of foreign firms). Tokyo: Ministry of Finance Printing Office. [AF87/88]

———. 1991a. *Dai 4 kai kaigai toushi toukei souran* (The 4th statistics on Japanese direct investment abroad). Tokyo: Ministry of Finance Printing Office. [OLD89]

———. 1991b. *Dai 24 kai gaishi-kei kigyou no doukou* (The 24th survey of Japanese affiliates of foreign firms). Tokyo: Ministry of Finance Printing Office. [AF89]

———. 1992a. *Dai 21 kai wagakuni kigyou no kaigai jigyou katsudou* (The 21st survey of foreign affiliates of Japanese firms). Tokyo: Ministry of Finance Printing Office. [OLD90]

———. 1992b. *Dai 25 kai gaishi-kei kigyou no doukou* (The 25th survey of Japanese affiliates of foreign firms). Tokyo: Ministry of Finance Printing Office. [AF90]

———. 1993a. *Dai 22 kai wagakuni kigyou no kaigai jigyou katsudou* (The 22nd survey of foreign affiliates of Japanese firms). Tokyo: Ministry of Finance Printing Office. [OLD91]

———. 1993b. *Dai 26 kai gaishi-kei kigyou no doukou* (The 26th survey of Japanese affiliates of foreign firms). Tokyo: Ministry of Finance Printing Office. [AF91]

———. 1994a. *Dai 5 kai kaigai toushi toukei souran* (The 5th statistics on Japanese direct investment abroad). Tokyo: Ministry of Finance Printing Office. [OLD92]

———. 1994b. *Dai 27 kai gaishi-kei kigyou no doukou* (The 27th survey of Japanese affiliates of foreign firms). Tokyo: Ministry of Finance Printing Office. [AF92]

———. 1994c. *Results of the basic survey of business structure and activity, 1992.* Vol. 3, *Report by subsidiary companies.* Tokyo: Shadan Houjin Tsuusan Toukei Kyoukai. [NEW91]

———. 1994d. *White paper on international trade: Japan 1994.* Tokyo: Japan External Trade Organization.

Lawrence, Robert Z. 1993. Japan's low levels of inward investment: The role of inhibitions on acquisitions. In *Foreign direct investment,* ed. Kenneth A. Froot, 85–111. Chicago: University of Chicago Press.

Mataloni, Raymond J., Jr. 1994. U.S. multinational companies: Operations in 1992. *Survey of Current Business* 74 (June): 42–62.

Nihon Boueki Kai 1990. *Sougou shousha no taigai chokusetsu toushi, shiryou hen* (Outward foreign direct investment by general trading companies, data volume). Tokyo: Nihon Boueki Kai. [GTC]

United Nations. 1992. *1990 International trade statistics yearbook.* Vol. 1, *Trade by country.* New York: United Nations. [UN90]

———. 1993. *1992 International trade statistics yearbook.* Vol. 1, *Trade by country.* New York: United Nations. [UN92]

U.S. Department of Commerce. Bureau of Economic Analysis. 1994. *U.S. direct investment abroad: Operations of U.S. parent companies and their foreign affiliates. Revised 1991 estimates.* Washington, D.C.: Government Printing Office. [FAUSF91]

Comment Michael G. Plummer

Like its U.S. companion piece, this chapter takes a nationality-based accounting approach to international transactions, using the new technique to calculate, inter alia, net sales by Japanese to foreigners, value added by foreign affiliates of Japanese firms (FAJFs), and value added by Japanese affiliates of foreign firms (JAFFs), in the aggregate and by sector. By concentrating on the nationality of firms rather than on their location (as is traditionally done), the authors are able to give a more accurate picture of the evolving competitiveness and characteristics of Japanese firms, providing new insights into a number of old questions.

This approach has many exciting applications, particularly for the private sector and policy circles. For example, Ford Motor Company recently launched its Ford 2000 strategy, which involves a major reorganization of its domestic and international operations to develop a truly global company. Moreover, its competitors are embracing variations of the same corporate strategy. This globalization of the automobile industry underscores the increasing irrelevance of geography-based accounting to formulate implicit proxies of competitiveness in a critical sector. Clearly, nationality-based accounting creates a far more accurate picture of the international competitiveness of American and Japanese firms.

Unfortunately, from a policy perspective, the results of Kimura and Baldwin end up reinforcing a number of accepted stereotypes about Japan and its firms that have generated repeated trade disputes, threats of retaliation against Japan, and the recurrent possibility of trade war. I would like to outline below a few of the more salient policy issues that relate to the paper, in anticipation of erroneous interpretation of the results. In citing numbers between the Japanese and U.S. papers, I ignore the important differences and shortcomings in data collection. After all, such imperfections will generally be ignored by policy-

Michael G. Plummer is assistant professor of economics and director of the master's programs in the Graduate School of International Economics and Finance, Brandeis University.

makers in discussing the issues, an inevitable and heavy burden that applied economists must shoulder, albeit with regrets.

First, net sales of Japanese firms to foreigners are not only positive but huge, growing from $139 billion (U.S. dollars) in 1987 to $377 billion in 1992, far exceeding and growing more rapidly than the usually cited Japanese (cross-border) merchandise trade balance ($80 and $106 billion, respectively). This compares to a $72 billion *deficit* and $61 billion surplus in the case of net sales by Americans to foreigners in 1987 and 1991 (corresponding to deficits in the cross-border merchandise trade balance of $160 and $74 billion, respectively) found in the U.S. companion paper. These results reinforce the view of Japan as the quintessential mercantilist; it could be argued that not only is Japan a closed market at home but Japanese firms tend only to "buy Japanese."

Second, a related issue is that of the asymmetry between Japanese inward and outward direct foreign investment. The share of foreign affiliates in Japanese economic activity is far smaller than that of Japanese affiliates abroad, as well as compared to other developed countries. For example, in 1991, in terms of value added, JAFFs accounted for only 1.1 percent of manufacturing value added by Japanese firms, whereas the comparable figure for FAJFs was 8.6 percent and for foreign affiliates in the United States 13.3 percent. A number of critics have stressed that the intractable trade and other commercially oriented imbalances of Japan are related to direct and indirect restrictions on inward direct foreign investment; they will, perhaps, find more ammunition from the nationality-based approach.

Finally, at the sectoral level, the role of Japan as a "strategic" protectionist could also be supported through a selective interpretation of the data. For example, JAFFs have a relatively large share of total sales of Japanese firms in areas where Japan is thought to have a comparative disadvantage (with the exception of textiles). But "strategic" sectors like electrical machinery and transport equipment show huge discrepancies: JAFFs as a percentage of total Japanese sales grew from only 4 percent to 4.4 percent from 1987 to 1992 in the former and actually fell from an extremely low 0.59 percent to 0.55 percent over the same period in the latter. For the same years and sectors, these figures compare to rises from 11 to 13 percent and from 9 to 16 percent for FAJFs. Expect these discrepancies to get worse with any increases in the value of the yen and trade frictions.

While some of these numbers seem to provide ample grist for the Japan-bashing mill, it is important to keep in mind a number of caveats in interpreting them. My intent here is not to be an apologist but rather to try to ensure that the results are understood in the spirit in which they were derived: as an important step toward the development of a nationality-based accounting system rather than as a new weapon of (trade) war.

First, aside from the obvious differences in the surveys being used between the U.S. and Japanese papers and, in particular, the biases inherent in the MITI survey, nationality-based accounting in these papers is applied to only two countries, and hence, we have an important identification problem: who is the outlier? In fact, the authors—one Japanese, one American—perhaps "suffer" from having (intellectual and locational) comparative advantages in each of these two countries, which happen to be at the forefront of economic confrontation in the global economy. If instead we were comparing, say, Germany, Korea, the United States, and Japan, who would be the outlier? Who would be the "mercantilist"? This problem underscores the importance of expanding the country coverage.

Second, as is noted in part in the U.S. paper, the activities of FAJFs have been affected by the international commercial policy environment. Trade frictions between Japan and its most important trading partners in the developed world have led, perhaps, to a "premature" globalization of Japanese industry in order to reduce geography-based bilateral trade discrepancies. Any tendency for FAJFs to buy from Japanese suppliers would, therefore, be logical: the preference is to produce in Japan, so when they are "pushed" offshore, they include as much Japanese value added as possible. Interestingly, what might seem to be antimarket policies leading to lower geography-based imbalances could actually lead to lower nationality-based imbalances. As FAJFs become more accustomed to the foreign environment, local sourcing will naturally increase, thereby reducing net sales by the Japanese to foreigners.

Third, we are limited to four years in these studies and, hence, are not able to get a historical perspective on the issues. As is well known, relatively large increases in U.S. direct foreign investment began after World War II, whereas the upsurge in Japanese direct foreign investment is far more recent. In order to confirm that Japan is "special," we would have to know what the United States (and preferably other countries) was like at a similar phase of structural adjustment. Now, this is not to say that the authors should therefore extend their analysis back 50 years—though this would be nice!—as data limitations would preclude such an extension.

Although it is important to be careful in interpreting the results of Kimura and Baldwin, it is clear that their approach effectively complements the existing balance-of-payments approach. Moreover, it holds considerable potential in rendering global computational general equilibrium models and derived measures of national sectoral competitiveness more realistic. In short, I am convinced that the Kimura and Baldwin approach is a seminal contribution to the literature.

3 Internationalized Production in World Output

Robert E. Lipsey, Magnus Blomström, and Eric D. Ramstetter

3.1 Introduction

Internationalized production, that is, the operations of multinational firms outside their home countries, represents a separation between the geographical location of production and the ownership of production. It is an extension of the activities and influence of residents of a country outside the geographical borders of the country.

Much of the literature on multinationals is based on the idea that they possess firm-specific assets that are immobile among firms but mobile across geographical boundaries. To the extent that that is the case, the profitability of R&D and the incentive to invest in it or in other activities that contribute to the accumulation of firm-specific assets depends on the size of the worldwide market for the firm's output rather than on the size of the firm's home-country markets. A judgment about the quality of a firm's management or of the management of a country's firms in general would take into account firms' worldwide operations rather than only those in the firms' home countries.

In this paper, we compare the geographical view and the ownership view of production for a number of countries and try to assess the overall importance of

Robert E. Lipsey is professor emeritus of economics at Queens College and the Graduate Center of the City University of New York and a research associate and director of the New York office of the National Bureau of Economic Research. Magnus Blomström is professor of economics at the Stockholm School of Economics and a research associate of the National Bureau of Economic Research. Eric D. Ramstetter is research professor at the International Centre for the Study of East Asian Development, Kitakyushu, Japan.

The authors are indebted to Qing Zhang and Ewa Wojas for skillful research assistance and to the National Science Foundation, HSFR of Sweden, and a PSC-CUNY grant from the City University of New York for support. This paper is part of the NBER's research program in International Trade and Investment. Any opinions expressed are those of the authors and not necessarily those of the NBER, the National Science Foundation, HSFR, or the City University of New York.

the internationalized production that separates the two views. The geographical measure for a country reflects the capabilities of the combination of the geographically immobile factors of production located in the country with home and foreign firms' mobile factors. The ownership measure for a country reflects the capabilities of the mobile factors controlled by the country's firms, combined with various countries' immobile factors. We make the comparisons in two ways, from the home-country side and from the host-country side. The home-country view compares the production of a country as a geographical unit with the overseas, and in a few cases, the worldwide production of firms based in that country. The host-country view compares the production of the country as a geographical unit with that part of production controlled by foreign firms.

Although it is not our focus here, the ownership basis could also be used to compare groups of firms, such as Japanese-, U.S.-, and British-based multinationals, or large and small multinationals, or those based in developed countries with those based in developing countries. In each case, the output of the group of firms would reflect their command over geographically mobile assets. However, in a world where access to immobile assets, such as natural resources, is not available on a nondiscriminatory basis, a home country's immobile assets may contribute to the capabilities of firms based in a country.

A series of previous papers has compared export market shares and the composition of exports of countries with those of firms based in those countries (Kravis and Lipsey 1985, 1987, 1992; Blomström and Lipsey 1989a, 1989b, 1993; Blomström 1990; Lipsey, Blomström, and Kravis 1990; Lipsey 1995b). These export market share comparisons have several advantages over other measures. One is that production for export may be more footloose, less subject to host-government manipulation or control, and therefore more revealing about economic factors than shares in host-country markets. Another advantage of export market shares is that it is relatively easy to define the denominators of the share ratios. These might be total world exports, or developed-country exports, or exports of manufactured goods or particular products. Quite comprehensive trade data are collected and published by the United Nations, using classifications of commodities fairly comparable from one country to another.

On the other hand, export sales account for a minority of production, and a small minority for some countries' affiliates. They are uninformative about competition in services, many of which cannot be exported and must be produced where they are consumed. Even within manufacturing, usually classified as producing tradables, a concentration on export shares gives a high weight to those products that are most tradable and a low weight to less tradable goods. The effects of skills in advertising and marketing that enable American manufacturers of soft drinks and breakfast cereals to enter many markets would probably not be evident in export market shares.

Another problem with exports as a measure is that exports, unlike value added, for example, can be duplicative. The same product can appear as parents' exports of components to an affiliate and in affiliate exports of a finished product. The same type of duplication characterizes the world trade data that are the denominators for export shares.

The obvious candidates for nonduplicative measures are value added and gross product originating in a country, a sector of the economy, an industry, or a set of firms. The denominators for such share measures are available for almost all countries for aggregates and major industry groups, although the quality of the data declines as one moves to narrower industry classifications. The numerators present worse problems, especially for measures of the shares of groups of firms spanning national borders. Very few countries report value added for their own multinationals' worldwide operations or for any operations outside home-country borders. However, on the inward side, a number of countries have coded their industrial censuses to distinguish establishments controlled by foreign firms, thus providing foreign firms' shares of geographically defined host-country production, by industry of establishment. For the United States, the first example of this type of establishment-based inward investment data was the results of the Bureau of Economic Analysis (BEA)–Census of Manufactures match for 1987 (U.S. Department of Commerce 1992c), although enterprise-based data go back to 1974. On the outward side, there have been several reports on value added by U.S. affiliates, but the first comprehensive estimates covering a substantial period, with industry and country detail, appeared in Mataloni and Goldberg (1994).

While gross output shares are informative about the control of production, they do not measure market shares. A firm or group of firms could have control over a market by supplying it through exports, or through control of downstream activities such as wholesaling or retailing, where the share in production would be much smaller than the share in final sales. Information on market shares is rarely available on any national or world basis for consumption in general, although there are some data for individual industries. It is possible, for example, to learn what portion of world sales of passenger automobiles is accounted for by American companies or Japanese companies around the world. The data on pharmaceutical sales collected by IMS could presumably be used to measure the degree of control of these markets by each company or group of companies. The share of each major producer in sales of transport aircraft is also known. What is not readily available is such data for all industries and data on the size of markets for groups of products, needed to calculate market shares.

The broadest summary of our conclusions is that the share of internationalized production (i.e., production by multinational firms outside their home countries) in world output was about 7 percent of world output in 1990 and had grown somewhat over the preceding two decades. However, there was a great variety of experience among individual countries. Most notable in the home-country histories has been the big decline in the share of U.S. internationalized production. That decline almost offset the increases in internationalized production in other countries. The host-country data show a mixed picture for the individual countries, with increasing importance of foreign-owned multinationals' production in some countries and decreasing importance in others.

Section 3.2 of this paper examines the internationalization of production from the home-country side. It compares the production of four countries—the United States, Japan, Germany, and Sweden—with the internationalized, and in some cases, the worldwide production of firms based in those countries. In section 3.3, internationalized production is examined through host-country reports on production by foreign-owned firms. Section 3.4 estimates the aggregate importance of internationalized production in world output, and section 3.5 summarizes our findings.

3.2 Production Viewed from the Home-Country Side

3.2.1 United States

Some hints of the role of U.S.-based multinationals in world output can be derived from data on the gross product of U.S. multinationals. Changes in the share of nonbank majority-owned affiliates of U.S. firms in world output outside the United States and in their importance relative to U.S. output are described in table 3.1. Nonbank American affiliates in foreign countries accounted for about 3 percent of output in the world outside the United States at what was probably their peak share, and that share fell by about a third between 1977 and 1993, after rising during the previous decade. The extent of internationalization of U.S.-owned production (the ratio of affiliate production overseas to output in the United States) jumped from less than 5 percent in 1966 to over 8 percent in 1977 before a long decline that brought the ratio back down to less than 6 percent in 1993.

Within the United States there was a similar decline in the importance of parent companies in total output. The share of U.S. nonbank parents in U.S. business output outside banking[1] fell from 32 percent in 1977 to 26 percent in 1989, and the share in total output fell from 25 to 20 percent (table 3.2). However, the decline in the U.S. multinational share within the United States came later than in the share outside and was not quite as sharp as the decline outside the United States. Among the three years for which data are available, 1982 was the peak. The parent share in U.S. multinational production remained close to three-quarters, rising somewhat from 1977 to 1982 and then falling to not far above the 1977 level in 1989.[2] Thus, the role of U.S. multinational firms in production was declining both at home and abroad, a little more rapidly abroad.

1. Business output excludes output produced in the government and household sectors.

2. Parent gross output estimates are available only for benchmark years beginning in 1977.

Table 3.1 **U.S. and U.S. Affiliate[a] Gross Product as a Percentage of U.S. and World GDP**

	U.S. Affiliate Gross Product as a Percentage of			U.S. GDP as a Percentage of World GDP	
Year	U.S. GDP	World GDP Outside United States	World GDP	Nominal[b]	In 1985 World Prices
1960	n.a.	n.a.	n.a.	36.5	26.9
1966	4.89	2.67	1.73	35.4	26.7
1970	6.88	2.46	1.81	26.3	24.0
1977	8.16	3.13	2.26	27.7	22.2
1982	7.10	2.80	2.01	28.3	20.6
1989	6.15	2.31	1.68	27.3	20.7
1990	6.49	2.29	1.69	26.1	20.4
1991	6.29	2.20	1.63	25.9	19.8
1992	6.09	2.11	1.56	25.6	19.8
1993	5.72	2.07	1.52	26.5	

Sources: Howenstine (1977, table 1), Mataloni and Goldberg (1994, table 6), Mataloni (1995, table 6), United Nations (1993), World Bank (1995), and Penn World Tables (5.6).

[a]Nonbank majority-owned foreign affiliates of nonbank U.S. parents.

[b]Converted to U.S. dollars by current exchange rates.

Table 3.2 **Gross Product of Nonbank U.S. Parents and Their Foreign Affiliates**

	Gross Product (million U.S. $)		U.S. Parent Share (%) in Gross Product of			
Year	Parents	Parents and Affiliates	U.S. Nonbank Business[a]	United States	U.S. Multinationals	U.S. Multinational Share (%) in World GDP
1977	490,529	651,665	32.3	24.8	75.2	9.15
1982	796,017	1,019,734	33.0	25.3	78.1	9.16
1989	1,044,884	1,364,878	25.9	20.1	76.6	7.16

Sources: Mataloni and Goldberg (1994, tables 1 and 3) and World Bank (1995).

[a]Excluding banks, government and government enterprises, private households, imputed rental income on housing, rental income of persons, business transfer payments, subsidies, and the statistical discrepancy.

A rough picture of the worldwide role of these firms shows a much larger share in world production for U.S. multinationals (parents and affiliates combined) than in production outside the United States for their affiliates alone. The U.S. multinational share was much greater in U.S. production than in foreign production, and U.S. production was still, in 1989, over a quarter of world output.

The trend in the share of the United States as a geographical area in world output is shown in table 3.1. The U.S. share declined substantially from 1960 and 1966 to 1970, but during the period for which we can compare the United States as a country with U.S. firms, starting in 1977, there was virtually no

Table 3.3 U.S. Parent Share of U.S. Business GDP,[a] 1989

Industry	Percentage
All industries	26
Petroleum extraction and refining	8
Manufacturing[b]	61
Services	6
All other[c]	16

Source: Mataloni and Goldberg (1994, table 3).

[a]Excluding production in the banking, government, and household sectors.

[b]Excluding petroleum and coal product manufacturing.

[c]Including agriculture, mining, except petroleum, construction, wholesale and retail trade, transportation and public utilities, and finance.

further change in the U.S. role. Thus, this history includes two very different periods for the United States and for U.S. firms. From the first half of the 1960s to the mid-1970s, the United States as a geographical entity had a declining share of world output, while U.S. firms' production outside the United States had a rising share of world output and a large rise relative to domestic U.S. output. After the mid-1970s, the United States as a country held on to a quite steady share of world production, while the U.S. multinational share of world output was falling, U.S. affiliate output was declining relative to geographical U.S. output and their own parents' domestic output, and the parents' share of domestic U.S. output was falling.

One reason why the share of U.S. multinationals in production outside the United States is so low is that much of the world's production takes place in sectors in which multinationals do not operate, such as government and households, or from which foreign firms are often barred or limited, such as transportation, communication, public utilities, and certain services. Even within the private business sector in the United States, the role of U.S. parents varies greatly across industries, as can be seen in table 3.3. Multinational home, or parent, operations account for a majority of U.S. production in the petroleum and manufacturing sectors, but for only a small part of production in the rest of the economy.

For the internationalized production of U.S. firms (production by affiliates in foreign countries) we can make comparisons to world totals by industry only for "industry" as contrasted with "services," the latter including agriculture and finance, and the former including mining; manufacturing; transportation, communication, and public utilities; construction; and wholesale and retail trade. This crude industrial origin breakdown is shown in table 3.4. The share of U.S. affiliates in service output outside the United States was negligible but stable, while the share in this very broadly defined "industry" category declined by almost 20 percent.

Table 3.4 **Shares of Nonbank Majority-Owned Foreign Affiliates of U.S. Firms in "Industry" and "Services" Output, Outside the United States**

	Affiliate Share (%) in Non-U.S. GDP	
Year	Industry[a]	Services[b]
1977	8.07	.16
1982	7.67	.16
1989	6.67	.17

Sources: Mataloni and Goldberg (1994, table 8) and United Nations (1993).

[a]Mining; manufacturing; transportation, communication, and public utilities; construction; and wholesale and retail trade.

[b]Agriculture, finance (except banking), insurance and real estate, and other services.

3.2.2 Japan

The next largest home country for which some production-related indicators are available is Japan. However, the Ministry of International Trade and Industry (MITI) surveys of multinational firms provide data on sales, the value of production, and intermediate expenditures. It is therefore possible to estimate value added by subtracting intermediate expenditures from sales (which we use) or from the value of production.

A major problem with the MITI surveys is that the coverage rates are low, vary sharply over time, and differ substantially from variable to variable even within a single year, causing large fluctuations in reported value added. A rough attempt, explained in appendix A, is made here to adjust the data for changes in coverage. The adjusted estimates indicate more stable growth in the value added of both parents and affiliates and more stable shares for multinationals in corporate value added in Japan (table 3.5A). After the adjustment, the multinational parent share of total corporate value added in Japan shows a downward trend, from around 30 percent in the early 1980s to less than a quarter at the end of the decade. Ratios of affiliate value added to Japanese corporate value added fluctuated between 4 and 6.5 percent, with no clear trend, but there was a large increase in manufacturing affiliates and something of a decline in trade affiliates, a much larger group at the beginning of the 1980s.

Multinational shares of Japanese GDP are, of course, smaller than their shares of corporate value added, but the two series show similar trends (table 3.5B). While Japanese multinational value added has fallen relative to Japanese GDP, Japan's share of world GDP has risen so much that the Japanese multinational share of world GDP and the Japanese affiliate share of world GDP outside Japan have both increased greatly.

While Japanese multinational affiliate value added grew less rapidly after 1986 than before, the stock of Japanese foreign direct investment (FDI) rose more rapidly. This divergence in trends may indicate that there was a deteriora-

Table 3.5A Japanese Multinationals' Value Added and Ratios to Corporate Value Added in Japan

	Parents			Affiliates		
Fiscal Year[a]	All Industries	Manufacturing	Trade	All Industries	Manufacturing	Trade
	Adjusted Value Added[b] (million U.S. $)					
1980	241,693	192,607	24,809	45,450	13,516	26,341
1983	293,608	225,400	29,433	57,547	14,187	34,264
1986	495,035	381,200	46,151	99,618	35,262	57,189
1987	n.a.	n.a.	n.a.	88,627	34,561	45,457
1988	542,116	438,504	45,432	95,734	43,791	44,018
1989	473,534	346,479	47,286	119,497	50,267	56,368
1990	601,583	451,925	56,059	151,879	68,886	68,889
1991	716,941	485,841	95,740	176,302	79,554	84,530
1992	661,076	537,301	56,542	180,918	88,760	82,786
	Ratios of Adjusted Value Added to Corporate Value Added in Japan (%)					
1980	31.11	58.43	11.02	5.85	4.10	11.70
1983	32.80	61.40	11.67	6.43	3.86	13.58
1986	29.53	60.54	9.53	5.94	5.60	11.81
1987	n.a.	n.a.	n.a.	4.09	4.21	7.23
1988	23.92	51.56	7.10	4.22	5.15	6.88
1989	23.70	44.64	8.93	5.98	6.48	10.65
1990	24.06	48.37	8.16	6.07	7.37	10.03
1991	24.96	47.15	11.85	6.14	7.72	10.46
1992	21.27	50.52	6.35	5.82	8.35	9.29

Source: Lipsey, Blomström, and Ramstetter (1995, tables A-3, A-4, and A-5).
[a]Fiscal years ending 31 March of the following calendar year.
[b]See appendix A for an explanation of how adjusted estimates are calculated.

tion in profitability of Japanese FDI, or that adjustment for the falloff in the coverage rates of the MITI surveys in recent years is not sufficient, or that the adjustment in 1986 (a year of particularly poor coverage) was too large.

3.2.3 Other Countries

For other home countries we have no information on affiliate production, and only for a few countries do we have data even on affiliate sales.

Since 1976, German affiliate sales have approximately doubled relative to German GDP and world GDP outside Germany, eventually reaching around 30 percent of German GDP and about 2 percent of world GDP outside Germany (table 3.6). However, sales are substantially larger than production. If the difference between sales and production is as large for Germany as for the United States, German firms' internationalized output may have reached 11 to 12 percent of German home output, up from 6 percent, and the German affiliate share of world production might have risen from about 0.4 percent to about 0.8 percent.

Table 3.5B Japanese Multinationals' Share of World GDP, World GDP Outside Japan, and Japanese GDP

Year	Parents and Affiliates Relative to World GDP	Affiliates Relative to World GDP Outside Japan	Parents and Affiliates Relative to Japanese GDP	Parents and Affiliates Relative to Corporate Value Added in Japan	Japanese GDP Relative to World GDP
	Multinational Shares Based on Adjusted Value Added (%)				
1980	2.58	.45	27.11	36.97	9.53
1983	3.04	.55	29.60	39.23	10.26
1986	4.10	.80	29.95	35.48	13.68
1987	n.a.	.64	n.a.	n.a.	14.72
1988	3.50	.62	22.01	28.14	15.88
1989	3.11	.74	20.65	29.68	15.05
1990	3.56	.83	25.70	30.14	13.87
1991	4.06	.95	26.69	31.10	15.22
1992	3.61	.92	22.94	27.09	15.73

Sources: Table 3.5A and World Bank (1980, 1993, 1995).
Note: World GDP and Japanese GDP as estimated by the World Bank.

Table 3.6 Sales of German Foreign Affiliates

		Sales of German Affiliates as a Percentage of		
Year	Sales (billion U.S. $)	German GDP	World GDP Outside Germany	World GDP
1976	68.71	15.4	1.16	1.08
1977	81.56	15.8	1.23	1.14
1982	172.83	26.4	1.65	1.55
1985	191.58	30.9	1.64	1.55
1989	373.40	31.6	2.08	1.96
1990	463.35	30.9	2.37	2.20
1991	477.85	27.8	2.37	2.19
1992	531.47	27.0	2.50	2.29
1993	535.29	28.1	2.49	2.27

Sources: Germany, Deutsche Bundesbank (1991) and earlier issues, Germany, Deutsche Bundesbank (1995, table 1) and earlier issues, Lipsey (1989), and World Bank (1980, 1993, 1995).

For Sweden we have data on sales for both parents and foreign affiliates, shown in table 3.7. There has been no clear trend in the world production share of Swedish multinationals as a whole during the period for which we have data since a large rise from 1970 to 1974. There was a very strong upward trend in the internationalized production share (the production share of Swedish affiliates), especially in the last few years, and a large shift in shares from parent sales to affiliate sales. The Swedish geographical output share shows little trend over the whole period.

Table 3.7 **Sales of Swedish Parent Firms and Their Foreign Affiliates**

	Sales (million U.S. $)			Share (%) in					
				World GDP of			Swedish GDP of		
Year	All Parents	Parents with Foreign Production Affiliates	Manufacturing Affiliates (Net Sales)[c]	Sales of Multinationals with Foreign Production Affiliates	Affiliate Net Sales	Swedish GDP	Affiliate Net Sales	Parent Sales	Swedish Multinational Sales of Affiliate Net Sales[c]
1965	n.a.	n.a.	1,426	n.a.	.07	1.12	6.5	n.a.	n.a.
1970	(10,817)[a]	7,997	2,598	.35	.09	.85	10.1	31.00	24.52
1974	24,102	17,818	5,849	.45	.11	1.10	10.0	30.54	24.71
1978	(32,179)[b]	24,736	10,535	.41	.12	1.09	11.4	26.80	29.87
1986	46,959	39,220	22,097	.42	.15	.93	16.6	29.49	36.04
1990	n.a.	50,962	45,370	.46	.22	1.09	19.7	22.18	47.10

Sources: Swedenborg, Johansson-Grahn, and Kinwall (1988, tables 2.4, C.4A, and C.4B), Andersson, Fredriksson, and Svensson (1996), and World Bank (1980, 1993, 1995). Data are translated into U.S. dollars using exchange rates from International Monetary Fund (1995).

[a]Estimated by assuming same ratio to sales of parents with only foreign production affiliates as in 1974.

[b]Estimated by assuming same ratio to sales of parents with only foreign production affiliates as average of 1970 and 1978.

[c]Sales minus imports.

The four home countries for which we have some data on internationalized production or sales present quite different histories. Internationalized production by U.S. multinationals reached its peak relative to aggregate output outside the United States in the middle or late 1970s and now accounts for a smaller share than in 1966. It has also declined substantially relative to U.S. GDP since 1977. U.S. multinationals and U.S. multinational parents have declined in importance relative to world output and U.S. output, respectively, after a peak in the early 1980s. Within U.S. multinationals, affiliate output declined relative to parent output after 1977 but regained most of its share during the 1980s, with little overall change over a dozen years.

Internationalized production by Japanese multinationals, as far as can be gathered from the incomplete data available, has doubled relative to total world output outside Japan but remains much smaller than that of American firms. Relative to all Japanese corporate output, internationalized production has changed little, but internationalized production in manufacturing has roughly doubled in comparison to Japanese manufacturing output. Japanese multinational parents have lost ground within Japan, in manufacturing and in all industries, and Japanese multinationals have declined in importance relative to total corporate output and total Japanese GDP.

For Germany and Sweden we have information only on sales and for Germany only on sales from internationalized production. If output followed the trend of sales, German internationalized production has risen substantially since the mid-1970s. Swedish internationalized production, to judge by sales, has grown the fastest, tripling since 1965 and almost doubling since 1978 relative to world output.

Internationalized production has apparently increased, relative to world output, in three of the four countries. However, because of the much larger initial importance of U.S. internationalized production, the decline for U.S. firms has pretty well offset the increases in the three other countries over the past decade and a half.

3.3 Production Viewed from the Host-Country Side

A different view would be obtained by examining host-country reports on production owned by foreign firms. The great advantage of the host-country view is that the data for production by foreign-owned firms are usually from the same sources as, and comparable to, data for production in general and production by domestically owned firms.

Host-country data do present additional adding-up problems since they are usually calculated in each host-country's own currency. Our solution to that problem is to calculate foreign-owned production shares in each country's home currency and then apply these shares to measures of real GDP in each country such as those calculated by Summers and Heston (1991).

One advantage of home-country data is that outward direct investment is more concentrated among countries than is inward investment, so that we could cover roughly half of internationalized production with data from only three countries. The drawback is that no other countries collect such data on their companies' activities overseas. While inward direct investment is much less concentrated, many more countries collect data on the activities of inward direct investors.

There are several comparisons we can make between foreign-owned and total production in a country. One is to compare foreign-owned production with GDP, as a measure of the importance of such production in a country's total output. Since GDP is the only denominator for which we have an appropriate translation to a common currency for aggregation across countries, we calculate these ratios of foreign-owned to total production for all countries.

Many sectors are essentially closed to production by foreign firms, including various types of governmental and household production. One can therefore also think of measuring foreign shares in "eligible" sectors, such as the business or corporate sector of each economy.

Since the importance of internationalized production varies greatly among sectors of the economy, it is also of interest to examine shares in individual sectors. In most countries, manufacturing is the only sector for which data are available. That and the petroleum sector are probably the most internationalized of all.

3.3.1 Developed Host Countries

United States

The trend within the United States, since 1974, has been that the share of production accounted for by foreign-owned firms has increased steadily, almost tripling over that period. By 1993, the foreign-owned firm share had reached 4.5 percent of total output and 6 percent of output in the nonbank business sector, excluding not only banks but also government and household production not open to foreign firms (table 3.8).

The foreign presence has always been much larger in petroleum and manufacturing than in other sectors of the U.S. economy. From less than 5 percent in 1974, the foreign-owned share grew to something in the neighborhood of 15 percent in 1993, a little faster growth than in other sectors. Foreign-owned manufacturing by itself tripled in importance relative to U.S. total and nonbank business output, reaching 3 percent of the latter in 1993.

The growth in the foreign firm share in U.S. output has taken place during a period after the rapid growth in the U.S. multinational share of world output described earlier. Thus, while U.S. domestic output was growing relative to U.S. multinational worldwide output, foreign firm U.S. output was growing faster than that of U.S.-owned firms.

Table 3.8 United States: Share of Foreign Firms in Output, 1974–93

	Share (%) in					
	Total GDP of		Nonbank Business GDP of		U.S. Manufacturing GDP	
Year	Total Foreign-Owned Output	Foreign-Owned Manufacturing Output	Total Foreign-Owned Output	Foreign-Owned Manufacturing Output	Excluding Petroleum and Coal Products	Including Petroleum and Coal Products and All Petroleum[a]
1974	1.64	.76	2.17	1.01	3.13	4.79
1977	1.78	.84	2.27	1.07	3.57	5.21
1978	1.92	.91	2.48	1.18	3.91	5.68
1979	2.23	1.06	2.89	1.38	4.59	6.65
1980	2.62	1.14	3.43	1.50	5.27	8.15
1981	3.26	1.55	4.18	1.99	7.22	10.48
1982	3.29	1.50	4.29	1.96	7.29	10.45
1983	3.27	1.54	4.33	2.04	7.57	10.44
1984	3.41	1.63	4.38	2.09	7.94	10.62
1985	3.34	1.55	4.31	2.00	7.85	10.51
1986	3.33	1.54	4.34	2.01	7.93	10.00
1987	3.48	1.66	4.54	2.17	8.60	10.73
1988	3.89	1.85	5.04	2.41	9.46	11.69
1989	4.25	2.08	5.56	2.72	10.87	13.28
1990	4.31	2.16	5.67	2.84	11.70	14.30
1991	4.50	2.20	5.96	2.91	12.20	14.59
1992	4.42	2.23	5.90	2.97	12.62	15.02
1993	4.58	2.26	6.10	3.02	12.84	15.18

Source: Lipsey, Blomström, and Ramstetter (1995, table B-1).

[a]Of which more than three-quarters was in petroleum and coal products.

United Kingdom

The United Kingdom is a major recipient of direct investment and is one of the countries that has distinguished foreign-owned manufacturing enterprises in its Census of Production for a fairly long period. The share of foreign-owned firms in U.K. manufacturing production has hovered in the neighborhood of 20 percent since 1977, with the latest years' shares a little above the earliest ones, but without a clear trend (table 3.9). The lowest foreign share, 17 to 18 percent, was reached in 1986, and there was a substantial rise after that to 22 to 23 percent in 1990 and 1991.

Since manufacturing has been declining relative to other industries in the United Kingdom, the stable foreign share in manufacturing meant a decline in the share of foreign-owned manufacturing in the economy as a whole. That share fell by about a third from 1979 to 1986 and then recovered somewhat but never reached more than 80 percent of the share in 1977 and 1979. We do

Table 3.9 **United Kingdom: Share of Foreign-Owned Manufacturing Enterprises in Manufacturing and Total Output**

	Share (%) of Foreign-Owned Enterprises in		
	Manufacturing		
Year	Net Output	Gross Value Added at Factor Cost	Aggregate GDP[a]
1977	19.87	19.76	6.62
1979	21.29	21.41	6.79
1981	18.55	18.30	5.15
1983	18.97	18.61	5.05
1984	20.30	20.15	5.27
1985	18.84	18.67	4.85
1986	17.71	17.31	4.53
1987	19.05	18.79	4.81
1988	18.52	18.23	4.76
1989	21.48	21.06	5.53
1990	22.39	21.77	5.67
1991	22.54	21.71	5.32

Source: Lipsey, Blomström, and Ramstetter (1995, table B-2).
[a]Share of net output of foreign-owned manufacturing firms.

not have data to tell whether information for all industries would show that same stability as in manufacturing or a declining share.

Canada

Canada, another important host country for multinationals, also provides long series of information on the operation of foreign firms. From the 1960s through the mid-1980s, foreign firms accounted for about a third of total sales in all industries and all nonfinancial industries, and more than half in manufacturing industries. The peak shares seem to have been reached around 1970, but there was little change until the late 1980s. The share of foreign-owned firms had dropped substantially by 1988, but it then increased slightly. Taken together, these figures suggest a declining importance of foreign-owned firm sales in Canada since the 1960s and 1970s.

The comparison of our crudely estimated value added in foreign-owned operations with total Canadian GDP gives a somewhat different picture. The share in total national output of foreign-owned production, in manufacturing and in all industries, reached a peak in the mid-1970s. Then it declined, to the point that over the whole period from 1967 to 1993 there was some decline in the foreign-owned share of total Canadian output (table 3.10).

Norway

By all the available measures, the foreign-owned share in Norway's output has declined over the past 15 years and particularly during the 1980s, after an

Table 3.10 **Canada: Share of Foreign-Owned Firm Value Added in GDP**

Year	Estimated Share (%) of Foreign-Owned Firm Value Added in Total GDP: Foreign-Owned Firms in		
	All Industries[a]	Nonfinancial Industries[a]	Manufacturing[b,c]
1967	16.5	16.1	14.1
1968	17.0	16.7	14.3
1969	16.6	16.3	14.1
1970	16.3	15.9	13.2
1972	16.6	16.3	13.6
1974	18.0	17.6	14.5
1978	n.a.	17.1	n.a.
1983	16.2	14.7	11.5
1988	15.6	13.9	11.1
1990	14.8	13.2	n.a.
1992	14.3	12.8	n.a.
1993	15.1	13.5	n.a.

Source: Lipsey, Blomström, and Ramstetter (1995, table B-3).

[a]Sales or operating revenue multiplied by 0.3, using approximation to ratios for U.S. majority-owned affiliates in Canada, which were as follows (%): 1977, 32.8; 1982, 31.5; 1989, 30.1; and 1991, 26.6 (from Mataloni and Goldberg 1994).

[b]Sales or operating revenue multiplied by 0.4, using approximation to 1972 Canadian ratios for foreign-owned manufacturing establishments, which were as follows (%): foreign-owned establishments, all activities, 38.6; and foreign-owned establishments, manufacturing activity, 41.7.

[c]Enterprise basis. On an establishment basis the ratio for 1972 is 11.3, and that for 1991 is 10.5.

earlier increase (table 3.11). Within manufacturing there was a rise in the foreign share in 1973 and another large rise in 1979, followed by a sharp drop, by over a half, to the low point in 1985. Since then there has not been any strong trend.

The dates of the major changes in the foreign-owned share, coinciding with large increases in oil prices, suggest that relative price changes may have played a major role in these fluctuations. That could be the case if there was substantial foreign ownership in petroleum refining and large changes in refining margins or margins in other downstream petroleum-related output, since these would enter manufacturing value added.

Whatever the source of these fluctuations, they seem also to have been associated with corresponding fluctuations in the importance of the manufacturing sector in aggregate national output. That relationship is shown by the fact that the fluctuations in the foreign share of GDP were wider than those in the foreign share of manufacturing output. For example, when the foreign share of manufacturing output rose by a quarter from 1972 to 1974, the foreign share in GDP rose by a third. And when the foreign share in manufacturing fell by 54 percent from 1979 to 1986, the foreign share in GDP fell by 65 percent.

The trend in foreign ownership of Norwegian production seems quite clear. Foreign-owned production has been declining in importance both within man-

Table 3.11 Norway: Share of Foreign-Owned Manufacturing Establishments in Manufacturing and Total Output

	Manufacturing Value Added at Factor Prices: Foreign-Owned as a Percentage of		Manufacturing Value Added at Purchasers' Prices: Foreign-Owned as a Percentage of
	Total Manufacturing Value Added at Factor Prices (1)	Aggregate GDP (2)	Aggregate GDP[a] (3)
	Foreign Ownership 50 Percent or More, Four Industries[b]		
1952	40.27		1.60
1957	36.62		1.38
1961	29.04		1.19
	Foreign Ownership 50 Percent or More, All Manufacturing		
1962	6.43		1.59
1962	6.35	1.51	
	Foreign Ownership 20 Percent or More, All Manufacturing		
1962	11.59		2.87
1962	11.79	2.80	
1972	14.69	3.10	2.91[c]
1973	18.46	4.01	3.77[c]
1977	17.23	3.43	3.08
1980	14.36	2.40	2.20
1982	13.29	1.93	1.82
1985	9.41	1.28	1.24
1986	11.27	1.60	1.54
1987	10.74	1.53	1.47[d]
1989	13.58	1.87	1.80[d]
1990	11.18	1.43	1.38[d]

Source: Lipsey, Blomström, and Ramstetter (1995, table B-4).

[a]Estimated by multiplying col. (2) by the ratio for all Norwegian manufacturing of value added at market prices to value added at factor prices (the ratio of col. [3] to col. [2] of Lipsey, Blomström, and Ramstetter 1995, table B-4).

[b]Electrochemical; other chemical, except oil refining; basic metals, except iron and steel; and electrotechnical.

[c]Extrapolated from 1975 by col. (2).

[d]Extrapolated from 1986 by col. (2).

ufacturing and for the economy as a whole ever since the peak share reached in 1973 or 1974. In addition, there is evidence of a decline in the foreign share during the 1950s in the four industries for which foreign ownership data are available, industries that were growing relative to the average within the declining manufacturing sector.

Sweden

The trajectory of foreign ownership of Swedish industry appears to have been quite different from that for Norway, although the severe reduction in

Table 3.12 Sweden: Share of Foreign-Owned Firms in Manufacturing and Total Production

	Value Added in Foreign-Owned Production as a Share (%) of					
	Value Added in All Corresponding Enterprises				GDP:	
	Manufacturing Establishments in Enterprises with Foreign Ownership		Enterprises with Foreign Ownership		Manufacturing Establishments in Enterprises with Foreign Ownership	
Year	>50	≥20%	>50%	≥20%	>50%	≥20%
1971	6.2	n.a.	5.3	8.1	1.65	n.a.
1972	6.3	10.9	5.3	8.3	1.68	2.91
1973	6.4	10.7	5.9	9.7	1.80	3.00
1974	6.7	11.0	5.8	9.0	2.05	3.38
1975	6.4	10.2	5.3	7.8	1.84	2.93
1976	6.9	11.0	5.2	7.8	1.90	3.04
1977	7.0	11.7	5.4	8.5	1.84	3.09
1978	7.5	12.5	5.3	8.5	1.89	3.13
1979			6.1	9.5		
1986			13.5			
1990			17.0			

Source: Lipsey, Blomström, and Ramstetter (1995, tables B-5 and B-6).

availability of data after 1978 makes inferences rather uncertain. Most of the measures show little change in the share of foreign-owned enterprises in manufacturing or in total production from 1971 through 1976 or 1977, but if there was any change, it was toward an increase in foreign shares, especially after 1978 (table 3.12). After 1979 very little is available on value added, but the one series that does continue shows more than a doubling of the foreign share by 1986 and 1990. That impression is reinforced by the foreign shares in employment. The employment share of foreign-owned enterprises rose similarly (Lipsey, Blomström, and Ramstetter 1995, table B-6), a little faster in manufacturing than in all industries, but both confirming the impression of rapid growth in the foreign share of Swedish production during the 1980s.

Japan

The data on production by foreign firms in Japan suffer from many of the same defects as the data on Japan-based multinationals. In particular, they are based on voluntary surveys with low and fluctuating degrees of coverage. Response rates have varied between a high of 59 percent and a low of 31 percent but fell between 45 and 55 percent in 11 out of the 15 years for which coverage is known. The definition of foreign ownership has also changed over time: 25 percent equity ownership in 1977–81, 50 percent in 1982–91, and 33 percent in 1991–92.

While those changes of definition might not have a major effect on measures of production in most host countries, minority-owned operations are of much greater importance in Japan than elsewhere. The 1991 change from 50 percent to 33 percent as the criterion for foreign control does not appear to have made a large difference, but the earlier increase from 25 percent to 50 percent may have been much more important.[3]

A way of estimating the effect of the strict criterion on estimated foreign ownership shares in Japan is to compare data for all U.S.-owned affiliates in Japan with data for majority-owned affiliates, both from U.S. outward investment surveys. Such a comparison is not possible for value added because those estimates cover only majority-owned affiliates. However, it is possible for a crude proxy for value added: the sum of employee and net income, both components of value added. The ratios of all affiliates to majority-owned affiliates for this proxy in three of the benchmark survey years are as follows (U.S. Department of Commerce 1981, 1985a, 1992b):

	1977	1982	1989
All industries	3.63	3.22	2.21
Manufacturing	2.95	3.86	2.61

In table 3.13 we present, first, estimates of foreign shares in corporate value added and in Japanese GDP according to the 50 percent foreign ownership criterion, the official one from 1982 through 1991. The 33 percent criterion introduced in 1991 added only about 4 percent to the foreign share in manufacturing and a little more than 10 percent to the overall foreign share, mainly because it added over 40 percent to the foreign share in trade.

The second part of the table gives two estimates of the foreign share by the 10 percent ownership criterion used in the U.S. data. The low estimate is based on the assumption that only U.S. firms held any minority interests above 10 percent in Japanese firms. The high estimate assumes that minority holdings by other countries bear the same relation to majority and 50 percent holdings as in U.S. investment.

The 10 percent criterion would put foreign shares higher, as far as we can judge: somewhere between 1.5 and 2.5 percent of GDP, according to the low estimate, and 2.5 to 3.5 percent, by the high estimate. The foreign share of corporate value added ranges from about 2 to over 3 percent in the low estimate and from almost 3 to around 6 percent in the high estimate, with fairly clear downward trends. Foreign shares are, and have mostly been, around 4 percent in manufacturing judged by the low estimate but 6 or 7 to over 10 percent according to the high estimate. Both, but particularly the high estimate, suggest a decline in the foreign share since the early or mid-1980s.

The data point to an important characteristic of value added as a production measure: its sensitivity to cyclical and exchange rate fluctuations. The fall in

3. For a discussion of some of the difficulties with Japanese data, see Weinstein (1997).

Table 3.13 **Japan: Share of Foreign-Owned Firms in Corporate Value Added and in GDP, by Various Ownership Criteria and Methods of Estimation**

Year	Foreign Share (%) of Corporate Value Added in Japan: All Industries		Foreign Share (%) of Corporate Value Added in Japan: Manufacturing		Foreign Share (%) of Japanese GDP: All Industries	
Foreign Ownership Criterion: 50 Percent or More						
1977	1.75		2.91		1.10	
1978	1.62		2.91		1.00	
1979	1.35		2.39		0.90	
1980	1.37		2.38		0.93	
1981	1.53		2.83		1.06	
1982	1.53		2.83		1.05	
1983	1.90		3.88		1.35	
1984	1.54		3.07		1.09	
1985	1.11		2.27		0.80	
1986	1.66		3.69		1.22	
1987	1.51		3.33		1.19	
1988	1.53		3.27		1.25	
1989	1.51		3.14		1.20	
1990	1.35		2.78		1.13	
1991	1.34		2.83		1.14	
1992	1.16		2.61		0.97	
Foreign Ownership Criterion: 10 Percent or More						
	Low	High	Low	High	Low	High
1977	3.61	6.36	4.35	8.58	2.27	4.00
1978	3.40	5.75	4.59	9.13	2.09	3.54
1979	2.92	4.68	4.04	7.91	1.94	3.11
1980	2.82	4.62	4.15	8.34	1.93	3.16
1981	2.90	5.04	4.63	10.40	2.01	3.49
1982	2.89	4.91	4.84	10.92	1.99	3.38
1983	3.18	5.49	5.67	13.57	2.26	3.90
1984	2.67	4.02	4.76	9.40	1.88	2.83
1985	2.26	3.00	4.10	7.33	1.63	2.17
1986	2.64	3.99	5.27	10.18	1.94	2.93
1987	2.30	3.35	4.71	8.46	1.81	2.63
1988	2.28	3.38	4.61	8.74	1.85	2.75
1989	2.29	3.32	4.53	8.21	1.83	2.65
1990	2.08	3.01	4.16	7.57	1.73	2.51
1991	2.01	2.87	4.03	7.18	1.70	2.43
1992	1.67	2.32	3.63	6.16	1.40	1.93

Sources: Lipsey, Blomström, and Ramstetter (1995, table B-7) and appendix B of this paper.

Table 3.14 **Australia: Share of Foreign-Owned and Foreign-Controlled Establishments in Mining, Manufacturing, and Total Output**

	Foreign Share (%) of Sector Value Added and GDP			
	By Control		By Ownership	
Industry and Year	Sector	GDP	Sector	GDP
Mining				
1971–72	55.0	1.87		
1972–73	57.7	1.88		
1973–74	60.2	2.03		
1974–75	60.1	2.27	51.8	1.96
1976–77	59.0	2.29		
1981–82	57.9	2.36	51.2	2.09
1982–83	56.6	2.51	50.4	2.24
1984–85	51.5	2.39	44.7	2.08
Manufacturing				
1972–73	n.a.	n.a.	31.2	6.82
1982–83	34.6	5.87	32.9	5.57
1986–87	33.3	5.38	30.9	5.00

Source: Lipsey, Blomström, and Ramstetter (1995, tables B-8 and B-9).

foreign firm value added from 1983 to 1985 probably represents the effects of the sharp rise in the exchange value of the U.S. dollar, as U.S. affiliates, especially those in trade, cut margins to preserve their markets in Japan.

Although Japan's government restrictions on inward FDI, extremely restrictive until the early 1970s, were largely eliminated in 1980, foreign firms' shares of Japanese production are still relatively low, leading some (e.g., Encarnacion 1992) to suggest that private barriers to FDI have replaced public barriers. Others (e.g., Ramstetter and James 1993) argue that these trends are a result of general entry barriers (e.g., high land costs) and the low priority accorded the Japanese market by many Western multinationals in this period.

Australia

Time series for foreign firms' shares in Australian output appear to be confined to mining and manufacturing, and even these cover only the period from the early 1970s to the mid-1980s. The mining sector is the one for which the longer span of years can be observed, and it is also the sector most dominated by foreign firms. Within that sector, the foreign share of production rose until the mid-1970s and then declined, the latest ratio, for 1984–85, being the lowest of the period (table 3.14). However, there was no real indication of a trend before that. The share of GDP originating in foreign-owned mining production did appear to have an upward trend, however, because the mining sector, though quite small, increased in importance during these years.

The foreign share in the much larger, but relatively shrinking, manufacturing sector declined somewhat over the period for which we have data, but the share of foreign-owned manufacturing production in total output declined substantially. Thus, there is little doubt that the foreign share in Australian production as a whole declined, given that foreign production in these two major industries fell from about 9.5 percent to about 7.5 percent of GDP.

Of the seven developed host countries for which we have data from national sources on production by inward investors, only two, the United States and Sweden, have undergone substantial growth in foreign-owned shares in their production, mainly during the 1980s. The growth was particularly large in manufacturing for the United States, although the shares have not reached high levels compared with those in other countries. For Sweden, we do not have data by industry for the period of high growth in the foreign share.

The opposite trend, for manufacturing at least, characterized Norway and Canada. In Norway, the foreign share in manufacturing was cut substantially after rising in the 1970s, and the contribution of foreign-owned manufacturing to GDP fell far more steeply, as manufacturing declined in importance in the whole economy. In Canada, the foreign share of production, which reached a peak in the mid-1970s, fell substantially until 1988 and then recovered a bit by 1993, but the final shares were below the levels of the 1960s. Japan, the United Kingdom, and Australia are harder to characterize by any particular trends. Thus, among these seven countries, there is no strong consensus regarding the direction of changes in the importance of foreign-owned production. The strongest case for a trend is that of the United States, which absorbed an unprecedented share of the world's direct investment during the 1980s, but that may have been a temporary episode not likely to be repeated.

3.3.2 Developing Host Countries

Our data for developing countries are less complete. Table 3.15 presents the data we have assembled on foreign firm shares of value added in Asia's developing economies.[4] Across countries these shares vary in a wide range, from very close to zero in India and in China's industrial sector for a number of years to well over 50 percent for some years in Malaysia and all years in Singapore. In the three countries for which data covering all industries are available for a reasonably long period of time (India, Malaysia, and Taiwan), there is a pronounced downward trend in Malaysia due in large part to declines of foreign shares in agriculture and mining (Ramstetter 1995, 123). There are no such strong trends in India and Taiwan, but in Taiwan foreign shares were, in the late 1980s, high relative to the past.[5] In India and Korea, foreign firm shares

4. The data for China refer to gross value of output for industry, including intermediate expenditures. Figures on sales and the gross value of output, including intermediate expenditures, are provided in the appendix tables of Lipsey et al. (1995).

5. Ratios of foreign firm sales to Taiwanese total output indicate that high foreign shares continued into 1991 (see Lipsey et al. 1995, table C-8). The two value-added estimates for foreign firms in 1990 and 1991 are inconsistent and seem inconsistent with the sales data as well.

Table 3.15 **Selected Asian Developing Economies: Share of Foreign Firms in Value Added**

	All Industries					Manufacturing					
				Taiwan				Malaysia		Taiwan	
Year	India	Korea	Malaysia	1	2	India	Korea	1	2	1	2
Ownership definition	b	b	a	b	b	b	b	a	a	b	b
Output measure		c		g	c		c	c		g	c
Industry coverage			e			d		e	f		h
1968	n.a.	n.a.	n.a.	n.a.	n.a.	n.a.	n.a.	n.a.	48.2	n.a.	n.a.
1969	n.a.	n.a.	63.5	n.a.	n.a.	n.a.	n.a.	57.6	55.1	n.a.	n.a.
1970	n.a.	n.a.	60.2	n.a.	n.a.	n.a.	n.a.	68.5	53.1	n.a.	n.a.
1971	n.a.	n.a.	56.6	n.a.	n.a.	n.a.	n.a.	60.8	58.1	n.a.	n.a.
1972	n.a.	n.a.	54.2	n.a.	n.a.	n.a.	n.a.	58.3	56.4	n.a.	n.a.
1973	n.a.	n.a.	55.5	n.a.	n.a.	n.a.	n.a.	53.8	53.0	n.a.	n.a.
1974	n.a.	2.73	57.1	6.1	n.a.	n.a.	9.5	57.4	53.5	18.0	n.a.
1975	1.75	3.83	50.0	6.4	n.a.	7.6	13.6	52.1	48.4	19.3	n.a.
1976	1.95	4.66	46.2	6.5	n.a.	n.a.	16.0	47.1	51.7	17.8	n.a.
1977	1.82	5.54	43.0	7.1	n.a.	n.a.	18.4	43.8	44.7	19.3	n.a.
1978	1.86	5.32	41.0	8.0	n.a.	n.a.	17.0	44.4	44.2	21.1	n.a.
1979	1.89	n.a.	40.3	8.4	10.4	7.0	n.a.	51.0	42.0	22.1	30.5
1980	1.71	n.a.	39.4	6.7	8.9	7.0	n.a.	49.7	n.a.	17.9	25.3
1981	n.a.	n.a.	39.6	6.1	8.5	n.a.	n.a.	48.6	n.a.	16.0	24.7
1982	1.26	n.a.	37.4	5.7	6.6	5.2	n.a.	47.4	n.a.	14.9	18.5
1983	1.23	n.a.	36.9	6.8	6.3	5.1	n.a.	44.2	36.0	16.2	17.0
1984	1.68	n.a.	34.0	8.8	11.3	5.8	10.7	38.2	32.9	21.9	28.7
1985	1.75	n.a.	31.4	5.7	7.8	6.1	11.6	34.3	32.2	13.4	18.5

1986	1.79	n.a.	31.3	7.1	6.9	6.4	12.0	36.3	33.4	15.6	15.6
1987	1.78	n.a.	32.9	8.0	7.8	6.3	n.a.	39.5	35.0	16.7	17.5
1988	n.a.	n.a.	32.0	11.4	10.5	n.a.	n.a.	40.6	36.8	22.9	22.2
1989	n.a.	n.a.	30.9	12.6	12.2	n.a.	n.a.	40.4	40.1	22.8	23.4
1990	n.a.	n.a.	30.1	14.0	7.8	n.a.	n.a.	40.5	42.0	20.4	28.7
1991	n.a.	n.a.	30.1	7.8	11.0	n.a.	n.a.	43.1	43.4	10.0	23.6
1992	n.a.	n.a.	n.a.	n.a.	n.a.	n.a.	n.a.	n.a.	n.a.	n.a.	n.a.

	Industry				Manufacturing				
		Guangdong			Indonesia		Singapore		
Year	China: Upper Limit	Upper Limit	Actual	Hong Kong	Total	Nonoil	1	2	Thailand
Ownership definition				a	b	b	a	a	b
Output measure	i	i	i				j	k	l
Industry coverage									m
1974	n.a.	n.a.	n.a.	n.a.	n.a.	n.a.	n.a.	n.a.	15.5
1975	n.a.	n.a.	n.a.	n.a.	19	21	62.7	n.a.	n.a.
1976	n.a.	n.a.	n.a.	n.a.	25	28	64.1	n.a.	n.a.
1977	n.a.	n.a.	n.a.	n.a.	26	29	65.2	n.a.	n.a.
1978	n.a.	n.a.	n.a.	n.a.	23	26	63.4	n.a.	n.a.
1979	n.a.	n.a.	n.a.	n.a.	21	25	67.3	n.a.	n.a.
1980	0.48	1.9	n.a.	n.a.	22	28	67.4	65.4	n.a.
1981	0.58	n.a.	n.a.	n.a.	22	28	67.7	66.0	n.a.
1982	0.68	n.a.	n.a.	n.a.	20	26	66.6	65.8	n.a.
1983	0.78	n.a.	n.a.	12.8	19	24	63.2	66.4	n.a.

(*continued*)

Table 3.15 (continued)

Year	Industry				Manufacturing				
		Guangdong			Indonesia		Singapore		
	China: Upper Limit	Upper Limit	Actual	Hong Kong	Total	Nonoil	1	2	Thailand
1984	1.01	n.a.	n.a.	13.0	14	19	63.1	67.9	n.a.
1985	1.21	4.6	n.a.	10.7	13	18	64.8	67.0	n.a.
1986	1.46	n.a.	n.a.	12.8	14	18	65.9	73.5	13.3
1987	2.02	n.a.	n.a.	13.5	15	18	72.4	74.0	n.a.
1988	2.72	n.a.	n.a.	14.3	14	17	71.7	72.4	n.a.
1989	3.44	n.a.	n.a.	14.6	16	19	73.6	74.4	n.a.
1990	4.38	24.3	8.34	16.2	15	19	72.7	74.2	14.8
1991	5.66	29.1	27.0	17.3	n.a.	n.a.	72.2	72.9	n.a.
1992	7.11	33.6	31.8	17.1	n.a.	n.a.	70.2	69.5	n.a.
1993	10.16	43.8	33.2	n.a.	n.a.	n.a.	n.a.	n.a.	n.a.

Source: Lipsey, Blomström, and Ramstetter (1995, tables C-1 through C-11).

Notes: Ownership definition: (a) foreign firms defined as firms with 50 percent or higher foreign ownership shares and (b) foreign firms defined to include firms with minority foreign ownership shares.

Output measure: (c) value added estimated as total sales less expenditures for raw materials and parts; (g) estimates given by the original source equal to total income less expenditures for raw materials and parts, electricity, and other intermediate consumption; (i) gross value of output, including intermediate expenditures; (j) gross value added; (k) net value added; and (l) ratios to national accounts measures of value added.

Industry coverage: (d) foreign firm manufacturing data refer to the sum of textiles, chemicals, and engineering (metals and machinery) only; (e) data from surveys of limited companies; (f) data from industrial surveys; (h) data exclude paper and printing, precision machinery, and miscellaneous manufacturing; (m) data refer only to firms promoted by the Board of Investment—including nonpromoted foreign firms, the foreign share was 30.6 percent in 1990 (many nonpromoted firms had been promoted firms earlier).

were much larger in manufacturing than in all industries. Foreign shares in Malaysia and Taiwan generally followed a U-shaped pattern, being relatively high in the mid- to late 1970s, bottoming out in the early to mid-1980s, and rising again in the late 1980s and early 1990s.

For the remaining countries (China, Hong Kong, Indonesia, Singapore, and Thailand), data are available only for industry or manufacturing. A very strong upward trend is observable in China, though the figures here represent only an upper limit on foreign joint venture shares, and the data for Guangdong Province indicate that there are substantial differences between the upper limit and the actual share in some years. Nonetheless, there is no doubt that foreign shares in China have increased dramatically in recent years and have reached moderately high levels in Guangdong Province, mainly in firms owned by overseas Chinese.[6] Upward trends are present in Hong Kong and Singapore, and a downward trend in Indonesia. In Thailand, shares of foreign firms promoted and surveyed by the Thai Board of Investment have not changed much over time, but it is also clear that these firms accounted for only about one-half of all foreign firm production in Thailand in 1990.

On balance, it appears that foreign firm shares of manufacturing production have increased somewhat in Asia's developing economies. The fact that Asian manufacturing has grown extremely rapidly in the past two decades, combined with constant or rising shares of foreign firms in these industries, means that the share of Asian manufacturing operations of foreign multinationals in world production has been increasing. Moreover, if one could account for the production of the growing number of Asian manufacturing multinationals in their home markets, the increase in the share of Asian multinationals in world production would likely be seen to be even more pronounced. As the Malaysian data indicate, internationalized production has long played an important role in Asian primary industries as well, though this role has become smaller in recent years in Malaysia.

We also have some information on the activities of multinationals in Latin America (table 3.16). In the two largest economies, Brazil and Mexico, as well as in Uruguay, foreign-owned firms play an important role in manufacturing production. In Brazil, foreign-owned production accounted for about 29 percent of manufacturing gross output in 1980, the only year for which data on all foreign affiliates are available. Little change has taken place in the share of U.S. affiliates (dominated by majority-owned affiliates), which accounted for approximately half of all foreign affiliate manufacturing output in Brazil in the beginning of the 1980s. If the growth of other foreign firms was like that of U.S. majority-owned foreign affiliates, there have been only small changes in the foreign manufacturing share in Brazil since the mid-1970s.

In Mexico, we find no significant change in the role of multinationals during

6. In 1992, 23 percent of the gross value of industrial production in Guangdong occurred in overseas Chinese firms (Lipsey et al. 1995, 41).

Table 3.16 **Three Latin American Countries: Share of Foreign-Owned Production in Manufacturing Output**

	Brazil		Mexico			
			Total Foreign			
Year	Total Foreign	U.S. MOFAs[a]	A	B	U.S. MOFAs[a]	Uruguay
1970		n.a.	34	28.7		n.a.
1975		n.a.	31			n.a.
1977		10.5			9.2	n.a.
1978		n.a.			n.a.	18.0
1980	28.5			27.2		n.a.
1982		12.3			8.5	n.a.
1988		n.a.			n.a.	28.0
1989		12.9			13.0	n.a.
1990		10.3			13.0	29.0
1991		9.2			n.a.	n.a.

Source: Lipsey, Blomström, and Ramstetter (1995, tables C-12 through C-14).
[a]In 1982, U.S. majority-owned foreign affiliates (MOFAs) accounted for 85 percent of manufacturing employment in all U.S. affiliates in Brazil and 60 percent in Mexico.

the 1970s, and if U.S. majority-owned foreign affiliates can represent all foreign affiliates in Mexico as we assumed they did in Brazil, the role of the multinationals remained unchanged in Mexican manufacturing in the 1980s. In 1970, 28.7 percent of Mexican manufacturing value added was produced by foreign-owned firms. In 1980, the last year for which figures for total foreign-owned production are available, that share was almost unchanged (27.2 percent). Looking only at U.S. majority-owned foreign affiliates in Mexican manufacturing, we see a downward trend until 1982, but then it shifted dramatically. Between 1982 and 1990, the share of these affiliates in Mexican manufacturing value added increased by 53 percent (from 8.5 to 13.0 percent). However, this seems to be a result of policy changes in Mexico after the debt crisis in 1982. Mexico abandoned its strict restrictions on FDI dating from the 1970s, which, among other things, prevented majority-ownership in new investments, and American firms seem to have responded to that change. In 1982, U.S. majority-owned foreign affiliates accounted for 60 (55) percent of the employment (sales) of all U.S. affiliates in Mexican manufacturing, and by 1990, this share had increased to 71 (66) percent.

The foreign share in Uruguay has also increased steadily since the 1970s. Almost 30 percent of the country's manufacturing output was produced by foreign firms in 1990. Given that Uruguay is a financial center for the Southern Cone, one would expect the foreign share of service industry production to be even higher.

In sum, it seems safe to guess that approximately 30 percent of our three Latin American countries' manufacturing output today is produced by foreign-

Table 3.17 **Estimate of Internationalized Production from the Home-Country Side**

Year	Affiliate (Internationalized) Output of Firms from Four Home Countries as a Percentage of World GDP[a] (1)	Share (%) of Four Home Countries in World Stock of Outward FDI[b] (2)	Share of Internationalized Output in World GDP[c] (3)
1960		49.6	
1970	2.5	(55)	4.5
1975		57.1	
1977	3.1	(57)	5.4
1980		56.5	
1982	3.2	(55)	5.8
1985		54.2	
1988	3.3	(53)	6.2
1990	3.4	51	6.7

[a]Roughly estimated from country tables.

[b]Lipsey (1995b, table E-7). Figures in parentheses are straight-line interpolations, rounded to two significant digits.

[c]Including four home countries. Calculated as (col. [1] ÷ col. [2]) × 100.

owned multinationals. The foreign share has been essentially unchanged in Mexico since 1970. It increased somewhat in Brazil during the 1970s but fell back again during the 1980s. In Uruguay, the trend has been upward since 1978, but the economy is small compared to the others. Thus, taking the three countries together, there has been little change in the foreign manufacturing share since the early or mid-1970s. During this period, these Latin American countries' manufacturing sectors have been growing more slowly than those of the Asian countries discussed above, but still faster than the world average. This suggests that the share of internationalized production in world output has been increasing somewhat for these developing countries as well.

3.4 Measuring World Internationalized Production

3.4.1 From Home-Country Data

Home-country data on affiliate production were available for four countries—the United States, Japan, Germany, and Sweden. Judging from data on stocks of direct investment, it appears that these four countries have accounted for about half or more of all outward investment stocks since 1960. If we assume that shares of world internationalized production are proportionate to shares of outward investment stocks, we can estimate how much of aggregate world output is from internationalized production, as shown in table 3.17.

The share in world output of affiliates of multinationals from the four home countries reporting affiliate sales or output has changed little since 1977. However, these countries' share of the stock of total world outward direct investment has declined since then. Given our assumptions, we can roughly estimate that the share of internationalized, or affiliate, production has risen from about 4.5 percent to between 6.5 and 7 percent of world output since 1970.

Of course, the share of production accounted for by the multinationals from these countries, including parent (noninternationalized) as well as affiliate (internationalized) production, is much larger. In the United States, Japan, and Sweden, it was probably about 12 percent in 1980 and a little less at the end of the 1980s.

We have no information as to what part of the world's multinational production is represented by these three countries' firms. If we assumed, with no justification, that the parents account for the same share of world output as their affiliates do of the stock of FDI (48 percent in 1980 and 41 percent in 1990), we would estimate that multinationals accounted for about 25 percent of world output at the beginning of the 1980s and somewhat more at the end. That is almost certainly a maximum estimate because these countries probably account for more of internationalized (affiliate) production than of home production.

3.4.2 From Host-Country Data

We aggregate the internationalized output in the seven developed countries we cover by taking ratios of foreign-owned (internationalized) production to aggregate GDP in each country, calculated in national currencies at current prices, and applying these ratios to GDP in current-year international prices for each country. The results are shown in appendix tables 3C.1 and 3C.2 and summarized in table 3.18.

Foreign-owned production increased its share of total output in the group of countries surveyed by a little over a quarter from 1977 to 1991, judged by the middle estimate that assumes minority ownership in Japan only by U.S. multinationals. The increase was not continuous, to judge from the five countries with data for the most years (appendix table 3C.1), but the upward trend is clear.

The shares of internationalized production in these countries as a group ranged from about 3.5 to 4.5 percent. The share of foreign-owned production in Japan was far below the average for these countries. By the broadest measure, Japan does not stand out at the beginning of the period, but by the end it appears to have lower foreign shares in production than is typical.

Since most host countries report foreign-owned shares only in manufacturing, it is difficult to judge the implications of these numbers, which mix data for all industries in some countries with data only for manufacturing in other countries. The second part of each panel in table 3.18 is a more consistent version, limited to manufacturing output, where possible. For manufacturing

Table 3.18 Growth in Foreign-Owned Shares of Production in Seven Developed Host Countries, 1977–91

Industry	Percentage
Growth in Foreign-Owned Shares in Host-Country Output	
All industries[a]	
Assuming minority ownership in Japan only by U.S. multinationals	+27.7
Assuming minority ownership in Japan by all foreign multinationals	+21.1
Manufacturing[b]	
Assuming minority ownership in Japan only by U.S. multinationals	+15.5
Assuming minority ownership in Japan by all foreign multinationals	+13.7
Growth in Foreign-Owned Host-Country Output as a Percentage of World Output	
All industries[a]	
Assuming minority ownership in Japan only by U.S. multinationals	+21.6
Assuming minority ownership in Japan by all foreign multinationals	+15.3
Manufacturing[b]	
Assuming minority ownership in Japan only by U.S. multinationals	+10.0
Assuming minority ownership in Japan by all foreign multinationals	+ 8.3

Source: Appendix tables 3C.1 and 3C.2.
[a]Seven countries, 1977–86; six countries, 1986–91.
[b]Seven countries, 1977–86; six countries, 1986–90.

production there is not such a large upward trend. There was little change for the first decade or so and then a fairly continuous increase from 1985 to 1989 before another dip. However, the share in 1991 was substantially above those for the late 1970s (appendix table 3C.2).

The share of internationalized production in these countries in world output reflects its growth within the seven countries, but also the rate of growth of these seven countries relative to the world as a whole. The growth in shares of world output was between 16 and 27 percent, the broader measure producing the smaller increase. The increases in the shares of world output are smaller than those for shares in country output because these countries were growing less quickly than the world as a whole. The contrast is even stronger for shares of internationalized manufacturing production in these countries in aggregate world output. These grew by between 8 and 10 percent. There did seem to be some upward trend, especially in the last few years, but it was not a strong one.

The slower growth of these countries than of the world partly reflects the implicit weighting in these calculations, which is by the size of internationalized aggregate or manufacturing production. Even within the group of seven countries, that weighting tends to raise the importance of the slow-growing United States and lower that of the fast-growing Japan.

From these calculations, we can gather that there has been some long-term growth in the importance of internationalized production in the developed countries relative to their total output and to world output.

We have also aggregated the internationalized output in the nine developing countries we cover, using the same method as for developed countries. There

Table 3.19 Share of Foreign-Owned Total and Manufacturing Production in Nine Developing Countries in Their Real Output and in Real World Output

	Share (%) of Foreign-Owned Production in Real Output[a] of			Share (%) in Real World Output[a] of Foreign-Owned Production in		
Year	Seven Countries	Nine Countries A	Nine Countries B	Seven Countries	Nine Countries A	Nine Countries B
			Total Production			
1975	1.79			0.22		
1977	2.17		3.38	0.26		0.59
1980[b]	1.73		3.11	0.24		0.55
1983[c]	1.83	2.99	3.03	0.27	0.46	0.56
1989[d]	2.38	3.29	(3.33)	0.38	0.59	(0.72)
1990[d]	2.79	3.41	(3.46)	0.46	0.64	(0.78)
			Manufacturing Production			
1975	1.65			0.21		
1977[e]	2.00		3.25	0.24		0.52
1980[b]	1.60		3.01	0.22		0.53
1983[f]	1.71	2.89	2.93	0.25	0.52	0.54
1989[d]	2.04	3.01	(3.05)	0.33	0.58	(0.60)
1990[d]	2.34	3.03	(3.07)	0.38	0.59	(0.61)

Sources: Text tables and Penn World Tables (5.6).

Note: Seven countries are China, India, Indonesia, Malaysia, Mexico, Singapore, and Taiwan. Nine countries A also include Brazil and Hong Kong. Nine countries B also include Brazil and Korea. Numbers in parentheses are extrapolated from 1983 by figures for nine countries A.

[a]Real GDP in current international prices.

[b]For Malaysia, 1979, and for Korea, 1978.

[c]For Brazil and Mexico, 1982, and for Korea, 1978.

[d]For India, 1987.

[e]For India, average of 1975 and 1979.

[f]For Brazil, 1982 and for Korea, 1984.

appears to have been a fall in the share of internationalized production in the developing countries' own output from 1977 to 1983, following an earlier rise (table 3.19). Then there was large growth in the share after 1983. Relative to aggregate world output there was little change from 1977 to 1983, after an earlier increase, but a very large rise after that, suggesting growth of over 50 percent relative to world output up to 1990. The growth was probably even faster after that because foreign investment in China accelerated in the 1990s. The increase in foreign-owned production was much larger relative to world output than relative to these countries' own output because these countries were growing faster than the rest of the world.

Even more than for the developed host-country data, the data for foreign-owned production in developing countries are limited to the manufacturing sector. The same ratios, confined as far as possible, to the manufacturing sector, are shown in the second panel of table 3.19. The time pattern for manufacturing alone relative to the countries' output is similar to that for the hybrid values in the first panel, with a rise to 1977, a decline to the early 1980s, and then another increase. However, there is no clear trend over the whole period. In contrast, the shares of world output do show an upward trend. The difference between the trends in shares of country output and in shares of world output results from the fact that the ratios are dominated by Asian countries that were growing much faster than the rest of the world.

If we add the foreign-owned manufacturing production in developed and developing host countries, we find that there was some rise over the period since 1977 in the share of world output, as indicated by column (1) of table 3.20.

These numbers understate the share of internationalized output in total output for two reasons. One is that they cover only manufacturing output, and the other is that they include only 16 host countries. To make up for the limitation to manufacturing we use estimates of the share of manufacturing in total internationalized output, as reported by five host countries (col. [2]).

Dividing the manufacturing output share measures of column (1) by these ratios, we estimate shares of world GDP for total internationalized output of the 16 host countries (col. [3]). Since these 16 host countries accounted for about 60 percent of all the inward stock of FDI (col. [4]), we can make an estimate of the share of internationalized production in the whole world by assuming that the share of world internationalized production of these 16 countries was equal to their share of the inward direct investment stock. The corresponding estimates for the share of internationalized production in the output of all host countries are in column (5).

This calculation from the host-country side implies a substantial growth in the share of internationalized production in world output, as does the calculation from the home-country side in column (6), but here almost all the growth is after 1985. The shares estimated from host-country data are smaller, but the growth is faster, over a third from 1977 to 1990 as compared with about a quarter in the estimates from home-country data.

3.5 Summary and Conclusions

The difference between a geographical and an ownership view of production is measured by the amount of internationalized production: that is, production in enterprises owned by nonresidents of the country where the production is located. That internationalized production is also one aspect of the much talked about "globalization" of production, for any one country and for the world as a whole.

The internationalization of production can be measured from two sides: that of the home country and that of the host country. Viewed from the home country, the question is, How much of production owned or controlled by home-country residents takes place outside the geographical boundaries of the home

Table 3.20 Estimates of Internationalized Production from the Host-Country Side

	Internationalized Manufacturing Output in 16 Host Countries as a Percentage of World GDP[a] (1)	Foreign-Owned (Internationalized) Manufacturing Output as a Percentage of Total Foreign-Owned Output: 5 Host Countries[b] (2)	Total Internationalized Output in 16 Host Countries as a Percentage of World GDP[c] (3)	Share (%) of 16 Host Countries in World Stock of Inward FDI[d] (4)	Share (%) of Internationalized Output in World GDP	
					Estimated from Host-Country Side[e] (5)	Estimated from Home-Country Side[f] (6)
1970						4.5
1977	1.55	65.4	2.37	(60.2)	3.9	5.4
1980	1.48	60.1	2.46	60.2	4.1	
1982						5.8
1985[g]	1.49	57.7	2.58	62.0	4.2	
1988						6.2
1990	1.88	59.6	3.15	59.5	5.3	6.7

[a] Appendix table 3C.2 for developed countries, and table 3.19 for developing countries. We use the conservative estimate from table 3C.2, assuming that only U.S. firms have minority ownership in Japan.

[b] Lipsey, Blomström, and Ramstetter (1995).

[c] (Col. [1] ÷ col. [2]) × 100.

[d] United Nations (1994, annex table 3).

[e] (Col. [3] ÷ col. [4]) × 100.

[f] Table 3.19.

[g] 1986 for developed countries, and 1983 for developing countries.

country? Viewed from the host country, the question is, How much of production located in the host country is owned or controlled by residents of other countries?" For the world as a whole, the two views, if measured perfectly, are identical.

Using host-country data, mostly limited to manufacturing, we estimated that the share of internationalized, or affiliate, output in world production increased from 4 percent in 1977 to over 5 percent in 1990, with most of the gain taking place in the late 1980s. The affiliate share of world production estimated from home-country data rose from 4.5 percent in 1970 to 5.4 percent in 1977 and to almost 7 percent in 1990. Since home-country data require fewer assumptions to move from the sample to a world total, we would be inclined to accept them as the best estimates and treat those from the host-country side as mainly a check on the orders of magnitude involved.

The general impression of a much greater importance of internationalized output stems from the contrast between shares of such production in goods industries, particularly manufacturing, and in services. Internationalized output by U.S. and Japanese firms was almost 6 percent of world output in "industry" in 1989, but less than 0.2 percent of the output of "services." "Industry" is defined here to include manufacturing, mining, transportation, communication, public utilities, construction, and trade, and it accounted for about 35 percent of world output in 1989, down from 41 percent in 1970. "Services" accounted for 58 percent, as compared with 49 percent in 1970. Since the United States and Japan account for about three-quarters of the outward direct investment stock of the four countries for which data are available (including also Germany and Sweden), we might guess that the four countries combined account for about 7.5 percent of world output of "industry." Since the four countries own about half of the world's outward investment stock, all internationalized production amounted to something in the neighborhood of 15 percent of world "industry" output.

In the "services" sector, which covers all except agriculture and industry, the internationalized share of production for these four countries' firms was negligible, somewhere between a quarter of 1 percent and a half, but closer to a quarter, with no strong trend.

Another reason for the impression of a much greater role of internationalized or globalization is that our calculations are not intended to describe the total output of multinationals, but only the part that is outside their home countries. Most output by multinationals takes place in their home countries. For example, U.S. multinational firms produced three-quarters of their output in the United States in 1977, and a little more than that fraction in 1989. Japanese multinationals produced 84 percent of their output at home in 1980, and almost 80 percent in 1992. A very rough calculation suggests that multinationals (parents and affiliates) accounted for about 22 percent of world output both at the beginning and at the end of the 1980s.

Given all the attention that globalization has received from scholars, international organizations, and the press, these numbers are a reminder of how large a proportion of economic activity is confined to single geographical locations and home-country ownership. Internationalization of production is clearly growing in importance, but the vast majority of production is still carried out by national producers within their own borders.

Appendix A
Adjusting the MITI Survey Data on Japanese Multinationals

Estimates for Japanese parents and their foreign affiliates are based on data obtained from the Ministry of International Trade and Industry's surveys of parents and affiliates, the only source that provides estimates of production-related activities of Japanese multinationals for more than one year. The coverage of these surveys is incomplete and varies from year to year as well as from variable to variable. This appendix explains the methods used in this paper to compensate for these variations in coverage.

The coverage problems can be most clearly seen by comparing the MITI surveys with generally more comprehensive surveys by a private publishing company, Toyo Keizai (table 3A.1). The number of parents identified by MITI is usually slightly larger than the number surveyed by Toyo Keizai, but because reply rates were low, the number of replying parents is far lower. Moreover, the number of firms reporting even such a basic indicator as sales is smaller than the number of replies for several years. Since we wish to calculate value added, the fact that the number of firms reporting intermediate expenditures is smaller in many years than the number reporting sales is a concern.

For affiliates, reply rates are generally much higher than for parents, but here again the number of firms reporting sales is often lower than the number of replying firms, and the number of firms reporting intermediate expenditures is still smaller in most years (table 3A.1, note c). Moreover, although the number of affiliates to which MITI has sent out questionnaires and the number of affiliates included in the Toyo Keizai surveys were roughly equal in 1988, in subsequent years the number of affiliates to which MITI sent out questionnaires increased much more slowly than the number of affiliates in the Toyo Keizai surveys. Thus, by 1992, the number of affiliates in the Toyo Keizai surveys was 31 percent larger than the number of affiliates receiving MITI questionnaires and 2.3 times as large as the number of affiliates reporting sales to MITI. The Toyo Keizai estimates of affiliate employment are far larger than MITI estimates in the years for which comparisons are possible. One reason the Toyo Keizai estimates are higher is that they apparently cover a large num-

Table 3A.1 **Japan: Comparison of MITI and Toyo Keizai Surveys**

	Parent Samples (number of firms)					Affiliate Samples (number of firms)				Affiliate Employment (thousands)	
	MITI Surveys[b]					MITI Surveys[c]					
Fiscal Year[a]	Sent Out (1)	Replies (2)	Sales (3)	Intermediate Expenditures (4)	Toyo Keizai Survey Replies[d] (5)	Sent Out (6)	Replies (7)	Sales (8)	Toyo Keizai Survey Replies[d] (9)	MITI Surveys[c] (10)	Toyo Keizai Surveys[d] (11)
1980	3,247	1,401	1,256	1,180	n.a.	n.a.	3,853	3,288	6,270	739	n.a.
1983	3,331	1,271	1,161	1,153	n.a.	n.a.	4,383	3,705	7,351	709	n.a.
1984	3,301	1,617	1,488	n.a.	n.a.	n.a.	4,962	4,962	7,684	926	n.a.
1985	3,385	1,413	1,293	n.a.	n.a.	n.a.	5,343	5,343	8,187	1,057	n.a.
1986	3,425	1,144	1,031	832	n.a.	7,112	4,579	4,519	8,146	962	n.a.
1987	3,708	1,718	1,511	n.a.	2,329	8,367	6,647	6,647	8,933	1,168	1,544
1988	3,525	1,771	1,606	1,441	3,165	9,576	7,544	7,544	9,859	1,326	1,672
1989	3,331	1,563	1,360	1,359	3,191	8,804	6,362	6,362	11,484	1,157	1,941
1990	3,529	1,776	1,616	1,553	3,284	10,210	7,986	7,986	12,522	1,550	n.a.
1991	3,368	1,789	1,630	1,325	3,331	10,835	8,505	7,620	13,522	1,621	2,277
1992	3,378	1,594	1,439	1,296	3,290	10,844	7,108	6,243	14,238	1,404	2,416

Sources: MITI (various years-a–c) and Toyo Keizai (various years-a–e).

[a]Fiscal years ending 31 March of the following calendar year. MITI estimates refer to the end of the fiscal year. Toyo Keizai estimates refer to the same calendar year (June–July for 1983–89, December for 1990–91, and October for 1992); figure for 1980 estimated as number of firms in June 1981 minus firms established from 1980 forward.

[b]Data refer to parent firms owning at least 10 percent of a foreign affiliate.

[c]Data refer to directly owned affiliates with 10 percent or larger Japanese ownership shares and indirectly owned affiliates that are majority owned by directly owned affiliates. Data for 1982 and 1984–85 exclude indirectly owned affiliates—indirectly owned affiliates accounted for 7 percent of the number of replying affiliates and 3 percent of affiliate employment in 1980; 9 and 5 percent, respectively, in 1983; and 8 and 4 percent, respectively, in 1986. Sample sizes for intermediate expenditures are not calculable for affiliates but, as in the case of parents, are thought to be much smaller than for sales in some years. For example, for directly owned affiliates in 1983, the sales sample was 3,368 but the intermediate expenditure sample was only 2,704.

[d]Since 1990 Toyo Keizai surveys have covered affiliates with Japanese ownership shares of 10 percent or more; before 1990 the cutoff is unclear.

ber of smaller affiliates that may be excluded from the MITI surveys.[7] The relatively stable growth rates of affiliate employment implied by the Toyo Keizai surveys are much more believable than the wild gyrations implied by the MITI surveys.

Unfortunately, the Toyo Keizai publications do not attempt to compile sales (the only production-related indicator included in these surveys). We can compare the MITI data with U.S. BEA data on Japanese affiliates operating in the United States, from surveys that are legally mandatory and adjusted to compensate for known variations in coverage. This comparison covers 22 to 27 percent of the number of Japanese affiliates abroad reporting sales and 40 to 55 percent of affiliate sales in 1983–92 (tables 3A.1, 3A.2, and 3A.4).

For sales, the variable for which coverage is among the best in the MITI surveys, MITI estimates were larger than BEA totals in 1983–84 and 1986–88, and BEA estimates were larger in other years (table 3A.2). For most years, the differences between the two estimates were under 10 percent, the exceptions being 1987 and 1990–92, with the MITI estimate being much lower in 1992. BEA numbers of affiliates were smaller than MITI's sales samples in 1983 and 1986–88, but the BEA numbers grew much faster thereafter. BEA estimates of Japanese affiliate employment were generally far larger than corresponding MITI estimates. Thus, it appears that estimates of sales are much closer in the two sources than estimates of the number of affiliates or affiliate employment.

MITI estimates of value added in Japanese affiliates in the United States are much larger than corresponding U.S. estimates of gross product originating in them, implying that MITI estimates of intermediate purchases are much lower. Moreover, although ratios of value added to sales calculated from U.S. data are relatively stable, rising slowly from 6 percent in 1980 to 13 percent in 1992, corresponding ratios calculated from MITI data varied from 15 percent to 58 percent. MITI's recently initiated business structure surveys indicate that corresponding ratios for majority-owned affiliates worldwide in 1991 (the only year available as yet) were close to the low end of the MITI estimates but slightly higher than U.S. estimates, 20 percent in all industries, 35 percent in manufacturing, and 15 percent in trade (MITI 1994). Thus, if the coverage of affiliates in the United States is representative of the MITI multinational survey coverage in general, estimates of sales appear to have been reasonably reliable in the 1980s, but poor coverage appears to have had a particularly adverse effect on more recent sales estimates, on estimates of intermediate purchases, and therefore on calculated value added.

Adjustments to the MITI estimates of sales and value added, presented in tables 3A.3 and 3A.4, attempt to compensate for (1) fluctuations in coverage over time and (2) the particularly low and variable coverage of intermediate expenditures. The first step involves adjusting the sales series to compensate

7. E.g., in 1992, average affiliate employment reported to MITI was 220 (MITI, various years-a), while the figures in appendix table 3A.1 indicate an average of 170 employees per affiliate in the Toyo Keizai sample.

Table 3A.2 **Japan: Sales and Value Added of Japanese Affiliates in the United States**

	Sales (billion yen)			Value Added (billion yen)			Value Added/Sales			
Year	All Industries	Manufacturing	Trade	All Industries	Manufacturing	Trade	All Industries	Manufacturing	Trade	No. of Affiliates, All Industries[a]
					MITI Surveys[b]					
1983	27,414	2,358	24,700	8,872	1,168	7,424	0.32	0.50	0.30	833
1984	36,781	5,660	30,136	n.a.	n.a.	n.a.	n.a.	n.a.	n.a.	n.a.
1985	25,199	3,862	20,654	n.a.	n.a.	n.a.	n.a.	n.a.	n.a.	n.a.
1986	25,969	4,845	20,600	15,060	2,989	11,691	0.58	0.62	0.57	1,107
1987	27,278	5,600	21,000	5,731	1,597	3,926	0.21	0.29	0.19	1,717
1988	31,222	7,249	22,659	4,657	2,020	2,362	0.15	0.28	0.10	1,957
1989	41,491	11,706	28,672	7,109	3,282	3,448	0.17	0.28	0.12	1,720
1990	40,071	11,196	27,459	10,516	4,539	5,024	0.26	0.41	0.18	2,070
1991	37,654	10,072	26,342	16,810	5,965	10,025	0.45	0.59	0.38	1,935
1992	31,576	9,313	20,474	15,540	5,518	8,828	0.49	0.59	0.43	1,602
					U.S. BEA Surveys[c]					
1980	17,822	844	15,918	1,050	n.a.	n.a.	0.06	n.a.	n.a.	709
1983	25,318	1,526	22,502	1,866	n.a.	n.a.	0.07	n.a.	n.a.	799
1984	34,280	2,485	29,920	2,938	n.a.	n.a.	0.09	n.a.	n.a.	833
1985	27,198	1,994	23,781	2,422	n.a.	n.a.	0.09	n.a.	n.a.	870
1986	24,462	1,754	21,620	2,014	n.a.	n.a.	0.08	n.a.	n.a.	953
1987	23,604	1,958	19,160	2,212	550	1,068	0.09	0.28	0.06	1,159
1988	30,891	3,603	23,752	3,223	1,031	1,199	0.10	0.29	0.05	1,378
1989	42,903	6,722	30,585	4,966	1,698	1,701	0.12	0.25	0.06	1,817
1990	45,114	8,656	31,504	5,001	2,127	1,531	0.11	0.25	0.05	2,233
1991	42,989	8,630	28,952	5,325	2,002	2,208	0.12	0.23	0.08	2,472
1992	41,769	8,517	27,971	5,382	2,104	2,349	0.13	0.25	0.08	3,124

Sources: MITI (various years-a, various years-b), Lowe (1990), U.S. Department of Commerce (1985b, 1990, 1992a, 1994, various years), and Zeile (1994).

[a]For MITI multinational firm surveys, number of firms reporting sales.

[b]For definitional notes, see table 3A.1.

[c]Data refer to nonbank affiliates with 10 percent or more foreign ownership and their largest ultimate beneficial owners in Japan. Value-added data refer to gross product estimates by the source. Original U.S. dollar figures converted to Japanese yen using exchange rates in the MITI multinational firm surveys.

Table 3A.3 **Japan: Sales and Value Added Estimates for Japanese Parents**

	Sales (billion yen)			Value Added[a] (billion yen)			Value Added/Sales		
Year	All Industries	Manufacturing	Trade	All Industries	Manufacturing	Trade	All Industries	Manufacturing	Trade
				Unadjusted					
1980	184,591	79,864	94,551	42,898	37,116	4,213	0.23	0.46	0.04
1983	219,431	91,489	111,945	62,678	51,422	5,669	0.29	0.56	0.05
1984	321,584	172,747	121,143	n.a.	n.a.	n.a.	n.a.	n.a.	n.a.
1985	272,219	114,664	126,028	n.a.	n.a.	n.a.	n.a.	n.a.	n.a.
1986	217,855	91,544	104,722	70,778	57,098	5,785	0.32	0.62	0.06
1987	267,807	119,331	120,473	n.a.	n.a.	n.a.	n.a.	n.a.	n.a.
1988	304,582	138,219	128,843	75,266	58,627	5,786	0.25	0.42	0.04
1989	315,548	125,004	159,502	56,922	46,803	4,958	0.18	0.37	0.03
1990	364,494	154,233	160,167	87,828	62,488	9,527	0.24	0.41	0.06
1991	363,258	151,615	158,758	152,800	79,611	34,965	0.42	0.53	0.22
1992	327,024	144,363	143,852	90,908	79,087	6,721	0.28	0.55	0.05
				Adjusted[b]					
1980	227,620	98,480	116,591	51,154	40,765	5,251	0.22	0.41	0.05
1983	279,407	116,495	142,542	65,768	50,490	6,593	0.24	0.43	0.05
1984	336,296	180,650	126,685	n.a.	n.a.	n.a.	n.a.	n.a.	n.a.
1985	317,390	133,692	146,940	n.a.	n.a.	n.a.	n.a.	n.a.	n.a.
1986	298,872	125,587	143,666	72,696	55,979	6,777	0.24	0.45	0.05
1987	301,680	134,424	135,711	n.a.	n.a.	n.a.	n.a.	n.a.	n.a.
1988	317,155	143,925	134,161	72,210	58,409	6,052	0.23	0.41	0.05
1989	349,072	138,284	176,448	74,818	54,744	7,471	0.21	0.40	0.04
1990	376,041	159,119	165,241	85,154	63,970	7,935	0.23	0.40	0.05
1991	363,273	151,622	158,765	95,317	64,593	12,729	0.26	0.43	0.08
1992	352,708	155,701	155,150	82,482	67,039	7,055	0.23	0.43	0.05

Source: See tables 3A.1 and 3A.2.

Note: See table 3A.1 for definitional details.

[a]Value added estimated as sales less intermediate expenditures. For 1988 and 1990–91, intermediate expenditures are estimated as IV/IR, where IV = value of imports and IR = ratio of imports to intermediate expenditures. Due to apparent differences in sample sizes across these variables and rounding errors, this induces errors in the value-added calculations not present for other years.

[b]See appendix A text for details on the calculation of adjusted values.

Table 3A.4 **Japan: Sales and Value Added Estimates for Japanese Affiliates**

	Sales (billion yen)			Value Added (billion yen)			Value Added/Sales		
Year	All Industries	Manufacturing	Trade	All Industries	Manufacturing	Trade	All Industries	Manufacturing	Trade
				Unadjusted[a]					
1980	37,940	6,510	30,979	11,136	3,205	7,706	0.29	0.49	0.25
1983	49,914	7,218	41,345	17,157	3,953	12,179	0.34	0.55	0.29
1984	68,933	13,442	52,564	n.a.	n.a.	n.a.	n.a.	n.a.	n.a.
1985	50,953	9,949	38,151	n.a.	n.a.	n.a.	n.a.	n.a.	n.a.
1986	48,166	11,362	35,510	27,478	7,483	19,118	0.57	0.66	0.54
1987	54,809	13,060	39,877	12,673	3,747	7,963	0.23	0.29	0.20
1988	68,427	17,621	48,128	10,440	5,082	4,644	0.15	0.29	0.10
1989	93,178	22,267	66,044	16,038	6,856	7,957	0.17	0.31	0.12
1990	99,806	26,195	69,149	25,926	11,233	11,586	0.26	0.43	0.17
1991	88,737	25,365	58,337	40,887	14,984	22,851	0.46	0.59	0.39
1992	79,007	25,114	48,785	39,347	15,185	21,166	0.50	0.60	0.43
				Adjusted[b]					
1980	44,834	7,693	36,608	9,619	2,861	5,575	0.21	0.37	0.15
1983	57,392	8,300	47,539	12,891	3,178	7,675	0.22	0.38	0.16
1984	72,350	14,108	55,169	n.a.	n.a.	n.a.	n.a.	n.a.	n.a.
1985	54,173	10,578	40,562	n.a.	n.a.	n.a.	n.a.	n.a.	n.a.
1986	54,190	12,783	39,951	14,629	5,178	8,398	0.27	0.41	0.21
1987	55,408	13,203	40,313	11,198	4,367	5,743	0.20	0.33	0.14
1988	68,422	17,620	48,124	12,752	5,833	5,863	0.19	0.33	0.12
1989	99,224	23,712	70,330	18,881	7,942	8,906	0.19	0.33	0.13
1990	103,452	27,152	71,675	21,498	9,751	9,751	0.21	0.36	0.14
1991	94,510	27,015	62,132	23,439	10,577	11,238	0.25	0.39	0.18
1992	88,363	28,087	54,561	22,573	11,075	10,329	0.26	0.39	0.19

Source: See tables 3A.1 and 3A.2.

[a]See table 3A.1 for definitional notes regarding the multinational firm surveys. Note also that data for 1984 and 1985 exclude indirectly owned affiliates that accounted for 7 percent of all affiliate sales in 1983 and 8 percent in 1986.

[b]For details on calculation of adjusted figures see appendix A text.

for changes in coverage from year to year. To estimate the marginal effect of changes in coverage rates, worldwide affiliate sales and parent sales were estimated as functions of sales by affiliates in the United States taken from BEA data and the applicable coverage rate. The idea here is to use the strong correlations between parent sales, affiliate sales, and sales of affiliates in the United States to remove trend effects independent of variance in reply rates, and then measure the effect of changing reply rates. The resulting ordinary least squares regressions for 1980 and 1983–92 are as follows:

$$\underset{}{SP_t} = \underset{(0.69)}{-29736} + \underset{(5.60)}{4.1794}\,(SAU_t) + \underset{(3.34)}{442766}\,(NPS_t / NP_t),$$

$$\text{Adj. } R^2 = 0.920,\ DW = 0.83,$$

$$SA_t = \underset{(2.07)}{-19945} + \underset{(15.7)}{2.1625}\,(SAU_t) + \underset{(2.19)}{28653}\,(NAS_t / NA_t),$$

$$\text{Adj. } R^2 = 0.961,\ DW = 1.10,$$

where NA is number of affiliates in the Toyo Keizai surveys, NAS is number of affiliates reporting sales to MITI, NP is number of parents sent MITI questionnaires, NPS is number of parents reporting sales, SA is worldwide affiliate sales, SAU is BEA estimates of sales of Japanese affiliates in the United States, SP is parent sales, and t is a subscript indicating year t. Figures in parentheses are t-statistics. Durbin-Watson (DW) statistics are uncomfortably low, especially in the parent equation, where first-order autocorrelation is definitely indicated, but the small samples involved make it difficult to correct this problem with any degree of confidence, and these estimates are used as is.

Aggregate adjusted sales (SAADJ and SPADJ for affiliates and parents, respectively) are then calculated as the sum of reported sales and the product of the coefficient on the reply rate from the above equations and the difference between the maximum observed reply rate and the actual reply rate:

$$SAADJ_t = SA_t + (0.765 - NAS_t / NA_t)(442{,}766),$$

$$SPADJ_t = SP_t + (0.484 - NPS_t / NP_t)(28{,}653).$$

The use of the maximum observed reply rate as opposed to one (implying 100 percent coverage) reflects a primary concern with compensating for variations in coverage rates rather than for the levels of coverage rates. To obtain estimates for the manufacturing and trade sectors (sector being indicated by subscript i), sectoral shares from reported sales data are multiplied by adjusted sales estimates:

$$SAADJ_{it} = (SAADJ_t)(SA_{it} / SA_t),$$

$$SPADJ_{it} = (SPADJ_t)(SP_{it} / SP_t).$$

The second step is to calculate value added from the adjusted sales figures. Since the levels and volatility of ratios of value added to sales in the MITI data seem clearly unrealistic, adjusted value-added estimates are derived by first adjusting the ratios of value added to sales downward somewhat and reducing their volatility, and then multiplying these adjusted ratios by the corresponding adjusted sales estimates. Because the average of MITI estimates for the years 1988–90 is relatively low and closer to other corresponding estimates, this average is taken as a base, and adjusted ratios of value added to sales are calculated as an 80–20 weighted average of this base and reported ratios. The resulting calculations are as follows:

$$\mathrm{VSADJ}_{it} = 0.8(\mathrm{VSB}_{i}) + 0.2(\mathrm{VS}_{it}),$$

$$\mathrm{VADJ}_{it} = (\mathrm{VSAADJ}_{it})(\mathrm{SPADJ}_{it}),$$

where VSB is the base (average 1988–90) ratio of value added to sales (for affiliates, 0.19 in all industries, 0.34 in manufacturing, and 0.13 in trade; for parents, 0.22 in all industries, 0.40 in manufacturing, and 0.05 in trade), VADJ is adjusted value added, VS is the reported ratio of value added to sales, and VSADJ is the adjusted ratio of value added to sales.

The resulting adjusted estimates for sales and value added are thought to be more realistic than the unadjusted figures in that fluctuations due to changes in the coverage of MITI surveys are somewhat compensated for. The resulting adjusted figures are correspondingly subject to far less variation than the unadjusted values.

Finally, there is also a problem encountered when trying to calculate multinational shares of Japanese value added or sales (or total output including intermediate expenditures) at the sector level. If one calculates the ratio of parent sales to total output on a national accounts basis for the trade sector, the resulting ratios are 1.68 to 2.25 (tables 3A.3 and 3A.5). If one uses the Ministry of Finance's corporation statistics to calculate parent shares of sales, these ratios fall to the 0.29–0.40 range. In other words, either differences between the definition of total sales and total output (i.e., inventory changes) or differences in accounting by establishments (national accounts data) or enterprises (corporation and multinational firm statistics) are extremely large. Due to the control of a large number of nontrade establishments by large trading firms in Japan, the latter is probably by far the larger factor. This makes the use of the corporation statistics preferable for sectoral-level analysis, but use of these data may lead to overestimation of multinational shares because estimates of value added based on corporation statistics are below national accounts estimates of GDP.

Table 3A.5 **Japan: Sales or Total Output and Value Added**

	Sales or Total Output (billion yen)			Value Added (billion yen)			Value Added/Sales		
Year	All Industries	Manufacturing	Trade	All Industries	Manufacturing	Trade	All Industries	Manufacturing	Trade
				All Corporations in Japan[a]					
1980	662,415	229,489	313,737	164,405	69,773	47,667	0.25	0.30	0.15
1983	766,836	260,240	360,230	200,482	82,230	56,508	0.26	0.32	0.16
1984	811,901	283,075	378,607	211,635	89,955	60,201	0.26	0.32	0.16
1985	857,031	295,821	392,407	231,619	95,000	62,497	0.27	0.32	0.16
1986	860,670	272,667	404,049	246,152	92,463	71,117	0.29	0.34	0.18
1987	953,937	300,878	448,820	273,814	103,733	79,388	0.29	0.34	0.18
1988	1,035,465	326,172	471,390	301,925	113,274	85,200	0.29	0.35	0.18
1989	1,093,531	345,425	484,382	315,698	122,623	83,630	0.29	0.35	0.17
1990	1,200,607	375,069	529,832	353,891	132,240	97,218	0.29	0.35	0.18
1991	1,256,101	387,860	550,597	381,881	137,005	107,446	0.30	0.35	0.20
1992	1,230,330	368,516	535,788	387,752	132,702	111,163	0.32	0.36	0.21
				National Accounts Estimates (Establishments)[b]					
1980	544,284	242,496	55,396	239,951	70,232	36,792	0.44	0.29	0.66
1983	614,674	264,895	61,900	279,169	81,416	41,774	0.45	0.31	0.67
1984	647,176	279,496	64,698	300,429	89,245	41,977	0.46	0.32	0.65
1985	674,321	287,810	65,896	320,258	94,673	42,836	0.47	0.33	0.65
1986	675,725	275,271	67,189	334,450	96,262	43,567	0.49	0.35	0.65
1987	696,821	274,715	70,158	349,516	99,297	45,540	0.50	0.36	0.65
1988	746,587	296,560	74,306	373,137	106,649	48,010	0.50	0.36	0.65
1989	810,513	322,246	78,391	398,238	114,455	50,377	0.49	0.36	0.64
1990	877,125	348,072	84,913	426,559	123,443	54,501	0.49	0.35	0.64
1991	924,561	366,078	90,286	451,873	131,336	57,830	0.49	0.36	0.64
1992	926,688	351,620	92,326	461,334	129,570	59,273	0.50	0.37	0.64

Sources: Japan, Economic Planning Agency (various years) and Japan, Ministry of Finance (various years).

[a]Data refer to fiscal years ending 31 March of following calendar year. Data in "sales or total output" columns refer to sales. Value added is estimated as sales less cost of sales plus labor costs.

[b]Data refer to calendar years. Data in "sales or total output" columns refer to total output, including intermediate expenditures. Value added is evaluated at producer prices.

Appendix B

Table 3B.1 **Estimating Foreign-Owned Production in Japan, Including Minority-Owned Firms**

Year	Exchange Rate[a] (yen per U.S.$) (1)	Value Added in Foreign Majority-Owned Firms[b] (billion yen) (2)	U.S.-Owned Affiliates in Japan: Sum of Employee Compensation and Net Income: U.S. Dollars (million): Total[c] (3)	U.S. Dollars (million): Majority Owned[c] (4)	Yen (billion): Total (5)	Yen (billion): Majority Owned (6)	Yen (billion): Minority Owned (7)	Ratio: Total to Majority Owned (3)/(4) (8)	Gross Product of Majority Owned[d] (billion U.S.$) (9)	Ratio: Gross Product to Sum of Employee Compensation and Net Income in U.S. Majority-Owned Affiliates (9)/(4) (10)	Estimated Value Added in Foreign-Owned (≥ 10%) Firms: High[e] (2)*(8) (11)	Low[f] (2)+[(7)*(10)] (12)
1977	268.51	2,045	5,523	1,522	1,483	409	1,074	3.629	3,065	2.014	7,421	4,208
1978	210.44	2,041					(1,108)	(3.547)		(2.019)	7,238	4,278
1979	219.14	1,988					(1,141)	(3.464)		(2.024)	6,887	4,298
1980	226.74	2,245					(1,175)	(3.382)		(2.029)	7,593	4,629
1981	220.54	2,725					(1,209)	(3.300)		(2.034)	8,992	5,184
1982	249.08	2,843	7,236	2,249	1,802	560	1,242	3.217	4,587	2.040	9,147	5,376
1983	237.51	3,812	8,300	2,876	1,971	683	1,288	2.886		(1.984)	11,001	6,368
1984	237.52	3,262	8,467	3,247	2,011	771	1,240	2.608		(1.929)	8,506	5,654
1985	238.54	2,572	9,476	3,511	2,260	838	1,423	2.699		(1.874)	6,942	5,238
1986	168.52	4,075	13,478	5,597	2,271	943	1,328	2.408		(1.818)	9,813	6,490
1987	144.64	4,136	15,487	6,991	2,240	1,011	1,229	2.215		(1.763)	9,162	6,302
1988	128.15	4,627	18,830	8,532	2,413	1,093	1,320	2.207		(1.708)	10,212	6,881
1989	137.96	4,757	19,949	9,042	2,752	1,247	1,505	2.206	14,940	1.652	10,495	7,243

(continued)

Table 3B.1 (continued)

			U.S.-Owned Affiliates in Japan							Ratio: Gross Product to Sum of Employee Compensation and Net Income in U.S. Majority-Owned Affiliates	Estimated Value Added in Foreign-Owned (≥ 10%) Firms	
			Sum of Employee Compensation and Net Income									
			U.S. Dollars (million)		Yen (billion)							
Year	Exchange Rate[a] (yen per U.S.$) (1)	Value Added in Foreign Majority-Owned Firms[b] (billion yen) (2)	Total[c] (3)	Majority Owned[c] (4)	Total (5)	Majority Owned (6)	Minority Owned (7)	Ratio: Total to Majority Owned (3)/(4) (8)	Gross Product of Majority Owned[d] (billion U.S.$) (9)	(9)/(4) (10)	High[e] (2)*(8) (11)	Low[f] (2)+[(7)*(10)] (12)
1990	144.79	4,778	20,506	9,209	2,969	1,333	1,636	2.227	14,565	1.582	10,639	7,365
1991	134.71	5,131	22,707	10,629	3,059	1,432	1,627	2.136	16,517	1.554	10,961	7,659
1992	126.65	4,497	21,673	10,851	2,745	1,374	1,371	1.997	15,747	1.451	8,982	6,486
1993	111.20		24,396	12,688	2,713	1,411	1,302	1.923	17,958	1.415		

Note: Numbers in parentheses were interpolated on a straight line.

[a]International Monetary Fund (1995).

[b]Lipsey, Blomström, and Ramstetter (1995, table B-7).

[c]U.S. Department of Commerce (1981, 1985a, 1992b) and corresponding annual volumes.

[d]Mataloni and Goldberg (1994) and Mataloni (1995).

[e]Assuming the same ratio of total to majority-owned in all countries as in United States.

[f]Assuming only U.S. firms had minority holdings.

Table 3B.2 Estimating Foreign-Owned Manufacturing Production in Japan, Including Minority-Owned Firms

			U.S.-Owned Manufacturing Affiliates in Japan									
			Sum of Employee Compensation and Net Income									
			U.S. Dollars (million)		Yen (billion)						Estimated Value Added in Foreign-Owned (≥ 10%) Firms	
Year	Exchange Rate[a] (yen per U.S.$) (1)	Value Added in Foreign Majority-Owned Firms[b] (billion yen) (2)	Total[c] (3)	Majority Owned[c] (4)	Total (5)	Majority Owned (6)	Minority Owned (7)	Ratio: Total to Majority Owned (3)/(4) (8)	Gross Product of Majority Owned[d] (billion U.S.$) (9)	Ratio: Gross Product to Sum of Employee Compensation and Net Income in U.S. Majority-Owned Affiliates (9)/(4) (10)	High[e] (2)*(8) (11)	Low[f] (2)+[(7)*(10)] (12)
1977	268.51	1,548	2,810	952	755	256	499	2.952	1,468	1.542	4,569	2,317
1978	210.44	1,604					(594)	(3.134)		(1.553)	5,027	2,526
1979	219.14	1,548					(689)	(3.316)		(1.563)	5,134	2,625
1980	226.74	1,663					(784)	(3.499)		(1.573)	5,818	2,897
1981	220.54	2,178					(879)	(3.681)		(1.584)	8,017	3,570
1982	249.08	2,183	5,277	1,366	1,314	340	974	3.863	2,178	1.594	8,433	3,736
1983	237.51	3,188	5,513	1,575	1,309	374	935	3.500		(1.579)	11,159	4,665
1984	237.52	2,762	6,087	1,988	1,446	472	974	3.062		(1.565)	8,457	4,285
1985	238.54	2,159	6,819	2,113	1,627	504	1,123	3.227		(1.550)	6,967	3,899
1986	168.52	3,414	8,851	3,210	1,492	541	951	2.757		(1.535)	9,413	4,873
1987	144.64	3,455	10,728	4,226	1,552	611	941	2.539		(1.520)	8,771	4,885
1988	128.15	3,701	12,575	4,701	1,611	602	1,009	2.675		(1.505)	9,900	5,219

(continued)

Table 3B.2 (continued)

			U.S.-Owned Manufacturing Affiliates in Japan								Ratio: Gross Product to Sum of Employee Compensation and Net Income in U.S. Majority-Owned Affiliates	Estimated Value Added in Foreign-Owned (≥ 10%) Firms	
			Sum of Employee Compensation and Net Income										
			U.S. Dollars (million)		Yen (billion)								
Year	Exchange Rate[a] (yen per U.S.$) (1)	Value Added in Foreign Majority-Owned Firms[b] (billion yen) (2)	Total[c] (3)	Majority Owned[c] (4)	Total (5)	Majority Owned (6)	Minority Owned (7)	Ratio: Total to Majority Owned (3)/(4) (8)	Gross Product of Majority Owned[d] (billion U.S.$) (9)		(9)/(4) (10)	High[e] (2)*(8) (11)	Low[f] (2)+[(7)*(10)] (12)
1989	137.96	3,852	13,450	5,147	1,856	710	1,146	2.613	7,668		1.490	10,066	5,559
1990	144.79	3,674	13,867	5,090	2,008	737	1,271	2.724	7,305		1.435	10,009	5,498
1991	134.71	3,882	14,384	5,680	1,938	765	1,173	2.532	7,932		1.396	9,831	5,519
1992	126.65	3,463	13,418	5,686	1,699	720	979	2.360	7,883		1.386	8,172	4,821
1993	111.20		14,896	6,597	1,656	734	922	2.258	8,993		1.363		

Note: Numbers in parentheses were interpolated on a straight line.

[a]International Monetary Fund (1995).

[b]Lipsey, Blomström, and Ramstetter (1995, table B-7).

[c]U.S. Department of Commerce (1981, 1985a, 1992b) and corresponding annual volumes.

[d]Mataloni and Goldberg (1994) and Mataloni (1995).

[e]Assuming the same ratio of total to majority-owned in all countries as in United States.

[f]Assuming only U.S. firms had minority holdings.

Appendix C

Table 3C.1 **Share of Foreign-Owned Production in Seven Developed Countries in Their Real Output under Three Assumptions about Foreign Minority Ownership in Japan**

	Omitting Minority Ownership in Japan			Assuming Minority Ownership in Japan Only by U.S. Multinationals			Assuming Minority Ownership in Japan by Foreign Multinationals in Same Proportion to Majority Ownership as for United States		
Year[a]	Seven Countries	Six Countries	Five Countries	Seven Countries	Six Countries	Five Countries	Seven Countries	Six Countries	Five Countries
				Share (%) of Foreign-Owned Production in Real Output[b]					
1977	3.28	3.10	3.12	3.50	3.33	3.35	3.83	3.67	3.70
1979	(3.59)[c]	3.39	3.42	(3.79)[c]	3.60	3.63	(4.00)[c]	3.83	3.87
1980	(3.74)[d]		3.56	(3.93)[d]		3.76	(4.16)[d]		4.02
1981			3.77			3.97			4.28
1982			3.67			3.88			4.18
1985			3.65			3.83			3.95
1986	3.76	3.64	3.65	3.91	3.80	3.81	4.13	4.02	4.03
1989		4.24	4.24		4.38	4.38		4.57	4.57
1990	(4.34)[e]	4.20	4.21	(4.47)[e]	4.35	4.35	(4.64)[e]	4.53	4.54
1991	(4.34)[e]	4.21	4.21	(4.47)[e]	4.35	4.35	(4.64)[e]	4.53	4.53
				Share (%) of Foreign-Owned Manufacturing Production in Real Output[b]					
1977	2.47	2.34	2.35	2.55	2.42	2.43	2.79	2.66	2.68
1979		2.47	2.48		2.57	2.58		2.80	2.82

(continued)

Table 3C.1 (continued)

Year[a]	Omitting Minority Ownership in Japan			Assuming Minority Ownership in Japan Only by U.S. Multinationals			Assuming Minority Ownership in Japan by Foreign Multinationals in Same Proportion to Majority Onwership as for United States		
	Seven Countries	Six Countries	Five Countries	Seven Countries	Six Countries	Five Countries	Seven Countries	Six Countries	Five Counties
1980	(2.49)[c]	2.35	2.37	(2.60)[c]	2.46	2.47	(2.84)[c]	2.70	2.73
1981	(2.58)[d]		2.45	(2.70)[d]		2.57	(3.05)[d]		2.93
1982			2.31			2.44			2.82
1985			2.33			2.45			2.66
1986	2.46	2.38	2.36	2.55	2.47	2.46	2.84	2.77	2.76
1989			2.85			2.95			3.21
1990	(2.94)[e]	2.83	2.81	(3.03)[e]	2.93	2.92	(3.26)[e]	3.18	3.17
1991	(2.87)[e]		2.75	(2.95)[e]		2.84	(3.17)[e]		3.08

Sources: Text tables, appendix B, and Penn World Tables (5.6).

Note: Seven countries are Australia, Japan, Norway, Sweden, the United Kingdom, the United States, and Canada. Six countries exclude Australia. Five countries exclude Australia and Sweden.

[a]In 1977, average of 1974 and 1979 for Canada. In 1978, U.K. figure for 1977. In 1979, figure for Sweden from 1978. In 1980, U.K. figure for 1979. In 1982, U.K. figure for 1981. In 1987, figure for Sweden from 1986. In 1988, figure for Norway from 1987. In 1991, figures for both Norway and Sweden from 1990.

[b]Real GDP in current international prices.

[c]Extrapolated from 1977 by figures for six countries.

[d]Extrapolated from 1979 by figures for five countries.

[e]Extrapolated from 1986 by figures for five countries.

Table 3C.2 **Share of Foreign-Owned Production in Seven Developed Countries in World Output under Three Assumptions about Foreign Minority Ownership in Japan**

	Omitting Minority Ownership in Japan			Assuming Minority Ownership Only by U.S. Multinationals			Assuming Minority Ownership by Foreign Multinationals in Same Proportion to Majority Ownership as for United States		
Year[a]	Seven Countries	Six Countries	Five Countries	Seven Countries	Six Countries	Five Countries	Seven Countries	Six Countries	Five Countries
	Share (%) in World Output[b] of Foreign-Owned Production								
1977	1.22	1.12	1.11	1.31	1.21	1.19	1.43	1.33	1.32
1979	(1.33)[c]	1.22	1.21	(1.41)[c]	1.30	1.29	(1.49)[c]	1.38	1.37
1980			1.22			1.29			1.38
1981			1.30			1.37			1.48
1982			1.25			1.32			1.42
1985			1.26			1.32			1.36
1986	1.38	1.29	1.27	1.43	1.35	1.33	1.51	1.42	1.40
1989		1.50	1.48		1.55	1.53		1.62	1.59
1990	(1.57)[d]	1.48	1.45	(1.62)[d]	1.53	1.50	(1.68)[d]	1.59	1.57
1991	(1.55)[d]	1.45	1.43	(1.59)[d]	1.50	1.48	(1.65)[e]	1.56	1.54
	Share (%) in World Output[b] of Foreign-Owned Manufacturing Production								
1977	0.93	0.85	0.84	0.96	0.88	0.87	1.04	0.97	0.95
1979		0.89	0.88		0.93	0.92		1.01	1.00
1980	(0.90)[c]	0.82	0.81	(0.93)[c]	0.86	0.85	(1.02)[c]	0.95	0.94
1981			0.85			0.89			1.01
1982			0.79			0.83			0.96
1985			0.80			0.84			0.92

(*continued*)

Table 3C.2 (continued)

	Omitting Minority Ownership in Japan			Assuming Minority Ownership Only by U.S. Multinationals			Assuming Minority Ownership by Foreign Multinationals in Same Proportion to Majority Ownership as for United States		
Year[a]	Seven Countries	Six Countries	Five Countries	Seven Countries	Six Countries	Five Countries	Seven Countries	Six Countries	Five Countries
1986	0.90	0.84	0.82	0.93	0.88	0.86	1.04	0.98	0.96
1989			0.99			1.03			1.12
1990	(1.06)[d]	0.99	0.97	(1.10)[d]	1.03	1.01	(1.18)[d]	1.12	1.09
1991	(1.02)[d]		0.93	(1.05)[d]		0.96	(1.13)[d]		1.04

Sources: Text tables, appendix B, and Penn World Tables (5.6).

Note: Seven countries are Australia, Japan, Norway, Sweden, the United Kingdom, the United States, and Canada. Six countries exclude Australia. Five countries exclude Australia and Sweden.

[a]In 1977, average of 1974 and 1979 for Canada. In 1978, U.K. figure for 1977. In 1979, figure for Sweden from 1978. In 1980, U.K. figure for 1979. In 1982, U.K. figure for 1981. In 1987, figure for Sweden from 1986. In 1988, figure for Norway from 1987. In 1991, figures for both Norway and Sweden from 1990.

[b]Real GDP in current international prices.

[c]Extrapolated from 1977 by figures for six countries.

[d]Extrapolated from 1979 by figures for five countries.

[e]Extrapolated from 1986 by figures for five countries.

References

Andersson, Thomas, Torbjörn Fredriksson, and Roger Svensson. 1996. *Multinational restructuring, internationalization, and small economies: The Swedish case.* London and New York: Routledge.

Blomström, Magnus. 1990. Competitiveness of firms and countries. In *Globalization of firms and the competitiveness of nations,* ed. John Dunning, Bruce Kogut, and Magnus Blomström. Lund: Lund University Press.

Blomström, Magnus, and Robert E. Lipsey. 1989a. The export performance of Swedish and U.S. multinationals. *Review of Income and Wealth* 35 (3): 245–64.

———. 1989b. U.S. firms in Latin American service industries. *World Development* 17 (11): 193–201.

———. 1993. The competitiveness of countries and their multinational firms. In *Multinationals in the global political economy,* ed. Lorraine Eden and Evan Potter. London: Macmillan.

Encarnacion, Dennis J. 1992. *Rivals beyond trade: America versus Japan in global competition.* Ithaca, N.Y.: Cornell University Press.

Germany. Deutsche Bundesbank. 1991. *Statistische Beihefte zu den Monatsberichten der Deutsche Bundesbank.* Frankfurt am Main: Deutsche Bundesbank, March.

———. 1995. *Kapitalverflechtung mit dem Ausland.* Frankfurt am Main: Deutsche Bundesbank, May.

Howenstine, Ned G. 1977. Gross product of foreign affiliate of U.S. companies. *Survey of Current Business* 57 (2): 17–28.

International Monetary Fund. 1995. *International financial statistics yearbook.* Washington, D.C.: International Monetary Fund.

Japan. Economic Planning Agency. Various years. *Annual report on national accounts,* 1983–94 issues. Tokyo: Ministry of Finance Printing Bureau.

———. Ministry of Finance. Various years. *Hojin kigyou toukei shiho* (Corporation statistics quarterly), April–June issues 1978–93.

———. Ministry of International Trade and Industry (MITI). 1994. *Results of the Basic Survey of Business Structure and Activity, 1992.* Vol. 1, *Summary report* (in Japanese). Tokyo: Shadan Houjin Tsusan Toukei Kyoukai.

———. Various years-a. *Kaigai jigyou katsudou kihon chousa: Kaigai toushi toukei souran* (A comprehensive survey of foreign investment statistics), nos. 1 (1980 survey), 2 (1983 survey), 3 (1986 survey), 4 (1989 survey), 5 (1992 survey). Tokyo: Toyo Hoki (no. 1); Keibun (nos. 2, 3); Ministry of Finance Printing Bureau (nos. 4, 5).

———. Various years-b. *Wagakuni kigyou no kaigai jigyou katsudou* (Overseas activities of national firms), nos. 15 (1984 survey), 16 (1985 survey), 18/19 (1987 and 1988 surveys), 21 (1990 survey), 22 (1991 survey). Tokyo: Keibun (nos. 15, 16); Ministry of Finance Printing Bureau (nos. 18/19, 20, 21, 22).

———. Various years-c. *Gaishikei kigyou no doukou* (Trends in foreign-owned firms), nos. 12, 13, 14, 15, 16–17, 18, 19, 20–21, 22–23, 24, 25, 26, 27. Tokyo: Ministry of Finance Printing Bureau (nos. 12, 13, 14, 22–23, 24, 25, 26, 27); Toyo Hoki (nos. 15, 16–17, 18); Keibun (nos. 19, 20–21).

Kravis, Irving B., and Robert E. Lipsey. 1985. The competitive position of U.S. manufacturing firms. *Banca Nazionale del Lavoro Quarterly Review,* no. 153 (June): 127–54.

———. 1987. The competitiveness and comparative advantage of U.S. multinationals, 1957–1984. *Banca Nazionale del Lavoro Quarterly Review,* no. 161 (June): 147–65.

———. 1992. Sources of competitiveness of the United States and of its multinational firms. *Review of Economics and Statistics* 74 (2): 193–201.

Lipsey, Robert E. 1989. The internationalization of production. NBER Working Paper no. 2923. Cambridge, Mass.: National Bureau of Economic Research, April.

———. 1995a. Outward direct investment and the U.S. economy. In *The effects of taxation on multinational corporations,* ed. Martin Feldstein, James R. Hines, Jr., and R. Glenn Hubbard, 7–33. Chicago: University of Chicago Press.

———. 1995b. The transnationalization of economic activity. Report to the Division on Transnational Corporations and Investment, UNCTAD. Geneva: United Nations Conference on Trade and Development, January.

Lipsey, Robert E., Magnus Blomström, and Irving B. Kravis. 1990. R&D by multinational firms and host country exports. In *Science and technology: Lessons for development policy,* ed. Robert E. Evenson and Gustav Ranis. Boulder, Colo.: Westview.

Lipsey, Robert E., Magnus Blomström, and Eric Ramstetter. 1995. Internationalized production in world output. NBER Working Paper no. 5385. Cambridge, Mass.: National Bureau of Economic Research, December.

Lowe, Jeffrey H. 1990. Gross product of U.S. affiliates of foreign companies, 1977–87. *Survey of Current Business* 70 (6): 45–53.

Mataloni, Raymond J., Jr. 1995. U.S. multinational companies: Operations in 1993. *Survey of Current Business* 75 (6): 31–51.

Mataloni, Raymond J., and Lee Goldberg. 1994. Gross product of U.S. multinational corporations, 1977–91. *Survey of Current Business* 74 (2): 42–63.

Ramstetter, Eric. 1994. Comparisons of Japanese multinationals and other firms in Thailand's nonoil manufacturing industries. *ASEAN Economic Bulletin* 11 (1): 36–58.

———. 1995. Characteristics of multinational firms in Malaysia: A time-series perspective. In *Projections for Asian industrializing region (IV),* ed. Mitsuru Toida and Daisuke Hiratsuka, 95–171. Tokyo: Institute of Developing Economies.

Ramstetter, Eric D., and William E. James. 1993. Transnational corporations, Japan–United States economic relations, and economic policy: The uncomfortable reality. *Transnational Corporations* (UNCTAD) 2 (3): 65–93.

Summers, Robert, and Alan Heston. 1991. The Penn World Table (Mark 5): An expanded set of international comparisons, 1950–1988. *Quarterly Journal of Economics* 106 (2): 327–68.

Swedenborg, Birgitta, Göran Johansson-Grahn, and Mats Kinwall. 1988. *Den Svenska industrins utlandsinvesteringar, 1960–1986.* Stockholm: Industriens Utredningsinstitut.

Toyo Keizai. Various years-a. *Kaigai shinshutsu kigyou soran* (A comprehensive survey of firms overseas), 1982–92 issues. Tokyo: Toyo Keizai.

———. Various years-b. *Kaigai shinshutsu kigyo soran: Kokubetsu hen* (A comprehensive survey of firms overseas, by country), 1993–94 issues. Tokyo: Toyo Keizai.

———. Various years-c. *Gyoshubetsu kaigai shinshutsu kigyo soran* (A comprehensive survey of firms overseas, by industry), 1988–90 issues. Tokyo: Toyo Keizai.

———. Various years-d. *Kaishabetsu kaigai shinshutsu kigyo soran* (A comprehensive survey of firms overseas, by company), 1991/92 and 1992 issues. Tokyo: Toyo Keizai.

———. Various years-e. *Kaigai shinshutsu kigyo soran: Kigyoubetsu hen* (A comprehensive survey of firms overseas, by firm), 1993–94 issues. Tokyo: Toyo Keizai.

United Nations. 1993. *MSPA handbook of world development statistics.* New York: United Nations, Department of Economic and Social Information and Policy Analysis, Macroeconomic and Social Policy Analysis Division, Long-Term Socio-Economic Perspectives Branch.

———. 1994. *World investment report, 1994: Transnational corporations, employment, and the workplace.* New York and Geneva: United Nations Conference on Trade and Development, Division on Transnational Corporations and Investment.

U.S. Department of Commerce. Bureau of Economic Analysis. 1981. *U.S. direct invest-*

ment abroad: 1977. Washington, D.C.: U.S. Department of Commerce, Bureau of Economic Analysis, April.

———. 1985a. *U.S. direct investment abroad: 1982 Benchmark survey data.* Washington, D.C.: U.S. Department of Commerce, Bureau of Economic Analysis, December.

———. 1985b. *Foreign direct investment in the United States: Operations of U.S. affiliates of foreign companies, revised estimates 1977–80.* Washington, D.C.: Government Printing Office.

———. 1990. *Foreign direct investment in the United States: 1987 Benchmark survey, final results.* Washington, D.C.: Government Printing Office.

———. 1992a. Gross product of U.S. affiliates of foreign direct investors, 1987–90. *Survey of Current Business* 72 (11): 47–54.

———. 1992b. *U.S. direct investment abroad: 1989 Benchmark survey, final results.* Washington, D.C.: Government Printing Office, October.

———. 1992c. *Foreign direct investment in the United States: Establishment data for 1987.* Washington, D.C.: Government Printing Office, June.

———. Various years. *Foreign direct investment in the United States: Operations of U.S. affiliates of foreign companies, revised estimates,* 1983–86 and 1988–91 issues. Washington, D.C.: Government Printing Office.

Weinstein, David E. 1997. Foreign direct investment and *keiretsu:* Rethinking U.S. and Japanese policy. In *The effects of U.S. trade protection and promotion policies,* ed. Robert C. Feenstra, 81–116. Chicago: University of Chicago Press.

World Bank. 1980. *World tables: The second edition* [1980]. Baltimore: Johns Hopkins University Press.

———. 1993. *World tables, 1993.* Baltimore: Johns Hopkins University Press.

———. 1995. *World tables, 1995.* Baltimore: Johns Hopkins University Press.

Zeile, William J. 1994. Foreign direct investment in the United States: 1992 Benchmark survey results. *Survey of Current Business* 74 (7): 154–86.

Comment Raymond J. Mataloni, Jr.

This paper by Blomström, Lipsey, and Ramstetter examines the changing role of multinational companies (MNCs) in the world economy using time-series estimates of their production of goods and services (MNC gross product). The first half of the paper examines MNC production from the home-country perspective by measuring production shares for home-country-based MNCs; these include parent company shares of home-country GDP, foreign affiliate shares of foreign-host-country GDP, and whole MNC shares of gross world product. The second half examines MNC production from the host-country perspective, calculating the foreign-country-based MNC share of host-country GDP. The research is significant in both its scope and methods; the authors have compiled an extensive collection of data on MNC production in terms of both the number of countries and the number of years covered, and they use a variety of ratios to uncover meaningful trends.

My comments will deal primarily with the share of world production accounted for by home-country MNCs, first because it is the broadest measure,

Raymond J. Mataloni, Jr., is an economist in the research branch of the International Investment Division, Bureau of Economic Analysis, U.S. Department of Commerce.

but more important because it deals with a central theme of this conference: How do you measure the competitiveness of a nation's companies in an increasingly integrated global economy? This share should reflect the "competitiveness" of home-country MNCs, in the sense that it reflects the quality of their geographically mobile corporate assets (such as management, production techniques, and designs); however, because all world markets are not equally accessible for a given country's firms, the share will also be influenced by barriers to direct investment and the additional costs to foreign versus domestic production. This ownership-based measure of a nation's companies' standing in the global economy differs from the other ownership-based measure presented at this conference (the Baldwin and Kimura framework) because it encompasses MNC production for all customers—home-country and foreign alike.

The paper presents the home-country MNC share of world production for two countries (the United States and Japan) because they are the only ones for which all of the necessary data are available. (No other countries are known to produce estimates of parent company production.) Over the period examined—roughly speaking, the 1980s—there were markedly different changes in this share for the two groups of MNCs. The share of world production accounted for by Japanese MNCs increased from 1.5 to 4.1 percent while that accounted for by U.S. MNCs *declined* from 8.7 to 6.7 percent. Although it is quite possible that these divergent changes partly reflect changes in the relative competitiveness of Japanese and U.S. MNCs, there are other factors that may have contributed. The bulk of my comments will deal with those other factors and I hope, in doing so, will offer possible future improvements to this measure.

The first factor, other than changes in competitiveness, is the convention of introducing all existing domestic operations to the parent company universe once a company undertakes its first foreign direct investment. When a large domestic company suddenly becomes a multinational by establishing as little as one foreign affiliate, it usually causes a sizable increase in the aggregate parent company data and only a minor (if not negligible) increase in the aggregate foreign affiliate data. For example, suppose that a large U.S. company such as General Motors were a purely domestic manufacturer and that it had U.S. production valued at $50 billion. If GM suddenly became a U.S. parent by establishing a Canadian affiliate with production valued at $100 million, U.S. MNC gross product would be increased by $50.1 billion, of which only $100 million (or well under 1 percent) reflected an actual expansion of production. Thus large changes can occur in aggregate MNC production data that have little to do with actual expansion—or heightened competitiveness—of given MNCs.

It is likely that the "new parent company" effect had a much greater impact on the Japanese MNC data than on the U.S. MNC data. The 1980s was a period of great expansion in Japanese direct investment abroad and was accompanied by a rise in the number of Japanese parent companies. During 1980–88, the number of Japanese parent companies showed a net increase of 210 companies (up 12 percent). By comparison, the U.S. parent company universe was much more stable, showing a net increase of only 71 companies (up 3 percent) during 1982–89. Perhaps consequently, Japanese parent companies accounted for the bulk (92 percent) of the growth in the share of world production accounted for by Japanese MNCs. In fact, had the Japanese parent share of worldwide GDP remained unchanged, while the Japanese foreign affiliate share increased as it did, the share of world production accounted for by Japanese MNCs would have only increased marginally (from 1.5 to 1.7 percent). To the extent that the rise in Japanese parent company production reflected additions to the parent company universe rather than expansion by existing parent companies, the rise in the Japanese MNC share of world production is unrelated to heightened competitiveness of given Japanese MNCs.

The phenomenon of new MNCs causing large increases in the parent company data, by bringing well-established domestic operations into the MNC universe, can cause analytical problems that cannot readily be controlled, or adjusted, for by data users. Any solution (if one exists) must come from the data producers.

Exchange rate changes are the second factor, other than rising competitiveness, that may have significantly boosted the Japanese MNC share of world production (measured in U.S. dollars) during the 1980s. The home-country MNC shares of world production were calculated in U.S. dollars. During the period for which the Japanese shares were calculated—1980 to 1988—the Japanese yen appreciated 62 percent relative to the U.S. dollar. Because the yen's appreciation was significantly greater against the dollar than against other foreign currencies, it boosted the dollar value of both Japanese parent production (translated from yen to dollars) and Japanese foreign affiliate production (translated from foreign currency to yen to dollars). Because Japanese parents accounted for 93 percent of Japanese MNC production worldwide in 1988, the exchange rate effect on the dollar value of their production alone would have increased the dollar value of Japanese MNC production by roughly 58 percent (93 percent of 62 percent).

During the roughly comparable period for which the U.S. shares were calculated—1982 to 1989—the dollar depreciated about 20 percent against other currencies, on average, which boosted the dollar value of U.S. foreign affiliate production. However, because foreign affiliates accounted for only 23 percent of U.S. MNC production worldwide in 1989, the exchange rate changes increased the dollar value of U.S. MNC production by only 5 percent, roughly (23 percent of 20 percent).

There are perhaps two ways that the comparison of Japanese and U.S. MNC shares of world production can be made more reflective of actual changes in the underlying competitiveness of those companies. First, to exclude the effects of exchange rate changes, the shares could be computed in base-period exchange rates. Researchers in the International Investment Division of the Bureau of Economic Analysis (BEA) may eventually be able to produce such estimates for U.S. MNCs. We are currently studying the effects of exchange rate (and price) changes on U.S. MNC gross product and evaluating the utility of developing alternative measures that exclude the effects of these changes. Second, it may be possible to exclude the effects of new parent companies entering the MNC universe. The most restrictive solution would be to exclude parent companies from the analysis and to compare the foreign affiliate production shares of world GDP excluding the home country. Another possible solution would be to produce a subset of data for "well established" MNCs and to restrict the analysis to this group. (Obviously, this could be done only with the cooperation of the statistical agencies that produce the data.) Neither of these "solutions" is perfect in that something is lost for whatever is gained; in the first case, the parent company perspective is lost, and in the second, the meaningful effects of new MNCs on the foreign affiliate data are lost.

In addition to the statistical issues just mentioned, there may also be a conceptual limitation to the MNC world production shares. Despite growing openness in the world economy, MNCs retain a competitive advantage at home. They can be shielded from cross-border foreign competition through tariff or nontariff barriers and from local foreign competition through explicit barriers to foreign direct investment or less tangible barriers such as language and cultural differences or restrictive market structures (such as the Japanese *keiretsu* system). These advantages could have a major effect on the MNC world production shares because an overwhelming share of global MNC production occurs in the home country (77 percent for U.S. MNCs in 1989 and 93 percent for Japanese MNCs in 1988). Therefore, when examining the world production shares for any two countries' MNCs, it is important to consider the relative openness of their domestic markets.

I would like to end by noting steps that BEA has taken to maintain and I hope expand its MNC gross product estimates in order to facilitate this type of research. Since the release, in the February 1994 *Survey of Current Business,* of the U.S. MNC gross product estimates used in this paper, the bureau has released revised 1991 estimates of gross product by majority-owned foreign affiliates in the June 1994 *Survey,* as well as revised 1992 and preliminary 1993 estimates in the June 1995 *Survey.* In addition, annual estimates of U.S. parent company, and thus worldwide U.S. MNC, gross product may soon be available. Those estimates are currently available only in benchmark survey years (the last of which covered 1989) because the necessary data items are not collected in the annual surveys. The bureau has proposed adding the necessary data items to its annual surveys following the 1994 benchmark survey. If these changes are approved, U.S. parent, foreign affiliate, and worldwide U.S. MNC gross product will be available annually from 1994 forward. Worldwide U.S. MNC gross product estimates are an important addition to the statistical information on MNCs that can enhance our understanding of direct investment, the operations of multinational companies, and the relevance of geography-based and ownership-based measures of international transactions.

4 Accounting for Outward Direct Investment from Hong Kong and Singapore: Who Controls What?

Linda Low, Eric D. Ramstetter, and
Henry Wai-Chung Yeung

4.1 Introduction

Hong Kong and Singapore provide a unique opportunity to examine the implications of different methods of classifying investments by multinational corporations. On the one hand, classifying investments by country of ownership, that is, by country of the owner of the investing parent firm, has gained increasing acceptance and is now widely used in the compilation of U.S. and Singaporean data, for example. This method differs from classification by country of capital source when the investing firm is owned by a firm from a country other than the country of capital source and seems clearly advantageous when, for example, investments are channeled through holding companies in tax havens like the Netherlands Antilles and the Cayman Islands. In Hong Kong and Singapore, a significant amount of investment is also channeled from foreigners through local holding companies to other foreign countries. In these two economies, however, there is also a large amount of outward investment made by foreign-controlled companies that have long histories in one or both of these economies. Moreover, such firms are often largely controlled and operated by long-term residents of the host economy who are empowered to take a wide range of decisions, including decisions to invest abroad. These characteristics, combined with the increasing sophistication of local firm management in each of these host economies, mean that foreign-controlled overseas investors may

Linda Low is associate professor of business policy at the National University of Singapore. Eric D. Ramstetter is research professor at the International Centre for the Study of East Asian Development, Kitakyushu, Japan. Henry Wai-Chung Yeung is lecturer in the department of geography at the National University of Singapore.

The authors thank Robert E. Baldwin, Robert E. Lipsey, Rachel McCulloch, conference participants, and participants in a preconference held in December 1994, for comments on earlier versions of this paper. The authors bear all responsibility for any remaining errors.

sometimes have more in common with locally controlled overseas investors than with their foreign parents. One possible implication of such behavior is that accounting by country of ultimate beneficial owner may be less enlightening than accounting by geographic source of investment in some cases.

The purpose of this paper is thus to illustrate, by examining the Hong Kong and Singapore examples, the nature of the problems encountered when trying to decide how to classify foreign investors by ownership. The paper outlines the rationales behind various classification rules (section 4.2) and summarizes the published information on outward investments from Hong Kong and Singapore by ownership (section 4.3). It then examines several cases of outward investment by foreign-controlled firms from these economies (section 4.4) and summarizes the major results that emerge (section 4.5).

4.2 Economics and Accounting for Sources of Foreign Direct Investment

What must be considered when foreign direct investment (FDI) is classified by its sources, and what are the implications of various classification schemes? Broadly stated, there are two primary ways of classifying FDI by source, classification by country of capital source and classification by country of ownership. Classification by country of capital source may be viewed as having its logical basis in international economics, which has emphasized the importance of cross-border transactions, especially international trade. Moreover, accounting by country of capital source is the traditional way in which international transactions have been handled in the balance of payments. The advantages of this accounting method include its suitability for a focus on the relationships among international transactions and economic activity (e.g., employment) in a specific location and its relative ease of implementation, as one needs only to measure cross-border transactions. On the other hand, there are also several drawbacks, the most important of which are difficulties encountered when a large amount of entrepôt activity is involved. In this context, accounting for the large amounts of outward investment from so-called paper companies in tax havens is the entrepôt activity of primary concern. However, the principal question involved in accounting for any entrepôt activity is the same: Just where is it most reasonable to view a given activity, be it trade or investment, as originating?

Accounting by country of ownership is a method of accounting that has been devised primarily as a means of dealing with the problem of entrepôt investments. Indeed, in its simplest form, accounting by country of ownership can be thought of as a means of understanding sometimes large outward investments from relatively small tax havens and is based on the premise that it makes little sense to attribute such investments to the tax havens themselves. Although the distinction may not be very important economically in the cases of portfolio investments, in the case of direct investments it is potentially significant. FDI is distinguished from portfolio investment in that it implies a greater degree of foreign control and in the case of FDI, most of the economic effects of that investment are thought to result, not from the capital flow involved, but from the transfer of knowledge-based, intangible assets (e.g., production technology, marketing networks, management know-how, and other similar assets) that accompanies the capital flow.[1] If the nature of these intangible assets depends on the country of the investing parent firm, it then becomes important to establish the source of investment because investments from different home economies may be expected to have different characteristics.[2] Correspondingly, in relatively simple cases, for example when a 100 percent U.S.-owned firm in the Cayman Islands undertakes an investment in Thailand, for most purposes it is clearly more reasonable to attribute such investment to the country of the owner than to the geographic source. However, this accounting can soon become quite complicated, especially in highly developed entrepôt centers like Hong Kong and Singapore, and this paper seeks to illuminate some of the gray areas involved in such cases.

One of the gray areas involves multiple ownership. For example, in Hong Kong and Singapore there are several cases of outward investment by firms that are the result of joint ventures between firms from two or more home economies. Furthermore, these joint ventures often involve several partners, none of which has a majority holding. In such cases, it is clearly impossible to unambiguously classify such FDI by country of ultimate beneficial owner.[3] A second gray area surrounds the issue of management control. In sophisticated entrepôts like Hong Kong and Singapore, one rarely sees simple entrepôt investments. Much of the reason for this is that high costs of doing business in these two city-states make it relatively expensive to establish and maintain paper companies in these two economies. On the other hand, firms in these economies, both local and foreign, are often very sophisticated, and there can be large benefits from entrepôt investment that involves a crucial resource contribution from the affiliate through which the investment is being conducted. At the extreme, such entrepôt investments may be entirely planned and managed by the staff of the affiliate with minimal assistance from the company's foreign parent. In such cases, the distinction between geography-based and ownership-based classifications may become clouded because the characteristics of the geographic source of investment may have more bearing on the nature of intangible assets transferred through such investments than do the characteristics of the ultimate parent firm. On the other hand, even if a high degree

1. See Caves (1982), Dunning (1993), and Markusen (1991), among others, for related theoretical analyses.

2. E.g., Kojima (1990) and Ozawa (1979) have argued that Japanese FDI is different from U.S. and European investments in a number of ways.

3. Moreover, given the international convention of defining FDI as a foreign investment where foreign ownership shares exceed a given minority percentage (usually 10 to 25 percent), there is substantial potential to double count such investments, attributing them to more than one home economy.

of autonomy is observed in the investing firm, this autonomy may only be a result of corporate organizational strategy, and one may argue that it is still preferable to classify such investments by country of ultimate beneficial owner.

In any case, the general lack of empirical analysis of this topic makes it of some interest to evaluate (1) how much of the outward FDI from Hong Kong and Singapore is by foreign-controlled firms and (2) how much of the outward FDI by foreign-controlled firms is by firms that exhibit a good deal of local control.

4.3 An Overview of Outward Direct Investment from Hong Kong and Singapore

According to traditional geography-based accounting, Hong Kong and Singapore were rather minor sources of the world's outward FDI flows throughout the 1980s, though they were among the major investors from the developing world. Between 1981–84 and 1988–90, the world experienced a more than fivefold increase in average annual FDI outflows, with shares of Asian economies rising from 13.8 to 24.8 percent (table 4.1). Japan and Taiwan accounted for the bulk of this increase; the combined shares of the two economies rose from 11.5 to 22.2 percent. Shares for Hong Kong and Singapore were larger than those for most other developing economies and regions as early as 1981–84 (1.2 and 0.3 percent, respectively) and remained rather stable throughout this period. Hence the absolute level of outward FDI flows from these economies increased markedly in this period.[4] In more recent years, Hong Kong has seen its share increase from 1.4 percent in 1988–90 to 5.3 percent in 1991–93, mainly as a result of its large contributions to the FDI boom in China. Singapore's outward FDI flows and shares of the world total have actually declined somewhat in this recent period. In summary, Hong Kong and Singapore were the among first Asian countries outside of Japan to make substantial outward investments, and high levels of FDI from these economies, combined with rapid growth in outflows from Korea and Taiwan, have made Asia's newly industrializing economies (NIEs) an increasingly important source of FDI in recent years.

4.3.1 Hong Kong

In view of Hong Kong's rather large outward FDI, it is perhaps surprising that the Hong Kong government does not keep any comprehensive records on outward FDI. Thus, before trying to evaluate how much of Hong Kong's outward FDI is undertaken by foreign-controlled firms, it is first necessary to esti-

4. Since, as noted in table 4.1, 1981–84 figures for Hong Kong exclude investments in China, the growth of the Hong Kong share is exaggerated somewhat. Note that this is also true for Malaysia, but China's share of Malaysia's FDI is much smaller than its share of Hong Kong's FDI.

Table 4.1 **Estimated Outward Flows of Direct Foreign Investment by Investing Economy**

Investing Economy	1981–84	1985–87	1988–90	1991–93
World	41,610	97,061	214,022	198,506
Africa	289	105	81	120
Asia	5,743	16,161	53,073	37,094
Japan	4,755	13,483	42,140	20,573
Asian NIEs	741	2,130	9,809	14,368
Hong Kong	489	1,529	3,090	10,504
Korea	88	109	425	1,153
Singapore	119	208	856	653
Taiwan	46	283	5,438	2,058
Other Asia	246	548	1,124	2,153
China	68	574	820	1,638
Malaysia	178	−88	211	344
Pakistan	−1	3	19	−6
Sri Lanka	0	1	2	5
Thailand	2	57	71	172
Europe	23,986	52,074	123,745	108,568
Latin America	245	325	687	1,374
Middle East	197	411	668	1,371
North America	10,117	24,312	31,800	48,944
Oceania	1,034	3,672	3,968	1,034

Sources: Data come from International Monetary Fund (various years) balance-of-payments data or are adjusted to be, in principle, consistent with those data. For Thailand, 1993 data come from Thailand, Bank of Thailand (various years). For Hong Kong and Malaysia, estimates are based on data from selected recipients of outward FDI from these economies (see table 4.2). For these two countries, note that 1981–84 figures exclude FDI in China, while figures for subsequent years include it; this exclusion is large for Hong Kong but not large for Malaysia. In any case, figures for both these economies are underestimates as FDI in only a few selected host economies is covered.
Note: Figures are in millions of U.S. dollars.

mate the magnitude of Hong Kong's outward FDI. To estimate the size of total outward FDI from Hong Kong, we have collected data on inward FDI from nine of the major recipients of Hong Kong's outward FDI. Since definitions differ greatly among host countries, an attempt has been made to adjust the data to be consistent, in principle, with balance-of-payments estimates of FDI flows, such as those presented in table 4.1 (see table 4.2 for details). According to these estimates, since the mid-1980s China has emerged as by far the largest host to Hong Kong's FDI, its share of stocks in the nine economies rising from 9 percent in 1984 to 54 percent in 1988 and 75 percent in 1993. Viewed from the Chinese side, Hong Kong's share of total inward FDI stocks in China rose from 11 percent in 1984 to 49 percent in 1988 and 61 percent in 1993.

Note also that there is significant investment from China to Hong Kong, with stocks of Chinese FDI in Hong Kong's manufacturing industries alone rising from $365 million (U.S. dollars) at year-end 1985 to $534 million at year-end 1992, these amounts representing 18 and 11 percent, respectively, of the total FDI stocks in Hong Kong's manufacturing.[5] Furthermore, it seems likely that Chinese investments in Hong Kong's service industries are several times larger than investments in manufacturing, though we have no hard figures to support this assertion. The observation of significant Chinese FDI in Hong Kong is consistent with the often-heard assertion that much of what the Chinese record as FDI from Hong Kong is in fact investment originating in local Chinese firms but circulated through Hong Kong in order to benefit from the incentives offered to foreign investors. In this respect, Hsueh and Woo (1991, 484; see also Shih 1989) indicate that at least 40 percent of Hong Kong's investment in China is from China-involved companies in Hong Kong and that China's banking groups are a large source of this investment. Moreover, there is also significant indirect FDI in China by foreign-controlled firms in Hong Kong, with Wong, Chen, and Nyaw (1991, xxix) citing Chinese figures that 30 percent of Hong Kong's FDI is of foreign origin. Although certainly not comprehensive, these figures suggest that accounting by country of ultimate beneficial owner would substantially reduce estimates of Hong Kong's FDI in China.

Similarly, indirect FDI through Hong Kong is also an important element of Hong Kong's FDI in other economies. Table 4.2 indicates that after China, Singapore was the second largest host to Hong Kong FDI in 1993, followed by the United States, Malaysia, Thailand, Indonesia, and Taiwan. Stocks were much smaller in the Philippines and Korea and even smaller in most other host economies for which spotty information was obtained.[6] This ordering represents a change from 1984, when Malaysia was the largest host, followed by Singapore and more distantly by the United States. In other words, these estimates indicate that Singapore and Malaysia, and to a lesser extent the United States, have historically been the most important destinations of Hong Kong's FDI, while Thailand and Indonesia, as well as China, have been more important in recent years.[7]

Some of the earliest outward investment from Hong Kong occurred in the nineteenth century when some British-controlled banks in Hong Kong extended their operations to Southeast Asia in order to serve increasing British

5. Data on FDI stocks come from Hong Kong, Industry Department (1993) and are translated into U.S. dollars using end-of-period exchange rates from International Monetary Fund (1995).

6. The only other host economies in which substantial FDI stocks from Hong Kong are known to exist are Canada ($1,261 million in 1990) and Australia ($556 million in 1990; International Monetary Fund 1995; United Nations 1993, 1994). In the United Kingdom, FDI stocks from developing Asian economies rose from $1,712 million in 1987 to $3,771 million in 1991 (United Kingdom, Central Statistical Office 1991), and we suspect that a substantial portion of this FDI is from Hong Kong. Japanese figures on approved FDI also indicate rather large FDI stocks from Hong Kong ($613 million as of 31 March 1993), but on a worldwide basis, actual stocks at year-end 1992 were only 58 percent of total approved stocks as of 31 March 1993, so actual FDI stocks are likely much smaller than approved stocks (International Monetary Fund, various years; Japan, Ministry of Finance 1993).

7. For details on Hong Kong's investment in Southeast Asia, see Yeung (1994, 1995, 1996).

Table 4.2 Estimated Flows and Stocks of FDI from Hong Kong to Selected Host Economies

Host	1984	1985	1986	1987	1988	1989	1990	1991	1992	1993
				Stocks of FDI from Hong Kong (million U.S. $)						
Subtotal	3,832	4,692	6,036	8,420	11,113	14,509	17,689	22,171	31,827	49,200
China	341	1,151	2,284	3,882	5,978	8,055	9,969	12,456	20,269	36,684
Indonesia	275	272	298	337	393	459	632	876	1,192	1,442
Korea	31	38	46	86	104	116	131	137	150	162
Malaysia	1,208	1,308	1,491	1,370	1,322	1,464	1,510	1,938	2,429	2,186
Philippines	43	48	48	67	126	163	198	239	253	301
Singapore	986	881	765	1,000	1,197	1,480	1,806	2,127	2,568	3,016
Taiwan	162	181	214	301	418	585	722	825	950	1,070
Thailand	213	236	273	304	414	637	911	1,365	1,937	2,109
United States	574	576	617	1,073	1,161	1,549	1,808	2,210	2,078	2,229
				Hong Kong's Share of Total FDI Stocks (%)						
Subtotal	2.3	2.5	2.7	2.9	3.0	3.2	3.4	4.0	5.3	7.4
China	11.1	24.4	34.6	43.6	49.4	52.0	52.5	53.3	59.0	60.7
Indonesia	9.2	8.2	8.3	8.5	8.7	8.8	10.0	11.2	12.5	12.5
Korea	2.8	2.9	2.6	3.6	3.2	2.9	2.8	2.4	2.4	2.4
Malaysia	13.5	13.6	14.8	13.0	11.8	11.3	9.9	10.1	10.2	7.8
Philippines	5.6	6.1	5.3	5.5	5.9	6.0	6.1	6.3	6.3	6.3
Singapore	10.0	8.1	6.1	6.5	6.3	6.7	6.6	6.6	6.6	6.6
Taiwan	11.2	10.1	10.1	10.6	11.0	10.8	10.7	10.3	10.7	10.9
Thailand	9.5	9.9	10.2	10.1	10.1	10.8	10.8	13.1	15.4	15.0
United States	0.4	0.4	0.3	0.4	0.4	0.4	0.4	0.5	0.5	0.5

Sources: China, State Statistical Bureau (various years), Hill (1988, 1991), Indonesia, Bank Indonesia (various years), Indonesia, BKPM (1993), International Monetary Fund (various years, 1995), Korean Foreign Trade Association (1992), Malaysia Industrial Development Authority (various years), Malaysia, Ministry of Finance (various years), Pangestu (1991), Philippines, Central Bank of the Philippines (various years), Republic of China, Central Bank of China (various issues), Republic of China, Investment Commission (1993, various years), Samudram (1995), Singapore, Department of Statistics (1993a, 1994), Thailand, Bank of Thailand (various years), U.S. Department of Commerce (1990, 1994), Zhang (1993).

Notes: In principle, estimates are obtained by first calculating total FDI flows and stocks, where stocks are defined as cumulative flows from 1970 forward. Second, Hong Kong shares are multiplied by these totals to obtain a proxy for FDI from Hong Kong that is in principle consistent with balance-of-payments estimates. Note, however, that calculation methods differ significantly among host economies. Contact the authors for more details.

business involvement in these Southeast Asian economies. In more recent years, Hong Kong has also been a springboard for investment by foreign-controlled companies in Southeast Asia as well as in China. One indication of this is the fact that a large number of firms have chosen Hong Kong as headquarters for their Asian operations.[8] A more concrete indication of the extent to which Hong Kong's FDI in Southeast Asia is indirect FDI can be obtained

8. According to a small-scale survey by the Industry Department in 1985, 163 of 470 affiliates of foreign multinationals in Hong Kong were operational headquarters in charge of the Asian region. An enlarged survey in 1990 found that 572 of 2,310 affiliates were operational headquarters, with half of the operational headquarters being affiliates of U.S. firms (Wilson 1992).

Table 4.3 **Ratios of Selected Indicators for Hong Kong- and Singapore-Owned Establishments in Singapore's Manufacturing Sector Classified by Country of Ultimate Beneficial Owner to the Same Indicators Classified by Capital Source**

Indicator	1980	1981	1982	1983	1984	1985	1986
Hong Kong–owned establishments							
Establishments	0.86	0.90	0.87	0.90	0.86	0.86	0.81
Employees	0.57	0.68	0.72	0.74	0.67	0.73	0.72
Output	0.48	0.54	0.42	0.54	0.42	0.43	0.42
Value added	0.49	0.58	0.51	0.62	0.53	0.53	0.54
Sales	0.49	0.56	0.42	0.53	0.42	0.44	0.41
Exports	0.42	0.52	0.37	0.45	0.31	0.37	0.38
Fixed investment	0.39	0.46	0.56	0.52	0.36	0.16	0.30
Singapore-owned establishments							
Establishments	1.05	1.05	1.05	0.99	0.98	0.98	0.98
Employees	1.12	1.12	1.10	0.97	0.96	0.96	0.95
Output	0.93	0.77	0.73	0.67	0.72	0.72	0.73
Value added	1.07	1.04	1.02	0.90	0.86	0.91	0.81
Sales	0.94	0.77	0.73	0.68	0.72	0.72	0.73
Exports	1.00	0.64	0.61	0.53	0.58	0.62	0.62
Fixed investment	1.09	1.07	1.04	0.96	0.90	0.94	0.84

Sources: Singapore, Department of Statistics (various years); Singapore, Economic Development Board (1994).

Note: Original indicators are in number of establishments, number of employees, and millions of Singapore dollars.

from Singapore's Census of Industrial Production for 1980–86. Comparisons indicate that classification by country of ultimate beneficial owner reduces the estimates of the importance of Hong Kong–owned establishments in Singaporean manufacturing significantly (table 4.3). Reductions of shares are relatively small in terms of the number of firms or employment but much larger in terms of output, sales, value added, exports, or investment, with estimates often being cut in half or even more. In addition, Hill (1988) indicates that British companies based in Hong Kong account for a large portion of Hong Kong's FDI in Indonesia, while firm-level data from Toyo Keizai (1994) show that a number of Japanese investments are routed through Hong Kong–based affiliates.[9] In contrast to these examples, Hong Kong's FDI position in the United States was larger, often much larger, when classified by country of ultimate beneficial owner in 1989–92, though this was reversed in 1993.[10] Thus, although the available data are limited, there is a clear indication that classifying

9. See subsection 4.4.2 for examples of indirect investment in Thailand. Casual thumbing through the Toyo Keizai surveys indicates substantial indirect investment in China and other Southeast Asian economies as well.

10. The ratio of Hong Kong's FDI position (stocks) classified by ultimate beneficial owner to the FDI position classified by country of each member of the parent group was 3.6 in 1989, 1.5 in 1990, 1.1 in 1991, 1.4 in 1992, and 0.8 in 1993 (U.S. Department of Commerce 1994).

Hong Kong's FDI by country of ultimate beneficial owner greatly reduces such FDI, especially in Asia.

4.3.2 Singapore

The data on outward FDI for Singapore are much more comprehensive than those for Hong Kong and are consistent in suggesting that much of the outward FDI from this economy is also from foreign-controlled firms. The share of foreign-controlled companies in total FDI stocks fell from 48 percent in 1981 to a low of 26 percent in 1985 and then increased to a peak of 58 percent in 1989, before it fell back to 51 percent in 1991 (table 4.4). The large increase in this share in the late 1980s came as a result of increased investment by wholly foreign-owned firms, whose share of the total grew from 17–25 percent in 1981–88 to 45 percent in 1989.

Another similarity with Hong Kong is that neighboring Asian economies have received the bulk of outward FDI from Singapore. Malaysia is by far the largest recipient of Singapore's FDI, accounting for 60 percent of these FDI stocks in 1981, 50 percent in 1984, and 23 percent in 1991 (table 4.4). Hong Kong has been the second largest destination of Singapore's FDI, its share of the total rising from 11 percent in 1981 to 20 percent in 1985 before falling off to 12 percent in 1991. Australia has traditionally been the third largest destination with shares of 4 to 8 percent, while the United States has seen its share rise from 2–3 percent through 1987 to 4–6 percent since. Shares for the Netherlands and New Zealand have also increased rapidly in recent years, reaching double-digit levels in some years. No other individual economy had shares of more than 3 percent.

Despite these similarities, there are also some conspicuous contrasts between Hong Kong and Singapore related to outward FDI. For example, although most outward FDI by locally controlled firms comes from the private sector in Hong Kong, government-linked companies dominate outward FDI by locally controlled firms in Singapore (Singapore, Economic Development Board 1993). Another difference is the relatively conspicuous role the government plays in Singapore's economy, in particular, the government's active promotion of the development of corporate regionalization strategies and outward FDI in recent years.

The breakdown by country of FDI by foreign-controlled companies reveals relatively small shares for Asian economies, 40 percent in 1991, compared to a similar breakdown of FDI by local companies, 61 percent (table 4.5). For foreign-controlled companies, shares of Malaysia (18 percent) and Hong Kong (8 percent) are notably low compared to corresponding shares for local companies (28 and 17 percent, respectively). Indeed, the only listed Asian economies for which shares are higher in foreign-controlled companies are Japan (1.6 vs. 0.2 percent) and Thailand (4.0 vs. 2.6 percent); however, for the other Asia category, the differential is even larger (4.9 vs. 1.0 percent). For Europe and the United States also, shares tend to be larger in local-controlled firms (17

Table 4.4 Singapore's Direct Investment Stocks Abroad by Ownership of Investing Firm and Country of Investment

Variable	1981	1982	1983	1984	1985	1986	1987	1988	1989	1990	1991
Total outward FDI stocks[a]											
Cumulative flows (IMF)	1,177	1,829	1,933	2,129	2,653	3,047	3,481	3,716	4,600	5,495	6,706
Outward FDI stocks (DOS)	1,678	2,087	2,233	2,399	2,257	2,598	2,962	2,994	5,289	7,784	8,553
Outward FDI stocks by ownership of investing firm[b]											
Foreign-controlled firms	799	988	1,007	1,004	585	744	1,125	1,095	3,047	3,867	4,372
Wholly foreign	293	380	526	552	384	547	742	711	2,395	n.a.	n.a.
Majority foreign	507	608	481	452	201	198	383	384	652	n.a.	n.a.
Local-controlled firms	878	1,099	1,226	1,395	1,672	1,854	1,836	1,899	2,242	3,917	4,181
Majority local	298	303	350	329	710	742	772	713	667	n.a.	n.a.
Wholly local	580	796	876	1,067	962	1,111	1,064	1,186	1,575	n.a.	n.a.
Outward FDI stocks of all investors by host economy[b]											
Asia	1,290	1,587	1,662	1,805	1,721	1,837	1,909	1,964	3,014	3,839	4,293
Brunei	4	6	9	49	53	50	54	57	67	n.a.	53
China	0	0	0	0	58	94	101	79	109	n.a.	153
Hong Kong	182	317	357	391	461	498	540	545	835	938	1,057
Indonesia	40	40	44	56	65	68	59	60	82	n.a.	175
Japan	0	0	1	1	5	6	16	17	29	n.a.	78
Malaysia	1,007	1,162	1,163	1,209	972	986	1,008	1,031	1,424	1,803	1,957

Philippines	18	16	18	18	22	23	14	23	53	n.a.	61
Taiwan	13	15	25	27	33	38	26	54	148	n.a.	222
Thailand	10	10	8	9	21	30	45	46	143	n.a.	285
Other Asia	16	21	38	45	32	45	45	52	124	n.a.	472
Europe	51	58	58	72	89	167	358	303	305	938	841
Netherlands	1	1	12	11	12	14	165	111	−90	1,179	527
United Kingdom	50	57	43	44	46	82	48	49	114	n.a.	197
Other Europe	0	0	2	17	31	72	145	143	281	n.a.	61
Other regions	337	442	513	523	447	594	695	727	1,970	3,007	3,419
Australia	63	91	121	132	177	176	218	166	331	410	433
New Zealand	n.a.	n.a.	n.a.	n.a.	n.a.	n.a.	n.a.	n.a.	832	n.a.	933
United States	32	44	48	54	66	65	69	108	293	n.a.	413
Other countries	243	307	333	325	186	335	390	424	514	n.a.	1,640

Note: Figures are in millions of Singapore dollars.

[a]From International Monetary Fund (1995, various years).

[b]From Singapore, Department of Statistics (1991, 1993a, 1993b, 1993c).

Table 4.5 Singapore's Direct Investment Stocks Abroad by Capital Source, Country, and Industry of Investment, 1991

Variable	All Industries	Manufacturing	Construction	Commerce	Transport	Finance	Real Estate	Business Services	Other Industries
Outward FDI stocks of foreign-controlled companies by host economy									
All countries	4,370	705	12	367	48	2,629	284	288	37
Asia	1,742	640	3	330	16	506	139	81	27
Brunei	6	0	0	6	0	0	0	0	0
China	27	22	0	6	0	0	0	0	0
Hong Kong	341	18	0	19	0	172	98	21	12
Indonesia	46	24	2	3	0	11	2	3	1
Japan	68	16	0	1	1	15	0	35	0
Malaysia	793	312	0	238	14	196	19	3	12
Philippines	28	14	0	4	0	1	6	3	0
Taiwan	43	7	0	27	0	9	0	0	0
Thailand	175	134	0	5	1	4	14	16	1
Other Asia	214	94	0	21	0	99	0	0	0
Europe	122	25	0	15	4	72	2	1	4
Netherlands	−57	9	0	0	0	−65	0	0	0
United Kingdom	113	1	0	14	1	96	2	0	0
Other Europe	65	15	0	1	3	42	0	1	4
Other regions	2,507	41	9	22	28	2,050	144	206	6
Australia	214	30	7	9	2	26	135	0	5
New Zealand	818	4	0	7	0	805	1	0	0
United States	157	6	0	2	3	0	4	141	0
Other countries	1,318	1	2	3	23	1,219	3	64	2

Outward FDI stocks of local companies by host economy									
All countries	4,181	1,019	69	609	94	1,921	272	101	95
Asia	2,551	864	40	561	80	621	235	69	81
Brunei	47	1	7	3	0	37	0	0	0
China	125	73	0	27	19	2	0	4	1
Hong Kong	716	226	7	81	15	262	103	20	2
Indonesia	129	32	11	0	29	44	6	0	6
Japan	9	0	0	6	3	0	0	0	0
Malaysia	1,164	427	9	298	6	231	113	13	67
Philippines	34	13	0	0	0	16	0	0	4
Taiwan	179	46	3	108	0	20	0	1	0
Thailand	109	19	2	39	3	8	7	31	1
Other Asia	40	27	0	0	5	0	6	1	0
Europe	719	28	29	3	2	641	0	3	13
Netherlands	584	0	0	0	0	582	0	2	0
United Kingdom	83	8	0	1	2	59	0	1	13
Other Europe	52	20	29	2	1	0	0	1	0
Other regions	911	127	0	46	11	659	37	30	1
Australia	219	18	0	34	2	155	9	0	1
New Zealand	115	0	0	0	3	93	0	19	0
United States	256	92	0	10	2	122	21	10	0
Other countries	320	18	0	1	5	289	7	1	0

Source: Singapore, Department of Statistics (1993b).

Note: Figures are in millions of Singapore dollars.

and 6 percent, respectively) than in foreign-controlled firms (3 and 4 percent, respectively). On the other hand, the substantial recent investments in New Zealand and in the other country category appear to have come primarily from foreign-controlled firms.

Contrary to the popular impression that local manufacturing firms facing high labor costs have been the major investors abroad, Singapore's outward FDI is dominated by investments in financial services, with this activity accounting for 60 percent of the FDI stocks of foreign-controlled firms and 48 percent of the FDI stocks of local firms (table 4.5). For foreign-controlled firms, the largest shares of these financial service investments are in other countries (46 percent) and New Zealand (31 percent), followed distantly by Malaysia (7 percent) and Hong Kong (7 percent). For local firms, the largest shares are in the Netherlands (30 percent), other countries (15 percent), Hong Kong (14 percent), and Malaysia (12 percent). Shares of Australia, New Zealand, and the United States are also relatively large at 5 to 8 percent. Thus, both foreign-controlled and local firms have apparently undertaken somewhat similar patterns of investment in that financial service investments in developed economies, Malaysia, Hong Kong, and other countries are a significant element of both types of investment.[11]

Investment patterns of the two groups of investors are also similar in that manufacturing is the second largest sector of investment, accounting for 16 percent of the FDI by foreign-controlled firms and 24 percent of the FDI by local firms (table 4.5).[12] For both foreign-controlled and local firms, the vast majority of such investments are concentrated in Asia, 91 and 85 percent, respectively. For foreign-controlled firms, Malaysia (44 percent), Thailand (19 percent), and other Asia (13 percent) are by far the dominant destinations of such investments, with shares in other Asian countries being much smaller (4 percent or less). The pattern for local firms is similar in that Malaysia is the largest destination (42 percent) but differs in that it is much more diversified with notably larger shares in Hong Kong (22 percent), China (7 percent), and Taiwan (5 percent) but lower shares in Thailand and other Asia (2 to 3 percent). These differences suggest that a relatively large amount of investment by local firms in manufacturing seeks to exploit the so-called Chinese connection, while a relatively large amount of FDI by foreign-controlled firms seeks to

11. We speculate that the large investments in other countries are concentrated in tax havens such as the Bahamas, the Cayman Islands, and the Netherlands Antilles, though we have no concrete evidence of this.

12. Note also the correlation between the data in table 4.4, which indicate that foreign-controlled firms accounted for 41 percent of Singapore's manufacturing FDI in 1991, and the data in table 4.3, which suggest that classification by country of ultimate beneficial owner reduces the scope of activities by Singapore-owned establishments for many years in the 1980–86 period, with exports, sales, and output being the activities most affected. Although these two data sources are not consistent in that the latter sample includes a large number of local establishments that do not invest abroad, they are consistent in suggesting that a large portion of manufacturing activity that would be considered Singaporean if country of capital source were the basis for classification would not be Singaporean if country of ultimate beneficial owner were the basis of classification.

expand operations in neighboring Southeast Asian economies, especially Thailand.[13]

Among the remaining industries listed in table 4.5, commerce (8 percent of the total), business services (7 percent), and real estate (6 percent) were the only industries with shares of total FDI stocks exceeding 1 percent for foreign-controlled firms. Among these investments, commerce investments in Malaysia, business service investments in Japan and the United States (and to a lesser extent Hong Kong and Thailand), and real estate investments in Australia and Hong Kong are conspicuous. For local companies, construction (15 percent) and real estate (6 percent) were the only industries with shares of total FDI stocks greater than 2 percent. Here construction investments are concentrated in other Europe (43 percent) and four Asian economies (Brunei, 10 percent; Hong Kong, 10 percent; Indonesia, 16 percent; and Malaysia, 13 percent). Thus, outside of the main sectors of investment (finance and manufacturing), differences in the patterns of outward FDI by foreign-controlled firms and local firms are relatively pronounced.

Although revealing, the above estimates of FDI stocks do not cover investments by primarily local individuals, sole proprietors, and partnerships. Another survey was carried out by the Singapore Manufacturers' Association between February and March 1993. Of its 323 respondents, half were small to medium-size firms.[14] The survey confirmed Malaysia as the traditional favorite spot for Singapore investors, with 34 percent of the respondents reporting that they had operations in that economy. Relatively large shares of the respondents also reported having affiliates in Indonesia (16 percent), China (11 percent), and Thailand (10 percent), but no other economy had over 5 percent of the respondents reporting investments. Thus these data also suggest that the geographical orientation of local investors venturing abroad is different from that of foreign-controlled firms.

4.4 Characteristics of Hong Kong's and Singapore's Outward Investors

The data in section 4.3 indicate that ownership-based estimates of outward FDI from Hong Kong and Singapore would be far smaller than geography-based estimates. The large differences in geography-based and ownership-based classifications, combined with the often complex nature of outward FDI by foreign-controlled firms in these economies, suggests that a closer examination of the criteria underlying these different classifications is warranted. In this context, we are primarily concerned with the issue of control of investment decisions in foreign-controlled firms undertaking outward investment from

13. One of the authors has personally encountered several examples of investment in Thailand through affiliates in Singapore and Malaysia during a recent survey of intrafirm trade and networking in multinationals operating in Thailand.

14. The results of this survey are quoted from the *Straits Times*, 30 April 1993.

these two economies. Parallel to the discussion in section 4.2 above, concern with control stems from recognition that control-related issues underlie many of the arguments in favor of using ownership-based classifications, combined with recognition that evaluation of the origin of control of investment decisions as well as evaluation of the implications of the origin of that control is sometimes extremely complex in these firms.

To examine these issues more closely, we have assembled survey information on foreign-controlled investors in Hong Kong with the aim of ascertaining just how management decisions, including decisions to invest, are made in the surveyed firms.[15] In addition, we have generated a rather comprehensive list of investors from Hong Kong and Singapore in Thailand that makes some more general evaluations of the two groups of investors possible.

4.4.1 Outward Investors from Hong Kong

Table 4.6 presents a synopsis of 20 case studies of foreign-controlled firms that have undertaken outward investment from Hong Kong.[16] These companies reflect a diverse mix of organizational approaches to multinational operations by the ultimate foreign parent firms through their regional headquarters based in Hong Kong. The case-study firms tend to be relatively old, with only three established after 1985 and nine in the 1970s or earlier. By industry, four firms are primarily involved in manufacturing, six in trade or distribution, one in finance, six in other services, and three in a combination of manufacturing, trade, and service operations. All but one of the 20 firms have affiliates in Singapore; about half of the firms have affiliates in Malaysia (11 firms), Indonesia (9 firms), and Thailand (9 firms); and one-fifth of the firms have affiliates in the Philippines.

In order to highlight some basic characteristics of these firms, the ASEAN affiliates of the 20 foreign-owned firms are classified by degree of autonomy of the Hong Kong–based investor as well as by source of finance and method of control used for operations in the ASEAN affiliates (table 4.7). Perhaps of most interest in this context is that the majority of these affiliates (30/56 or 26/42) are controlled by relatively autonomous Hong Kong firms. If one looks at the sample of 56 affiliates for which information on the source of finance could be obtained, the vast majority (80 percent) are seen to rely primarily on finance through the internal capital reserves of the foreign-controlled firms (regional headquarters) based in Hong Kong. Furthermore, reliance on this source of finance is even more pronounced in affiliates of relatively autonomous firms (90 percent) compared to parent-controlled firms (69 percent). Hong Kong

15. Originally, we had hoped to have parallel coverage of investors from Hong Kong and Singapore, but difficulties in obtaining interviews with Singapore-based firms have precluded this.

16. These cases are abstracted from a larger project in which one of the authors has interviewed more than 110 headquarters firms in Hong Kong and another 60 odd subsidiaries or affiliates in Indonesia, Malaysia, Singapore, and Thailand. For confidentiality reasons, company names are not revealed.

Table 4.6 Characteristics of Case-Study Foreign-Owned Firms in Hong Kong

Company	Year Established	Main Business	Country of Ultimate Parent Firm	Country of ASEAN Operation[a]
A	1975	Electronic manufacturing	Netherlands	S
B	n.a.	Solder chemical manufacturing	United States	S
C	1983	Computer software solutions	United States, Thailand	I, M, S, T
D	1980	Electronic components, distributor	United States	M, S
E	n.a.	Power supplies, distributor	United States	S
F	1971	General insurance	Netherlands, United Kingdom	I, M, P, S, T
G	1987	Distribution, testing services	United Kingdom	M, S, P, T
H	1972	Travel services	Australia	S, T
I	1975	Pharmaceuticals manufacturing and trade	Sweden	I, M, S, T
J	1964	Market research	United States	I, M, P, S, T
K	1983	Software distribution	United Kingdom	M, S
L	1990	Software distribution	United States	S
M	1836	General insurance	United States	S
N	1984	Lead frame manufacturing	Germany, Netherlands	M, S
O	1965	General insuarnce	Indonesia	I
P	1959	Furniture manufacturing	United States	I, M, S, T
Q	1981	Merchant banking	United Kingdom	I, M, S, T
R	1977	Chemical products, transportation	Singapore	I, M, S, T
S	1989	Electronic components trading	Singapore	S
T	1981	Department store trading, sourcing	Belgium	I, S, P, T

Source: Field interviews by Henry Yeung.

[a]I = Indonesia, M = Malaysia, P = Philippines, S = Singapore, and T = Thailand.

capital markets and the ultimate parent companies were the second and third most frequently used sources of finance for affiliates of parent-controlled firms, but these sources were not used at all by the affiliates of autonomous firms. This limited sample thus suggests somewhat different financial strategies in the two groups of firms.

A second variable examined here is the method of controlling the ASEAN affiliates used by the Hong Kong–based, foreign-owned firms (table 4.7). Most of the 42 affiliates in this sample were controlled by the Hong Kong headquarters in one of three ways: cost control (26 percent), periodic reports to headquarters (24 percent), and periodic inspections by top executives from headquarters (14 percent). Autonomous firms tend to rely more on these methods, especially reports to headquarters, than do controlled firms, though the ranking

Table 4.7 Source of Finance, Method of Control, and Extent of Ultimate Control for ASEAN Subsidiaries of a Sample of Foreign-Owned Firms in Hong Kong

Source of Finance or Method of Control	Controlled	Autonomous	Total
Source of finance (number of firms)	26	30	56
Regional headquarters, Hong Kong	18	27	45
Capital market, Hong Kong	4	0	4
Family reserve, Hong Kong	0	1	1
Host-country partners	1	2	3
Ultimate parent company	3	0	3
Source of finance (% of firms)	100.00	100.00	100.00
Regional headquarters, Hong Kong	69.23	90.00	80.36
Capital market, Hong Kong	15.38	0.00	7.14
Family reserve, Hong Kong	0.00	3.33	1.79
Host-country partners	3.85	6.67	5.36
Ultimate parent company	11.54	0.00	5.36
Method of control (number of firms)	16	26	42
Production, market planning from headquarters	2	1	3
Inventory, quality control by headquarters	0	2	2
Cost control by headquarters	4	7	11
Broad guidelines from corporate groups	0	1	1
Centralized decision making from headquarters	1	2	3
Inspections by top management from headquarters	2	4	6
Reports from local managers to headquarters	3	7	10
Sourcing information from headquarters	0	1	1
No specific ways	1	0	1
Mutual exchange of information	2	1	3
Annual meetings	1	0	1
Method of control (% of firms)	100.00	100.00	100.00
Production, market planning from headquarters	12.50	3.85	7.14
Inventory, quality control by headquarters	0.00	7.69	4.76
Cost control by headquarters	25.00	26.92	26.19
Broad guidelines from corporate groups	0.00	3.85	2.38
Centralized decision making from headquarters	6.25	7.69	7.14
Inspections by top management from headquarters	12.50	15.38	14.29
Reports from local managers to headquarters	18.75	26.92	23.81
Sourcing information from headquarters	0.00	3.85	2.38
No specific ways	6.25	0.00	2.38
Mutual exchange of information	12.50	3.85	7.14
Annual meetings	6.25	0.00	2.38

Source: Field interviews by Henry Yeung.

of these methods is markedly similar in both groups. Among other methods, reliance on inventory and quality control, guidelines from corporate groups, and information sourcing are observed in a few affiliates of autonomous firms but not in controlled firm groups. On the other hand, affiliates of controlled firms use production and market planning, mutual exchange of information, and annual meetings more than do autonomous firm groups. Thus, to a certain extent, there is a regional division of control in which ASEAN subsidiaries report to regional headquarters based in Hong Kong rather than directly to their ultimate parent companies.

Among foreign-owned firms in Hong Kong that have been given substantial autonomy in running the group's operations in the Asia Pacific region, four broad types are observed in this sample: recently acquired firms, firms with strong local entrepreneurial involvement, customer-oriented firms, and relocated holding companies. This typology is based on the limited sample used here and is by no means exhaustive. Moreover, there are overlaps in organizational structures among the different types of firms. The examples below illustrate how these four types of firms have come to have a good deal of control over their operations, including investment decisions.

The sample contains two autonomous firms that were recently acquired by ultimate foreign parent companies, companies D and J. As has been explained by previous researchers (e.g., Dicken, Forsgren, and Malmberg 1994) these kinds of firms often do not experience much change in their internal operating systems because their management structures tend to be embedded, and these two firms generally fit this pattern. Company D was first established in Hong Kong in early 1980 (table 4.6), but it was acquired as a wholly owned subsidiary by its American ultimate parent company in August 1993. Even after the takeover the firm has continued to be run by its present ethnic Chinese president who continues to make decisions for the parent firm's operations in Asia. The company is now owned by a holding company registered in the British Virgin Islands, which is, in turn, wholly owned by the U.S. parent and owns 100 percent of the firm's operations in Hong Kong, China (Beijing, Shanghai, and Shenzhen), Korea, Singapore, and Malaysia.

Company J has been a market leader in the field of market research in Asia, with offices spanning the entire Asia Pacific region (Australia, Canada, China, Indonesia, Japan, Korea, Malaysia, New Zealand, the Philippines, Singapore, Taiwan, Thailand, the United States, and Vietnam). Ever since its establishment in 1964, the firm has been a multinational, with operations in several countries and employees of several nationalities. In the early 1980s, the firm merged with a British research company that owned 30 percent of the firm until the management of the company bought itself out in the late 1980s. After a period as an employee-owned firm, it then merged with the largest U.S. research firm of its type in early 1994. The first merger did not bring significant changes to the group's corporate structure, which was characterized by a large degree of decentralization. However, since the merger with the U.S. firm, the firm's Hong Kong–based executive committee has tried to exert more influence over the firm's foreign affiliates.

Firms with strong local entrepreneurial involvement can exercise significant control over their foreign investment activities, despite being foreign owned, as illustrated by two of the cases considered here, companies N and P. Company N is a joint venture between a Hong Kong (ethnic Chinese) entrepreneur (40 percent shareholding) and a large German conglomerate (60 percent shareholding) in which the Hong Kong entrepreneur is an expert in the plating industry. The firm is also the regional headquarters for the Far East and is currently in charge of operations in Singapore and Malaysia. Corresponding to the ownership structure of the Hong Kong company, operations in Singapore and Malaysia are both 60–40 joint ventures between the holding company in Germany and the Hong Kong entrepreneur, who is also the managing director for all three Asian firms. The Hong Kong office, as the regional headquarters, has the autonomy to make most of its own operational, marketing, and investment decisions provided it follows the general guidelines laid down by the German head office and reports strategic changes in operations. Daily operations of plants in Singapore and Malaysia are financed by the regional headquarters based in Hong Kong and are managed by top executives sent from Hong Kong who are encouraged to develop their own markets. The relative autonomy given to subsidiaries is due to the German parent's decentralization policy, whereby parent control is only exercised in financial areas such as budgeting, borrowing from banks, and distribution of profits, and is also reflected in the ownership structure of the parent itself, which has been turned into a trustee holding company and is governed by an executive board of directors.

Company P is a wholly owned subsidiary of probably the world's largest home furnishing company based in the United States, and as in company N, Hong Kong is the financial and administrative center for manufacturing operations worldwide. Knockdown furniture components are manufactured in the Far East, and final assembly of these components is completed by related firms in the United States and European countries. The majority of sales by manufacturing plants in the Far East is thus intrafirm trade. Experienced supervisors from existing plants in ASEAN countries are transferred to help set up new plants in the region as they are initiated. Regional management control is in Singapore, where the chief executive officer (CEO) and the chairman (both former Hong Kong Chinese) are based. All financial matters in ASEAN subsidiaries must be reported to and controlled by the CEO who reports to the U.S. parent at annual meetings. The Hong Kong office thus exercises control over the accounting of financial matters, while the CEO in Singapore controls investment decisions and the ultimate source of capital is usually the firm's registered holding company in the British Virgin Islands. Hong Kong has been chosen as the operational headquarters mainly for tax purposes and for its accessibility.

The two customer-oriented firms in the sample, companies C and T, tend to exercise their control in a slightly different way. Namely, because frequent contacts with key clients at the highest possible level are required, top-level executives are often sent from the ultimate parent companies to Hong Kong and given authority to make in situ investment decisions, though this does not necessarily mean that investment capital comes from regional headquarters based in Hong Kong. Company T, for example, is wholly owned by its Belgian parent and is one of more than 40 offices and subsidiaries worldwide, mainly in the form of wholly owned subsidiaries. It specializes in apparel sourcing, primarily for major garment companies (90 percent of its business) and also for department stores. The Hong Kong office is the regional headquarters for the Far East and controls all subsidiaries throughout the Asia Pacific region, which must report to the regional headquarters, though these subsidiaries make many decisions independently. There are four offices in the ASEAN region and eighteen throughout the rest of Asia. The regional headquarters in Hong Kong has been given complete control over operations within Asia, and according to the Belgian managing director in Hong Kong, there is no interference with decision-making processes from the parent.

Company C is a multiparty joint venture among IBM Hong Kong/China (25 percent, financed through IBM Hong Kong/China based in Hong Kong), a New Zealander managing director and chairman (37.5 percent), and a Thai banker (37.5 percent). Neither IBM nor the Thai banker are involved in day-to-day operations. The group controlled by the Hong Kong firm is now one of the largest computer software companies in Asia. It prefers to establish joint ventures when investing in the ASEAN region, the exception being in Singapore, where there is a wholly owned affiliate. In these joint ventures, the firm seeks out reputable local businessmen or companies as partners to strengthen its competitive advantages in host-economy markets. Management control is primarily exercised by the managing director/chairman in Hong Kong, though local general managers are put in charge of day-to-day operations. Because joint ventures are preferred, the sources of investment in ASEAN affiliates are often economies other than Hong Kong, with differences among joint ventures depending on the host country and the partner initiating the investment. For example, in Thailand, although ownership of the Thai office is shared among the three parties, it is controlled by the local general manager and is financed from Thailand instead of Hong Kong. In contrast, the establishment of the Malaysian firm was initiated by IBM in order to facilitate support of IBM mainframe systems.

There are two firms in the sample, companies G and Q, that can be classified as relocated holding companies. As companies have tried to grapple with the uncertainties surrounding the return of Hong Kong to China in 1997, many have chosen to relocate their holding companies abroad, often to tax havens such as Bermuda, the British Virgin Islands, and Panama, or in the case of multinationals that had migrated to Hong Kong from other economies, back to the original home economy (primarily the United Kingdom). The two examples considered here fall into the category of firms that were originally British, then incorporated in Hong Kong, but have since moved their headquarters back to the United Kingdom. However, both firms have maintained their Hong Kong operations at more or less the same level since the relocation.

Company G is a regional subsidiary of its international ultimate parent company, which, as an international service and marketing group, operates in over 80 countries worldwide and employs some 48,000 people. The firm has a long history in Asia and other international markets, with some of its businesses dating back more than 150 years. In a period of three to six years, the group had carried out what they called "business streaming" on a worldwide basis. As a result of this business streaming, all overseas affiliates have to report to a headquarters of that stream, usually based in London. Within this organizational structure, the Hong Kong firm is responsible for the group's operations in Hong Kong, China, Taiwan, Macau, the Philippines, Vietnam, Cambodia, and Laos, focusing on three core businesses, distribution of motors, marketing of premier consumer goods, and international services (insurance, shipping, testing, and buying). The firm and its affiliates in China and Taiwan apparently have control of most daily matters but are often referred to the London parent on strategic matters, including most investment decisions. The Hong Kong firm is the international head office for the group's global buying service operation and controls the sourcing of apparel and general merchandise from developing and newly developed countries for major department stores and other buyers, primarily in the United States, Europe, and Australasia. Another of the Hong Kong firm's functions is as regional headquarters for the group's testing services in the Asia Pacific region. All major decisions in ASEAN subsidiaries are reported to the Hong Kong firm and frequently reported to the London parent, but the Hong Kong firm has large influence on actual decisions as its familiarity with regional issues is valued highly by the parent.

Company Q is the merchant banking arm of a large British bank formerly incorporated in Hong Kong that has transferred its holding company back to London. The Hong Kong firm is the regional headquarters for the Asia Pacific region and is seeking to become the market leader in merchant and investment banking with strong financial support from the holding company. Although the Hong Kong firm and its Asian operations are wholly owned by the holding company in London, it is run rather independently. Key investment decisions are made at board meetings usually held in Hong Kong. The parent is represented at board meetings, and directors can raise questions on investment proposals. Outside of these meetings, however, the parent exercises little control over how these investment proposals are executed. One reason is that the holding company is much more concerned with the commercial banking arm of the group. Investment projects are financed from various sources in Hong Kong or local capital markets. It appears that ownership has very little relation to outward direct investments and control of these investments. The Malaysian office, for example, is managed autonomously, with the Malaysian director reporting to the CEO in the Hong Kong firm as well as the CEO in the bank's Malaysian branch.

These case studies thus indicate that there is often a high degree of autonomy exercised by foreign-owned Hong Kong firms investing in Southeast Asia, and it is evident that several foreign-owned companies are using Hong Kong not only as a "stepping stone" to penetrate the lucrative and emerging Asian markets but also as a regional center of decision making and control in its own right. This might suggest that the geography of ownership often does not correspond to the geography of control. On the other hand, even among the relatively autonomous firms, there are a number of examples where autonomy is a result of a conscious decentralization strategy by the parent firm. In other words, the very lack of a correlation of the geography of ownership and the geography of control may be dictated by the parent firm.

4.4.2 Investors from Hong Kong and Singapore in Thailand

There are a number of published corporate directories in Thailand that have made it possible to classify 95 Thai affiliates of Hong Kong and Singapore investors by whether the Hong Kong or Singapore investor can be identified as foreign controlled or not (see table 4.8 for some summary statistics; the firm list on which other observations are based is available from the authors). It should be noted that a few of the firms not identified as foreign controlled are probably foreign controlled but it simply has not been possible to identify them as such. On the other hand, we are reasonably sure that all the affiliates identified as foreign controlled (the results of indirect investment) are indeed ultimately owned by a firm or individual that is not from Hong Kong or Singapore.

The most conspicuous pattern observed from these data is that 59 percent of the affiliates of Hong Kong firms and 64 percent of the affiliates of Singapore firms are actually controlled by investors outside of Hong Kong and Singapore. This finding is consistent with the data presented in section 4.3 that suggested a large portion of the FDI from Hong Kong and Singapore is of the indirect variety.[17] These data also suggest that, in terms of the number of investors at least, the shares of indirect investment are similar in Hong Kong and Singapore. If measured in terms of sales, however, the shares are somewhat different, with 18 foreign-controlled affiliates accounting for 68 percent of the sales of the 33 Hong Kong affiliates for which sales data were available, but 29 foreign-controlled affiliates accounting for only 50 percent of the sales of the 50 Singapore affiliates for which data were available.

Also, as indicated by the numbers in section 4.3 and the Hong Kong case

17. Because the sample is biased toward large investors and investors from Japan, it is likely to overstate the relative importance of indirect investors. At the same time, however, the sample is reasonably comprehensive, and this bias is not likely to be large.

Table 4.8 A Sample of Thai Affiliates of Firms Based in Hong Kong and Singapore

	Industry				Major Foreign Country						Ownership Shares					
Measure	Manuf.	Trade	Trade plus Manuf. or Other	Other	Hong Kong	Singapore	Japan	Other OECD	Other Countries	Unknown	Hong Kong or Singapore	Foreign Total	Local	Year of Start-Up	1991 Employment[a]	1991 Sales[b]
Affiliates of foreign-controlled Hong Kong firms																
Number in sample	2	5	7	8	0	0	16	4	2	0	22	22	22	22	20	18
Mean											34.0	49.6	4.4	1980	465	28.378
Sample standard deviation											19.3	16.8	11.3	8	949	36.011
Affiliates of Hong Kong firms not known to be foreign controlled																
Number in sample	7	7	0	1	4	0	0	1	1	9	15	15	15	15	6	15
Mean											44.2	46.7	0.0	1983	1,092	15.743
Sample standard deviation											18.1	16.5	0.0	8	1,218	10.058

Affiliates of foreign-controlled Singapore firms																
Number in sample	6	10	12	9	1	0	30	6	0	0	37	37	37	37	29	29
Mean											33.7	58.6	1.6	1986	214	13.449
Sample standard deviation											23.2	25.5	6.3	7	374	14.388
Affiliates of Singapore firms not known to be foreign controlled																
Number in sample	5	12	1	3	0	9	0	0	0	12	21	21	21	21	7	21
Mean											35.1	38.2	0.0	1978	337	18.722
Sample standard deviation											24.5	22.8	0.0	12	394	20.566

Sources: Data taken from published lists of firms operating in Thailand; primary sources are International Business Research (Thailand) (1994), Advanced Research Group (1992), SEAMICO Business Information and Research (1993), and Toyo Keizai (1992, 1993). The former two publications cover most large and medium-size firms in Thailand, and the majority of these firms with sales of U.S.$4 million or more are included in one of these lists. The third source covers so-called supporting industries and includes some smaller firms. The last source covers only Japanese firms. Hence the sample is biased toward large firms and firms with ultimate parents in Japan. In addition to these primary sources, which provided the information on the Thai firms, a number of secondary sources, namely, Datapool (1993), American Chamber of Commerce in Thailand (1992), and Thai-Canadian Chamber of Commerce (1994), were used to obtain supplemental information on ultimate parents.

[a]Number of employees.

[b]In millions of U.S. dollars.

studies above, these investments are in a wide range of activities. By industry, the largest number of firms were in trade (36 percent) and another large group combined trade with manufacturing (19 percent) or other activities (2 percent). The remaining sample firms were evenly divided between manufacturing (21 percent) and other activities (22 percent), primarily services. If one compares foreign-controlled investors and investors not known to be foreign controlled, the shares of trade combined with other activities and other industries are larger for foreign-controlled investors than for investors not known to be foreign controlled, while the reverse is true in manufacturing and trade alone, for both Hong Kong and Singapore investors.[18] In contrast, the differences between investors by country are less consistent, suggesting that distinguishing the level of foreign control may be more important for understanding investment patterns than distinguishing the geographical source of investment.

Another interesting characteristic is that affiliates of Hong Kong and Singapore firms are rarely characterized by high foreign ownership shares, with only 13 percent of the sample firms having total foreign ownership shares of 90 percent or greater and 29 percent with shares of 50 percent or greater. Low foreign ownership shares are due in part to Thai policies that restrict foreign equity shares in a number of activities, but there are many ways around these equity restrictions, and the sources used to construct table 4.8 suggest that high foreign ownership shares are generally more common among foreign affiliates in Thailand.[19] In this sample, there is also a tendency for total foreign ownership shares to be larger in affiliates of foreign-owned investors, with the differences being largest in the Singaporean case.

However, when comparing affiliates of foreign-owned investors and other affiliates, the more pervasive difference is the relatively large gap between total foreign ownership shares and Hong Kong/Singapore investor ownership shares in the case of affiliates of foreign-owned investors. In other words, indirect investment from Hong Kong or Singapore is often accompanied by investment from other foreign firms, most often those in the investing firm group. This pattern is especially common among Japanese investors in this sample. A related pattern of some significance in this case is the tendency for many Japanese affiliates to receive equity investment from other affiliates located in Thai-

18. Comparisons of shares for foreign-controlled firms vs. firms not known to be foreign controlled are as follows: in manufacturing only for Hong Kong affiliates, 2/22 vs. 7/15, for Singapore affiliates, 6/37 vs. 5/21; in trade only for Hong Kong affiliates, 5/22 vs. 7/15, for Singapore affiliates, 10/37 vs. 12/21; in trade and other activities (including manufacturing) for Hong Kong affiliates, 7/22 vs. 0/15, for Singapore affiliates, 12/37 vs. 1/21; and in other activities only for Hong Kong affiliates, 8/22 vs. 1/15, for Singapore affiliates, 9/37 vs. 3/21.

19. E.g., defining "foreign firms" as firms with 10 percent or more of their equity coming from foreign investors, 20 percent of 516 foreign firms listed in Advanced Research Group (1992) had ownership shares of 90 percent or greater and 29 percent had shares of 50 percent or greater. In a 791-firm sample from SEAMICO Business Information and Research (1993), these shares were 26 and 44 percent, respectively. Finally, of the 533 Japanese affiliates listed in Toyo Keizai (1993) that had their equity financed by Japanese parents only, these shares were 20 and 34 percent.

land.[20] The combination of investment from foreign affiliates and indirect investment through Thai affiliates is perhaps best understood as a way to secure ownership control in the presence of equity restrictions. On the other hand, the combination of indirect investment through Hong Kong and Singapore affiliates and investment from other foreign sources, usually Japanese parents, indicates that these Hong Kong and Singapore affiliates are acting as integrated parts of a worldwide network. Interviews with a few Japanese firms in Thailand that received equity investment from related firms in other Asian economies (mainly Hong Kong and Singapore, but also some from Malaysia) also indicated that this type of investment pattern is often the result of deliberate efforts by parent firms to spur regional integration and coordination among foreign affiliates.

Finally, there are clear differences between the Hong Kong and Singapore economies, notably the more dominant role of foreign multinationals (e.g., Ramstetter 1994) and the relatively small size of the local entrepreneurial class in Singapore (e.g., Lee and Low 1990), that might lead one to think that investment patterns from the two economies would differ greatly in a place like Thailand. However, this sample suggests that the patterns are quite similar in a number of respects.

4.5 Conclusions

This paper has surveyed information on outward investors from Hong Kong and Singapore with the aim of illuminating the implications of accounting for outward FDI by geographical source or by country of ultimate beneficial owner. By any measure it is clear that a very large portion of the FDI from these economies comes from foreign-controlled firms and hence that traditional, geography-based estimates of FDI from these economies greatly exceed corresponding ownership-based estimates. Examination of case studies from Hong Kong indicated a tendency for investment decisions to be relatively autonomous in four types of foreign-controlled Hong Kong firms: recently acquired firms, firms with strong local entrepreneurial involvement, customer-oriented firms, and relocated holding companies. On the other hand, evidence from some of these case studies and a sample of Thai affiliates of foreign-controlled Hong Kong or Singapore investors suggested that many of the investors were acting as parts of an integrated network of foreign investors, even when the foreign-controlled investor in Hong Kong and Singapore had a large degree of control over investment decisions. Moreover, if the Thai sample is representative, it does not appear that autonomous foreign-controlled investors constitute a majority among foreign-controlled investors in Hong Kong and Singapore.

20. Note that 38 percent (329) of the 872 Thai affiliates of Japanese firms listed in Toyo Keizai (1993) received equity investment from affiliates of Japanese investors located outside of Japan, including other affiliates located in Thailand.

References

Advanced Research Group. 1992. *Thailand company information 1992–93.* Bangkok: Advanced Research Group.

American Chamber of Commerce in Thailand. 1992. *Handbook directory 1992.* Bangkok: American Chamber of Commerce in Thailand.

Caves, Richard E. 1982. *Multinational enterprise and economic analysis.* Cambridge: Cambridge University Press.

China. State Statistical Bureau. Various years. *China statistical yearbook,* 1985–94 issues. Beijing: State Statistical Bureau.

Datapool. 1993. *Singapore 1000 1993,* 2 vols. Singapore: Datapool.

Dicken, Peter, Mats Forsgren, and Anders Malmberg. 1994. The local embeddedness of transnational corporations. In *Globalization, institutions, and regional development in Europe,* ed. Ash Amin and Nigel Thrift, 23–45. Oxford: Oxford University Press.

Dunning, John H. 1993. *Multinational enterprises and the global economy.* Workingham, England: Addison-Wesley.

Hill, Hal. 1988. *Foreign investment and industrialization in Indonesia.* Singapore: Oxford University Press.

———. 1991. Multinationals and employment in Indonesia. ILO Multinational Enterprises Programme Working Paper no. 67. Geneva: International Labour Office.

Hong Kong. Industry Department. 1993. *1993 Survey of overseas investment in Hong Kong's manufacturing industries.* Hong Kong: Industry Department.

Hsueh, Tien-tung, and Tun-oy Woo. 1991. The changing pattern of Hong Kong–China economic relations since 1979: Issues and consequences. In *Industrial and trade development in Hong Kong,* ed. Edward K. Y. Chen, Mee-Kau Nyaw, and Teresa Y. C. Wong, 464–96. Hong Kong: University of Hong Kong, Center of Asian Studies.

Indonesia. Bank Indonesia. Various years. *Annual report,* 1974/75–1992/93 issues. Jakarta: Bank Indonesia.

Indonesia. BKPM (Investment Coordinating Board). 1993. *Monthly report,* April issue. Jakarta: BKPM.

International Business Research (Thailand). 1994. *Million baht business information Thailand 1993.* Bangkok: International Business Research.

International Monetary Fund. 1995. *International financial statistics yearbook.* Washington, D.C.: International Monetary Fund, September. CD-ROM.

———. Various years. *Balance of payments statistics yearbook,* June 1988 computer tape, 1988–93 issues. Washington, D.C.: International Monetary Fund.

Japan. Ministry of Finance. 1993. *Zaisei Kinyu Toukei Geppo* (Financial and monetary statistics monthly), no. 500 (December). Tokyo: Ministry of Finance.

Kojima, Kiyoshi. 1990. *Japanese direct investment abroad.* Monograph Series, no. 1. Mitaka, Tokyo: International Christian University, Social Science Research Institute.

Korean Foreign Trade Association. 1992. *Major statistics of Korean economy,* 1992 issue. Seoul: Korean Foreign Trade Association.

Lee (Tsao) Yuan and Linda Low. 1990. *Local entrepreneurship in Singapore: Private and state.* Singapore: Times Academic Press.

Malaysia. Ministry of Finance. Various years. *Economic report,* 1979/80–1992/93 issues. Kuala Lumpur: Ministry of Finance.

Malaysia Industrial Development Authority. Various years. *Statistics on the manufacturing sector,* 1988, 1989, January–December 1989, 1985–90, and 1988–92 issues, and similar unpublished mimeographs for 1987–91. Kuala Lumpur: Malaysia Industrial Development Authority.

Markusen, James R. 1991. The theory of the multinational enterprise: A common analytical framework. In *Direct foreign investment in Asia's developing economies and structural change in the Asia-Pacific region,* ed. Eric D. Ramstetter, 11–32. Boulder, Colo.: Westview.

Ozawa, Terutomo. 1979. *Multinationalism, Japanese style: The political economy of outward dependency.* Princeton, N.J.: Princeton University Press.

Pangetsu, Mari. 1991. Foreign firms and structural change in the Indonesian manufacturing sector. In *Direct foreign investment in Asia's developing economies and structural change in the Asia-Pacific region,* ed. Eric D. Ramstetter, 35–64. Boulder, Colo.: Westview.

Philippines. Central Bank of the Philippines. Various years. *Annual statistics,* 1990 and 1991 issues. Manila: Central Bank of the Philippines.

Ramstetter, Eric D. 1994. Characteristics of foreign multinationals in selected Asian economies. Paper prepared for the Fourth Convention of the East Asian Economic Association, Taipei, 26–27 August.

Republic of China. Central Bank of China. Various issues (quarterly). *Balance of payments, Taiwan district, Republic of China,* 1958–82 summary (published 1983), December issues 1981–91. Taipei: Central Bank of China.

———. Investment Commission. 1993. *Statistics on: Overseas Chinese and foreign investment, technical cooperation, outward investment, outward technical cooperation, indirect mainland investment, the Republic of China. Taipei: Investment Commission, 31 December.*

———. Various years. *A survey of overseas Chinese and foreign firms and their effects on national economic development* (in Chinese), 1974–91 issues. Taipei: Investment Commission.

Samudram, Muthi. 1995. Return of Hong Kong to China and Asian industrializing region. Kuala Lumpur: Malaysia Institute of Economic Research. Mimeograph.

SEAMICO Business Information and Research. 1993. *Directory of supporting industries 1993.* Bangkok: SEAMICO Business Information and Research.

Shih, Ta-Lang. 1989. The PRC's Hong Kong–based conglomerates and their role in national development. In *Global business: Asia-Pacific dimensions,* ed. Erdener Kaynak and Kam-Hon Lee, 368–87. London: Routledge.

Singapore. Department of Statistics. 1991. *Singapore's investment abroad 1976–1989.* Singapore: Singapore National Printers.

———. 1993a. Data on inward and outward foreign direct investment downloaded from the PATS (Public Access Time Series) database on July 22. Singapore: Department of Statistics.

———. 1993b. Direct investment abroad of local companies. Occasional Paper Series. Singapore: Department of Statistics.

———. 1993c. *Singapore's investment abroad 1990.* Singapore: Singapore National Printers.

———. 1994. *Yearbook of statistics 1993.* Singapore: Singapore National Printers.

———. Various years. *Report on the Census of Industrial Production,* 1980–86 issues. Singapore: Singapore National Printers.

———. Economic Development Board. 1993. *Your partners in regionalisation: Singapore government agencies.* Singapore: Economic Development Board.

———. 1994. *Report on the Census of Industrial Production,* 1980–92 issues. Singapore: Economic Development Board, 31 December. Mimeographs with revised series.

Thai-Canadian Chamber of Commerce. 1994. *Handbook and directory 1994.* Bangkok: Thai-Canadian Chamber of Commerce.

Thailand. Bank of Thailand. Various years. Foreign investment data mimeographs, undated [September 1983, July 1986, July 1987, July 1988, July 1989, July 1990, July 1991, July 1992, August 1992, April 1993, April 1994, September 1994]. Bangkok: Bank of Thailand.

Toyo Keizai. 1992. *Kaigai Shinshutsu Kigyou Souran, Kokubetsu Hen, 1992* (A comprehensive survey of firms overseas, 1992). Tokyo: Toyo Keizai.

———. 1993. *Kaigai Shinshutsu Kigyou Souran, Kokubetsu Hen, 1993* (A comprehensive survey of firms overseas, compiled by country, 1993). Tokyo: Toyo Keizai.

———. 1994. *Kaigai Shinshutsu Kigyou Souran, Kaishabetsu Hen, 1994 Nenban* (A comprehensive survey of firms overseas, compiled by company, 1994). Tokyo: Toyo Keizai.

United Kingdom. Central Statistical Office. 1991. *Business monitor MA4.* London: Government Statistical Service.

United Nations. Center on Transnational Corporations. 1992. *World investment directory 1992: Foreign direct investment, legal framework and corporate data.* Vol. 1, *Asia and the Pacific.* New York: United Nations.

———. 1993. *World investment directory 1992: Foreign direct investment, legal framework and corporate data.* Vol. 3, *Developed countries.* New York: United Nations.

———. 1994. *World investment directory: Foreign direct investment, legal framework and corporate data.* Vol. 4, *Latin America and the Caribbean, 1994.* New York: United Nations.

U.S. Department of Commerce. 1990. Foreign direct investment in the United States, balance of payments and direct investment position estimates, 1980–86. Washington, D.C.: U.S. Department of Commerce, Bureau of Economic Analysis. Computer diskette.

———. 1994. Foreign direct investment in the United States, direct investment position and related capital and income flows, 1987–93. Washington, D.C.: U.S. Department of Commerce, Bureau of Economic Analysis. Computer diskette.

Wilson, John C. 1992. Hong Kong as regional headquarters. Paper presented at the ASEAN-China Hong Kong Forum on Hong Kong's Role in the Asian Pacific Region in the 21st Century, Hong Kong, 28–29 February.

Wong, Teresa Y. C., Edward K. Y. Chen, and Mee-Kau Nyaw. 1991. The future of industrial and trade development in the Asian Pacific: An overview. In *Industrial and trade and development in Hong Kong,* ed. Edward K. Y. Chen, Mee-Kau Nyaw, and Teresa Y. C. Wong, ix–xxxiii. Hong Kong: University of Hong Kong, Center of Asian Studies.

Yeung, Henry Wai-Chung. 1994. Hong Kong firms in the ASEAN region: Transnational corporations and foreign direct investment. *Environment and Planning A* 26: 1931–56.

———. 1995. The geography of Hong Kong transnational corporations in the ASEAN region: Some empirical observations. *Area* 27 (3): 318–34.

———. 1996. The historical geography of Hong Kong investments in the ASEAN region. *Singapore Journal of Tropical Geography* 17 (1): 66–82.

Zhang, Xiaoning James. 1993. The role of foreign direct investment in market-oriented reforms and economic development: The case of China. *Transnational Corporations* 2 (3): 121–48.

Comment Rachel McCulloch

The move from economic theory to empirical analysis always requires a leap of faith. Key concepts that shine out clearly in theoretical modeling rarely find

Rachel McCulloch is the Rosen Family Professor of International Finance at Brandeis University.

neat counterparts in the data. In the case of foreign direct investment (FDI), the difficulty is not simply one of incomplete or inaccurate data, although this is often a formidable hurdle. The deeper problem arises because there is only a loose correspondence between conveniently measurable characteristics of firms and the economic phenomena to be investigated. Even data that are complete and accurate can leave much to be desired, and what are the "correct" data cannot always be specified in advance of the question to be answered using those data.

In their investigation of FDI from Hong Kong and Singapore, Low, Ramstetter, and Yeung (LRY) offer a rare opportunity to look behind the numerical indicators to the actual business operations the data are intended to capture. The authors' focus is the appropriate statistical treatment of outward direct investments of corporate parents in Hong Kong and Singapore that are themselves foreign-controlled subsidiaries of firms based elsewhere. Such investments may be classified by geographical source or by ultimate ownership. Because of the important role played by foreign-controlled firms, using an ownership definition of source greatly reduces the measured extent of outward FDI originating in Hong Kong and Singapore. Which accounting measure provides the more accurate statistical picture? To address this question, the authors combine information from published statistics with case studies of outward FDI by foreign-controlled Hong Kong parents and of Thai affiliates controlled by parent firms in Hong Kong and Singapore.

Who Is in Control?

Theory distinguishes FDI from other types of international capital flows on the basis of foreign managerial control over host-country operations. The standard empirical proxy for control is a required minimum equity participation in the host-country enterprise. Given the arbitrary character of the proxy, it is not surprising that the required minimum varies across countries, or that the observed degree of control bears little relationship to the statistical measure. The equity participation yardstick also allows joint ventures to be "controlled" simultaneously by source firms in several countries or, as Baldwin and Kimura (chap. 1 in this volume) point out, to be attributed to more than one industry. Moreover, because measurement of FDI almost always relies on cross-border flows, standard data fail to capture equity positions financed by subsidiaries' local borrowing in the host country.

The authors examine 20 cases of ASEAN investments by foreign-owned Hong Kong companies to determine the degree of autonomy of the Hong Kong parent in its outward investment activities. Of these 20, eight are judged to have a substantial degree of autonomy in making decisions with regard to outward investment. But the significance of this finding is unclear. The Hong Kong companies in the sample are all headquarters firms. Each thus has a specific role to play in the parent firm's global management structure as the locus of corporate decision making for the region. Observing a decision-making function in the area of outward FDI does not make the case for autonomy as long as the top management at the regional headquarters can be replaced should their actions fail to satisfy the needs of the parent. What is observed for these eight is better described as decentralization of a particular function rather than autonomy in an economic sense.

If the question to be answered is whose business interests these investments serve, ultimate ownership may be the appropriate criterion for classifying investments regardless of the location where particular decisions are made. Any systematic differences in the apparent autonomy of Hong Kong subsidiaries may simply reflect differences in management structure (as suggested by LRY's study of Thai affiliates). However, the authors note that the "autonomous" subsidiaries fall into several categories. This finding suggests the interesting further hypothesis that certain types of companies are better served by a decentralized management structure.

Whose Firm-Specific Assets?

The criterion of control focuses on where decisions are made, and for whose benefit. A different possible reason to classify FDI by source is the assumption that the firm-specific assets (FSAs) associated with FDI are related to characteristics of the investing firm's home base. For geographical sources that are notable mainly as tax havens, for example, the Netherlands Antilles, it is clear that any FSA (other than perhaps a certain type of financial know-how) is linked more to the ultimate beneficial owner. But what about a geographical source like Hong Kong or Singapore, one that is financially advantaged but also an important locus for business decision making?

Recent theory views FDI as a cross-border intrafirm conduit for hypothesized FSAs that can be used profitably in advantageous locations abroad. But how are such FSAs identified and measured? Empirical research has shown that differences in the extent of FDI across manufacturing industries is explained in part by industry ratios of R&D to sales and advertising to sales, that is, by expenditures used to create and maintain FSAs. In fact, these ratios are proxies for current or recent *additions* to FSAs rather than for their current importance. Moreover, anecdotal FSAs have less to do with technology in the formal sense than with accumulated practical know-how relevant for successful organization of production, quality control, and marketing.

The Hong Kong case studies summarized in the paper suggest that a foreign-owned parent may be a significant independent source of FSAs even when managers lack decision-making power in the area of outward investment. In fact, the choice of Hong Kong as a regional headquarters site by a significant fraction of all multinationals investing there may reflect the ready availability of certain types of region-specific know-how. Presumably, the FSAs transmitted to Asian affiliates will be a blend of firmwide assets (brand identification, marketing linkages, technology in the narrow sense) and Asia-specific assets (language, culture).

The paper's approach of going behind the data through the use of case studies is very illuminating for any user of FDI data. Although it cannot resolve the underlying conceptual problems, the use of case studies allows users to be more fully aware of the implications of choosing one data series rather than another. The paper also provides an interesting perspective on the classification scheme proposed by Baldwin and Kimura (chap. 1 in this volume). To add together U.S. trade with foreigners and sales to foreigners of U.S. subsidiaries abroad, it is first necessary to decide which U.S. subsidiaries to include in the calculation. For example, a number of foreign subsidiaries in Mexico have U.S. parents that are themselves controlled by Japanese parents. According to the Baldwin and Kimura methodology, these Mexican enterprises should be classified as Japanese, but the conceptually "right" answer is not obvious. And a practical problem in implementing the Baldwin-Kimura approach is that while the United States, unlike Hong Kong, does collect data on outward FDI, the U.S. data do not separate outward FDI on an ownership basis.

5 Accounting for Chinese Trade: Some National and Regional Considerations

K. C. Fung

5.1 Introduction

In this paper I examine various conceptual and data issues related to trade and investment in China. This topic is interesting because China is the most dynamic, fastest growing economy in the world. Despite cycles of inflation and contraction, real GDP in China has grown at almost 10 percent annually over the period 1979–92. For the coastal provinces, from Guangdong in the south up through Fujian, Jiangsu, Zhejiang to Shandong in the north, the annual growth rate averaged over 12 percent for the same period (Ho 1993). This economic performance has led many to predict that China will one day be the next economic superpower (Survey of China 1992). For example, Larry Summers (1992) once extrapolated that if the growth differential between China and the United States during the 1980s persists, China could surpass the United States to become the largest economy in the world in 11 years. He further pointed out that if the per capita income of China reached that of Taiwan, China's GDP would exceed that of all Organization for Economic Cooperation and Development (OECD) countries. According to estimates by the

K. C. Fung is associate professor at the University of California, Santa Cruz, and associate director at the Hong Kong Centre for Economic Research.

Funding from the Hong Kong Centre for Economic Research, the National Bureau of Economic Research, and the University of California Pacific Rim Research Grant is gratefully acknowledged. The author has benefited from conversations with many academics from the University of Hong Kong (particularly Stephen Cheung and Richard Wong), Chinese University of Hong Kong (Sung Yun-Wing and Ho Yin-Ping), Hong Kong Baptist College (Tsang Shu-Ki), and Hong Kong University of Science and Technology (Leonard Cheng); with officials in the Hong Kong government; with private sector research economists and businesspeople in Hong Kong; and with many researchers at the Chung-Hua Institution for Economic Research in Taiwan. Richard Wong, Steven Parker, Christine Wong, Larry Lau, Anne Krueger, Marc Noland, Ron McKinnon, Donald Wittman, and Dan Friedman have provided comments and pointed to some useful sources of data. Hitomi Iizaka, Changhua Rich at UC-Santa Cruz, and S. F. Lee at Hong Kong University have all been excellent research assistants for this project.

Table 5.1 **China's Foreign Merchandise Trade**

Year	Total	Exports	Imports
1978	20.7	9.8	10.9
1979	29.4	13.7	15.7
1980	38.1	18.1	20.0
1981	44.0	22.0	22.0
1982	41.6	22.3	19.3
1983	43.6	22.2	21.4
1984	53.5	26.1	27.4
1985	69.7	27.4	42.3
1986	73.8	30.9	42.9
1987	82.7	39.4	43.2
1988	102.8	47.5	55.3
1989	111.7	52.5	59.1
1990	115.4	62.1	53.4
1991	135.7	71.9	63.8
1992	165.6	85.0	80.6
1993	195.8	91.8	104.0

Source: China, State Statistical Bureau (1994).
Note: Figures are in billions of U.S. dollars. Exports are valued on a f.o.b. basis, imports on a c.i.f. basis.

International Monetary Fund (IMF) (1993), based on purchasing-power-parity exchange rates, China has the third highest GDP in the world, behind only the United States and Japan. Some argue that China's economic performance since the economic reform era has brought about one of the biggest improvements in human welfare anywhere at any time (Survey of China 1992).[1]

Since December 1978, when the history-making third plenary session of the eleventh Central Committee of the Chinese Communist Party decided to abandon the Stalinist strategy for growth and opted for a program of open door policies and reforms, there has been a tremendous increase in China's foreign trade activities. In the prereform era, China had traded relatively little with the outside world, given its size. By 1992, China's total foreign trade volume ranked eleventh in the world, a jump from thirty-second in 1979. Using China's official statistics, table 5.1 shows the changes over time in China's trade.[2]

1. As China grows in importance, the amount of research into various aspects of China has also exploded; see, e.g., Lau (1995), Wong (1995), Wong, Heady, and Woo (1993), and McKinnon (1991). However, work on the foreign trade of China and direct investment in the country has been relatively sparse. Exceptions are, e.g., Sung (1991), Liu et al. (1992), Lardy (1994), Fung (1997, 1996), Fung and Iizaka (1998), and Fung and Lau (1996). Baldwin and Nelson (1993), Bergsten and Noland (1993), Feenstra (1995), Ito and Krueger (1993), and Noland (1990) contain recent research related to trade and trade policies with Taiwan or Hong Kong.

2. As Lardy (1992) points out, even different agencies within the Chinese government report Chinese data differently. For example, Ministry on Foreign Economic Relations and Trade export statistics on processing include only the processing fees earned from such exports, which are less than 10 percent of the value of the exports. By contrast, China's customs statistics include the entire value of these exports.

The money value of China's merchandise exports of $85 billion (U.S. dollars) in 1992 was more than eight times the $9.8 billion in 1978. In nominal terms, this means a compound growth rate of 16.8 percent per year. For imports, the $80.6 billion in 1992 was more than seven times the $10.9 billion in 1978. This translates into nominal growth of 15.4 percent. This is almost twice as fast as the growth of global trade for the same period. According to the OECD (1993), China was sixteenth by its share of global exports in 1990, with a share of 1.6 percent of world exports. But if we add Hong Kong and Taiwan to mainland China (Greater China), Greater China's rank was fifth, behind only the United States, Japan, Germany, and France.

Beyond the very rapid growth of China's economy and trade and the country's new role as a global player, there are other reasons why I want to look into data concerning China's trade. First, Chinese trade data are often at odds with the data of its trading partners. Trade data discrepancies are actually quite common, but the situation with China is particularly striking. In 1992, for example, according to Chinese statistics exports to the United States were $8.6 billion and imports from the United States were $8.9 billion. This translates into a small U.S. *surplus* of $0.3 billion. But U.S. trade statistics show that imports from China were $25.7 billion and exports were $7.4 billion, resulting in a U.S. trade *deficit* of $18.3 billion. From an economic standpoint, bilateral trade imbalance is not generally a cause for concern, but political factors often cause trade imbalances to fuel trade frictions. Trade data discrepancies between China and its trading partners heighten these trade tensions.

A significant part of the discrepancy in trade data related to China is due to Chinese trade with and via Hong Kong, its small but prosperous southern neighbor. According to China's customs statistics, 44 percent of China's 1992 exports went to Hong Kong and 26 percent of China's 1992 imports came from Hong Kong. Using these figures, Hong Kong is China's largest trading partner.

Because of its strategic location, its modern facilities in banking, finance, insurance, transportation, and other services, and the fact that there is a sound legal framework in place, Hong Kong is China's main gateway to the West, and vice versa. Much of Hong Kong's role in China's trade is to act as a middleman. This means that a lot of trade involving Hong Kong is entrepôt trade: reexport and transshipment. Even after 30 June 1997, when Hong Kong will become officially a part of China, Hong Kong will remain a separate customs territory and a separate member of the General Agreement on Tariffs and Trade (GATT)—more accurately, the World Trade Organization (WTO)—according to the 1984 Sino-British Joint Declaration and also according to the promise that China had made to GATT. In other words, the problems with China's trade data due to a separate Hong Kong are not likely to go away in the near future.

Until very recently, China's official trade data counted exports to Hong Kong for consumption in Hong Kong and exports to Hong Kong to be reexported elsewhere both as exports to Hong Kong. Similarly, U.S. goods reexported via Hong Kong to China are not always counted as U.S. exports to China in U.S.

data. We will look at China's trade by taking into account its important *reexport* character.[3] One example of this complication is that using Chinese data, Hong Kong was the largest exporter to China from 1987 to 1992. But in 1993, when Chinese authorities began to trace the origin of Chinese imports more seriously, Hong Kong dropped to fourth largest exporter behind Japan, the United States, and Taiwan (Sung 1994).

Another source of the problem with China's trade statistics is the markup that the Hong Kong middleman adds to reexports to and from China. This added value is attributed to the exporting country but in fact should be attributed to Hong Kong. Thus, in addition to reexports, trade data with China should be adjusted by taking the reexport markup into account. Reexports and reexport markups affect China's trade with *all* countries and regions, including the three on which we will focus in this paper, Hong Kong, Taiwan, and the United States. Furthermore, both reexports and reexport markups are large and thus significantly affect Chinese trade data.

Another interesting aspect of China's trade is that a large part of it is fueled by foreign direct investment (FDI), particularly investment by Hong Kong and Taiwan in Guangdong and Fujian. Exports and imports related to investment are not unique to China, but such FDI-related trade is especially important in the Greater China region. In Chinese trade data, both geography and foreign ownership play an important role.

For geographical and historical reasons, China's trade with Taiwan is of special interest. According to 1992 Chinese trade data, Taiwan is China's fourth largest export market, behind Hong Kong, Japan, and the United States. Cold war politics and the historical rivalry between the Chinese Nationalists and the Chinese Communist Party caused most direct trade to be banned between Taiwan and mainland China. In 1978, mainland China wanted to reestablish mail, travel, and trade. Taiwan initially responded with a continuation of the "three no's policy": no contact, no negotiations, no compromise (Kao 1993). However, by 1985, Taiwan no longer interfered with indirect exports, though indirect imports were still to be subject to control. Taiwan's control of indirect imports would later be relaxed. Taiwan's official policy is still that all trade and investment must be carried out indirectly. A substantial portion of trade between mainland China and Taiwan is indirect reexport trade via Hong Kong.

In addition to reexports, which also form a large part of China's trade with its other trading partners (e.g., the United States), China-Taiwan trade is further characterized by forms of direct trade, such as transshipment, that are illegal from the Taiwanese standpoint.[4] Because of this illegal trade, statistics from Taiwan concerning China-Taiwan trade are also inaccurate. Based on the limited information we have, illegal trade is a large part of trade between mainland China and Taiwan.

3. Sung (1991) and, more recently, Lardy (1994), Fung (1997), and Fung and Iizaka (1998) were among the first to highlight quantitatively the importance of reexports in China's trade.

4. Kao (1993), Sung (1994), and Fung (1997) discuss the issue of transshipment.

From the U.S. side, trade with China represents both an opportunity and an increasing concern. China can be a large and growing market for American business; at the same time, the United States is worried about trade barriers in the Chinese market and the export potential of the Chinese. These worries have fueled several trade disputes. Some of the disputes have focused on the different ways that both sides look at trade data. For the United States, reexports and reexport margins are the dominant factors complicating the trade data.

In this paper I focus mainly on China's trade with and via Hong Kong, Taiwan, and the United States. There will also be special attention paid to the southern provinces of Guangdong and Fujian, where most FDI from Hong Kong and Taiwan takes place. Hong Kong and Taiwan deserve special attention because of their roles in FDI, reexport, and transshipment. U.S.-China trade is of interest because it highlights how different trade-accounting methods in data can lead to trade problems between important economic powers. In the next section, I examine and update the recent evolution of the Chinese foreign trade regime. In section 5.3, I look at the role of Hong Kong reexports in China's trade and discuss reexports and reexport margins in the context of trade with Hong Kong, Taiwan, and the United States. In section 5.4, I cover the importance of FDI-related trade, using first Hong Kong data, then official national Chinese data, and finally data from the provinces of Guangdong and Fujian. In section 5.5, I examine transshipment and other forms of illegal trade. There is some indication that smuggling is important for some segment of U.S.-China trade. Concluding remarks are given in section 5.6.

5.2 China's Evolving Foreign Trade Regime

Various writers have written about China's trade system (Sung 1991; Lardy 1992; Ho 1993; Fung 1997). In this section, we update and condense their work. Before 1978, the Ministry of Foreign Trade (MOFT) completely controlled China's foreign trade system. Under a mandatory trade plan, 15 product-specific national foreign trade corporations (FTCs) operated China's trade. International trade was just an extension of the domestic planning process. The Soviet style of material balances was used to construct the basic economic plan, which coordinated the flow of raw materials and intermediate goods among industries. The production of each good was equated to the intermediate and final demands by other major state enterprises. The plan used imports to fill the difference between planned demand and domestic production. Exports needed to pay for imports were then identified, first using goods of which there were excess supplies. The State Planning Commission set preliminary annual and long-term targets for broad categories of imports and exports. Then, on the basis of the State Planning Commission's targets, MOFT prepared more detailed plans and sent these plans to the FTCs.

Based on the foreign trade plan, the FTCs purchased goods from domestic enterprises at fixed prices, sold them abroad, and sent all foreign exchange to the Bank of China, which was the sole organization allowed to handle foreign exchange. The FTCs bought fixed quantities of foreign goods for domestic use at fixed prices and paid foreign suppliers with foreign exchange obtained from the Bank of China. World market prices had little impact on the Chinese domestic prices of tradable goods. Since the renminbi (the mainland Chinese currency) was overvalued, the FTCs usually suffered a loss on exports but earned a profit on imports.

In 1979, provincial and municipal governments and some large state enterprises were allowed to establish their own foreign trade enterprises. In March 1982, China's trade regime was further reformed. MOFT, the Import-Export Administration Commission, the Foreign Investment Administration Commission, and the Ministry of Foreign Economic Relations were consolidated into the Ministry of Foreign Economic Relations and Trade (MOFERT), with the latter organization supervising the 15 national FTCs and the local foreign trade bureaus. Recently, MOFERT has been reorganized into the Ministry of Foreign Trade and Economic Cooperation (MOFTEC) and given the responsibility to formulate and implement China's foreign trade policies.

In 1984, the State Council ended the monopoly power of the national FTCs and reduced the scope of foreign trade planning. The number of FTCs increased dramatically. In addition to the new national FTCs under the control of central government ministries and other state organizations, almost every provincial and municipal government had its own network of FTCs.

With decentralization, the number of FTCs increased from 15 in 1978, to more than 1,000 by the mid-1980s, to about 6,000 by the latter half of the 1980s. The new FTCs did not have to report to MOFERT. Unfortunately, there were some unscrupulous activities, and some new FTCs were unable to fulfill their contracts (e.g., some were unable to purchase the promised domestic goods for export). Since China had a long-standing reputation of fulfilling foreign contracts, the increasing failure to meet contractual obligations became a major concern not only to China's trading partners but also to the Chinese central authority.

These events led to a retrenchment in mid-1988. As many as 2,000 FTCs were dissolved, reorganized, or stripped of their right to conduct foreign trade. By the end of 1991, there were roughly 4,000 FTCs.

The scope of mandatory planning for foreign trade was also significantly reduced. The old foreign trade system was replaced by a system that combined mandatory planning, guidance planning, and the market. The 1984 trade reform assigned mandatory exports and imports (i.e., trade specified in quantitative terms) to designated national FTCs and allowed other FTCs to conduct their trade both within and outside the guidance plans. Unlike mandatory plans, guidance plans were generally specified in value terms. In addition to being more flexible, these plans allowed FTCs to take market demand and supply into account when deciding the mix of tradables within each broad product group.

The mandatory export plan covered about 3,000 items before 1979, but by 1988 the number fell to 112. By the end of the 1980s, exports under mandatory or guidance plans accounted for about 34 percent of total exports. Compared to the export system, the import system remained relatively unreformed in the 1980s. There were import licensing and high tariffs on protected products. In addition, almost all importers faced a series of complicated approval procedures. However, in the process of reforming the foreign trade system, the scope of mandatory planning for imports was also reduced. By 1991, no more than 40 percent of China's imports were under mandatory or guidance plans. In addition, as a consequence of a U.S. market access Section 301 case in 1992 and China's desire to join the WTO, China has made progress in making its trade regime more transparent.

In 1992, the Chinese government took important steps to reform its trade policy (World Bank 1993). A large number of trade documents previously unavailable to foreigners were published. Several steps were also taken to liberalize imports. The Customs Tariff Commission of the State Council reduced a large number of tariff rates. Rates were cut on 225 tariff lines, beginning on 1 January 1992. In addition, special import regulatory duties that had been instituted for 14 products in 1985 were lifted as of 1 April 1992.[5]

5.3 Issues Related to Reexports

The only data source on reexports that I am aware of are the official statistics of the Hong Kong government. Reexports, as defined by the Hong Kong government, occur when imports to Hong Kong are consigned to a buyer in Hong Kong who takes legal possession of the goods. These imports must clear customs (that is why Hong Kong has such statistics). Buyers in Hong Kong add a markup and then reexport the goods elsewhere. They may also undertake minor processing of the imports before reexporting them. However, they do not change the fundamental character or nature of the goods (no substantial transformation) so that *no* Hong Kong origin is supposed to be conferred. If the process substantially changes the imports, then they become goods "made in Hong Kong," and exports of these goods are regarded as exports of Hong Kong goods. They are then classified in official Hong Kong statistics as "domestic exports" rather than "reexports." Sung (1991) and, more recently, Lardy (1994) and Fung (1997) were among the first to consider the issue of reexports in the context of Hong Kong–China trade.

Reexports cost more than direct exports since they typically need additional loading, more customs clearing, and further insurance. The middleman also adds a markup before reexporting. In 1988, the Hong Kong Trade Development Council carried out a large-scale survey of Hong Kong traders. One find-

5. However, the effects of these measures have been essentially to bring the average tariff level back to pre-1987 levels (see World Bank 1993).

Table 5.2 Reexports in Hong Kong Trade

Reexport Category	1992	1993
1. Total reexports	690.8	823.2
2. Reexports to China	212.1	274.6
3. Reexports of Chinese origin	403.8	474.0
4. Reexports not involving China	95.1	96.5

Source: Hong Kong Government (1993).

Note: Figures are in billions of HK dollars. Rows 2, 3, and 4 sum to more than row 1 because reexports of Chinese origin back to China have been counted twice in rows 2 and 3.

ing was that the reexport markup on Chinese goods was 16 percent and the markup on other countries' goods was 14 percent. Another survey conducted by the Hong Kong Census and Statistics Department indicated that the reexport markup for all reexports in 1990 was 13.4 percent but the markup for Chinese goods was much higher. The department, however, did not publish the exact markup figure for Chinese goods in this survey. The higher markup for Chinese goods probably reflects the lower quality control on goods in China and Chinese producers' lack of information about overseas markets. Hong Kong middlemen thus need to do more repackaging and to look harder for markets for Chinese products.[6]

5.3.1 China–Hong Kong Trade

The bulk of trade between Hong Kong and China involves reexports. Hong Kong reexports registered significant growth in 1993. The value of reexports was HK$823 billion in 1993, about 19 percent higher than in 1992.[7] As reexports grew rapidly while domestic exports by Hong Kong declined, the share of reexports in total Hong Kong exports rose from 75 percent in 1992 to 79 percent in 1993.

China was the most important *source* of goods reexported through Hong Kong. In 1993, Chinese goods reexported via Hong Kong amounted to HK$474 billion, or 58 percent of total reexports (table 5.2). A large proportion of the reexports from China were products of outward processing commissioned by Hong Kong companies in China.[8] The major reexport items from China were clothing, telecommunications and sound recording equipment, footwear, and textile yarn and fabrics. China also remained the largest *market* for Hong Kong's reexports, accounting for HK$275 billion, or 33 percent in

6. Another interpretation is that the higher markup of Chinese goods reflects transfer pricing by mainland Chinese traders based in Hong Kong. I am indebted to Larry Lau for suggesting this interpretation.

7. The exchange rate between the HK and U.S. dollars is fixed. In 1993, the rate was U.S.$1 = HK$7.7.

8. I discuss trade related to outward processing in section 5.4.

Table 5.3 **Hong Kong Reexports by Major Market**

	1992	1993	Growth Rate in 1993 (%)
All markets	690.8 (100)	823.2 (100)	19
China	212.1 (31)	274.6 (33)	29
United States	148.5 (21)	180.3 (22)	21
Japan	37.5 (5)	44.2 (5)	18
Germany	33.1 (5)	40.8 (5)	23
United Kingdom	20.6 (3)	24.5 (3)	19
Taiwan	26.2 (4)	21.9 (3)	−16
Rest of the world	212.9 (31)	236.9 (29)	11

Source: Hong Kong Government (1993).

Note: Reexports values are in billions of HK dollars. Numbers in parentheses are shares of the reexports.

value terms of all goods reexported through Hong Kong in 1993 (table 5.3). Reexports to China consisted mainly of textile yarn and fabrics, textile madeup articles, motor vehicles, electrical machinery, telecommunications and sound recording equipment, industrial machinery, and plastic materials. The other major market for Hong Kong's reexports was the United States (accounting for HK$180 billion, or 22 percent of the total value in 1993).

Besides reexports, the Hong Kong government collects data on retained imports (imports for domestic consumption), which are defined as total imports by Hong Kong minus reexports. A more accurate definition would be total imports minus reexports adjusted for the reexport markup.[9]

If we take the average markup on Chinese goods to be around 16 percent, the amount of retained imports from China becomes negligible or *negative* in recent years (table 5.4). This implies that the markup for Chinese goods must be higher than 16 percent. However, we do not have much information on what the actual percentage is. In my interviews with Hong Kong businessmen in July 1994, a figure of 25 percent was suggested several times. Hong Kong officials who had presented cases in GATT also suggested that the markup was 25 percent. For the rest of this paper, we use an average reexport markup of 25 percent for Chinese goods.

Data on Hong Kong's exports to China also are complicated by the existence

9. See Sung (1991) for an early discussion.

Table 5.4 Hong Kong Imports from China

Year	Adjusted[a] Retained Imports	Unadjusted Retained Imports
1977	1,377	1,286
1979	2,268	2,076
1981	3,715	3,325
1983	4,048	3,588
1984	4,686	4,075
1985	4,546	3,790
1986	5,966	4,842
1987	7,428	5,591
1988	7,948	5,084
1989	8,801	4,698
1990	5,624	−549
1991	4,212	−3,913
1992	2,457	−7,975
1993	1,147	−11,108

Source: Hong Kong Government (various years, b).
Note: Values are in millions of U.S. dollars.
[a]Adjusted for 25 percent reexport markup.

of reexports. But, given that Hong Kong government statistics provide data on Hong Kong's *domestic exports,* we can rely on these as figures for exports of Hong Kong goods to China.

5.3.2 China–Taiwan Trade

As previously noted, Taiwan forbids Taiwanese firms from trading directly with China, so all trade is supposed to occur indirectly. Most of this indirect trade takes place via Hong Kong. Trading via Hong Kong is often referred to as "triangular trade." There is also indirect trade between Taiwan and mainland China via Japan, Singapore, Guam, and other third parties (Kao 1993). In terms of trade data, neither Taiwanese sources nor mainland sources are entirely accurate. The mainland data are again contaminated by lumping trade with Hong Kong and reexports together. In Taiwanese data, trade with China shows up mainly as trade with Hong Kong and other third parties. Table 5.5 shows Taiwanese indirect trade via Hong Kong, using Hong Kong data. There is also illegal direct trade that is not recorded properly in Taiwanese trade statistics. Trade with mainland China is heavily influenced by periods of contraction in China. The significant decrease of indirect trade between Taiwan and the mainland in 1982–83 and in 1986 was due mainly to mainland China's deflationary policies during those periods.

5.3.3 China–U.S. Trade

Chinese export statistics reported all exports to Hong Kong, whether for Hong Kong consumption or for reexport to the United States via Hong Kong

Table 5.5 **Trade between Taiwan and Mainland China via Hong Kong**

Year	Taiwan to Mainland	Mainland to Taiwan
1979	21	55
1980	242	78
1981	390	76
1982	208	89
1983	168	96
1984	425	127
1985	987	116
1986	811	144
1987	1,226	289
1988	2,242	478
1989	2,896	586
1990	3,278	765
1991	4,679	1,129
1992	6,288	1,119

Source: Hong Kong Government (various years, a).
Note: Figures are in millions of U.S. dollars.

Table 5.6 **U.S. Exports to China Adjusted for Reexports**

Year	U.S. Source	Reexports to China via Hong Kong		Total Adjusted Exports	
1993	8.77	2.79	(3.18)	11.56	(11.95)
1992	7.47	2.06	(2.35)	9.53	(9.82)
1991	6.29	1.50	(1.71)	7.79	(8.00)
1990	4.81	1.16	(1.32)	5.97	(6.13)
1989	5.76	1.16	(1.32)	6.92	(7.13)

Sources: Hong Kong Government (various years, a) and U.S. Department of Commerce (various years).
Note: Figures are in billions of U.S. dollars. Numbers in parentheses are unadjusted for reexport markup.

as exports to Hong Kong. Chinese import statistics do take country of origin into account, but inconsistently. U.S. import data distinguish country of origin, including reexports, but U.S. export data deal with exports to Hong Kong inaccurately. This is because reexports, by definition, change legal possession, and U.S. exporters do not always know the final destination of the U.S. goods.

In calculating U.S. exports to China, we should add reexports of American goods via Hong Kong to China to recorded exports to China (although this may overstate the error because the U.S. data may capture some exporters who know and declare that the final destination of the goods is China even when they are first shipped to Hong Kong). Table 5.6 illustrates the importance of taking reexports into account when using U.S. export data.

The amount of U.S. goods reexported to China via Hong Kong is not trivial.

Table 5.7 Adjusted U.S.–China Bilateral Trade Balance (U.S. Source)

Year	Unadjusted Balance	Adjusted Trade Balance	
1993	−22.76	−15.63	(−19.59)
1992	−18.26	−12.58	(−15.91)
1991	−12.68	−8.50	(−10.97)
1990	−10.43	−7.17	(−9.11)
1989	−6.18	−3.38	(−4.91)

Sources: See table 5.6.

Note: Figures are in billions of U.S. dollars. Numbers in parentheses are not adjusted for re-export margins.

On average over 1989–93, reexports were *30.0 percent* of U.S. direct exports to China. Another important issue is the role of the reexport margin. Hong Kong middlemen raise the value of the U.S. goods shipped via Hong Kong. The average markup on non-Chinese goods is 14 percent. Reexports and total exports not discounted by the markup are given in parentheses in table 5.6.

U.S. imports take reexports into account. While there are severe difficulties in tracing the country of origin (Krueger 1995), this problem is not unique to trade with China. We assume that U.S. data for imports from mainland China are by and large correct, or at least no worse than other published sources. But we do need to take the reexport margin into account. For Chinese goods, we take a markup of 25 percent, as discussed earlier. The adjusted trade balance, taking both reexports and reexport margins into account, is

Adjusted U.S. trade balance with China

= (Direct exports of U.S. goods to China

+ Reexports of U.S. goods to China via Hong Kong

– 14% reexport margin)

– (Direct imports of Chinese goods to the U.S.

+ Reexports of Chinese goods to the U.S. via Hong Kong

– 25% Reexport margin).

Using the adjusted figures, U.S.-China bilateral trade deficits are shown in table 5.7. The adjusted trade deficits, using U.S. and Hong Kong data, are quite different from the unadjusted, published deficits. If we use deficits adjusted for both reexports and reexport margins, the deficits have to be revised downward by 31.1, 33.0, 31.3, and 45.3 percent for the years 1992, 1991, 1990, and 1989, respectively. This gives a four-year average of 35.2 percent.[10]

10. This downward revision is larger than those reported in Lardy (1994) primarily because of the use of a different reexport margin. West (1995) also reported different adjustments because she used different markups for different periods and she also took into account other minor adjust-

Table 5.8 **Adjusted U.S. Trade Deficit with China**

Year	Adjusted Chinese Data		Adjusted U.S. Data		Chinese Source	U.S. Source
1989	2.14	(3.7)	3.38	(4.91)	−3.5	6.18
1990	5.84	(7.8)	7.17	(9.11)	−1.4	10.43
1991	7.42	(9.9)	8.50	(10.97)	−1.8	12.68
1992	12.12	(15.5)	12.58	(15.91)	−0.3	18.26
1993	20.95	(24.9)	15.63	(19.59)	6.3	22.76

Sources: See table 5.6 and China, General Administration of Customs (various years) and Hong Kong Government (1993).

Note: Figures are in billions of U.S. dollars. Numbers in parentheses are not adjusted for reexport margins.

Table 5.8 shows six different U.S. trade imbalances with China: published U.S. data, which show a growing trade deficit; published Chinese data, which show a U.S. surplus until 1993, when reexports were beginning to be considered; Chinese data adjusted for reexports only (in parentheses); Chinese data adjusted for both reexports and reexport margins; U.S. data adjusted for reexports only (in parentheses); and U.S. data adjusted for both reexports and reexport margins. The most reliable amount should be the U.S. data adjusted for both reexports and reexport margins. However, as noted earlier, this correction overstates the problem, since some U.S. firms that export to China via Hong Kong may know in advance the final destination and may declare this on their customs forms.

If we compare the adjusted Chinese data with the U.S. published data, we see that the discrepancies are diminishing over time. As percentages of the published U.S. data, the adjusted Chinese data are 34.6, 56.0, 58.5, 66.4, and 92.1 percent from 1989 to 1993, respectively. If we use adjusted U.S. data as the benchmark, as a percentage the differences between U.S. adjusted data and Chinese adjusted data are 36.7, 18.6, 12.7, 3.66, and −34.0 percent from 1989 to 1993. It is interesting that by 1992, the difference between the two adjusted numbers is negligible. This gives us indirect confirmation that our adjustments are not completely off the mark.

5.4 Issues Related to FDI-Related Trade

5.4.1 China–Hong Kong Outward Processing Trade

The Hong Kong Census and Statistics Department began to compile statistics on domestic exports and reexports to China related to outward processing in the third quarter of 1988 and statistics on imports from China related to outward processing in the first quarter of 1989. According to the Hong Kong government, outward processing arrangements are made between Hong Kong

ments (such as the low-level threshold; i.e., U.S. customs does not report export transactions that are under U.S.$2,500).

Table 5.9 **Hong Kong Domestic Exports to China of an Outward Processing Nature as a Share of Total Domestic Exports to China, by Product Group (percent)**

Product Group	1989	1990	1991	1992	1993
Textiles	84.8	84.2	83.7	87.4	86.8
Clothing	85.1	87.9	89.6	93.2	94.2
Plastic products	83.9	86.1	79.6	77.5	81.5
Machinery and electrical appliances	56.7	62.2	58.6	59.7	54.0
Electronic products	94.6	94.4	92.5	92.7	94.7
Watches and clocks	98.5	97.3	98.1	98.5	98.6
Toys, games, and sporting goods	96.4	96.9	96.1	91.9	97.2
Metals and metal products	64.2	71.1	73.5	69.0	65.1
All products	76.0	79.0	76.5	74.3	74.0

Source: Hong Kong Government (various years, a).

companies and manufacturing entities in China under which the companies concerned subcontract all or part of the production processes relating to their products to the Chinese entities. Raw materials or semimanufactures are exported to China for such processing. The Chinese entity involved can be a local enterprise, a joint venture, or some other form of business involving foreign investment (Hong Kong Government 1994). Almost four-fifths of Hong Kong manufacturers have transferred production to China. About 25,000 factories in the Pearl River Delta region of Guangdong are engaged in outward processing for Hong Kong companies, while 3 to 4 million workers are directly or indirectly employed by these firms (Ash and Kueh 1993). In 1993, the entire labor force in manufacturing in Hong Kong was only 0.5 million. Employment in China for outward processing of Hong Kong goods is then between six to eight times that in Hong Kong. Tables 5.9, 5.10, and 5.11 document, respectively, the extent of domestic exports, imports, and reexports related to Hong Kong processing in China.

From tables 5.9, 5.10, and 5.11, we see that 74 percent of Hong Kong's domestic exports to China were related to outward processing in 1993. The highest amount of outward processing was in watches and clocks, with 98.6 percent. For the five years between 1989 and 1993, the overall percentage is fairly consistent, hovering between 74.3 and 79 percent. For imports from China, there is an increase from a low of 58.1 percent in 1989 to a high of 73.8 percent in 1993. As with domestic exports, watches and clocks had the highest outward processing ratio in 1993. For Hong Kong's reexports to China, table 5.11 shows that in 1993, 42.1 percent of all products were for outward processing. Compared to domestic exports and imports, this lower ratio is due to the low outward processing character of bulkier reexports such as machinery and electrical appliances and metal and metal products (26.1 and 35.8 percent in 1993, respectively). Bulkier items tend to be produced outside of Hong Kong and reexported via Hong Kong to China without further processing. As

Table 5.10 **Hong Kong Imports from China of an Outward Processing Nature as a Share of Total Imports from China, by Product Group (percent)**

Product Group	1989	1990	1991	1992	1993
Textiles	12.8	18.2	20.5	23.0	27.3
Clothing	84.5	87.4	86.6	84.4	83.1
Plastic products	73.4	78.0	84.8	89.3	90.4
Machinery and electrical appliances	77.8	73.3	78.7	81.0	76.4
Electric products	85.2	88.7	89.7	92.7	91.5
Watches and clocks	94.6	94.9	96.4	94.3	95.8
Toys, games, and sporting goods	94.1	94.8	92.1	96.9	91.6
Metals and metal products	30.2	32.5	29.6	43.6	52.3
All products	58.1	61.8	67.6	72.1	73.8

Source: Hong Kong Government (various years, a).

Table 5.11 **Hong Kong Reexports to China of an Outward Processing Nature as a Share of Total Reexports to China, by Product Group (percent)**

Product Group	1989	1990	1991	1992	1993
Textiles	71.5	75.9	77.1	81.9	81.0
Clothing	87.3	86.5	84.1	76.0	80.2
Plastic products	58.0	68.7	58.3	64.5	63.0
Machinery and electrical appliances	24.9	31.2	26.7	27.3	26.1
Electric products	43.1	52.9	46.9	41.4	35.7
Watches and clocks	93.5	96.9	96.3	97.7	98.7
Toys, games, and sporting goods	60.1	73.2	66.8	80.1	79.9
Metals and metal products	37.8	46.4	48.1	34.8	35.8
All products	43.6	50.3	48.2	46.2	42.1

Source: Hong Kong Government (various years, a).

regards Hong Kong's reexports of Chinese origin to overseas markets (not shown in the tables), 74, 78, and 81 percent were products of outward processing arrangements commissioned from Hong Kong in 1991, 1992, and 1993, respectively (Hong Kong Government 1994).

Hong Kong's outward processing arrangements with China involve a combination of assembly by Chinese firms and production in China by Hong Kong–owned firms.[11] Technically, this trade is not all related to FDI but is a combination of FDI and Hong Kong *subcontracting*. However, in practice, outward processing often involves situations in which the Hong Kong investor has de facto (though not necessarily legal) control of the operations.

We can compare the above outward processing activities with the extent of intrafirm trade involving U.S. multinationals. In essence, we compare intrafirm

11. I discuss the different types of foreign investment in China immediately following the section on outward processing from Hong Kong.

Table 5.12 Intrafirm Exports and Intrafirm Imports as a Share of Total U.S. Exports and Imports with U.S. Parents, 1989 (percent)

Industry	Exports	Imports
Textile products and apparel	11.42	10.98
Rubber and plastics	23.88	6.23
Machinery	20.41	18.25
Electric and electronic equipment	22.16	15.45
Primary and fabricated metals	7.26	2.93
All industries	24.64	15.46

Sources: U.S. Department of Commerce (1992) and U.S. Bureau of the Census, *Statistical Abstract of the United States* (Washington, D.C.: U.S. Bureau of the Census, 1991).

trade between Hong Kong parents and their affiliates in China to that between U.S. parents and their affiliates outside the United States. But the comparison is not exact because Hong Kong outward processing can involve some local mainland Chinese enterprises. The industries also are not entirely comparable across countries. Unlike Hong Kong, the United States does not have statistics related to intrafirm trade on reexports. Nor do we expect reexports to be an important share of total trade for the United States.

From tables 5.9, 5.10, and 5.12, we see that Hong Kong–China intrafirm activity is significantly larger for most industries. For all products, 76 percent of Hong Kong's domestic exports were related to outward processing in 1989, while the percentage of intrafirm exports for the United States was only 24.6 percent. On the import side, the corresponding figures for Hong Kong and the United States were 58.1 and 15.5 percent, respectively. Using this comparison as an index of economic integration, Hong Kong is clearly more integrated with China than the United States is with the rest of the world. Next we compare the outward processing activities of Hong Kong in China to intrafirm trade between the United States and Mexico.

Table 5.13 reports related-party imports to the United States from Mexico in 1991. "Related-party trade" is defined in Section 402 (g) (1) of the Tariff Act of 1930, as amended, to include transactions between parties with various types of relationships, including "any person directly or indirectly owning, controlling, or holding with power to vote, 6 percent or more of the outstanding voting stock or shares of any organization" (U.S. Department of Commerce 1993). Related-party trade includes imports into the United States by U.S. companies from their foreign subsidiaries as well as imports by U.S. subsidiaries of foreign companies from their parent companies. I assume that imports into the United States by Mexican firms are small relative to imports by U.S. firms.

Related-party imports in textiles were more intense between the United States and Mexico than outward processing imports between Hong Kong and China, though for clothing, the figure for Hong Kong was much higher

Table 5.13 U.S. Related-Party Imports from Mexico, 1991

Product	Share of Related-Party Imports in Total Product Imports (%)
Textile yarns, fabrics, madeup articles	58.49
Articles of apparel and clothing accessories	47.15
Articles of plastics	59.33
Machinery, electrical and others	85.04
Toys and sports equipment	85.28
Electronic products and parts	89.53
Metals and metal products	43.87
All products	63.2

Source: U.S. Department of Commerce (1993).

(tables 5.10 and 5.13). For metals and metal products, the U.S. import figure was, however, higher than that for Hong Kong. Loosely speaking, FDI-related trade in 1991 was somewhat larger between Hong Kong and China than between the United States and Mexico (for all products, the percentage was 67.6 percent for Hong Kong–China vs. 63.2 percent for U.S.-Mexico). If we take FDI-related trade as one index of economic integration, then Hong Kong and China are more integrated than the United States and Mexico.

5.4.2 China's FDI-Related Trade

China's customs statistics contain information about imports and exports related to FDI (or trade related to foreign-invested firms). FDI arrangements include three types of enterprises: Sino-foreign contractual joint ventures, Sino-foreign equity joint ventures, and wholly foreign-owned enterprises. Contractual joint ventures, sometimes called cooperative ventures, are flexible arrangements that may take almost any form as long as the arrangement is acceptable to both parties. Usually the foreign partner contributes funds, equipment, and technology, and the Chinese partner supplies land, factory buildings, labor, and raw materials.[12] Legally, China discourages subcontracting in joint ventures, hoping for more transfer of technology and management skill.[13]

In addition to statistics on trade associated with FDI, there is also information about imports and exports related to foreign subcontracting, compensation trade, and processing and assembling operations (see China, General Administration of Customs, various years).[14] FDI arrangements are those in which the

12. See Sung (1991), Ash and Kueh (1993), and Fung (1997) for further discussion of the three types of enterprises.

13. But according to my own interviews with Hong Kong businessmen, in practice subcontracting seems to be quite common among joint ventures as well.

14. Ash and Kueh (1993), Sung (1991), and Fung (1997) discuss these activities.

Table 5.14 Foreign-Investment–Related Trade in Mainland China

Trade Category	1992		1993	
Imports				
Total	24.36	(100)	34.37	(100)
Processing and assembling	12.64	(51.89)	12.97	(37.73)
Equipment imported for processing and assembling	1.207	(4.96)	1.324	(3.85)
Equipment and materials imported as investment by FDI	8.018	(32.92)	16.63	(48.38)
Compensation trade	0.250	(1.02)	0.330	(0.96)
Materials or components imported by FDI for manufacturing products for domestic use	2.243	(9.21)	3.121	(9.08)
Exports				
Total	15.60	(100)	16.28	(100)
Processing and assembling	15.30	(98.09)	15.96	(98.07)
Compensation trade	0.298	(1.91)	0.314	(1.93)

Source: China, General Administration of Customs (various years).

Note: Figures are in billions of U.S. dollars. Numbers in parentheses are shares of foreign-investment–related imports and exports.

foreign investors have some legal control of the enterprises. In subcontracting, the Chinese partner has legal control of the operations.[15] In processing and assembling, the foreign entity gives its manufacturing operation to a Chinese partner, providing the necessary materials and selling the finished products abroad. In return, the Chinese partner gets subcontracting fees for conducting the prescribed operations (usually no more than 10 percent of the value of the finished products; see Lardy 1994). In compensation trade, the foreign partner provides the Chinese partner with equipment and receives products in return. Outputs from subcontracting have to be exported. Outputs from FDI can be sold domestically (Sung 1991). In this paper, foreign investment refers to both FDI and foreign subcontracting. Until recently, investments from Hong Kong and Taiwan tended to concentrate on subcontracting, while investments from the United States and Japan tended to concentrate on FDI (Fung 1997; Fung and Iizaka 1998). Table 5.14 decomposes Chinese imports and exports associated with different kinds of foreign investments (both FDI and foreign subcontracting) for the years 1992 and 1993.

According to China's customs statistics, 33.0 percent of 1993 Chinese imports were related to FDI and subcontracting while 17.7 percent of exports were related to subcontracting.[16] The bulk of imports associated with foreign investment were processing and assembling (37.7 percent of imports related to

15. But in practice, the Chinese partner manufactures according to the orders given by the foreign partner, who arguably has real control.

16. These figures are calculated by dividing foreign-investment–related imports and exports by China's total imports and exports for 1992 and 1993.

Table 5.15 **Trade by FDI Enterprises in Guangdong Province (Customs Source)**

Enterprise Category	1989	1992	1993
Imports			
Total	4.85	13.95	19.80
Sino-foreign contractual joint venture	1.14	3.32	5.88
Sino-foreign equity joint venture	3.11	7.43	9.28
Foreign-owned enterprise	0.61	3.19	4.64
Exports			
Total	3.53	10.79	14.37
Sino-foreign contractual joint venture	0.71	2.40	3.35
Sino-foreign equity joint venture	2.26	5.69	6.88
Foreign-owned enterprise	0.56	2.70	4.14

Source: China, General Administration of Customs (various years).
Note: Figures are in billions of U.S. dollars.

foreign investment in 1993) and equipment and materials imported as investment by FDI (48.4 percent of imports related to foreign investment in 1993).[17]

We can further focus on trade activity related to foreign investment in two provinces where foreign investment from Hong Kong and Taiwan is most intense: Guangdong and Fujian. There are two sets of data on trade related to foreign investment in these two provinces, one from China's customs statistics and the other from the statistical yearbooks of the respective provinces.[18] The customs data show imports and exports related to the three types of foreign enterprises. Imports and exports of these foreign firms are growing rapidly. For example, in Guangdong, total exports from foreign firms grew by 33.1 percent while imports grew by 41.9 percent in 1993 (table 5.15).[19] Trade (both imports and exports) related to foreign-owned enterprises is an increasing share of total FDI-related trade in both provinces. In Fujian, 55.5 percent of FDI exports and 49.0 percent of imports were from foreign-owned enterprises in 1993 (table 5.16). Since the tour by Deng to southern China in early 1992, there has been a rush of FDI to China from Hong Kong and Taiwan firms. Part of the general increase in imports and exports in 1993 may reflect this trend.

The *Guangdong Statistical Yearbook* and the *Fujian Statistical Yearbook* have different classifications from the customs statistics, and the classifications of these yearbooks also differ from one another. The provincial yearbooks attempt to separate out FDI and foreign subcontracting. According to these yearbooks, in 1991, 45 percent of Guangdong's exports were associated with either

17. On the export side, exports by foreign-invested firms amounted to U.S.$25.2 billion, or 27.5 percent of Chinese total exports (Lardy 1994). Total exports associated with foreign investment (both FDI and subcontracting) in 1993 were 45 percent of total Chinese exports.

18. China, Provincial Government of Guangdong (various years) and China, Provincial Government of Fujian (various years). Ash and Kueh (1993) also contains discussions of trade related to foreign investment in Guangdong and Fujian.

19. Growth rates are not shown in tables 5.15 and 5.16.

Table 5.16 **Trade by FDI Enterprises in Fujian Province (Customs Source)**

Enterprise Category	1989	1992	1993
Imports			
Total	0.760	2.50	3.57
Sino-foreign contractual joint venture	0.047	0.106	0.201
Sino-foreign equity joint venture	0.591	1.31	1.63
Foreign-owned enterprise	0.120	1.09	1.75
Exports			
Total	0.490	1.93	2.49
Sino-foreign contractual joint venture	0.047	0.0908	0.123
Sino-foreign equity joint venture	0.363	0.929	0.984
Foreign-owned enterprise	0.086	0.910	1.382

Source: China, General Administration of Customs (various years).
Note: Figures are in billions of U.S. dollars.

Table 5.17 **Foreign-Investment–Related Trade of Guangdong Province (Guangdong Source)**

Trade Category	1988	1989	1990	1991
Imports				
Guangdong imports	5.11	4.83	5.75	8.51
FDI enterprise	1.13	1.95	3.30	4.51
Exports				
Guangdong exports	7.48	8.17	10.6	13.7
Processing and assembling	0.347	0.578	0.583	0.800
Compensation trade	0.06	0.06	0.078	0.095
FDI enterprise	1.20	2.28	3.72	5.33

Source: China, Provincial Government of Guangdong (various years).
Note: Figures are in billions of U.S. dollars.

subcontracting or FDI (table 5.17). The bulk of it was from FDI enterprises (38.9 percent). In Fujian, 9.4 percent came from subcontracting (table 5.18). But there is no record of exports by foreign-invested firms in the *Fujian Statistical Yearbook.* Furthermore, if we look at the reported FDI exports from the statistical yearbook and compare these exports with those in the customs statistics, the data differ quite significantly. In general, data from the customs statistics are more reliable.

Another interesting question about foreign firms in China is where their products are going.[20] If they are made under subcontracting arrangements, then they are exported. But if they are produced by the three types of foreign enterprises, they can be intended for domestic use or for export. In 1994, the Chung-Hua Institution for Economic Research reported the results of a large-scale

20. For a comparison of U.S. firms and Japanese firms in China, see Fung and Iizaka (1998).

Table 5.18 **Foreign-Investment–Related Trade of Fujian Province (Fujian Source)**

Trade Category	1988	1989	1990	1991
Imports				
Fujian imports	1.43	1.59	1.90	2.61
Processing and assembling	0.15	0.16	0.16	0.25
Equipment and materials imported by foreign-invested enterprises	0.23	0.17	0.24	0.28
Compensation trade	0.005	0.01	0.004	0.005
Components imported by FDI for manufacturing products for domestic use	0.01	0.08	0.01	0.02
Exports				
Fujian exports	1.42	1.83	2.45	3.15
Processing and assembling	0.12	0.18	0.21	0.29
Compensation trade	0.01	0.01	0.01	0.005

Source: China, Provincial Government of Fujian (various years).
Note: Figures are in billions of U.S. dollars.

Table 5.19 **Markets for Manufactured Products Produced by Foreign Firms in Mainland China, 1992**

	Market						
Firm	Mainland China	Taiwan	Hong Kong	Europe	Japan	United States	Others
Hong Kong/Macau	35.4	12.0	13.2	7.0	7.5	14.1	10.8
United States	69.5	0.0	2.8	3.6	1.9	15.6	6.6
Taiwan	59.6	0.9	22.3	4.1	2.2	4.8	6.1
Singapore	55.2	1.0	9.7	9.0	4.2	8.0	12.9

Source: Chung-Hua Institution for Economic Research (1994).
Note: Figures are percentages of the value of sales.

survey in China on this issue. Table 5.19 indicates the export markets of the foreign firms.

From table 5.19, we see that most products of foreign firms are destined for the domestic Chinese market. U.S. firms have the highest domestic percentage, with a figure close to 70 percent. Hong Kong has the lowest percentage, with 35 percent. About 16 percent of the value of U.S. goods produced in China is for sale back to the United States. For Hong Kong firms, export markets are evenly spread over the United States, Hong Kong, and Taiwan, with the U.S. market being most important. For Taiwanese firms, after China, the largest market is Hong Kong. But it seems strange that only 0.9 percent of the sales go back to Taiwan. One reason may be that, again, exports have to go through Hong Kong before they go to Taiwan. In sum, the picture here is that foreign-invested firms sell most of their goods in China. This illustrates the growing importance of the domestic Chinese market. For both U.S. and Hong Kong firms, the United States is the next largest market.

5.5 Issues Related to Illegal Trade

5.5.1 China-Taiwan Illegal Trade

As mentioned earlier, the Taiwanese government still has an official policy of no direct contact with mainland China. Much of the indirect trade occurs via Hong Kong as reexports. But Taiwan's import controls on the mainland's products have gradually been liberalized. By the end of 1990, indirect imports of 92 items were permitted, including all agricultural and industrial raw materials (Kao 1993).

Transshipment (using the Hong Kong government's definition) means that goods are consigned directly from the exporting country to a buyer in the importing country, though the goods are transported via Hong Kong and are usually loaded into another vessel for further journey. Since transshipment is a form of direct trade, it is illegal from Taiwan's standpoint. Transshipment is not a part of Hong Kong trade because nobody has legal possession of the goods in Hong Kong.[21] The goods do not clear customs. According to Sung (1994), Taiwan's customs allow exporters to leave final destinations open and specify Hong Kong as the port from which goods will be transported elsewhere. In Taiwan's trade statistics, such exports are entered under exports to Hong Kong. When the cargo arrives in Hong Kong, the shipping company can pick a mainland port as the final destination.

Transshipment is different from transit shipment, which means that goods do not change vessels and just pass through Hong Kong on their way to the final destination. Exporters from Taiwan claim that their goods are going to Hong Kong when they leave Taiwan and then claim in Hong Kong that they are going to the mainland (Sung 1994). Unlike transshipment, this method of direct trade is risky since it involves lying to the Taiwanese government. The Hong Kong government has data on transshipments by *weight* but does not keep records on cargo in transit. The value of transshipments is not known because transshipped goods do not go through customs. Table 5.20 reports reexports and transshipments via Hong Kong between Taiwan and mainland China.

As early as 1980s, fishing boats were conducting direct barter trade between Taiwan and Fujian. Fujian legalized this trade in 1985. But the Taiwanese government considers such trade illegal smuggling. Researchers at the Chung-

21. This definition of transshipment is different from the term "transshipment" used in popular discussions of Chinese trade. In the popular press, "transshipment" is often used in the context of false declaration of origins and misuse of quotas, particularly Multifiber Arrangement (MFA) quotas.

Table 5.20 **Reexports and Transshipments via Hong Kong: Taiwan and China**

Year	Reexports		Transshipments	
1989	2,897	(587)	33,283	(6,662)
1990	3,283	(766)	43,757	(12,447)
1991	4,685	(1,130)	272,475	(87,610)
1992	6,336	(1,128)	527,427	(211,026)

Sources: Hong Kong Government (various years, b) and Hong Kong Government, *Hong Kong Shipping Statistics* (Hong Kong: Census and Statistics Department, various years).

Note: Reexports are in millions of U.S. dollars; transshipments are in tons. Numbers without parentheses are reexports and transshipments from Taiwan to China via Hong Kong. Numbers in parentheses are reexports and transshipments from China to Taiwan via Hong Kong.

Table 5.21 **Taiwan's Exports to Mainland China**

Year	Reexports via Hong Kong	Reexports via Others	Direct Exports		Total	
1988	2,242 (3.6)	960	116	[236]	3,318 (5.5)	[3,438] (5.7)
1989	2,896 (4.4)	1,241	642	[793]	4,779 (7.2)	[4,930] (7.4)
1990	3,278 (4.9)	1,405	1,361	[1,525]	6,044 (9.0)	[6,208] (9.2)
1991	4,679 (6.1)	2,005	3,189	[3,399]	9,873 (13.0)	[10,083] (13.3)
1992	6,288 (7.2)	2,695	5,392	[4,705]	14,375 (17.6)	[13,688] (16.8)

Sources: Kao (1993), Sung (1994), and Taiwan, Ministry of Finance (various years).

Note: Figures are in millions of U.S. dollars. Numbers in parentheses are percentages of total Taiwanese exports. Numbers in brackets are alternative estimates from Sung (1994).

Hua Institution for Economic Research estimated that in the late 1980s such smuggling of mainland Chinese goods to Taiwan was about one-third of Hong Kong reexports of Chinese goods to Taiwan (Kao 1993). For 1989, this estimate puts the value of such illegal trade at U.S.$195 million.

Table 5.21 reports Taiwanese exports to China via Hong Kong, exports via other places (Singapore, Japan, Guam, etc.), and illegal direct exports (including transshipment, transit shipment, minor trade, etc.). Total Taiwanese exports to mainland China are significantly higher than "legal" trade alone. In 1991 and 1992, the percentages of illegal trade were 31.3 and 36.5 percent, respectively. In 1992, illegal exports (direct exports) were between 52 and 60 percent of legal exports (reexports through Hong Kong and elsewhere). As indicated in table 5.22, the corresponding figure for imports was between 44 and 76 percent.

Table 5.22 **Taiwan's Imports from Mainland China**

Year	Reexports via Hong Kong	Reexports via Others	Direct Imports		Total	
1988	478 (1.0)	205	n.a.	[14]	683 (1.4)	[697] (1.43)
1989	586 (1.1)	251	93	[37]	930 (1.8)	[874] (1.69)
1990	765 (1.4)	328	320	[70]	1,413 (2.6)	[1,163] (2.14)
1991	1,129 (1.8)	484	595	[501]	2,208 (3.5)	[2,114] (3.35)
1992	1,119 (1.6)	479	698	[1,219]	2,296 (3.2)	[2,817] (3.93)

Sources: Kao (1993), Sung (1994), and Taiwan, Ministry of Finance (various years).
Note: Figures are in millions of U.S. dollars. Numbers in parentheses are percentages of total Taiwanese imports. Numbers in brackets are estimates by Sung (1994).

5.5.2 Other Forms of Illegal Trade

While illegal trade between Taiwan and China arises primarily from the policies of the Taiwanese government, there are also other more standard forms of illegal trade such as smuggling and tariff evasion, as documented by Sung (1991), Lardy (1994), and West (1995). In 1993, Chinese customs seized a record of U.S.$0.41 billion in smuggled products, an increase of almost 80 percent over the 1992 level. From 1981 to early 1993, more than 10,000 cases of smuggling at sea were discovered.[22]

Geographically, smuggling as a form of illegal trade is now a *national* rather than regional phenomenon. In the past, smuggling was confined mainly to southern coastal areas. In recent years, it has spread all the way up to the coast of Shandong and Dalian. However, it is unclear whether the increase in reported smuggling reflects improved enforcement or greater incidence of smuggling.

Smuggling is most popular for products whose import is restricted by the government, either by tariffs or other barriers. From an economic standpoint, this illegal trade may be regarded as induced by inefficient governmental interventions.[23] Commonly smuggled items include color television sets, cars, cigarettes, motorcycles, air conditioners, steel products, and polyester fibers. In the first quarter of 1993, cars and cigarettes were reported to be the number one and number two smuggled goods.[24]

One can often get an idea of how significant smuggling is by comparing

22. West (1995) contains a more detailed discussion.
23. Some of the governmental interventions in U.S.-China trade are imposed by the U.S. government. In textile and clothing, trade is regulated via the MFA. In high-technology trade, the U.S. government imposes some export controls (Richardson 1993).
24. See West (1995) for further discussion.

bilateral trade statistics, preferably by quantity and, with some care, also by value. For example, according to South Korean customs, between January and April 1993 South Korea exported 26,688 cars to China, but Chinese customs statistics show only 166 cars imported from South Korea for the same period. One can infer that some of the "missing" cars have been smuggled into China to avoid Chinese customs (West 1995).

In the first quarter of 1994, about 35 percent of the major reported smuggling cases involved the use of fake customs certificates, seals, and customs officers' signatures. There are also false declarations of origin (Lardy 1994). It has been reported that a Thai certificate of origin can be obtained for as little as $100 (Sung 1991). The U.S. Trade Representative (USTR) reported that U.S. Customs Service officers have found Chinese goods illegally labeled in at least 25 other nations, including Honduras, Panama, and Hong Kong.

5.6 Conclusion

In this paper I try to clarify various conceptual and data issues related to China's trade. China's trade is characterized by at least *three* features: high incidence of reexports via Hong Kong, high incidence of trade related to foreign investment, and high incidence of "illegal" trade, most notably with Taiwan. There are also indications that illegal trade in the form of smuggling and evasion of trade barriers is spreading to China's trade with all its trading partners.

In 1993, 67 percent of China's exports were reexported via Hong Kong, and 34 percent of China's imports were reexports via Hong Kong from the rest of the world. These reexports complicate China's trade data with all its trading partners, and not until 1993 did China differentiate these reexports from trade with Hong Kong. If we take these reexports and reexport margins into account, bilateral U.S.-China trade deficits (using U.S. trade data) must be adjusted downward by about 35 percent. Reexport and reexport margins affect not only Chinese trade data but also make other countries' trade data with China inaccurate.

Much of China's trade is also foreign investment related. According to Chinese data, in 1993, 45.2 and 33 percent of Chinese exports and imports, respectively, were due to foreign firms and foreign subcontracting.[25] In 1991, according to Guangdong data, about 44 percent of Guangdong's exports were associated with foreign investments. Furthermore, there are good reasons to believe that this figure is understated.

With respect to China–Hong Kong trade, 74.0 percent of China's imports from Hong Kong were related to outward processing in 1993. For China's exports to Hong Kong, the corresponding figure was 73.8 percent. Of the reex-

25. In 1993, exports associated with subcontracting alone were 17.7 percent while exports associated with FDI were 27.5 percent.

ports of Chinese goods to overseas markets via Hong Kong, 81.0 percent were commissioned by Hong Kong firms, while 42.1 percent of reexports via Hong Kong to China were due to outward processing.

"Illegal" trade between mainland China and Taiwan was primarily induced by Taiwan's policy banning direct trade. Most of the legal exports from Taiwan to mainland China occur as reexports via Hong Kong. In 1992, illegal direct exports from Taiwan to mainland were between 52 and 60 percent of legal indirect exports. There are also some indications that other forms of illegal trade such as smuggling may be spreading. But other than a few isolated figures, it is difficult to get accurate estimates of illegal trade.

References

Ash, R., and Y. Y. Kueh. 1993. Economic integration within Greater China: Trade and investment flows between mainland China, Hong Kong and Taiwan. Hong Kong: Lingnan College. Mimeograph.

Baldwin, R., and D. Nelson. 1993. The political economy of U.S.-Taiwanese trade and other international economic relations. In *Trade and protectionism,* ed. T. Ito and A. Krueger, 307–33. Chicago: University of Chicago Press.

Bergsten, F., and M. Noland, ed. 1993. *Pacific dynamism and the international economic system.* Washington, D.C.: Institute for International Economics.

China. General Administration of Customs. Various years. *China customs statistics,* 1989, 1992, 1993 issues. Hong Kong: Economic Information Agency.

———. Provincial Government of Fujian. Fujian Foreign Economic Relations and Trade Commission. Various years. *Fujian Tongji Nianjin* (Fujian statistical yearbook). Fujian, China: Provincial Government of Fujian.

———. Provincial Government of Guangdong. Guangdong Foreign Economic Relations and Trade Commission. Various years. *Guangdong Tongji Nianjin* (Guangdong statistical yearbook). Guangdong, China: Provincial Government of Guangdong.

———. State Statistical Bureau. 1994. *Statistical yearbook of China.* Beijing: State Statistical Bureau.

Chung-Hua Institution for Economic Research. 1994. *A comparative study of foreign investments in mainland China* (in Chinese). Taipei: Chung-Hua Institution for Economic Research.

Feenstra, R. 1995. A model of business group. Paper presented to NBER preconference on U.S. Trade Protection and Trade Promotion, Cambridge, Mass.

Fung, K. C. 1996. Mainland Chinese investments in Hong Kong: How much, why and so what. *Journal of Asian Business* 12: 21–39.

———. 1997. Trade and investment: Mainland China, Hong Kong and Taiwan. Hong Kong: City University of Hong Kong Press.

Fung, K. C., and Hitomi Iizaka. 1998. Japanese and U.S. trade with China: A comparative analysis. *Review of Development Economics* 2(2): 181–90.

Fung, K. C., and Lawrence J. Lau. 1996. U.S.–China bilateral trade balance: How big is it really? Stanford, Calif.: Asia/Pacific Research Center, Institute for International Studies, Stanford University. Occasional paper.

Ho, Yin-Ping. 1993. China's foreign trade and the reform of the foreign trade system. In

China review 1993, ed. Joseph Cheng Yu-Shek, and Maurice Brosseau. Hong Kong: Chinese University Press.

Hong Kong Government. 1993. *1993 Economic background.* Hong Kong: Financial Services Branch, Economic Analysis Division.

———. 1994. *First quarter economic report 1994.* Hong Kong: Financial Services Branch, Economic Analysis Division.

———. Various years, a. *Hong Kong external trade.* Hong Kong: Census and Statistics Department.

———. Various years, b. *Review of overseas trade.* Hong Kong: Census and Statistics Department.

International Monetary Fund. 1993. *World economic outlook.* Washington, D.C.: International Monetary Fund.

Ito, T., and A. Krueger, eds. 1993. *Trade and protectionism.* Chicago: University of Chicago Press.

Kao, Charng. 1993. A study of the economic interactions among Taiwan, Hong Kong, and mainland China (in Chinese). Taipei: Chung-Hua Institution for Economic Research. Mimeograph.

Krueger, A. 1995. Customs union versus free trade area. Stanford, Calif.: Stanford University. Mimeograph.

Lardy, N. 1992. Chinese foreign trade. *China Quarterly,* no. 131 (September): 691–720.

———. 1994. *China in the world economy.* Washington, D.C.: Institute for International Economics.

Lau, L. 1995. The role of government in economic development: Some observations from the experience of China, Hong Kong and Taiwan. Stanford, Calif.: Stanford University. Mimeograph.

Liu, P. W., R. Y. C. Wong, Y. W. Sung, and P. K. Lau. 1992. *China's economic reform and development strategy of Pearl River delta.* Hong Kong: Nanyang Commercial Bank. Research report.

McKinnon, R. 1991. *The order of economic liberalization,* 2d ed. Baltimore: Johns Hopkins University Press.

Noland, M. 1990. *Pacific Basin developing countries: Prospects for the future.* Washington, D.C.: Institute for International Economics.

Organization for Economic Cooperation and Development (OECD). 1993. Economic integration between Hong Kong, Taiwan and the coastal provinces of China. OECD Economic Study. Paris: Organization for Economic Cooperation and Development.

Richardson, J. David. 1993. *Sizing up export disincentives.* Washington, D.C.: Institute for International Economics.

Summers, L. 1992. The rise of China. *International Economic Insights,* May/June, pp. 13–15.

Sung, Yun-Wing. 1991. *The China–Hong Kong connection.* Cambridge: Cambridge University Press.

———. 1994. Subregional economic integration: Hong Kong, Taiwan, South China and beyond. Paper presented to the 21st Pacific Trade and Development Conference, Hong Kong.

A survey of China. 1992. *Economist,* 28 November.

Taiwan. Ministry of Finance. Department of Statistics. Various years. *Monthly statistics of exports and imports.* Taipei: Ministry of Finance.

U.S. Department of Commerce. Bureau of the Census. 1993. *U.S. merchandise trade: Related party imports from North American trading partners 1991.* Washington, D.C.: U.S. Department of Commerce, Bureau of the Census.

———. Bureau of Economic Analysis. 1992. *U.S. direct investment abroad: 1989 Benchmark survey, final results.*

———. Various years. *U.S. foreign trade highlights.* Washington, D.C.: U.S. Department of Commerce, Bureau of Economic Analysis.
West, L. 1995. Reconciling China's trade statistics. IPC Staff Paper no. 76. Washington, D.C.: U.S. Department of Commerce, Bureau of the Census. Mimeograph.
Wong, C., C. Heady, and W. T. Woo. 1993. *Economic reform and fiscal management in China.* Manila: Asian Development Bank.
Wong, R. Y. C. 1995. China's economic reform—The next step. *Contemporary Economic Policy* 13: 18–27.
World Bank. 1993. *China: Foreign trade reform.* Washington, D.C.: World Bank.

Comment Marcus Noland

It's a dirty job but someone had to do it, and K. C. Fung has written a very useful paper plowing through the accounting morass of China's burgeoning trade. I will simply elaborate on three issues: valuation, trade between Taiwan and China, and transshipment and smuggling.

Valuation

The issue of Hong Kong reexport margins is particularly salient because of the asymmetrical role Hong Kong plays in intermediating imports and exports in U.S.-China trade. The reason is that U.S. exports to China are concentrated in products such as aircraft, chemicals, and logs in which Hong Kong firms do not play much of an intermediation role and the products are shipped directly from the United States to China. In contrast, Chinese exports to the United States are concentrated in light manufactures in which Hong Kong firms are more active in ancillary manufacturing activities such as packaging, and indeed many of these exports originate from Hong Kong–owned plants in China.

In any event, policy reforms and the real exchange rate changes of the late 1980s have led to a relocation of light manufactures production from Hong Kong and Taiwan to China. Again, it would be interesting to evaluate the "shifting surplus" story depicted in table 5C.1 in light of Fung's accounting adjustments.

Taiwan Trade

Trade between Taiwan and China is booming. In March 1995, Hong Kong replaced the United States as Taiwan's largest export destination for the first time ever. In May 1995, the Taiwanese government announced that it would begin to permit direct shipping across the Taiwan Straits to the mainland. Trade was $14.4 billion in 1993 based on Chinese government figures, $13.74 according to the ROC Board of Trade; some 30,000 Taiwan businesses have an

Marcus Noland is a senior fellow at the Institute for International Economics and visiting professor at Johns Hopkins University.

Table 5C.1 Bilateral U.S.-Chinese Economic Area Trade Balances

Year	Chinese Economic Area	People's Republic of China	Hong Kong	Taiwan
1987	−25.9	−2.8	−5.9	−17.2
1988	−20.6	−3.5	−4.6	−12.6
1989	−22.6	−6.2	−3.4	−13.0
1990	−24.4	−10.4	−2.8	−11.2
1991	−23.7	−12.7	−1.1	−9.8
1992	−28.4	−18.3	−0.7	−9.3
1993	−31.4	−22.8	0.3	−8.9
1994	−37.4	−29.5	1.7	−9.6
1995	−39.6	−33.8	3.9	−9.7

Source: U.S. Department of Commerce.
Note: Figures are customs valuation, in billions of U.S. dollars.

estimated $20 billion (give or take $5 billion) invested in China. (Again, figures are highly uncertain because of circumvention of Taiwanese capital controls.) Taiwanese firms are beginning to set up R&D facilities, as well as production facilities, on the mainland. And, indeed, the Taiwanese are probably the biggest investors in China.

This poses a real political dilemma for the Taiwanese authorities. On the one hand, trade with and investment in the mainland is the logical result of shifting comparative advantage. On the other hand, increased contact poses a potential security threat in the narrow sense and loss of independence in a deeper sense. The Taiwanese government has become concerned about dependence, and in 1992 the government introduced a new monitoring system based on customs data released by the Hong Kong government on growth rate and market share of 30 leading imports and exports transshipped through Hong Kong. The 100-point system is divided into cold, cool, normal, warm, and overheated. The government has also introduced a "Look South" policy of encouraging investment diversion away from the mainland and toward Southeast Asia, but it is not obvious that the policy is having much effect.

Some interesting surveys of the activities of Taiwanese firms in China have been done. In 1992, the Ministry of Economic Affairs found that 18.5 percent of firms primarily sold their output within the People's Republic of China, 12.1 percent exported back to Taiwan, and the remainder primarily exported the output to third markets, supporting the shifting surplus story. Indeed, the worsening intellectual property rights disputes between the United States and China can in some part be seen as a case of Taiwan offloading its pirate activities (at least with respect to compact disks) to China.

A subsequent survey in 1993 by the Chung-Hua Institution for Economic Research found that 63.75 percent of Taiwanese firms in China primarily procured intermediates from Taiwan, while 20 percent indirectly purchased parts from Chinese suppliers.

With respect to financing, nearly three-quarters of Taiwanese plants in China are financed from Taiwan (72.25 percent), 17.2 percent get their financing from Chinese financial institutions, 7.0 percent are financed by banks in third countries, and 1.45 percent get financing from Chinese subsidiaries of third-country banks. In 1993 the first Taiwanese firm, Tsann Kuen Enterprise Ltd., an appliance maker, listed on a mainland stock exchange (Shenchen).

Transshipment

Last, on the issue of transshipment and smuggling, there is one channel that Fung does not mention. South Korean firms currently tranship through China to North Korea and then back again. This trade is in the hundreds of millions of dollars and growing rapidly, though how it continues is obviously contingent on North Korea–South Korea relations. Also, there is significant smuggling across the North Korea–China border. Again, observers have put the magnitude in the hundreds of millions of dollars.

The real money is in textile and apparel transshipment, however, and I believe that Fung has grossly underestimated the quantitative importance and policy relevance of this issue. In an earlier version of the paper, transshipment to circumvent the Multifiber Arrangement was brushed off in two sentences, with the statement that the estimated $2 billion in illegal textile imports into the United States is an inflated figure from a textile producer group. My understanding is that figure comes from the U.S. Customs Service.

China circumvents its bilateral textile and apparel quotas, mainly by transshipping products through third countries that are also covered by bilateral quotas. In other words, the Chinese substitute their products for the unfulfilled quotas of third countries. A Treasury study also put the value of these transshipments at $2 billion. The main transshipment points are the high-wage locations of Hong Kong, Taiwan, Macau, and Singapore. Textile and apparel imports from these four countries were $8.5 billion in 1993. In other words, the Treasury figure implies that nearly 25 percent were transshipped.

A bilateral agreement on this issue was signed in January 1994. Government sources indicate that the problem appears to be getting worse, however. According to the Customs Service (not the textile lobby!), there appears to be roughly $10 billion in Chinese textiles and apparel floating around the world not properly accounted for.

For example, Chinese customs officials reported $13 billion in exports to 120 countries in 1992. Eighty-one countries alone reported $23.7 billion of imports from China in the same year. (The Ministry of Foreign Trade and Economic Cooperation reports $7.7 billion in textile and apparel exports in 1992, making the discrepancy even bigger.)

China reports $6.4 billion in textile and apparel exports to Hong Kong in 1992. Hong Kong reports $8.6 billion in consumption imports (a enormous figure), and $9.7 billion in reexports. Even allowing for high reexport markups, these discrepancies are huge.

The Customs Service found that half of the 36 fastest growing apparel suppliers to the U.S. market had no significant domestic production for export but reported a significant increase in imports from China. Kenya, for example, has recently experienced a 790 percent growth rate in apparel imports from China, and a 212 percent growth in exports to the United States. Other countries, including Belize, the Czech Republic, Ecuador, and Qatar, exhibit similar triple-digit growth rates. All in all, the Treasury Department estimates that at least $200 million of illegally transshipped apparel is coming into the United States through these countries.

Transshipping is currently subject to criminal prosecution, and the Customs Service and the Justice Department have launched an ambitious campaign to prosecute transshippers. There was recently a major conviction involving a Chinese state-owned firm.

Transshipping is potentially a big issue. Growing imports from China put downward pressure on the wage rates of low-skilled American workers. Moreover, the United States and China clash over issues such as China's desultory human rights record and arms proliferation. This is a combination that is likely to spell trouble for U.S.-China relations and could have a big impact on things like China's accession to the World Trade Organization.

Conclusion

When asked about an apparent musical plagiarism, Ringo Starr reportedly replied, "When you steal, steal from the best." I will give a paper next month in Hong Kong called "China in the World Economy." I am sure that I will be able to make good use (with proper attribution, of course) of "Accounting for Chinese Trade: Some National and Regional Considerations."

6 Imported Inputs and the Domestic Content of Production by Foreign-Owned Manufacturing Affiliates in the United States

William J. Zeile

In recent years, foreign multinational firms have come to occupy a conspicuous position in U.S. manufacturing industries. Growth in the market share of foreign-owned manufacturing affiliates has been substantial, reflecting the dramatic surge in inward direct investment that occurred in the late 1980s. Recent data on the establishment-level operations of foreign-owned manufacturers, for example, indicate that from 1987 to 1991 the share of total U.S. manufacturing shipments accounted for by foreign-owned establishments increased from less than 10 percent to 15 percent; in such manufacturing industries as fabricated metal products, industrial machinery, and transportation equipment, the share of shipments by foreign-owned establishments doubled (U.S. Department of Commerce 1992, 1994).

This growing presence has prompted questions concerning the degree to which the output sold by foreign-owned manufacturers represents actual production within the borders of the United States. Concerns have been expressed in some quarters, for example, that foreign-owned manufacturing affiliates may be little more than final assembly operations set up to increase penetration of the U.S. market, with most of the value added in production taking place abroad. To the extent that these affiliates displace production by domestically owned firms, it is feared, they may reduce domestic employment and factor rents both in the industries in which they compete and in upstream industries supplying materials and components to domestically owned firms. Fears have also been expressed that, to the extent that they source their inputs from

William J. Zeile is an economist in the International Investment Division, Bureau of Economic Analysis, U.S. Department of Commerce.

Views expressed in this paper are those of the author and do not necessarily reflect those of the Department of Commerce. The author is indebted to Betty L. Barker, R. David Belli, David Hummels, J. David Richardson, Obie G. Whichard, and other conference participants for their comments.

abroad, affiliates may contribute to increased import dependency in intermediate product sectors deemed to be of national importance.

Such concerns, while relatively new in the United States, have long been voiced in other countries that have been host to substantial foreign direct investment. In the case of developing countries, a related concern has been the possibility that foreign-owned manufacturers, relying on foreign sources for their intermediate inputs, might impede the development of indigenous suppliers through backward linkages.[1] Does the evidence for the United States support these concerns? At the end of our analysis, our answer is "only mildly, if at all."

Earlier work at the Bureau of Economic Analysis (BEA) suggests that the domestic content of production by foreign-owned manufacturing affiliates operating in the United States has been quite high, at least in the aggregate. For manufacturing affiliates in 1987, Lowe (1990) estimates an aggregate ratio of domestic content to sales of 91 percent, with imports accounting for 16 percent of affiliate purchases of intermediate inputs. Similar results at the aggregate level are reported in Zeile (1993) for manufacturing affiliates in 1991: the share of domestic content in total output is estimated to be 88 percent, with imports accounting for 17 percent of purchased inputs.

In the latter article, however, estimates from BEA's tabular data on affiliates aggregated by industry and country of ownership indicate that the import content of purchased inputs for affiliates is quite high in a number of specific industries, particularly for Japanese-owned affiliates. An outstanding question from this research is the degree to which the high import content observed for particular groups of affiliates may reflect finished goods imports associated with the affiliates' secondary activities in wholesale trade, rather than intermediate goods imports used in their strictly manufacturing operations.

Expanding on this earlier research, this paper presents detailed measures of the domestic content and sourcing behavior of foreign-owned U.S. manufacturing affiliates, based on affiliate-level data collected in BEA's 1992 benchmark survey of foreign direct investment in the United States.[2] The benchmark survey provides new information on the intended use of affiliate imports that can be used to construct a sample limited to affiliates whose imports consist mainly of intermediate goods used in manufacturing. The benchmark survey data also include information on the geographic origin of affiliate imports that is not collected in BEA's annual surveys.

The paper begins with a discussion of three measures related to the content of affiliate production and their construction from the benchmark survey data. Industry-level measures are presented for affiliates in 24 manufacturing indus-

1. Much of the existing empirical literature on the domestic content of production by foreign-owned firms is concerned with the issue of Hirshmanian linkages. For a summary of this literature, see Caves (1982, 270–72) and Dunning (1993, 445–73).

2. Data from the benchmark survey aggregated by industry of affiliate and country of ownership appear in U.S. Department of Commerce (1995).

tries, in comparison with similar measures for domestically owned manufacturing firms. The relation between the three content measures and affiliate age is also examined, using data constructed for a panel of affiliates in selected manufacturing industries. The paper then turns to an examination of differences in the content of affiliate production by investing country. Finally, the paper examines differences in import sourcing among affiliates of the major investing countries, in terms of the importance of intrafirm imports and the geographic origin of imports.

6.1 Measuring the Content of Affiliate Production

In its benchmark and annual surveys of foreign direct investment in the United States, BEA collects data on the consolidated operations of U.S. affiliates of foreign companies.[3] The data collected include balance sheet and income statement items, employment data, and data on the U.S. merchandise exports and imports shipped by or to affiliates. From data related to factor payments and certain other costs, BEA calculates the value added of affiliates.[4] Total output can be computed from the reported data as sales plus the change in end-of-year inventories. The value of intermediate inputs purchased by affiliates can be computed as the difference between total output and value added.

These data can be used to construct three measures that reveal information about the content of affiliate production. The first measure is the domestic content of affiliate total output, expressed as follows:

(1) Domestic content of total output

$$= (\text{Total output} - \text{Imports}) / \text{Total output}$$

$$= (\text{Valued added} + \text{Total purchased inputs} - \text{Imports}) / \text{Total output}$$

$$= (\text{Value added} + \text{Domestically sourced inputs}) / \text{Total output}.$$

As the final expression shows, domestic content can take the form of either internal production by the affiliate or production by the affiliate's domestic suppliers. In both cases, value is added within the borders of the affiliate's host country.

Dunning (1993) refers to two distinct decisions a foreign-owned affiliate

3. A U.S. affiliate is defined as a U.S. business enterprise in which a single foreign person owns or controls, directly or indirectly, 10 percent or more of the voting securities of an incorporated U.S. business enterprise or an equivalent interest in an unincorporated U.S. business enterprise. The 10 percent ownership threshold used in this definition conforms with International Monetary Fund (IMF) and Organization for Economic Cooperation and Development (OECD) standards on the definition of foreign direct investment.

4. The gross product (value added) of affiliates is calculated from the income side as the sum of employee compensation, profit-type return, net interest paid, indirect business taxes, and capital consumption allowance.

makes that affect its linkages with the domestic economy: the "make or buy" decision and the "import or procure locally" decision.

The make-or-buy decision determines the degree to which an affiliate internalizes the production of its intermediate inputs through vertical integration. Vertical integration at the affiliate level can be measured by the share of value added in total output:

$$\text{(2)} \qquad \text{Vertical integration} = \text{Value added} / \text{Total output}.$$

Assuming that all of the labor and other primary factors contributing to the affiliate's value added are supplied domestically, a higher degree of vertical integration implies higher domestic content.[5]

The import-or-procure-locally decision determines the import content of the affiliate's purchased intermediate inputs, which can be measured as

$$\text{(3)} \quad \text{Import content of purchased inputs} = \text{Imports} / \text{Total purchased inputs}.$$

Ceteris paribus, a higher share of imports in the affiliate's purchased inputs implies lower domestic content.

It should be noted that measures (1) and (3) capture direct (or first round) imports only—by construction, they exclude any imports (direct or indirect) that may be embodied in the inputs purchased from domestic distributors or manufacturers, data for which are not available. The measures also fail to count as "foreign" any purchases of services from abroad, as the data for affiliate imports cover merchandise imports only.

As an added caveat, measures (1) and (3) will be distorted to the extent that the data on affiliate imports include additions to the affiliates' capital stock (which, not being intermediate inputs, would not appear in the denominator of the measures) or goods for resale without further manufacture (which are part of the sales data used to construct the denominator, but which are not related to manufacturing production). Some affiliates classified in manufacturing may have substantial imports of goods for resale without further manufacture due to secondary activities in wholesale trade.[6]

Affiliate activities in secondary industries can also create distortions in the measure of vertical integration, insofar as the data on value added and total

5. An interesting question that challenges this assumption is how one should treat the contribution to value added provided by the depreciation of machinery and equipment that were imported. This question must remain an academic one, however, given the absence of data on the share of affiliate capital stock originating from imports.

6. In BEA's surveys of foreign direct investment in the United States, each affiliate is assigned to the industry in which it has the largest sales, based on a breakdown of its sales by BEA International Surveys Industry Classification code. Whereas sales and employment for an affiliate can be disaggregated by each industry in which it reports sales, the data for the other financial and operating items collected in the surveys are necessarily all assigned to the single industry in which the affiliate is classified. Data from the 1992 benchmark survey indicate that manufacturing sales accounted for 85 percent of total sales by affiliates classified in manufacturing. Sales in wholesale trade accounted for a little more than 6 percent of total sales by manufacturing affiliates.

output used to compute the measure are consolidated data covering all of an affiliate's operations, which may be diverse. Thus, in comparisons between affiliates classified in the same manufacturing industry, a lower measure of "vertical integration" observed for a particular affiliate could simply reflect the existence of substantial secondary activities in wholesale trade (where the ratio of value added to total output is relatively low) rather than any difference in the structure of the affiliate's purely manufacturing operations. Similarly, changes over time in this measure could reflect changes in the composition of an affiliate's secondary activities rather than changes in the structure of its manufacturing output.

For this paper, the three content measures described above have been constructed for a sample of foreign-owned U.S. affiliates in 24 manufacturing industries, using preliminary data from the 1992 benchmark survey of foreign direct investment in the United States. The data from this survey include new detail on the intended use of affiliate imports. Specifically, all affiliates required to complete a detailed "long" form (i.e., affiliates with assets, sales, or net income exceeding $50 million) were asked to provide a dollar breakdown of their merchandise imports according to three categories: goods intended for further manufacture by the affiliate, goods intended for resale without further manufacture, and capital goods intended as additions to the affiliate's plant and equipment.

To minimize the potential distortions associated with wholesale trade activity or imports of capital goods, the sample is confined to manufacturing affiliates that reported on the long form and had imports that mainly consisted of goods intended for further manufacture. ("Mainly" was defined by a share of over 50 percent.) The sample consists of 701 affiliates (out of a total of 2,752 affiliates classified in manufacturing and 878 manufacturing affiliates that reported on the long form). The collective sales of these 701 affiliates account for two-thirds of total sales by all affiliates classified in manufacturing.[7]

Limiting our analysis to this relatively "pure" sample of manufacturing affiliates, we can be reasonably confident that the measures constructed provide the intended information on the content of manufacturing production. A necessary trade-off, however, is the sacrifice of information on a number of large affiliates that have substantial operations in both manufacturing and wholesale trade. The sample excludes, for example, some of the largest affiliates producing motor vehicles since (in the data used to compute the content measures) their manufacturing operations cannot be segregated from their large-scale operations as wholesale distributors of vehicles produced abroad by their parent companies.[8]

7. As shown in appendix table 6A.1, affiliates in the sample account for a majority of affiliate sales in all but 2 of the 24 manufacturing industries for which the content measures have been constructed.

8. Some of the largest affiliates with operations in automobile manufacturing are actually classified in wholesale trade (where their sales are largest) rather than in manufacturing.

For purposes of comparison, the three content measures have also been constructed at the industry level for U.S. parent companies of foreign affiliates, using data from BEA's 1989 benchmark survey of U.S. direct investment abroad.[9] In the absence of industry-level data on imported inputs by all U.S. businesses, the data for U.S. parent companies provide the best available measures of the domestic and import content of production by domestically owned U.S. companies. Because U.S. parent manufacturing companies in 1989 accounted for about 60 percent of the production by all U.S. companies in manufacturing, the measures for these parent companies can be taken as indicative of the content of production for domestically owned manufacturing firms in general.[10]

6.2 Industry-Level Results

In the aggregate, foreign-owned manufacturing affiliates in the United States display a high level of domestic content in production, just slightly below that for domestically owned U.S. manufacturing companies. Table 6.1 shows that, for all affiliates in the sample combined, the domestic content of total output is 89 percent, compared to 93 percent for domestically owned companies. Of the 89 percent share, 32 percent represents value added by the affiliates; the remaining 57 percent consists of intermediate inputs purchased domestically. The share of imports in purchased inputs is 16 percent. These results are consistent with the aggregate estimates reported for earlier years in Lowe (1990) and Zeile (1993).[11]

Among the 24 manufacturing industries, the domestic content share of affiliate output is greater than 90 percent in 16 industries; in 13 of these industries, the domestic content measure for affiliates is within 5 percent of the measure

9. In its benchmark and annual surveys of U.S. direct investment abroad, BEA collects financial and operating data for both U.S. parent companies and their foreign affiliates. The latest benchmark survey data cover the year 1989. In nonbenchmark survey years, the data collected for U.S. parent companies do not include all of the items required to compute the content measures examined in this paper. For further discussion, see Mataloni and Goldberg (1994), which presents industry-level measures of content for U.S. parent companies in each of the benchmark survey years 1977, 1982, and 1989.

10. The use of domestically owned U.S. firms as a comparison group for foreign-owned U.S. affiliates fits in with the theme of this volume, as the comparison is between firms with a common geographic location distinguished by country of ownership. Alternatively, it would be useful to compare the domestic content and sourcing behavior of foreign-owned U.S. affiliates with that of foreign affiliates of U.S. parent companies. Unfortunately, data are not available to construct comparable measures of domestic and import content for U.S.-owned foreign affiliates. Specifically, the data collected in BEA's annual and benchmark surveys of U.S. direct investment abroad include only imports by foreign affiliates that originate in the United States, not their total imports.

11. As noted above, these measures may overstate the domestic content of affiliate output insofar as they fail to capture any imports embodied in the affiliates' purchases from domestic suppliers. This limitation, however, also applies to the measure of domestic content for domestically owned U.S. manufacturing companies, the reference group used for comparison.

for domestically owned companies (cols. [1] and [7] of table 6.1). The high domestic content level in these industries reflects a marked propensity for affiliates to procure most of their intermediate inputs from domestic suppliers: in all 16 industries, imports account for less than one-sixth of the affiliates' intermediate input purchases (col. [3]).[12] Even so, affiliates in these industries tend to rely on imports substantially more than their domestically owned counterparts (col. [9]).[13] In 7 of the 16 industries, the import content share for affiliates is more than twice as high as the very low share for domestically owned companies.

While the domestic content of affiliate output is generally high, it is relatively low—less than 80 percent—in five industries: construction, mining, and materials handling machinery; computer and office equipment; household audio and video, and communications, equipment; electronic components and accessories; and motor vehicles and equipment.[14] (In each of these industries, the domestic content measure for affiliates is at least 15 percent lower than that for domestically owned companies.) These industries, which can all be categorized as "machinery type" industries, share the characteristic of having intermediate inputs that consist mainly of manufactured components (which may be subject to product differentiation across suppliers) rather than commodity-type bulk materials (which generally can be procured most cheaply from domestic suppliers due to transportation costs). In all five industries, imports account for more than one-third of the intermediate inputs purchased by affiliates. In four of these industries, more than 60 percent of the imported inputs are sourced from the affiliates' foreign parent companies or other foreign firms with which the parents are affiliated (table 6.2).

The measure of domestic content for affiliates is lowest in the computer and motor vehicle industries, with domestic content in each case constituting slightly less than two-thirds of affiliate output. In both industries, the low domestic content share reflects a relatively low level of vertical integration in affiliate production (the share of value added in total output being one-third lower than that for domestically owned companies) coupled with a high reliance on imports for the affiliates' intermediate inputs. Imports account for more than 50 percent of the purchased inputs of affiliates in the computer industry and for more than 40 percent of the purchased inputs of affiliates in

12. Across the 24 industries shown in table 6.1, the coefficient of correlation between the domestic content of total output and the import content of purchased inputs for foreign-owned affiliates is −0.99. The correlation between the measures of domestic content and vertical integration for affiliates is much weaker, the correlation coefficient being 0.41 (barely significant at the 95 percent confidence level).

13. The sole exception appears in printing and publishing, where the domestic content measure for affiliates is actually higher than that for domestically owned companies.

14. It should be noted that a substantial portion of the sample data in "motor vehicles and equipment" represents affiliates producing motor vehicle parts and accessories.

Table 6.1 **Measures of Domestic Content of Production, Vertical Integration, and Import Content of Purchased Inputs for Foreign-Owned Manufacturing Affiliates in 1992 and Domestically Owned U.S. Manufacturing Companies in 1989**

	Foreign-Owned Affiliates[a]			Domestically Owned Companies[b]			Ratio of Measure for Affiliates to Measure for Domestically Owned Companies		
Industry	Domestic Content/ Total Output (%) (1)	Value Added/ Total Output (%) (2)	Imports/ Total Purchased Inputs (%) (3)	Domestic Content/ Total Output (%) (4)	Value Added/ Total Output (%) (5)	Imports/ Total Purchased Inputs (%) (6)	Domestic Content/ Total Output (7)	Value Added/ Total Output (8)	Imports/ Total Purchased Inputs (9)
Manufacturing[c]	89.3	32.3	15.9	93.2	37.6	10.9	0.96	0.86	1.45
Food and kindred products	93.3	21.1	8.5	98.1	31.6	2.8	0.95	0.67	3.09
Textile products and apparel	93.6	34.4	9.7	97.2	38.1	4.5	0.96	0.90	2.18
Paper and allied products	93.8	32.9	9.3	98.0	42.6	3.4	0.96	0.77	2.73
Printing and publishing	99.2	38.0	1.3	97.7	39.7	3.9	1.02	0.96	0.34
Industrial chemicals and synthetics	92.5	35.0	11.6	93.5	40.2	10.8	0.99	0.87	1.07
Drugs	90.0	40.1	16.8	96.1	52.1	8.1	0.94	0.77	2.07
Other chemicals	92.9	26.2	9.7	96.5	33.1	5.3	0.96	0.79	1.82
Rubber products	91.8	35.3	12.7	94.6	39.2	8.9	0.97	0.90	1.43
Miscellaneous plastics products	91.5	21.0	10.7	98.1	34.8	2.9	0.93	0.60	3.65
Glass products	92.9	40.6	11.9	97.8	50.1	4.5	0.95	0.81	2.64
Stone, clay, and concrete products	96.1	34.4	5.9	97.4	37.2	4.2	0.99	0.93	1.42
Primary ferrous metals	93.0	29.1	9.9	95.6	35.7	6.8	0.97	0.82	1.45

Primary nonferrous metals	81.4	24.3	24.6	91.3	38.9	14.2	0.89	0.62	1.73
Fabricated metal products	94.7	33.5	8.0	96.8	33.2	4.8	0.98	1.01	1.65
Construction, mining, and materials handling machinery	75.5	28.6	34.3	90.6	32.7	13.9	0.83	0.88	2.47
Other nonelectrical machinery	87.0	29.4	18.5	94.6	38.9	8.8	0.92	0.76	2.09
Computer and office equipment	63.8	29.9	51.7	87.4	44.8	22.9	0.73	0.67	2.26
Household audio and video, and communications, equipment	72.4	34.3	42.0	89.4	36.1	16.6	0.81	0.95	2.53
Electronic components and accessories	72.4	30.3	39.6	87.4	43.3	22.3	0.83	0.70	1.78
Other electric and electronic equipment	93.0	35.0	10.8	96.1	39.1	6.3	0.97	0.90	1.71
Motor vehicles and equipment	66.4	17.5	40.8	82.5	27.3	24.0	0.80	0.64	1.70
Other transportation equipment	90.7	31.9	13.6	97.4	44.9	4.8	0.93	0.71	2.87
Instruments and related products	94.5	43.8	9.8	95.0	48.1	9.7	0.99	0.91	1.01
Other manufacturing	91.4	45.9	15.9	97.3	37.9	4.4	0.94	1.21	3.62

[a]Calculated from preliminary data from BEA's 1992 benchmark survey of foreign direct investment in the United States. The data employed cover U.S. affiliates of foreign companies that had total assets, sales, or net income exceeding $50 million at the end of 1992. They cover affiliates classified in manufacturing, excluding those affiliates whose imports were not primarily used for further processing or manufacture by the affiliates.

[b]Calculated from data on the operations of U.S. parent companies classified in manufacturing, from BEA's 1989 benchmark survey of U.S. direct investment abroad.

[c]Excludes petroleum refining, which, in the data for many large affiliates, is integrated with oil and gas extraction.

Table 6.2 **Measures Relating Intrafirm Imports, Total Imports, and Total Purchased Inputs of Foreign-Owned Manufacturing Affiliates, 1992**

Industry	Total Imports/ Total Purchased Inputs (%)	Intrafirm Imports/ Total Imports (%)	Intrafirm Imports/Total Purchased Inputs (%)
Manufacturing	15.9	67.0	10.6
Food and kindred products	8.5	31.7	2.7
Textile products and apparel	9.7	41.8	4.1
Paper and allied products	9.3	56.0	5.2
Printing and publishing	1.3	9.5	0.1
Industrial chemicals and synthetics	11.6	20.7	2.4
Drugs	16.8	96.4	16.2
Other chemicals	9.7	86.8	8.4
Rubber products	12.7	90.3	11.5
Miscellaneous plastics products	10.7	95.2	10.2
Glass products	11.9	52.6	6.2
Stone, clay, and concrete products	5.9	33.5	2.0
Primary ferrous metals	9.9	47.1	4.7
Primary nonferrous metals	24.6	68.8	16.9
Fabricated metal products	8.0	71.4	5.7
Construction, mining, and materials handling machinery	34.3	65.4	22.5
Other nonelectrical machinery	18.5	74.2	13.7
Computer and office equipment	51.7	90.7	46.9
Household audio and video, and communications, equipment	42.0	47.3	19.9
Electronic components and accessories	39.6	80.8	32.0
Other electric and electronic equipment	10.8	76.8	8.3
Motor vehicles and equipment	40.8	96.4	39.3
Other transportation equipment	13.6	86.1	11.7
Instruments and related products	9.8	62.1	6.1
Other manufacturing	15.9	33.0	5.3

Note: Intrafirm imports are imports by affiliates from their foreign parent groups.

motor vehicles. In both cases, more than 90 percent of the imports are intrafirm imports shipped from the affiliates' foreign parent groups.

6.3 Relation to Age

Given the large influx of new foreign investment that occurred in the late 1980s, it is appropriate to ask whether the relatively low domestic content observed for affiliates in some machinery-type industries can be attributed to an immature phase in their U.S. production operations. Many have argued that foreign direct investment in manufacturing typically begins with affiliates undertaking final assembly operations that rely heavily on components and parts sourced from the foreign parent or other established suppliers abroad. Over time, these affiliates are expected to increase their domestic content, both through vertical expansion of their production operations and through increased procurement from domestic suppliers.[15]

To investigate whether domestic content is related to the age of affiliate operations, a panel was created from the 238 sample affiliates classified in machinery-type industries.[16] The panel consists of 119 affiliates that existed in 1987 (the earliest year for which affiliate-level data are readily accessible) and were fully operational in each of the years 1988–92.[17]

As a first step in this investigation, the panel can be used to determine whether, at a given moment in time, older affiliates have higher domestic content than newer affiliates. Table 6.3 presents industry-level comparisons of the three content measures in 1992 for affiliates in the panel (termed "old" affiliates) and nonpanel sample affiliates that entered the direct investment universe sometime after 1987 (termed "new" affiliates). The results shown appear to contradict the expectation that older affiliates have higher domestic content than their younger counterparts. In all but two of the nine machinery-type industries, the domestic content of total output is lower (and the import content of purchased inputs is correspondingly higher) for "old" affiliates than for "new" affiliates. This finding can probably be attributed to the fact that foreign direct investment in the United States has predominantly taken the form of acquisitions of existing companies rather than the sort of "greenfield" investment to which the expected association between affiliate age and domestic content really applies.[18]

Although domestic content does not appear to be positively associated with age in same-year comparisons *among* affiliates, there is a marked tendency in some industries for affiliate domestic content to increase over time. For affiliates in the panel, table 6.4 shows an upward trend in the domestic content of total output (accompanied by a downward trend in the import content of purchased inputs) in four of the nine machinery industries. In the other five

15. McAleese and McDonald (1978) find support for this hypothesis in the case of foreign-owned "greenfield" manufacturing enterprises in Ireland.

16. Machinery-type industries are defined as all industries in electrical and nonelectrical machinery, transportation equipment, and instruments. Of the 24 industries listed in table 6.1, 9 are classified as machinery-type industries.

17. The panel excludes some affiliates that existed in 1987 but did not have sales or value added in one or more of the years 1988–91. Because affiliate-level estimates of value added exist only for the years 1988 forward, 1988 is the earliest year for which the three content measures can be constructed for affiliates in the panel.

18. Data from BEA's annual survey of new foreign direct investment in the United States indicate that acquisitions of existing manufacturing enterprises accounted for more than 80 percent of the outlays by foreign direct investors to acquire or establish U.S. manufacturing enterprises in each of the years 1980–91.

Table 6.3 **Measures of Content for Machinery-Type Industry Affiliates Segregated by Age, 1992**

	Number of Affiliates in Sample			Domestic Content/Total Output (%)			Value Added/Total Output (%)			Imports/Total Purchased Inputs (%)		
Industry	Total	"Old" Affiliates	"New" Affiliates	Total	"Old" Affiliates	"New" Affiliates	Total	"Old" Affiliates	"New" Affiliates	Total	"Old" Affiliates	"New" Affiliates
Construction, mining, and materials handling machinery	20	9	11	75.5	78.7	73.7	28.6	27.3	29.3	34.3	29.3	37.1
Other nonelectrical machinery	56	33	23	87.0	85.8	88.5	29.4	28.0	31.0	18.5	19.8	16.7
Computer and office equipment	12	5	7	63.8	51.3	72.3	29.9	33.9	27.2	51.7	73.7	38.0
Household audio and video, and communications, equipment	12	8	4	72.4	71.9	78.7	34.3	33.8	40.3	42.0	42.4	35.6
Electronic components and accessories	30	12	18	72.4	66.5	76.2	30.3	30.8	30.0	39.6	48.5	34.0
Other electric and electronic equipment	28	15	13	93.0	92.5	94.0	35.0	32.6	39.8	10.8	11.2	10.0
Motor vehicles and equipment	34	13	21	66.4	64.6	69.4	17.5	16.4	19.4	40.8	42.4	38.0
Other transportation equipment	18	9	9	90.7	85.1	97.3	31.9	33.6	29.9	13.6	22.5	3.8
Instruments and related products	28	15	13	94.5	95.3	87.7	43.8	45.0	34.7	9.8	8.5	18.8

Note: "Old" affiliates are affiliates in 1992 sample that existed in 1987 and were fully operational in 1988–92. "New" affiliates are affiliates in 1992 sample that entered BEA's data after 1987; they include some affiliates that were in existence in 1987 but were not fully operational in one or more of the years 1988–91.

Table 6.4 **Time Series of Measures of Content for "Old" Machinery-Type Industry Affiliates, 1988–92**

Industry	1988	1989	1990	1991	1992
Domestic Content/Total Output (%)					
Construction, mining, and materials handling machinery	70.5	73.4	75.5	88.2	78.7
Other nonelectrical machinery	83.7	81.9	84.8	84.4	85.8
Computer and office equipment	–[a]	47.7	40.5	46.4	51.3
Household audio and video, and communications, equipment	64.0	67.4	68.4	75.7	71.9
Electronic components and accessories	63.8	78.0	69.1	68.9	66.5
Other electric and electronic equipment	78.8	91.6	91.6	91.8	92.5
Motor vehicles and equipment	45.9	52.1	60.7	63.6	64.6
Other transportation equipment	69.5	78.2	83.3	81.8	85.1
Instruments and related products	93.5	94.8	94.7	95.5	95.3
Value Added/Total Output (%)					
Construction, mining, and materials handling machinery	28.2	25.7	24.6	29.0	27.3
Other nonelectrical machinery	27.8	28.3	29.7	27.5	28.0
Computer and office equipment	–[a]	42.5	38.7	38.5	33.9
Household audio and video, and communications, equipment	27.0	31.9	33.6	35.3	33.8
Electronic components and accessories	29.9	30.6	24.5	25.4	30.8
Other electric and electronic equipment	23.4	33.0	33.0	33.0	32.6
Motor vehicles and equipment	12.2	10.1	14.7	16.5	16.4
Other transportation equipment	23.7	30.2	34.7	27.0	33.6
Instruments and related products	35.9	38.7	40.1	41.8	45.0
Imports/Total Purchased Inputs (%)					
Construction, mining, and materials handling machinery	41.1	35.8	32.5	16.6	29.3
Other nonelectrical machinery	22.5	25.3	21.6	21.5	19.8
Computer and office equipment	–[a]	90.9	97.0	87.0	73.7
Household audio and video, and communications, equipment	49.3	47.9	47.6	37.6	42.4
Electronic components and accessories	51.7	31.7	41.0	41.7	48.5
Other electric and electronic equipment	27.7	12.6	12.5	12.2	11.2
Motor vehicles and equipment	61.6	53.2	46.1	43.6	42.4
Other transportation equipment	40.0	31.2	25.6	24.9	22.5
Instruments and related products	10.2	8.4	8.8	7.7	8.5

Note: Measures constructed from data for a fixed panel of affiliates that existed in 1987 and were fully operational in 1988–92.

[a]Suppressed to avoid disclosure of data of individual companies.

industries, the domestic and import content measures are either stable or display no sustained trend.[19]

19. In seven of the nine industries, the import content of purchased inputs decreases in 1988–89, perhaps reflecting a lagged response to the substantial depreciation of the U.S. dollar in international currency markets in 1985–88. In 1985–88, the multilateral-trade-weighted value of the U.S. dollar in real terms depreciated 33 percent. In contrast, in 1988–92—the period covered by the

For panel affiliates in the motor vehicles and equipment industry, the domestic content of total output increases every year, from 46 percent in 1988 to 65 percent in 1992. This increase mainly reflects a large and sustained decrease in the import share of the affiliates' purchased intermediate inputs, from 62 percent in 1988 to 42 percent in 1992. It also appears to reflect a mild increase in the vertical integration of affiliate production.

6.4 Comparisons by Investing Country

We now turn to an investigation of differences among foreign-owned manufacturing affiliates by country of ownership. The domestic content and sourcing behavior of affiliates are compared across six major investing countries: Canada, France, Germany, Switzerland, the United Kingdom, and Japan.[20] Affiliates with owners in these six countries collectively account for 550 of the 701 affiliates in the sample.

Comparisons among the investing countries' affiliates are made in terms of the three content measures normalized by industry. To normalize, each content measure for a given affiliate was divided by the corresponding aggregate content measure (shown in table 6.1) for domestically owned companies in the affiliate's industry.

Table 6.5 presents the unweighted mean values of the normalized content measures for affiliates of each country. Mean values are also shown for the countries' affiliates in two industry subgroups: machinery-type industries and other industries. A mean value equal to one indicates that the content measure for affiliates, on average, is equal to that for domestically owned companies in comparable industries. For affiliates of each investing country, a *t*-test was performed to determine whether the sample mean of the normalized content measure is significantly different from one.

Supplementing the summary statistics in table 6.5, appendix table 6A.2 presents the aggregate content measures for affiliates of selected investing countries in individual machinery-type industries. The presentation in this table is necessarily selective in order to ensure the confidentiality of data for individual companies.

Among the six investing countries, affiliates with owners in Japan and Germany stand out in table 6.5 as having substantially lower domestic content, and a substantially higher import content of purchased inputs, than domestically owned companies in comparable industries. The difference is particularly

panel data—the real depreciation of the dollar was a relatively modest 5 percent. Data on the real exchange rate appear in *Economic Report of the President* (1997, table B-108).

20. The 1992 benchmark survey data for all affiliates indicate that manufacturing affiliates with ultimate beneficial owners in these six countries account for more than 80 percent of the total value added of affiliates classified in manufacturing. In terms of affiliate value added, the United Kingdom ranks as the leading investing country in manufacturing, followed by Canada, Japan, Germany, France, and Switzerland.

Table 6.5 **Mean Values of Normalized Content Measures for Manufacturing Affiliates of All Countries and Six Major Investing Countries, 1992**

Industry Type	All Countries	Canada	France	Germany	Switzerland	United Kingdom	Japan	Other Countries
				Domestic Content/Total Output (%)				
All industries[a]	0.94***	0.97*	0.96**	0.92***	0.93***	0.99	0.90***	0.94***
	(0.16)	(0.14)	(0.13)	(0.19)	(0.14)	(0.11)	(0.18)	(0.16)
Machinery-type industries[b]	0.89***	1.07***	0.94	0.84***	0.91**	0.99	0.80***	0.94**
	(0.21)	(0.09)	(1.90)	(0.22)	(0.14)	(0.16)	(0.21)	(0.17)
Other industries	0.96***	0.94***	0.97*	0.97	0.95**	0.99	0.98*	0.94***
	(0.13)	(0.14)	(0.09)	(0.14)	(0.13)	(0.08)	(0.10)	(0.16)
				Value Added/Total Output (%)				
All industries	0.81***	0.83***	0.87**	0.88**	0.89**	0.89***	0.69***	0.82**
	(0.65)	(0.37)	(0.35)	(0.50)	(0.36)	(0.37)	(0.80)	(0.91)
Machinery-type industries[b]	0.80***	0.96	0.83**	0.85**	0.97	0.91*	0.68***	0.75***
	(0.59)	(0.33)	(0.27)	(0.40)	(0.40)	(0.27)	(0.86)	(0.37)
Other industries	0.82***	0.79***	0.90	0.89	0.85**	0.88**	0.70***	0.84*
	(0.68)	(0.38)	(0.39)	(0.55)	(0.33)	(0.41)	(0.74)	(1.01)
				Imports/Total Purchased Inputs (%)				
All industries[a]	2.02***	2.45***	1.94**	2.20***	2.23**	1.17	1.85***	2.52***
	(3.48)	(4.48)	(3.02)	(2.44)	(3.42)	(1.95)	(2.30)	(5.15)
Machinery-type industries[b]	1.91***	0.41***	2.21	3.10***	2.27**	0.92	2.27***	1.38
	(2.09)	(0.56)	(3.37)	(2.81)	(1.98)	(1.33)	(1.69)	(1.68)
Other industries	2.08***	2.99***	1.78	1.64**	2.21	1.29	1.48*	2.86***
	(4.01)	(4.89)	(2.84)	(2.01)	(4.02)	(2.17)	(2.70)	(5.77)
				Number of Affiliates				
All industries	701	77	49	83	46	117	178	151
Machinery-type industries	238	16	18	32	16	37	84	35
Other industries	463	61	31	51	30	80	94	116

Note: The measures were normalized at the affiliate level by dividing the content measure for each affiliate by the aggregate content measure for domestically owned companies in the industry of the affiliate. Numbers in parentheses are standard deviations.

[a]Industries listed in table 6.1.

[b]Industries listed in table 6.3.

*Significantly different from one at the 90 percent confidence level.

**Significantly different from one at the 95 percent confidence level.

***Significantly different from one at the 99 percent confidence level.

pronounced in machinery-type industries, with the import content of purchases by Japanese- and German-owned affiliates averaging two to three times that of their domestically owned counterparts.[21] In both machinery-type and other industries, Japanese-owned affiliates display a relatively low share of value added in total output, averaging about 30 percent less than that for domestically owned companies.

Examining the averages for the other major investing countries, we find that Swiss-owned affiliates also display lower domestic content than domestically owned companies, with the difference being significant in both machinery-type and other industries. In contrast, the average measure of domestic content for British-owned affiliates is barely distinguishable from that for domestically owned companies. The difference is also insignificant for French-owned affiliates in machinery-type industries, due to the large variance in the domestic content measure across individual affiliates.

For Canadian-owned affiliates, the results of the comparison with domestically owned companies are mixed. In machinery-type industries, Canadian-owned affiliates actually display a significantly higher measure of domestic content than their domestically owned counterparts, reflecting a significantly lower reliance on imports for their intermediate inputs. In other industries, however, Canadian-owned affiliates display significantly lower domestic content, with an average import content share three times as high as that for domestically owned companies. The high import content share in non-machinery-type industries appears to be related to the relatively low transportation costs involved in shipping bulk materials from the affiliates' home country, owing to Canada's unique proximity across the U.S. border. It may also reflect Canada's relative abundance of natural resources. An examination of the data for individual industries revealed that the share of imports in purchases by Canadian-owned affiliates is particularly high in such materials-intensive industries as paper and allied products, miscellaneous plastics products, and primary nonferrous metals—in each of these industries, virtually all of the affiliates' imports originate in Canada.

In the results just summarized, affiliates of each of the six major investing countries were compared with domestically owned companies in comparable industries. Each can also be compared with affiliates of the other investing countries. Direct comparisons among the investing countries *across the sample affiliates* are summarized in table 6.6, which reports the results of simple correlations between the normalized content measures and a set of dummy variables for each of the major investing countries. The correlations were taken across the full sample of 701 affiliates and across two subsamples consisting of the affiliates in machinery-type industries and all other industries. Each entry in

21. Appendix table 6A.2 shows that the domestic content measure for Japanese-owned affiliates is uniformly low in most machinery-type industries, with the share of imports in their purchased inputs exceeding 40 percent in five industries.

Table 6.6 Simple Correlations across Affiliates between Normalized Content Measures and Dummy Variables for Major Investing Countries, 1992

Industry Type	Number of Observations	Canada	Germany	United Kingdom	Japan
		Domestic Content/Total Output (%)			
All industries	701	0.063*	−0.052	0.137***	−0.150***
Machinery-type industries	238	0.237***	−0.105	0.196***	−0.317***
Other industries	463	−0.072	0.007	0.095**	0.074
		Value Added/Total Output (%)			
All industries	701	0.006	0.036	0.052	−0.110***
Machinery-type industries	238	0.072	0.036	0.084	−0.149**
Other industries	463	−0.018	0.038	0.039	−0.090*
		Imports/Total Purchased Inputs (%)			
All industries	701	0.044	0.019	−0.109***	−0.028
Machinery-type industries	238	−0.193***	0.224***	−0.204***	0.126*
Other industries	463	0.089*	−0.039	−0.090*	−0.075

Note: Dummy variables for France and Switzerland are insignificant in all correlations.

*Statistically significant at the 90 percent confidence level.

**Statistically significant at the 95 percent confidence level.

***Statistically significant at the 99 percent confidence level.

the table can be interpreted as the correlation between the particular measure and the identity of the investing country vis-à-vis all other investing countries.

The correlations across the full sample reveal that Japanese-owned affiliates tend to have significantly lower domestic content than affiliates of other investing countries. For German-owned affiliates, the correlation is also negative, but insignificant. British-owned affiliates, in contrast, tend to have significantly higher domestic content and a significantly lower share of imports in their purchases.

In machinery-type industries, Canadian- as well as British-owned affiliates tend to have higher domestic content, with each displaying a relatively low propensity to source their intermediate inputs through imports. Japanese-owned affiliates show a marked tendency to have lower domestic content; they also tend to have a relatively high share of imports in their purchased inputs, although here the correlation is not as strong as that for German-owned affiliates.[22]

In all three sets of industries, Japanese-owned affiliates stand out as unique among affiliates in displaying a lower degree of internalization (and a correspondingly higher reliance on outsourcing) in production, as indicated by a significantly lower share of value added in total output.

The results can be summed up by remarking that Japanese- and British-owned affiliates appear to occupy two polar extremes in terms of the three content measures, with domestic content being relatively low for Japanese-owned affiliates and relatively high for British-owned affiliates. In machinery-

22. The relatively low correlation between the normalized import content measure and the dummy variable for Japanese ownership appears to reflect the fact that the industries in which Japanese-owned affiliates have very high import content are those in which domestically owned firms also have high import content, so that the ratio between the two is not very high. Based on the industry-level data in table 6.1, the coefficient of correlation across the 24 industries between the normalized and unnormalized versions of the import content measure is only 0.15, whereas the coefficient of correlation between the two versions of the domestic content measure is 0.98.

As an alternative to the correlations reported in table 6.6, regressions were run on the unnormalized measure of import content, with the import content of domestically owned companies in the affiliate's industry entered as a control variable. With this specification, the dummy variable for Japanese ownership is positive and significant at the 99 percent confidence level, both for the full sample and for the reduced sample of affiliates in machinery-type industries. The estimated regression equation for the 238 affiliates in machinery-type industries is as follows:

$$\underset{}{\text{MCNTAF}} = 8.43 + \underset{(3.64)}{0.78}\ \text{MCNTUS} + \underset{(4.55)}{14.27}\ \text{JPNDMY}, \qquad R^2 = 0.18,$$

where MCNTAF is the import content measure for the affiliate, MCNTUS is the import content measure for domestically owned companies in the industry of the affiliate, and JPNDMY is a dummy variable for Japanese ownership. The t-statistics for the independent variables appear in parentheses.

The same regressions were run using dummy variables for the other five major investing countries. For these countries, the significance levels of the dummy variables in the regressions do not differ substantially from those reported in table 6.6 for the correlations using the normalized import content measures.

type industries, German- and Canadian-owned affiliates can also be positioned at the poles occupied, respectively, by Japanese- and British-owned affiliates.

While a formal investigation of the reasons behind these differences by investing country is beyond the scope of this paper, we can speculate on some possible factors. First, we note that the differences observed for Japanese- and British-owned affiliates may partly reflect differences in the means by which their direct investment occurred. Data from BEA's survey of new foreign direct investment in the United States suggest that British investment in manufacturing has almost exclusively taken the form of acquisitions of existing U.S. companies, whereas Japanese investment has included substantial outlays for the establishment of new enterprises (table 6.7).[23] One would expect the domestic content of production to be substantially higher for an affiliate created through acquisition of an existing firm (which may involve only a transfer of management to a foreign headquarters office) than for a newly established affiliate (which represents an extension of the parent firm's production overseas to a location within the borders of the host country).

Second, the higher domestic content observed for British- and Canadian-owned affiliates may be related to the fact that these two countries share a common language and legal system with the United States. For the other major investing countries, the differences in language and legal institutions may very well constitute a barrier that makes it more costly for their affiliates to contract with U.S. suppliers for their intermediate inputs.

Finally, some of the observed differences in the content measures may reflect differences between the investing countries in established methods of organizing production. The finding, for example, that Japanese-owned affiliates tend to have a lower share of value added in total output is consistent with the observation that Japanese companies rely heavily on subcontracting in their production.[24] Japanese companies also tend to forge long-term bonds with their suppliers, which may be a factor contributing to the relatively high import content observed for their U.S. affiliates.

6.5 Import Sourcing by Investing Country: Geography and Ownership

Differences by major investing country can also be perceived in the import-sourcing behavior of affiliates, both in terms of the share of imports related to

23. Data by investing country on outlays to establish new U.S. manufacturing enterprises are readily accessible only for the years 1987 forward. The data from BEA's survey of new investment are maintained separately from, and for a variety of reasons cannot readily be integrated with, the operating data on affiliates from BEA's annual and benchmark surveys of foreign direct investment in the United States, which were used to construct the content measures for this paper. Unfortunately, it is not possible to segregate the operating data for affiliates according to whether the affiliates were originally acquired or newly established.

24. A discussion of this and other features of Japanese business organization appears in Aoki (1990).

Table 6.7 **Outlays by Foreign Direct Investors to Establish New U.S. Manufacturing Enterprises as a Percentage of Their Total Outlays to Acquire or Establish U.S. Manufacturing Enterprises, 1987–92**

Year	All Countries	Canada	France	Germany	Switzerland	United Kingdom	Japan
1987	4.3	1.4	2.3	4.3	8.3	0.0	18.0
1988	6.8	1.0	0.6	5.0	1.9	0.3	11.5
1989	7.6	0.4	0.7	1.6	12.2	7.4	20.1
1990	4.6	13.3	0.9	1.6	7.2	1.1	8.3
1991	15.6	2.5	5.6	0.3	2.5	0.3	10.6
1992	23.8	11.5	0.3	20.8	9.6	13.6	38.0
Average, 1987–92							
Unweighted	10.5	5.0	1.7	5.6	7.0	3.8	17.8
Weighted[a]/1/	7.6	2.7	1.8	4.8	7.8	3.6	14.2

Source: The data used for this table are from BEA's annual survey of new foreign direct investment in the United States. Aggregate results from this survey for 1987–93 are reported in "U.S. Business Enterprises Acquired or Established by Foreign Direct Investors in 1993," *Survey of Current Business* 74 (May 1994): 50–61.

[a]Calculated as the percentage of cumulative investment outlays in 1987–92 accounted for by outlays on new establishments. Investment outlays for each year were deflated using the GDP deflator then summed over the years 1987–92.

ownership (i.e., intrafirm imports) and in terms of the geographic origin of the affiliates' imports.

For sample affiliates of the six major investing countries, table 6.8 presents aggregate figures on the share of imports sourced from the affiliates' foreign parent groups (their foreign parent companies plus other foreign companies with strong ownership ties to the parents)[25] in comparison with the share of imports originating in the investing country. In the table, affiliates with owners in Switzerland and Japan stand out as sourcing about nine-tenths of their imported inputs through intrafirm trade (line 1). Close to 90 percent of the imports by Japanese-owned affiliates originate in Japan, whereas about 75 percent of the imports by Swiss-owned affiliates originate in Switzerland (line 2).[26] Imports from the investing country also account for a dominant share of the imports by German- and Canadian-owned affiliates, with about three-fourths of the imports by German-owned affiliates representing intrafirm trade. In contrast, only about one-third of the imports by French- and British-owned affiliates originate in the investing country, and less than one-half of the imports by French-owned affiliates are sourced through intrafirm trade.

As shown in table 6.9, a large share of the imports by British- and French-owned affiliates are sourced from OECD countries other than the investing country (which can be taken to represent other "developed" countries). The share of imports originating in other OECD countries is particularly high for British- and French-owned affiliates in non-machinery-type industries, about 40 percent in each case. In machinery-type industries, almost one-half of the imports by French-owned affiliates are sourced from the developing and newly industrializing countries of East Asia. By way of contrast, Japanese-owned affiliates in machinery-type industries rely on Japan for 90 percent of their imported inputs, sourcing less than 5 percent of their imports from other East Asian countries.

6.6 Conclusion

The measures of content discussed in this paper, though subject to some limitations due to the consolidated nature of company data reports, are a useful aid to furthering our understanding of the relationship between foreign ownership and manufacturing production within the borders of the United States.

The measures reveal that domestic content for foreign-owned manufactur-

25. In addition to inputs actually produced by the affiliates' foreign parent companies, such intrafirm imports may include materials and components procured by the parents from unaffiliated suppliers for shipment to the affiliates.

26. As shown in line 3 of table 6.8, intrafirm imports by affiliates (which include imports from all members of a given affiliate's foreign parent group) need not originate in the country of ownership: e.g., only 52 percent of the intrafirm imports by British-owned affiliates are shipped from the United Kingdom. Line 4 shows that intrafirm imports do not account for all affiliate imports from the country of ownership; however, for five of the six major investing countries, more than 90 percent of the affiliates' imports from their respective home countries are through intrafirm trade.

Table 6.8 **Measures of Intrafirm Imports and Imports Sourced from Country of Ownership for Affiliates of Major Investing Countries**

Measure	Canada	France	Germany	Switzerland	United Kingdom	Japan
1. Intrafirm imports as a percentage of total imports by the investing country's affiliates	54.5	39.2	73.4	90.2	62.6	86.8
2. Imports from investing country as a percentage of total imports by the investing country's affiliates	65.7	29.5	69.4	76.4	35.3	88.1
3. Intrafirm imports from investing country as a percentage of total intrafirm imports by the investing country's affiliates	94.4	69.2	87.4	85.4	52.2	95.6
4. Intrafirm imports from investing country as a percentage of total imports from investing country by the investing country's affiliates	78.8	92.1	95.8	99.2	93.1	94.7

Note: Intrafirm imports are imports by affiliates from their foreign parent groups.

Table 6.9 **Geographic Origin of Imports by Manufacturing Affiliates of Major Investing Countries, 1992**

	Country of Ownership					
Origin	Canada	France	Germany	Switzerland	United Kingdom	Japan
Geographic Origin of Imports by Investing Country's Affiliates in All Manufacturing Industries						
All countries	100.0	100.0	100.0	100.0	100.0	100.0
Investing country	65.7	29.5	69.4	76.4	35.3	88.1
Other OECD countries[a]	16.6	31.1	25.7	18.5	40.2	4.0
Other Asia and Pacific[b]	2.5	23.5	2.9	–[c]	11.2	4.7
Latin America and other Western Hemisphere[d]	13.3	13.1	–[c]	3.3	10.2	–[c]
Other	1.9	2.8	–[c]	–[c]	3.0	–[c]
Geographic Origin of Imports by Investing Country's Affiliates in Machinery-Type Industries						
All countries	100.0	100.0	100.0	100.0	100.0	100.0
Investing country	–[c]	15.4	71.3	69.7	31.9	90.2
Other OECD countries[a]	1.7	–[c]	24.8	25.1	32.7	2.2
Other Asia and Pacific[b]	–[c]	44.8	2.4	–[c]	33.9	4.8
Latin America and other Western Hemisphere[d]	0.0	–[c]	1.5	–[c]	1.5	–[c]
Other	0.0	0.0	0.0	0.0	0.0	–[c]
Geographic Origin of Imports by Investing Country's Affiliates in Other Manufacturing Industries						
All countries	100.0	100.0	100.0	100.0	100.0	100.0
Investing country	59.3	44.7	65.6	79.2	36.1	67.2
Other OECD countries[a]	20.4	39.6	27.4	15.7	41.9	21.5
Other Asia and Pacific[b]	1.2	0.7	3.8	0.2	6.2	4.1
Latin America and other Western Hemisphere[d]	16.7	9.1	–[c]	–[c]	12.2	–[c]
Other	2.4	5.9	–[c]	–[c]	3.7	–[c]

[a]For affiliates of the investing country identified in the column heading, includes the other five major investing countries. Does not include Mexico, which became a member nation of the OECD in 1994.

[b]Excludes Japan, Australia, and New Zealand, which are member nations of the OECD.

[c]Suppressed to avoid disclosure of data of individual companies.

[d]Includes Mexico.

ing affiliates is generally very high but is substantially lower than that of domestically owned companies in a few machinery-type industries involving the assembly of manufactured components. In most such industries, domestic content for older affiliates has tended to increase over time.

An examination of the content measures by investing country reveals that Japanese- and German-owned affiliates tend to have lower domestic content, whereas British- and Canadian-owned affiliates tend to have higher domestic content, with the differences being particularly pronounced in machinery-type industries. Examining the geographic pattern of affiliate sourcing, Japanese-owned affiliates display a high tendency, whereas British-owned affiliates display a low tendency, to source their intermediate inputs from their respective home countries.

Appendix

Table 6A.1 Data by Industry on Sample of Affiliates Used in Study

Industry	Number of Affiliates in Sample	Share of Affiliate Sales Represented by Sample[a]
Manufacturing[b]	701	65.8
Food and kindred products	63	40.3
Textile products and apparel	32	59.7
Paper and allied products	29	82.8
Printing and publishing	25	78.2
Industrial chemicals and synthetics	41	65.6
Drugs	29	96.5
Other chemicals	31	81.5
Rubber products	6	4.3
Miscellaneous plastics products	25	54.3
Glass products	9	53.2
Stone, clay, and concrete products	39	79.2
Primary ferrous metals	31	72.8
Primary nonferrous metals	29	91.4
Fabricated metal products	48	72.2
Construction, mining, and materials handling machinery	20	55.8
Other nonelectrical machinery	56	66.3
Computer and office equipment	12	66.6
Household audio and video, and communications, equipment	12	55.7
Electronic components and accessories	30	69.0
Other electric and electronic equipment	28	50.2
Motor vehicles and equipment	34	60.9
Other transportation equipment	18	67.8
Instruments and related products	28	81.6
Other manufacturing	26	64.0

Note: Sample consists of affiliates reporting in the 1992 benchmark survey that had total assets, sales, or net income exceeding $50 million at the end of 1992, excluding those affiliates whose imports were not used primarily for further processing or manufacture by the affiliates.

[a]Sales by affiliates in sample as a percentage of sales by all affiliates covered in the 1992 benchmark survey.

[b]Excludes petroleum refining.

Table 6A.2 **Measures of Domestic Content of Production, Vertical Integration, and Foreign Sourcing of Purchased Inputs for Foreign-Owned Affiliates in Selected Machinery-Type Industries, by Major Investing Country, 1992**

		Foreign-Owned Affiliates			Ratio of Measure for Affiliates to Measure for U.S. Companies[a]		
Industry and Investing Country	Number of Affiliates	Domestic Content/ Total Output (%)	Value Added/ Total Output (%)	Imports/Total Purchased Inputs (%)	Domestic Content/ Total Output	Value Added/ Total Output	Imports/Total Purchased Inputs
Construction, mining, and materials handling machinery	20	75.5	28.6	34.3	0.83	0.88	2.47
Japanese-owned affiliates	8	54.7	16.2	54.1	0.60	0.50	3.90
Affiliates of all other investing countries	12	89.0	36.6	17.4	0.98	1.12	1.25
Other nonelectrical machinery	56	87.0	29.4	18.5	0.92	0.76	2.09
German-owned affiliates	14	79.1	28.4	29.2	0.84	0.73	3.31
Swiss-owned affiliates	7	85.3	37.6	23.5	0.90	0.97	2.67
British-owned affiliates	9	94.5	35.3	8.5	1.00	0.91	0.96
Japanese-owned affiliates	13	86.9	32.6	19.5	0.92	0.84	2.21
Affiliates of all other investing countries	13	84.0	18.8	19.7	0.89	0.48	2.24
Computer and office equipment	12	63.8	29.9	51.7	0.73	0.67	2.26
Japanese-owned affiliates	7	55.9	26.8	60.2	0.64	0.60	2.63
Affiliates of all other investing countries	5	89.6	40.2	17.5	1.02	0.90	0.76

(continued)

Table 6A.2 (continued)

		Foreign-Owned Affiliates			Ratio of Measure for Affiliates to Measure for U.S. Companies[a]		
Industry and Investing Country	Number of Affiliates	Domestic Content/ Total Output (%)	Value Added/ Total Output (%)	Imports/Total Purchased Inputs (%)	Domestic Content/ Total Output	Value Added/ Total Output	Imports/Total Purchased Inputs
Household audio and video, and communications, equipment	12	72.4	34.3	42.0	0.81	0.95	2.53
Japanese-owned affiliates	3	59.6	17.7	49.1	0.67	0.49	2.96
Affiliates of all other investing countries	9	73.1	35.1	41.5	0.82	0.97	2.51
Electronic components and accessories	30	72.4	30.3	39.6	0.83	0.70	1.78
Japanese-owned affiliates	15	69.7	30.1	43.3	0.80	0.69	1.95
Affiliates of all other investing countries	15	75.1	30.6	35.9	0.86	0.71	1.61
Other electric and electronic equipment	28	93.0	35.0	10.8	0.97	0.90	1.71
French-owned affiliates	6	96.0	42.7	7.0	1.00	1.09	1.11
German-owned affiliates	3	69.1	35.6	48.0	0.72	0.91	7.59
Japanese-owned affiliates	10	89.0	29.8	15.7	0.93	0.76	2.48
Affiliates of all other investing countries	9	94.1	34.5	9.1	0.98	0.88	1.43

Motor vehicles and equipment	34	66.4	17.5	40.8	0.80	0.64	1.70
Japanese-owned affiliates	22	62.9	15.8	44.0	0.76	0.58	1.83
Affiliates of all other investing countries	12	85.7	27.3	19.6	1.04	1.00	0.82
Instruments and related products	28	94.5	43.8	9.8	0.99	0.91	1.01
French-owned affiliates	3	95.4	40.8	7.7	1.00	0.85	0.80
German-owned affiliates	4	88.2	35.0	18.1	0.93	0.73	1.87
British-owned affiliates	8	97.1	47.2	5.4	1.02	0.98	0.56
Japanese-owned affiliates	6	82.7	29.2	24.5	0.87	0.61	2.53
Affiliates of all other investing countries	7	90.2	39.2	16.1	0.95	0.81	1.67

[a]Ratio of measure for affiliates of given investing country to aggregate measure for domestically owned U.S. companies in industry of the affiliates.

References

Aoki, Masahiko. 1990. Toward an economic model of the Japanese firm. *Journal of Economic Literature* 28 (March): 1–27.

Caves, Richard E. 1982. *Multinational enterprise and economic analysis.* Cambridge: Cambridge University Press.

Dunning, John H. 1993. *Multinational enterprises and the global economy.* Workingham, England: Addison-Wesley.

Economic report of the president. 1997. Washington, D.C.: Government Printing Office, February.

Lowe, Jeffrey H. 1990. Gross product of U.S. affiliates of foreign companies, 1977–87. *Survey of Current Business* 70 (June): 45–53.

Mataloni, Raymond J., Jr., and Lee Goldberg. 1994. Gross product of U.S. multinational companies, 1977–91. *Survey of Current Business* 74 (February): 42–63.

McAlesse, Dermot, and Donogh McDonald. 1978. Employment growth and the development of linkages in foreign-owned domestic manufacturing enterprises. *Oxford Bulletin of Economics and Statistics* 40 (November): 321–39.

U.S. Department of Commerce. Bureau of Economic Analysis. 1992. *Foreign direct investment in the United States: Establishment data for 1987.* Washington, D.C.: Government Printing Office, June.

———. 1994. *Foreign direct investment in the United States: Establishment data for manufacturing, 1991.* Washington, D.C.: Government Printing Office, November.

———. 1995. *Foreign direct investment in the United States: 1992 Benchmark survey, final results.* Washington, D.C.: Government Printing Office, September.

Zeile, William J. 1993. Merchandise trade of U.S. affiliates of foreign companies. *Survey of Current Business* 73 (October): 52–65.

Comment David L. Hummels

This paper seeks to improve what we know about the domestic content of production for foreign-owned manufacturing affiliates. The domestic content of production may have important welfare effects, especially if there are technological externalities in the linkages between manufacturing affiliates and upstream suppliers of components. This is an important issue if foreign-owned affiliates choose to locate in the United States to avoid trade restrictions on final assembled goods while contributing little to the domestic economy in the way of linkages.

Previous studies of the domestic content of foreign-owned affiliates found domestic content to be high and reliance on imports for intermediate inputs to be low. Early work suffered from two problems. First, inclusion of retail enterprises in the affiliate data failed to distinguish between imports intended for furthering manufacturing and those intended for direct sale without additional

David L. Hummels is assistant professor of economics at the University of Chicago Graduate School of Business.

processing. Second, excessive aggregation masked the importance of foreign inputs in certain high-technology sectors. The contribution here is to separate affiliates engaged primarily in retail trade from those that engage in domestic manufacturing and also to disaggregate affiliates by sector, age, and nation of origin in order to pick out characteristics that seem to matter for import behavior.

The author provides a commendably rich array of data for readers to examine, too much to consider properly here. I will focus on some of the main results of this disaggregation, and their implications. In most sectors, domestic content seems to be quite high in absolute terms and close to the domestic content of production for U.S.-owned firms (see table 6.1). However, domestic content is much lower among machinery-type firms.

Of the many numbers in table 6.1, the last columns showing the ratios of domestic content, value added, and import usage for foreign-owned to U.S.-owned firms are most useful. Without knowing the location of world input supplies, or the importance of nontraded inputs in production, it is not possible to say what an "appropriate" quantity of domestic content would be. However, it might be instructive to examine the measures of imported to total inputs in the context of a baseline of expected import dependence. One way is to use a gravity model of trade that relates trade volumes to relative world shares in production and consumption. That is, if the United States produces a large world share of an input, we would expect import dependence (among both affiliates and domestic firms) to be lower for industries that use that input.

Regarding the finding that machinery-type industries have relatively low levels of domestic content, there is good and bad news. The bad news is that if any sector were likely to be important for linkages through upstream suppliers, we would expect it to be machinery. So this finding may be a matter of some concern. The good news is that the low levels of domestic content are mostly due to foreign-owned affiliates creating only a small amount of value added.

Why is this good news? Well, if upstream linkages are important, it helps domestic component suppliers very little if foreign-owned affiliates are entirely self-contained. Put another way, if value added is a good indicator of vertical integration, affiliates with high value added require few inputs from domestic suppliers—there will be no linkages. It may be that foreign-owned affiliates begin life heavily dependent on foreign suppliers for components and gradually switch to domestic suppliers. As these affiliates locate domestic sources of component production over time, their low degree of vertical integration may offer more profound effects for upstream linkages.

Unhappily, the data on domestic content over time casts some doubt on this proposition. Tables 6.3 and 6.4 show that young firms (defined as those established or acquired since the 1987 benchmark study) appear to have higher domestic content than do older firms. However, these older firms do show a tendency to move toward greater domestic content over time. The author ascribes this result to the predominance of acquisitions, rather than greenfield investment, as a method of foreign direct investment. This seems plausible, but I will offer some additional explanations.

First, it may be that there is some trend in the relative cost of domestic versus foreign sourcing. For example, appreciation in the yen or mounting protectionism make the use of domestic sources more attractive. If new entrants are relatively free to choose domestic rather than foreign supply sources, they will immediately choose a higher domestic content mix. Because of existing contracts, older firms will adjust to changing costs more slowly and have lower domestic content initially. Over time, however, these differences will disappear as older firms move to increase domestic content as well.

A second possibility is that domestic content is increasing because entire supply networks, and not just final stages of production, are moving to the United States. That is, domestic content as measured by the location of the plants is increasing, but domestic content as measured by ownership (say, U.S. vs. Japanese) is not.

Finally, the author separates affiliates by country of origin and finds that Japanese affiliates tend to be low-end outliers with respect to domestic content, while firms from the United Kingdom are high-end outliers. It is difficult to tell why this is exactly. It may indicate fundamentally different behavior on the part of Japanese firms, or it may merely reflect that Japanese firms are younger and tend to engage in greenfield investments in machinery-type industries. It may be useful to see whether these results are due to auto industry effects and also to see how U.S. affiliates abroad behave.

As a final note on geographic differences, there are some very interesting results in tables 6.8 and 6.9 on the locations from which foreign-owned affiliates source their inputs. Many countries engage in bilateral sourcing; for example, Japanese parents in Japan send components to Japanese affiliates in the United States. However, France and the United Kingdom are notable for their reliance on third-country sources. It would be interesting to further study which third countries in particular are being used and how this varies over industries. Canada and Mexico are unique in their geography and trade relationships with the United States. It would be interesting to examine the degree to which foreign-owned affiliates in these countries are used as component suppliers for affiliates in the United States. As NAFTA data become available, it will be worthwhile to measure the degree to which these countries are being used to jump trade barriers and achieve higher North American content.

7 Comparing Wages, Skills, and Productivity between Domestically and Foreign-Owned Manufacturing Establishments in the United States

Mark E. Doms and J. Bradford Jensen

Over the past 20 years, there has been a several-fold increase in the foreign ownership of U.S. assets. This increase has generated interest, sometimes concern, over the effects of foreign direct investment (FDI) on the economy (see Graham and Krugman 1989; Froot and Stein 1991; McCulloch 1993). The interest has focused on the nature of employment opportunities provided by foreign-owned plants and their contribution to productivity. How do foreign plants compare to domestically owned plants in terms of wages and productivity? If foreign companies can overcome the costs of entering the U.S. market, this might signal that these companies have specific advantages, such as superior product design, greater production efficiency, and advanced marketing skill, relative to their domestically owned competitors. As a result, these foreign companies might outperform domestically owned plants in a number of respects, including productivity and wages. Alternatively, foreign firms might keep most of their high value-added operations in their home countries, with their U.S. operations consisting primarily of lower value-added assembly operations. In this case, foreign-owned establishments in the United States would have relatively low skilled workers, and hence relatively low wages, and not necessarily high productivity. Whichever case predominates, these arguments suggest that establishments owned by multinational corporations, regardless of

Mark E. Doms is an economist in the Industrial Output Section of the Board of Governors of the Federal Reserve System. J. Bradford Jensen is research scientist at the H. John Heinz III School of Public Policy and Management at Carnegie Mellon University and executive director of the Carnegie Mellon Census Research Data Center.

The authors thank Betty Barker and the Bureau of Economic Analysis for access to the Foreign Direct Investment Survey. They thank Keith Head, Robert McGuckin, William Zeile, conference participants, and the editors for helpful suggestions. The views expressed in this paper are the authors' and do not necessarily reflect those of the Census Bureau or the Federal Reserve Board of Governors.

country of ownership, might differ from establishments owned by companies with only domestic operations.

We compare the operating characteristics of foreign-owned and domestically owned plants using detailed data from a large number of U.S. manufacturing establishments. We present evidence on how foreign-owned plants compare to domestically owned plants in terms of employment, wages, productivity, capital intensity, and technology. Previously, researchers have identified differences between foreign-owned plants and domestically owned plants using more aggregated data. Using industry-level data, Howenstine and Zeile (1992) suggest that foreign-owned plants pay higher wages than domestically owned establishments. Further, foreign-owned plants account for a larger share of employment in industries that are capital intensive and skilled labor intensive. This research uses industry-level data, which might hide considerable plant-level heterogeneity within the class of foreign- and domestically owned plants.

The heterogeneity across establishments within industries is substantial. In fact, within-industry variance in wages and productivity exceeds the interindustry variance (for wages, see Davis and Haltiwanger 1991; and for productivity, see Baily, Hulten, and Campbell 1992). Thus, using plant-level data to examine differences across plants within an industry offers advantages over industry-level data. Howenstine and Zeile (1994) use plant- and subindustry-level data from the Annual Survey of Manufactures for 1989 and 1990 and find that foreign-owned plants are larger, more capital intensive, and more productive and pay higher wages than domestically owned plants. Globerman, Ries, and Vertinsky (1994) use Canadian plant-level data and examine the economic performance of foreign affiliates in Canada. They find that foreign affiliate plants are more productive than Canadian-owned plants but that when other plant characteristics (size, capital intensity, share of nonproduction workers, and share of male workers) are controlled for, these differences disappear. Further, Globerman et al. do not find statistically significant differences in performance between foreign-owned Canadian plants by country of ownership.

In this paper, we make use of newly available manufacturing plant-level data for 1987 (approximately 115,000 observations) that allow us to control for industry, size, age, and location and more rigorously test for differences between the operating characteristics of foreign- and domestically owned plants than previous research. Our initial results suggest that even controlling for four-digit industry, state, plant age, and plant size, foreign-owned plants are more productive, rely relatively more on capital than labor, and pay higher wages than domestically owned plants.

To investigate the sources of the observed differences between foreign- and domestically owned plants, we suggest a more useful categorization of ownership. We classify plants based on the nationality of ownership, firm size, and whether U.S.-owned plants belong to firms that have significant assets outside the United States. This allows us to compare plants of foreign multinationals to plants of U.S. multinationals, plants of large domestically oriented firms, and plants of small U.S. firms. When we compare across these four categories, we find different results. As a group, the U.S. multinationals are the most productive, biggest, and most capital intensive and pay the highest wages. The foreign multinationals follow closely in terms of pay and productivity, followed by large domestically oriented plants.

These results suggest that multinational firms, whether foreign or domestic, have the most productive, most capital intensive, highest paying plants. Thus, comparing foreign-owned plants to all domestic plants is in some ways comparing apples and oranges. Plants owned by multinationals tend to be much bigger than the average plant in the United States and have the characteristics associated with size. Thus, it is true that foreign-owned plants have desirable characteristics relative to the whole of U.S. manufacturing. However, when compared to plants owned by U.S. multinationals, foreign-owned plants do not compare as favorably. Further, the results are consistent with the theory that firm-specific advantages, like productivity, enable firms, whether U.S. or foreign, to overcome the barriers to direct foreign investment.

The rest of the paper is organized as follows. In the next section we describe the 1987 Foreign Direct Investment Survey–Census of Manufactures link and our four firm classifications. Section 7.2 focuses on regression results comparing foreign- and domestically owned establishments for basic operating characteristics of establishments—wages, worker mix, productivity. Section 7.3 extends the analysis of section 7.2 by segregating domestic firms into three categories. Sections 7.4 and 7.5 examine the differences by country of ownership and the use of advanced manufacturing technologies in foreign-owned plants. Section 7.6 concludes.

7.1 Data Description

This section describes the data used in the subsequent analysis. The data set used in this paper is a combination of several establishment-level data sets: the 1987 Census of Manufactures (CM), 1987 Central Administrative Offices and Auxiliary Establishment Survey, 1988 Survey of Manufacturing Technology (SMT), and the 1987 Bureau of Economic Analysis (BEA) Foreign Direct Investment Survey. Through a joint project between BEA and the Bureau of the Census, the 1987 FDI Survey was linked to the 1987 Standard Statistical Establishment List, of which the 1987 CM, 1988 SMT, and Auxiliary Reports are subsets.[1] The CM provides information on shipments, value added, capital, production workers, nonproduction workers, wages, and other types of production information. The CM has this data for approximately 200,000 establish-

1. For more information on the Census-BEA link, see U.S. Department of Commerce (1992).

ments. The SMT provides information on the use of 17 advanced manufacturing technologies for a sample of approximately 10,000 manufacturing establishments.

In this paper we examine how labor productivity, the mix of production workers and nonproduction workers, and the wages of production and nonproduction workers vary according to whether establishments are domestically or foreign owned. Some of these variables require accurate measures of nonproduction workers. One problem that arises is that nonproduction workers involved in production might not be physically located at manufacturing establishments. Instead, some nonproduction workers might be located at manufacturing auxiliary establishments. Manufacturing auxiliaries are those establishments that do not manufacture goods but are the locations for such things as R&D labs, headquarters, and data-processing centers. The measurement problem that arises is that in some firms these auxiliary functions are performed at manufacturing sites while in other firms these functions are performed at auxiliary establishments. If the nonproduction workers located at auxiliaries are excluded, then labor productivity will be biased upward, and nonproduction worker wages will most likely be biased downward since auxiliaries tend to pay above average wages. One reason why the issue of nonproduction workers is of particular interest in this paper is that the mix of workers in manufacturing operations gives some indication of the activities being performed in the country.

We present results with and without adjustments for auxiliary employment.[2] We use data from the 1987 Central Administrative Offices and Auxiliary Establishment Survey to make the auxiliary adjustments. First, for each firm we compute the total number of nonproduction workers and their salaries (each firm might have more than one manufacturing auxiliary) located in manufacturing auxiliaries. Second, we distribute these auxiliary workers and their wages across all manufacturing establishments of the firm. The proportion of auxiliary workers and auxiliary wage bill that an establishment receives depends on the share of the firm's nonproduction workers that establishment has. For instance, if an establishment has 30 percent of the firm's nonproduction workers who are employed at manufacturing establishments, we allocate to that plant 30 percent of the firm's auxiliary workers.

The FDI data that we currently have access to provide the country of ultimate beneficial ownership for the enterprise to which each establishment belongs. In the FDI Survey, "a U.S. affiliate is a U.S. business enterprise that is owned 10 percent or more, directly or indirectly, by a foreign person." Unfortunately, we do not have degree of foreign ownership. Therefore, in the analysis that follows, we treat all foreign-owned establishments equally.

In our analysis, there is significant sample attrition in terms of the number

2. This assuages, to some extent, a criticism of work that uses U.S. establishment-level manufacturing data, namely, that nonproduction workers are being undercounted in multiplant firms.

of establishments and, to a much lesser degree, in terms of manufacturing employment. The 1987 population of manufacturing establishments in the United States was approximately 350,000. About 200,000 of these establishments were mailed a 1987 Census of Manufactures form that requested information on shipments, labor, wages, and capital. The production data for the other 150,000 records, known as administrative records, are imputed and therefore cannot be used in our analysis. Administrative records almost always have fewer than five employees. The next largest source of attrition is the dropping of records with impute flags. An impute flag is set if any one of the following four variables was not reported by the establishment: employment, salaries and wages, materials, and total value of shipments. We dropped all records with impute flags. These records tend to be below average in terms of size. Table 7.1 reports the number of establishments, employment, average employment, and average earnings for the 1987 CM and some basic statistics for our final sample.

We also make use of the 1987 Large Company Survey (ES9100). The ES9100 is mailed to all enterprises with more than 500 employees. We use the ES9100 to identify whether domestically owned firms have significant foreign assets. Firms are asked to report "all assets in foreign countries, and U.S. possessions, regardless of type." Unfortunately, we do not know the nature of these assets. We divide foreign assets by total assets, and if the ratio of foreign to total assets is greater than 10 percent, we classify the firm as having foreign exposure (or as a U.S. multinational, for short).[3] If the ratio is less than 10 percent, we classify the firm as being a large U.S. firm without foreign exposure (or a large domestic firm). Unfortunately, the ES9100 is only mailed to firms with more than 500 employees, so there is a significant number of establishments for which we do not have foreign asset information. We classify firms with fewer than 500 employees as small U.S. firms. Table 7.1 also presents the breakdown of establishments by domestic ownership type.

7.2 U.S.-Owned Establishments Compared to Foreign-Owned Establishments

We begin by comparing the plant characteristics of U.S.-owned establishments to foreign-owned establishments. The discussion of foreign ownership of manufacturing facilities has typically focused on the nature of employment opportunities. Some suggest that foreign-owned plants undertake a set of activities different from that pursued by domestic plants and therefore use a different class of workers, pay lower wages, and are less productive than domestically owned plants. Other theories of FDI suggest that foreign-owned plants

3. Note that this definition differs from BEA's definition of a "parent" multinational. BEA defines a parent as any U.S. enterprise that owns 10 percent or more of a foreign entity. We do not observe the nature of the foreign assets in the ES9100. For more analysis of the sensitivity of this definition of U.S. "multinational" see Doms and Jensen (1997).

Table 7.1 Basic Sample Statistics: Comparison between Samples and Populations

Sample or Population	Number of Establishments	Total Employment	Average Employment per Establishment	Average Annual Earnings[a]
1987 CM manufacturing population	358,941	17,716,649	49.4	19.08
Total sample	115,139	12,420,340	107.9	21.44
Foreign population	7,077	1,180,686	168.8	26.55
Foreign sample	4,463	853,338	191.2	24.95
Domestic population	351,864	16,535,963	47.0	18.92
Domestic sample	110,676	11,567,002	104.5	21.30
Small domestic	87,030	3,902,625	44.8	20.78
Large domestic	15,920	4,229,001	265.6	21.87
U.S. multinational	7,726	3,435,376	444.6	25.90

[a]In thousands of dollars per employee.

belong to firms that have specific advantages that enable them to invest in new markets. These advantages include superior product design, greater production efficiency, and advanced marketing skill. We investigate these claims by comparing measures of average annual wages, skill mix, capital-labor ratios, and productivity between foreign-owned establishments and domestically owned establishments. Table 7.2 provides more precise definitions of the operating characteristics that we use in our comparisons.

In table 7.1 we saw that foreign-owned plants are larger than domestically owned plants. Table 7.3 reports plant means and standard deviations for the operating characteristics of each class of plant. We see that foreign-owned plants do differ from domestically owned plants. Foreign-owned plants pay higher wages to both production workers and nonproduction workers. Production workers in domestic plants average about $18,760 in earnings in 1987, while production workers in foreign plants average about $22,290 in 1987.

The difference in earnings of nonproduction workers is not as large. Without taking auxiliary employment into account, foreign plants pay nonproduction workers about $32,100 a year and domestically owned plants pay about $30,370. When we adjust for nonproduction worker employment at auxiliary establishments, the difference between domestically owned and foreign-owned establishments declines. What is the source of these earnings differentials?

One possibility is differences in human capital. Beyond paying higher wages, foreign-owned establishments are more nonproduction worker intensive than domestic plants, whether auxiliary employment is included or not. Foreign-owned plants use a higher share of nonproduction, or skilled, workers. This in itself would not explain the wage differential for the different categories of workers. But if, in addition to using more nonproduction workers,

Table 7.2 **Variable Definitions**

Variable Name	Definition
	A. Dependent Variables
Production worker wages	Annual salaries (thousand $) for production workers/ number of production workers
Nonproduction worker wages (1)	Annual salaries (thousand $) for nonproduction workers/ number of nonproduction workers
Nonproduction worker wages (2)	Same as Nonproduction worker wages (1) except with an adjustment made for employment and payroll in auxiliaries
Production workers/Total employment (1)	Number of production workers/total employment
Production workers/Total employment (2)	Number of production workers/total employment, where total employment is adjusted for auxiliary employment
Capital/Employment (1)	Book value of machinery and building assets (thousand $)/total employment
Capital/Employment (2)	Book value of machinery and building assets (thousand $)/total employment, where total employment is adjusted for auxiliary employment
Value added/Employment (1)	Value added (thousand $)/total employment
Value added/Employment (2)	Value added (thousand $)/total employment, where total employment is adjusted for auxiliary employment
TFP-R	Natural logarithm of total factor productivity calculated from using the residual from a value-added Cobb-Douglas production function[a]
TFP-FS	Natural logarithm of total factor productivity calculated using a factor share method[b]
	B. Independent Variables
Plant size	Categorical variable band on total plant employment (TE): Size class 1: $1 \leq TE < 50$ Size class 2: $50 \leq TE < 100$ Size class 3: $100 \leq TE < 250$ Size class 4: $250 \leq TE < 500$ Size class 5: $500 \leq TE < 1{,}000$ Size class 6: $1{,}000 \leq TE < 2{,}500$ Size class 7: $2{,}500 \leq TE$ (omitted category)
Plant age	Categorical variable based on year of first CM appearance: Age class 63: First appearance in census is 1963 Age class 67: First appearance in census is 1967 Age class 72: First appearance in census is 1972 Age class 77: First appearance in census is 1977 Age class 82: First appearance in census is 1982 Age class 87: First appearance in census is 1987 (omitted category)
Plant industry	Dummy variables representing four-digit industry

(*continued*)

Table 7.2 (continued)

Variable Name	Definition
	B. Independent Variables
Plant location	Dummy variable representing state in which plant is located

[a]The residual measure is calculated using a Cobb-Douglas specification with capital, labor, and materials (including parts, fuels, and services) included as inputs. The regression coefficients are from four-digit industry regressions.

[b]The factor share method is calculated using the median factor shares of capital, labor, and materials (including parts, fuels, and services) from the four-digit industry. This method is similar to that used in Baily et al. (1992).

Table 7.3 **Variable Means by Foreign and Domestic Ownership**

Variable	Domestic	Foreign
Production worker wages (thousand $)	18.76	22.29
	(8.13)	(8.57)
Nonproduction worker wages (1) (thousand $)	30.37	32.10
	(15.74)	(12.44)
Nonproduction worker wages (2) (thousand $)	32.49	32.94
	(11.06)	(10.58)
Production workers/Total employment (1)	0.73	0.68
	(0.19)	(0.21)
Production workers/Total employment (2)	0.72	0.63
	(0.20)	(0.22)
Capital/Employment (1) (thousand $)	39.34	103.10
	(91.1)	(218.40)
Capital/Employment (2) (thousand $)	36.84	91.83
	(75.9)	(193.49)
Value added/Employment (1) (thousand $)	56.50	109.48
	(77.9)	(160.35)
Value added/Employment (2) (thousand $)	53.75	96.55
	(66.73)	(137.77)
TRP-R	.02	.06
	(.29)	(.28)
TFP-FS	.04	.06
	(.36)	(.36)

Note: See table 7.2 for variable definitions. Numbers in parentheses are standard deviations.

foreign-owned plants also used more skilled or more educated workers within a category, this might explain the observed higher wages within categories. Supporting this claim is Troske (1994), who finds that worker characteristics account for a significant portion of observed cross-plant wage differentials in a sample of plants from the 1987 CM. Unfortunately, we do not have any additional information on the workers in our establishments. Another possibility is that foreign-owned plants pay a wage premium to deter unionization. Although we cannot test this hypothesis, we include controls for state and industry.

Foreign-owned plants are more capital intensive and more productive. Foreign-owned plants average approximately $103,000 in capital assets per employee (without adjusting for auxiliary employment), while domestic plants average about $40,000 in capital assets per employee. After adjusting for auxiliary employment, the differential is still quite large, though reduced. Foreign-owned plants have higher labor productivity (which might be due to the higher capital-labor ratio at foreign plants) and higher total factor productivity (TFP), which takes into account the higher capital-labor ratio.

These results suggest that foreign plants differ significantly from domestic plants. However, other studies, such as Howenstine and Zeile (1992, 1994), show that foreign-owned plants are concentrated in industries that are more capital intensive, pay higher wages, and are more productive. Thus, the observed differences described above could be due to industry composition effects. Column (1) of table 7.4 presents regression results comparing foreign-owned plants to domestically owned plants without industry, location, age, or size controls.[4] The regression coefficients in column (1) of table 7.4 tell the same story as the means reported in table 7.3. Foreign-owned plants are significantly more capital intensive, are more productive, and pay higher wages, but this may be due to composition effects. To control for possible composition effects, we include controls for plant size, industry, plant age, and plant location.[5] In column (2), we present regression results that control for these other plant characteristics. When we include controls for plant size, industry (four-digit), plant age, and plant location (state), the observed differences between foreign-owned and domestically owned plants decrease but persist.

The equations controlling for size, age, industry, and location still show that foreign-owned plants pay about 7 percent more to production workers and 1 to 2 percent more to nonproduction workers. Foreign-owned plants are about 30 percent more capital intensive and have about 20 percent higher labor productivity than domestically owned plants of the same age and size, in the same location and industry. In terms of TFP, foreign-owned plants are about 2 to 4 percent more productive. Further, foreign-owned plants use fewer production workers than domestically owned plants.

4. The regression coefficients reported in col. (1) of table 7.4 are from a regression of the dependent variable on an intercept term and a dummy variable that is one if the establishment is foreign owned. These results represent the mean differences between foreign-owned plants and domestically owned plants. See the appendix for a more detailed description of the specification.

5. The regression coefficients reported in col. (2) of table 7.4 are the coefficients from a dummy variable representing whether a plant is foreign owned. The specification also includes controls for plant size, plant age, plant industry, and plant location. We include as controls seven plant-size dummy variables based on employment at the plant. We choose this form of controls as it allows more flexibility than imposing a linear restriction by including a continuous measure of plant employment. We control for plant age by including a categorical variable representing the first CM in which the plant appears. We also include dummy variables for four-digit industry and state. See the appendix for a more detailed description of the specification.

Table 7.4 **Differences between Domestically and Foreign-Owned Establishments**

Dependent Variable	Foreign Owned No Controls (1)	Foreign Owned With Controls (2)	Foreign Owned Controls + K/L[a] (3)
log Production worker wages	.190	.073	.038
	(.007)	(.006)	(.006)
log Nonproduction worker wages (1)	.104	.012	−.020
	(.008)	(.008)	(.008)
log Nonproduction worker wages (2)	.130	.026	−.005
	(.008)	(.008)	(.008)
Production workers/Total employment (1)	−.052	−.020	−.018
	(.003)	(.003)	(.003)
Production workers/Total employment (2)	−.084	−.031	−.029
	(.003)	(.003)	(.003)
log Capital/Employment (1)	.941	.332	
	(.018)	(.015)	
log Capital/Employment (2)	.877	.308	
	(.017)	(.014)	
log Value added/Employment (1)	.537	.211	.134
	(.010)	(.009)	(.008)
log Value added/Employment (2)	.473	.186	.118
	(.010)	(.009)	(.008)
TFP-R	.041	.037	
	(.004)	(.005)	
TFP-FS	.024	.023	
	(.006)	(.006)	

Note: The numbers are regression coefficients from linear models that do and do not control for establishment size, four-digit industry, plant age, and state. The omitted group is domestically owned establishments. Number of observations is approximately 115,000. Numbers in parentheses are standard errors.

[a]K/L = capital-labor ratio (capital intensity).

Following Globerman et al. (1994), we also include the capital-labor ratio as a control variable. Globerman et al. find that when they include size, capital intensity, and percentage of males in the plant,[6] the observable labor productivity difference between Canadian and foreign-owned plants becomes statistically insignificant. We report the results of including capital intensity among the controls in column (3) of table 7.4.[7] The differences are reduced, but the differential for productivity is still positive and statistically significant. Including the capital-labor ratio also reduces the observed wage premium to produc-

6. We cannot replicate the percentage of males in the plant as we do not know the composition of workers by gender in the plant.

7. We do not include the capital-labor ratio in the TFP regressions as the capital and labor inputs are already controlled for in a less restrictive manner.

tion workers, but it is still positive and statistically significant at about 3.8 percent.

These results suggest that the differences between foreign- and domestically owned plants are partially the result of industry, size, age, and location effects. Including controls for these effects reduces the observed differences between domestically and foreign-owned plants. However, the differences do not disappear. Even after controlling for these effects, foreign-owned plants still have superior operating characteristics relative to domestic plants.

The results suggest that some of the fears expressed over FDI are unwarranted. Foreign-owned plants are more capital intensive, are more productive, pay higher wages, and use a higher proportion of nonproduction workers than the average U.S.-owned plant. Further, although some of the differences between foreign-owned and domestically owned plants are the result of industry composition effects, foreign-owned plants still have superior operating characteristics compared to domestically owned plants controlling for industry, state, age, and size. While these results are suggestive of the impact of foreign-owned plants on the domestic economy, the results do not speak to the potential sources of the different operating characteristics. In section 7.3 we further decompose the plants by ownership type to investigate potential sources of the differences in operating characteristics.

7.3 Foreign-Owned Establishments Compared to U.S. Multinational Establishments

In section 7.2 we compared foreign-owned plants to all domestically owned plants. For some purposes, this is the relevant comparison. However, in trying to uncover the sources of these differences, a more detailed comparison might prove fruitful. According to theories of multinational investment, firms that engage in FDI have some firm-specific advantages that allow them to overcome the hurdles of FDI. Thus, we might expect that plants owned by foreign multinational corporations would be more productive than the average domestically owned plant. However, if this theory of FDI is correct, we would expect to find that plants owned by U.S. multinational corporations would also have these superior characteristics. To investigate this possibility, we further divide our sample and compare plants owned by U.S. multinationals to foreign-owned plants.

We divide plants into four categories: (1) plants owned by foreign companies, (2) plants owned by U.S. firms with fewer than 500 employees, (3) plants owned by U.S. firms with more than 500 employees without significant foreign assets, and (4) plants owned by U.S. firms with more than 500 employees and foreign assets comprising more than 10 percent of total assets. For ease of exposition, we call the first group "foreign-owned plants," the second group "small U.S. firm plants," the third group "large domestic firm plants," and the fourth group "U.S. multinationals."

Table 7.5 Differences between Foreign-Owned Establishments and Domestic Establishments by Domestic Plant Type

	Plant Type		
Dependent Variable	Foreign Owned	Large Domestic Firm	Small U.S. Firm
log Production worker wages	−.029	−.069	−.152
	(.007)	(.005)	(.005)
log Nonproduction worker wages (1)	−.004	−.025	−.020
	(.010)	(.007)	(.007)
log Nonproduction worker wages (2)	−.039	−.050	−.095
	(.010)	(.007)	(.007)
Production workers/Total employment (1)	−.021	.008	−.006
	(.003)	(.002)	(.002)
Production workers/Total employment (2)	.009	.036	.056
	(.003)	(.003)	(.002)
log Capital/Employment (1)	−.062	−.212	−.605
	(.017)	(.013)	(.012)
log Capital/Employment (2)	−.006	−.156	−.488
	(.017)	(.013)	(.012)
log Value added/Employment (1)	−.082	−.166	−.446
	(.010)	(.008)	(.007)
log Value added/Employment (2)	−.026	−.110	−.329
	(.010)	(.007)	(.007)
TFP-R	−.036	−.042	−.111
	(.006)	(.004)	(.004)
TFP-FS	−.024	−.024	−.073
	(.007)	(.005)	(.005)

Note: All numbers are regression coefficients from linear models that control for establishment size, four-digit industry, plant age, and state. Number of observations is approximately 115,000. Omitted plant type is U.S. multinational. Numbers in parentheses are standard errors.

In table 7.5 we present regressions comparing plant characteristics for the four plant types (plants of U.S. multinationals is the omitted category). Plants of U.S. multinationals pay the highest wages to both production and nonproduction workers. Production workers are paid 2.9 percent less at foreign-owned plants, 6.9 percent less at large domestic firm plants, and 15.2 percent less at small U.S. firm plants relative to U.S. multinationals. Nonproduction workers at U.S. multinationals do not enjoy as large a pay premium as production workers; the differential ranges from 0.4 percent lower at foreign-owned plants to 2.0 percent lower at small U.S. firm plants (when auxiliary employment is not included), and 3.9 percent lower at foreign-owned plants to 9.5 percent lower for small U.S. firm plants (when auxiliary employment is included).[8]

8. The nonproduction wage differential increases when auxiliary employment is included because large firms tend to have more auxiliary employment and auxiliaries have above average wages.

Plants owned by U.S. multinationals are also the most capital intensive. The capital-labor ratio of foreign-owned plants is 6.2 percent lower than that of U.S. multinational plants. Plants of large domestic firms have a 21.2 percent lower capital-labor ratio, and plants of small U.S. firms have a 60.5 percent lower capital-labor ratio. When employment at auxiliary establishments is included in total employment, the results change. With auxiliary employment included, foreign-owned plants are not statistically different from plants of U.S. multinationals in terms of capital-labor ratios. Plants of large and small U.S. firms still have lower capital-labor ratios, although the differences have decreased to 15.6 percent lower and 48.8 percent lower, respectively. The addition of auxiliary employment increases employment for plants of U.S. multinationals the most. Thus, the capital-labor ratio at these plants decreases relative to the other plant classes when auxiliary employment is included.

In terms of labor productivity and TFP, plants of U.S. multinationals are the most productive. Labor productivity (without adjusting for auxiliary employment) is 8.2 percent lower at foreign-owned plants than at plants of U.S. multinationals. Labor productivity is even lower at plants of large domestic firms, 16.6 percent lower, and lower still at plants of small U.S. firms, 44.6 percent lower. When auxiliary employment is included, the differentials decrease but are still significant. For TFP, the story is much the same. Foreign-owned firms have 3.6 percent lower TFP than plants of U.S. multinationals. For plants of domestic firms, plants of large firms have 4.2 percent lower TFP and plants of small firms have 11.1 percent lower TFP. Again, when auxiliary employment is included, the productivity differentials decrease but are still significant.

These results, and the results from section 7.2, suggest that while foreign-owned plants do indeed have different, and in many ways superior, characteristics compared to the average U.S.-owned plant, there is considerable heterogeneity within the class of U.S.-owned plants. When we divide U.S.-owned plants and look at plants of U.S. multinationals, we see that they compare favorably with foreign-owned plants and with all other domestically owned plants. Further, the results suggest that the plants of multinationals, whether U.S. or foreign, are the most alike and possess superior operating characteristics. These results suggest that plants of multinational corporations are the most productive, are the most capital intensive, and pay the highest wages. This finding is consistent with the notion that multinationals possess firm-specific advantages, whether superior product design, greater production efficiency, or advanced marketing skill, that enable them to overcome the barriers to FDI.

7.4 Comparing Plant Characteristics Based on Country of Ownership

We also break out the plants by country of ownership. Vernon (1993) suggests that in the past researchers have found it useful to distinguish multinational enterprises according to their national bases. He further suggests that this dimension will become less useful in the future. We examine differences in the operating characteristics of foreign-owned plants by country of ownership.

Table 7.6 presents the wage, labor mix, capital-labor ratio, and productivity results. One interesting feature is that no country compares favorably with plants owned by U.S. multinationals. Further, plants owned by Japanese firms do not seem to perform as well as might be expected based on popular perceptions. Plants owned by Japanese firms have the lowest labor productivity of foreign-owned plants and the lowest and second lowest measured TFP.[9] These data are from 1987. Much of the Japanese investment in the United States was done in the early 1980s. While we control for plant age, using the year of the first CM that the plant appears in as a proxy for age, this might not adequately control for age effects.[10] Thus, it is possible that the low productivity numbers for Japan reflect start-up costs. In terms of labor market characteristics, Japan and Australia are again relatively poor performers. Both pay their production workers less than other foreign-owned plants. While plants owned by multinationals from these countries exhibit lower productivity and production worker wages relative to plants owned by other multinationals, they compare favorably to nonmultinational domestically owned plants.

7.5 Technology Use at Foreign- and Domestically Owned Plants

We examine the use of advanced technologies at foreign-owned and domestically owned plants. One potential advantage of FDI is technology transfer. If foreign plants are more technologically advanced than domestic plants, these plants might produce technological spillovers. We use data from the Survey of Manufacturing Technology to examine technology use in domestically and foreign-owned plants. The SMT provides information on the use of 17 advanced manufacturing technologies for a sample of approximately 10,000 manufacturing plants.[11] We use the number of technologies reported as present in a manufacturing plant as a measure of the technology intensity at that plant.

Table 7.7 presents results for regressions with the number of technologies as the dependent variable comparing domestically owned and foreign-owned establishments. On average, foreign plants do use more technologies than domestic plants. However, when we control for industry, location, plant size, and plant age, the difference is reduced and marginally significant. When we control for the capital-labor ratio at the plant, the difference is negligible. Table 7.8 presents results for the comparison with plants owned by U.S. multinationals. We see that plants owned by U.S. multinationals are the most technology-

9. The other country whose plants seem to perform relatively poorly is Australia.

10. We use the first census a plant appears in to proxy for the age of the plant. This identifies a plant birth to prior to one of six five-year censuses: birth prior to the 1963, 1967, 1972, 1977, 1982, or 1987 CM. A problem that arises with this definition is that it pertains to new facilities, commonly referred to as "greenfield" plants. The definition does not measure how long the facility has been operated by a particular firm. Unfortunately, we do not know how long a plant has been owned by a foreign firm.

11. For more information on the design and coverage of the SMT, see Dunne and Schmitz (1992).

Table 7.6 **Cross-Country Comparisons**

Establishment Ownership	log Production Worker Wages	log Non-production Worker Wages (1)	log Non-production Worker Wages (2)	Production Workers/ Total Employment (1)	Production Workers/ Total Employment (2)	log Capital/ Labor (1)	log Capital/ Labor (2)	log Value Added/ Employee (1)	log Value Added/ Employee (2)	TFP-R	TFP-FS
Australia	−.157	.094	.007	−.029	.013	.077	.164	−.192	−.106	−.068	−.095
	(.038)	(.053)	(.052)	(.018)	(.018)	(.095)	(.094)	(.056)	(.056)	(.030)	(.038)
Canada	−.036	−.025	−.067	−.027	.008	−.036	.033	−.059	.010	−.013	−.017
	(.015)	(.021)	(.020)	(.007)	(.007)	(.038)	(.037)	(.022)	(.022)	(.012)	(.015)
France	−.054	−.001	−.081	−.022	.020	−.219	−.136	−.121	−.037	−.015	.021
	(.020)	(.030)	(.029)	(.010)	(.010)	(.051)	(.051)	(.030)	(.030)	(.016)	(.020)
Germany	.011	.046	.006	−.026	−.004	.130	.173	−.015	.029	−.032	−.035
	(.018)	(.025)	(.025)	(.009)	(.009)	(.046)	(.046)	(.027)	(.027)	(.015)	(.018)
Japan	−.058	−.028	−.039	.018	.059	.001	.080	−.207	−.177	−.102	−.078
	(.019)	(.027)	(.026)	(.009)	(.009)	(.047)	(.047)	(.028)	(.028)	(.015)	(.019)
Netherlands	−.047	−.027	.032	.016	.002	.077	.051	.049	.024	−.020	−.019
	(.024)	(.033)	(.032)	(.011)	(.011)	(.059)	(.059)	(.035)	(.035)	(.019)	(.023)
Other	.016	.049	−.009	−.006	.035	−.056	.021	−.101	−.025	−.041	−.042
	(.015)	(.022)	(.021)	(.007)	(.007)	(.039)	(.039)	(.023)	(.023)	(.012)	(.015)
Sweden	.041	−.008	−.039	−.055	−.020	−.117	−.048	−.154	−.084	−.025	−.027
	(.030)	(.043)	(.042)	(.014)	(.015)	(.076)	(.076)	(.045)	(.045)	(.024)	(.030)
Switzerland	−.028	.003	.004	−.006	−.005	.058	.031	.064	.038	−.004	.016
	(.024)	(.033)	(.032)	(.011)	(.011)	(.059)	(.059)	(.035)	(.035)	(.019)	(.023)
United Kingdom	−.042	−.032	−.071	−.042	−.007	−.172	−.114	−.097	−.038	−.039	−.013
	(.011)	(.016)	(.015)	(.005)	(.005)	(.027)	(.027)	(.016)	(.016)	(.009)	(.011)
U.S. small firm	−.151	−.020	−.095	−.007	.056	−.607	−.489	−.447	−.329	−.112	−.073
	(.005)	(.007)	(.007)	(.002)	(.002)	(.012)	(.012)	(.007)	(.007)	(.004)	(.005)
U.S. large domestic firm	−.069	−.025	−.051	.008	.036	−.214	−.157	−.167	−.110	−.042	−.024
	(.005)	(.007)	(.007)	(.002)	(.002)	(.013)	(.013)	(.008)	(.008)	(.004)	(.005)

Note: All coefficients are relative to U.S. multinational firms. All numbers are regression coefficients from linear models that control for establishment size, four-digit industry, plant age, and state. Number of observations is approximately 15,000. Numbers in parentheses are standard errors.

Table 7.7 **Differences between Domestically and Foreign-Owned Establishments**

Dependent Variable	Foreign Owned No Controls	Foreign Owned With Controls	Foreign Owned Controls + K/L[a]
Number of technologies	.930 (.189)	.268 (.152)	.055 (.149)

Note: The numbers are regression coefficients from linear models that do and do not control for establishment size, four-digit industry, plant age, and state. The omitted group is domestically owned establishments. Number of observations is approximately 6,800. Numbers in parentheses are standard errors.

[a]K/L = capital-labor ratio (capital intensity).

Table 7.8 **Differences between Foreign-Owned Establishments and Domestic Establishments by Domestic Plant Type**

	Plant Type		
Dependent Variable	Foreign Owned	Large Domestic Firm	Small U.S. Firm
Number of technologies	−.229 (.165)	−.309 (.106)	−1.03 (.109)

Note: All numbers are regression coefficients from linear models that control for establishment size, four-digit industry, plant age, and state. Number of observations is approximately 6,800. Omitted plant type is U.S. multinational. Numbers in parentheses are standard errors.

intensive plants. Foreign-owned plants use fewer technologies than plants owned by U.S. multinationals. Plants owned by large domestic firms also use fewer technologies than plants of U.S. multinationals, and plants of small U.S. firms use even fewer technologies.

These results suggest that foreign-owned plants are more technology intensive than the average domestically owned plant and, thus, offer the possibility of more technology transfer than the average U.S. plant. The results are also consistent with the notion that multinationals, whether foreign or domestic, use the most technology-intensive means of production.[12]

7.6 Conclusions

The results presented in this paper show that foreign-owned manufacturing plants in the United States in 1987 have superior operating characteristics rela-

12. Using the SMT subsample, we reran all of the regressions reported in tables 7.4 and 7.5, both with and without the number of technologies as a control variable. The results do not change, in general, even with the inclusion of the technology control variable.

tive to the average U.S.-owned plant. Foreign-owned plants pay higher wages, are more capital intensive, are more technology intensive, and are more productive than the average U.S. plant. There do not appear to be large differences among foreign-owned plants based on country of ownership.

This being said, the results also suggest that it is not the fact that the plants are foreign owned that is important to plant operating characteristics, rather it is the fact that the plants are owned by multinational corporations that seems important. Plants owned by U.S. multinationals exhibit the best operating characteristics, followed by plants of foreign multinationals. The combined class of multinationals is significantly different from both plants owned by large domestically oriented U.S. firms and plants owned by small U.S. firms. These results are consistent with the notion that multinationals possess some firm-specific advantages that enable them to overcome the barriers of FDI.

Appendix

In this appendix we present a more detailed description of the specifications we estimate in table 7.4. We use the same general set of specifications throughout the paper. Below, we also present more of the coefficient estimates from the specifications in table 7.4.

For column (1)—no controls—in table 7.4, we estimate

$$Y_i = \alpha + \beta \text{ Foreign owned}_i + \varepsilon_i,$$

where Y_i is the dependent variable listed in the table. Table 7A.1 contains the full set of regression coefficients.

For column (2)—with controls—in table 7.4, we estimate

$$Y_i = \alpha + \beta \text{ Foreign owned}_i + \Gamma X_i + \varepsilon_i,$$

where X_i includes dummy variables for plant size, plant age, state, and industry (see panel B of table 7.2). Table 7A.2 contains an extended set of regression coefficients for this specification. (We suppress the industry and state results to conserve space and to avoid disclosure issues.)

For column (3)—with controls and capital-labor ratio—in table 7.4, we estimate

$$Y_i = \alpha + \beta \text{ Foreign owned}_i + \delta \text{ Capital/Labor}_i + \Gamma X_i + \varepsilon_i,$$

where X_i includes dummy variables for plant size, plant age, state, and industry (see panel B of table 7.2). Table 7A.3 contains an extended set of regression coefficients for this specification.

Table 7A.1 Differences between Domestically and Foreign-Owned Establishments

Independent Variables	log Production Worker Wages	log Non-production Worker Wages (1)	log Non-production Worker Wages (2)	Production Workers/ Total Employment (1)	Production Workers/ Total Employment (2)	log Capital/ Labor (1)	log Capital/ Labor (2)	log Value Added/ Employee (1)	log Value Added/ Employee (2)	TFP-R	TFP-FS
R^2	.007	.001	.002	.003	.007	.024	.021	.025	.021	.001	.000
Intercept	2.843	3.290	3.306	.732	.718	3.009	2.983	3.781	3.756	.022	.036
	(.001)	(.002)	(.002)	(.001)	(.001)	(.004)	(.003)	(.002)	(.002)	(.001)	(.001)
Foreign owned	.190	.104	.130	−.052	−.084	.941	.877	.537	.473	.041	.024
	(.007)	(.008)	(.008)	(.003)	(.003)	(.018)	(.018)	(.010)	(.010)	(.004)	(.006)

Note: The numbers are regression coefficients from linear models that include an intercept and a foreign-owned dummy. Numbers of observations is approximately 115,000. Numbers in parentheses are standard errors.

Table 7A.2 **Differences between Domestically and Foreign-Owned Establishments**

Independent Variables	log Production Worker Wages	log Non-production Worker Wages (1)	log Non-production Worker Wages (2)	Production Workers/ Total Employment (1)	Production Workers/ Total Employment (2)	log Capital/ Labor (1)	log Capital/ Labor (2)	log Value Added/ Employee (1)	log Value Added/ Employee (2)	TFP-R	TFP-FS
R^2	.317	.144	.150	.245	.260	.407	.395	.318	.290	.024	.032
Foreign owned	.073	.012	.026	−.020	−.031	.332	.308	.211	.186	.037	.023
	(.006)	(.008)	(.008)	(.003)	(.003)	(.015)	(.014)	(.009)	(.009)	(.005)	(.006)
Size class 1 (1–49)	−.482	−.306	−.303	.040	.087	−.983	−.902	−.508	−.426	−.088	−.093
	(.021)	(.029)	(.028)	(.010)	(.010)	(.053)	(.052)	(.031)	(.031)	(.017)	(.021)
Size class 2 (50–99)	−.472	−.188	−.180	.042	.083	−.841	−.770	−.456	−.384	−.080	−.086
	(.021)	(.029)	(.028)	(.010)	(.010)	(.053)	(.053)	(.031)	(.031)	(.017)	(.021)
Size class 3 (100–249)	−.412	−.179	−.162	.042	.075	−.703	−.650	−.381	−.326	−.063	−.071
	(.021)	(.029)	(.028)	(.010)	(.010)	(.053)	(.053)	(.031)	(.031)	(.017)	(.021)
Size class 4 (250–499)	−.348	−.160	−.134	.046	.066	−.587	−.555	−.289	−.256	−.037	−.033
	(.021)	(.029)	(.028)	(.010)	(.010)	(.054)	(.053)	(.032)	(.031)	(.017)	(.021)
Size class 5 (500–999)	−.263	−.138	−.102	.045	.056	−.405	−.391	−.182	−.167	−.016	−.017
	(.021)	(.030)	(.029)	(.010)	(.011)	(.055)	(.055)	(.033)	(.032)	(.017)	(.022)
Size class 6 (1,000–2,499)	−.162	−.061	−.044	.023	.029	−.274	−.271	−.107	−.103	−.000	−.007
	(.023)	(.032)	(.031)	(.010)	(.011)	(.058)	(.058)	(.035)	(.034)	(.018)	(.023)
First census 63	.112	.128	.126	−.022	−.023	.184	.185	.025	.025	−.013	−.046
	(.003)	(.005)	(.005)	(.002)	(.002)	(.009)	(.009)	(.005)	(.005)	(.003)	(.003)
First census 67	.093	.110	.113	−.012	−.014	.166	.165	.042	.040	.000	−.031
	(.005)	(.007)	(.006)	(.002)	(.002)	(.012)	(.012)	(.007)	(.007)	(.004)	(.005)
First census 72	.075	.105	.105	−.008	−.009	.135	.136	.027	.027	−.004	−.028
	(.004)	(.006)	(.006)	(.002)	(.001)	(.010)	(.010)	(.006)	(.006)	(.003)	(.004)
First census 77	.049	.075	.072	−.005	−.005	.108	.112	.018	.020	−.001	−.024
	(.004)	(.005)	(.005)	(.002)	(.002)	(.009)	(.009)	(.006)	(.005)	(.003)	(.004)
First census 82	.028	.038	.036	−.002	−.001	.066	.070	.010	.013	−.001	−.014
	(.003)	(.005)	(.005)	(.002)	(.002)	(.008)	(.009)	(.005)	(.005)	(.003)	(.003)

Note: The numbers are regression coefficients from linear models that control for establishment size (size class 7 omitted), plant age (census class 87 omitted), four-digit industry (results not reported), and state (results not reported). Numbers of observations is approximately 115,000. Numbers in parentheses are standard errors.

Table 7A.3 **Differences between Domestically and Foreign-Owned Establishments**

Independent Variables	log Production Worker Wages	log Non-production Worker Wages (1)	log Non-production Worker Wages (2)	Production Workers/ Total Employment (1)	Production Workers/ Total Employment (2)	log Value Added/ Employee (1)	log Value Added/ Employee (2)	TFP-R	TFP-FS
R^2	.367	.168	.177	.246	.261	.421	.391	.024	.178
Foreign owned	.038	−.020	−.005	−.018	−.029	.134	.118	.038	.074
	(.006)	(.008)	(.008)	(.003)	(.003)	(.008)	(.008)	(.005)	(.005)
log Capital/Labor (1)	.107	.094		−.009		.231		−.001	−.152
	(.001)	(.002)		(.001)		(.002)		(.001)	(.001)
log Capital/Labor (2)			.096		−.010		.223		
			(.001)		(.001)		(.002)		
Size class 1 (1–49)	−.377	−.213	−.217	.032	.079	−.280	−.225	−.089	−.242
	(.020)	(.028)	(.002)	(.010)	(.010)	(.029)	(.029)	(.017)	(.019)
Size class 2 (50–99)	−.382	−.109	−.107	.035	.076	−.261	−.212	−.081	−.215
	(.020)	(.028)	(.028)	(.010)	(.010)	(.029)	(.029)	(.017)	(.019)
Size class 3 (100–249)	−.337	−.113	−.100	.037	.069	−.218	−.182	−.064	−.179
	(.020)	(.028)	(.028)	(.010)	(.010)	(.029)	(.029)	(.017)	(.019)
Size class 4 (250–499)	−.285	−.105	−.081	.041	.060	−.153	−.132	−.038	−.123
	(.020)	(.029)	(.028)	(.010)	(.010)	(.029)	(.029)	(.017)	(.019)
Size class 5 (500–999)	−.220	−.100	−.065	.041	.052	−.088	−.080	−.017	−.079
	(.021)	(.030)	(.029)	(.010)	(.010)	(.030)	(.030)	(.017)	(.020)
Size class 6 (1,000–2,499)	−.133	−.036	−.019	.021	.027	−.044	−.043	−.001	−.049
	(.022)	(.031)	(.031)	(.011)	(.011)	(.032)	(.031)	(.018)	(.021)
First census 63	.093	.110	.108	−.021	−.021	−.018	−.016	−.012	−.018
	(.003)	(.005)	(.005)	(.002)	(.002)	(.005)	(.005)	(.003)	(.003)
First census 67	.075	.094	.098	−.011	−.012	.003	.003	.000	−.005
	(.004)	(.007)	(.006)	(.002)	(.002)	(.006)	(.006)	(.004)	(.004)
First census 72	.061	.093	.092	−.007	−.008	−.005	−.004	−.004	−.007
	(.004)	(.006)	(.006)	(.002)	(.002)	(.005)	(.005)	(.003)	(.004)
First census 77	.038	.065	.062	−.005	−.004	−.007	−.005	−.001	−.007
	(.004)	(.005)	(.005)	(.002)	(.002)	(.005)	(.005)	(.003)	(.003)
First census 82	.021	.032	.029	−.002	−.000	−.005	−.002	−.000	−.003
	(.003)	(.005)	(.004)	(.002)	(.002)	(.005)	(.005)	(.003)	(.003)

Note: The numbers are regression coefficients from linear models that control for establishment size (size class 7 omitted), plant age (census class 87 omitted), four-digit industry (results not reported), and state (results not reported). Number of observations is approximately 115,000. Numbers in parentheses are standard errors.

References

Baily, M., C. Hulten, and D. Campbell. 1992. Productivity dynamics in manufacturing plants. *Brookings Papers on Economic Activity, Microeconomics,* pp. 187–249.

Davis, S., and J. Haltiwanger. 1991. Wage dispersion between and within U.S. manufacturing plants, 1963–1986. *Brookings Papers on Economic Activity, Microeconomics,* pp. 115–80.

Doms, M., and J. B. Jensen. 1998. The productivity, skills, and wages of multinational corporations in the U.S.: Does country of ownership matter? Revision of paper prepared for the conference Beyond Us and Them: Foreign Ownership and U.S. Competitiveness, Georgetown University, Washington, D.C., September 1995.

Dunne, T., and J. Schmitz. 1992. Wages, employer size-wage premia and employment structure: Their relationship to advanced technology usage at U.S. manufacturing establishments. Center for Economic Studies Discussion Paper no. 92–15. Washington, D.C.: Center for Economic Studies.

Froot, K., and J. Stein. 1991. Exchange rates and foreign direct investment: An imperfect capital markets approach. *Quarterly Journal of Economics* 106 (4): 1191–217.

Globerman, S., J. Ries, and I. Vertinsky. 1994. The economic performance of foreign affiliates in Canada. *Canadian Journal of Economics* 27 (1): 143–56.

Graham, E., and P. Krugman. 1989. *Foreign direct investment in the United States.* Washington, D.C.: Institute for International Economics.

Howenstine, N., and W. Zeile. 1992. Foreign direct investment in the United States: Establishment data for 1987. *Survey of Current Business* 72 (October): 44–78.

———. 1994. Characteristics of foreign-owned U.S. manufacturing establishments. *Survey of Current Business* 74 (January): 34–59.

McCulloch, R. 1993. New perspectives on foreign direct investment. In *Foreign direct investment,* ed. K. Froot, 37–53. Chicago: University of Chicago Press.

Troske, K. 1994. Evidence on the employer size-wage premium for worker-establishment matched data. Washington, D.C.: U.S. Bureau of the Census, Center for Economic Studies. Mimeograph.

U.S. Department of Commerce. Bureau of Economic Analysis and Bureau of the Census. 1992. *Foreign direct investment in the United States: Establishment data for 1987.* Washington, D.C.: Government Printing Office.

Vernon, R. 1993. Where are the multinationals headed? In *Foreign direct investment,* ed. K. Froot, 57–79. Chicago: University of Chicago Press.

Comment Keith Head

Doms and Jensen ask and answer the question, How do foreign plants compare to domestically owned plants in terms of wages and productivity? Their answer can be summarized as follows. Workers at foreign-owned manufacturing plants generate about 50 percent more value added and receive 20 percent higher wages than employees at the average domestically owned plant. However, most of the premiums in productivity and wages can be explained by observable

Keith Head is assistant professor in the Faculty of Commerce at the University of British Columbia.

differences in the attributes of the plants, rather than in the form of a pure "ownership" effect. Furthermore, the unexplained part of the premiums does not appear to derive from their "foreignness"; rather, it appears that plants owned by multinational corporations pay more and have higher productivity. In fact, employees at plants owned by large U.S.-owned multinationals receive the highest average wages. Doms and Jensen have provided a clear and convincing answer to the question they posed; however, they do not explore the policy implications of their work. In particular, do their results justify policies designed to attract foreign direct investment (FDI)?

In 1994 the state of Alabama helped convince Mercedes Benz to locate a plant there by offering an incentive package of approximately $230 million. This topped a previous record set by Kentucky when its $147 million package drew an auto plant from Toyota.[1] For initial employment levels of 1,500 and 3,000, respectively, these plants cost the host governments around $150,000 and $50,000 per job. What can Doms and Jensen's results tell us about the return on these outlays? To start, let us assume that the only benefit to the host economy is the higher incomes received by the workers employed at these plants. The present value, assuming a discount rate of 0.05, of a 20 percent wage premium over the sample average $25,000 annual earnings in manufacturing is $100,000. This suggests that the Kentucky bid might have been reasonable but Alabama overpaid.

The 20 percent wage premium is the raw increase to wages without any controls. After accounting for the industry, state, plant size and age, and capital intensity of foreign-owned plants, the wage premium falls to 4 percent, or a present value of $20,000. At this premium level, neither incentive package appears to make sense. Which number should the state governor use? It might be argued that the exact mechanisms underlying the wage premium do not matter—just the overall result. However, the governor could allocate the funds to alternative projects designed to improve the attributes of existing firms. For instance, some form of general investment subsidy could be used to increase their size and capital intensity. If such opportunities exist, then perhaps the governor should consider only the premium attributable to foreign multinational management.

The simple calculations above made two key assumptions that should now be critiqued. First, I assumed that the wage premium constituted a welfare gain for the host economy. Second, by focusing solely on the jobs at the particular investment, we omit the potential for external effects. Namely, the foreign plant may generate spillovers that benefit other local manufacturers. These spillovers might induce subsequent investment by the same firm or its suppliers. These factors could make us revise our estimates of the benefits of FDI upward if the wage premium does not represent a welfare improvement or downward if there are substantial positive spillovers.

1. More details on both incentive packages can be found in the *New York Times*, 4 October 1994.

What causes foreign-owned plants to pay higher average wages? To answer this question it is useful to consider some alternative hypotheses. First, suppose foreign-owned plants employ different, but technically equal, management methods. Then we would expect no difference in productivity and would interpret a wage premium as evidence of a compensating differential to induce domestic workers to accept foreign management. Alternatively, suppose workers are indifferent as to ownership but foreign firms really do possess superior techniques. Then we would expect a productivity premium, but wages would be determined by the alternative opportunity of working for a domestic firm. The finding of both wage and productivity premiums might argue for a superior technology that imposes costs on the workers for which they must be compensated.

The high wage premium paid by U.S. multinational-owned plants suggests that the compensation does *not* reflect aversion to foreign control per se. It could be that the higher wages paid by foreign and domestic multinationals reflect the outcome of a bargaining game in which workers share the extra rents generated by the superior technologies used by multinational-owned plants. An alternative interpretation consistent with high productivity and wages would be that multinational plants use production processes that require higher levels of effort from their employees. One reason might be that multinationals have a greater stake in maintaining a reputation for product quality. Alternatively, the multinational may use technologies that make intensive use of more highly skilled—and hence, better paid—workers.

If the wage premium represents compensation for higher effort or greater skills, individual workers may not benefit from employment at a multinational. In one case they have to work harder, in the other case they probably gave up high-paying jobs at other firms. Even if individual workers do not receive a net benefit from working at a multinational plant, the local government may value the increase in the income tax revenues it can obtain as a result of higher average wages. If the skill intensity story is correct, attracting a multinational-owned plant would tend to draw an inflow of skilled workers from other states that might be viewed as a desirable development in its own right.

Defenders of large incentive packages would probably argue that the most critical flaw in the calculations I made on the return to attracting foreign investors is the omission of "job creation" beyond the direct employment of the firm. They would probably point to complementary investments by supplier firms and to the likelihood of future expansion by Mercedes and Toyota. Indeed, Toyota is expected to increase its employment in Kentucky to 6,000, and there are already a couple dozen new Japanese-owned parts suppliers in the state.

In addition, superior technologies employed by multinational plants may spill over to domestic firms, causing additional productivity and wage increases beyond those at the assembly plants themselves. These externality issues could be addressed using the Doms and Jensen data set if it can be extended to include a time-series dimension. With better estimates of the magnitudes of the indirect effects of multinational investments, we could obtain more precise measures of their value to host governments. Even with more precise quantifications of the potential benefits to host-country governments, competition between states may bid away most of the benefits after subtracting the cost of the incentive package. It seems likely that there will be a push for policy reforms designed to curb the tendency of local governments to overbid for investments. The results of Doms and Jensen provide a useful component in evaluating potential agreements on investment incentives.

8 The Significance of International Tax Rules for Sourcing Income: The Relationship between Income Taxes and Trade Taxes

John Mutti and Harry Grubert

As multinational corporations play a greater role in global economic activity, the incentives such firms face in choosing particular locations for production become important determinants of the geographic-based measures of output discussed elsewhere in this volume. International trade economists have long paid attention to the role of tariffs and other trade taxes on the pattern of trade and international investment. This paper assesses how rules for sourcing income in different locations affect parent income tax liabilities and correspondingly create incentives to export or to produce abroad.

From an early postwar perspective, income taxes were presumed to have little influence on the location of real output across countries: a general tax imposed on an internationally immobile resource was borne by that factor and represented a windfall loss that did not alter the pattern of production. In a world of increasingly mobile capital and labor, that perspective became less warranted. In the 1960s and 1970s academicians and policymakers tried to assess the influence of home- and host-country tax and tariff rates on the location of production, investment, and trade internationally (see Bergsten, Horst, and Moran 1978).

The current paper pursues a related but less obvious issue, the way that rules to determine the source of income for tax purposes also can have important effects on the form in which taxable income is reported and economic activity is located. In particular, two issues are evaluated in more detail: the ability to regard a portion of export income as foreign source (sales source rules) and the treatment of royalties received from abroad as foreign-source income. The potential benefits from these source rules have become particularly important

John Mutti is professor of economics at Grinnell College. Harry Grubert is an international economist at the U.S. Department of the Treasury.

The views expressed here do not necessarily represent those of the U.S. Treasury Department.

due to U.S. tax policy changes adopted in the 1980s and to the growing role of U.S. production and trade in goods that require intangible intellectual property.

The U.S. computer software industry provides good examples of the conflicting incentives that exist. Relatively similar transactions can be carried out as trade in goods, trade in services, or production by foreign affiliates. How a company chooses to structure these often substitutable transactions will depend on several policy measures: host-country tariffs on software imports, foreign income tax rates and the opportunity to deduct royalty payments from taxable income, foreign withholding rates on royalties, the way U.S. taxes are imposed on foreign-source income, and the U.S. income tax rate. The incentives created by these tax and trade provisions may result in fundamentally similar transactions being characterized quite differently when different industries and countries are involved.

This paper demonstrates several implications of rules that govern whether export income, service income, and royalties are regarded as domestic or foreign-source income, a determination relevant in calculating a firm's foreign tax credit position. The relative significance of these source rules is demonstrated in a set of stylized calculations that show how domestic and foreign policies affect a firm's after-tax returns under various assumptions about the importance of tangible and intangible capital in production. A brief section considers some related examples and issues that arise as a result of source rules applied in foreign countries, which also affect the incentives U.S. firms face.

The empirical significance of the incentives identified above is treated in the final section of the paper. Background information is provided with respect to two issues. First, because these incentives apply to active business income but not to passive income from portfolio investments, a general overview of U.S. income earned abroad is presented. It indicates that the focus on active income is not misplaced or directed at an inconsequential part of U.S. investment activity. Second, because the benefits from characterizing income as foreign source depend on a firm's ability to claim credit for foreign taxes paid, the foreign tax credit position of U.S. multinational corporations is briefly discussed. Finally, work that evaluates the response to these tax incentives is reviewed. While such tax benefits might result only in income shifting, with no effect on the location of economic activity, some evidence suggests that these provisions influence real economic activity as well.

8.1 Basic Approaches in Taxing Foreign-Source Income

The United States, together with Japan and the United Kingdom, applies a worldwide system that taxes all of the income its residents receive regardless of the source of that income across countries. To avoid double taxation of foreign-source income, the United States grants a credit for foreign income taxes paid, where the credit is limited to the amount of the U.S. tax liability on foreign income. The amount of foreign income to declare is defined by U.S. rules, not by foreign rules that determine the foreign tax actually paid.

U.S. law provides for an overall foreign tax credit limitation that does not distinguish by country of origin. The foreign tax paid on a dividend received from an active business in a high-tax country may offset the U.S. tax due on a dividend received from a low-tax country. The United States does, however, separate different types of income into different baskets. Interest income received from a tax haven country that imposes a low withholding tax cannot be combined with dividends received from a country that imposes a high income tax, which otherwise would shield the interest income from U.S. taxation.

Consider the following example that demonstrates the calculation of a U.S. multinational corporation's foreign tax credit limitation and total tax liability. Suppose a firm receives $1,000 of foreign-source income, has paid a foreign income tax of $385, and also has domestic-source income of $1,000. Given a U.S. income tax rate of 35 percent, the foreign tax credit limitation is $350, calculated as the U.S. tax liability on total income (.35 × $2,000) multiplied by the share of income that is foreign source (0.5). In this case the firm owes no residual U.S. tax on its foreign-source income, has excess foreign tax credits of $35, and pays U.S. tax of $350 on its domestic-source income. It pays total income taxes of $735.

If source rules allow the firm to characterize a larger share of its income as foreign source, the firm benefits by being able to claim a larger foreign tax credit, and it avoids U.S. taxation of that recharacterized income. For example, if the firm can treat an additional $100 as foreign-source rather than domestic-source income, the foreign tax credit limitation becomes $385. The firm now can claim all of the foreign tax paid as a credit against the U.S. tax liability on foreign-source income, and its U.S. liability on domestic-source income is $315. It pays total income taxes of $700, a decline of $35 compared to the previous example.

If the circumstances above are changed so that foreign income taxes paid are $285 rather than $385, then the foreign tax limitation remains $350, the foreign tax credit is $285, and the residual U.S. tax due is $65. Being able to characterize more income as foreign source provides no advantage because a residual tax will be due on any additional foreign-source income received by this firm, which is in an excess limit position. Therefore, whether a firm has excess foreign tax credits is a key factor in determining the effects of source rules under the U.S. system of taxing worldwide income.

8.2 U.S. Rules for Sourcing Income

The following discussion presents three alternative types of transactions that are economically similar but are treated differently under U.S. tax law. The three alternatives include the export of a good from the United States, the export of a service from the United States, and the transfer of technology to an affiliate who provides the good or service in the foreign market. An important part of the difference in tax treatment is attributable to rules that determine what part of the income earned is regarded as domestic source and what part as foreign source. The computer software industry is used as a point of reference in the discussion because the three different types of transactions all represent plausible ways of selling software abroad. The different incentives identified, however, apply to other industries as well.

8.2.1 Exports of Goods

Begin by considering the exportation of a good from the United States. Suppose a U.S. company develops a new computer program in the United States and exports prepackaged software to foreign users. The profit it earns depends on the revenue received from the foreign buyer, Rev_f, the tariff rate that must be paid to import the good into the foreign market, τ, the variable cost of goods sold, Cost, and the U.S. income tax rate imposed on export earnings, t_x:

$$\Pi = (1 - t_x)[\text{Rev}_f /(1 + \tau) - \text{Cost}].$$

To apply this simple framework, assume initially that all capital is equity financed, and ignore the distinction between tangible and intangible assets.

The U.S. income tax rate may be lower than the rate imposed on domestic income if the firm takes advantage of the foreign sales corporation (FSC) provisions of the tax code. Under the combined taxable income administrative pricing rule, 15 percent of the corporation's taxable income from exports sold through the FSC is exempt from federal income tax. The exempt income is intended to reflect the FSC's activity abroad in selling the exported goods. An alternative approach, the gross receipts method, results in exempt income equal to about 1.19 percent of gross receipts. Because the benefit from this latter rule declines as the firm's profit margin increases, firms with profit margins greater than 8 percent will find the combined taxable income method more advantageous. In fact, that is the most commonly selected method, and it is particularly relevant for the high-technology examples considered here. In 1987 FSCs reported gross export receipts of $84.3 billion and net exempt income of $2.1 billion. The effective tax rate on U.S. export income, then, will be lower than the statutory corporate tax rate.

If the U.S. firm is in an excess foreign tax credit position, it may benefit even more under provisions of the sales source rules. These rules specify how firms are to determine the source of income (domestic or foreign) from the sale of inventory property. As shown above, if a firm that has excess credits can declare additional foreign-source income, it can claim a larger foreign tax credit and the additional foreign-source income escapes U.S. taxation.

If the exported goods are sold through an FSC and the combined taxable income method is used to determine FSC income, generally no more than 25 percent of the combined taxable income of the FSC and the U.S. exporter can be treated as foreign-source income. In combination with the FSC exemption, that would allow 40 percent of the firm's export income to escape U.S. taxation. If the goods are not sold through an FSC, however, the firm can often use rules to source 50 percent of the export profits abroad. Thus, firms are more likely to forgo operating an FSC if they are in an excess credit position, since they will gain a larger benefit from the other provisions of the sales source rules.

The importance of the sales source rules is indicated by the U.S. Department of the Treasury (1992) calculation that U.S. firms' tax liabilities would rise \$1.8 to \$2.1 billion in their absence. A more recent estimate suggests a lower tax benefit, roughly half this size (Rousslang 1994). This latter calculation indicates that fewer firms actually claim 863(b) income on Form 1118 than would be predicted on the basis of firms in excess credit positions.

For those companies that do claim 863(b) income, the benefit from a lower U.S. tax rate on export earnings rewards U.S. production. This benefit will be more significant the larger the profit margin on goods exported. Conversely, a higher foreign tariff rate discourages U.S. production. In the case of computer software, tariffs on prepackaged software range from zero in many countries to 85 percent in India. The total value of U.S. merchandise exports reported in 1993 was \$2.3 billion.[1]

8.2.2 Exports of Services

An alternative transaction to consider is the U.S. provision of a service to a foreign buyer. In the case of computer software, this item is reported by the Commerce Department as computer and data-processing services, and in 1993 total sales were \$1.8 billion. Such a transaction might involve development of a program or analysis carried out in the United States, which is then delivered to the foreign customer. The profit the firm earns is represented by the revenue it receives from the foreign buyer, the cost of providing the service, and the U.S. tax rate:

$$\Pi = (1 - t_{us})[\mathrm{Rev}_f - \mathrm{Cost}].$$

Several factors distinguish this case from the exportation of a good. The delivery of a service is not ordinarily subject to a tariff. The treatment of the income earned by providing the service may be less favorable, however. The United States regards such services provided by domestic establishments as domestic-source income and subject to U.S. tax. Exports of software services do not qualify for FSC treatment,[2] although exports of master disks could benefit from the sales source rules in calculating the foreign tax credit. In general, the relevant U.S. tax rate for providing services will exceed the effective rate on income from exports of goods.

1. This figure recorded under HS 8524905000 includes both prepackaged software valued at the price at which it is sold to the foreign buyer and also the value of the medium (tape, disk, etc.) used to send software that will require customizing or assistance in installation abroad or to send a master disk that will allow foreign reproduction. In the latter two cases the value of the medium typically represents a small fraction of the value of the intangible knowledge being transferred.

2. Architectural and engineering services and export management services qualify for FSC treatment. Receipts from exports of patents and other intangibles do not qualify as foreign trade gross receipts (U.S. Department of the Treasury 1990, 7), although exports of masters for the distribution of copyrighted movies, tapes, and records do qualify.

8.2.3 Direct Investment Abroad and Affiliate Production

Suppose a U.S. company develops a new technology in the United States. If it licenses the technology for use in the United States (or exploits the technology itself domestically), the royalty payment (additional income) is treated as domestic-source income and is subject to U.S. tax. If instead the company licenses the new technology to a foreign producer or produces abroad in a foreign affiliate, the royalty it receives is considered foreign-source income.[3]

The profit the parent firm receives after payment of foreign taxes but before the determination of any residual U.S. tax can be represented in this situation as

$$\Pi = (1 - t_f)(1 - w_d)(\text{Rev}_f - \text{Cost} - R) + (1 - w_r)R,$$

where all profits are repatriated, Rev_f represents the revenue that the foreign affiliate is receiving in the foreign market, Cost is the variable cost of production in the foreign country, R is the royalty paid to the parent, t_f is the foreign income tax rate, w_d is the dividend withholding rate, and w_r is the royalty withholding rate. Assume statutory and effective tax rates are identical. If the parent is in an excess foreign tax credit position and U.S. and foreign rules for defining income and allowable expenses are the same, then the foreign tax paid will be the final tax burden and no residual U.S. tax is paid. A firm operating in a low-tax country does not lose that tax advantage, while a firm operating in a high-tax country pays taxes that exceed the comparable burden on domestic-source income.

If the parent firm is in an excess limit position and owes a residual tax to the U.S. government, then the parent's after-tax income derived from its foreign operation is

$$\Pi = (1 - t_{us})(\text{Rev}_f - \text{Cost}).$$

For a firm operating in a high-tax country, this represents an advantage over the situation depicted in the previous paragraph because the higher foreign tax burden generates credits that can shield other foreign-source income the parent earns. Conversely, if the firm operates in a low-tax country but profits are repatriated when earned, the additional U.S. tax due eliminates the tax advantage gained from foreign production in that location. A firm in excess limit, however, may have an incentive to pay a lower royalty. That strategy allows it to gain the benefits of deferring the U.S. tax liability on the income it earns and retains in a low-tax country. The present discussion ignores the opportunity to

3. This presentation assumes that when the firm transfers technology to its affiliate to produce abroad, the affiliate will pay a royalty to the parent. As established in 1984 under Section 367(d) of the Internal Revenue Code, transferring an intangible as described above cannot be used as a tax-free method of capitalizing a foreign affiliate. Tax legislation in 1986 provides that transferring an intangible shall result in a commensurate royalty payment to the parent.

defer that tax liability and does not evaluate the possible benefits from retaining income abroad because the source rule issues discussed above are most relevant to firms in an excess credit position.

In the case of the software industry, the Bureau of Economic Analysis (BEA) judges that sales of computer-related services by foreign affiliates are by far the dominant method of serving foreign markets. In contrast to the exports of goods or services from the United States, which were roughly $2 billion each, total service sales by affiliates in computer and office equipment manufacturing and in professional and commercial equipment were $40 billion in 1993 (Sandheimer and Bargas 1994). Therefore, royalties are likely to be one of the primary forms in which this activity appears in U.S. tax and balance-of-payments tabulations.

8.3 Comparisons of Alternative Tax Treatment

Table 8.1 summarizes the issues discussed above by comparing the after-tax return to capital earned under several alternative tax treatments. The stylized cases assume that the same revenues are earned from foreign sales in all situations. Variable costs of production are assumed to be the same whether production takes place at home or abroad. Two different cases are presented to reflect a difference in the relative importance of variable cost as a share of total cost. The two values chosen, 40 percent and 65 percent, represent differences among export industries that can be inferred from Internal Revenue Service

Table 8.1 **After-Tax Returns from Alternative Transactions to Serve the Foreign Market**

	Variable Cost/Total Cost		Royalties/Foreign-Source Income	
	.40	.65	.40	.20
Case	(1)	(2)	(3)	(4)
Export of goods				
No tariff, no benefits	9.75	9.75		
Tariff, no benefits	8.27	7.20		
FSC benefits, excess limit	8.94	7.80		
Sales source rules, excess credit	10.50	9.16		
Export of services				
U.S. taxation	9.75	9.75		
Affiliate production				
Excess credit, high tax			9.86	8.64
Excess credit, low tax			13.75	13.45
Excess limit, high tax			9.75	9.75
Excess limit, low tax			9.75	9.75

Assumptions: $t_{us} = .35$, $\tau = .10$. High-tax case: $t_f = .45$, $w_d = .10$, $w_r = .10$; low-tax case: $t_f = .10$, $w_d = .025$, $w_r = .025$.

(1993): in industries such as pharmaceutical drugs the cost of goods sold as a share of business receipts is represented by the 40 percent figure, while in various nonelectrical machinery industries the 65 percent value is observed.

Assume that the firm finances its spending on tangible and intangible capital with equity. The importance of intangible capital can only be approximated in rough terms. The 1989 benchmark survey of U.S. direct investment abroad reports the relative importance of parent receipts from affiliates of direct investment income, royalties, and other direct investment services (U.S. Department of Commerce 1992). Royalties may not represent the entire return to intangible capital if some of the return appears as higher direct investment earnings (Grubert 1998). Also, receipts for other services (or charges for parent headquarter expenses) may represent a source of return comparable to royalties in some sectors, but from a tax perspective they represent U.S. domestic-source income. Those payments are more important in several service sectors, including computer and data-processing services, but they are less important in manufacturing. Two cases are considered, one where intangibles account for 40 percent of foreign operating income (before the deduction of royalty payments), and one where they account for 20 percent.

The U.S. income tax rate is assumed to be 35 percent. Operations in two different foreign countries are presented, one with an income tax rate of 45 percent, to represent a high-tax country such as Japan, and one with an income tax rate of 10 percent, to represent low-tax countries such as Singapore, Hong Kong, and Ireland. In the high-tax case the dividend and royalty withholding rates are both 10 percent, while in the low-tax alternative both rates are 2.5 percent. In both cases the tariff rate imposed on imports from the United States is 10 percent.

First compare the tax consequences of exporting a good versus exporting a service. The base case for exports of goods assumes no tariff and no special tax treatment of export income, and the rate of return is calibrated to be the same (9.75 percent) as when a service is exported. The imposition of a tariff reduces the net revenues to exporters of goods, making that way of serving the foreign market less attractive.[4] FSC benefits are not sufficient to offset the effect of the tariff; when the gross profit margin is small, as in column (2), even applying advantageous sales source rules for a firm with excess foreign tax credits results in a lower return. This outcome reflects a relationship familiar from the effective protection literature: a relatively low tariff imposed on a good where value added accounts for a small share of its price can yield a very high effective rate of protection. Because exports of services are not subject to foreign tariffs, that form of serving the foreign market may appear more attractive, as in column (2).

The tax consequences from affiliate production abroad depend importantly

4. This reasoning assumes the firm currently has excess capacity to produce both at home and abroad, and a higher tariff creates an incentive to expand foreign production at the given foreign market price.

on the foreign tax credit position of the U.S. parent. For a firm in an excess credit position the benefit from being able to treat royalties as foreign-source income is determined by the importance of intangibles in the firm's production and by the host-country tax rate that is avoided when the royalty is a deductible expense. Note in column (3), where high royalties are paid, that the deterrent effect of operating in a country with a high income tax rate is offset by the opportunity to pay royalties, which are subject to a low withholding rate. The parent benefits from being able to use its excess credits to offset any residual U.S. tax due. In column (4) the firm has less intangible income, and the effect of the high foreign income tax rate is not offset by the opportunity to pay royalties. Thus, a high-technology firm that receives more of its return from foreign operations in the form of royalties is more likely to gain from operating an affiliate in a high-tax host country.[5]

In the case of a firm without excess foreign tax credits, a residual tax is due in the United States regardless of the host-country tax rate or the extent to which royalties are paid. Production in a high-tax country is not penalized because the opportunity to use the additional foreign tax credits generated by production there means the U.S. firm does not bear the burden of the higher host tax rate.

If the United States were to treat royalties as domestic-source income, the U.S. firm with excess foreign tax credits would not benefit from bringing home lightly taxed foreign-source income free from U.S. tax. The rates of return previously reported in table 8.1 would drop substantially: for the case of a firm paying out a higher share of royalties, returns fall from 9.86 percent to 7.97 percent in the high-tax host country and from 13.75 percent to 11.70 percent in the low-tax host country. Perhaps such a policy shift would give U.S. parents an incentive to declare fewer royalties and instead to make larger overhead charges for R&D, an item that appears in the BEA category "other direct investment services." While such an entry generally would be regarded as U.S.-source income, it typically has not been subject to a high foreign withholding tax.

The negative effect on U.S. firms is not, however, as disadvantageous as if a high-tax foreign government did not recognize royalties as deductible business expenses. In that situation if the same withholding rate were levied on all payments to the parent, then all of the foreign-source income would become subject to the higher foreign income tax rate. The rate of return would fall from 9.86 percent to 6.75 percent.

In summary, source rules that treat royalties and portions of export income as foreign source influence the attractiveness of production at home or abroad.

5. This example ignores any requirement that the parent firm allocate some portion of its U.S. R&D expenses against its foreign source income. Section 861 of the Internal Revenue Code addresses such allocations, but its implementation has varied considerably over time. Allocating expenses to foreign-source income reduces the size of the foreign tax credit that can be claimed. For a parent firm in an excess credit position the parent's loss equals the amount of the allocation times the U.S. tax rate.

Because services provided to foreigners generally are domestic-source income rather than foreign-source income, firms in an excess credit position may find it attractive to structure those transactions in another form. Few general presumptions emerge because the relative advantages of different locations or transactions depend importantly on host-country trade and tax policies, too.

8.4 Foreign Rules for Sourcing Income

U.S. firms are also influenced by foreign rules for sourcing income. In the case of U.S. exports of goods and services, the purchasing country may claim that some part of the income earned is sourced in that country, even if the provider has no permanent business establishment there.[6] Consider situations that involve services, where a host country pays for oil core logs to be analyzed or an economic consulting report to be prepared, but the work is done outside of the country. In the case of a service provided to a related party, many host-country governments will prohibit that party from deducting the payment from its foreign taxable income. If the payment is not to a related party, Colombia, for example, treats the income as domestic source and subject to Colombian income taxation and withholding taxes (McLure et al. 1990).

When a foreign government claims the right to tax service income, it may have no way of verifying what costs are incurred in providing the service. Therefore, it may levy a tax on the gross payment to the foreigner. That approach is similar to imposing a withholding tax on gross interest or royalty payments where no attention is paid to expenses incurred in earning that income. The present example differs from a royalty or interest payment, however, because in this case the U.S. government does not recognize that any foreign-source income is earned. If the U.S. firm already is in an excess credit position, it can make no use of the additional foreign tax credits generated. In terms of the stylized example above, imposing a tax of 9.1 percent on the gross value of the service payment would reduce returns by exactly the same amount as the 10 percent tariff on U.S. exports reported earlier. The penalty on the U.S. producer again arises because the foreign tax is deductible but not creditable. For a higher foreign tax rate, the provision of services becomes even less attractive.

Host-country taxation of this income represents a trade barrier that discriminates against foreign service providers, since those individuals will also face home-country taxation of what the home country regards as domestic-source income. Are there circumstances, however, in which this treatment will have the same neutral effect on trade that arises under the destination principle of border tax adjustment that is applied to indirect taxes?

Under that principle, an indirect tax is imposed on imports and rebated on exports. As shown by various authors (Baldwin 1970; Feldstein and Krugman

6. Tax laws provide no consistent rationale for determining the source of income in such situations. E.g., in the insurance industry income usually is attributed to the country in which the insured risk is located, even though the actuaries who evaluate the risk or the individuals who bear the risk are located elsewhere.

1990) the goal of such border tax adjustment is to leave unaltered the relative prices of domestic and foreign goods both in the home market and in foreign markets. Suppose domestic prices in countries A and B are initially the same before the imposition of an indirect tax by country A. The price of the domestic good becomes $P_a(1 + t)$, and under a destination principle that imposes the same tax on imports, the price of the foreign good becomes $P_b(1 + t)$. Relative prices do not change. Similarly, the price of foreign goods remains P_b in other markets, and when country A rebates the tax on exports, its price remains P_a. Again, relative prices do not change. To impose an indirect tax in order to be able to gain the benefit of destination principle treatment misinterprets the consequences of making border tax adjustments and mistakenly infers there is some benefit available.

A uniform value-added tax levied on all goods has the same economic effect as a general income tax levied on all income. Making the same border tax adjustment for both taxes would call for imposing the income tax on imports and rebating it on exports. Therefore, the distorting effect of the service tax described above arises not because it is imposed on imports but because it is not rebated on exports.

Note that the tax in the service example is an income tax on an individual or corporation, not an indirect tax on computer programs or consulting reports. Therefore, it does not fall within the standard conditions for border tax adjustment under the General Agreement on Tariffs and Trade (GATT). Historically, the GATT has not allowed rebates of direct taxes at the border, and in fact a GATT panel ruled against the U.S. DISC (domestic international sales corporation) program on the grounds that it effectively taxed export income at a lower rate than domestic income and therefore represented an export subsidy.

The new General Agreement on Trade in Services (GATS) is a possible forum to address issues of double taxation or border tax adjustments applied to direct taxes. In the Uruguay Round negotiations the United States strongly opposed such a move (Matthews 1995). Without considering the precise rationale for the U.S. position, recognize there are significant administrative issues to address in verifying what income taxes have been paid in the production of a particular product. Another reason for caution in introducing this issue before the GATS may the existence of ambiguities in the application of the national treatment standard to income tax systems. Determining what constitutes comparable treatment can be difficult. For example, would levying a withholding tax on foreigners in lieu of imposing an income tax on them be construed as resulting in a heavier burden on some foreigners in some years?

8.5 Foreign-Source Income, Taxation, and Firm Response

How important are the incentives created by the two source rules identified above? To address that question, first consider several general measures that indicate the relative importance of various items of foreign-source income. Special attention to active business income reported in the general basket is warranted because it is used in calculating the foreign tax credit limitation relevant to royalties and allocated export income. A related issue is the likelihood that a firm will have a potential excess of foreign tax credits and thereby benefit from these two source rules. Based on data from 1990, foreign tax credit positions across industries are reported. Finally, efforts to evaluate the effects on firm behavior of the sales source rules and the treatment of royalties are discussed.

8.5.1 The Importance of Active Business Income

Table 8.2 provides a summary of several balance-of-payments entries for investment income and for other payments among affiliated enterprises. In spite of the widely reported surge in portfolio investment as individual savers have bought shares of stock in foreign companies and mutual funds, direct investment receipts are substantial and have risen more rapidly than other private receipts over the decade from 1986 to 1996. Therefore, source rules that govern the calculation of the foreign tax credit limitation for U.S. multinational corporations can have quantitatively significant economic effects.

Royalties grew particularly rapidly between 1986 and 1990, and by 1996 they nearly equaled $30 billion. Over three-fourths of U.S. receipts come from affiliates rather than unrelated parties. That arrangement is not surprising because two unrelated parties may not easily predict or agree on the future profits likely to be generated by an intangible. Affiliation avoids the need to make that sort of forecast. Changes in the tax law discussed above may have given U.S. firms a greater incentive to receive royalties, too. Receipts from other private services are a much larger number than royalties, and from 1990 to 1996 they have grown slightly more rapidly than royalties. In contrast to royalties, however, less than 30 percent are accounted for by receipts from affiliates.

These figures are not directly equivalent to items that appear in the general basket for calculating the foreign income tax limitation. First, only the portion of direct investment earnings repatriated to the United States is subject to a residual U.S. tax or relevant in determining the foreign tax credit limitation. Second, not all foreign-source income declared by U.S. taxpayers appears in the general basket, and therefore it may not be combined with royalties and export income in calculating the foreign tax credit limitation.

With respect to the first point, table 8.2 contains the BEA measure of distributed earnings. The corresponding payout ratio shows considerable variation: it exceeds 70 percent in 1986, 1988, and 1989, but it is less than 40 percent in 1995 and 1996.[7] Predicting future behavior is not straightforward.

7. The BEA series reflects the new convention adopted in 1992 to exclude unrealized capital gains from retained earnings and total earnings. The high payout ratio in 1986 may reflect the desire to repatriate more highly taxed foreign-source income in order to combine it with other income subject to low foreign taxes that subsequently would be treated in separate baskets. For general discussion of the determinants of dividend remittances, including nontax factors such as the potential importance of foreign investment opportunities or parent financial requirements, see Hines and Hubbard (1990) and Altshuler and Newlon (1993).

Table 8.2 Investment Income and Related Service Flows: United States, 1984–96

Category	1984	1985	1986	1987	1988	1989	1990	1991	1992	1993	1994	1995	1996
Income receipts on U.S. assets abroad	104,756	93,679	91,186	100,511	129,366	153,659	163,324	141,408	125,852	129,844	154,510	196,880	206,400
Direct investment receipts	31,262	30,547	31,968	39,608	52,092	55,368	58,740	52,198	51,912	61,241	70,911	90,349	98,890
Earnings	35,593	34,621	35,129	41,918	53,394	55,183	56,958	50,945	50,729	59,559	68,402	86,998	95,514
Distributed earnings	18,687	19,780	26,077	25,264	41,744	43,257	36,553	33,945	34,441	28,847	38,265	32,991	37,629
Other private receipts	68,267	57,633	52,806	55,592	70,571	92,638	94,072	81,186	66,826	63,495	79,498	101,836	102,866
U.S. government receipts	5,227	5,499	6,413	5,311	6,703	5,653	10,512	8,023	7,114	5,108	4,101	4,695	4,644
Royalties and license fees	6,177	6,678	8,113	10,183	12,146	13,818	16,634	17,819	19,656	20,304	22,661	27,383	29,974
Affiliated	n.a.	n.a.	6,174	7,897	9,501	10,961	13,250	14,106	15,718	15,707	17,793	21,670	23,760
Other private services	19,255	20,035	27,303	28,701	30,709	36,204	39,540	47,024	50,294	54,517	61,093	66,850	73,569
Affiliated	n.a.	n.a.	8,385	8,494	9,568	12,296	13,622	14,539	16,581	16,740	18,651	20,272	22,810

Sources: Michael Mann, Daniel Atherton, Laura Brokenbaugh, Sylvia Bargas, "U.S. International Sales and Purchases of Private Services," *Survey of Current Business* 76 (November 1996): 70–112; Christopher Bach, "U.S. International Transactions, Revised Estimates for 1974–96," *Survey of Current Business* 77 (July 1997): 43–99; and unpublished information from the U.S. Department of Commerce.

Note: Figures are in millions of dollars.

With respect to the second point, data reported by the Internal Revenue Service are useful in interpreting the general picture derived from BEA data, even though the calendar-year definitions are not the same. Foreign-source income declared by corporations claiming a foreign tax credit in 1990 was $99.6 billion, while deferred income retained abroad was $34.9 billion. Active foreign-source income reported in the general basket was $73.6 billion; the foreign tax credit limitation was $24.7 billion and the foreign tax credit claimed was $22.6 billion, leaving a residual U.S. tax liability of $2.1 billion. Part of the $99.6 billion received by U.S. corporations was passive foreign-source income (such as interest received), and another part was financial service income. These separate categories of income may be subject to a higher residual rate of U.S. taxation because they cannot be combined with other foreign-source income that has been subject to a high foreign rate of taxation. For example, in the case of passive income of $4.3 billion, the foreign tax credit limitation was $1.462 billion and the foreign tax credit claimed was $385 million; these figures imply an effective foreign income tax rate of 9 percent. In the case of financial service income, the corresponding numbers were a $2.432 billion limitation, a $1.536 billion foreign tax credit claimed, and an effective foreign tax rate of 21.5 percent.

The total foreign tax credit limitation for all corporate income was $29.6 billion, and the foreign tax credit claimed was $25.0 billion. The items in the general basket cited above account for a large share of the U.S. tax liability on foreign-source income (83 percent) but a smaller share of the residual tax collected by the U.S. government after allowing for foreign tax credits (43 percent). While other items are important from the standpoint of tax administration, the incentives examined in this paper apply to a significant part of U.S. activity abroad.

8.5.2 The Excess Credit Position of U.S. Parent Firms

By reducing the U.S. statutory tax rate and establishing separate income baskets to calculate the foreign tax credit limitation, the Tax Reform Act of 1986 made it much more likely that U.S. parent firms would be in excess credit positions with respect to income in the general basket. Tax return data analyzed by Altshuler and Newlon (1993) from the set of U.S. companies with positive foreign-source income indicate that the percentage of income reported by firms in excess credit positions was 35 percent in 1982 and 42 percent in 1984. The postreform figure for 1990 shows that 65 percent of the income declared in the general basket was by firms with excess foreign tax credits. Therefore, a much wider set of firms can benefit from favorable source rules than was true a decade earlier. Whether this figure declines in the future depends in part on how costly firms find it to shift income or operations out of high-tax countries or whether foreign countries reduce their tax rates in competition with the United States.

The extent to which benefits are available from declaring additional foreign-source income varies considerably across industries. Based on 1990 data table 8.3 shows the amount of foreign-source income declared by industry and the extent to which aggregate tax payments exceeded the foreign tax credit limitation for firms in the industry. Column (3) shows the percentage of foreign-source income accounted for by firms in an excess credit position, and column (4) presents the average effective tax rate on active foreign-source income.

Note the unique position of the office and computing machinery industry. Not only does it account for nearly half of all the excess credits reported by nonpetroleum manufacturing parents, but the proportion of industry income accounted for by firms with excess credits exceeds 95 percent. That industry, however, should not be regarded as typical of all high-technology industries where returns to intangibles are an important part of total revenue. Other high-technology industries such as drugs and electronics owe a residual U.S. tax. Some industries may be more reliant on production and sales in high-tax countries, while other industries are more footloose and can locate production in low-tax countries but still serve high-tax markets. Furthermore, the average effective tax rate is an endogenous variable, determined by the mix of repatriated income subject to different tax rates, and some industries may have a lower cost of adjusting the form of their repatriations in order to reduce their overall tax burden.

The Altshuler-Newlon study also reports the likelihood that a firm's foreign tax credit position changes from excess credit to excess limit or vice versa. Comparing 1980 to 1982 and then 1982 to 1984, they find that 52.4 percent and then 58.1 percent of income was reported by firms whose tax credit positions did not shift. That leaves a significant share of firms whose positions did shift, perhaps due to exogenous changes in policy or to random shocks over the business cycle or to tax-motivated adjustments by the firm. While a firm might have less incentive to alter its exports or foreign production if an excess credit position were only transitory, how should observed shifts in the firm's foreign tax credit position be interpreted? Knowing a firm's expected or more permanent ex ante foreign tax credit position would allow a more accurate assessment of the role of taxes. Altshuler and Newlon create such a proxy in their study of multinational repatriation practices, a good precedent for other work. If firms assign a high probability to having excess credits, even firms in excess limit will respond to the source rule incentives discussed above.

8.5.3 The Sales Source Rules

The sales source rules do not provide a neutral incentive to all U.S. exporters. Rather, the incentive only arises when the firm is a multinational corporation with foreign affiliate operations that generate excess foreign tax credits. The greater the profit rate per dollar of sales, the greater the benefit to multinational exports. Because such multinational corporations also may pay high royalties, however, they may not consider sales source rule benefits to be the most desirable strategy to absorb foreign tax credits.

Table 8.3 **Excess Credit Positions of U.S. Corporations, 1990**

Industry	Foreign Source Income (1)	Excess Credit (2)	Share of Income Reported by Firms in Excess Credit (3)	Average Effective Foreign Tax Rate (4)
Food	2,914	26	37.8	34.8
Paper	1,454	−16	13.6	32.9
Industrial chemicals	4,840	59	68.4	34.8
Drugs	3,867	−46	34.2	32.9
Other chemicals	2,616	104	30.2	37.6
Primary metals	1,107	14	33.0	34.6
Fabricated metals	1,173	23	72.3	35.9
Office and computing machinery	10,875	516	95.5	38.8
Other nonelectrical machinery	1,551	117	62.7	40.2
Electrical machinery and electronics	4,222	−153	47.6	29.6
Motor vehicles	4,314	181	99.4	38.2
Other transport equipment	1,105	39	21.5	36.7
Instruments	2,552	95	68.0	37.3
Other manufacturing	4,429	106	44.5	36.1
Total manufacturing, except petroleum	47,019	1,066	62.8	36.0

Source: U.S. Department of the Treasury, Office of Tax Analysis, unpublished information.

Note: All dollar values are in millions.

Rousslang's review of the sales source rules provides direct observation of which firms actually claimed these benefits. Thirty-six percent of the allocated export income was claimed by firms in excess credit positions, although those firms accounted for 73 percent of the tax saving. By claiming additional foreign-source export income, many firms converted their position from one of potential excess credits to one of excess limit. Industries that gained an above average tax benefit, measured as a share of export sales, appear to be paper and publishing, drugs and toiletries, office and computing machinery, electrical machinery and electronics, and instruments.[8] Note that this list includes the three manufacturing industries in table 8.3 that were not in excess credit in 1990. In those industries the tax incentive to expand exports further is much smaller on average.

Rousslang projects the potential effect of the sales source rules by calculating the marginal reduction in the cost of capital from this tax benefit, multiplying the resultant price effect by the relevant export demand elasticity, and finally allowing for subsequent adjustment of the exchange rate. Such a procedure is standard practice when the effect of a tax policy change is difficult to disentangle from other influences, although its accuracy depends on the appropriate elasticities being known.

If the experience of individual firms were to be evaluated to verify such projections, what effects would demonstrate the influence of the sales source rules? One possibility is that the tax benefit from exporting would cause the U.S. parent to serve foreign markets by greater export production rather than affiliate production abroad. Under that scenario the ratio of exports to affiliate sales is likely to rise, especially if the foreign market is fixed in size and greater exports necessarily cause a reduction in affiliate sales. Another possibility, however, is suggested by a complementary relationship between exports and affiliate sales (Lipsey and Weiss 1981; Grubert and Mutti 1991). In this situation, a U.S. export may be an input with few close substitutes in foreign production, but the output produced abroad may be sold in markets where there are many substitutes available. Thus, a lower tax on U.S. exports or a lower tax on foreign profits both promote exports and affiliate sales. Where output will be affected most cannot be predicted a priori when affiliate sales represent a mixture of sales in a protected home market and in more competitive world markets.

For example, in a regression to explain the ratio of U.S. exports to total affiliate sales, based on the Commerce Department's 1982 benchmark survey of direct investment abroad used in Grubert and Mutti (1991), a higher foreign corporate income tax rate reduces the export share:

8. This calculation is based on Rousslang's figure for the foreign tax credits absorbed in each industry divided by U.S. multinational exports in that industry, as reported in U.S. Department of Commerce (1992).

$$\ln[\text{Exports}/\text{Affiliated sales}] = \underset{(2.42)}{12.69} + \underset{(3.19)}{4.37}\ \ln(1+\text{Tax}) - \underset{(-.86)}{.17}\ln \text{GDP}$$
$$- \underset{(-2.06)}{.64}\ \text{Trade barrier}$$
$$- \underset{(-2.27)}{1.02}\ \ln \text{GDP}/\text{Capita} + \underset{(1.69)}{2.06}\ \text{Transport},$$
$$F_{5,27} = 4.69, \qquad R^2 = .37$$

where Tax is the host-country corporate tax rate, Trade barrier is a World Bank categorization of progressively more restrictive host country trade policy, Transport is a dummy for sales within North America, and the numbers in parentheses are *t*-statistics. The regression also appears credible in demonstrating that exports will be lower where trade barriers are higher and where production in the host country is more likely due to a larger market and higher labor productivity. Using the next available benchmark survey for 1989 for the same set of countries, however, the tax coefficient is insignificant. That outcome does not indicate that taxes are unimportant but only that there is not a differential effect on exports and affiliate sales.

This distinction can be seen by considering the two separate demand equations:

$$\ln(\text{Exports}) = a_0 + a_1\ \ln(1-\text{Tax}) + a_2\ \ln \text{GDP} + \cdots,$$
$$\ln(\text{Affiliate sales}) = b_0 + b_1\ \ln(1-\text{Tax}) + b_2 \ln \text{GDP} + \cdots,$$

and then subtracting the second from the first to give

$$\ln(\text{Exports}/\text{Affiliate sales}) = (a_0 - b_0) + (a_1 - b_1)\ln(1-\text{Tax}) + (a_2 - b_2)\ln \text{GDP} + \cdots$$

In 1989 higher foreign corporate income taxes still have a negative effect on affiliate sales (a statistically significant estimate of b_1), but the effect on exports is too imprecisely estimated for the difference between the two to be significant.

Kemsley (1995) relies on a similar ratio approach to assess the sales source rules, but he obtains different results. Based on a time-series analysis of Compustat data for individual firms he identifies two trends in the post-1986 period: exports relative to affiliate sales have risen, and a larger share of firms appear to be in excess credit positions. He estimates that firms in excess credit positions account for this increased reliance on exports to serve foreign markets. Average export sales in his sample are $80 million per firm, and he projects that in the absence of the sales source benefits a firm would export $70 million less.

This strong effect may be due to systematic differences across firms in the products they make, the country markets they serve, and the tax rates applicable in those markets. For example, exporters may successfully develop markets in high-tax countries, but their sales may be more attributable to tastes or income levels in those countries than to tax factors. Therefore, Kemsley also estimates an aggregate cross-sectional relationship similar to the one reported above.[9] He again reports a strong effect from the sales source rules: in countries with higher tax rates a larger share of the market is served by exports and this relationship is more pronounced in 1989 than in 1982.[10] Because the causation in this relationship still is ambiguous, it is premature to claim a precise measure of the sales source rules' effectiveness.

8.5.4 Royalties as Foreign-Source Income

Royalty receipts are much larger than allocated export income under the sales source rules, and at least in absolute terms a greater influence on multinational operations can be expected. By paying royalties a firm can increase its after-tax return from operating in high-tax countries. The tax saving is greater for firms that would be in excess credit than for those in excess limit. Under what circumstances will this tax saving affect the location of real economic activity?

If the foreign market can only be served by affiliate production and if the technology developed for the home market can be costlessly applied to produc-

9. By looking at two different benchmark years, Kemsley explicitly considers changes in the cost of exporting from the United States. The two demand equations become

$$\ln(\text{Exports}) = a_0 + a_1 \ln P_x + a_2 \ln P_f + a_3 \ln \text{GDP} + \cdots,$$

$$\ln(\text{Affiliate sales}) = b_0 + b_1 \ln P_x + b_2 \ln P_f + b_3 \ln \text{GDP} + \cdots,$$

where P_x represents the price of exporting from the United States, which is affected by the U.S. tax rate on export income, and P_f represents the price of affiliate production in the foreign country, which is affected by the host-country tax rate for firms in excess credit. If changes in export and foreign prices are presumed to have symmetric effects, then the ratio of export to affiliate sales appears as

$$\ln(\text{Exports / Affiliate sales}) = (a_0 - b_0) + e \ \ln(P_x / P_f) + (a_3 - b_3)\ln \text{GDP},$$

where the elasticity of substitution, e, requires that $a_1 + a_2 = b_1 + b_2$, a testable constraint from parameters estimated in the two separate demand equations (Leamer and Stern 1970).

10. The dominance of the substitution effect in Kemsley's sample of firms may be attributable to a different conceptual measure, aside from the difference in data source and time frame: by focusing only on multinational exports to unrelated parties, which thereby excludes 43 percent of multinational exports, possible complementarities between U.S. and foreign production are less likely to be observed. In the cross-sectional study, treating only the ratio between exports and affiliate sales may obscure the causal relationship involved. For example, affiliate production may be lower in countries with high tax rates, which would cause the ratio of exports to affiliate sales to rise even in the absence of a separate effect on exports from the sales source rules. Because Kemsley does not report separate export and affiliate demand estimates, or the corresponding separability tests noted above, reasons why his results differ from Grubert and Mutti cannot be clearly identified. Possible explanations are differences in the definition of the tax variable (average effective tax rates vs. statutory tax rates) and differences in the set of countries included in the analysis.

tion in the foreign market, then the royalty represents a pure rent. A change in the tax treatment of the royalty merely changes the distribution of the rent without altering the firm's operations in the country. If the firm can exploit the technology elsewhere and still serve the same foreign market, however, favorable tax treatment of the royalty can alter the incentive to produce in a country. In particular, treating royalties as foreign-source income reduces the disadvantage of producing in a high-tax country where the cost of equity-financed investment otherwise is higher.

Two relationships are relevant in assessing the empirical response to this tax incentive. One is the tendency for firms to pay larger royalties from high-tax locations. Aggregate data from the 1989 benchmark survey show this effect quite strongly, for various representations of royalty payments as the dependent variable and for various potentially relevant tax effects. The relevant tax variable is somewhat ambiguous because the tax price of paying a royalty depends on the foreign tax credit position of the parent and the alternative forgone (retaining income abroad, paying a dividend, paying interest, etc.). Also, if royalties are represented relative to assets or sales, the foreign tax rate influences the denominator as well, implying a different functional form.

Estimates based on the aggregate data used above for all affiliates in a host country give the following results:

$$\text{Royalty/sales} = \underset{(2.38)}{.009} - \underset{(-3.28)}{.040}\, w_r - \underset{(-2.48)}{.028}\ln(1-t), \quad F_{2,27} = 8.50,\ R^2 = .34;$$

$$\text{Royalty/sales} = \underset{(2.18)}{.010} - \underset{(-3.19)}{.040}\, w_r + \underset{(-2.01)}{.032}\, t, \quad F_{2,27} = 7.12,\ R^2 = .30;$$

$$\text{Royalty/sales} = \underset{(4.40)}{.017} - \underset{(-3.99)}{.038}\, w_r - \underset{(-.37)}{.0006}\, t - \underset{(-3.74)}{.083}\,\text{High} + \underset{(4.31)}{.23}\,\text{High} * t,$$

$$F_{4,25} = 11.89,\ R^2 = .60;$$

where w_r is the withholding rate imposed on royalties, t is the effective income tax rate, High is a dummy equal to one for those countries where the effective tax rate exceeds 0.34, and the term High $*$ t multiplies this dummy by the tax rate. Royalties as a share of affiliate sales are larger in countries where the foreign income tax rate is higher and the royalty withholding rate is lower. The final equation suggests that firms operating in countries where the foreign tax rate exceeds the U.S. rate are particularly likely to be those that can adopt the strategy of paying higher royalties. This relationship is demonstrated more completely in an analysis of firm-specific data by Grubert (1998), which controls for firm characteristics such as R&D expenditures and also treats other repatriation decisions the firm makes.

This effect on financial practices also may affect the firm's real operations.

Using firm-specific tax return data for 1990, Grubert and Mutti (1995) found that probit estimates of the likelihood of a firm's locating in a given country were quite sensitive to the host-country corporate income tax rate. The size of this deterrent tax effect fell by roughly 20 percent when a variable was included that interacted the relevant tax rate with a firm's expenditure on research and development per dollar of assets. That is, the opportunity to pay royalties is greater for companies that have larger stocks of intangible, intellectual property (represented by research and development expenditures), and firms that can pay higher royalties face less of a penalty operating in high-tax countries. The empirical estimates from 1990 data suggest that the opportunity to treat royalties as foreign-source income does encourage investment in high-tax locations. Subsequent analysis based on 1992 data, however, did not find this relationship to be significant. Establishing the robustness of potential effects of source rules on the location of real activity apparently will require additional data and analysis.

8.6 Conclusions

This paper extends an earlier literature by Horst (1971) and others from the 1970s that demonstrated how low tax rates and the opportunity to defer the repatriation of foreign income created an incentive to locate production abroad rather than export from the United States. The focus here is on a different set of tax provisions that also may influence the location of production internationally. Rather than analyze the level of foreign tax rates, however, the paper evaluates U.S. rules for sourcing income, a determination that is important in calculating the foreign tax credit limitation. These source rules have become increasingly important because a much larger proportion of the income earned abroad by U.S. exporters and by U.S. subsidiaries is reported by parents in excess foreign tax credit positions.

The ability to characterize income as foreign source is especially beneficial to firms with excess credits because income that is subject to little taxation abroad also may be free of U.S. taxation. The stylized examples demonstrate that while the effects of these provisions are not as transparent as the effects of statutory tax rates, they create significant incentives to report taxable income in certain forms. The sales source rules provide an important benefit by allowing roughly half of export income to be regarded as foreign source. Treating royalties as foreign source may provide an even greater benefit to affiliate production, though, since royalties reduce the affiliate's foreign tax burden and may create no U.S. tax liability when the parent is in an excess credit position. That potentially large effects on firm profits lead to large changes in real economic activity cannot be conclusively demonstrated. Tentative evidence suggests that U.S. exports increase as a result of the sales source rules, and foreign production in high-tax locations is encouraged by treating royalties as foreign-source income.

References

Altshuler, Rosanne, and Scott Newlon. 1993. The effects of U.S. tax policy on the income repatriation patterns of multinational corporations. In *Studies in international taxation,* ed. A. Giovannini, R. G. Hubbard, and J. Slemrod, 77–115. Chicago: University of Chicago Press.

Baldwin, Robert. 1970. *Nontariff distortion of international trade.* Washington, D.C.: Brookings Institution.

Bergsten, Fred, Thomas Horst, and Theodore Moran. 1978. *American multinationals and American interests.* Washington, D.C.: Brookings Institution.

Feldstein, Martin, and Paul Krugman. 1990. International trade effects of value-added taxation. In *Taxation in the global economy,* ed. A. Razin and J. Slemrod, 263–82. Chicago: University of Chicago Press.

Grubert, Harry. 1998. Taxes and the division of foreign operating income among royalties, interest, dividends, and retained earnings. *Journal of Public Economics,* in press.

Grubert, Harry, and John Mutti. 1991. Taxes, tariffs and transfer pricing in multinational corporate decision making. *Review of Economics and Statistics* 73 (2): 285–93.

———. 1995. Do taxes influence where U.S. corporations invest? Mimeograph.

Hines, James, and Glenn Hubbard. 1990. Coming home to America: Dividend repatriations by U.S. multinationals. In *Taxation in the global economy,* ed. A. Razin and J. Slemrod, 161–200. Chicago: University of Chicago Press.

Horst, Thomas. 1971. The theory of the multinational firm: Optimal behavior under different tariff and tax rates. *Journal of Political Economy* 79 (5): 1059–72.

Internal Revenue Service. 1993. *Statistics of income 1990 sourcebook: Corporation income tax returns.* Washington, D.C.: Internal Revenue Service.

Kemsley, Deen. 1995. The effect of taxes on the choice between exports and foreign production. Mimeograph.

Leamer, Edward, and Robert Stern. 1970. *Quantitative international economics.* Boston: Allyn and Bacon.

Lipsey, Robert, and Merle Yahr Weiss. 1981. Foreign production and exports in manufacturing industries. *Review of Economics and Statistics* 63 (4): 488–94.

Matthews, Kathleen. 1995. The U.S. tax implications of GATT. *Tax Notes International,* 13 March, pp. 900–901.

McLure, Charles, John Mutti, Victor Thuronyi, and George Zodrow. 1990. *The taxation of income from business and capital in Colombia.* Durham, N.C.: Duke University Press.

Nutter, Sarah. 1994. Statistics of income studies of international income and taxes. *SOI Bulletin* 13 (3): 10–31.

Rousslang, Donald. 1994. Sales source rules for U.S. exports: How much do they cost? *Tax Notes International,* 24 February.

Sandheimer, John, and Sylvia Bargas. 1994. U.S. international sales and purchases of private services. *Survey of Current Business* (September): 98–138.

U.S. Department of Commerce. Bureau of Economic Analysis. 1992. *U.S. direct investment abroad: 1989 Benchmark survey, final results.* Washington, D.C.: Government Printing Office.

U.S. Department of the Treasury. 1990. *Report on the FSC legislation.* Washington, D.C.: U.S. Department of the Treasury.

———. 1992. *Report on the sales source rules.* Washington, D.C.: U.S. Department of the Treasury.

Comment Kristen L. Willard

One of the persistent questions in international economic research is, Why do some firms choose to develop multinational production facilities while others expand internationally through direct export or licensing arrangements? Despite decades of research into the issue, the profession has arrived at few unequivocal conclusions. Rather, we have learned that the organization of a firm's global expansion efforts may be influenced by many competing factors, including but not limited to standard international trade issues, such as comparative advantage and tariffs; standard industrial organization issues, such as market concentration; and of course taxes. Indeed, the explicit question of the extent to which tax burdens may affect the location of investment has received an increasing amount of attention in the wake of the 1986 tax reform. (See Hines 1996 for a review of the literature.)

This paper contributes to the discussion of the relationship between tax policy and multinational production decisions in two important ways. First, in the tradition of Ault and Bradford (1990), this paper documents the rules governing the sourcing of foreign income for U.S. corporations, providing a much needed resource on such complications as the use of foreign sales corporations, sales source rules for recharacterizing export income as foreign source, and the treatment of royalty income.

Through the use of the extended example of the U.S. computer industry selling computing services abroad, the reader can see the conflicting incentives inherent in the source rules. Moreover, it also becomes clear that firms able to easily recharacterize the nature of a transaction—for example, from a product export to service income—may avoid taxation in a manner unintended by policymakers. This may be particularly relevant in technology-intensive industries: the sale of computer software may be indistinguishable from the provision of some computer service, from the clients' perspective. However, since tariffs are rarely imposed on service provision, this recharacterization gives new meaning to the idea of tariff jumping.

The second contribution of the paper is that the authors provide some comparisons of the likely magnitude of incentive effects from various combinations of these rules and in so doing generate some empirically testable implications of source rules on investment. For instance, higher foreign tariff rates discourage U.S. production relative to licensing or investment in foreign production capacity; hence, reductions in foreign tariff rates should increase domestic production, all else equal. In addition, for excess credit firms, affiliate production when royalties can be classified as foreign-source income is particularly attractive in low-tax locations. Finally, since the value of the tax incentives are closely tied to the domestic tax rate, researchers may be able to mea-

Kristen L. Willard is assistant professor of finance and economics at Columbia University Graduate School of Business.

sure the sensitivity of firms to these incentives by considering individual firm reliance on various methods of global expansion and production before and after changes in the U.S. tax rate, as happened in 1986.

In using these benchmark numbers to generate empirical implications, the reader should be aware that the authors make some incidence assumptions. For instance, in calculating the residual profit from exporting goods subject to an import tariff, the authors have implicitly assumed that consumers in the foreign market bear the full burden of the tariff. This is a reasonable assumption only insofar as the good in question is provided by a firm in a competitive market. The incidence of import tariffs imposed on the product of firms with significant market power is likely to be substantially different, requiring a revision of the return calculation. Since intraindustry trade between oligopolies is an increasingly important aspect of international trade flows, this incidence assumption needs to be considered carefully by researchers confronting data having derived testable implications from the relative returns calculations presented by the authors.

Unfortunately, this work is not as broadly applicable as the researcher interested in international tax policies might guess given the title of section 8.1: "Basic Approaches in Taxing Foreign-Source Income." The paper does not, as that phrase implies, attempt to review the range of approaches to taxing foreign-source income around the globe. Rather, the paper is a more narrowly focused exploration of the U.S. system of sourcing rules. Since few other countries have similar rules, researchers must be careful not to extrapolate too much from U.S. experience, summarized so nicely here, for the differences typically extend beyond the details of tax rates. Fully one-third of the countries in the world impose taxes only on income derived from local activities (so-called territorial taxation). Because foreign-source income plays no role in local tax collections, these countries experience no distortions or complications arising from necessarily arbitrary definitions (Hines and Willard 1994).

Even among those countries that do tax worldwide income of their residents, the U.S. practice of defining foreign-source income appears atypical. Japan and the United Kingdom, for instance, allow host-country definitions of income to prevail for their multinational firms. This U.S.-centric view of taxation is notable, for instance, in the discussion of host-country taxation of service income. Mutti and Grubert argue that this type of income taxation amounts to a trade barrier because "those individuals will also face home-country taxation of what the home country regards as domestic-source income." This conflict will clearly never arise for countries that allow host-country definitions to prevail in determining the source of income.

Nevertheless, with this caveat in mind, the paper by Mutti and Grubert provides a good stepping-off point for understanding the U.S. approach to foreign-source income and gives the reader a good understanding of the marginal decisions that can be distorted by policy rules defining the source of income.

References

Ault, Hugh J., and David F. Bradford. 1990. Taxing international income: An analysis of the U.S. system and its economic premises. In *Taxation in the global economy,* ed. Assaf Razin and Joel Slemrod, 11–46. Chicago: University of Chicago Press.

Hines, James R. 1996. Tax policy and the activities of multinational corporations. NBER Working Paper no. 5589. Cambridge, Mass.: National Bureau of Economic Research.

Hines, James R., and Kristen L. Willard. 1994. Trick or treaty: Bargains and surprises in international tax negotiations. Mimeograph.

9 The Effect of U.S. State Tax and Investment Promotion Policy on the Distribution of Inward Direct Investment

Deborah L. Swenson

9.1 Introduction

Foreign investment plays an increasingly significant role in the U.S. labor market. By 1992, foreign investment provided more than 5 percent of all U.S. employment, although there was significant variation among the different states. For example, as table 9.1 indicates, while foreign employment represented almost 12 percent of all employment in Delaware and Hawaii, in Montana and South Dakota it accounted for little more than 2 percent of employees. Foreign investment is often seen as desirable for its employment benefits alone. However, it is widely believed that foreign investment may provide other advantages such as knowledge spillovers to host locations as well.[1] In this context, it is not surprising that state governments during the 1980s intensified their efforts to capture a larger fraction of these new investments. It is natural to ask how successful these states were in altering investment outcomes. It is also important to ask how this investment responded to differences in factor market conditions both across the nation and within regions.

The responsiveness of foreign investment to differences in tax and promotion policies intranationally as well as internationally, however, remains a matter of debate. Uncertainty arises in part from the number of ways to measure the volume of foreign investment. Measures include capital investment, the number of new plant investments, and the new employment generated. The more important reason for uncertainty is the difficulty of measuring and characterizing the significance of fiscal and promotion policies. While one may readily observe the existence of various investment inducements, it is difficult to provide an accurate view of the magnitude of the benefits conferred by these

Deborah L. Swenson is assistant professor of economics at the University of California, Davis, and a faculty research fellow of the National Bureau of Economic Research.

1. This argument applies particularly to "greenfield" investment.

Table 9.1 Growth in Foreign Employment by State, 1980–92

State	1992 Employment[a]		Foreign Percentage[b]		1980–92 Percentage Change[c]
	Foreign	U.S.	1980	1992	
Total	4,705.5	93,022	2.08	5.06	2.98
Connecticut	81.7	1,354	2.36	6.03	3.67
Maine	24.1	428	3.15	5.63	2.48
Massachusetts	113.6	2,508	1.79	4.53	2.74
New Hampshire	27.7	427	2.85	6.49	3.64
Rhode Island	12.3	376	1.62	3.27	1.65
Vermont	7.5	212	2.77	3.54	0.77
Delaware	35.8	302	3.29	11.9	8.56
Maryland	74.8	1,727	2.10	4.33	2.23
New Jersey	216.3	2,962	3.67	7.30	3.63
New York	340	6,552	2.41	5.19	2.78
Pennsylvania	215.3	4,496	2.31	4.79	2.48
Illinois	246.4	4,575	2.22	5.39	3.17
Indiana	126.2	2,226	2.00	5.67	3.67
Michigan	140.4	3,394	1.74	4.14	2.4
Ohio	212.6	4,228	1.85	5.03	3.18
Wisconsin	81.8	2,052	2.78	3.99	1.21
Iowa	32.6	1,062	1.5	3.07	1.57
Kansas	27.4	926	1.28	2.96	1.68
Minnesota	94.1	1,896	1.64	4.96	3.32
Missouri	77.2	2,025	1.44	3.81	2.37
Nebraska	16	626	0.72	2.56	1.84
North Dakota	5.3	217	0.88	2.44	1.56
South Dakota	5.8	248	0.37	2.34	1.97
Alabama	60.7	1,380	1.5	4.4	2.9
Arkansas	30.8	815	1.69	3.78	2.09
Florida	194.9	4,666	1.65	4.18	2.53
Georgia	154.3	2,518	2.89	6.13	3.24
Kentucky	69.4	1,260	1.67	5.51	3.84
Louisiana	62.1	1,325	2.41	4.69	2.28
Mississippi	23.8	771	1.02	3.09	2.07
North Carolina	191.3	2,698	2.59	7.09	4.5
South Carolina	111.1	1,267	4.11	8.77	4.66
Tennessee	121.7	1,933	2.3	6.30	4
Virginia	119.9	2,321	1.58	5.17	3.59
West Virginia	34.1	510	2.75	6.69	3.94
Arizona	52.6	1,298	1.29	4.05	2.76
New Mexico	13.6	462	1.4	2.94	1.54
Oklahoma	43.8	980	1.5	4.47	2.97
Texas	324.4	6,090	2.16	5.33	3.17
Colorado	61	1,355	1.46	4.50	3.04
Idaho	13.5	344	0.97	3.92	2.95
Montana	5.4	254	0.55	2.13	1.58
Utah	22.7	638	1.62	3.56	1.94
Wyoming	5.5	154	1.38	3.57	2.19

Table 9.1 (continued)

State	1992 Employment[a]		Foreign Percentage[b]		1980–92 Percentage Change[c]
	Foreign	U.S.	1980	1992	
California	521.8	10,614	2.06	4.92	2.86
Nevada	23	576	1.15	3.99	2.84
Oregon	43	1,063	0.90	4.05	3.15
Washington	78.7	1,870	1.18	4.21	3.03
Alaska	9.7	179	5.05	5.42	0.37
Hawaii	53	451	3.74	11.7	8.01

Source: Data are taken from the Bureau of Economic Analysis benchmark surveys.

[a]Number of employees in thousands.

[b]Foreign percentage of overall employment in each state.

[c]Percentage change in state employment that is provided by foreign affiliates.

programs. Finally, the implementation of programs is not exogenous. Hence, in determining the value of a new program, further analysis of the governmental unit is important.

This study examines U.S. state employment data between the years 1980 and 1992 to determine the effect of state policies on the interstate distribution of employment by foreign firms. The focus on employment is motivated in part by the fact that little work to date has examined the role of fiscal policies in changing the distribution of foreign employment. In addition, since many state policies are justified by their positive employment effects, it is important to assess the significance of these claims.

Two tools are used to identify the effect of state policies on foreign employment. First, contrary to most treatments of investment, this paper does not assume that all states are equal competitors for foreign investment. Instead, states are assumed to compete most intensely with their neighbors. In other words, there should be a higher degree of substitutability among states within a region than between states located in different regions of the United States. Therefore, tax and factor market variables are measured relative to each state's region rather than to the nation as a whole. Second, foreign firms operating in the United States ultimately face one of two different tax treatments of their U.S.-based income when they repatriate their U.S. earnings to their home countries. The implication of this treatment dichotomy is that some countries will respond more vigorously to interstate tax differences than others. This dichotomy will be used as a further discriminant in testing for fiscal effects.[2]

The findings of this paper are as follows. Tax effects are not apparent in the

2. This method is introduced in the context of state data by Hines (1996), which studies cross-sectional data on foreign plant, property, and equipment in 1987. In contrast, this paper will study panel data concerning foreign employment.

employment of all nonbank foreign affiliates. However, tax effects are evident once the focus of attention is shifted to foreign manufacturing employment. Presumably, manufacturing employment is more responsive to interregional tax differences since proximity to final markets is less important than it is for nonmanufacturing activity. Further controls for tax system differences facing investors of different nationalities indicate that the intraregional distribution of investment is affected by state taxes. In contrast, state promotion efforts, such as the opening of state investment promotion offices overseas, provide no measurable stimulus to foreign investment. The failure to identify a significant effect for state promotion efforts may arise for any of a number of reasons. It is possible that the interstate subtleties of these state efforts are not easily captured by indicator variables that denote their presence. On the other hand, some states may implement such programs precisely because they are attempting to overcome intrinsic disadvantages in attracting investment. For example, a state whose industrial base has recently deteriorated may institute new policies that succeed in attracting new investment. The effects may not be readily apparent, however, since the policy brings the state back to the national average for states with similar observable characteristics. In addition, if a state adds a new policy tool but it is matched by neighboring states in its region, no net effect may be observed. Finally, it must be recognized that investment responds not only to tax and fiscal variables but also to nontax factors that enhance the attractiveness of one state over others. It is possible that the lack of a positive finding reflects that fact that foreign investors will not be attracted to a state on the basis of information programs unless the state has attractive characteristics.

The organization of this paper is as follows: Section 9.2 describes investment incentives and briefly reviews some previous work on the issue. Section 9.3 provides a model that relates investment decisions to the tax and promotion environment. Description of the data and discussion of relevant employment and fiscal trends are presented in section 9.4. Estimation proceeds in section 9.5, and section 9.6 concludes.

9.2 Background on Investment Incentives

It is natural to expect that, all else equal, increases in state taxes deter investment while state investment promotion efforts encourage investment. However, much research on state taxation finds that investment is only minimally responsive to tax policy.[3] That corporate tax rates or average tax payments are not shown to consistently deter investment may mean in part that the revenues collected are used for the provision of infrastructure or services valued by busi-

3. Carlton (1983) is unable to find any significant evidence that state taxes exerted a negative effect on investment. In contrast, Helms (1985) and Wasylenko and McGuire (1985), when looking at employment changes, and Bartik (1985) and Papke (1987, 1991), when looking at industry-specific effective tax rates, discover significant tax effects. Extensive surveys of previous findings are provided by Bartik (1991) and Wasylenko (1994).

nesses. Nonetheless, numerous states during the 1980s made major changes to their tax systems, claiming that they would help to attract and retain investment and consequently raise state employment levels.

More recently, a number of papers have examined the responsiveness of foreign investment to state tax policies. Coughlin, Terza, and Arromdee (1991), Woodward (1992), Friedman, Gerlowski, and Silberman (1992), and Luger and Shetty (1985) study international investment in U.S. states as it relates to state promotion attempts, measured by promotion expenditures, promotion offices and unitary taxes, and an effort index. Dynamic aspects of interstate competition are explored in Head, Ries, and Swenson (1994). This paper creates investment-specific measures of the fiscal incentives to be gained by investors selecting the various states and finds that while state investment promotion measures increased the investment received by one state over the others, in the aggregate states neutralized each other's efforts through emulation. Ultimately, states received the same amount of investment that they would have received in the absence of all programs. In order to identify the tax sensitivity of foreign plant, property, and equipment expenditure, Hines (1996), Slemrod (1990), and Swenson (1994) utilize investor nationality to determine the strength of country response to host-country taxation. Hines's results, which consider the interstate distribution of investment, show that states with higher taxes attract smaller shares of foreign capital equipment and plant investments.

In the international context, there is additional work that has examined the responsiveness of investment to taxes and factor markets. Wheeler and Mody (1992) study the international location of manufacturing investment and investment in the electronics industry. They find that risk and factor conditions, such as wage differences across countries, are important determinants of investment location. Grubert and Mutti (1991) and Hines and Rice (1994) give greater attention to tax conditions. Both studies show that foreign investment is responsive to tax differences. The relationship they note is nonlinear, with particularly low rates of tax creating the greatest location incentives.

However, there are a number of advantages to studying the distribution of foreign investment within the United States, rather than examining the international distribution of investment. To begin with, since almost all states use the federal method for calculating corporate income, the computation of profits by state is less complicated than the calculation of profits across countries. After the computation of profit, each state assesses corporate income taxes on this profit according to apportionment formulas that seek to determine how activities in that state contributed to the firm's overall profits.[4] In contrast, a firm's international tax payments are based on the profits it is deemed to have earned in various countries. In this context, differences in tax rates can create incentives to shift income between country jurisdictions for tax purposes as a means

4. The most common apportionment formula gives a one-third weight to payroll, sales, and capital. However, in recent years some states are increasing the relative weight placed on sales.

of reducing a foreign firm's tax liability for a given amount of real activity. For example, a multinational can, subject to some limitations, use the location of its financing to affect the amount of profit that is deemed earned and taxable in different locations. In marked contrast, a multinational operating in the United States cannot alter the amounts it pays to New Jersey versus Kansas, for example, by choosing different states for its debt or equity finance. A second advantage to the study of interstate tax differences is that interstate tax payments are not subject to the same timing issues that are present in the payment of international taxes. Foreign firms tend to become liable for home taxes when they repatriate income from host locations to the home country. As a result, it is financial movements, rather than income earning, that triggers tax payments. In the case of state taxes, taxes are based on current-year profits, rather than the timing of intrafirm financial flows that move across borders.

9.3 A Model of Investment

The objective of this paper is to determine the responsiveness of the interstate distribution of foreign employment to wage and fiscal differences between the states. In order to model this decision, we begin with the assumption that foreign firms distribute a fixed amount of new employment, L, across U.S. states.[5] From the perspective of each individual firm i, labor is allocated to U.S. states in a fashion that maximizes the firm's overall U.S. profits after tax,

$$\Pi_i = f(v_s, \tau_s, p_s). \tag{1}$$

Profits earned by each firm depend on the vector of factor prices in each state, v_s, a vector of each state's tax and promotion efforts, τ_s, and finally a vector of final goods prices, p_s. This profit function governs how much labor, L_s, the firm deploys in each state. Changes in labor demand can now be written as

$$\Delta L_s = \sum_j \beta_j * \Delta v_{sj} + \gamma * \Delta p_s + \delta * \Delta \tau_s . \tag{2}$$

However, since we are examining the geographic distribution of investment, we will now rewrite equation (2) in a way that characterizes changes of employment in state s, relative to overall foreign employment in the United States. It is assumed that there is a single price for final output on national markets, allowing us to remove the price term, Δp_s:

$$\Delta(L_s / L) = \beta_w * \Delta(w_s / w) + \delta * \Delta(\tau_s / \tau). \tag{3}$$

Each of the terms in equation (3) represents the change in the variable in a particular state relative to the average change across all states. Another assump-

5. As is demonstrated by Wheeler and Mody (1992), the *amount* of investment located in the United States will depend, in part, on conditions in the United States relative to other countries. However, we assume that the *distribution* of investment within the United States is unaffected by the international location of non-U.S. investment.

tion that is implicit in equation (3) is that the only factor price that is relevant to the demand for labor is the wage by state. Because the capital market is assumed to operate at the national level, market integration implies that firms will not face interstate differences in the cost of capital. Since it is unlikely that labor markets are integrated to the same degree, the same is not assumed to be true of labor markets. Variants of equation (3) will be used as the basis for estimation.

However, further explanation of the tax coefficient is required. First, the notion that a state will receive less foreign employment if it raises its corporate taxes relative to other states is based on two factors. Naturally, a higher corporate tax rate will subject firms operating in state s to the direct effect of lower after-tax profits. In addition, almost all states use apportionment formulas to determine what fraction of a firm's U.S. earnings will be subject to corporate tax in that state. Each state collects taxes on accounting profits, Π_i^a, that are usually calculated in a similar manner for all states. Total state taxes owed by each firm, Tax_i, are then determined as follows:

$$\text{(4)} \qquad \text{Tax}_i = \Pi_i^a \sum_s \tau_s [\theta_{sL}(L_{is} / L) + \theta_{sK}(K_{is} / K) + \theta_{ss}(S_{is} / S)].$$

The tax collected by each state is determined by the state's tax rate and by its apportionment formula. The apportionment formula determines the taxation of a firm's income according to a set of weights, θ, that are typically based on the firm's employment payroll, L, capital stock, K, and sales, S, within the state. The weights sum to one: $\theta_{sL} + \theta_{sK} + \theta_{ss} = 1$. As a result, if a firm increases its employment in a state, it increases the income that is subject to tax within that state. This factor creates an additional deterrent to placing employment in higher tax states.[6]

9.4 Data and Foreign Employment Trends

Between the Commerce Department benchmark surveys of foreign investment conducted in 1980 and 1992, employment by foreign nonbank affiliates in the United States more than doubled. Foreign nonbank affiliates provided slightly more than 2 million jobs in 1980. The number had risen to 4.7 million by 1992. Tables 9.2A and 9.2B provide further snapshots of foreign employment in the years 1980 and 1992, including a state and country breakdown of that employment. It is interesting to note that the rate of growth within a state is not uniform across investors. In part, these differences probably reflect the relative industry strengths of the investors of different nationalities.

This study uses employment data from these benchmark surveys for the

6. In recent years some states have worked to mitigate this disincentive to employment by changing the weights of their apportionment formulas to weight sales more heavily and the payroll and capital factors less heavily.

Table 9.2A **Distribution of Employment across States, by Country, 1980**

State	Country							Total
	Canada	France	Germany	Netherlands	Switzerland	United Kingdom	Japan	
Total	290	206.3	375.9	186.7	157.8	428.2	115.3	2,033.9
Connecticut	2.3	4.4	5.8		1.9	13.5	0.1	34.9
Maine	6.8			0.5		1	0.08	14.5
Massachusetts	6	1.9	10.3	2.2	1.8	13.8		47.9
New Hampshire	2.6	1.6	2.5	0.7		1.5	0.8	12.3
Rhode Island	0.5	0.5	1.3		0.984	2	0.04	6.9
Vermont	1.5			0.01	1.7	0.1		6.3
Delaware	0.5		0.9		0.02	5.3	0.006	8.7
Maryland	9	7.3	8.3	3.3	2.4	5.4	1.3	40.9
New Jersey	5.2	11.4	26.8	9.6	21.1	22.4	7.1	120.5
New York	21.4	18.7	23.3	10.9	19.7	44.8	10.9	179.3
Pennsylvania	13	12.9	31.8	2.9	8	31.7	2.2	114.6
Illinois	16.8	6.9	17	11	16.2	24.9	8.1	112.4
Indiana	5.7	5.5	12.4	9.2	2.7	6.9	1	47.3
Michigan	16	10.1	13.2	2.4	2.9	13.5	2.8	65.3
Ohio	9	13.2	15.6	4	12.3	23.9	1.3	84.2
Wisconsin	11.4	10.7	7.2	4.1	2.9	18.7	0.3	58.8
Iowa	6	0.7	2.6	1.3	1.6	5.4	0.3	19.6
Kansas	1.6	2.8	3.1	0.7	0.4	2.9	0.1	13.8
Minnesota	14.3	1.7	3.8	1.3	2.6	5.8	0.4	30.9
Missouri	6.6	1.1	6.6	2.3	2.6	5.4	0.7	30.3
Nebraska	0.8			0.3	1.3	1		5.2
North Dakota	1.3	0.03			0.02	0.08		2.4
South Dakota	0.5		0.04		0.03	0.3		1.1

Alabama	2.9	3.4	2.8	1.3	1.9	6.3		22.7
Arkansas	1.5	2	1.2		0.5	4.8		14.8
Florida	7.7	9.8	11.9	2.9	4.1	14.4	2	65.9
Georgia	10.4	7.1	8.1	6.2	2.1	15	5	67.4
Kentucky	5.2	1.1	5.1		0.5	5.9	0.4	23.2
Louisiana	4.9	2.2	8.8	8.5	2	6.7	0.4	39.6
Mississippi	2.1	0.9	1.8	0.8	0.9	2	0.2	9.5
North Carolina	11.1	4.5	12.6	8.7	3.1	17.5	0.8	67.5
South Carolina	3	8.9	11	10.3	2.5	10.3	2.6	54.2
Tennessee	3.9	3.5	4.6	12.5	5.8	7.4	1.6	44.1
Virginia	3	4.5	8.1	2.1	3	11.5	0.7	37.2
West Virginia	6	1	3.3		0.2	2		19
Arizona	3.1	0.7	4.4	0.3	0.6	1.6	0.3	14.4
New Mexico	1.8	0.1	2.3		0.07	1.9	0.02	7.1
Oklahoma	2.7	1.6	5.5		1.4	3	0.2	19.4
Texas	16.2	12.1	29.8	21.8	7.3	19.2	4.1	136.1
Colorado	4.6	2.8	3.3	1	1	4.1	0.4	19.9
Idaho	0.7		0.08			0.9	0.04	3.7
Montana	0.6	0.3	0.3			0.09	0.07	1.8
Utah	1.6	0.5	1.5		0.2	0.6	0.04	9.5
Wyoming	1.4		0.3		0.1	0.2		3
California	25.6	14.8	44.9	21.7	11.3	32.7	34.8	219.6
Nevada	0.9	0.5	0.9	0.02	0.1	0.7		4.6
Oregon	2.2	1.9	2.1	0.6	0.5	1.2		10.2
Washington	4.2	2.5	3.6	1.2	2.2	3.3	2.6	21.1
Alaska	0.8		0.005		0.006		4.6	8.3
Hawaii	0.8			0.08	0.09	0.5	9	15.5

Note: Table reports numbers of employees in thousands. The "total" column may contain a number higher than the sum of the country columns because the "total" column includes foreign employment from countries not listed individually.

Table 9.2B **Distribution of Employment across States, by Country, 1992**

State	Country								Total
	Canada	France	Germany	Netherlands	Switzerland	United Kingdom	Australia	Japan	
Total	587.9	358.7	519.5	306.1	295.1	961.4	137.8	728.2	4,705.5
Connecticut	6.4	8.7	13.9	14.1	6.9	16.7	1.2	5.1	81.7
Maine	11	0.9	0.9	1.3	0.7	5.3	0.1	0.8	24.1
Massachusetts	14.9	11.3	11.1	3.4	5.3	34.7	3.2	13	113.6
New Hampshire	7.5	1.5	3	1.2	1.2	8.2	0.8	1.8	27.7
Rhode Island	1.8	0.4	1.9	0.6	1.4	4.4	0.3	0.7	12.3
Vermont	2.4	0.5	0.8	0.4	1.1	0.8		1	7.5
Delaware	17.5	0.5	1.3	0.6	0.5	5.1		0.8	35.8
Maryland	12	6.6	8.1	7.2	5.8	13.6	1.5	7.8	74.8
New Jersey	19.2	16	29	13.9	27.7	40.5	1.6	31.6	216.3
New York	41.1	28.6	39	31.4	21	81.6	4.6	45.1	340
Pennsylvania	25	21.3	30.8	20.8	8.8	58.6	5.8	16.1	215.3
Illinois	27	13.3	26.6	14.3	27.2	53	6.4	46.2	246.4
Indiana	13.7	15.6	12.8	9.5	4.9	17.7	1.3	32	126.2
Michigan	19.9	10	23.3	4.2	4.5	25.4	9.5	3	140.4
Ohio	16.6	15.9	15.7	15.5	16.7	52.1	1.7	46.7	212.6
Wisconsin	12.8	5.3	15	8.5	8.3	15.9	1.8	4	81.8
Iowa	5.8	3.4	3.4	2.6	1.7	6.2	0.1	3.2	32.6
Kansas	6.2	2.6	2.6	1.6	2.2	6.1	0.5	2.4	27.4
Minnesota	10.7	3.4	12.7	5.3	6.1	19.4	17.5	5.2	94.1
Missouri	16.1	6.7	6.8	4.6	6.6	15.9	1.1	6.9	77.2
Nebraska	1.5	1.8	3.1	1.2	1.3	3.7	0.4	1.4	16
North Dakota	1.8	0.8	0.2	0.3	0.1	0.8	0.1	0.8	5.3
South Dakota	1.5	0.1	0.7	0.9	0.1	1.4		0.4	5.8

Alabama	7.6	12.8	4	1.6	4.2	8.8	1.9	7.8	60.7
Arkansas	5.8	2.7	0.9	1.8	1.7	4.4	1.4	4.9	30.8
Florida	20.4	18	18.1	9.6	8.3	42.7	4.8	22.1	194.9
Georgia	21.2	12.7	13.1	10.4	10.1	34.5	5.3	21	154.3
Kentucky	10.7	4.7	7.9	2.4	1.8	12.8	1.2	19.1	69.4
Louisiana	10	3.6	7	7.3	2.6	11.6	1	2.3	62.1
Mississippi	4.3	2.2	2.3	0.7	2.7	3.8	1	2	23.8
North Carolina	29	14	29.5	6.7	12.6	43	1.6	13.3	191.3
South Carolina	8.4	15	17.4	18.3	5.1	14	0.6	11.7	111.1
Tennessee	16.9	9.6	7.3	6.2	6.9	30.7	4.7	20.3	121.7
Virginia	15.3	8.5	15.1	4.9	5.7	23.3	0.6	15	119.9
West Virginia	7.1	2.1	7.1	2.8	3.2	7		1.9	34.1
Arizona	10.2	3.9	3.3	1.7	2	7.8	17.5	7.5	52.6
New Mexico	1.3	1.2	2.4	1.5	0.3	1.9	1.8	1.8	13.6
Oklahoma	1.7	5.4	2.5	1.8	1.1	7.1	0.4	4	43.8
Texas	2.4	23.2	26.7	22.4	16.5	66.5	9.1	33.8	324.4
Colorado	0.6	3.6	5.5	2.9	4.3	11	1.5	7.9	61
Idaho	1.3	0.4	7.5	0.2	1	2.8	0.1	0.2	13.5
Montana	1.7	0.3	0.6	0.2	0.2	0.9	0.8	0.3	5.4
Utah	2.4	0.7	3.8	1.4	1.5	6	0.3	1.9	22.7
Wyoming	0.6	1.3	0.7	0.4		1.5			5.5
California	35.9	31.2	48.1	27.3	28.9	97.5	17.3	147.9	521.8
Nevada	4.9	0.7	2.8	2.9	0.3	2.9	1.9	4.4	23
Oregon	4.1	1.4	9.4	0.9	1.5	6.1	1.2	12.2	43
Washington	8.9	2.9	11.2	3.7	5.8	13.1	3.5	16.9	78.7
Alaska	1.8	0.1	0.1	0.5	0.2	2.5	0.4	2.6	9.7
Hawaii	0.5	0.6	0.5	0.8	1.6	1.1	3.3	35.7	53

Note: Table reports numbers of employees in thousands. The “total” column may contain a number higher than the sum of the country columns because the “total” column includes foreign employment from countries not listed individually.

analysis in section 9.5.[7] Although employment data are available on an annual basis, the dependent variables used in the next section measure the change in employment between the 1980 and 1987 surveys and the change between the 1987 and 1992 surveys. There are a number of reasons for looking at the data at this lower frequency. First, we assume that foreign employment will adjust to changes in the fiscal and factor environments with a lag. Since it is not clear how long the lags should be, and it is not clear that the rate of adjustment to factor markets is the same as it is to fiscal changes, we examine the changes over longer time frames. Second, mergers and acquisitions were a large component of foreign investment expenditures, especially in the late 1980s. Many of these mergers were large, involving the acquisition of control over large labor forces, some of which might be reduced in subsequent selloffs. By looking at lower frequency data, we intend to capture a smoother picture of trends in foreign employment. The statistics that are of most importance to this study are those detailing investment at the state level, disaggregated by the country of investor origin.

The data on state fiscal characteristics and on policy changes are collected from a number of sources. Fiscal policies were first identified with the aid of the *Directory of Incentives for Business Investment and Development in the United States* (National Association of State Development Agencies [NASDA] 1991). Next, data on state characteristics and on state fiscal collections and expenditures were added from Census Bureau collections. Finally, the timing of changes in fiscal policies were identified through the periodical *Site Selection.*

At first glance, the fiscal environment is notable for its stability. Table 9.3A presents information on some variables of interest. For example, the range of corporate tax rates remained virtually unchanged over the 1982–90 period. The average state tax rate on corporate income did rise, but only from 6.36 to 6.71 percent. But these averages obscure some of the activity that was taking place during this interval. As table 9.3B demonstrates, though the average corporate tax rate changed only slightly, 18 states raised their rates while 7 states lowered theirs. The simultaneous changes in opposing directions mean that relative corporate taxes across states were changing and can be used to examine investment decisions.

A second tax of interest is the sales and use tax rate on manufacturing inputs. This tax applies to firm purchases of inputs, whether sourced from within or outside of the state of operation, and can lead to a significant increase in the cost of materials. Concern over this factor caused the state average sales and use tax on manufacturing inputs to be reduced by almost a third, from 1.89 to 1.27 percent (table 9.3A). State differences in the treatment of sales and use tax on manufacturing inputs are further captured in table 9.3B. Half of all states

7. U.S. Department of Commerce (1985, 1990, 1994). Data are studied from the reported samples of all nonbank affiliates and of manufacturing affiliates.

Table 9.3A **National Summary Statistics on State Taxes and Promotion Variables**

Variable	1982	1990
Corporate tax rates (%)		
Minimum	0.0	0.0
Maximum	12.0	12.0
Average	6.36	6.71
Standard deviation	2.84	2.80
Sales and use tax rates on manufacturing inputs (%)		
Minimum	0.0	0.0
Maximum	7.5	6.0
Average	1.89	1.27
Standard deviation	2.62	2.03
State corporate income tax provisions[a] (number of states)		
R&D tax credit	12	17
Investment tax credit	16	17

Source: NASDA (1991).

Note: Calculations are based on all 50 states.

[a]Not all states that offered a provision in 1982 continued to offer it in 1990.

Table 9.3B **National Summary Statistics on Changes in State Fiscal Offerings, 1982–90**

Change[a]	Number of States
Corporate tax rates	
States raising their corporate tax rates	18
States lowering their corporate tax rates	7
States with no corporate tax	4
Sales and use tax rates on manufacturing inputs	
States raising their sales tax rates	25
States lowering their sales tax rates	0
States lowering their taxes on manufacturing inputs	7
States with no sales tax on manufacturing inputs	21
States raising their sales tax rates that exempted sales of manufacturing inputs	6

Source: NASDA (1991).

Note: Calculations are based on all 50 states.

[a]Changes are based on comparison of 1990 and 1982 statistics.

raised their sales taxes on general sales. At the same time 21 states levied no sales and use tax on manufacturing inputs. Of those states that raised their sales taxes, almost one-fourth exempted manufacturing inputs from these increases. The pattern of changes in sales tax rates generally, and in sales and use tax rates on manufacturing inputs specifically, is consistent with a policy that taxes less elastic sales activity at a higher rate than more elastic manufacturing activity, which can avoid the tax by moving to another location.

Another characteristic of the 1980s evidenced in *Site Selection* is that states changed the activities they targeted most directly. High technology was cited as a sector that states wished to foster, and this was reflected in the adoption of R&D credits, raising the number of states offering such credits from 12 to 17. The number of states offering investment tax credits rose overall from 16 to 17, but the identity of those states changed. Similarly, although 19 states had foreign investment promotion offices in both 1982 and 1990, the identity of some of those states changed. Since a number of states opened additional offices, the number of offices rose from 27 worldwide in 1982 to 45 in 1990.

A final cut on the data is provided in table 9.4. Here, fiscal variables are summarized on a regional basis, where the regional classifications conform to regional definitions presented in U.S. Department of Commerce, Bureau of Economic Analysis publications. The corporate tax rate on a regional basis ranges from a low of 4.1 percent to a high of 8.83 percent. Although states can make slight changes in their definitions of income that could potentially offset high tax rates, it appears that this was not the case in practice. The variation in corporate taxes collected as a fraction of value added in the region is highly correlated with the corporate tax rate.

Large dispersion is also seen in the rate of sales taxes across regions. However, the range of sales and use taxes on manufacturing inputs varies even more widely, as some regions, notably the Mideast and Great Lakes, have rates very close to zero, while other regions, such as the Far West and Southwest, offer no reductions for manufacturing inputs as compared with general sales. Two other policies that may be of interest to foreign investors are the availability of foreign trade zones and the existence of foreign investment promotion offices. Here too, we see great regional heterogeneity. Some regions, such as New England, have almost no foreign investment promotion offices, while other regions, such as the Southeast, average more than one per state.

Overall, the distribution of these variables across regions suggests that states may be competing not with the nation as a whole but with their neighbors. If states within a region are more similar, then tax policies that are implemented may actually result in the shifting of employment within a region. In contrast, tax effects may be much less pronounced among regions, since dissimilar regions will not be in competition with each other unless massive fiscal efforts are used to diffuse the general inclination to select one region over the others based on the suitability of factor conditions.

9.5 Estimation

In this section we examine the responsiveness of the interstate distribution of foreign employment to wage and fiscal differences between the states. The dimensions of the geographical responsiveness are tested by two cuts on the

Table 9.4 **Regional Fiscal Variables, 1991**

Variable	New England	Mideast	Great Lakes	Plains	Southeast	Southwest	Rocky Mountain	Far West
Corporate tax rate (%)	8.83	8.44	5.31	7.45	6.35	7.08	5.01	4.10
	(1.34)	(0.83)	(2.90)	(3.93)	(1.35)	(2.55)	(3.04)	(4.58)
Sales tax rate (%)	4.58	5.08	5.40	5.10	5.19	2.32	3.66	4.87
	(2.53)	(2.83)	(0.96)	(0.78)	(1.11)	(2.65)	(2.38)	(3.32)
Manufacturing sales	1.25	0.08	0.03	1.57	2.19	2.32	1.80	4.87
tax rate (%)	(3.06)	(0.18)	(0.67)	(2.28)	(2.93)	(2.68)	(2.49)	(3.32)
Tax per capita ($)	1,192	1,377	1,114	1,006	979	1,057	967	1,227
	(354)	(231)	(139)	(248)	(97)	(178)	(157)	(225)
Corporate tax/Value	2.29	2.79	1.58	1.91	1.73	1.89	2.12	1.29
added (%)	(0.91)	(0.77)	(0.91)	(1.10)	(0.70)	(1.98)	(1.84)	(1.79)
Foreign offices[a]	0.167	1.6	2.6	0.57	1.16	0.5	0.2	0.25
	[0–1]	[0–4]	[0–5]	[0–2]	[0–3]	[0–2]	[0–1]	[0–1]
Foreign trade zones[a]	1.5	4.6	4.2	1.5	3.25	7.5	1.0	4.5
	[0–3]	[1–12]	[2–7]	[0–2]	[0–10]	[1–22]	[0–2]	[2–8]

Note: Regional groupings are calculated according to the groupings used in U.S. Department of Commerce, Bureau of Economic Analysis publications: New England = CT, ME, MA, NH, RI, VT; Mideast = DE, MD, NJ, NY, PA; Great Lakes = IL, IN, MI, OH, WI; Plains = IA, KS, MN, MO, NE, ND, SD; Southeast = AL, AR, FL, GA, KY, LA, MS, NC, SC, TN, VA, WV; Southwest = AZ, NM, OK, TX; Rocky Mountain = CO, ID, MT, UT, WY; Far West = CA, NV, OR, WA; not included = AK, HI. Numbers in parentheses are standard deviations.

[a]Average number of facilities by region. Numbers in brackets provide numerical range for the states within each region.

data. First, the data are tested to see whether the *interregional* distribution of investment reflects wage and fiscal conditions. Second, the data are examined to see whether the *intraregional* distribution of investment responds to intraregional factor and wage conditions. Further tests are then performed to see whether different types of foreign investment respond more vigorously than others. In particular, it may be that manufacturing employment exhibits different responsiveness to wage and factor conditions than does other nonbank affiliate investment. This possibility is tested through applications of the tests to the subsample of foreign manufacturing employment data.

9.5.1 The Interregional Employment Distribution of All Nonbank Affiliates

In order to estimate the responsiveness of investment to differences across regions, comparison variables are created that normalize the change in the value of a particular variable in each region by the change in that variable nationally. These averages are weighted by population so that the effects of small states are not overrepresented in the regional variables. The estimating equation takes the following form:

$$(5) \qquad \Delta(L_r / L) = \alpha + \beta_w * (w_r / w) + \delta * \Delta(\tau_r / \tau) + \gamma * (Z_r / Z) + \varepsilon_r .$$

The change in a country's employment in region r is related to changes in wages in that region relative to the nation and changes in taxes relative to the nation. The change in employment may also be affected by other characteristics of the region, which are contained in the vector Z. The comparison variables differ when interregional employment is being tested as opposed to intraregional investment. In order to avoid simultaneity bias, the wage variable presented is the relative level of wages across regions rather than the relative change in wages across regions.

It is possible that foreign firms choose the regions in which they will place their investments based on interregional differences. This idea is implicit in the estimation presented in table 9.5, which measures changes in employment by region as a function of the weighted average corporate tax and weighted average wage of the region. These changes are measured between the benchmark survey years 1980 and 1987 and between 1987 and 1992. Columns (1) and (2) test whether employment is proportional to regional activity as measured by either population or value added. In either specification these scale variables are shown to be highly significant. Column (3) tests whether either of these scale factors is more significant as a determinant of the interregional distribution of foreign employment. When both measures are included population remains highly significant while value added loses its significance. This suggests that value added entered significantly in specification (2) only because it proxied for population.

Specification (4) augments the regression with variables representing the weighted average wage in the region and the weighted average corporate tax

Table 9.5 **Employment Changes across Regions**

	Dependent Variable: Change in Foreign Employment by Region							
Variable	(1)	(2)	(3)	(4)	(5)	(6)	(7)	(8)
Region population	0.76		1.17	0.69	0.73	0.66	0.75	0.69
	(0.17)		(0.45)	(0.19)	(0.20)	(0.21)	(0.20)	(0.23)
Region value added		0.11	−0.08					
		(0.03)	(0.08)					
Region average wage				0.01	0.01	0.01	0.02	0.01
				(0.01)	(0.01)	(0.01)	(0.02)	(0.01)
Region average corporate tax				0.19	0.31	0.57		
				(1.38)	(1.39)	(1.71)		
Region change in corporate tax							4.31	1.80
							(9.20)	(10.15)
Region job credit programs					8.09		8.92	
					(9.57)		(9.77)	
Regional foreign investment offices						1.20		0.35
						(3.12)		(2.86)
Adjusted R^2	0.12	0.08	0.12	0.11	0.11	0.11	0.11	0.11

Note: Numbers in parentheses are standard errors. Regression constant terms not reported. Regional variables are calculated as average of region. Each regression has 144 observations.

rate in the region. Contrary to expectation, both variables enter with a positive sign, though neither coefficient is significant. While a nonpositive coefficient is expected on wages, the positive coefficient on the corporate tax variable could be consistent with the "benefits" view of taxation. As long as the government is providing benefits that are valued by investors, higher corporate taxes can be consistent with rising levels of employment in a region. To examine the effect of including a specific benefit, regression (5) adds regional job creation credit programs as a variable, since it is a benefit that one would assume is directly related to employment decisions. While the expected positive coefficient is found, it is not significant. Moreover, the coefficient on the corporate tax rate remains positive.

Further specifications were tested that included benefit measures such as investment tax credits and R&D credits. The results are not displayed since they were as unpromising and insignificant as the result shown in column (5). If the benefits view of taxation is driving the insignificant positive coefficient found on the regional corporate tax rate, the successful combination of benefits is not discernable in this data set.

Regression (6) examines another variable that might enhance foreign employment in a region, the presence of foreign investment promotion offices. We find a weak positive correlation between foreign employment decisions and the presence of such offices.

Finally, regressions (7) and (8) try a different specification of the corporate tax rate by region. Here, the corporate tax rate variable is taken to be the weighted average *change* in the region's corporate tax rate. The coefficients again go against the common presumption that corporate tax increases decrease employment. However, no conclusions can be drawn, since these estimates are not statistically significant. As in the two previous specifications, these regressions are augmented alternatively by a job creation credit variable and a foreign investment promotion office variable. The coefficients on these variables remain equally insignificant.

It is too early to draw conclusions from the results in table 9.5. It is clearly possible that taxes and wages exert a significant effect on employment and that the regressions fail to capture these effects. However, one hypothesis is suggested. In particular, it appears that the interregional distribution of all affiliate investment is based purely on population, and by association ultimate product markets. The lack of any decisive effect of corporate taxes or wages on employment may reflect the fact that foreign affiliates locate their employment as a means of gaining proximity to final markets. If this proximity is sufficiently valuable, then they will distribute themselves evenly across U.S. regions in a fashion that is proportionate to population.[8]

8. The proximity arguments made here are similar in character to descriptions of international incentives for proximity in Brainard (1997).

9.5.2 The Interregional Employment Distribution of Manufacturing Affiliates

Unless transportation costs are extremely high or customers in final markets require frequent changes in product specifications, it is not necessary to locate production near final markets. Hence, we repeat the tests that were performed, this time on the narrower sample of foreign employment involved in manufacturing.[9] Since the 1980 benchmark survey does not present foreign employment in manufacturing, the manufacturing data examined span the years 1987–92.

The first three columns of table 9.6 examine whether region size as measured by population or value added exerts a significant influence on the level of manufacturing employment placed in that region. The value-added variable has a positive coefficient but is not significant. The population variable is negative and insignificant, alone or in combination with the value-added variable. It appears that the location of foreign manufacturing employment within a region is not strongly influenced by population or manufacturing density as exhibited by value added. Regressions (4) and (5) now augment the specification with regional wages and taxes. Column (5) includes country dummies, while column (4) does not. The wage variables have a negative coefficient that is not significant. Regional variation in corporate tax rates now enters with a negative and significant sign. Column (6) measures the corporate tax with its change rather than its level, but the change does not enter significantly.

Finally, columns (7) and (8) include two indicators of state investment promotion effort. In contrast with the data on all nonbank affiliates, these variables enter with negative signs. In the case of the job creation credit program, the negative coefficient is significant. Interestingly, at the same time, the measured effect of wages in column (7) now approaches marginal significance. One interpretation would be that states with poor-quality labor forces are more likely to adopt job creation programs. The presence of the program provides an indicator variable for interregional variation in labor quality. Once one controls for this quality heterogeneity, it becomes more possible to identify the effects of wage variation.

In summing up, there are two primary differences in the interregional employment regressions performed on the manufacturing subsample relative to the full sample of nonbank affiliates. First, corporate taxes exert an identifiable negative effect on manufacturing, but not on overall affiliate activity. This is consistent with the previous conjecture that much foreign investment is located with proximity to final markets and customers in mind. To the extent that manufacturing can locate at greater distance from final markets, tax differences

9. In aggregate, foreign employment in manufacturing was less than half of total nonbank affiliate employment of foreign firms.

Table 9.6 **Manufacturing Employment Changes across Regions**

	Dependent Variable: Change in Foreign Employment by Region							
Variable	(1)	(2)	(3)	(4)	(5)	(6)	(7)	(8)
Region population	−0.66		−0.49	−0.49	−0.49	−0.19	−0.63	−0.61
	(0.11)		(0.43)	(0.43)	(0.38)	(0.39)	(0.38)	(0.39)
Region value added		0.02	0.07	0.07	0.07	0.04	0.10	0.13
		(0.02)	(0.09)	(0.09)	(0.08)	(0.07)	(0.07)	(0.08)
Region average wage				−.002	−.002	.004	−.009	−.002
				(.006)	(.006)	(.006)	(.006)	(.006)
Region average corporate tax				−2.94	−2.94		−3.21	−3.09
				(1.42)	(1.25)		(1.22)	(1.24)
Region change in corporate tax						19.2		
						(6.05)		
Region job credit programs							−16.1	
							(7.55)	
Regional foreign investment offices								−3.75
								(2.62)
Country dummies	Yes	Yes	Yes	No	Yes	Yes	Yes	Yes
Adjusted R^2	0.20	0.12	0.24	0.12	0.24	0.29	0.29	0.26

Note: Numbers in parentheses are standard errors. Regression constant terms not reported. Regional variables are calculated as average of region. Each regression has 72 observations (8 countries, 9 regions).

will exert a greater influence. In addition, the effects of apportionment may also be evident here. Payroll is one component of most states' apportionment formulas. As such, this weight factor should discourage firms from locating manufacturing in states with high corporate tax rates. The difference in tax coefficients between the two samples are suggestive that these effects are operating.

The second interesting distinction in the manufacturing subsample reinforces the notion that the distribution of manufacturing employment is subject to different influences. Overall population was identified as the primary determinant of the changes in regional employment by all foreign nonbank affiliates. In the manufacturing subsample, population has a negative effect, if any. This is further evidence that manufacturing activities do not need to be located near customers while other operations do require proximity. At the same time, value added by state has a slight positive influence. This finding is potentially indicative of the presence of agglomeration economies in manufacturing.

9.5.3 The Intraregional Employment Distribution of Manufacturing Affiliates

Our examination now moves to the more disaggregated analysis of the distribution of employment between states within regions, where each state's employment is compared with employment within its region, r. These results are presented in table 9.7. In portions of this table, identity of the foreign investor is used as a further discriminant to identify the effect of taxes on investment. The estimating equation takes the following form:

$$(6)\quad (L_{cs} / L_{cr}) = \alpha + \beta_w * (w_s / w_r) + \delta * (\tau_s / \tau_r) + \gamma'(Z_s / Z_r) + \lambda_c + \varepsilon_{cs}.$$

Column (1) provides a benchmark. In considering the relative employment of different states within a region, value added in a state relative to other states in the region is a decisive factor. This factor is consistent with agglomeration stories of investment in which investment benefits from positive spillovers in either labor markets or in markets for intermediate inputs. This finding will not be discussed further since it is consistent throughout table 9.7.

The relative corporate tax rate in column (1) exhibits no discernable effect on the distribution of manufacturing employment. However, as is explained in Hines (1996), the nationality of the investor has important implications for the effect of U.S. taxes on investment. Investors who are headquartered in exemption countries pay no home-country taxes on their U.S. earnings. In comparison, investors who are headquartered in foreign tax credit countries may have a smaller reduction in their after-all-tax profits as a result of high taxes paid to a U.S. state. It is not purely true that all foreign tax credit investors will be unaffected by state tax differences. Firms that are in excess credit positions may not be able to use all their credits generated by state taxes. In this case higher taxes will deter investment by these firms, too. However, the result remains that exemption country investors should be more negatively influenced

Table 9.7 Manufacturing Employment

	Dependent Variable: Employment Relative to Region						
	(1)	(2)	(3)	(4)	(5)	(6)	(7)
Relative value added	1.15	1.14	1.16	1.15	1.16	1.17	1.17
	(0.18)	(0.16)	(0.18)	(0.17)	(0.16)	(0.16)	(0.16)
Relative population	−0.31	−0.30	−0.29	−0.30	−0.29	−0.33	−0.33
	(0.19)	(0.17)	(0.19)	(0.19)	(0.17)	(0.17)	(0.17)
Relative corporate tax rate	0.03	0.07	0.04	0.032	0.71	0.70	0.73
	(0.12)	(0.12)	(0.12)	(0.12)	(0.13)	(0.12)	(0.13)
Relative corporate tax rate*exemption		−0.93	−0.93		−0.93	−0.93	−0.96
		(0.09)	(0.09)		(0.11)	(0.09)	(0.11)
Relative pay			−0.37		−0.46		
			(0.43)		(0.43)		
Relative job credit program offer				−0.03	−0.06		
				(0.04)	(0.06)		
Relative job credit program offer* exemption					0.03		
					(0.07)		
Relative use tax						0.04	0.01
						(0.03)	(0.05)
Relative use tax* exemption							0.04
							(0.06)
N	376	376	376	365	365	376	376
Adjusted R^2	0.36	0.50	0.50	0.38	0.51	0.50	0.50

Note: Numbers in parentheses are standard errors. Regression constant terms not reported.

by U.S. corporate taxes than the average investor who is governed by a foreign tax credit system. This hypothesis is tested in column (2) through an interaction variable that multiplies the relative corporate tax rate variable by a dummy variable that indicates exemption investors. As predicted, the results show that corporate tax variation within a region has a strong negative effect on exemption investors.

The effect of the job credit program is tested in a similar fashion in regressions (4) and (5). Job creation credits reduce state corporate taxes payable by firms. Therefore, foreign investors from exemption countries should derive equivalent, if not larger, benefits from job creation credits. Since these credits usually reduce a firm's state tax payments, it is expected that the job credit program variables will have the opposite sign of the corporate tax variables. The coefficient estimates on this interaction term are of the expected sign, but there are no significant effects, and the values of the credit to the two types of investors are not statistically distinguishable.

Finally, in manufacturing, sales and use tax is a component that may increase the cost of investment. To measure the effect of these sales and use taxes on the intraregional distribution of employment, regression (6) adds a variable that measures the sales and use tax on manufacturing inputs relative to the sales and use taxes applied to manufacturing inputs purchased by firms in other states of the region. No significant effect is found. However, the data present another opportunity to test whether the earlier exemption distinction was a spurious correlation that represented other characteristics of the exemption investors. Column (7) adds a regressor that multiplies the relative sales and use tax variable by the exemption dummy. There should be no effect here since, unlike taxes on corporate income, sales and use taxes are not deductible by firms from foreign tax credit countries. In other words, sales and use taxes do not have differential effects on the overall tax payments of firms from exemption as opposed to nonexemption countries. This spurious exemption variable has no measurable effect. This suggests that the earlier findings regarding the corporate tax reflect differential responsiveness to corporate tax rates rather than unmeasured differences that separate the exemption from the foreign tax credit investors.

As a second check on the robustness of the results, the regional groupings were changed to conform to the regional definitions presented by the Bureau of the Census. There were no discernable differences between the results presented in table 9.7 and the results generated with changes in the regional groupings.

In considering intraregional employment effects in manufacturing, three conclusions emerge. First, the strong coefficients on value added as opposed to population suggest that agglomeration economies are one of the important factors determining the distribution of employment in manufacturing. Second, when corporate tax effects are measured among the set of countries that are expected to respond most vigorously, intraregional differences in corporate taxes appear to reduce employment in the states that have the highest taxes relative to their regions. Finally, the failure to find any correlation between the intraregional distribution of employment and sales and use taxes on manufacturing does not prove that these taxes have no effect. As table 9.4 showed, different regions center on different levels of sales and use tax on manufacturing equipment. Since this variable has a potentially strong effect on manufacturing investment, states within regions may bring their taxes into conformity with the rates that their neighbors have. If this occurs, no effect would be found, since state policymakers have set their tax rates in a way that minimizes loss of employment to other states in their region, leaving inadequate variation within regions to identify any effects econometrically.

9.6 Conclusions

Our results suggest that the geographical distribution of foreign employment across U.S. states is in fact sensitive to both fiscal and labor market conditions in some but not all situations. The distinction that is of most relevance here is whether the foreign employment is in manufacturing or in the broader category of all nonbank affiliates. Both the interregional and the intraregional distribution of foreign employment in manufacturing appear to respond to tax differences. Regions whose taxes are higher than average for the country, or states whose taxes are high relative to their region, appear to deter investment. By way of contrast, the distribution of all nonbank employment does not appear to be sensitive to tax differences. This may reflect the activity mix of the two sectors. If the activity of nonmanufacturing firms in the nonbank affiliate category is directed toward functions such as sales and services, then these activities need to be located in close proximity to final markets. This is consistent with the finding in this study that the broadly defined category of employment appears to be evenly distributed across regions in a fashion that corresponds to population. In contrast, the location of manufacturing is positively related to the current levels of business activities in states, as opposed to the populations themselves.

The differential tax sensitivity of these two types of employment suggests that fiscal policy oriented toward the more general investment levels is likely to be unsuccessful. The finding that foreign employment may in fact be more responsive to intraregional differences than to intranational differences has two implications for state policymakers. First, in crafting promotion policies, the most intense competition is found among one's neighbors. Therefore, it is not necessary for states to copy actions that are taken by states in other regions. Second, some observers claim that in the international context it will be difficult for nations to maintain high corporate tax rates when far lower tax rates are offered by tax havens. These results suggest that firms' real activities are not perfectly elastic in the face of fiscal differences.

While this study finds that foreign manufacturing employment is affected by broad measures of corporate tax, the inclusion of other state promotion tools does not produce identifiable effects. One might suspect that we are unable to find measurable effects because these promotion policies are, for the most part, denoted by indicator variables that cannot capture the full degree of interstate heterogeneity that is present. A more serious problem is that the failure to measure results on this front may very well be due to the fact that states' use of investment promotion tools is endogenous. On the positive side, attractive states may open investment promotion offices since they expect large investments and these investment offices abroad help coordinate foreign firms' planning. On the negative side, states that have failed in the past may implement programs to augment employment. Here, the use of indicator variables for the programs will yield what appear to be negative effects. Yet another possibility is that no successful program will go without imitation. This possibility is explored in Head et al. (1994) in the case of foreign trade zones. If this is the case, imitation removes the differentials in the explanatory variables that are needed to identify the effects of these programs. In order to identify the impact of these promotion variables, future research is needed to model and measure states' use of promotion tools.

References

Bartik, Timothy J. 1985. Business location decisions in the United States: Estimates of the effects of unionization, taxes, and other characteristics of states. *Journal of Business and Economic Statistics* 3:14–22.

———. 1991. Who benefits from state and local economic development policies? Kalamazoo, Mich.: W. E. Upjohn Institute for Employment Research.

Brainard, S. Lael. 1997. An empirical assessment of the proximity-concentration tradeoff between multinational sales and trade. *American Economic Review* 87 (4): 520–44.

Carlton, Dennis. 1983. The location and employment choices of new firms: An econometric model with discrete and continuous endogenous variables. *Review of Economics and Statistics* 65 (3): 440–49.

Coughlin, Cletus C., Joseph V. Terza, and Vachira Arromdee. 1991. State characteristics and the location of foreign direct investment within the United States. *Review of Economics and Statistics* 68 (4): 675–83.

Friedman, Joseph, Daniel A. Gerlowski, and Jonathan Silberman. 1992. What attracts foreign multinational corporations? Evidence from branch plant location in the United States. *Journal of Regional Science* 32 (4): 403–18.

Grubert, Harry, and John Mutti. 1991. Taxes, tariffs and transfer pricing in multinational corporate decision making. *Review of Economics and Statistics* 73 (2): 285–93.

Head, C. Keith, John C. Ries, and Deborah L. Swenson. 1994. The attraction of foreign manufacturing investments: Investment promotion and agglomeration economies. NBER Working Paper no. 4878. Cambridge, Mass.: National Bureau of Economic Research.

Helms, L. Jay. 1985. The effect of state and local taxes on economic growth: A time series cross section approach. *Review of Economics and Statistics* 67 (4): 574–82.

Hines, James R., Jr. 1996. Altered states: Taxes and the location of foreign direct investment in America. *American Economic Review* 86 (5): 1076–94.
Hines, James R., Jr., and Eric M. Rice. 1994. Fiscal paradise: Foreign tax havens and American business. *Quarterly Journal of Economics* 109 (1): 149–82.
Luger, Michael I., and Sudhir Shetty. 1985. Determinants of foreign plant start-ups in the United States: Lessons for policymakers in the southeast. *Vanderbilt Journal of Transnational Law* 18 (2): 223–45.
National Association of State Development Agencies (NASDA). 1991. *Directory of incentives for business investment and development in the United States,* 3d ed. Washington, D.C.: Urban Institute Press.
Papke, Leslie E. 1987. Subnational taxation and capital mobility: Estimates of tax-price elasticities. *National Tax Journal* 40 (2): 191–204.
———. 1991. Interstate business tax differentials and new firm location. *Journal of Public Economics* 45 (1): 47–68.
Slemrod, Joel. 1990. Tax effects on foreign direct investment in the United States: Evidence from a cross-country comparison. In *Taxation in a global economy,* ed. Assaf Razin and Joel Slemrod, 79–117. Chicago: University of Chicago Press.
Swenson, Deborah L. 1994. The impact of U.S. tax reform on foreign direct investment in the U.S. *Journal of Public Economics* 54:243–66.
U.S. Department of Commerce. Bureau of Economic Analysis. 1985. *Foreign direct investment in the United States: Operations of U.S. affiliates of foreign companies, revised 1982 estimates.* Washington, D.C.: Government Printing Office.
———. 1990. *Foreign direct investment in the United States: 1987 Benchmark survey, final results.* Washington, D.C.: Government Printing Office.
———. 1994. *Foreign direct investment in the United States: 1992 Benchmark survey, preliminary results.* Washington, D.C.: Government Printing Office.
Wasylenko, Michael. 1995. Has the relationship changed between taxes and location decisions? *National Tax Association Proceedings of the 86th Annual Conference 1994,* pp. 107–12.
Wasylenko, Michael, and Therese McGuire. 1985. Jobs and taxes: The effect of business climate on states' employment growth rates. *National Tax Journal* 38 (4): 497–512.
Wheeler, David, and Ashoka Mody. 1992. International investment location decision: The case of U.S. firms. *Journal of International Economics* 33 (1–2): 57–76.
Woodward, Douglas P. 1992. Locational determinants of Japanese manufacturing start-ups in the United States. *Southern Journal of Economics* 58 (3): 690–708.

Comment Michael Wasylenko

At a lively debate some years ago on the elasticity of demand for money, one person challenged the group to name one controversial issue in economics that was resolved through empirical work. Each empirical researcher has his or her favorite examples, but most would agree that resolving issues takes replication

Michael Wasylenko is professor of economics and senior research associate of the Center for Policy Research at the Maxwell School of Syracuse University.

of results over several studies using a variety of data sets before one can speak confidently about the size and statistical significance of the coefficients.

Through replication, a strong consensus has recently emerged among researchers studying location decisions about the effect of state and local business taxes on plant locations. State and local taxes affect location decisions of manufacturers but have less or even no impact on the location decisions of nonmanufacturing industries. Another consistent finding is that in the United States the smaller a region over which the location decision is made, the more likely it is that taxes and other fiscal variables will influence location decisions. Those empirical results suggest that intraregional business location decisions are more susceptible to the influences of fiscal variables than are interregional business location choices.

The findings cited above seem to apply to domestic and foreign location decisions in the United States (Wasylenko 1995; Ondrich and Wasylenko 1993), although there are many more studies of location decisions of domestic plants (or employment) than of specifically foreign plants (or employment). For manufacturing firms, the elasticity of employment or location with respect to business taxes appears to be between −0.5 and −0.8, depending on the time period of the study, on whether employment or plants are used as the left-hand-side variable, and on whether aggregate or micro data are used in the analysis.

Agglomeration economies, or plants locating in groups to take advantage of technological transfers, information, proximity to suppliers, or to a workforce, have consistently and strongly determined plant locations in empirical work. Put differently, regions with plants in a particular industry are likely to attract more plants in the same or a similar industry.

The results reported in Deborah Swenson's paper are roughly consistent with the results reported in other papers. Her paper makes a contribution to the literature on the location of foreign direct investors. However, several points should be made about the data and the modeling used in her paper.

Use of Aggregate versus Micro Data

Total employment in foreign-owned plants, which is an aggregate of new plants, plant expansions, mergers, acquisitions, equity increases, joint ventures, and other direct investments, is explained in her paper. Investors typically exercise more choice over where to locate new plants than they would over acquisitions of existing plants and other forms of investment. Therefore, findings on the variables that attract foreign investment to a state have typically been stronger when new plants or "greenfield" investments are analyzed than when other forms of investment are commingled with new plants in the analysis. Empirical results based on greenfield investments may describe what foreign investors actively seek, while the results based on aggregate data describe what investors do when financial and other considerations enter the location decision. Policymakers with an interest in shaping the state business climate would want to know what investors actively seek in a location. Studies using aggregate data might then be less interesting to policymakers.

Tax Variables

While Swenson is careful to acknowledge and to account to the extent possible for several of the complications of the tax code as it applies to foreign investors, there are several points about the tax variables worth reemphasizing. Moreover, the measurement of the tax variables is not pushed as far as one would like in her paper.

Worldwide unitary taxation was used at one time or another in 13 states during the 1980–87 period. However, during that time period many of these states abandoned worldwide unitary taxation. These changes in the tax structure might be important in the analysis of the 1980–87 time period, and her study does not take into account the nature of the unitary tax system in the states. After 1987, however, only five states used worldwide unitary taxation, and the changes in this policy were few and not influential. Thus, in the latter period of the study, the variation in the unitary tax structure among states may be differenced away in her estimation and not important in her analysis of the 1987–92 period. But in the earlier period worldwide unitary taxation could have changed location decisions in the aggregate.

Formulas that are used to apportion corporate income among states vary among states. States do use the three-factor formula based on sales, payroll, and property; however, some states double weight the sales factor, while others allow firms to choose among several apportionment formulas. Again, these variations might difference out of the model if states do not alter their apportionment formulas over the time periods. If apportionment formulas change, however, they could influence the amount of manufacturing investment in the states.

Moreover, states do not typically use the three-factor formula to apportion income in some nonmanufacturing industries, such as finance. This is not taken into account in her model and reasoning.

Effective tax rates are preferred to nominal corporate tax rates as measures of tax burdens. In fact, one would like to have measures of marginal effective tax rates in states. Investment tax credits in New York State, for example, give New York a relatively low marginal effective tax rate, although the state's nominal corporate tax rate is higher than average. In her paper, Swenson uses nominal tax rates, which are likely to mismeasure the marginal tax rates of foreign investors.

However, her analysis accounts for the different state tax circumstances that investors from different home countries face. She distinguishes between home-country territorial and residential tax systems, where investors in territorial countries pay U.S. taxes and no taxes to their home country. An investor from a residence-based tax country might effectively pay no U.S. corporate taxes (upon repatriation of the income), unless he were in an excess credit position in his home country.

Swenson accounts for some variation in the rate of manufacturing sales and use taxes. However, the administration of this tax complicates greatly the accurate measurement of the sales and use tax rate as it affects manufacturers. For example, Ohio exempts business machinery and equipment from sales taxes, but still 30 percent of all sales tax revenue in Ohio is derived from business purchases. The reason is that Ohio uses an administrative list approach, where a specific set of items is sales tax exempt, instead of granting a sales tax exemption to all material and equipment purchased by a firm (the integrated plant approach to levying the exemption). Thus, the findings in her papers that sales and use tax exemptions for business equipment do not influence locations may occur because investors are aware that the sales tax rate itself is a less important determinant of their sales tax burdens than is the administration of the tax. Put another way, there may be quite a bit of measurement error in the sales tax exemption variable used in the paper.

Fiscal Incentives

A generic problem that affects all attempts to analyze the effects of fiscal incentives is measuring accurately the size of fiscal incentive packages or programs. Swenson, for instance, attempts to account for whether a state has a foreign trade office in a country, but there are no easily available measures of the staffing and activity in the office. To emphasize this point, Japan has a Japanese External Trade Organization (JETRO) within the United States. There are eight regional offices, each with a large staff to promote Japanese exports as well as to help small to medium-size U.S. businesses export to Japan. Moreover, JETRO offices arrange exchange programs with universities in the United States for civil servants in Japanese ministries. This example highlights the range of activities that an office in another country could undertake. More important, the size of each state's foreign office in other countries is not measured in Swenson's analysis.

Similar arguments can be made for a host of fiscal incentive programs, which have typically limited participation to new firms or to small firm start-ups and made available everything from loan guarantees to direct loans. The wide variation in the formulation of fiscal incentives among states as well as the wide range of eligibility criteria for firms to qualify for the incentive packages complicates the measurement of these incentive programs and makes it difficult to estimate their effectiveness. As a result, what we can say with confidence about the effectiveness of these programs is limited. Moreover, as Swenson also notes, the presence of fiscal incentive programs in themselves may be an attempt to compensate for inherent weaknesses in the business climate of a state (and thus endogenous to employment growth) rather than an exogenous source of employment growth.

Comments on Specific Regressions

While she does not say so, I assume that a time effect was included as a variable when two different time periods are pooled in the analysis. Carroll and Wasylenko (1994) have shown that fiscal variables have different effects over time because different levels of state competition in different time periods can drive state fiscal systems to look more similar over time. As fiscal variables become more alike among states, fiscal variables become more neutral as determinants of location. (This latter point is also made by Swenson.)

It would be interesting to know the results of her model when it is run on all states without deflating the equations by their regional averages, as in table 9.7. By running all states (weighted appropriately by population to correct for the size of the state), one could learn about the sensitivity of the results when states are compared to averages within their respective regions relative to when states are simply pooled without comparisons to regional averages.

In summary, this is a good paper. Nonetheless, research in this area has moved beyond aggregate analysis and has employed microlevel plant location data. Better measures of the fiscal variables would also help identify their effectiveness with more accuracy.

References

Carroll, Robert, and Michael Wasylenko. 1994. Do state business climates still matter? Evidence of a structural change. *National Tax Journal* 47 (March): 19–38.

Ondrich, Jan, and Michael Wasylenko. 1993. *Foreign direct investment in the United States: Issues, magnitudes, and location choices of new manufacturing plants.* Kalamazoo, Mich.: W. E. Upjohn Institute.

Wasylenko, Michael. 1995. Has the relationship changed between taxes and location decisions? *National Tax Association Proceedings of the 86th Annual Conference 1994,* pp. 107–12.

10 A Measure of the Current Account Related to the Well-Being of Japan: Generational Accounts in the Open Economy

Eric O'N. Fisher

10.1 Introduction

An article entitled provocatively "Hollywood 1, Japan 0" appeared recently in the national press (Sterngold 1995). It reported that the president of Matsushita Electric Industrial Company paid a brief visit to the chairman of the American entertainment conglomerate MCA early in April 1995 and informed him coldly that Matsushita had sold its controlling interest in MCA to Seagram's, a Canadian firm. This foreign direct investment was the single largest purchase of an American corporation by a Japanese firm; Matsushita had acquired MCA for $6.6 billion in 1990 and sold 80 percent of its stake for $5.7 billion in 1995. During the same period, the comparable return from holding an open position in yen was greater than 13 percent per year. How do investment decisions like this one affect Matsushita's shareholders? Also, if this kind of foreign direct investment is typical of the flow of capital out of Japan in the past two decades, what are the macroeconomic implications of the continuing Japanese external surplus of the past 15 years?

This chapter answers these questions in two ways. First, it describes two new measures of a country's external surplus that are based in economic theory. One is called the *aggregate generational current account,*[1] and the other pre-

Eric O'N. Fisher is associate professor of economics at The Ohio State University.

The author thanks Jon Haveman, conference participants, and two anonymous referees for helpful comments on an earlier draft of this chapter. He also thanks Eric Ramstetter, Hajime Miyazaki, Masao Ogaki, Takeshi Kohno, Nao Ikemoto, Masanori Hashimoto, Bob Lipsey, Guy Stevens, and the Osaka University Institute for Social and Economic Research for help in collecting and interpreting the data used in this chapter. The author will make available at cost a diskette containing all the data and forecasts of exogenous variables used in constructing the statistics reported in this chapter.

1. Fisher (1995) defines the aggregate generational current account, and Fisher and Woo (1997) calibrate this statistic for the postwar Korean economy. The term "aggregate generational current account" is a bit of a misnomer because in practice one ignores the generational heterogeneity that

sents a generational cross section of the net foreign assets of Japanese residents. Both extend the important work of Auerbach, Gokhale, and Kotlikoff (1991) to the open economy. Second, it uses data from Japan's balance of payments in the past two decades to calibrate these measures. The value of Japan's external assets, measured at market prices, has been somewhat higher than that of its net international investment position, measured at historical prices. This fact is true because the surge in Japanese outward investment occurred in the first part of the past decade. Although Japanese investments in real estate in the United States have suffered some spectacular recent losses,[2] Japan's overseas assets have enjoyed large capital gains because securities prices in world markets have risen sharply in the past 15 years.

The measures calculated in this chapter are intuitively related to the well-being of the Japanese. The aggregate generational current account is the entire profile of the annual change in the expected present value of net foreign assets broadly defined. Thus it captures changes in the expected present value of the goods and services that a country can import from abroad. For domestic residents, one aggregate generational current account profile is ex ante Pareto superior to another if, at all time horizons, the present value of the stock of net foreign assets is greater for the former than the latter. For example, consider a one-off capital gain that increases the present value of Japan's net foreign assets. This change raises the expected utility of some Japanese residents and thus, with an appropriate internal redistribution of wealth, permits a Pareto improvement for all current and future residents. On the other hand, consider an increase in Japan's expected official transfers to abroad, perhaps as a part of a commitment to pay for the Allies' military expenses in the Gulf War. Such a transfer implies an analogous Pareto worsening for the residents of Japan.[3]

The aggregate generational current account is constructed in two big steps. First, one determines the market value of net foreign assets. Second, one capitalizes expected transfers from abroad. The sum of these two after any history is a country's net foreign assets position defined broadly. The present value of

is at the heart of Auerbach, Gokhale, and Kotlikoff's measure. The phrase "a utility-theoretic measure of the external surplus" is perhaps too pompous. I have elected to use the phrase "aggregate generational" to place my work firmly within the tradition started by those authors and continued recently by Ablett (1996). Auerbach, Gokhale, and Kotlikoff (1994) give a nice overview of the literature on generational accounts.

2. On 12 May 1995, the front page of the *New York Times* reported that Mitsubishi Estate Company, the holding company that had purchased an 80 percent stake in Rockefeller Center for $1.4 billion, was filing for bankruptcy. The *Survey of Current Business* (May 1994, tables 5.1 and 5.2) shows that real estate purchases represented about 15 percent of Japanese direct investment into the United States in 1992 and 1993. This is a small fraction of Japan's purchases of dollar-denominated securities in those years.

3. The utility generated by the provision of public goods has not as yet been incorporated into the calculation of generational accounts. Thus the appropriate comparison here is between a world in which the Japanese enjoy the benefits of global military security without having to pay unilateral transfers and one in which the Japanese enjoy these benefits and also shoulder some concomitant financial burdens.

this stock of assets puts the current account into an intertemporal framework.[4] Finally, first differences of this present value show how the stock of external assets evolves across time and through history. If the aggregate generational current account is consistently positive, as is the case for Japan in the 20 years between 1973 and 1992, then a country's net foreign assets are increasing more rapidly than world interest rates over a long horizon. In a dynamically efficient world economy, such a situation represents the expectation of a higher future standard of living owing to expected investment income from abroad.

The aggregate generational current account thus uses two standard techniques of generally accepted accounting principles: first, it evaluates net foreign assets at market value, not historical cost; and, second, it forces the economist to use an accrual accounting method to evaluate foreseeable international commitments. From a theoretical perspective, both of these practices make enormous sense. Of course, the difficulty in constructing theoretically meaningful economic statistics is that they are only as good as the assumptions one uses to compute them.

In this chapter, I assume that no Japanese transfer to abroad is enduring. Thus the consistently negative balance for unilateral transfers on current account does not reflect the expectation of an enduring Japanese commitment to a larger geopolitical role. If this assumption is wrong, then I have overestimated the level of Japan's net foreign assets. Also, I have evaluated Japan's net foreign assets only in four regions: the United States, Western Europe, the Communist bloc, and Australia. Japan has played a historically important role in several rapidly growing Asian economies. Since I have excluded these countries from my analysis, I may have underestimated the value of Japan's net foreign assets. Further, I have used equity prices, bond prices, and exchange rates from the United Kingdom only to revalue all of Japan's Western European assets. If the rates of return on European assets in general have been higher in the past 20 years, then I have underestimated the level of Japan's net foreign assets. Finally, I have assumed that Japan's assets in the United States have borne market rates of return. If Japanese investors suffer consistently large losses from real estate holdings, then I have overestimated slightly their net foreign assets in the United States.

This chapter also presents a generational cross section of the net foreign assets of Japan in 1992. Using data on household savings and borrowing rates, I construct the portfolios of net foreign assets of 19 different age cohorts. Different groups hit their years of peak savings in different years. Thus some generations benefited quite substantially from the large capital gains that Japan's overseas investments experienced in the past decade, while others had not yet

4. Since nominal interest rates include a component for expected inflation, the present value of the stock of net foreign assets deflates these assets both for inflation and the opportunity cost of holding real balances. Ulan and Dewald (1989) correct the U.S. stock of net foreign assets for inflation and for market value effects, but they do not consider the full implications of the dynamic pattern of asset accumulation.

accumulated sufficient wealth to have gained much from that boom. For example, this generational profile of net foreign assets shows that Japanese residents in their forties and fifties stand to lose proportionally most from a drop in dollar-denominated bond prices, whereas older generations lose less because they do not hold as large portfolio shares in dollar-denominated assets.

The broad picture that emerges from the data is that the market value of Japan's overseas assets was about 30 percent higher in 1992 than the Bank of Japan's official estimates. The rate of return on European assets was quite high, whereas assets held in the United States bore positive but not stellar returns. Since Japan held about $680 billion in net foreign assets in 1992, the degree of interdependence between Japan and the world economy is probably greater now than at any other time in history.

The rest of this chapter consists of four sections. Readers interested in the theoretical arguments showing that the conventional current account is ill defined should focus closely on section 10.2. Section 10.3 presents rough calculations of the market value of Japan's net foreign assets from 1973 through 1992. That section calibrates a benchmark using the status quo ex ante in the world economy in 1992. Section 10.4 presents the generational cross section of the distribution of these assets. Then it analyzes the effects on the welfare of Japan of three different scenarios: a continued strong yen, higher dollar interest rates, and rapid Chinese economic growth. Section 10.5 presents a brief conclusion. The chapter ends with a data appendix.

10.2 An Illustrative Model

Consider a country trading in a larger world economy. There are two generations, and the world economy lasts for two periods: the present and an uncertain future. Uncertainty is summarized by a random variable whose realization is denoted by $\theta \in \Theta$, the latter denoting the set of all possible future states of the world. This random variable summarizes both intrinsic and extrinsic uncertainty in the market, and its distribution is common knowledge. Intrinsic uncertainty is related to production, consumption, and government policy decisions, while extrinsic uncertainty captures the notion that market equilibria may be subject to a degree of randomness independent of the fundamentals of the world economy.

In the domestic economy, there is one representative agent in each generation. Agent 0 lives for one period only, and agent 1 lives for two periods. Let x_0^1 be the vector describing agent 0's consumption bundle; a subscript denotes a person and a superscript denotes a time period. Since x_0^1 has several elements, one can think of it as consisting of many different goods and services, both traded and not traded, that influence the utility of agent 0. Likewise, the state-contingent consumption profile of agent 1 is $[x_1^1, x_1^2(\theta)]$. Preferences for the people in the domestic economy are summarized by $u_0(x_0^1)$, a utility function for agent 0, and $E\{u_1([x_1^1, x_1^2(\theta)])\}$, an expected utility function for agent 1, where the expectation is taken with respect to the information available in the first period.

Let a_0^1 be the value of agent 0's initial assets, y_0^1 her income, and g_0^1 the domestic government's net transfers to her. Net transfers from the domestic government are positive if the agent's subsidies exceed her tax obligations. Likewise, a_1^1 is the initial wealth of agent 1, $(y_1^1, y_1^2(\theta))$ that agent's income profile, and $(g_1^1, g_1^2(\theta))$ his state-contingent government net transfers. It will be convenient to denote the ex post interest rate by $i(\theta)$.

Assume that asset markets are complete. Then a rational expectations equilibrium will entail that agents choose consumption plans that maximize expected utility subject to the usual budget constraints. Let c_0^1 and $(c_1^1, c_1^2(\theta))$ be solutions to these problems. Agent 1's consumption plans depend in general on risk aversion, expected domestic and foreign transfers, and the profile of earned income. Now let $s_1^1 - a_1^1 = y_1^1 + g_1^1 - c_1^1$ be the increment to agent 1's assets. Since $-a_0^1 = y_0^1 + g_0^1 - c_0^1$, the conventional current account in period 1 is $b^1 = s_1^1 - (a_0^1 + g_0^1) - (a_1^1 + g_1^1)$, the excess of domestic savings over investment. Likewise, the conventional current account in period 2 is $b^2(\theta) = -[a_1^2(\theta) + g_1^2(\theta)]$, where $a_1^2(\theta) = [1 + i(\theta)]s_1^1$ is the law of motion for agent 1's assets. Thus the *conventional current account profile* is

$$(1)\qquad [b^1,\ b^2(\theta)] = [s_1^1 - (a_0^1 + g_0^1) - (a_1^1 + g_1^1),\ -\ (a_1^2(\theta) + g_1^2(\theta))].$$

The essence of Fisher's (1995) argument is that the term $s_1^1 - a_1^1$ is not well defined. Consider a fixed level of initial wealth for agent 1. Then one can always increase b^1 by raising net transfers from abroad by one dollar and then imposing a offsetting state-contingent decrease in transfers in the amount of 1 + $i(\theta)$ in the next period. This change in the timing of transfers has no effect on the present value of the wealth of any agent after any history, and the consumption and utility of each agent is unchanged in any state of the world. But the conventional current account surplus has risen. Since the equilibrium allocations of the agent in the world economy are unchanged, agents' expected utilities are not affected after any history. This argument is the essence of a general proof showing that the conventional current account can take on any value in all but the final period of any economy. In an economy with an infinite horizon, the conventional current account is arbitrary in every period! Since each agent's expected utility is not affected by the timing of these transfers, changes in the conventional current account profile need not be related at all to changes in the welfare of domestic residents.

How should one interpret the rescheduling of these unilateral transfers from abroad? If this country has a valued fiat asset, then the government improves the conventional current account simply by delaying payments to abroad and promising foreigners principal and interest in the next period. Thus this year's net interest payments from abroad and conventional current account have increased. If the economy has no such asset, then the timing of transfers from abroad is a rescheduling of sovereign debt that leaves the present value of debt service unchanged in every state of the world. This "infusion of foreign official capital" leaves the present value of the equity of any international creditor unchanged, but it allows the conventional current account of the debtor country to be anything.

Rescheduling taxes and transfers among the agents in the domestic economy does not influence the current account. Kotlikoff (1993) shows that a one dollar decrease in g_1^1 that is offset by a future increase of $1 + i(\theta)$ in the next period lowers current savings s_1^1 just as much as the decrease in g_1^1. Of course, this delayed transfer affects no agent's utility after any history. Still, the conventional current account is not affected. Thus rescheduling internal taxes and transfers is another policy tool allowing the government to make its internal deficit any number it wants in all but the final period!

What is a well-defined measure of the external surplus? Let $\tilde{a}_0 = d_0^1 + f_0^1 + t_0^1$ be the present value of agent 0's assets, where d_0^1 denotes assets located domestically, f_0^1 net assets abroad, and t_0^1 the expected value of all current and future transfers from abroad. Since this definition includes expected foreign transfers, $\tilde{a}_0$ is thus broader than a_0^1. Also, there is no superscript on this quantity because these assets incorporate the present value of all current and expected future transfers from abroad that accrue to agent 0. This definition is thus independent of time. Likewise, let

$$\tilde{a}_1 = d_1^1 + f_1^1 + t_1^1 + E\{(1 + i(\theta))^{-1} t_1^2(\theta)\},$$

where the expected value of transfers accruing to agent 1 is explicit.

Further, let $f^1 = f_0^1 + f_1^1$ be the present value of private net foreign assets of all current and future agents in the domestic economy at time 1. For a creditor country, $f^1 > 0$ might be the market value of equity owned reflecting past savings decisions of the economy. Likewise, let $t^1 = t_0^1 + t_1^1 + E\{(1 + i(\theta))^{-1} t_1^2(\theta)\}$ be the aggregate values of net foreign assets net expected transfers from abroad. These transfers are assets in a broad sense because they reflect the capitalized value of foreign economic aid. Both these aggregates are indexed by a time superscript because they represent the aggregate value of current and future net foreign assets, conditional on the history of the world economy up until time 1. These aggregates are independent of agents because they sum across all current and future agents in the domestic economy.

In this simple economy, the profile of net foreign assets evolves according to the realization of the state of nature in the second period. Since there is only one (current and future) domestic agent in the second period, the present value of the aggregates $f^2(\theta) = [1 + i(\theta)]^{-1} f_1^2(\theta)$ and $t^2(\theta) = [1 + i(\theta)]^{-1} t_1^2(\theta)$ should cause no confusion. Again, these aggregates depend only on time since the history of the world economy evolves through time. If the expected value of net foreign assets was zero in the status quo ex ante,[5] the *aggregate generational current account profile* is

5. This assumption is not innocuous. The aggregate generational current account is defined as a flow, just as the conventional current account is. In practical applications, one takes first differ-

$$[\tilde{b}^1,\ \tilde{b}^2(\theta)] = [f^1 + t^1,\ (f^2(\theta) - f^1) + (t^2(\theta) - t^1)]. \tag{2}$$

The aggregate generational current account is the (history dependent) change in the expected present value of net foreign assets, broadly defined, across all generations alive and not yet born. This definition shows that a country's welfare includes a component capturing the expected transfer of real resources from abroad. In a more general model, equation (2) would sum across an infinite sequence of generations of domestic residents.[6]

Equation (2) defines the aggregate generational current account as the change in the history-dependent stock of net foreign assets. In practical applications, it is natural to construct annual changes in order to facilitate comparisons with the conventional current account. But, in this and many other economic models, the demarcation of a period serves two functions: it keeps track of calendar time and differentiates between agents. Generational accounts are really indexed by the agents in an economy, and this fact has important implications for how to use them.[7] Since the aggregate generational current account is the increase in the present value of assets owned abroad, a surplus in this measure indicates that net foreign assets have risen more rapidly than the nominal interest rate. Thus current and future generations can expect a larger inflow of goods and services than was the case before.

The aggregate generational current account is useful for two purposes. First, it determines the extent to which a country's standard of living depends on receipt of goods and services from abroad. For example, if $\tilde{b}^2(\theta) > 0$, then agent 1 owns net foreign assets whose market value is larger than the initial net foreign asset position of the economy. This increase is larger than the loss in net foreign assets that occurred when agent 0 liquidated her portfolio, and it represents a high rate of domestic savings, realized capital gains, or unexpected transfers from abroad. There is an inherent legal asymmetry between net assets located abroad, $f_1^2(\theta) + t_1^2(\theta)$, and those located at home, $d_1^2(\theta)$. Domestic assets are the liabilities of a corporate entity subject to some domestic juridical authority; thus disputes arising because of ownership rights can be settled fairly readily. Foreign assets, however, are riskier precisely because there is no simple means for the resolution of conflicts between creditors and

ences of the present value of the stock of net foreign assets. We have thus assumed implicitly that the stock defined in eq. (2) can be interpreted as a flow because the economy's original valuation of net foreign assets was zero.

6. Let $\tilde{a}_h$ be the expected present value of the assets of domestic agent h born at some time in the distant future. If there is no explicit program of foreign aid and no bequest motive in the economy, then domestic assets, foreign assets, expected foreign transfers, and thus $\tilde{a}_h$ would all be zero. In this important case, the profile of the aggregate generational current account is simply the change in the present value of the economy's net foreign asset position. Then the analogue of eq. (2) reports the profile of the present value the economy's conventional current account with assets computed at market value.

7. This important subtlety is recognized by Kotlikoff (1993). I think it has been the source of some confusion in the theoretical and practical interpretations of generational accounts for the closed economy. See the interesting and though-provoking debate in Bohn (1992a), Drazen (1992), and Bohn (1992b).

debtors. Thus $\tilde{b}^2(\theta) > 0$ indicates that the domestic economy has become increasingly dependent on assets located abroad in maintaining its standard of living.

Second, the aggregate generational current account shows how changes in policy or exogenous variables affect the welfare of domestic residents. Consider a change in the stochastic processes describing expectations such that neither component of equation (2) decreases and at least one component increases after every relevant history. Such a change has at least three interpretations. First, there has been a capital gain in the market value of net foreign assets, and thus some agent in the home country can expect to enjoy increased consumption now or later. Second, the interest differential has narrowed at all horizons, raising the value of foreign bonds or decreasing the value of domestic liabilities of fixed maturity. Third, the domestic currency has experienced a real depreciation, lowering the value of liabilities denominated in the domestic currency. The crucial point is that each of these phenomena can be interpreted in terms of an increase in the expected utility of a representative agent in the domestic economy. Since equation (2) is defined using domestic aggregates, there exist lump-sum (domestic) taxes such that all agents in the home country are better off.

There is no simple relationship between the conventional government deficit and the aggregate generational current account.[8] Since the conventional government deficit is not well defined, this fact should come as no surprise. Of course, if foreigners do not acquire domestic assets, then government deficits involve only an internal redistribution of wealth among the generations in a country. Then they influence the aggregate generational current account only to the extent that they crowd out outward foreign investment. However, if foreigners do acquire domestic fiat assets, then an internal deficit causes the aggregate generational current account to increase. Thus part of the burden of the national debt is the present value of the interest payments to foreigners.

Another natural measure of an economy's net foreign asset position is the profile of net foreign assets owned by the current and future generations of its residents. In this simple model, the only interesting such cross section is

$$[f_0^1 + t_0^1,\ f_1^1 + t_1^1 + E\{(1 + i(\theta))^{-1} t_1^2(\theta)\}], \tag{3}$$

where the second term depends on the expected transfers from abroad to the agent in generation 1. This cross section must be taken at time 1 because there is no generational heterogeneity at time 2 in this simple model. These values simply divide an economy's net international investment position, measured at market values and inclusive of expected transfers from abroad, among the several current and future generations of domestic residents. Of course, this cross section allows specifically for the generational heterogeneity that is at the heart of Auerbach et al.'s (1991) analogous measure for the domestic economy.

8. Dewald and Ulan (1990) have made this point for the conventional current account.

Measuring (2) or (3) requires making explicit assumptions about the stochastic processes driving exchange rates, interest rates, and international transfer policies. Thus the aggregate generational current account is only as good as the assumptions that are used to construct it, and economists must face an essential paradox. Cash flow accounts, like the conventional current account, are measured quite precisely, but compelling theoretical arguments show that they are potentially devoid of economic meaning. On the other hand, accrual accounts, such as the aggregate generational current account are measured imprecisely, but they do have sound foundations in economic theory. So one is caught between Scylla and Charybdis. Is it nobler to accept an accurate measurement of a meaningless number or to attempt a rough measure of a useful economic concept? Recognizing that I must now make many heroic assumptions, I turn my attention to the latter endeavor using 20 years of data from the Japanese economy.

10.3 Japan's Aggregate Generational Current Account

The Bank of Japan reports regional balance-of-payments statistics in the April and November issues of *Balance of Payments Monthly.*[9] These data are reported in millions of current dollars, and they were the primary source for the historical statistics used to compile the aggregate generational current account for Japan. The data cover the period from 1973 to 1992 and describe regional balances with the United States, Western Europe, the Communist bloc,[10] and Australia. These groups of countries have historically represented more than three-quarters of the aggregate bilateral trade of Japan. Taiwan, Korean, Thailand, and Singapore form the only major trading group that was excluded. Since the data were all reported in current dollars, I used the realized nominal interest rate on long-term government bonds in the United States for all relevant present value calculations.

These regional balance-of-payments data are broken down into the current account and the capital account. In constructing the aggregate generational current account, I focused on inward and outward annual flows of long-term capital. The *Balance of Payments Monthly* reports changes in both assets and liabilities in these categories: direct investments, trade credits, loans, securities, external bonds, and others. I assumed that all assets were denominated in the currency of the host county and that all liabilities were denominated in yen.

Outward direct investment is subject to capital gains for two reasons. First, changes in the exchange rate of the host country influence the market value of assets located abroad. Second, movements in local asset market indexes reflect

9. Matsuoka and Rose (1994) give an excellent guide to Japanese economic statistics. Many Japanese publications have statistical sections with bilingual headings in Japanese and English.

10. This nomenclature is a vestige of the cold war. This group of countries includes Russia, several other Eastern European countries, the People's Republic of China, Cambodia, Vietnam, and other countries.

capital gains and losses in local securities markets. The measure reported in this chapter captures both of these sources of fluctuations in asset prices. Likewise, the market value of inward foreign direct investment into Japan fluctuates as the yen appreciates and depreciates and also as yen-denominated assets experience the vicissitudes of Japanese financial markets.

I assumed that assets and liabilities in the *Balance of Payments Monthly* falling under the four headings "trade credits," "loans," "external bonds," and "others" took the form of long-term debt. However, the aggregate called "securities" includes portfolio investments in both bonds and stocks. Indeed, it is difficult to find statistics that distinguish between portfolio investment in debt and equity. Although the Ministry of Finance reports regional portfolio investment in the August issue of *Zaisei Kinyu Tokei Geppo* (Monthly Statistics on Government Finance), it seems that these data do not differentiate between portfolio investment in bonds and in equity. Using data on Japanese investment into the United States reported in the *Survey of Current Business,* I assumed arbitrarily that 40 percent of the value of outward Japanese portfolio investment was in equities and the rest in bonds.[11] I imposed the condition that these shares were also true of inward portfolio investment into Japan.

The appropriate asset market deflator for long-term debt is an index of bond prices for the relevant currency denomination. Long-term interest rates on government debt are reported in the International Monetary Fund's *International Financial Statistics,* and it was assumed that the average duration of the bonds in question was 10 years. Then a simple formula allows one to construct a bond price index for four of the five regions.[12] These indexes are graphed in figure 10.1. That figure shows that the general drop in interest rates in the past decade was a source of capital gains for Japanese investors holding long-term debt denominated in dollars and sterling.

The International Monetary Fund's *International Financial Statistics* also reports price indexes for industrial shares in the markets of Japan, the United Kingdom, the United States, and Australia. Following Dewald and Ulan (1990), I revalued Japanese outward and inward foreign direct investment using local market indexes.[13] These indexes are graphed in figure 10.2. Thus Japanese investors holding equity in the United States and Europe enjoyed appreciable capital gains in the past decade.

11. The June 1990 issue of the *Survey of Current Business* (56, table 1) shows that Japanese investors acquired $115 billion of U.S. securities other than Treasury securities in 1988 and 1989. They acquired $69 billion in corporate and other bonds and $46 billion in corporate stocks in America those two years.

12. See Sharpe, Alexander, and Bailey (1995, 469–71) for a good discussion of duration and bond prices. I used bond prices in the United Kingdom as a proxy for European bond prices, and I assumed that all debt extended to the Communist bloc was denominated in dollars. Thus the bond index for the United States was also used to evaluate the market price of debt in the Communist bloc. If the average duration of debt is actually less than 10 years, then these indexes overstate the effects of interest rate changes on the prices of bonds.

13. The index for the Communist bloc is simply an index of nominal GDP in the People's Republic of China.

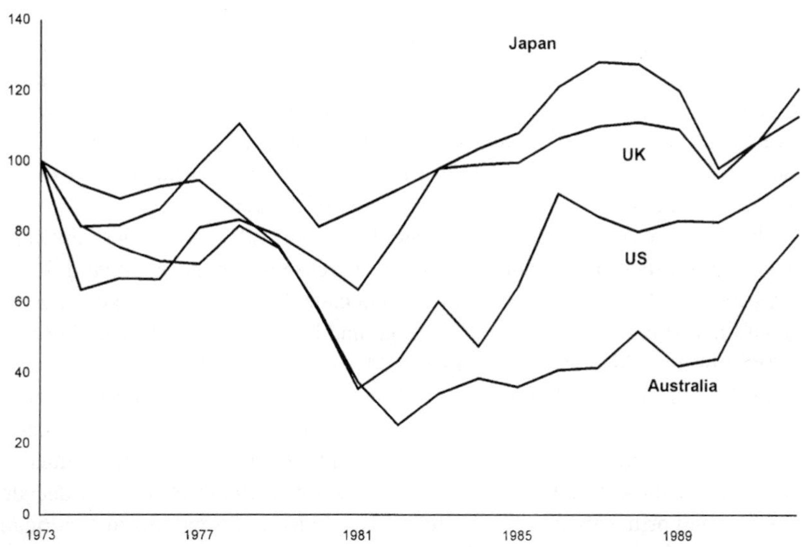

Fig. 10.1 Bond price indexes

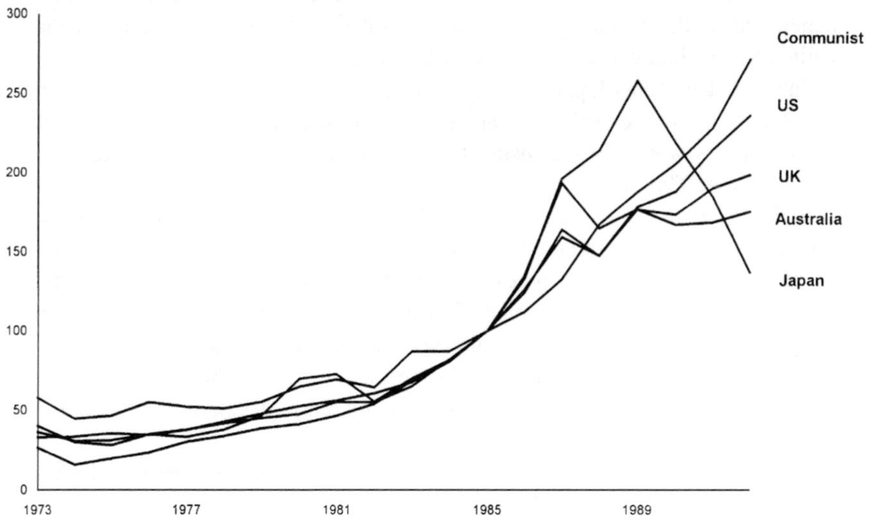

Fig. 10.2 Industrial share price indexes

The last effect that must be accounted for in constructing the market value of the net international position is the effect that currency prices have on the market value of direct or portfolio investment. I used the end-of-period exchange rates reported in *International Financial Statistics* to adjust the value of the stock of assets accordingly. These exchange rates are the dollar prices of the yen, the pound sterling, the Australian dollar, and the huan. The exchange rate indexes are graphed in figure 10.3. They confirm the general long-term appreciation of the yen against the dollar and the analogous depreciation of sterling, the Australian dollar, and the huan. Thus Japanese outward direct investment has suffered capital losses owing to exchange rate movements in each of these broad regions, while inward investment into Japan has experienced capital gains owing to the appreciation of the yen.

These indexes enable one to calculate the market value of Japanese outward and inward direct investment.[14] The rapid increase in Japanese outward direct investment first occurred early in the past decade. In 1982, the market value of Japan's net foreign assets was $12 billion, and by 1992, that figure had grown to $687 billion. Also, by 1992, Japan held 76 percent of its net foreign assets in the United States and 10 percent in Europe. The share of net foreign assets in Australia was 11 percent and that in the Communist bloc was 3 percent. Since the low volume of direct investment into Japan is well documented,[15] these shares show that Japan's outward foreign investment in the past decade was directed primarily into the United States. Indeed, movements in American asset prices have an increasingly important role in determining the market value of Japanese assets and thus influence Japan's aggregate generational current account. In essence, the well-being of Japanese residents is much more dependent, both absolutely and relatively, on macroeconomic factors in the United States than was the case two decades ago.

Table 10.1 presents Japan's aggregate generational current account. Column (1) shows the market value of Japan's international investment position; net foreign assets were adjusted using the price indexes and exchange rates displayed above. The market value of these net assets is about 60 percent higher than the Bank of Japan's own figure for 1992.[16] The surge in Japanese outward investment coincided with the boom in world equity markets after the recession of the past decade; thus Japan's overseas investments have shown strong capital gains. Still, the outward investments in Europe bore a better rate of return than those in the United States. Also, although the rate of return on holding yen-denominated assets was quite high in the past 15 years, the low volume of inward investment into Japan has limited the increase of Japan's liabilities vis-à-vis the rest of the world.

Column (2) of table 10.1 presents Japan's net transfers from abroad. Fisher

14. Let K_t^i be the market value in dollars of direct investment in country i at time t. Let I_t^i be the analogous increase in the dollar value of assets. I used the recursive relationship

$$K_{t+1}^i = K_t^i(P_{t+1}^i / P_t^i)(S_t^i / S_{t+1}^i) + I_{t+1}^i,$$

where P_t^i is the relevant asset price index and S_t^i is the dollar price of a unit of currency i both at time t.

15. See Lawrence (1993) for an extensive discussion.

16. Table 17 of the *Balance of Payments Monthly* for April 1993 states that the dollar value of Japan's external assets at the end of 1992 was $514 billion.

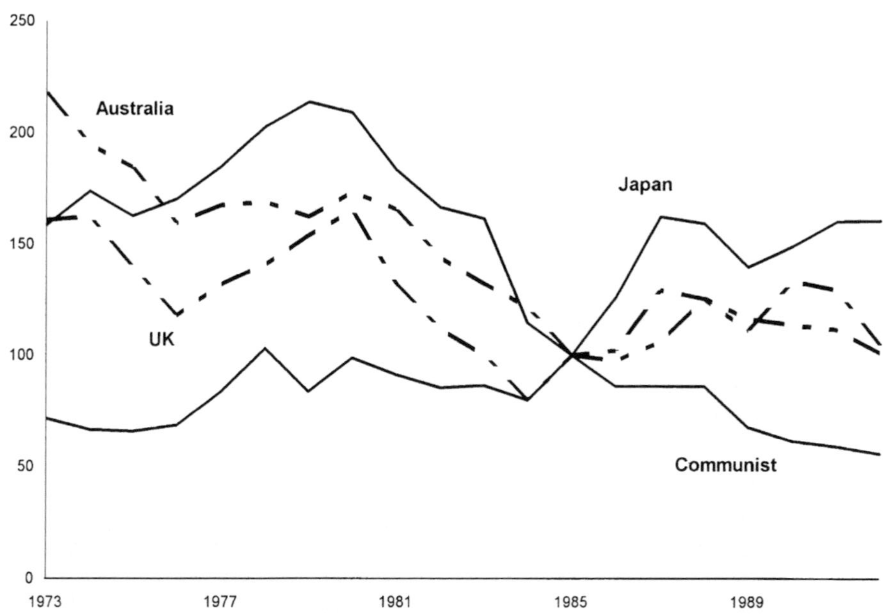

Fig. 10.3 Exchange rate indexes

and Woo (1997) computed the present value of capitalized transfers for Korea, but they made the assumption that military and economic transfers into Korea formed a part of the United States' long-run military policy. I have made the judgment here that Japan's transfers to abroad are not part of ongoing international commitments. This opinion reflects the role imposed by the United States on Japan in the postwar era. Indeed, the single large transfer of $12 billion in 1991 was a contribution to the Allies' defense of Kuwait. This compensation is precisely the kind of one-off payment showing that these unilateral transfers are not part of a continuing geopolitical role imposing long-run liabilities on the residents of Japan.

Column (3) in table 10.1 gives the present value of the net foreign assets of Japan under the assumption that the value of these assets was zero at the beginning of 1973. It is impressive that the dollar value of Japanese net foreign assets has grown more rapidly than the nominal interest rate in the past 20 years. Of course, such an accumulation reflects a rapid increase in the expected flow of goods and services into Japan in the future. The aggregate generational current account is given in column (4) of table 10.1; this column simply presents first differences of the data in the previous column. It shows that the rapid increase in the present value of Japanese net foreign assets first occurred in 1982. Thus the end of the last major recession marked the advent of Japan's sustained external surplus. This observation is confirmed by the data on the present value of the conventional current account reported in column (5). The

Table 10.1 **Japan's Aggregate Generational Current Account**

Year	Net International Investment Position at Market Values (1)	Transfers from Abroad (2)	Present Value of (1) + (2) (3)	Aggregate Generational Current Account (4)	Present Value of the Conventional Measure (5)
1973	4,580	−210	4,370	4,370	−136
1974	5,630	−203	5,079	709	−4,393
1975	4,792	−272	3,933	−1,146	−593
1976	4,336	−204	3,330	−603	2,965
1977	4,216	−194	3,011	−318	8,176
1978	7,596	−230	5,135	2,124	11,526
1979	15,072	−755	9,206	4,071	−5,629
1980	10,201	−1,288	5,237	−3,969	−6,155
1981	5,886	−1,405	2,362	−2,875	2,514
1982	11,809	−1,297	4,865	2,502	3,170
1983	26,257	−1,369	10,193	5,328	8,518
1984	49,737	−1,372	17,827	7,634	12,902
1985	96,186	−1,375	31,057	13,231	16,106
1986	199,459	−1,465	58,631	27,573	25,421
1987	297,586	−2,697	81,096	22,465	23,929
1988	370,651	−3,007	93,286	12,190	20,206
1989	448,088	−3,253	103,695	10,410	13,324
1990	582,268	−4,468	124,139	20,444	7,683
1991	661,101	−11,834	128,506	4,367	14,429
1992	687,291	−3,362	125,502	−3,004	21,571

Note: Figures are in millions of dollars.

aggregate generational current account and the present value of the conventional measure are highly correlated; they differ in years when large fluctuations in asset prices or exchange rates precipitate large changes in the market value of net foreign assets. At such times, the conventional current account surplus is a poor measure of the increase in the expected present value of resources imported from abroad in the future.

10.4 The Generational Pattern of Ownership of Net Foreign Assets

Who owns Japan's net foreign assets? The data in section 10.3 showed how the market value of Japan's net international investment position has evolved since 1973. But who has benefited from the large capital gains that Japan experienced on its outward investment in the past decade? And who owes the relatively small amount of yen-denominated liabilities that Japan has issued during the past 15 years? This section answers those questions by assuming that these assets and liabilities are allocated according to the patterns of saving and borrowing of Japan's residents during the past three decades.

Japan's savings rate rose and then fell in the past three decades; Horioka (1993) gives a good historical overview, and Ito and Kitamura (1994) show

how savings rates in Japan are influenced by public policy. The Statistics Bureau of Japan's Management and Coordination Agency presents time series on family income and expenditure in Japan. It gathers these data from a random sample of households of Japanese residents. I used data from the bureau's *Comprehensive Time Series Report on the Family Income and Expenditure Survey: 1947–1986* (1988) to construct the savings and borrowing rates of 13 different "generations" of Japanese residents.

A generation is a cohort of Japanese residents born during the five-year period whose central year is used as its label. I identify the first generation with 1906,[17] and subsequent generations occur quinquennially until 1966. For each year between 1966 and 1986, the Family Income and Expenditure Survey gives the total savings and liabilities of the average household in a generation, and it describes the number of households sampled. Thus I was able to compute the share of total savings and also total liabilities that accrued to any one generation in the sample. I used data from the years 1973, 1978, 1983, and 1988[18] to construct the savings and borrowing rates for each of the generations in my sample. In 1973, the generations born later than 1951 were assumed not yet economically active, and by 1988, the generations born after 1966, including those not yet born in 1991, were analogously inactive.

The savings rates were used to allocate new outward investment to the agents in the generations economically active in that year. Likewise, the borrowing rates were used to assign new yen-denominated liabilities among the generations active in that year. Since Japan's transfers to abroad have not been enduring, I allocated each year's unilateral transfers as a lump-sum tax whose burden was distributed uniformly on the agents who were economically active in that year. Then I was able to construct the market value of the net international investment position of each generation for each year between 1973 and 1992. These calculations are entirely analogous to those underlying the construction of the market value of Japan's net international investment position, inclusive of the burden of unilateral transfers to abroad, but new investment and new borrowing are assigned in each year according to the savings and borrowing rates of the economically active generations. These data are stocks of assets, and they are denominated in current dollars. Finally, I divided them by the number of people in each generation in 1993. Thus the data are presented in 1992 dollars per person.

Column (1) of table 10.2 presents the generational pattern of Japan's net international investment position, broadly defined. The calculations presented in table 10.2 make the assumption that a generation's mortality rate is 6 percent per quinquennium, independent of the age of the cohort. Column (1) is a benchmark showing that members of the oldest generation in 1992 own substantial net foreign assets. The generation born around 1926 has benefited from

17. My first generation is really people born before 1909 who are still alive in 1993, but I identify this group with the 1906 generation, those born between 1904 and 1908, inclusive. In contrast with Auerbach et al. (1991), I put males and females together.

18. I actually used data from 1986 as a proxy for those from 1988.

the capital gains in world securities markets more than those before and after it because its years of peak savings occurred at the time when Japan's external surplus first began to grow most rapidly and world asset markets were historically undervalued. The modest positions of the generations born around 1961 and 1966 reflect the fact they paid for Japan's contribution to the Persian Gulf War before they had begun to accumulate substantial net foreign assets. Generations born after 1966 have no net foreign assets because they are not economically active and I have assumed they have no liability for future transfer payments to abroad.

The calculations inherent in column (1) of table 10.2 allow me to make forecasts about the effects of three different policy scenarios on the welfare of these different generations. I examine three changes in exogenous variables from the 1992 benchmark: a strong yen, a rise in dollar interest rates, and rapid economic growth in China. The first situation entails an appreciation of the yen: a rise in the dollar price of the yen from 0.00816 (its value in 1992) to 0.0125 dollars per yen (near its current value in 1995). The second assumes that dollar interest rates rise from 7.01 percent per annum (its value in 1992) to 10.00 percent per annum. The third situation assumes that Chinese economic growth stays more robust than the world average; I modeled this as a 20 percent capital gain in the Japanese assets in the Communist bloc.

Columns (2), (3), and (4) of table 10.2 show the outcomes of each of these scenarios respectively. A strong yen causes a Pareto worsening for the Japanese

Table 10.2 Generational Pattern of Japanese Net Foreign Assets

Generation	Net Foreign Assets (1)	Yen Appreciation (2)	Higher Dollar Interest Rates (3)	Robust Chinese Growth (4)
1906	23,544	22,045	22,031	23,571
1911	23,563	22,077	22,050	23,590
1916	23,201	21,339	21,675	23,228
1921	22,531	20,100	20,976	22,559
1926	18,248	14,041	16,743	18,275
1931	13,633	9,211	12,367	13,657
1936	8,134	3,358	7,150	8,152
1941	4,566	(855)	3,717	4,581
1946	3,711	(1,016)	2,980	3,725
1951	1,832	(2,218)	1,276	1,843
1956	1,777	(832)	1,367	1,785
1961	1,397	(212)	1,111	1,403
1966	494	358	431	495
1971	0	0	0	0
1976	0	0	0	0
1981	0	0	0	0
1986	0	0	0	0
1991	0	0	0	0
After 1991	0	0	0	0

Note: Figures are in 1992 dollars per person.

because the real value of their liabilities have risen. Thus the present value of net foreign assets for every generation is lower, and generations in their middle age in 1992 suffer capital losses especially.[19] These generations have incurred liabilities to foreigners as Japan's traditional barriers to inward foreign investment have relaxed slightly in the past decade. Higher dollar interest rates are a capital loss on the dollar-denominated bonds that are such a large part of the net foreign assets of many generations. A rise in dollar rates is Pareto inferior to the benchmark. Still, this situation is not Pareto superior to the strong yen scenario; the generations born around 1911 and 1916 actually lose slightly more in this situation than they do under a strong yen. Finally, even if the Chinese economic boom continues, there will be little effect on the Japanese. This is so because Japan held only 3 percent of its net foreign assets in the Communist bloc in 1992. Capital gains on Chinese assets represent a slight Pareto improvement over the benchmark.

The important point in each of these three cases is that these generational profiles of assets illustrate in intuitive ways the effects that changes in macroeconomic variables have on the welfare of the Japanese. For example, the generational asset profiles worsen immediately when the yen appreciates. Since the trade balance adjusts over time, the conventional current account worsens only slowly in analogous historical situations. The aggregate generational current account shows that the real effects of a strong yen are the immediate capital losses sustained by Japanese investors owing net foreign assets. These losses are so obvious that they have become the standard grist of financial journalists in the last few months. The conventional current account barely captures such contemporaneous effects at all.

10.5 Conclusion

This chapter has presented a measure of the Japanese external surplus that has its foundation in economic theory. The Japanese have accumulated net foreign assets at a remarkable rate in the past 20 years, and their economic well-being is now inextricably tied into the smooth functioning of the world financial system. There have been other countries that have accumulated net foreign assets at a pace greater than the rate of interest over long periods: Britain in the nineteenth century and the United States in the twentieth century are two important examples. It is tempting to draw historical parallels between the overvaluation of the sterling after the First World War and the current strength of the yen. But I am not a bold or competent enough historian to predict that Japan will suffer a prolonged deterioration in its standard of living if the yen remains as strong as it is now. Still, a generational perspective on the external surplus shows that large movements in the real exchange rate have immediate effects on the market value of assets.

19. I am implicitly assuming a real appreciation of the yen. In a world with not traded goods, the negative income effect of the yen appreciation is not fully offset by a drop in all consumer prices.

Finally, it is important that international economists recognize that the conventional current account depends on the timing of cross-border payments. The International Monetary Fund's *Balance of Payments Manual* (1977) is a classic statement of careful cash-flow accounting principles, and I have relied on it in interpreting the capital account statistics that I have analyzed in this chapter. I am not advocating throwing out the baby with the bathwater because it is indeed obvious that the conventional current account is highly correlated with the aggregate generational current account. Thus the conventional measure does have practical economic significance, especially if one is willing to interpret the conventional current account within the discipline of an explicit economic model. But accurate cash-flow accounts are only part of a bigger picture, and I hope that this chapter spurs further research into accrual-based international accounts.

Appendix
Description of the Data

The data on the net foreign assets of Japan were constructed from the annual long-term capital transactions reported in the regional balance of payments summaries in the April issues of the Bank of Japan's *Kokusai Shushi Tokei Geppo* (Balance of Payments Monthly). The capital account covers six categories: direct investments, trade credits, loans, securities, external bonds, and others. The four regions selected were not entirely consistent across the 20 years of the sample. The geographic definitions for the United States and the Communist bloc are consistent. That for Europe actually covers the United Kingdom and the European Community in 1973 and 1974 and corresponds to the European Economic Community, including its new members as it enlarged, between 1975 and 1992. The data for Australia include New Zealand and South Africa until 1981, and they consist of the category "other OECD" from 1982 to 1988. After that they include Australia alone. The disaggregated Japanese capital account figures reverse the signs for assets (outward flows of capital) but not for liabilities in the years from 1973 to 1978. Since the aggregated figures always follow the usual convention (an increase in assets takes a negative sign), this inconsistency can be vexing. Future researchers beware!

In later years, *Kokusai Shushi Tokei Geppo* also includes a table on the external assets and liabilities of Japan. The text uses figures from this table when comparing the market value of Japan's net foreign assets with the official figures reported by the Bank of Japan.

Direct investments and 40 percent of the value of securities were revalued using the annual industrial share price indexes given in the International Monetary Fund's *International Financial Statistics*. The indexes were for Japan, the

United States, the United Kingdom, and Australia. The analogous series for the Communist bloc was an index of the national income of the People's Republic of China at market prices as reported in *International Financial Statistics.* The categories "trade credits," "loans," 60 percent of "securities," "external bonds," and "others" were revalued using a bond price index constructed from the annual interest rates on long-term government debt reported in *International Financial Statistics.* Again, the data are interest rates from Japan, the United States, the United Kingdom, and Australia. It was assumed that debt extended to the Communist bloc was denominated in dollars. The exchange rate indexes are the end-of-period dollar prices of foreign exchange for Japan, the United Kingdom, the People's Republic of China, and Australia, all taken from *International Financial Statistics.*

The data on household saving and borrowing rates are from the Statistics Bureau of Japan's Management and Coordination Agency's *Comprehensive Time Series Report on the Family Income and Expenditure Survey, 1947–1986* (table 8-2). I used the columns entitled "no. of tabulated households," "savings," and "liabilities" from the years 1973, 1978, 1983, and 1986 (as a proxy for 1988). The 1993 populations for the different generations are reported in the Statistics Bureau of Japan's Management and Coordination Agency's *Japan Statistical Yearbook, 1995* (table 2–9). The per capita asset figures assume implicitly all assets acquired between 1973 and 1992 by a given generation are held by the members of that generation living in 1993.

The text refers at several times to the U.S. Department of Commerce's *Survey of Current Business.* The data giving U.S. international transactions by area (September 1994, table 10) were the basis for allocating 60 percent of securities to bonds and the rest to equity. Tables 5.1 and 5.2 of the May 1994 issue report data on Japan's direct investment into the United States by industry in 1992 and 1993.

References

Ablett, John. 1996. Generational accounting—An Australian perspective. *Review of Income and Wealth* 42:91–105.

Auerbach, Alan J., J. Gokhale, and L. J. Kotlikoff. 1991. Generational accounts: A meaningful alternative to deficit accounting. In *Tax policy and the economy,* vol. 5, ed. David Bradford. Cambridge, Mass.: MIT Press.

———. 1994. Generational accounting: A meaningful way to evaluate fiscal policy. *Journal of Economic Perspectives* 8:73–94.

Bohn, Henning. 1992a. Budget deficits and government accounting. *Carnegie-Rochester Conference Series on Public Policy* 37:1–84.

———. 1992b. Budget deficits and government accounting: Reply to Allan Drazen. *Carnegie-Rochester Conference Series on Public Policy* 37:93–95.

Dewald, William G., and M. Ulan. 1990. The twin-deficit illusion. *Cato Journal* 9: 689–718.

Drazen, Allan. 1992. Problems of government accounting: A comment. *Carnegie-Rochester Conference Series on Public Policy* 37:85–92.

Fisher, Eric O'N. 1995. A new way of thinking about the current account. *International Economic Review* 36:555–68.

Fisher, Eric O'N., and YoungSoo Woo. 1997. Meaningful measures of the current account. *Review of International Economics* 5:452–66.

Horioka, Charles Y. 1993. Savings in Japan. In *World savings: An international survey,* ed. A. Heertje. Oxford: Blackwell.

International Monetary Fund. 1977. *Balance of payments manual,* 4th ed. Washington, D.C.: International Monetary Fund.

———. Various issues. *International financial statistics yearbook.* Washington, D.C.: International Monetary Fund.

Ito, Takatoshi, and Yukinobu Kitamura. 1994. Public policies and household saving in Japan. In *Public policies and household saving,* ed. J. Poterba, 133–60. Chicago: University of Chicago Press.

Japan. Bank of Japan. Foreign Department. Various issues. *Kokusai shushi tokei geppo* (Balance of payments monthly). Tokyo: Bank of Japan.

———. Management and Coordination Agency. Statistics Bureau. 1988. *Comprehensive time series report on the Family Income and Expenditure Survey: 1947–1986.* Tokyo: Statistics Bureau.

———. 1995. *Japan Statistical Yearbook, 1995.* Tokyo.

———. Ministry of Finance. Various issues. *Zaisei kinyu tokei geppo* (Monthly statistics on government finance).

Kotlikoff, Laurence J. 1993. *Generational accounting: Knowing who pays, and when, for what we spend.* New York: Free Press.

Lawrence, Robert Z. 1993. Japan's low levels of inward investment: The role of inhibitions on acquisitions. In *Foreign direct investment,* ed. K. A. Froot, 85–107. Chicago: University of Chicago Press.

Matsuoka, Mikhiro, and B. Rose. 1994. *The DIR guide to Japanese economic statistics.* Oxford: Oxford University Press.

Sharpe, William F., G. J. Alexander, and J. V. Bailey. 1995. *Investments,* 5th ed. Englewood Cliffs, N.J.: Prentice-Hall.

Sterngold, James. 1995. Hollywood 1, Japan 0. *New York Times,* 16 April 1995, sec. 4, p. 5.

Ulan, Michael, and W. G. Dewald. 1989. The U.S. net international investment position: Misstated and misunderstood. In *Dollars deficits and trade,* ed. J. A. Dorn and William A. Niskanen. Norwell, Mass.: Kluwer.

U.S. Department of Commerce. Economics and Statistics Administration. Bureau of Economic Analysis. Various issues. *Survey of Current Business.* Washington, D.C.: Bureau of Economic Analysis.

Contributors

Robert E. Baldwin
Department of Economics
1180 Observatory Drive
University of Wisconsin–Madison
Madison, WI 53706

Magnus Blomström
Stockholm School of Economics
P.O. Box 6501
S-113 83 Stockholm, Sweden

Mark E. Doms
U.S. Department of Commerce
Bureau of the Census
Washington, D.C. 20233

Eric O'N. Fisher
Department of Economics
Ohio State University
410 Arps Hall
1945 North High Street
Columbus, OH 43210

K. C. Fung
Department of Economics
University of California
Crown College
Santa Cruz, CA 95064

Harry Grubert
Office of International Tax Analysis
U.S. Department of the Treasury
1500 Pennsylvania Avenue NW
Washington, DC 20220

Keith Head
Faculty of Commerce and Business Administration
University of British Columbia
2053 Mail Mall
Vancouver, BC V6T 1Z2, Canada

David L. Hummels
Graduate School of Business
University of Chicago
1101 East 58th Street
Chicago, IL 60637

J. Bradford Jensen
U.S. Department of Commerce
Bureau of the Census
Washington, DC 20233

Fukunari Kimura
Faculty of Economics
Keio University
2-15-45 Mita, Minato-ku
Fuku, Tokyo 108, Japan

Robert E. Lipsey
National Bureau of Economic Research
50 East 42d Street, 17th Floor
New York, NY 10017

Linda Low
Department of Business Policy
National University of Singapore
10 Kent Ridge Crescent
Singapore 0511

Raymond J. Mataloni, Jr.
U.S. Department of Commerce
Bureau of Economic Analysis
1414 L Street NW (BE-50)
Washington, DC 20230

Rachel McCulloch
Department of Economics
Brandeis University
Waltham, MA 02254

John Mutti
Department of Economics
Grinnell University
Grinnell, IA 50112

Marcus Noland
Institute for International Economics
11 Dupont Circle NW
Washington, DC 20036

Michael G. Plummer
Department of Economics
Brandeis University
Waltham, MA 02254

Eric D. Ramstetter
International Centre for the Study of East Asian Development
11-4 Otemachi
Kokurakita-ku
Kitakyushu, 803, Japan

J. David Richardson
Department of Economics
Syracuse University
347 Eggars Hall
Syracuse, NY 13244

Guy V. G. Stevens
Board of Governors
Federal Reserve System
Washington, DC 20551

Deborah L. Swenson
Department of Economics
University of California, Davis
Davis, CA 95616

Michael Wasylenko
Dean's Office
Syracuse University
200 Eggers Hall
Syracuse, NY 13244

Kristen L. Willard
Graduate School of Business
Columbia University
101 Uris Hall
New York, NY 10027

Henry Wai-Chung Yeung
Department of Geography
National University of Singapore
10 Kent Ridge Crescent
Singapore 0511

William J. Zeile
U.S. Department of Commerce
Bureau of Economic Analysis
1441 L Street NW
Washington, DC 20230

Author Index

Subject Index

Four Musical Minimalists

The American composers La Monte Young, Terry Riley, Steve Reich and Philip Glass are widely regarded as pioneers of the aesthetic and the techniques of minimalism in musical composition during the 1960s and early 1970s. This book offers the most detailed account so far of their early works, putting extensive discussion of the music into a biographical perspective. The true musical minimalism of these years is placed in the wider context of their musical output as a whole, and considered within the cultural conditions of a period which saw not only the rise of minimalism in the fine arts but also crucial changes in the theory and practice of musical composition in the Western cultivated tradition.

KEITH POTTER is a Senior Lecturer in Music at Goldsmiths College, University of London, and is a regular contributor to *The Independent*.

Music in the Twentieth Century

GENERAL EDITOR Arnold Whittall

This series offers a wide perspective on music and musical life in the twentieth century. Books included range from historical and biographical studies concentrating particularly on the context and circumstances in which composers were writing, to analytical and critical studies concerned with the nature of musical language and questions of compositional process. The importance given to context will also be reflected in studies dealing with, for example, the patronage, publishing and promotion of new music, and in accounts of the musical life of particular countries.

Recently published titles

The Music of John Cage
James Pritchett
0 521 56544 8

The Music of Ruth Crawford Seeger
Joseph Straus
0 521 41646 9

The Music of Conlon Nancarrow
Kyle Gann
0 521 46534 6

The Stravinsky Legacy
Jonathan Cross
0 521 56365 8

Experimental Music: Cage and Beyond
Michael Nyman
0 521 65297 9
0 521 65383 5

The BBC and Ultra-Modern Music, 1922–1936
Jennifer Doctor
0 521 66117 X

The Music of Harrison Birtwistle
Robert Adlington
0 521 63082 7

Four Musical Minimalists:

La Monte Young,
Terry Riley,
Steve Reich,
Philip Glass

Keith Potter

PUBLISHED BY THE PRESS SYNDICATE OF THE UNIVERSITY OF CAMBRIDGE
The Pitt Building, Trumpington Street, Cambridge, United Kingdom

CAMBRIDGE UNIVERSITY PRESS
The Edinburgh Building, Cambridge CB2 2RU, UK http://www.cup.cam.ac.uk
40 West 20th Street, New York, NY 10011–4211, USA http://www.cup.org
10 Stamford Road, Oakleigh, Melbourne 3166, Australia

First published 2000

Printed in the United Kingdom at the University Press, Cambridge

Typeset in Adobe Minion 10.5/13.5 pt in QuarkXPress® [SE]

A catalogue record for this book is available from the British Library

Library of Congress cataloguing in publication data

Potter, Keith
Four musical minimalists / Keith Potter.
p. cm.
Includes bibliographical references (p.) and discography (p.).
Contents: La Monte Young – Terry Riley – Steve Reich – Philip Glass.
ISBN 0 521 48250 X (hardcover)
1. Young, La Monte, 1935– . 2. Riley, Terry, 1935– . 3. Reich, Steve, 1936– . 4. Glass, Philip, 1937– . 5. Composers – United States – Biography. 6. Minimal music – United States – History and criticism. I. Title.
ML390.P759 2000
780′.92′273 – dc21 00–11736 CIP

ISBN 0 521 48250 X hardback

For Kay,
and David Huntley (in memoriam)

Contents

Acknowledgements

First and foremost, I am indebted to the four composers who are the subjects of this book for their extensive assistance and considerable patience over the years during which it has been put together. Between 1984 and 1998, they have submitted themselves variously, but always generously, to many hours of interviewing and – in a field in which there are relatively few published sources, and in which the secondary source materials are frequently patchy, inaccurate and seldom scholarly – have additionally provided written and taped documentation on a sometimes extensive scale. Whenever their views and memories differ, I hope I have interpreted their collective statements sensitively as well as done justice to each of them individually; in several respects, they have been the ideal counterbalance to each other in the attempt to produce a fully informed historical account. Having stayed at the homes of three of my 'victims', I should also acknowledge their hospitality. Both in this respect, and for participating in interviews and spending many hours collecting and photocopying material and helping to check several versions of the chapter on Young, I must also thank Marian Zazeela, whose husband regularly enjoys the benefits of an unusually close artistic as well as personal partnership.

Among many others who have also submitted to interviewing, corresponded with me and in many others ways assisted, directly or indirectly, with research, I should like in particular to mention Jon Gibson. The only musician to have worked regularly with all four composers under scrutiny here, and himself a composer of minimalist music as well as one of its most talented and staunchest champions as a performer, he has been unfailingly and selflessly helpful. Among others, many of them participants in the early history of musical minimalism, whose knowledge and perspective – the latter sometimes very different from that of my subjects – have been shared with me directly, modifying and improving my understanding of the subject, John Adams, JoAnn Akalaitis, Glenn Branca, Rhys Chatham, Tony Conrad, Hugh Davies, Ruth Dreier, Paul Epstein, Henry Flynt, Daniel Goode, Tom Johnson, Jack Kripl, David Lang, Ruth Maleczech, Phill Niblock, Pauline Oliveros, Michael Parsons, Ann Riley, Howard Skempton and Janis Susskind must receive particular mention. Of those others who have offered assistance or advice at various stages, and in some cases commented on drafts of individual chapters, I should like to mention

Mark Cromar and Robert Davidson (whose unpublished dissertations have additionally proved considerable stimuli to my own work), Jeremy Peyton Jones and Andrew Poppy (the last two being chief among many former students with whom I have maintained an ongoing debate concerning the past practice and present state of musical minimalism), Dave Smith and Mark Swed. David Allenby, of Boosey and Hawkes, and Ramona Kirchschenman, of Dunvagen, are among many others who have helped in various ways. I should also like to place on record my gratitude to David Huntley, also of Boosey and Hawkes, whose unstinting advice and hospitality whenever I was in New York during the ten years before his untimely death in 1994 were a source of special pleasure to me.

Thanks must go, in addition, to Goldsmiths College, University of London, my long-time employers, who have not only given me the time to research and write this book but also provided a travel grant, as did the University of London itself. I should particularly thank Stanley Glasser, for many years Head of Music at Goldsmiths, for his faith that my endeavours in this area would eventually yield fruit in book form. As General Editor of the series of which this volume is part, I am pleased to acknowledge the patient advice of Professor Arnold Whittall, and also proud to admit to being his student many years ago. Penny Souster at Cambridge University Press has been equally persistent in her efforts to see this book through to completion; Ann Lewis, my copy editor, and Karl Howe, production and design manager, are among several others at CUP whom I should also thank. My parents – Ronald and Betty Phelps – will be surprised, and perhaps even pleased, that I have produced offspring of any kind after so many years of waiting. Many friends, both in London and in Dorset (where much of this book was written), have been encouraging and consoling, as appropriate. Finally, I should like to thank Kay Potter, my wife, for being the most supportive and long-suffering of all.

Music examples (some of them in the composers' own hand) are published either entirely by permission of the composer himself (in the case of La Monte Young and Terry Riley) or as follows:

Chapter Three: Examples 3.1–3.7, 3.12 and 3.15: copyright by Steve Reich, reproduced by kind permission of the composer. Examples 3.8, 3.16–3.18 and 3.20–3.25: copyright by Boosey and Hawkes Inc., New York, reproduced by kind permission. Examples 3.9–3.11, 3.13–3.14 and 3.19: copyright by Universal Edition, London, reproduced by kind permission.
Chapter Four: Example 4.1: copyright by Novello, reproduced by kind permission. Examples 4.2–4.8, 4.10, 4.11, 4.13–4.15 and 4.17–4.21: copyright by Dunvagen Inc., reproduced by kind permission.

Preface

This book is a story of four American composers all born within eighteen months of each other. Their pioneering roles in musical minimalism are alone sufficient to single them out. A degree of overlap in their associations and their activities makes it sensible to consider them as in some sense a group. The fact that such associations mainly involve the earlier parts of their lives, as tends to be the case with any group of composers termed a 'school' by music historians, is not, however, the only reason why this volume tells their story in detail only to the middle of the 1970s. More significant in this decision is an interpretation of their work which argues a gradual move away from what can reasonably be regarded as music driven by a minimalist aesthetic towards a diversity – not only of underlying intentions, but also of style and technique – that makes it almost impossible to consider their outputs of the last quarter of a century as a meaningful whole. Though this diversity is observable more clearly in the developments of Steve Reich and Philip Glass than of La Monte Young and Terry Riley, there is sufficient evidence in the outputs of the latter pair to make sense of their stories in this rather truncated form as well.

Young, Riley, Reich and Glass have been singled out as a group by other writers, though many leave out the admittedly more controversial Young. Of those who include all four names, several – including Tom Johnson and Michael Nyman, discussed below – have written insightful journalism about them, and in 1974 Nyman brought them together in the final chapter of his seminal book, *Experimental Music: Cage and Beyond.* In his own volume, *American Minimal Music,* originally published in 1980, Wim Mertens (a composer, like Johnson and Nyman) confined his discussion of actual compositions to these four Americans, though the most interesting parts of his text are probably those which discuss wider aesthetic issues. More recently, other writers mentioned in what follows here have brought the four together, sometimes expanding their lists with further, chiefly American names. Of these, Edward Strickland's 1993 volume, *Minimalism: Origins,* imaginatively structured as an A–Z of minimalism in art and music, is the only book-length study. References to articles by several other authors – some tackling the problems of defining musical minimalism more directly, and certainly more succinctly – are made in the present text and bibliography.

My own efforts naturally overlap in intention with those of Strickland. Like him, for instance, I stress the origins and early development of American minimalist music, allowing this to influence not only the cut-off date of *c.* 1976 but also my discussions of the outputs of Young and Riley, in particular, which concentrate on their earliest, pioneering work at the expense of what followed it. I devote much less space than Strickland does, however, to Minimalist art. By dealing with each of these four figures separately, I have tried to give more comprehensive accounts of their early lives. And, in particular, I also offer more detailed musical analysis, considering that the compositions concerned have previously not received the scrutiny I would argue they deserve. Such an approach strengthens the suggestion that each composer, while undeniably playing his part in a wider scenario, is ultimately to be understood as an individual with quite different personal and musical characteristics from those of his colleagues. This book is thus simultaneously a single story and four individual stories.

Given the negative connotations of its connecting aesthetic subject matter, it seems more than usually appropriate to make clear what this book strips away from a truly comprehensive account of musical minimalism. It makes no more than occasional references to the prehistories and 'proto-minimalisms' which others have, sometimes rightly, identified, whether in the music of past composers (Vivaldi, Satie, Ravel) or more recent ones (György Ligeti, Giacinto Scelsi). It does not attempt to deal with the range of other Americans who were in some sense part of the same movement as the four considered here: composer-performers such as Meredith Monk, to give just one example. It does not encompass the variety of possible interpretations of the origins, nature and purposes of minimalism in European musics. It does no more than hint at the growth of European, American or other territories of minimalism, or post-minimalism, since the mid-1970s, or give more than brief suggestions as to whether any or all of these can be considered part of a genuine diaspora emanating directly from the work of Young, Riley, Reich and Glass. It is neither comprehensive nor up-to-the-minute.

It is, rather, an attempt to write – while its subjects are available for extended consultation – a slice of history which seems, to its author, of peculiar fascination, both for itself and for what it tells us about the wider currents of musical, and cultural, development in the twentieth century. When compared to more recent activities, its stories may be likened in some respects to the Old Testament. Limited in provenance and applicability, their subjects' sometimes painful discoveries – and prophecies – nevertheless became vital building blocks for the more encompassing and more widely accepted – though in certain quarters also frequently challenged – revelations of a New Testament enshrined in the musical culture of our own time. Before I begin, however, a little further context for these four stories must be established by examining the term that ostensibly binds them together.

Introduction

What is minimalism in music? Why has a term borrowed from the language of art historians been applied by many writers to music? To what range of work have they actually applied it? How might the use of the term illuminate our understanding of the music involved? Do the composers involved see themselves as in any sense 'minimalists'? What are the term's disadvantages? And what aspects of the wider cultural context – the compositional movements arising at the point in musical history at which these concerns surface, the phenomenon of Minimalist art itself, the move from modernism to post-modernism – help put the stories unfolded here into a wider perspective? Such questions are addressed frequently in the four main chapters that follow and, for the moment, they can be introduced only briefly. Please also note that I have attempted to suggest the rather looser connotations of the term's deployment in a musical context by reserving the upper-case 'Minimalist' for the fine arts, and generally using the lower-case 'minimalist' for musical references. I have also preferred the epithet 'minimalist' (whether upper or lower case) to the overly reductive 'minimal'. Let us begin with the earliest-known applications of the term to music.

Unsurprisingly, most composers described as minimalist are impatient with the term. Of the four subjects of this book, only Young is reasonably happy with it, and then only as applied to his earliest efforts.[1] This is perfectly understandable, even merely on the grounds that no creative artist likes to be defined, and limited, by any term. In an essay entitled 'Paragraphs on Conceptual Art', to which further reference is made below, the artist Sol Le Witt somewhat naughtily concluded that all the labels currently in use to describe Minimalist art – his list also includes 'primary structures, reductive, rejective, cool, and mini-art' – were all 'part of a secret language that art critics use when communicating with each other through the medium of art magazines'.[2] An additional problem attaching to Minimalism arises from its already derogatory sounding suggestion of 'less than usual'. As the art critic Lawrence Alloway has pointed out, '[b]ecause there is no consensus on what is Enough, or Too Much, one cannot accurately characterize [such art] as minimal. . . . It is a weakness of "minimal" as a critical term that it assumes, or rather memorializes, a point in time when such work was less than expected'.[3]

Two music critics who themselves subsequently renounced commentary in favour of composition following a minimalist approach have vied for the dubious honour of being the first to adopt the word 'minimalist' for musical purposes. In March 1972, the American writer Tom Johnson used the term to describe a concert given by his compatriot Alvin Lucier.[4] Lucier's explorations of acoustic and psycho-acoustic phenomena are, in both provenance and sonic result, very different from the music of Riley, Reich and Glass, though they have more in common with Young's rigorous and scientific investigations of sound. But some of the aspects which Johnson identifies in this 'minimal, slow-motion approach' – here not only of Lucier himself, but also of his British pupil Stuart Marshall and his wife, the artist Mary Lucier – are also characteristic of the aesthetic informing the early works of Reich and Glass, in particular. In addition to the fact that 'very little happens in any of the pieces', Johnson notes that 'the most striking thing about the concert as a whole was its coolness'.

An early champion of Riley, Reich and Glass (though oddly less enthusiastic about Young), Johnson had, at the time of this Lucier article, recently covered the première of Reich's *Drumming*: a review he subsequently assessed as 'probably the first occasion that any of the minimalist composers were taken seriously by any of the New York press'.[5] Yet his articles on the music of these figures take a while to settle for minimalism as his term of choice to describe what they do. Just a week after the Lucier notice, a review of the latest sections of Philip Glass's *Music in Twelve Parts* to appear begins with the suggestion that '[o]ne of the most important new trends in music is the area I like to refer to as "hypnotic music"'.[6] A few months later – in a review which must represent one of the first occurrences of the names of Young, Riley, Reich and Glass together in a published article[7] – Johnson relates having heard the term 'New York Hypnotic School' several times, though he includes 'minimal' among his list of such music's attributes, along with 'flat, static . . . and hypnotic'. By June 1977 – when he wrote 'What Is Minimalism Really About?'[8] – Johnson had been deploying the term more regularly for some while, and it is clear that its use had caught on in the New York community in which he operated, as it had by then done elsewhere. The list of epithets in this now classic article forms a good basis for a more detailed consideration of musical minimalism's chief attributes: 'repetition . . . tiny variations . . . hyper-clarity . . . encouraging more subtle perceptions . . . making music less dramatic . . . [stemming] partly from certain Asian and African attitudes'. As one of the few composers besides Young to accept the 'minimalist' label willingly, Johnson has himself consistently celebrated his fascination with numbers, clearly audible processes and what may be called a self-reflexive approach in music combining a high degree of systematisation with a ready wit.

In October 1968, three-and-a-half years before Johnson's Lucier article, the writer Michael Nyman had employed the term 'minimal' in a round-up review, entitled 'Minimal music', including his fellow Englishman Cornelius Cardew's work then known as *The Great Digest*; the word 'minimal' is, though, in fact applied directly only to the also mentioned Henning Christiansen's *Springen.*[9] Cardew had espoused an aesthetic owing a good deal to John Cage, though his activities also engaged improvisation: something his mentor avoided as too redolent of self-expression, of what he called 'individual taste and memory'.[10] Again, the sound world of what later became known as *The Great Learning* and its provenance are far removed from most of the music covered in the present volume. The debt to Cage is, however, some connection in itself, as we shall see; while improvisation has been central to the work of Young and Riley.

Likewise an early champion of Young and the others – in his case, particularly of Reich, whose work he was among the first to present in Britain – Nyman eventually used the term 'minimalist' to describe not only the output of the Americans, but also the work of his own colleagues in the English 'experimental' movement: composers such as Gavin Bryars, Christopher Hobbs, Michael Parsons, Howard Skempton and John White, most of them at one time close associates of Cardew. In an interview which Nyman conducted with Reich in the summer of 1970,[11] when the composer was on his way to study African drumming in Ghana, there is some discussion of labelling, in the course of which Reich reveals a preference for 'pulse music', also the title of a then still fairly recent piece. Though he is described as working 'with an absolute minimum of musical material,' the term 'minimalism' is never used. In October 1971, Nyman suggested that some of the techniques used in English 'experimental music' of the period – the so-called 'systems music' influenced by Riley and Reich, in particular – had analogies with, among other movements, 'Minimal Art'.[12] Four months later, however, he managed to write an introduction to Reich's *Drumming* without ever mentioning 'minimalism'.[13]

Nyman's book *Experimental Music: Cage and beyond* – now a classic of twentieth-century compositional aesthetics, first published in the summer of 1974[14] – devotes a chapter to 'Minimal music, determinacy and the new tonality', in which Young, Riley, Glass and Reich (an order apparently based on their increasing importance as then perceived by the book's author) have pride of place. Nyman makes no attempt here to relate their music to any other movement besides Fluxus. But in putting these composers into a post-Cageian context, he raises the pertinent question of their precise relationship to Cage himself.

Cage was famously critical of musical minimalism, notably of its more rock-orientated manifestations. When Glenn Branca's earthily insistent – and I would say 'post-minimalist' – music for an orchestra of electric guitars was performed at the 1982 New Music America festival in Chicago, this now eminent experimental composer reportedly called it 'fascist':[15] an accusation which has also been levelled at earlier American minimalism – including that of Reich, notably, and rather interestingly, in Germany. Yet Cage's early, pre-chance compositions seem proto-minimalist: in their composer's search for a music based on rhythm and, more generally, lengths of time rather than pitch, for instance, and in their evident borrowing from non-Western musics equally concerned with timbre as well as the vitality of pulse-based methods.

More importantly, Cage's espousal of non-intention, which supplied the philosophical force that propelled his use of indeterminate techniques, links him with the aesthetic of minimalism, both in art and in music. The composer's associations with Abstract Expressionist painters such as Willem de Kooning, Franz Kline and Jackson Pollock have confused many accounts of where Cage's aesthetic preferences really lay. The 'action painting' of Pollock, for instance, represents a mid-twentieth-century *angst* with strong roots in the more 'Romantic' of earlier twentieth-century art forms, notably Cubism and Surrealism. For all its dalliance with automatism – which suggests comparisons with the minimalists' development of processes independent of their creator's control – the Abstract Expressionists' espousal of an essentially non-figurative, (post-)surrealist, aggressively abstract mode is the outcome of attempts to express the individual, often tortured, would-be unique personality of each artist. At least two painters associated with the movement – Barnett Newman and Ad Reinhardt – did, however, prefigure aspects of minimalism: Newman's so-called 'stripe' paintings, for example, clearly deal in drastic reduction.

Cage's artistic preferences were with Marcel Duchamp and Dada, and, in particular, with Jasper Johns and Robert Rauschenberg, probably the composer's closest friends in the art world. All these artists share one crucial concern with Cage which sets them apart from Abstract Expressionism, and which also makes both composer and artists significant, if not often acknowledged, models for Minimalist artists and composers. Like his artist friends, Cage devoted himself to finding ways of bypassing the already mentioned 'individual taste and memory' in order to discover something new and unpredictable to which access could not be gained through the application of the human imagination alone. In connection with this, it may be observed that Johnson's 'encouraging more subtle perceptions . . . making music less dramatic . . . [and] [stemming] partly from certain Asian and African attitudes' are as apt in application to Cage as they are to the minimalist composers.

With Cage, indeterminacy proved the key technique. The artists with whom he was most closely associated were similarly concerned with exploring new perceptions by expunging old values, especially the expressive ones; though, if anything, their work pointed up even more than Cage's the contradictions brought into play by drastic reduction. Rauschenberg's 'White Painting' of 1951 prefigured later minimalists not only in its reductiveness, but also in its use of commercial materials, by rolling house enamel on to a set of identical canvas panels. It was Cage himself who described the results as 'airports for lights, shadows, and particles',[16] drawing attention to the way in which they reflected back to the viewer not the singular, and illusory, void of their original conception but the multiple reflections of everyday life. Acknowledging the influence of Rauschenberg, in 1952 Cage produced what must in some sense be regarded as the ultimate minimalist statement; his infamous *4′33″* similarly reflects the world it confronts but over which it has no control.

Cage acted as a crucial father-figure both to younger composers in the 1950s and, more pervasively, to the artistic culture that flourished with particular vitality in the downtown Manhattan of the 1960s and 1970s that formed the seedbed for much of the musical developments described in this book. Of his better-known immediate associates, Morton Feldman had the closest connections with the painters who went beyond Abstract Expressionism, and the most immediately apparent links with the minimalist composers. In what is probably the most extended examination, in article form, of the relevance for music of the Minimalist aesthetic in art, Jonathan Bernard warns against interpreting '[t]he ostensibly sparse "event-density"' of the music of Feldman – or of Cage and Earle Brown – as minimalist, 'for in reality, the small number of events over time tends to focus the listener's attention intensely on each event, in all its particularity, thus resulting, from the minimalist point of view, in a music of parts rather than a whole'.[17] We shall explore later in this book some of the ramifications of what Bernard calls 'the opposition between arrangement and composition'[18] in minimalist music: in terms, for instance, of the dialectic between the continuing audibility of what I call the Basic Unit of a composition and the perceptual consequences of its working out.

Feldman's earlier compositions, meanwhile, with their deregulation of sounds from the periodicity of a beat, offer a world of unusual purity, in which technique was subordinated to sound, and the pieces became 'time canvases . . . prime[d] . . . with an overall hue of music'.[19] His later scores are not only sufficiently long to subvert their listener's sense of the passage of time while retaining developmental features, but also have a tendency to lock sounds into clearly audible, repeating metrical patterns: sometimes diatonic, often subtly changing, and thus creating ambiguities of musical time analogous to those found in Reich and Glass. The former was aware quite early on of Feldman's *Piece for Four Pianos* of 1957, the first of several pieces by its composer to release a freely unravelling multiple canon suggestive of a free kind of phasing. Reich feels, though, that only much later, after the composer's death in 1987, did he belatedly see the full significance of Feldman. Christian Wolff's early exercises in reductive rigour with only three notes in a whole piece (his Trio for flute, clarinet and violin of 1951, for instance, confines itself to a 'short stack' of perfect fifths, E, B and F♯) seem to have gone largely unrecognised by the subjects of this volume. This is somewhat surprising in view of the fact that several of their early associates – David Behrman, Tony Conrad, Henry Flynt and Frederic Rzewski among them – knew the composer and his music when they were Harvard students and Wolff himself a young Classics professor, during the early 1960s; some of them performed in pieces of his at that time.

Three consequences of the avoidance of 'individual taste and memory' help not only to expand Nyman's definition of an 'experimental' aesthetic built, in particular, upon Cage's example, but also to make additional connections with a working definition of musical minimalism. These are, firstly, the concern to avoid the creation of conventional time-objects by stressing process rather than product; secondly, the avoidance of previous notions of musical expression, in particular of music being in some sense about the composers themselves, their own preconceptions and predilections; and thirdly, the reconsideration of what we may call narrativity. The balance of these concerns varied from composer to composer. Reich and Glass, for instance, might well be argued to have been more involved, even in their early minimalist compositions, with the notion of a 'time-object', even with narrativity, than Young and Riley. But all four composers shared with Cage and other experimentalists the belief that their music should somehow go beyond what their own imaginations were inherently capable of inventing. Importantly, this applied to structure, in their case more than to material.

The art historian Irving Sandler is very clear that a seismic shift occurred in the arts around 1960. 'During the period from Johns's first show, in 1958', he writes, 'to the emergence of Pop Art, in 1962, the sensibility of the avant-garde underwent a pervasive change'.[20] A crucial contributor to this changing sensibility was the painter Frank Stella, whose black-stripe abstractions, also first exhibited in 1958, proclaimed a highly influential form of anti-Expressionism, and whose slogan '[w]hat you see is what you see'[21] became a watchword of the Minimalist sculptors in the 1960s. The art critic Kenneth Baker elaborates on this in ways which suggest close comparisons with both Cageian non-intention and the aesthetics of musical minimalism: 'Stella', he writes, 'shifted emphasis from the artist's activity as a metaphor for human self-definition to the viewer's activity of studying art objects for clues to the metaphysics of experience'.[22]

Yet any attempt to characterise briefly the cauldron of creative activity that followed Sandler's 'seismic shift' immediately comes up against its evident diversity. To confine matters to the so-called fine arts alone, a list of 1960s movements offered by Sandler himself includes 'Pop Art, New Perceptual Realism, Photo-Realism, Op Art, Minimal Art, Process Art, Earth Art and Conceptual Art'.[23] To these we should add the Fluxus movement and the wider range of performance-art activities with which it is frequently considered synonymous; as we shall see, Fluxus provides a further, and notable, 'hinge' between, in particular, Cage and Young. Despite this sometimes contradictory diversity, connections of many kinds can be made between individual items here, starting with the link between the Cage/Johns/Rauschenberg aesthetic and Pop Art. Johns famously took the American flag, targets and numbers as his departure points: 'things the mind already knows', as he put it, which 'gave me room to work on other levels'.[24] The Pop artists, such as Roy Lichtenstein and Andy Warhol, took more obviously commercial subject matter likewise redolent with meanings for their viewers, and made a whole movement out of its exploitation as potential art objects.

Pop Art's critiques, both of the modernist project and of the still new consumer society in which it functioned, should not be underestimated. Warhol and others may have 'contributed to the legitimation of . . . [the consumer] system through its aggressive appropriation of the images, techniques, and strategies associated with the ideology of consumption'.[25] Yet it did so not only by challenging modernism's insistence on purity and the new, but also via two other strategies which call into question the nature of its relationship with consumer society as well as the modernist art that rejected that society more clearly and wholeheartedly. One of these was Pop Art's rejection of narrative rhetoric while using materials – notably the comic strip – previously closely associated with narrative structure: a stance which has clear points in common with that of early minimalism. The other was Pop's blurring of the boundaries between the avant-garde and kitsch, to employ the terms used by the critic Clement

Greenberg in the course of his famous championing of a modernist art unsullied by commerce or the vernacular.[26] This led both to a questioning of the conceptual framework on which modernism and its continued existence was based, and, perhaps paradoxically, to a greater consciousness on the part of artists and their viewers of their historical position and roles. Here, close comparisons with musical minimalism are probably unwise, though, as we shall see, some regard even the early compositions of Riley, Reich and Glass as kitsch.

Neither should we underestimate a certain unity of purpose among at least some of the movements on Sandler's list in aesthetic projects related either to Cageian non-intention or to Minimalist refusal of reference, or to both. In 1967, Gene Davis declared that 'coolness, passivity and emotional detachment seem to be in the air. Pop, op, hard-edge, minimal art, and color painting share it in some degree'.[27] But in their negation of both aesthetic and social values, the Minimalist sculptors such as Carl Andre, Donald Judd, Robert Morris and Richard Serra pushed at the frontiers of art in ways which, again, only Cage equalled for sheer confidence in dismantling preconceived notions of what art should be.

One movement missing from Davis's list above with evident connections both to Minimalist art and minimalist music is the Conceptual Art of Sol Le Witt, who should be mentioned here due not least to his close association with Reich and, later, with Glass. Credited with the coining of the term 'conceptual art' – ironic, given his castigation of labels mentioned above – Le Witt developed his treatment of ideas as opposed to substances not only in his familiar grids of hollowed-out cubes but also in the already mentioned 1967 'Paragraphs on Conceptual Art', with which Reich's 1968 essay 'Music as a Gradual Process'[28] – a now classic statement of the minimalist aesthetic in music – has some parallels. Confronted, by Nyman in 1976, with the similarity, for instance, between his statement that 'once the process is set up and loaded it runs by itself' and Le Witt's 'all the planning and decisions are made beforehand' – both echoes of the Minimalist artists' 'elimination of transformative labor' – Reich argues that his own 'decisions weren't all made beforehand':[29] something which will be examined later, in my chapter on the composer. Both essays are, however, notable as statements of hard-line positions arguably already abandoned – in the composer's case, at least – by the time of writing.

In its instigation of developments which have led it to be considered the leading art movement of the 1960s, Minimalist art focused directly on the object itself. It experimented with the limits of art by asking how many of the elements traditionally associated with it could be taken away to leave something which could still be considered art. By 'eliminating transformative labor from his work',[30] as Baker puts it, Andre – perhaps the most widely known, and widely denigrated, Minimalist sculptor – presents his rectangular arrays of metal plates, modular sequences of blocks of wood (or even single blocks) and infamous piles of bricks for contemplation as art only because they are offered *as* art in a gallery space. In proposing that '[t]he thing . . . is not supposed to be suggestive of anything other than itself',[31] Minimalist art attempted to eliminate not only conventional notions of expression but also referentiality.

Frances Colpitt begins her book on what she calls 'Minimal art' with an unusually clear and concise set of defining and contextual characteristics, summarising the position outlined above:

> Minimal art describes abstract, geometric painting and sculpture executed in the United States in the 1960s. Its predominant organizing principles include the right angle, the square, and the cube, rendered with a minimum of incident or compositional maneuvering. Historically a reaction to what young artists saw as the autobiographical, gestural excesses of Abstract Expressionism, Minimal art, at the same time, pursues the formal innovations of Abstract Expressionism, particularly as laid out by the paintings of Jackson Pollock and Barnett Newman. Although Minimalism shares with Pop art anonymous design, deadpan flatness, and unadulterated or industrial color, and was in fact described as 'Imageless Pop' in 1966, the Minimalists eschewed any form of comment, representation, or reference.[32]

After so many artistic upheavals earlier in the twentieth century, Minimalist art succeeded, by doing away with all expressive baggage, in calling into question once again, yet at the same time freshly, just what the viewer was supposed to get out of art. The absence not only of conventional social symbology, but also of psychological symbology, was crucial. If Minimalist art had no subject matter – no social, practical or psychological value – did it indeed have any aesthetic value at all? Minimalist art's commitment to formal innovation throws down challenges which are heightened rather than cushioned by such art's resistance to metaphorical, as opposed to metaphysical, interpretation. Its focus on sensations based on the direct perception of objects forces the viewer to a radical reconsideration of those objects. Minimalist art also appears antagonistic to a capitalist culture based on values derived entirely from what is perceived to sell most easily. Even its reliance on the mass-production techniques of industrial technology must be viewed, in Duchampian terms, as the only valid response to the apparently inevitable subjection of art objects created with the artist's own imagination and own hands to the values of the market place. Minimalist art's hard-line stance of negation suggests that it operates as an alternative to the excesses of Abstract

Expressionism, but an alternative that is decidedly modernist in its stance.

All this suggests that the early phases of American musical minimalism described in the present book can likewise be interpreted as essentially modernist, along the radical, 'alternative' lines developed by Nyman's definition of an 'experimental' aesthetic. Like Cageian indeterminacy, they represent an American reaction to the serial models of modernism offered by European composers such as Pierre Boulez and Karlheinz Stockhausen, and by American serialists such as Milton Babbitt. All four subjects of this volume have criticised serialism, in particular, as irrelevant not only to their own concerns but also as a musical, and cultural, mistake; Reich and Glass have been particularly vitriolic in their comments on what might be called the establishment modernism of the European serialists working after the Second World War, and on the validity of pursuing, either aesthetically or technically, the achievements of the Second Viennese School. In 1986, Reich protested to Tim Page: 'Don't get me wrong. Berg, Schoenberg and Webern were very great composers. They gave expression to the emotional climate of their time. But for composers today to recreate the angst of "Pierrot Lunaire" in Ohio, or in the back of a Burger King, is simply a joke'.[33] In 1991, Glass was more directly critical of the activities of Boulez and the European serialists in the 1960s, speaking of 'a wasteland, dominated by these maniacs, these creeps, who were trying to make everyone write this crazy creepy music'.[34]

Such dismissals have been frequently paralleled by the denigrations poured on musical minimalism by composers, critics and others from the Western classical tradition. The aesthetic starting points for these sometimes even more barbed criticisms are wide-ranging. Conservative and anti-modernist commentators such as Samuel Lipman suggest that minimalism is 'merely a pop music for intellectuals'.[35] Adherents of high-modernist tendencies such as the so-called New Complexity would probably agree with one of their chief spokesmen, Richard Toop, when, quoting Roland Barthes, he asserts that '[t]he "transparent impenetrability" of recent music by composers such as Glass and Adams is, I believe, a result of their having acquiesced to the culture industry's demand for consumable objects, finished products, for "an art that inoculates pleasure (by reducing it to a known, coded emotion)"'.[36] It is true, though, that Toop's strictures are not meant to apply to all so-called minimalist compositions: he himself makes exceptions of 'the stubbornly nonconformist work of La Monte Young or Philip Corner'.[37] But even more open-minded writers like William Brooks have interpreted Riley's *In C* – still the emblematic example of musical minimalism – as an affirmation of mass culture comparable to Warhol,[38] whose initial rise to fame coincides with the period in which many other compositions discussed in this book were written. Not only, however, is it possible to interpret Warhol's Pop Art aesthetic quite differently (see above), but Riley's cunningly contrived lack of control over the materials he unleashes – in his earlier tape pieces as well as in his own improvisations – surely makes his explorations of sound dangerous as well as delightful.

Besides, matters are not as simple as such polar oppositions suggest. As we shall see, the minimalism of all four composers discussed here has some of its roots in European modernist achievements. While Riley's enthusiasm for free-atonal Schoenberg and the early works of Stockhausen, surprising though it may be, can be argued as merely a stage on the road typical of any composition student attempting to find an individual path, Young drew directly on both free-atonal and twelve-note Webern in the formation of the pioneering minimalism with sustained sounds which strongly influenced Riley's development of a modal, pulse-based style. And while Glass's extensive pre-minimalist output is mostly couched in a rather conservative brand of what is usually called neo-classicism, both his very earliest minimalist efforts and some of the music Reich was writing on the way to his own mature style deploy a dissonance level and technical procedures which owe clear debts to the Second Viennese School.

Just as Boulez and Cage found common ground in the late 1940s and early 1950s in their use of procedures the details of which were generated by forces outside their conscious control, so it is possible to make connections between integral serialism and minimalism: a commitment to the consequences of rigorous application of processes independent, to a significant degree, of the composer's note-to-note control is evidently the key here. Taking these ideas further, Parsons, an English 'experimental' composer with a serial pedigree, has developed a long-standing interest in exploring the relationships between systems in music and an English tradition of 'Systems art', in the work of artists such as David Saunders and Jeffrey Steele. Parsons has pointed to the new kinds of unity between material, sound and expression that such rigorous and, to some, fundamentally unmusical concern with process can bring about. 'The system liberates the medium', he quotes his close associate, Skempton, as saying, adding that 'the expressive quality of the sound itself is revealed'.[39] The involvement of these and other British composers and artists with repetition remains sufficiently severe to exclude the exploration of psychoacoustic effects: the illusions conjured by the combination of fast repetition and high dynamic level in Glass's music, or the optical illusions of Op Art such as Bridget Riley's. Op Art is denounced by Parsons as 'degenerate': an opinion with which Reich, despite his interest in psycho-acoustic phenomena, would seem to concur.

The most rigorous of the four American composers, Reich was likewise fascinated by a formalism generated by processes discovered and fed with musical material but then left to run their course. Transcending the limitations which inevitably conditioned the human imagination's ability to come up with new structures, as well as materials, this approach led naturally – indeed, with an inevitability clearly attractive to such a composer – to an acceptance of the results, just as Cage was happy to do with the consequences of indeterminacy. But while the processes Cage used were, like those of serialism, 'compositional ones that could not be heard when the piece was performed',[40] as Reich put it, what he himself wanted was 'a compositional process and a sounding music that are one and the same thing'. Minimalist music's purchase on perception is in this case a highly structural one, closely integrated with the process of composition itself. This is the main reason to agree with Bernard when he argues that 'the music of chance ultimately served the minimalists as a negative ideal, an example of what not to do, in their efforts to create a viable alternative to (what they came to see as) the needless and overly intellectual complexities of serialism'.[41] 'I don't know any secrets of structure that you can't hear',[42] wrote Reich, delighting in the transparency of his musical procedures. *4′33″* itself, though, cuts through the elaborate chance-derived schemes Cage devised for many of his other works to make the listener's perceptions operate with a different kind of focus. And Reich's discovery of phasing in fact has much in common with Cageian musical practice: the use of raw material drawn from everyday life, for instance, and its roots in the observation of a process happening independently of its composer's conscious control.

In the late 1960s, Glass shared a similar formalist concern, and neither he nor Reich was happy with the results of what he was doing until he had discovered a process of his own with a sufficient degree of rigour to be closely followable by the listener. Young's kind of rigour is different, but his obsession with exploring the innards of a complex sound continuum makes him the most uncompromising of the four composers; the fact that he is 'wildly interested in repetition, because [he thinks] it demonstrates control'[43] offers a further insight into his special and extreme position. As suggested above, the modernist credentials of Riley – whose early music comes nearer than that of anything Reich or Glass composed before the mid-1970s to suggesting a celebratory spirit untinged by more cerebral challenges – are perhaps less easy to argue. As we shall see, however, the critical dimensions inherent in his work go beyond obvious matters such as the transcendence, and subversion, of established modes of listening posed by his all-night concerts of the late 1960s and early 1970s.

Robert Carl[44] and Kyle Gann[45] provide a persuasive amplification of the view that the musical minimalism under discussion here can valuably be viewed from a modernist perspective. More recent interpretations – such as that of Björk, who celebrates minimalism's ability to 'shake off that armour of the brain'[46] which has, for her, constricted so many twentieth-century developments – suggest different origins and functions for musical minimalism. Again, though, distinctions between the minimalism of the 1960s and the (post-)minimalism of the 1990s need to be borne in mind; Björk was referring specifically to Arvo Pärt, whose religious aspirations for his work are shared by many other composers today – Henryk Mikołaj Górecki and John Tavener being just two of them – but, among the four subjects of this book, only by Young and Riley. Even the idea of minimalism as a necessary antidote to the ills of late twentieth-century society, however, has some common ground with another approach to the matter, despite the background of what follows in theories of modernism.

A further modernist interpretation of such early minimalism can be developed with the aid of a Formalist critique dating from much earlier in the twentieth century. In the 1920s, the Russian Formalist Viktor Schklovsky suggested that the goal of all art is its 'defamiliarisation' of things which have lost their impact, and even become invisible to us, through habit. 'Habitualisation', he wrote, 'devours objects, clothes, furniture, one's wife and the fear of war. . . . Art exists to help us recover the sensation of life, it exists to make us feel things, to make the stone *stony*. The end of art is to give a sensation of the object as seen, not as recognised. The technique of art is to make things "unfamiliar", to make forms obscure, so as to increase the difficulty and duration of perception'.[47]

Both serialism and indeterminacy had already sought to encourage new perceptions through the search for new kinds of musical material and its manipulation, and Cage's openness to the familiar as well as the unfamiliar had complemented this search for new vocabularies and grammars with something akin to Schklovsky's 'sensation of the object as seen, not as recognised'. Minimalism goes much further, however, in taking a fresh and more focused look at single pitches, modal fragments, regular rhythmic structures and – in its later developments – chords and simple chord progressions. By selecting some of the oldest and most familiar building blocks of music, and subjecting them to the radical scrutiny afforded by remorseless repetition, it takes on the challenge of revitalising the most hackneyed and debased musical currency available. Minimalism forces its listeners to reinterpret the familiar not only through the microscope of their own perceptions and sensations, but also via the energies generated by processes driven by the same forces – regular pulse and apparent forward motion – which had underpinned the goal-directed approaches of Western tonal musics of the previous few centuries.

Interpreted – by Mertens, for example – as fundamentally different from post-Renaissance Western music of the cultivated tradition in its activation of rhythmic repetition to reject teleology altogether, such music already has the potential to 'make forms obscure, so as to increase the difficulty and duration of perception'. Interpreted – as I would prefer to do – as encoding a much more complicated set of clashes and contradictions of the grammars available for such a simple vocabulary – of which this potential non-teleology is but one – musical minimalism has the capacity to harness the development of active modes of listening in order to 'complete the work'. Such a 'metaphysics of experience', to requote Baker, forces a radical reappraisal of familiar musical objects, conquering habit to make the aural equivalent of the stones *stony*. It also makes common cause with the arguments – probably first advanced, again, by Mertens – connecting the evolution of musical minimalism with post-modernist and post-structuralist concerns such as Barthes' declaration of the 'death of the author'.[48] While Glass's recent music reminds Toop of Susan Sontag's depiction of works 'to which the audience can add nothing',[49] perhaps even he would acknowledge the different approach which this composer's early music encourages. Some would say, however, that Glass's early scores require their listeners to make a contribution to the business of 'completing the work' so large as to call any meaningful input by their author into serious question, though I myself would not go that far.

Just as Minimalist art acted as a critique of a commercialised society and challenged its viewers to adopt new modes of perception, so minimalist music – whether excavating the innards of sound, like Young's work, constructing rigorously assembled sound objects, like the early works of Reich and Glass, or offering counterpoints in textures often sufficiently dense to frustrate any attempt to untangle them, as in Riley's output – required new modes of listening. Even Brian Ferneyhough – a scourge of musical minimalism, like many other kinds of modernist composers and their adherents – acknowledges a certain kinship based on the fundamentals of musical perception and on the greater focus modernists, and post-modernists, from Duchamp onwards have offered on the necessity for the viewer or listener to 'complete the work'. 'All music', as he points out, 'is many-layered. . . . Our ears impose upon us, with any listening process, a number of possible strategies which we're constantly scanning and assessing, and . . . finding a new distance or new perspective in relation to what we're hearing at that particular moment. It's one of the few possible justifications for minimalist music, for instance: that the maximalisation comes through the individual, rather than through the object'.[50]

Mertens' insistence on a fundamentally anti-teleological interpretation of such music seems, as I have already suggested, to limit its potential, despite what I have said above concerning the advantages of the new musical structures which the rigours of process have helped create. The harnessing to his argument of the view that, unlike the dialectical music of the Western classical tradition, minimalist music is 'non-representational and is no longer a medium for the expression of subjective feelings'[51] leads him, however, into some interesting, and wide-ranging, discussion of post-structuralist and post-modernist ideologies of the kind raised above, which could valuably be pursued in ways for which there is no space here, particularly in the context of more recent music.

In a 1990 article, Elaine Broad begins some elaboration of Mertens' position in terms of an aesthetic characterised by 'the conception of the *non-narrative work-in-progress*'.[52] Suggesting that '"stasis" is precisely the wrong word to describe a music that . . . depends so heavily upon time as a vehicle',[53] Bernard suggests, on the other hand, that – like those Minimalist artists (he cites Morris, Jo Baer, Dan Flavin, Agnes Martin and Le Witt) who deal with temporality via gradual and/or systematic progress through a series of possibilities – the minimalist composers draw attention to the passage of time by 'composing out' the possibilities of their material in a followable manner. Though he acknowledges the fact that what he calls 'the more recent work of Glass, Riley, and Reich' is 'brand[ed] "Post-Minimal"', Bernard himself does not seem to see the distinction being made with this label. He refers to it only to suggest that what he calls the 'serial principle' involved in such composing out applies equally well to the later music as to the earlier, and uses this as the justification for continuing to apply the term 'minimal' to both.

Arguments concerning the changing focus of these composers' music up to, and beyond, the mid-1970s are advanced at least somewhat by Timothy A. Johnson's 1994 attempt to discuss the term minimalism as aesthetic, style and technique. His suggestion that 'minimalism may be defined most fruitfully as a technique'[54] allows him to take technical aspects such as 'continuous formal structure' and 'repetitive rhythmic patterns' and trace their use in the music of Reich and others beyond the mid-1970s, surviving the abandonment of minimalism as he defines it aesthetically and stylistically. While his discussion runs into difficulties – for example, that of confusion between 'style' and 'technique' – his argument does something to clarify the notion of a 'post-minimalist' approach.

For the present writer, the differences between the work of these composers, and even of the more single-minded and maverick Young, from the mid-1970s onwards and what they produced in the years before that period is sufficiently significant to make the mid-1970s the cut-off point for the stories told here. While continuing to activate their music with the crucial ingredient of repetition – or, in Young's case, more often sustained sounds – all four composers have, in their more recent outputs, found ways of recuperating aspects which what we might call their earlier, hard-line minimalism had deliberately negated. Melodic profile, timbral variety and sheer sonic allure all added new dimensions that made their music richer and deeper, at least from a conventional Western classical perspective. While the first two of these aspects in principle encouraged the cultivation of a cleaner textural profile – a clear separation into melody and accompaniment, for instance – the increasing interest in texture *per se* brought with it less chance of hearing whatever processes were controlling its note-to-note details. Most significant of all, however, in this 'post-minimalist' music, is the arrival of a kind of harmonic motion: a development which naturally interacts in a variety of ways with the other new aspects, and with the ongoing energy of repetition itself, but which tends towards musical results in which harmonic progression, and sometimes a more encompassing narrative development across broader spans of time, becomes more important than audibility of the sorts of note-to-note processes more characteristic, in any case, of the earlier music.

At this point in the story, Young proves himself capable of highly idiosyncratic feats of fantasy with the melodies and chord sequences which he incorporates into a minimalist idiom still quite evidently his own. Riley's work takes on a surprising variety of styles, some redolent of the jazz to which he has always been closely attached, some more indebted to classical traditions, Western as well as his beloved Indian. Reich retains his contrapuntal concerns, dovetailing them with considerable ingenuity into the new forms he creates with this clearer harmonic profile. Harmonic motion and melodic ingenuity have allowed the especially prolific, and sometimes undiscriminating, Glass to write everything from large-scale operas to pop songs.

While it certainly seems necessary to distinguish these developments by the use of a different term – whether 'post-minimalist' or even 'post-modernist' – the extent to which even the earlier, more truly minimalist, output of the composers can be called 'static' has already been called into question. My own view is that the role of harmonic motion, of however putative a kind, proves crucial to an understanding of the music which these composers were writing in the early 1970s, and that various notions of hierarchy even play a part in their earliest minimalist compositions. The analyses which follow are designed, in part, to test out the arguments of Mertens and others for this music's essentially anti-teleological status. Particularly interesting here is Jonathan Kramer's concept of a 'vertical music' free of hierarchies as well as teleology.[55]

In deciding on just how to place such early minimalism in the context of twentieth-century musical history, the approach adopted by the Prague School of Linguisticians may assist us, in conjunction with Schklovsky's already mentioned 'defamiliarisation'. Experimentation with any particular new materials or ideas in itself over time becomes dulled by familiarity: a process which generally involves adding layers of increasing complexity to the original. To employ the terminology of these 1930s Czech successors to 1920s Russian Formalism, fresh stimulation will then need to be sought by placing in the background what had previously been foregrounded. The early outputs of Young, Riley, Reich and Glass may thus be interpreted as foregrounding the modal materials and repetitive formal schemes set aside by the fragmented discourses of serialism and indeterminacy, and also challenging the capacity of such materials and structures to come up with something quite different from the reassuring continuities of a neoclassicism which, surviving until beyond the 1950s, had long ago lost its cutting edge. Once this had been accomplished, a so-called 'post-minimalism' was then similarly required to counter the modernist reductiveness of early minimalism, foregrounding extended melodic materials and harmonic progressions more readily associated with earlier Western musics, and more obviously narrative structures.

Attention must be drawn to the vital significance for the development of all four of these composers of musics outside the Western classical tradition. Most obvious among these are the non-Western traditions to which Tom Johnson makes reference, which have had a powerful influence on the spiritual development, and lifestyle, of Young and Riley, and which have also influenced Reich and Glass. Jazz – in particular the so-called modal jazz developed by John Coltrane and others around the time that the four subjects of this book were finding themselves, musically speaking – has been a significant influence on all of them except Glass.

Minimalism – at least of the kinds being examined here, in both the fine arts and in music – is rooted in American culture. Among many others, John Rockwell has campaigned for the necessity of treating the history of music in the USA as 'a dialogue between the "cultivated" and the "vernacular"';[56] though he suggests that '[b]efore the 1960's, by and large, the vernacular side of the dialogue was mute, silenced by the academic, cultivated view of what music was and should be'. Russell Jacoby has argued that the Beat Generation of 1950s American writers (Allen Ginsberg, Jack Kerouac and so on), soaked in the jazz of their time, had a crucial role in the popularisation of High Art for Americans;[57] they certainly helped to produce the cultural climate in which Young and Riley first flourished in late 1950s San Francisco, just as they had also contributed to the Greenwich Village 'alternative' culture of a decade earlier.

Sally Banes argues that it was only when the work of the early 1960s artists of a younger generation 'circulated transgressive ideas in what would ultimately become acceptable packages'[58] that a true counter-culture was created by 'the first generation of postmodern artists':[59] her initial list includes the Judson Dance Theater and Poets' Theater, the Living Theater, Warhol and the film-maker Kenneth Anger. It is here – in the so-called 'downtown' scene of New York's Greenwich Village and SoHo in the 1960s and 1970s, and in the extent of its overlaps with the so-called hippie culture of which it formed part – that we find the wider cultural context of most immediately impinging relevance for the work of all four composers discussed here. The Manhattan artistic community that spawned many of the artistic developments which have fed into the continuing story of musical minimalism and 'post-minimalism' in part owed its existence to purely practical aspects: the low rents for large loft spaces available in downtown Manhattan in the 1960s and 1970s, for instance, and the (relatively) high technology that was beginning to become available, and affordable.

With its new version of the 'happy babble of overlapping dialogues – not just cultivated and vernacular, but European and American, white and black, male and female, East Coast and West Coast, Occidental and Oriental . . '.[60] that Rockwell identifies as the story of America's musical history, this 'downtown' community offered much more than radical art practice spiced with the *frisson* easily gained via a few 'vernacular' borrowings. As part of this wider range of endeavours, musical minimalism confronted the contradictions between the 'cultivated' tradition in its more radical guises and the 'vernacular' roots with which so many of its practitioners felt perfectly at ease.

More widely still, of course, there is the context of a specifically 'Sixties' counter-culture with roots on the USA's West Coast and ramifications which are international in scope, even though many of the hippie trappings famously associated with the Haight-Ashbury district of San

Francisco percolated out to give a powerfully American flavour to the developments which followed in the wake of this radical critique of capitalism. Ironic in the manner in which it helped spread specifically American values as well as fashions and mannerisms to an international community already primed by the Americanisation of the 1950s, and too quickly compromised by its remarkably easy commodification by the very institutions it had set out to undermine, that so-called counter-culture was nevertheless a very real force in a climate primed for change of every kind: social and political as well as cultural in the narrower senses of the term.

Though nurtured by the hothouse artistic community of 1960s and 1970s downtown Manhattan, musical minimalism was actually spawned in Young's California, while Riley, who brought about its second phase, has spent most of his life on the West Coast. It is typical of the contradictions seemingly inherent in this 'happy babble of overlapping dialogues' that it is the latter composer who simultaneously seems responsible for the early commercial breakthrough of minimalism via its assimilation into late 1960s rock culture, and today – along with the still less well-known Young – continues most evidently to uphold the spiritual values of a 1960s ethos engulfed by the subsequent waves of attack on its principles and practice.

In a cultural climate such as this, it might be argued that only those – like the already mentioned Greenberg or, to take a famous example from musical discourse, Theodor Adorno[61] – who preach an aesthetic completely antithetical to commercial contamination or who practise an art totally untainted by worldly constraints, such as the serialism of Milton Babbitt, can claim to be the true proponents of a critically modernist stance. Discussions of cultural realignment, meanwhile, to say nothing of such accusations of pre-emptory commercial capitulation, might suggest the characterisation of early, as well as later, minimalism as post-modernist rather than modernist in character.

A willingness to engage with 'vernacular' traditions is one of the few aspects widely accepted as a defining characteristic of post-modernism. We should be wary, however, of the conflicting arguments which continue to rage around any attempt to characterise post-modernism more fully, and in particular of the gulf that exists between what Hal Foster has called a 'post-modernism of reaction' and a 'post-modernism of resistance'.[62] While the former might involve an uncritical re-embracing of such matters as the commodification of culture, the latter, which Foster argues is the genuine post-modernism, requires the kinds of radical engagement characteristic – as I have argued elsewhere[63] – of Nyman's theory of 'experimental music'. Such a 'post-modernism of resistance' offers potentially fertile territory for any future that 'experimental music' might have. Already mentioned concepts such as that of the listener 'completing the work' would here extend naturally to others, such as Barthes' famous, and already mentioned, argument regarding the 'death of the author'.

For a composer of a younger generation, such as the American David Lang, the musical minimalism of the 1960s and 1970s which is the subject of this book can best be defined in political, rather than aesthetic, terms. His vision of it is as a weapon with which to challenge the hegemony that had been constructed around the serialism from which I argue minimalism itself in part derived. While it offers another perspective for viewing what that downtown culture, and musical minimalism itself, now represents, it also attempts to confront the consequences for those who come after it. Minimalism, he says,

> was a historic reaction to a sort of music which had a stranglehold on American musical institutions, and which none of us really liked. . . . What most people really hated was the way that this other world had theorised that it was the only music possible . . . I look at minimalism . . . as being just the battleground that was necessary to remove those forces from power: not to obliterate them or destroy them, but . . . to loosen up the power structure in America. And I think that [one reason why] Glass's music and Reich's music came out so severe, and so pared down, was that . . . it was a polemical slap in the face. . . . That battle's been fought. . . . My job is to sift among the ashes and rebuild something.[64]

1 La Monte Young

La Monte Young's career divides geographically into three parts: his childhood and undergraduate years mainly in Los Angeles; his time as a graduate student at Berkeley, in the San Francisco Bay Area; and the period that saw his establishment as both composer and performer, as well as concert organiser, teacher and much else, following his move to New York City. Young was almost twenty-three when he went to Berkeley; just twenty-five when he moved to settle permanently on the East Coast. In terms of his output as a minimalist, the story begins while he was still an undergraduate, and becomes of substance with a composition he took with him when he went to northern California to begin graduate studies. Young is not only the first true musical minimalist, but was producing radically innovatory work at a much younger age than Riley, Reich and Glass: some of his most important compositions were written when he was twenty-one and twenty-two.

Central to Young's development is his tendency to combine an involvement with improvisation – an involvement so extensive that the distinction between composition and improvisation sometimes becomes hard meaningfully to preserve – with a concern to establish a firm theoretical base for his music. The latter contributes to his slow rate of creative output as much as it productively intertwines with it. Not least among the effects of these things is a tendency to work on a composition over many years: extending its theoretical investigations, adding to its material, and testing ideas through improvisation. The best example of this is *The Well-Tuned Piano*, which originated in a tuning devised in 1964 and some improvisations made using it, and which, over thirty years later, is still open-ended, at least in principle. It makes little sense to abandon consideration of this in the mid-1970s; accordingly, the story of this major work will be taken beyond the present book's official cut-off date. Young also continues to use material originally conceived for use with the famous group he had with John Cale, Tony Conrad, Terry Jennings, Terry Riley, Marian Zazeela and others in the mid-1960s, which makes it difficult to establish clear lines of chronology and closure. Some aspects of Young's development – for instance, his move away from ensemble work and towards solo performances, to which the first sustained and successful period of work on *The Well-Tuned Piano* in 1974–5 contributes an important statement –

mark the mid-1970s as something of a watershed in his development. Yet many of the essentials of Young's aesthetic, style and techniques were firmly established by the mid-1960s, thus making detailed commentary beyond this period less important to an understanding of his significance.

Wim Mertens divided Young's output into the customary three periods.[1] Though not an entirely accurate reflection of the composer's development, they provide a useful point of departure. Mertens characterises the compositions of 1955–8 as 'serial music'; Young discovered what came to be called 'sustenance',[2] the use of long sustained sounds, while working with serial principles as a basic framework. Mertens' 'second period' covers the years 1959–61; this was the period when, under the influence of John Cage, Young moved away from conventionally notated compositions and into a range of performance art works that are commonly – though in Young's view erroneously – included as an integral component of the Fluxus movement which flourished in the early 1960s and beyond. The third and final period begins in 1962, characterised by Mertens as the 'actual repetitive period'. Mertens was writing in 1979, and other ways of dividing what is now a period of over three decades are available besides that which pinpoints the mid-1970s. One could, for example, argue that Young's more recent return to ensemble work – with The Forever Bad Blues Band and Big Band, both reincarnations of The Theatre of Eternal Music newly inspired by his old love, jazz – represents a new 'period', beginning in 1990. Yet it still seems sensible to view the obsessive concern with 'sustenance' and drones, which dominates almost everything the composer has done since the early 1960s, as one long development: emerging from his discovery of long tones in the 1950s, and separated from this by a short period of more theatrical – but still crucially related – activities.

No scores by Young are published in any conventional sense and few commercial recordings of his work exist.[3] For many years, he habitually made access to would-be interviewers extremely difficult and, to this day, all private tapes can be listened to only in his loft, while scores and documentation are lent extremely selectively. That documentation is extensive: no activity in his daily life, whether musical or otherwise, is too insignificant to escape the tape recorder, the photocopier or the filing cabinet. Between 1979 and 1985, the Youngs took advantage of the lavish sponsorship bestowed on them by the Dia Foundation in the ordering, notation and copying of some of this material. While the archive he jealously guards with the help of Zazeela – his constant companion – and several assistants is not as thoroughly catalogued as it would be in the hands of a professional librarian, it could form the basis of an extensive biography far beyond the aims of the present book.

Early years

La Monte Thornton Young was born in a log cabin in Bern, a Mormon hamlet in Bear Lake County, Idaho, on 14 October 1935. His parents – Dennis and Evelyn – were poor; when the composer was born, his father was a shepherd. Young relates that 'the very first sound that I recall hearing was the sound of the wind blowing under the eaves and around the log extensions at the corners of the log cabin'.[4] In an earlier interview, he describes this as 'very awesome and beautiful and mysterious; as I couldn't see it and didn't know what it was, I questioned my mother about it for long hours'.[5] Continuous sounds – man-made as well as natural – fascinated Young as a child: the humming harmonics of the step-down transformer at the local power plant; train whistles across the river; lathes and drill presses; wind, insects, water, trees. The telephone poles in Bern produced a continuous chord from which, much later, he recalled the four pitches he named the 'Dream Chord', basing many of his mature works on it. Southern California, in general – with its 'sense of space, sense of time, sense of reverie, sense that things could take a long time, that there was always time'[6] – helped Young to conclude from an early age, well before he encountered the ideas of Cage, that the external world was quite possibly more fascinating than art.

Young's early years in this Idaho dairy community dominated by Mormon values was not, however, bereft of musical experiences. The composer says that the harmonica was the first instrument he ever played; 'however, at the age of two, this was soon followed by singing and guitar lessons from my Aunt Norma, who sang in the local high-school operettas [and rodeos]. The songs I learned to sing at that time were cowboy songs'.[7] He played his maternal grandparents' piano a little. When he was aged three or so, the family moved to Montpelier, the nearest town to Bern, where he also had tapdancing lessons; at the age of four, he was singing and tapdancing at Montpelier's Rich Theater. The family moved to Los Angeles when Young was five, to Utah when he was ten, and then back to settle finally in the Los Angeles area when he was about fourteen. Young did not learn to read music until he was seven, when he began learning the saxophone, taking lessons from his father. His first performing experience on this instrument came via Mormon services. The saxophone – first alto, later tenor and, particularly, sopranino – was, though off and on, his main performing outlet until 1964. Between 1951 and 1954, he had lessons on the clarinet as well as saxophone with William Green at the Los Angeles Conservatory of Music.

Between September 1950 and June 1953 Young attended the

John Marshall High School in Los Angeles, a rough school which was nevertheless known for its music making and was capable of attracting at least a few artistic and intellectual high fliers. His harmony teacher, Clyde Sorenson, turned out to have been a pupil of Schoenberg at the University of California, Los Angeles; Sorenson, who played a recording of the Six Little Piano Pieces, op. 19, first introduced Young to Schoenberg's music. While in high school, he accompanied the dancing of an Apache friend, encountering native American music for the first time. As he points out, American Indian music, like the cowboy songs he learned in early childhood, is essentially static. But Young's most important high-school musical experiences came through jazz.

Jazz was Young's first love, and though not a direct influence on most of the first compositions he would now regard as his own, it dominated his musical activities as a teenager. It was later to have a considerable influence on his music. Almost the first thing he did on returning to Los Angeles in 1950 was to join a Dixieland band that played outside every morning before school classes began. He played extensively in his high-school and early college days; jazz was, he says, 'the burning thing'. John Marshall High School had a strong jazz tradition and high playing standards. Young's jazz-playing schoolfriends included Pete Diakinoff, a tenor saxophonist who advised him to study with Green and introduced him to the latest trends in bebop and cool jazz; and David Sanchez, known as 'Gordo', a precocious trombonist – and local gang leader – who had already been on the road with Perez Prado's band by the time he was in tenth grade (aged about fifteen). Young and his friends were often hired to play for dances, but never asked back since they were considered too modern. 'I stopped playing in dance bands for money, accepting dance gigs . . . because I only wanted to play pure jazz', he says.

From September 1953 – by which time he had moved out of the family home to live with his paternal grandmother – to June 1955, Young attended Los Angeles City College, studying counterpoint and composition both in school and privately with Leonard Stein, who had been Schoenberg's disciple and assistant. In February 1956, after further private work with Stein, he registered for a year at Los Angeles State College, additionally returning to Los Angeles City College for the fall semester of 1956. In January 1957, he enrolled for three semesters at the University of California at Los Angeles; here he majored in music, taking music theory, composition and ethnomusicology, and some English, finally obtaining his BA in June 1958. Composition studies were undertaken with Boris Kremenliev and John Vincent; Lukas Foss, then running one of the earliest free-improvisation groups, also encouraged him. He was, in addition, a pupil of Robert Stevenson, who taught him Baroque and sixteenth-century counterpoint and keyboard harmony.

At UCLA, Young encountered a fellow student called Dennis Johnson when he heard him practising Webern's Piano Variations, op. 27; the two became firm friends. Johnson – whose own compositions (only rarely publicly performed after his student days) would, for a while, also be influenced by Young – was to become, says Young, the only person in the late 1950s besides Jennings and Terry Riley to understand his music. Johnson's role, Young says, 'along with that of Terry Jennings, was extremely important in the formative years of minimalism in the late 1950s through 1961 and 62. Dennis developed some of the most original and feelingful ideas about music, including the social implications of concerts and venues, of anyone I had ever met'.[8] Johnson's idealism was to lead to the withdrawal of his work from public performance, since he ceased to believe that the concert arena had any worth for the presentation of serious music. In 1959 or 1960, he once described to Young an outline for a piece to be 'staged in some far away wooded countryside . . . heard only by those who just happened to come across it by happenstance'. The overall conception of this – and in particular the plan for the musical material to consist of a perfect fourth 'which would sound for a long time from some far away undiscoverable place' before falling a minor third and continuing at the new pitch – was evidently influential on Young's subsequent development.

At Los Angeles City College Young had continued his involvement with jazz, competing successfully against Eric Dolphy for the second-alto chair in the award-winning City College Dance Band; the first alto was a brilliant player called Lannie Morgan. (In the College Symphony Orchestra, Dolphy played first clarinet, Young second.) Young additionally played in the College Jazz Combo. He was invited by the pianist Don Friedman to join his trio, which ultimately led to the formation of Young's own group with the guitarist Dennis Budimir, the drummer Billy Higgins, and the bassist Hal Hollingshead, which played regularly at Studio One in downtown Los Angeles. Others sat in from time to time, including the trumpeter Don Cherry, whom Young already knew, and guitarists Buddy Matlock and Tiger Echols, the latter of whom became an important influence on Young's early blues playing. The earliest surviving recording of Young performing appears to be a 'demo' disc of 'All the things you are', made in the summer of 1955, on which he plays with this group. By that time, he was living in Hollywood with friends, plus his step-uncle Kenny Young, who moved in a social circle which included James Dean and Vampira.

Other jazz experience gained at this period included occasional performances as featured soloist with the Willie Powell Big Blues Band. Also playing in this primarily black and Mexican band was another white alto saxophonist, the then thirteen-year-old Terry Jennings: a pianist and clarinettist, but ultimately most brilliantly a saxophonist, who had recently entered John Marshall High School and whom Young had already heard on tape. Jennings was to become a close associate for many years. During jam sessions around Los Angeles, Young played sets with Ornette Coleman; both Cherry and Higgins later became members of Coleman's original free-jazz quartet.

When in school and college, Young had at first intended making a career in jazz. Stylistically, he seems to have been ahead of many of his playing colleagues; he favoured an approach, influenced in particular by the saxophone playing of Lee Konitz and Warne Marsh, which tended to fragment the beat. Though surviving tapes of his playing at this time suggest a move towards the kind of 'free jazz' Coleman was shortly to pioneer, Young began to feel jazz's limitations: 'Jazz is a form, and I was interested in other forms'.[9] His involvement with jazz peaked in 1955–6; Young's decision not to register for the fall semester of 1955 at City College was due partly to his wish to play more jazz sessions. A piece called *Annod* – a twelve-bar blues in a style influenced by the playing of Konitz and Miles Davis on George Russell's *Ezzthetic* (1948) and *Odjenar* (1949), and perhaps particularly by Johnny Carisi's 'Israel', one of Capitol Records' landmark 'birth-of-the-cool sides' with Davis, recorded in 1949–50 – was written some time between 1953 and 1955. *Annod*, which spells the name of a girlfriend (Donna Lee Lathrop) backwards, includes a ten-bar bridge that abandons melody and regular beat and employs a degree of polytonality; its composer claims it as a precursor of both his later use of sustained sounds and what he came to call the 'Dream Chord'.

By the time Young moved to UCLA in January 1957, he had for the moment abandoned serious saxophone playing 'and was really headed into composition. I never took up jazz in the same way ever again'. Jazz nevertheless returns as a direct influence on his work from about 1962, when he took up the sopranino. And he considers that 'many things about jazz absolutely never left me: for instance, the fact that I became so interested in improvisational forms'. In addition to the better-known influence of jazz on his later saxophone playing, he also began to develop a style of piano improvisation based on the standard twelve-bar blues. Called 'Young's Blues' by the composer, it was characterised at this stage by a continuous alternation of the chords in the left and right hands – for example, in a left-*right*, right-left, right, right-left pattern – which Young

Example 1.1 'Young's Blues', characteristic rhythmic structure

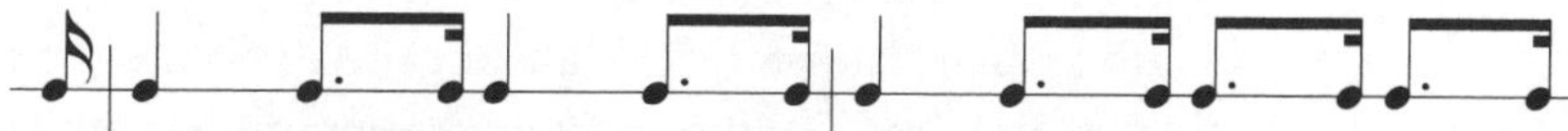

describes as 'ka chunk chunka chunk chunka':[10] see Example 1.1. The detailed evolution of this 'Young's Blues' style is far from clear. Riley recalls that Young's blues playing in the practice rooms at Berkeley in 1958–9 was at first in the form of 'funky bebop in the right hand over some sort of walking bass in the left hand'. Then, one day at Riley's house on Potrero Hill, he recalls Young playing in the later characteristic 'ka chunk chunka chunk chunka' style and saying, 'This is something new I'm working on'; after this, Riley never heard his friend play blues in any other way. Other evidence – for example, the testimony of the tenor saxophonist Michael Lara, a friend of the composer's from his Los Angeles City College days – suggests that 'Young's Blues' originated some four years earlier, or even as far back as 1953. But it was only fully developed much later when he began playing regularly with Jennings in New York.

The significance of jazz was in any case shortly to become intertwined with an influence equally compelling, and arguably even more important, in Young's later development: that of non-Western musics in general and North Indian classical music in particular. The realisation that a classical art form could also involve improvisation helped feed an interest in the creative potential of performing that had initially been nourished by jazz. In addition, the approach to harmony in both jazz and a variety of non-Western musics – very different from that of Western classical music – is clearly an important influence on Young's development of 'static' structures.

Young's education on the West Coast allowed him at least some contact with non-Western musics as early as 1957. Strolling one day, he heard Indian music broadcast across the UCLA campus: an experience which sowed the seeds of what was to become important to him a decade later, and eventually an overwhelming preoccupation. Young cites an early recording by Ali Akbar Khan (sarod) and Chatur Lal (tabla) – of two ragas, *Sind Bhairavi* and *Piloo* (heard on the radio and then purchased) – as particularly influential, since it 'essentially introduced the longest example then available of masterfully played Indian music'.[11] Perhaps at least as importantly, it provided him with his first opportunity to hear the drone instrument, the tambura, with its timbral harmonic array, played solo at the beginning of the recording by Shirish Gor. Young says that this experience had a profound effect on him, furthering his interest in sustained sounds and harmonics; the tambura eventually became the instrument he played in his studies of vocal music under Pandit Pran Nath. In 1961–2, two other Indian musicians – the shenai player Bismillah Khan and the South Indian flautist T. R. Mahalingam – became the major influences, along with John Coltrane, on Young's sopranino saxophone playing.

UCLA had a particularly good ethnomusicology department, with its own student gagaku orchestra and Japanese instructors; Young listened a lot, but did not attempt to play. The combination of precision and serenity found in gagaku, in the context of a sense of musical time quite different from that of most Western musics, has been acknowledged by him as a significant influence on *Trio for Strings*, in particular. Quite early on, he also heard plainchant and organum on records. Later, while at Berkeley, he visited a local Dominican monastery to hear chant. This, however, was only after he had pursued – to quite new, and extraordinary, conclusions – the dominant modernist musical aesthetic and technique of the day: serialism.

Towards serialism, and away from it

Young's earliest compositions were, he says, written in the style of Bartók, with some additional influence from Debussy. These include Variations for String Quartet (1954); 'after that', the composer reports, 'Leonard Stein announced to people that I was a composer'. He had also been attracted to serialism; he says that his schoolteacher's association with Schoenberg made him 'predisposed to the twelve-tone technique'.[12] Like Pierre Boulez and Karlheinz Stockhausen, however, Young preferred the freely atonal compositions of Schoenberg to his twelve-note ones. 'Farben', no. 3 of the Five Orchestral Pieces, op. 16, was singled out for comment: not surprisingly, since what he called its 'mirage-like motifs disappearing and reappearing over recurrent droning textures'[13] exhibit precisely the qualities – static, drone-based, essentially repetitive – of Young's later music. He had little interest in the more conventionally thematic approach of Schoenberg's twelve-note works.

It was Webern who was more useful to Young in pointing the way forward to a new 'static' music. On going to college, Young came to Webern largely through Stein, and investigated a post-Webernian idiom for himself. Webern's integration of serial technique and motivic materials interested Young more than the sorts of integral procedures being developed 'out of Webern' by the Europeans; so did the extent to which Webern's serial processes were audible. But it was the apparent contradiction between an aesthetic still rooted in the dynamism of classical forms and a resulting music that was often essentially static that probably fascinated him most. One technique of significance to Young, as to others, was Webern's tendency to repeat pitches at the same octave, as found, for instance, in the Symphony, op. 21, and the Variations for Orchestra, op. 30; though he seems not to have appreciated the potential of this until after he composed *Trio for Strings* in 1958. This brought greater structural clarity; it also suggested the constant repetition of material to create what Young saw as a non-developmental form of striking economy. Thinking along these lines, twelve-note music easily became understood as 'the same information repeated over and over and over again, in strictly permuted transpositions and forms, which recalls the thirteenth-century use of cantus firmus';[14] European Renaissance music had, after all, also been a strong influence on Webern. The latter's influence on Young was not, however, confined to the twelve-note works; in Webern's Six Bagatelles for String Quartet, op. 9, he heard 'little static sections, like a chime, or a music box, or time ticking off'. Webern and, more selectively, Schoenberg turned out to offer models as potent for the development of a 'static' music as did jazz and non-Western musics.

In developing his idea of minimalism using serialism as a direct inspiration in the creation of an innovative static style, Young by no means ignored the twelve-note method's usual function of generating non-tonal pitch material. As a result, his early but already highly individual approach to minimalism has more in common with other, more conventionally non-tonal, modernist musics than does the early minimalism of Reich or Glass. Yet while Young's compositions of 1956–8 adopt the basic principles of the twelve-note method, they soon depart quite radically from any of the styles to which the method had previously given rise. Webern may have used sparse textures; but Young quickly takes economy of material to such an etiolated extreme that the term 'minimalist' becomes the most natural word to describe it. The most striking difference between Young's music and earlier twelve-note and serial practice is its increasing reliance on sustained notes. His choice of intervallic vocabulary – rejecting thirds and sixths in favour of perfect intervals and major sevenths – is, however, also important. These tendencies culminate in *Trio for Strings*, the most remarkable work of this period; its extremity alone should guarantee its place in the history of musical minimalism.

In the evolution of Young's serial compositions from exercises in Second Viennese twelve-note music to the establishment of 'sustenance' as his own mature minimalism's chief concern, the extent and function of sustained sounds provide the main point of reference. These already play a role in the Five Small Pieces for String Quartet (2–16 November 1956), the earliest of Young's compositions to receive more than very occasional performance today. Young says that the Five Small Pieces, written when he 'was deep into my studies with Leonard Stein . . . were the first works that I composed using twelve-tone row technique'.[15]

The pervasive atonality of the Five Small Pieces, in which individual intervals nevertheless emerge as prominent, shows an obvious debt to Webern. But they also include, in their composer's own words, '[l]onger static sections of pulses and ostinato figures, and even a hint of the sustenance to come in my later works'. Interestingly, the subtitle of the Five Small Pieces – 'On Remembering a Naiad' – suggests the Romantic imagery conjured by Schoenberg's op. 16, no. 3 (subtitled 'Summer Morning by a Lake'), or by Webern himself in his own accounts of his compositions, rather than post-Webernian abstraction. Variations for alto flute, bassoon, harp and string trio (11 February 1957), apparently inspired in particular by the palindromic variation structures of the second movement of Webern's Symphony, op. 21, emphasises the perfect fourths and fifths and major sevenths that were to become characteristic of Young's later music; significantly, too, these intervals can be contemplated in the silences that surround them.

Young had not yet abandoned more conventional idioms. Other pieces from 1957 are simply exercises: the Prelude in F minor for piano, for instance (24 March), was written as 'a personal assignment in $\frac{5}{8}$ meter' for Stevenson's Baroque counterpoint class at UCLA; yet in 1989 Young numbered it among his favourite compositions. A Canon for two instruments (24 April), an assignment for Kremenliev, demonstrates the fledgling composer's 'enthusiasm for the contrapuntal disciplines as applied to serial technique and developed in the works of Schoenberg and Webern'. It was played on two pianos at UCLA by the composer and Johnson, but it can be performed by almost any two melodic instruments, or even as a piano solo. Even after he went to Berkeley, Young was responding to his teachers' requests to write, for example, 'a work in a Baroque dance form, but using a "modern" scale'. The result in this case – a *Sarabande* for piano (late 1958 or early 1959) using major-seventh chords with a minor third – actually emphasises the very intervals, major and minor thirds, which he had already made a characteristic of avoiding. This mixture of works is hardly surprising in a twenty-one-year-old or even twenty-three-year-old student. What *is* surprising is the significance Young today ascribes to even so obviously exercise-like a piece as the Prelude: it is a good example of his obsession with the significance of everything he does.

for Brass (the lower case f is deliberate), completed only four months after the Variations, is already a much more independent statement.

Example 1.2 *for Brass*, bars 54–66

Finished in June 1957, this is a single movement lasting, according to the score, thirteen-and-a-half minutes for an octet consisting of a pair each of French horns, trumpets, trombones and tubas. It is the first of Young's works to use sustained notes as more than an incidental feature. According to its composer in 1966, the middle section of *for Brass* introduces 'notes sustained easily for three or four minutes . . . [N]othing else would happen except other occasional long notes overlapping in time, and there would be rests for a minute or, at any rate, a few beats, and then another long note or chord would come in'.[16] Inspection of the score and a performance on tape reveal that this is rather an exaggeration. In the section in question, single notes, dyads and trichords, even a single four-part chord – presented just twice – are characteristically held for between twenty and thirty seconds, though some are shorter (see Ex. 1.2). Silences, too, vary only between about five and eight seconds in length.

Throughout *for Brass*, the intervals of the perfect fourth and fifth and the major seventh predominate, frequently presented by the pairs of the octet's instrumentation. The set on which the work is based emphasises these intervals. The opening two pairs of pitches (G♯, A, G♮ and D) also form what the composer was later to call the 'Dream Chord', and it is this which becomes the real building-block for the whole work; 'throughout the work', he has written, 'numerous examples of the Dream Chords are stated at various transpositions for the first time in my music'.[17] This was the chord inspired by his childhood experiences of the hum of telephone-pole wires. Young in fact formulated four 'Dream Chords', described in more detail below with respect to *The Four Dreams of China* (1962). Their characteristics – stress on secundal and quartal intervals, and avoidance of thirds, both major and minor, but particularly major – now became the basis of Young's harmonic vocabulary, as he began to formulate his 'own musical mode'. 'I began to realize', he has said, 'that this interval of a major third didn't convey any of the feelings that I was interested in'.

In the context of major sevenths such as C B, omission of the major third – either as E above C or G below B – also permitted what Young argues is 'the true character'[18] of the equal-tempered major seventh (eventually to be translated into the ratio 17:9 in *The Four Dreams of China*) to emerge unencumbered by 5:4 associations above the dominant G, or 3: 2 associations above the major third E. (There is a difference of only 1.05 cents between the equal-tempered and the just-tuned 17: 9 major sevenths, even less than the 1.96 cents' difference between the equal-tempered and the just-tuned 3: 2 perfect fifths.) Either, or both, of these associations tend to establish the more conventional tonally functional leading-note character of the 15: 8 major seventh. The notion that 'the major third sounded worn out and used up' was later to receive theoretical justification when Young began to investigate just intonation and the expression of intervals as ratios using prime numbers. More generally, the particular qualities contained in the simplest of intervallic relationships had, for him, already taken the place, both structurally and expressively, of those aspects of music – thematic, tonal, serial or whatever – which most other composers regard as their basic building-blocks.

Though the outer sections framing the slower middle one – forming what is basically a three-part arch structure with coda – are durationally less extreme, these basic methods obtain throughout. While even the held notes of the middle section, which forms an exact palindrome, are not as consistently long as those of the later *Trio for Strings*, they already signal the adoption of a technique which turns Webern's pulverisation of musical grammar to quite new ends. Though *for Brass* also fails to exploit low dynamics with the bare-faced consistency that characterises their use in the *Trio*, it remains an unusually radical and reductive statement for its time.

The other composition of significance in the evolution of the *Trio*'s style is *for Guitar*, completed on 21 June 1958, just before work on the *Trio* began. While not actually longer than those of *for Brass*, the long notes and silences of *for Guitar* are more consistent and pervasive. The application of these for the first time to an instrument incapable of sustaining a note for any length of time without fast repeated attack causes a quite different relationship to develop between sound and silence. *for Guitar* makes ingenious use of the possibilities the acoustic guitar offers for resonance; as a result, the work perpetually hovers in the territory between the decay of a sound and its total absence. The composer's own description of the work stresses the extension of what he calls 'my concept of abstract musical form which included identical and similar pitch constellations set in durational permutations occurring at points sometimes separated by long periods in expanded time structures'.[19] The outer main sections of *for Guitar*'s four-part-plus-coda structure may still be audibly relatable, partly through the use of the same registers on repetition; and the second section (much longer than the first) is another exact palindrome. But the use, particularly in the third section – which extends the 'abstraction' of *for Brass* without the aid of a palindromic structure – of similar overlapping techniques to those of the earlier composition frees both repetition and silence to work more comprehensively to confound any attempts to make sense of the music as a balanced, goal-directed whole.

In a work for a single instrument, Young is almost bound to focus on fewer pitches at once; in general, *for Guitar* is more reductive and more rigorous. As before, he tends to avoid thirds and sixths, though the bottom E and open G string of the guitar inspire the occasional minor tenth. While *for Brass* had formed 'Dream Chords' from pairs of characteristic intervals, *for Guitar* generates what its composer calls 'three-pitch subsets' of the 'Dream Chords' by dividing the basic set – of eleven notes this time – into small groups, rather as Webern did. The outer sections focus almost exclusively on secundal dissonances: both narrow seconds and wide sevenths and ninths. Young himself sees the beginning and end of *for Guitar* as being in E-Phrygian, though as Example 1.3 illustrates, foreign notes are soon added. The third section introduces a perfect fourth (G♯ C♯), a perfect fifth (C♯ G♯) and a range of longer single pitches. Despite the potential these offer for establishing a modality, the prevailing impression is much more elusive.

Young did not find a performer for *for Guitar* at the time of its composition and it remained unplayed until 1979, when Ned Sublette, who had

Example 1.3 *for Guitar*, bars 1–3

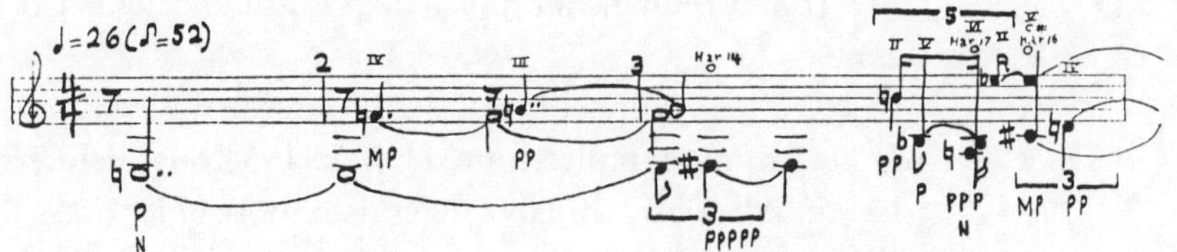

practised this extremely difficult work for three years, gave its première. A version using just intonation, made the year before this, was eventually performed by Jon Catler in 1986.

Trio for Strings

Trio for Strings was composed in Los Angeles with the help of experiments made on the pipe organ at UCLA's Royce Hall, one of the city's main concert venues, and copied in Berkeley, where the date of 5 September 1958 was added to the score. The work is cast in a single movement; an accurate observation of its metronome markings implies a performance of fifty-eight minutes. The most striking aspect of the work is, of course, its reliance on long sustained notes. Young has written that the *Trio* 'is the first work that I composed which is comprised almost entirely of long sustained tones. It is probably my most important early musical statement, and I feel it actually influenced the history of music since no one had ever before made a work that was composed completely of sustained tones'.[20] While long notes – and their counterpart, silences – had been important components of *for Brass* and *for Guitar*, in *Trio for Strings* they constitute the work's material and essence.

The opening viola note C♯, for instance, has been timed from an actual performance at 4′23″;[21] and though it lasts longer than the two notes by which it is surrounded – the first on violin, the second on cello – it proves to be by no means 'eccentric' in the context of the work as a whole. (Example 1.4 reproduces the first two pages of the score.) Silences, too, punctuate the texture quite frequently; though they are much shorter than many of the sustained notes, some last as many as forty seconds. As with *for Brass*, each instrument's sequences of pitches in the *Trio* are not designed to be played 'as individual "parts", but as contributions to a chordal unit whose components are of different durations'.[22] This makes the function of the lengthy silences clearer: they separate the chordal units so that they may be experienced as individual, isolated phenomena.

Some *scordatura* is necessary to achieve the full range; both viola and cello are required to tune to the B♭ a tone below their usual bottom pitch. Though the *Trio* employs, according to the score, 'an absolute scale of eleven perceptible dynamic gradations (*pppppp* to *fff*)', much of the work is extremely soft, as well as slow. Another important aspect of the *Trio* is the method of performance: '*senza* vibrato. Vibrato should not be used at any time, *ever*!' says the score. The effect should thus consistently be of a timbre from which all colour has been bleached. This is but one of many special challenges for the players that the *Trio* creates; the range of less familiar techniques includes *flautando* and *col legno*, as well as quite extensive use of harmonics. Young also requests 'the production of a smooth, steady bow stroke while also minimizing the audibility of the change of bow direction so that the long sustained tones sound as uninterrupted as possible'. Even – or perhaps especially – in this context, the instruction to make 'the difference between adjacent dynamic markings (e.g. *ppp* to *pp*) just perceptible' seems a tall order. The focus and concentration the work requires also has an effect on the listener's experience of the *Trio* in concert. 'The sculptural qualities of the sound', as Dave Smith says, 'are reinforced in performance by the statuesque appearance of the players'.[23]

The entire pitch material of the *Trio* is derived from a twelve-note set, the subdivisions of which form two-, three- and four-note groupings based on the 'Dream Chord'. Within these groupings, Young confines himself almost entirely to the intervals of the minor and major second, the perfect fifth and the possible inversions of these, again avoiding the major third. The only interval included in the work's articulation of these groupings besides those given above is, Young says, 'a very occasional augmented eleventh'. Such thirds as occur between groupings play no part in the harmonic articulation, and are in any case separated by substantial silences.

The basic pattern is established at the outset. A single note (in this case, the viola's C♯) is sustained throughout the unit; to this are added a further two notes (in this case an E♭ on the violin and a D on the cello), disposed in a strict durational symmetry about the held C♯. (See Ex. 1.5 for a graphic representation of this.) Examination of Examples 1.4 and 1.6 will show the sort of variations on this pattern which Young immediately establishes. The opening trichord (C♯ E♭ D) is followed by a group of four notes (F♯ B F♮ E). Here, an initial dyad (rather than a single note) is sustained throughout, while the third of the four pitches, F, is repeated prior to the entry of the final one, E, and again later. Then we have another trichord (B♭ A♭ A♮), consisting of an initial dyad to which a single pitch is added; and finally a fourth group consisting of a dyad (C G) on its own.

Example 1.4 *Trio for Strings*, pages 1–2

Subsequently, this set is fragmented into further representations of the 'Dream Chord' in a variety of ways. The next statement of the set, for example, presents an inverted form (I-9), whose initial trichord (B♭ A♭ A♮) turns out to be identical, in pitch-class, to that of P-0's third unit; each note enters separately according to a new, overlapping durational scheme. The second unit is also of three notes this time (F C F♯), returning to the simple symmetry of the opening. Instead of completing the presentation of I-9 with two further trichords, the F♯ from group 2 is repeated, overlapping with G♮ to form group 3. We are now left, again, with five pitches, divided, as before, into three (E♭ C♯ D; again, identical in pitch-class to the first group of P-0) and two (B E) to complete the statement of I-9 without the

Example 1.4 (*cont.*)

aid of any further durational symmetry. It should be observed that, like the rest of the *Trio*, this statement frequently fails to respect the registral dispositions of the set's initial presentation.

In a variety of spacings and transpositions, this set and its attendant 'Dream Chord' divisions provide all the material needed to fill out the whole structure of the *Trio*, each group of long sustained notes unfolding in turn for the listener's contemplation before a silence separates it from the next. While the means of elaboration vary considerably, the constant alternation of chordal unit and silence increases the audibility of a structure devoid, like Webern's, of tonality or modality. A music is offered in which a minimum of material is slowly laid out before the listener in such

Example 1.5 *Trio for Strings*, duration structure of first trichord

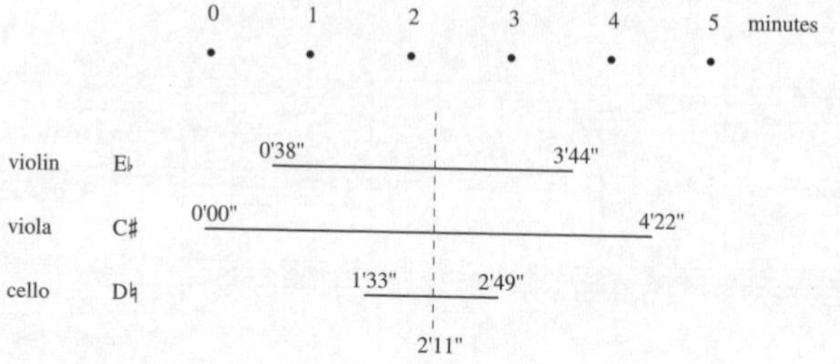

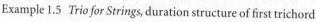

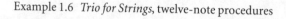

Example 1.6 *Trio for Strings*, twelve-note procedures

"Exposition"

a)

b)

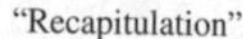

"Recapitulation"

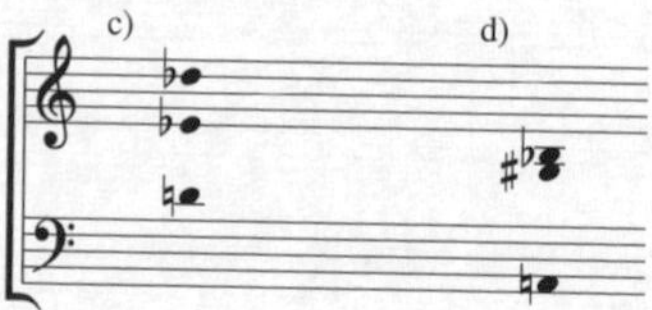

an extended form, the connections between units becoming in the process so fragile, that a totally new form of listening must be developed. *Trio for Strings* seems to be the ultimate 'static' music.

Or is it? When asked about the structural audibility of the *Trio*, Young talks not of allowing the listener to meditate on the minutiae of each unit's 'perfect' deployment of pitch stripped to bare essentials and suspended in time on a potentially endless stream of symmetries and asymmetries, but of the extent to which it may be heard in terms of the formal thinking which apparently helped him compose it: sonata form. He insists that the work has 'extraordinarily deep roots in Classicism, both of the West and of the East', and that it was conceived as an exposition–development–recapitulation–coda structure articulated not so much by the twelve-note organisation as by pitch centres and by development as well as repetition. To suggest that the 'exposition' consists of the first twelve notes, the initial unfolding of the set itself, certainly makes sense in terms of sheer duration, since the music moves so slowly that these notes take more than ten minutes to play. (Example 1.4, in fact, includes this 'exposition', reproduced complete.) And since this does indeed lay out the *Trio*'s basic material, it may not seem too far-fetched to describe the ensuing twenty minutes or so in terms of what Young calls 'a long kind of variations type of development section,' and the last fifteen or twenty minutes as 'a recapitulation of the exposition in a special set of permutations', followed by a coda which includes the thirty-one bars' duration of the concluding C G dyad in the cello – the longest single note or chord in the entire work.

We have already examined the opening of Young's 'development' section in analysing the statement of I-9. As an example of how the basic material of the 'exposition' is reworked in the 'recapitulation', let us take the opening's first and third chordal units. The first unit of the 'exposition' (Ex. 1.6a) consists of a 'major-second' dyad (C♯ E♭) underpinned by the note (D) a major seventh below its lower pitch ('one of my favourite voicings', says Young). The third unit (Ex. 1.6b) already presents this in a different, and transposed, form: the 'major-second' dyad has now become a minor seventh (B♭ A♭), and the underpinning note (A) is now just a semitone below. At the beginning of the 'recapitulation' (see Ex. 1.6c), the opening 'major-second' dyad has become a minor seventh (E♭ D♭), underpinned by the original pitch-class D now just a semitone below: in other words, the pitches of Example 1.6a in the voicing of Example 1.6b. Similarly, in Example 1.6d – the third unit of the 'recapitulation' – the minor-seventh dyad has become a 'major second' (G♯ B♭), underpinned by the original pitch-class A now a major seventh below: in other words, the pitches of Example 1.6b in the voicing of Example 1.6a.

If this hardly suggests the kind of evolutionary structural manoeuvres to be found in Beethoven, it surely makes it less surprising to learn that Milton Babbitt apparently admired Young at about this time, though he may not have seen any of the *Trio*. But its composer makes other claims for the work's links with the Western classical tradition. The *Trio* is, he avers, 'a rather tonal piece. It's in some sort of C . . . probably . . . C-minor . . . . It doesn't start there, but it gets there: in the cadence of the exposition and in the cadence of the recapitulation and in the cadence of the coda'. The first of these 'cadences' can be seen towards the end of Example 1.4: concluding on the C G open fifth of the cello. This is certainly the work's first clear consonance; Young himself speaks of it as concluding 'a kind of modal cadence', in which the preceding B♭ A♭ dyad, to which A is then added, produces an effect 'a little bit like a Landini cadence'.

While the glacial progress of this exposition in actual performance will be likely to produce an effect drastically different from its effect on the eye in the form of little more than a page of manuscript, the very attenuation created by the music's speed must surely help blur the listener's ability to distinguish between 'atonality' and 'modality'. Yet the result will, of course, hardly resemble the dynamic tonality of sonata practice. More interesting than the above details themselves, perhaps, is the fact that Young apparently thought about the material of *Trio for Strings* in this way. One might have expected that the purveyor of ideas as radical as those he was about to unleash on the New York avant-garde could have created a work of such stunning originality only by jettisoning the baggage of 'tradition' entirely. We should not forget the continuing influence in the *Trio* of jazz and Indian music and, in particular, that of Japanese gagaku, as well as whatever influence Western classical music still exerted on his thinking at this time. Modality, not atonality, was to provide Young with the key to his mature development, but his ability to synthesise elements from a wide range of musical traditions into multifaceted compositions is a hallmark of his development.

Now 'refined and perfected', as its composer calls it, the approach already identified in *for Brass* and *for Guitar* is here taken to extremes. In excluding 'almost any semblance of what had been generally known as melody', Young may not have entirely purged his music from past associations. But he had certainly created music with a degree of reductive focus – both of means and of expression – unusual, if not unique, in Western composition of the time. Edward Strickland has suggested that the 'dodecaphony' of the *Trio* could be argued as 'exclud[ing] the harmonic stasis theoretically afforded by tonal organisation'.[24] Yet the models Young had selected from the output of the Second Viennese School suggested that both free atonality and the twelve-note method could produce music much more static than anything propelled by the dynamism properly implied by 'tonal organisation'. Besides, Young had shown that it is possible to 'freeze out' the linearity implied in twelve-note theory, and often used as a prop in twelve-note practice, while continuing to use its basic techniques. Even the long silences, which Strickland also argues '[interrupt] the musical continuum',[25] call linearity into question in a context so removed from that of traditional musical discourse – not least in dynamic level – that what he calls a 'reciprocity' between sound and silence allows a new kind of continuity to develop. The *Trio for Strings* is undoubtedly Young's most important composition of this period, and the work which firmly establishes his place as the first composer to discover a truly minimalist language and to develop it in a totally individual way.

Young himself has described this revolution in terms of a move from 'ordinal' to 'cardinal'.[26] Serial technique, he argued, was essentially 'ordinal', being based on a linear sequence of pitches. The increasing emphasis 'on concurrent frequencies or harmony in my work', on the other hand, 'implied the possibility of the organization of the cardinal values both in regard to how many frequencies are concurrent and the relationship of the frequencies to each other'. The first stage, accomplished by the *Trio for Strings*, was to release the twelve-note method from its linear origins. The second was to continue the search for an 'absolute music . . . evolving from the universal truths of harmonic structure'[27] without the shackles that method inevitably imposed.

This 'cardinal' thinking was to lead to Young's investigation of tuning systems and new kinds of harmony in the 1960s. And though some of the thrust of this acoustic research appears very theoretical – Young has a firmer grasp of acoustic theory than most composers – it was rooted in the search for music one could unravel to an unusual extent by ear. The twelve-note compositions of Schoenberg, even Webern, and certainly those of the emerging younger generations had serial structures resistant to aural identification. By contrast, Young's emphasis on longer notes made 'harmonic analysis by ear a reality'.[28] And it was this desire to get inside the harmonies he was creating that led him to become dissatisfied with the imprecisions and limitations of the equal temperament which he had up to now accepted as the foundation for his work as a composer. The use of a circumscribed number of intervals – and in particular, his natural predilection for perfect fourths and fifths – was already leading him towards a Pythagorean approach to the harmonic series, and its attendant aesthetic. By investigating the possibilities of just intonation, Young was eventually to discover new 'integral relationships' which 'soon sound much more beautiful and harmonious and correct than their irrational equal-tempered approximations'. In 1984, he even produced a version of *Trio for Strings* using just intonation.

Could a modal, rather than Webernian, approach to pitch materials combine with the other elements Young had already selected from musics both Eastern and Western to provide a more permanent way forward for a new music? In the long term, the answer was emphatically yes. The use of long sustained notes and modal pitches derived from just intonation inspired by non-Western models gave Young 'other organizing factors' which became 'more interesting and pertinent' to his work. In the short term, however, Young became occupied with – and in certain respects sidetracked by – other concerns. The main influence on his output over the next two or three years was Cage.

Berkeley and Darmstadt: towards Cage, and away from him

In September 1958, Young moved north to the Bay Area and enrolled as a graduate student at the University of California at Berkeley. (He had seriously considered going to Princeton to study with Babbitt who, through the intervention of Stein, had apparently been enthusiastic about *for Brass* and *for Guitar*. Babbitt, though, had a bad car accident that year and was unable to teach for a while.) For two years, he studied composition – first with Seymour Shifrin, later with Charles Cushing and William Denny – as well as analysis (with Andrew Imbrie). For his first year Young had received a Woodrow Wilson Fellowship, and in his second year he became a teaching assistant.

He took with him to Berkeley the *Trio for Strings*, which he had been composing during the summer vacation. It was the first score he showed to Shifrin who – though more open-minded than some of his academic composing colleagues – was, not surprisingly, highly critical of its radical reinterpretation of Webernian principles and, given his own Schenkerian predilections, presumably doubtful about Young's attempts to create a music so patently devoid of voice-leading. He was sufficiently concerned for his new pupil, however, to arrange for a performance of the *Trio* at one of the 'musicales' for graduate composers held in his own home. Shifrin seems to have been unconvinced that Young could hear his own composition's structure; the performance was designed as a demonstration of the piece's unworkability.

The première of *Trio for Strings* was accordingly given privately that autumn by student players – Oleg Kavelenko, John Graham and Catherine Graff – to a very small audience. Nearly all its members were Young's fellow composition students in Shifrin's class, several of whom would later become well known for very different kinds of music; these included David Del Tredici (especially admired as a pianist at this time), Jules Langert, Pauline Oliveros and Loren Rush. 'Almost everyone thought that I had gone off the deep end',[29] Young recalls. Few of his colleagues, and none of his teachers, subsequently took Young very seriously; though it should be pointed out that Oliveros subsequently developed her own style of minimalism based on sustained sounds.

The only friend of Young who appears to have developed any real understanding at the time of what he was doing missed the *Trio*'s première. Terry Riley didn't register officially at Berkeley until the spring of 1959; though he visited the campus, at the suggestion of Rush, some time in October or November to check out its suitability for his own studies, he wasn't present at the performance. It was through this visit that Young and Riley first met; their friendship began to develop even before Riley officially became a fellow student. Riley's sympathetic recollections of Young at this time make clear that his image, as well as his music, was strikingly, bafflingly innovative. Young, he says, 'had one of the weirdest images of anybody I'd seen. You have to remember this is the '50s, when everybody was very straight-looking, and La Monte looked like he'd just drifted in out of the '60s . . . So he was the most psychedelic-looking person in the class'.[30]

By 1957–8, Young says, he 'was beginning to discover reasons for moving beyond the twelve-tone system'. At Berkeley, however, he continued to write several more fully notated scores in a style now owing much to 1950s serialism. The titles of his solo piano pieces of 1958–9 – *Studies I, II* and *III* – suggest the impact of Stockhausen, with whose work he was starting to become familiar. *Study I* (finished on 18 January 1959, and written for Del Tredici to play) was circumscribed by the conditions imposed by Shifrin, who had told Young after hearing the *Trio for Strings* that he was 'writing music like an eighty-year-old man',[31] and that he 'should be writing music with lines and climaxes, vitality and youth' in order to receive a grade. The piece used serial methods and sharp contrasts in order to show his teacher 'that I could indeed write music that more overtly included elements that have come to be considered the conventions of our tradition', but still contained sections of more spare, sustained sounds, as well as fast music 'somewhat inspired by Stockhausen's "as fast as possible" writing'. *Study II*, begun in the spring of 1959, also for Shifrin, remained unfinished.

Meanwhile, other interests were compelling Young's attention, and contributing to his 'reasons for moving beyond the twelve-tone system'. Between his two years at Berkeley, he went to Europe. On his way east, he stopped over in New York. There he met Richard Maxfield, whose tape music especially impressed him; Maxfield was shortly to become his teacher. But the object of Young's quest that long vacation was the 1959 Darmstadt Summer School, where he was to participate in Stockhausen's composition class. Stockhausen, Young says, 'had made a very powerful impression on me', and he wished to find out more. He had intended to go to Darmstadt with Dennis Johnson who, having accompanied him to New York, contracted pneumonia and had to abandon the trip. Young took with him scores of *Trio for Strings* and *Study I*.

Stockhausen, according to Young, praised the *Trio*, though – perhaps rather untypically – its composer waited nervously until his last day in Darmstadt before producing it for his inspection. Young does not seem to have been viewed very seriously by many of those at Darmstadt, though he got on well with a few of his fellow students, including Sylvano Bussotti, Cornelius Cardew (then Stockhausen's assistant), Friedrich Goldmann, Heinz-Klaus Metzger and Ernstalbrecht Stiebler. Stockhausen, however, seems to have approved of both *Study I* and of *Study III*, the latter of which Young composed during the course (it is dated 3 September 1959).

Stockhausen's ideas about the integration of pitch and time, in particular, seem to have struck Young as having greater potential than, say, Babbittian serialism. *Study III*, at some twelve minutes, was his longest and most substantial piano piece so far. It follows on from *Trio for Strings* in its use of sustained notes and long rests in conjunction with a serial structure, to which the Webern-influenced technique of repeating pitches at the same register is now rigorously applied. As with *Study I*, though, this texture is several times broken up by short, faster sections which reveal the influence of Stockhausen and make the piece far less minimalist than some of its predecessors. Even its Stockhausen-influenced aspects – the 'entire work is based on the number seven'[32] – failed to gain *Study III* anything more than a rather cool reception from apparently sophisticated colleagues, who considered it 'somewhat radical and abstract'. David Tudor was supposed to play the piece during a student composition concert, but the score mysteriously disappeared – and was only rediscovered too late. Tudor, though, began to perform Young's compositions in New York and in Europe the following year.

Young's major discovery at Darmstadt was in fact not Stockhausen but Cage. In what now seems a generous gesture – considering, not least, the battle then being waged between Stockhausen and Boulez for domination of the European avant-garde scene – Stockhausen devoted much time to Cage in his composition seminar that year. Though Cage himself was not present, he had made a significant impression at Darmstadt the year before; and in 1959, Tudor was again on hand to play his work, as well as that of Bussotti and others. Curiously, Young had not come to grips with either Cage's ideas or his music before. 'In those days', he said in 1966, 'there was no Cage on the West Coast, except on records. Dennis Johnson had played the recording of the Sonatas and Interludes for Prepared Piano for me maybe once, and Terry Jennings had a record of the String Quartet which we used to listen to, but I had to go to Europe to really discover Cage'.[33] In a later interview, he stressed the importance of the First String Quartet, 'Cage's best piece'.[34] Darmstadt even provided Young with his first exposure to Cage's lectures, in written form. The recording of the première of *Concert for Piano and Orchestra*, completed the previous year, was 'played on an impressive sound system'.[35]

In Young's 1966 interview with Richard Kostelanetz, Cage's influence on him is acknowledged by the composer himself in the form of two specific matters: 'the use of random digits'[36] and 'the presentation of what traditionally would have been considered a non- or semi-musical event in a classical concert setting'. To these we should add Cage's concern with the discovery of new sound sources. *Vision* and *Poem for Chairs, Tables,*

Benches, Etc. (or other sound sources) – two of the four main works Young composed during his final year in California before beginning the *Composition* series – use random numbers 'as a method for determining the inception and termination of the sounds'. They also constitute the composer's first 'algorithmic scores', as he calls them: rule-based compositions in which words, and sometimes other forms of notation, provide the instructions to the performers. The idea of 'live friction sounds', as he refers to it, used in *Poem*, is further explored in the other pieces of this period, notably *2 Sounds*. In all these, the influence of Cage manifests itself in aesthetic, as well as technical, matters.

Vision (12 November 1959) consists, according to its composer, 'entirely of unconventional sounds articulated on conventional instruments';[37] the work is scored for an ensemble of twelve instrumentalists, including a recorder player and four bassoonists. Its performers are ranged around the perimeter of the auditorium and the work is played in darkness. Each sound is precisely described in the score, but the duration and spacing of these sounds within a total time of thirteen minutes must be calculated with the aid of a random number book or telephone directory. Silence, with which the piece begins and ends, continues to be an important feature. The composer's tape of the Berkeley première in December 1959 bears out his assertion that *Vision* 'created a major stir with the audience and the faculty, since apparently nothing quite so radical had ever been heard at the University'.[38]

Poem (21 January 1960) was, in the mid-1960s, 'probably the most widely performed of all La Monte compositions', according to Cardew;[39] Cage and Tudor introduced it to New York before Young's own arrival there. The initial inspiration for the piece may have occurred in the Berkeley laundromat. 'I vividly remember trying out the large, heavy wooden benches', Young has written, 'which when pulled or pushed across the cement floor produced unimaginably beautiful sustained tones'.[40] One can detect Cage's influence on this work in Michael Parsons' observation that 'sounds of the kind specified in *Poem*, sometimes regarded as an affront to the ear, can actually be quite beautiful if one concentrates on listening to them'.[41] The score specifies in detail the techniques required for pushing and dragging 'ordinary, readily available furniture . . . across an engaging floor surface'. As in *Vision*, random numbers determine the number of events ('any number including zero'), the duration both of each event and of the performance as a whole ('any length including no length'), the points at which events begin and end, and the relationship of available sound sources to the duration scheme.

In the instructions for *Poem*, we can also see the influence of Cage on

Young. What is missing is almost as telling as what is prescribed. Since no rules are given concerning the size of the unit to be used to measure the duration of the events, this could, as Michael Nyman points out, be 'quarter of a second, hours, days, years',[42] thus enlarging the potential field of perception considerably. But since the composition may be 'any length including no length', chance may, as Nyman says, determine that nothing at all is perceived, thus taking the work into the realm of the purely conceptual. As Cardew observed, *Poem* 'developed into a kind of "chamber opera" in which *any* activity, not necessarily even of a sounding variety, could constitute one strand in the complex weave of the composition, which could last minutes, or weeks, or aeons. In fact it was quickly realized that all being and happening from the very beginning of time had been nothing more nor less than a single gigantic performance of *Poem*'.[43] *Poem* is then, as its composer suggests, 'the forerunner of my 1960 conceptual word pieces'[44] and of all Young's subsequent 'algorithmic scores' too.

The moving furniture of *Poem*, its composer discovered, was 'but one subset from an entire genre of live friction sounds, such as gong on cement, gong on wood floor, metal on wall, with which I worked at that time'. In *2 Sounds* (April 1960), Young extended these ideas with the aid of tape. The following account was given by Cardew in 1966, based on performances of the work for Merce Cunningham's ballet *Winterbranch* (1964) in London two years earlier. (Cage selected *2 Sounds* for Cunningham: evidence of Cage's continuing enthusiasm for Young's work.)

> The composer had provided two sounds on separate tapes, to be started at different points during the ballet. When the first sound starts you cannot imagine that any more horrible sound exists in the whole world. Then the second sound comes in and you have to admit you were wrong. That is an exaggerated account of the piece given by one of the managers of the dance company.[45]

Though the work could have used other 'friction sounds', the tape of *2 Sounds* recorded by Young consisted of tin cans scraped across window panes (which he improvised with Riley), and a drum stick scraped around a gong (which he improvised alone).

This single-minded attention to 'friction sounds' also marks the beginning of Young's attention to harmonics as the central, or even sole, focus of a musical experience. *Poem* and *2 Sounds* – both, when under their composer's control, frequently producing an ear-splitting roar – make possible the production of 'very unusual sets of harmonics', he says, 'which I enjoyed listening to for long periods of time'. Begun in earnest in *Trio for Strings*, and followed up in the compositions of 1959–60, Young's concern to 'give ourselves up to [sounds]',[46] to get 'inside of them to some extent so that we can experience another world', was occasionally to be deflected by other concerns over the next couple of years. But the work done with live friction sounds eventually contributed a great deal to the essential characteristics of Young's output from the early 1960s onwards.

2 Sounds, in particular, provides a link to another important dimension of Young's activities during his student years at Berkeley: his work with the choreographer and dancer Ann Halprin. In 1959–60, Young was musical co-director of her company, providing music for her dances in collaboration with Riley. Halprin made use of *Trio for Strings* for a dance entitled *Birds of America or Gardens Without Walls*, premièred in San Francisco on 29 November 1960, after Young had left for New York. But the music Young and Riley produced for her consisted largely of live friction sounds, *2 Sounds* being but one example. According to Riley, 'we were dragging things across glass to make these sounds. . . . Then we also used to drag garbage cans down stairs and stuff like this when she was dancing, to make really incredible clatters'.[47]

The many performances, both formal and informal, which they gave with Halprin's company included a concert at UCLA's Schoenberg Hall on 22 April 1960. On this return trip to Los Angeles, Young also played piano at a session at the home of Jennings's parents which was important for the further development of 'Young's Blues'; the group on this occasion consisted of Young on piano, Jennings (alto saxophone), Johnson (hichiriki) and Lara (tenor saxophone). Among the performances Young organised at Berkeley was a pair of concerts shortly after this – on 2 and 6 May 1960, entitled 'Collaboration Event: To' – mounted in conjunction with the Department of Architecture. These programmes included a performance, in an open courtyard, of *2 Sounds* with a further, subsequently discarded sound, that of triangles in buckets. The third performer, in these events, with Young and Riley, was the sculptor – and drummer – Walter de Maria, who had also played jazz with Young in the Bay Area.

One composition produced by Young in the context of his work with Halprin made a small but significant departure from this employment of continuous sounds. *Arabic Numeral (any integer), to H. F.* is also widely known as 'X for Henry Flynt', to whom it is dedicated. (A Harvard-trained mathematician, Flynt became a significant member of the circle around Young in New York.) The score requires a pianist to repeat a single loud cluster, using the forearms, a large number of times, at equal intervals of between one and two seconds. The curious title thus refers to the number of repetitions selected by the performer. This decision should be made in advance, the number then forming part of the title: for instance, '1698 (to

Henry Flynt) (April 1960)', to choose a taped performance of 3 March 1961 by the composer himself with which he seems especially happy. Though the piano is specified in the score, Young first performed the piece – in April 1960 at one of Halprin's rehearsals – using a drumstick on a gong. It may, according to the composer's worklist, be played by 'piano(s) or gong(s) or ensembles of at least forty-five instruments of the same timbre, or combinations of the above, or orchestra'.

In performance, it becomes clear that what are usually regarded as sounds of indefinite pitch in fact contain a rich variety of both acoustic and psycho-acoustic phenomena: harmonic partials, combination tones and so on. A further dimension of the piece's interest lies in 'the stress imposed on the single performer and through him on the audience',[48] as Cardew has put it. 'What the listener can hear and appreciate are the *errors* in the interpretation. If the piece were performed by a machine this interest would disappear and with it the composition'. *Arabic Numeral* is one of only two works by Young to use repetition, the method favoured by all the other composers discussed in this book, rather than the sustenance for which he has become famous; its employment of repetition predates Riley's early tape compositions by over two years and his *In C* by two more. Despite its untypical aspect, it is a particularly fine and characteristic example of Young's tendency 'to concentrate on and delimit the work to be a single event or object'[49] in contradiction to Cageian multiplicity.

In the summer of 1960, Young and Riley taught composition at Halprin's summer school in Marin County. Not surprisingly, their course was somewhat unconventional: Young says, for instance, that he required the students 'to go out and collect bugs and things, and put them in paper bags'. Here, he also delivered 'Lecture 1960'. This rather Cageian mixture of philosophical pronouncements and anecdotes – featuring Riley, Jennings and Johnson – is perhaps most notable for a statement that Cage would not have made:

> Often I hear somebody say that the most important thing about a work of art is not that it be new but that it be good. . . . I am not interested in good; I am interested in new – even if this includes the possibility of its being evil.[50]

Among those attending this summer school were Trisha Brown, Simone Forti (at that time married to Robert Morris) and Yvonne Rainer, all of whom subsequently became important choreographers and dancers. Forti's husband Morris – later to become a famous sculptor – was also present at the Marin County summer school; his own interest in performance art had been stimulated by Halprin and continued for several years. A tendency towards disciplinary 'crossover', encouraged by

Halprin's example, characterised all the members of this group. Young himself had been interested in poetry for some time, partly as a result of his relationship with the poet Diane Wakoski, with whom he lived for some while both in Berkeley and after he moved to New York. On 16 September, Wakoski and Young shared a poetry reading at the Millard Bookstore in San Francisco, at which he read some 'simultaneous poems' of his own, and also poems by Morris and others. Within weeks, Young together with a number of these colleagues had moved to New York City to seek their fortunes in the avant-garde art world there.

New York

In the autumn of 1960, not yet quite aged twenty-five, Young moved with Wakoski to New York City, which became his permanent home; after staying for a while in Brooklyn with the composer Joseph Byrd, whom Young had known from northern California, they found an apartment on Bank Street in the West Village. Young was still a student, having won the Alfred Hertz Memorial Traveling Scholarship (which he is sure Berkeley awarded him in order to get rid of such a subversive pupil); he had officially gone to New York to study electronic music with Cage and Maxfield. Yet Flynt is quite clear about the true motive for Young's move to New York. '[T]he avant-garde', he has written, 'was conducted in a messianic way. . . . In 1960–61 in New York, the role of solidifying the new wave was assumed by La Monte Young'.[51]

Besides, Cage was out of town; that autumn, Maxfield had taken over Cage's teaching at the New School for Social Research. Young studied with him for about a year. Maxfield was mainly a composer of tape music, and technically very much at the forefront of this field; he was a leading recording engineer at Westminster Records and also acted as musical director for the James Waring Dance Company. Disillusioned, apparently, by his lack of public success, he committed suicide in 1969. Young himself seems to have had little trouble achieving recognition in New York almost immediately. To some extent this was a matter of image: 'psychedelic' before such things existed, he was soon dressing in a black velvet suit and black cape. To some extent it was a matter of circumstance: early on, he fell in with other leading practitioners of the downtown avant-garde, including the artist George Brecht, the lighting designer Nic Cernovich, the composer and pianist Toshi Ichiyanagi, the poet Jackson MacLow, the graphic designer and avant-garde impresario George Maciunas, the filmmaker and conceptual artist Yoko Ono (then Ichiyanagi's wife) and the artist Larry Poons; Flynt – a philosopher, violinist and commentator on the avant-garde, among other things – also became an important member of this community. It was now enlarged by Young's Californian entourage.

Within scarcely two months of his arrival, Young became the founding musical director of the concert series in Ono's loft at 112 Chambers Street, having been introduced to Ono by Tudor. According to Young, this series 'was perhaps the first to take place in a loft in New York City, thus representing one of the beginnings of alternative performance spaces'. Eight pairs of programmes were presented by him between December 1960 and June 1961, with two concerts each devoted to a single composer or artist.[52] In only six months, Young helped establish a significant presence for several new kinds of music on the wider New York avant-garde scene. The first pair of programmes was devoted to the music of Jennings. Besides music, theatrical events and even installations were also included. Later programmes featured both musicians – including Maxfield and Ichiyanagi, as well as Young himself – and others, including Forti, MacLow and Morris. After this series, however, he resigned as Ono's concert organiser due to disagreements with her over programming.

By the time he arrived in New York, Young had already written several of the works which soon helped establish him as a leader of the avant-garde. These include not only *Arabic Numeral (any integer), to H. F.*, given its first public performance in New York on 14 May 1961, but also half the pieces eventually grouped under the title *Compositions 1960.* The theatrical and conceptual dimensions of these pieces were, in fact, partly a response to the stifling atmosphere of Berkeley, where Young's activities had been widely treated with derision. Together with the three *Piano Pieces for David Tudor* (which the composer has also included as part of *Compositions 1960*), the two *Piano Pieces for Terry Riley* (both sets also 1960), the *Compositions 1961* – all composed in New York – and a few other lesser-known works, these 'word pieces' or 'performance pieces' are probably Young's most famous, or infamous, creations.

Several of the fifteen *Compositions 1960* emphasise how what might at first appear essentially theatrical or conceptual may also be considered musical. *Composition 1960 #5* (8 June; some pieces are precisely dated, others not) – inspired by a trip to Mount Tamalpais, in Marin County – requires the performer to 'Turn a butterfly (or any number of butterflies) loose in the performance area'. In interview with Kostelanetz, Young agrees that performing this activity in a concert situation makes clear that even a butterfly makes a sound. More importantly, he says that 'a person should listen to what he ordinarily just looks at, or look at things he would ordinarily just hear'.[53] Other pieces go further in redefining the relationship between the audience and the performer. In *Composition 1960 #4* (3 June), the lights are turned off for a period of time previously announced; when they are turned back on, the audience may be told that it is they who have been the performers, though the score says that 'this is not at all necessary'. In *Composition 1960 #6* (2 July), performers onstage pretend to be the audience. Still other pieces seem more viable as poetry than as performance instructions. *Composition 1960 #15* (9:05 A.M., 25 December) reads: 'This piece is little whirlpools out in the middle of the ocean'. *Piano Piece for David Tudor #3* (14 November 1960) suggests merely that 'most of them were very old grasshoppers'. According to Cardew,[54] Cage once suggested that Wakoski was at least partly responsible for these pieces, a view Young attributes to the fact that Wakoski transcribed some of them for him. Wakoski now recalls that 'for La Monte, words, including poetic language, were sound events. I didn't influence him to write poetry – he was already describing ordinary events as poetry. We simply inspired each other to follow our own imaginations'.[55] Both she and – later and to a much greater extent – Zazeela worked tirelessly to help him realise his ideas and to promote himself. The pieces for Tudor were composed out of admiration for 'the foremost performer of new music',[56] who was now championing Young's work after encountering it at Darmstadt.

In *Piano Piece for David Tudor #1* (October 1960), the performer is asked to '[b]ring a bale of hay and a bucket of water onto the stage for the piano to eat and drink. The performer may then feed the piano or leave it to eat by itself. If the former, the piece is over after the piano has been fed. If the latter, it is over after the piano eats or decides not to'. The initial stage is simply – if, in a concert context, amusingly, even shockingly – theatrical. But then things become more complicated: whichever option is taken (and for that matter whichever option the piano may be deemed to have taken), the piece quickly moves into a surreal, unreal or conceptual space in which the piano itself is simultaneously the focus of an entirely new attention and the piece's only link with 'music'. *Composition 1960 #13* (9 November) instructs the performer to 'prepare any composition and then perform it as well as he can': an apparently straightforward activity. Flynt, however, once performed *#13* by selecting *#13* itself as the composition to be performed: an altogether more 'conceptual' response.

Other pieces from *Compositions 1960* offer direct connections to Young's more purely musical activities, both before and since. Probably the best example is *Composition 1960 #7* (July), which consists of the perfect fifth B F♯, notated on a staff, plus the words 'to be held for a long time'. The link with the composer's concern with sustained sounds is obvious, right down to the choice of a 'pure' interval which allows the listener to focus on aspects otherwise unnoticed. More clearly, because even more reductively, than any of Young's earlier works, *#7* opens up the world of psycho-acoustic events behind a simple acoustic phenomenon: combination tones, for instance, and the possibility of hearing the balance of partials within each note of the interval quite differently in different parts of the room. As Smith has said, the piece 'emphasises the harmonic series through the purity and reduction of material and points to Young's later work with precisely-tuned sinewave drones and voices'.[57] Just as the world had become conceptualised as 'a single gigantic performance of *Poem*', so *Composition 1960 #7* can be considered to encompass Young's entire output.

This can also be said of *Composition 1960 #10* (October) – dedicated 'to Bob Morris' – which consists of the instruction 'Draw a straight line and follow it', and its companion, *#9* (October), the score of which is a horizontal line drawn on a card. Though even more conceptual than *Composition 1960 #7*, these are readily translatable into everyday, theatrical or musical terms. Young's own realisation of *#10* involved sighting with plumb lines and making a chalk line along the floor. Howard Skempton once performed the piece by sustaining a single chord on the accordion for two-and-a-half hours. Young used to play *#9* by sustaining a single note. 'People said I was playing one note', he says, 'but I was trying to make it very clear that even if you try to play the same thing over and over, it will always be different'.

The following year, Young decided to translate the already apparent universality of 'Draw a straight line and follow it' into the direct working terms of his own output. Reckoning that in 1960 he had averaged completion of a new piece every thirteen days, he composed a similar quota for 1961 at a single sitting, on 6 January, by writing out 'Draw a straight line and follow it' twenty-nine times, giving each a date between 1 January and 31 December, and publishing the result in a miniature volume entitled *LY 1961*. This 'single, all-embracing metaphor',[58] as Nyman calls it, takes Young and his audience yet further into the realms of what Young termed the 'Theatre of the Singular Event', and towards what is often called 'conceptual art'. His metaphor of the 'line' can be taken as representative of the 'potential of existing time',[59] expressed in directly musical terms in the held B and F♯ of *Composition 1960 #7*. But in 'Draw a straight line and follow it', a line can also be taken, more ambiguously and even more provocatively, 'as a condensation of any number of mono-directional, undeviating linear activities – walking, education (perhaps), marksmanship, Catholicism, La Monte Young's career, etc'. He also performed all twenty-nine pieces by drawing a line and then attempting to draw over it twenty-eight times; 'and each time it invariably came out differently. The technique I was using at the time was not good enough'. While not the total triumph of perception over conception – this performance took place on 21 March 1961 at Harvard University, arranged by Flynt: that is, before most of these pieces had been 'composed' – this certainly demonstrates that Young was as willing to deal with challenging approaches to the passing of time as some of his other avant-garde colleagues, such as Cage and Dick Higgins.

Such matters may seem to connect Young with Cage once again; and indeed Cage was a potent influence on his junior colleague's abandonment, not merely of serialism, but of note-against-note composition in any conventionally understood sense in favour of a fresh look at what music might be and might signify. Neither does the influence all flow in one direction. Flynt argues that Cage's *0′ 00″* (1962) and *Variations III* (1963) can be seen as attempts to keep up with the example set by Young's word pieces, and even by Flynt's own anti-art lectures, such as the one he gave on 5 July 1962, on New York's Avenue D, which Cage attended.[60]

Young's move into conceptual art may have sprung from a Cageian base, but it already occupied new territory. Cage himself said in 1961 that 'La Monte Young is doing something quite different from what I am doing, and it strikes me as being very important. Through the few pieces of his I've heard, I've had, actually, utterly different experiences of listening than I've had with any other music'.[61] As Flynt has it, '[Cage's] compositions, and those of his colleagues, presupposed a quasi-scientific analysis of music as nothing but a collection of sounds defined by frequency, amplitude, duration, and overtone spectrum'.[62] 'Young', he claims, 'overthrew Cage's definition of new as extravagent [*sic*] confusion'. The composer's own view of the matter, at the time, was that (to quote a longer version of a statement already included above) whereas Cage's pieces 'were generally realized as a complex of programmed sounds and activities over a prolonged period of time with events coming and going, I was perhaps the first to concentrate on and delimit the work to be a single event or object in these less traditionally musical areas'.[63] The conceptual, in other words, was being investigated with newly minimal means.

Douglas Kahn expresses the issues with explicit reference to the two composers' relationship to conceptual art. For Cage, 'everything we do is music. . . . By means of electronics, it has been made apparent that everything is musical'.[64] Young, according to Kahn, 'was beginning to say, with respect to *Composition 1960 #5* [the butterfly piece], that any sound could be music as long as the existence of sound was conceivable; in other words, the arbitrary limitations of the human ear or technology (imagine the difficulty of placing a microphone on the butterfly) should not define the bounds of music'. Cageian multiplicity, focusing on perception and aided by electronics and chance operations, had given way not only to Youngian singularity, in which the conceptual played a much more important role; chance and, for the moment, electronics were replaced by an audacious imagination positively enlivened by practical restrictions. According to Flynt, by the time Young came to New York, 'For him Cage was already history then'.[65]

Young's 'unitary activities' had a certain amount in common with the Fluxus compositions of those such as George Brecht and Maciunas. Five of Young's 'conceptual word pieces' were performed at the Fluxus festival in Wiesbaden in September 1962, including what was billed as *'566' for Henry Flynt* and a string quartet version of *Composition 1960 #7*, the held-fifth piece, following a realisation for strings at the AG Gallery in New York the previous year. Several of his works – including *Trio for Strings* as well as *Compositions 1961* – were published by Fluxus from 1963 onwards.[66] Since then, his output of 1959–61 has been played all over the world in Fluxus-related contexts, including the periodic revivals that the movement has spawned; and his name frequently appeared on Maciunas's lists of Fluxus associates. Overlapping with the end of Young's series at Ono's loft, Maciunas mounted his own short but more intensive series, plus a show of Ono's paintings, at the AG Gallery. Young, according to his own account, had some influence on the choice of contributors to its fourteen events. Those not already represented at Ono's included Cage, de Maria and Higgins; Young had two programmes to himself, including the aforementioned *1960 #7* as the sole content of one.

By 1963, however, Young had largely detached himself from Fluxus, feeling much the same as Morris, who left the movement a year later: that Fluxus performances 'were nothing more than vaudeville, shallow revivals of the Dadaist performances of Hugo Ball and Tristan Tzara'.[67] The programming of his compositions in Fluxus contexts, by Maciunas and others, was done without their composer's consent. The work of Young and his circle in 1960–61 is, in any case, arguably pre-Fluxus and not part of Fluxus itself; Flynt suggests that the work of both Young and Cage 'has been submerged by Fluxus expansionism'[68] by subsequent chroniclers, including Maciunas himself, who seems to have been desperate to unite the whole post-Cage movement under his command, and thus set himself up as a rival to Young.

Cage, Young and Maciunas all made what Flynt calls a 'screaming claim to be new (along with an attempt to dictate the definition of the terms "new" and "avant-garde")'.[69] But the 'conceptual' aesthetic of Young and Flynt 'had nothing of the demand for political reconstruction of culture, or for unpretentiousness, which Maciunas incorporated in Fluxus'.[70] It was more sophisticated: Flynt argues for independence from the emotions, and, in his 'Essay: Concept Art', characterises this approach by referring to 'refinement, elegance, intellectuality'.[71] The titillation of Fluxus was to be avoided in favour of a fresh look at the potential of boredom: 'prolonged monotony in art – the position which would later be called minimalism'.[72]

Young remained, however, in sympathy with the belief – expressed at various times by both Cage and several Fluxus artists, though it is another matter whether they have acted on this – that 'art should aim for self-sufficient exploration and not for the saleable product'. This determined how he came to feel about those of his close associates – whether musicians or other artists – who, the composer believes, have 'made themselves saleable'. Young well understands the need to make a living, as befits someone who grew up in a family in which, he says, his father even had trouble finding the rent for a log cabin. From the mid-1960s, lists circulated of the composer's charges for performing his music: the shorter the proposed performance, the more astronomical was the fee. ('A purely conceptual business', he comments dryly.) In the early 1980s, as we shall see, he cultivated his own sources of funding his art with spectacular success. But Young remains in certain respects curiously purist, by conventional standards, despite his constant financial need not only for the technology to develop his work but also for assistance both professional and personal. The Youngs' present home – their old loft on Church Street – is close to one of the busiest road junctions in downtown Manhattan, and a stone's throw from the offices of Wall Street. Yet Young and Zazeela live there like hermits, largely aloof from the teeming world around them.

Young fairly soon relinquished the role of impresario, deciding that life was too short to spend so much time away from presenting his own work. The position of influence in the New York avant-garde art world that went with that role was in the process inevitably affected too. But before this, he responded with enthusiasm to the writer Chester Anderson's suggestion, some time in 1961, that he guest-edit a special issue of *Beatitude East* magazine (of which Anderson was editor) devoted to an anthology of the avant-garde art with which he was associated. *Beatitude East* folded and Anderson disappeared. The project itself suffered other vicissitudes too, but *An Anthology of Chance Operations/Concept art/Meaningless work/Natural disasters/Indeterminacy/Anti-art/Plans of Action/Improvisation/Stories/Diagrams/Poetry/Essays/Dance/Constructions/Compositions/Mathematics/Music* – to give it its full title – was finally published in 1963 by Young himself and Jackson MacLow, it was designed by Maciunas. A second edition appeared in 1970 under the auspices of Heiner Friedrich, a supporter of Young's work since the previous year, when this Munich-based gallery-owner underwrote the publication of the composer's *Selected Writings.*[73]

There were eventually twenty-five contributors to *An Anthology*, ranging from subsequently established Fluxus artists already mentioned, to Cage and his close associates, and several of Young's own circle including Flynt, Jennings, Johnson and Riley. Flynt's seminal 'Essay: Concept Art' – substantially revised in the second edition – has already been quoted. Morris withdrew his own contribution when the as yet unbound volumes of *An Anthology* were stored in his loft. Young himself is represented by ten of the *Compositions 1960*: *#2–7*, *9*, *10*, *13* and *15*, as well as the three pieces dedicated to David Tudor and one of the two dedicated to Riley. David Farneth's assessment of *An Anthology* as being 'among the most influential collections of music and performance art of the 1960s . . . represent[ing] an unprecedented breaking down of barriers between artistic media that had an important influence on the FLUXUS movement'[74] appears fully justified.

Amidst this 'conceptualism', Young's only other composition to rely on reductive repetition, besides *Arabic Numeral*, sits somewhat oddly. *Death Chant* (23 December 1961) was written in memory of the daughter born to MacLow and his wife Iris, who died when she was only three days old. It consists of a spare and bleak three-note dirge based on the minor mode on G, subjected to brief processes of addition and subtraction very similar to those used from around five years later by Glass. *Death Chant* is reproduced as Example 1.7. The work is scored for male voices, with percussive thigh slaps on the last, and later the first, beat of each bar; alternatively, a carillon or large bells may be used, transposed as necessary. It remains Young's only piece of 1960–62 to use staff notation except *Composition 1960 #7*, and was the composer's last fully notated work until *Chronos Kristalla* in 1990.

From composition to improvisation?

By the summer of 1961, Young was improvising regularly on the piano to accompany the alto saxophone playing of Jennings, who was now also living in New York. In doing so, he not only began the process of returning to music *per se*, but also began to establish the musical concerns which would occupy him from then onwards: in particular, the attempt to discover new ground on which composition and improvisation might meet with the aid of structures and approaches borrowed, at least in part, from the music of his youth – jazz. Jennings' abilities as an improviser especially impressed Young, causing him to develop a particular style of piano playing to accompany Jennings' saxophone. He also used a different form of this in more occasional performances with Flynt on violin.

As we have already seen, Jennings and Young had first experimented with this style of improvisation at least a year earlier. 'Young's Blues', as the composer called it, took the basic I–IV–I–V–IV–I blues structure, but prolonged each chord for as long as required; Young then provided a continuous, regular rhythmic accompaniment on each chord in turn, using the 'ka chunk chunka chunk chunka' manner he had already begun to use at least two years before that. Jennings, meanwhile, improvised a continuously flowing stream of notes over this in a manner influenced by Coltrane and shortly to be explored further by Young himself. 'The concept in that style of blues', Young has written, 'was to spend long periods of time on each chord change to emphasize the modal drone aspects of the music'.[75] The result was a 'static, modal, drone-style' combining the sustained approach of Young's early notated compositions with a jazz structure articulated through improvisation. *Young's Aeolian Blues in B♭ with a Bridge* – an improvisation by Jennings and Young, recorded that summer – appears typical. Sometimes the basic material of their improvisations is credited to Jennings, notably his *Tune in E* (1961), first recorded at the same session.

An important result of this was to suggest to Young that he could now return to the concerns first successfully explored in *Trio for Strings*, and pursued at least intermittently in the performance-art works, but now in the context of a modal form of pitch organisation. The change of pitch commitment proved crucial. By forsaking both Webernian atonality and serialism, and Cage's dismissal of harmony, and by returning to modality, he finally discovered an approach rich in potential precisely because of the accessibility it allowed to 'the profound feelings that have to do with these universal structures which consist of vibrational systems'. This essentially Pythagorean aesthetic was to serve Young as the basis for his work to the present day.

Playing piano for Jennings paved the way for Young's return to the saxophone in the spring of 1962. While his previous saxophone playing had been firmly based on the jazz of its time, the new approach, using a sopranino, followed the 'static, modal, drone-style' of his keyboard style; 'the piano', as Kyle Gagne puts it, 'in a sense was a transition between [Young's] reed styles'.[76] Coltrane's move from tenor to soprano saxophone a year or so earlier had popularised this instrument almost overnight.

Example 1.7 *Death Chant*, complete score. The composer's captions read: Line 1: Statement of The Theme with All Motivic Elements; Line 2: Statement of The Theme with All Motivic Elements Plus Retrograde; Lines 3–5: Statement of The Theme With All Motivic Elements Followed by Additive Permutations in Which The First Measure is Followed by The First and Second Measures, Which Are Followed by The First, Second and Third Measures, Which Are Followed by The First, Second and Third Measures, Which Are Followed by The First, Second, Third and Fourth Measures, and Then at The Unison, The Retrograde of All of The Material to This Point

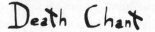

Death Chant

Dec. 23, 1961

Slow (♩=54-68)

♪= percussive slap on thigh
♩= male voices

dada dada di dada di di dada didi di
to be repeated
many times
or ad infinitum

Received on the death of Jackson and Iris's baby, Gwendolyn Malka Maclow.
B. Dec. 19, 61; d. Dec. 22, 61.

to be repeated
many times
or ad infinitum

Young had been an alto player; thus the choice of sopranino was more natural for him, since both these instruments are in E♭ (tenor and soprano are both in B♭). The essential ingredients of Young's sopranino saxophone improvisations were the repetition of modal pitch sequences at an extremely fast tempo over a continuous drone. The sopranino proved especially persuasive for this kind of playing, being even more redolent than

Example 1.7 (*cont.*)

Any of the above may be played on carillon or large bells. If carillon, use the pitches [notation] If bells, use any low pitches with the proper interval relationships. The carillonist or bell ringer should find the best way to produce the percussive sound for each performance situation.

Slower tempos may be used, especially in the case of bells.

The first measure

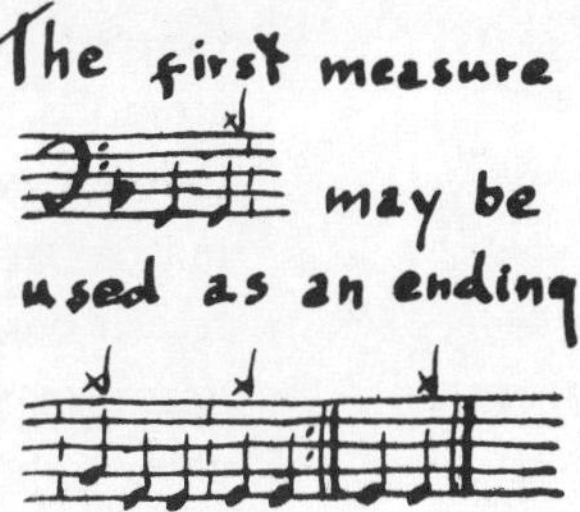

Coltrane's soprano of the Indian double-reed shenai; Dolphy, Young's student colleague, who now played with Coltrane, may have been another influence. To provide the drone he required, Young now set about establishing a regular group of like-minded performers around him, with whom he could work extensively: recording every rehearsal, listening and learning, modifying, elaborating. Though he usually now played saxophone, Young also continued to employ his piano blues style with this ensemble.

Byrd, de Maria, Jennings and Johnson – in any case only occasional members – were the sole musicians in this group who had been part of Young's original 'entourage' from California. All the others were new. Angus MacLise – a poet and composer of music for underground films, as well as a percussionist – was in fact the first to participate in Young's sopranino saxophone improvisations, in the spring of 1962; usually playing hand-drums, he was a regular member of the group until he left New York in February 1964, initially to go to India, eventually to Morocco. The earliest recorded example of Young's sopranino improvisation dates from 11 June 1962, when he was accompanied by MacLise and Forti, who sang what they called the 'drone tone'. Within days of this recording, however, Marian Zazeela – a painter, calligrapher and light artist recently graduated from Bennington College, whom Young got together with through working with MacLise – had moved into the composer's Bank Street apartment; she now replaced Forti as vocal drone in the group. Young and Zazeela were married on 22 June 1963, exactly a year after they began living together. Zazeela subsequently established her innovative and exquisite lighting designs as an indispensable dimension of all Young's concerts and, later, of their 'sound and light environments'.

This trio gave a series of seven concerts at the 10-4 Gallery on Fourth Avenue and 10th Street in the summer of 1962, joined towards the end by Billy Linich – also known as Billy Name, later an assistant to Andy Warhol – who remained in the group until some time the following year. Tony Conrad – who had met Young while visiting Berkeley a few years earlier – attended several of these concerts and joined the group as a violinist the following May, after he moved from Harvard to New York. His training as a mathematician was soon to prove useful to Young in establishing the theoretical basis for his work in just intonation. John Cale, who joined the group in September 1963, was a viola player from South Wales; he had gone to the USA to study with Aaron Copland at the Tanglewood Summer School. He decided to settle in New York, where he investigated the avant-garde scene and quickly became part of Young's ensemble.

The range of pitches covered by Young's sopranino playing was very wide – more than two octaves; but he sometimes employed just a few notes in a narrow microtonal range, using alternative fingerings. The intention behind both approaches was to create 'the impression of a sustained chord'. The speed of his playing – creating the effect of a continuous stream of sound, though in practice separated into bursts of wild, breathless tremolo lasting between about four and ten seconds, separated by short pauses and divided into sections by longer ones – is quite extraordinary; despite the influence of Coltrane, Young's performances have a character all their own.

The choice of modality employed and the ways in which it is spun out over what may seem exorbitant spans of time play important parts in this. The natural improviser's sheer joy of improvising is significant, too. 'I went more and more in the direction of improvisation as a creative outlet', Young says of this period. He himself refers to the style of these improvisations as a 'combination/permutation technique on one set of tones'. Ultimately, these performances are compelling because the fantasy of improvisation is held in tight check by highly reductive repetition. 'I am wildly interested in repetition', Young told Kostelanetz, 'because I think it demonstrates control'.[77] MacLise's drumming, also very fast, gives the music a rather fierce tension, though it, too, gives the impression of being highly controlled, in spite of its metrical freedom. The drone-based accompaniment – in which pitches are sustained for long periods, usually by upper strings and voices – makes a significant contribution as well. Most important, however, is Young's concern with exploring the innards of sound over extended time-periods.

In August 1963, Young and Zazeela moved from Bank Street in the West Village to a loft on Church Street, at the edge of the area later to become known as TriBeCa. Their loft – among the earliest of the artists' lofts of downtown Manhattan – was ideally suited for rehearsals and occasional private concerts, both sometimes taking all night: perhaps the beginnings of Young's interest in the even longer time-spans involved in the Dream House projects and the twenty-seven-hour day which he and Zazeela began observing in the 1960s and have now developed to a more flexible twenty-eight to thirty-six hours. (This routine – originally eighteen to nineteen hours awake, eight or nine hours sleeping – is, they argue, more in line with their natural body clocks.) This nucleus of musicians provided a vehicle not only for Young's improvisations using the sopranino saxophone – which turned out to be a fairly brief, if intense, obsession – but for the wider range of group work conducted under the title The Theatre of Eternal Music.

The Four Dreams of China *and the move towards just intonation*

The work that really began to bring Young's concerns into a new, much sharper focus was *The Four Dreams of China*. This marks the composer's discovery that the harmonic material which he had been using in his instrumental compositions of 1957–8 could be further rationalised to form four chords, each consisting of four pitches. The story goes that Young first notated these chords on a restaurant paper napkin during a car trip from San Francisco to New York City on 10 or 11 December 1962.

Example 1.8 reproduces the chords in full. Their simplest interpretation is in the form of four different orderings of the pitches C, F♮, F♯ and G (though of course any transposition could also be used). The third and fourth 'Dreams' present the pitches in close position, spanning a perfect fifth; either can be interpreted as an inversion of the other, the cluster of semitones being attached to the lower or the upper pitch of the larger interval. The first and second 'Dreams' spread the pitches out to span the interval of a tritone displaced by an octave, leaving a major-second cluster either closer to the lower pitch or the upper; again, these chords are related by inversion. *The Four Dreams of China* thus clarifies the harmonic basis upon which Young's early works using sustenance, notably *Trio for Strings*, had been written by a rigorous ordering of the intervals already emphasised in those compositions: the minor and major second, and the perfect fourth and fifth. Once again, the major third is avoided; even the interval framing the first and second 'Dreams', the augmented eleventh, is comparable to the occasional augmented elevenths to be found in *Trio for Strings.*

The Four Dreams of China, its composer has written, 'forms a structural, stylistic and harmonic link between my earlier, fully notated works composed of long sustained tones from the late 50s, and later works combining improvisation with predetermined rules and elements'.[78] The connection with *Trio for Strings* is especially close. 'As I listened to one of these sustained chords while composing the *Trio for Strings*', he writes, 'I received a powerful image of the sound and timelessness of China'. On 12 October 1962, the *Trio* received its live public concert première in New York's Judson Hall, performed by LaMar Alsop, Jack Glick and Charlotte Moorman.

As a concept – open-ended in its potential realisation and of no fixed duration – *The Four Dreams of China* forms a link with the 'conceptual' performance-art pieces of the previous few years. In performance, it becomes the first composition in which Young combined the style based on long sustained notes and silences with his, still new, re-embrace of improvisation. It could only be realised as group improvisations based on algorithmic scores which extrapolated particular characteristics of the chordal vocabulary it set out, and which provided both the materials and the structures from which those improvisations could proceed. This increased Young's concern to establish on a firmer footing the group with which he had already been playing sopranino saxophone. *The Four Dreams of China* not only provided the basis of much that he and the ensemble did

Example 1.8 *The Four Dreams of China*

over the next few years, but also led to the 'eternal music' of the Dream House installations.

One more element, however, was necessary to complete the ingredients for Young's mature style: the move into just intonation. His experimentation with this emerged naturally out of his involvement with modality and drones which had, in turn, arisen from a considerable experience of sustained sounds. 'What I found', he says, 'was that I was deeply and profoundly moved by great modal music, and that I really wasn't by harmonically unstructured music, equal-tempered music in particular'. A full appreciation of the possibilities inherent in tuning systems less compromised than equal temperament, he found, was complemented perfectly by his already established concern for sustained sounds, since the ear needs the time allowed by a drone to get inside a sound in the ways which interested him. Coltrane's exploration of freedom within harmonically well-defined limits in his modal period had an important effect on his developing style of harmonic-based music; Young cites the famous improvisations on 'My Favorite Things' as particularly important to him at this time, but has also argued that Indian classical music was an even more significant influence.

It was his increasing commitment to just intonation that caused Young's decision to give up the sopranino saxophone in favour of the voice. The fixed-pitch structure of the saxophone posed considerable problems for anyone wishing to break free of equal temperament. For a while, Young investigated the possibilities of adapting the instrument to his new musical needs. He bought some double reeds and attempted to turn his sopranino into a kind of shenai, which it already somewhat resembled. He considered having a modified version of the instrument specially built to incorporate the new tunings he wanted. Ultimately, though, he realised that the saxophone could never provide him with the flexibility of pitch he needed. '[W]ith the voice', on the other hand, he once wrote, 'I could sing anything I could hear'.[79] On 23 March 1964, he also began tuning the first piano to which he had ever had permanent access to a system of just intonation and improvising the earliest versions of what turned out to be another major project, *The Well-Tuned Piano.*

The move into just intonation caused Young to become something of a specialist in areas of acoustic theory which remain a closed book to many musicians. It is not possible to detail these investigations here, but their central relevance to the composer's thinking and his output to this day should be stressed, not least since it may do something to counter the impression of dilettantism given by casual acquaintance with the infamous pieces of 1959–61. Since the longer a note is sustained, the more its overtones become clear to the listener, it is hardly surprising that Young should have become obsessed with such theorising. Other matters of acoustic fact, too, relate the theory of acoustics directly to the concerns the composer had earlier developed quite intuitively: his distaste for the major third, for instance, is well founded, scientifically speaking, in that while equal temperament modifies the perfect fifth by only two cents, it alters the major third by 13.69 cents.

Young's adoption of ratio numbers soon began to focus and clarify his approach to intervals. 'I was beginning', he has written, 'to understand the musical implications of the overtone series more specifically as a set of rational numbers and that there were ways of getting around in the series by ear'.[80] The theoretical potential inherent in conceiving intervallic structures in terms of their Pythagorean base in prime numbers allowed him to develop those areas of particular interest to him – secundal and quartal harmonies based on the primes 2, 3 and 7, later also 31 – and to avoid the third-based areas based on the number 5. Ratios also nicely accommodate the composer's already established preference for 'algorithmic scores', which – in the later works – not only allow space for improvisation but can also be extremely precise in those areas of most interest to him. The exploration of intervallic relationships over sustained periods of time thus encourages close connections between theory and practice, 'inspiring a new vision of composition evolving from the universal truths of harmonic structure'.

The framing augmented elevenths of the first and second 'Dream Chords' as notated in Example 1.8 can only be considered the exact equivalent of the augmented elevenths to be found in *Trio for Strings* in equally tempered terms. As his preference for expressing the pitches of these 'Dream Chords' in ratios suggests, however, Young soon began to think in terms of just intonation, in which the precise quality of these intervals could be appreciated in ways which corresponded more closely to the 'universal truths of harmonic structure'. Thus the four pitches C, F♮, F♯ and G become 24:32:35:36, later becoming refined in the ratios 12:16:17:18. This permits the exploitation – in works such as *The Second Dream of The High-Tension Line Stepdown Transformer* (the 'Harmonic Version', 1962; the 'Melodic Version', 1984) – both of ratios which are further reductions of these to the simplest and purest intervals – 18:12 becomes 3:2, for example – and of ratios which remain reducible no further – 18:17, for example.

As the date of the 'Harmonic Version' of *The Second Dream* suggests, the basic materials, as well as the founding inspiration, of much of the composer's work in the last thirty-five years were conceived in the early 1960s. Two decades later, Young was regrouping the 'Dream Chords' to make *The Subsequent Dreams of China* (1980), and using this as the basis for *Orchestral Dreams* (1985), which exploits the octave displacements available with orchestral resources. The only commercially recorded performance of *The Second Dream* is of a realisation of the 'Melodic Version' for eight trumpets made in 1990. In 1966, he began work on a theoretical treatise entitled *The Two Systems of Eleven Categories* which remains unfinished and unpublished, just like the compositions *The Tortoise, His Dreams and Journeys* and *The Well-Tuned Piano*, both begun two years earlier. A mass of other theoretical explication – most of it published, if at all, only in the form of programme notes, etc. – has accompanied many of his musical projects.

Extended duration is not the only requirement for the exploration of the innards of sound along these lines. Young has also sometimes found it necessary to use levels of amplification which reach the threshold of pain in order to appreciate these harmonic partials with full clarity and intensity. In the autumn of 1967, the taped drones he had provided for three of Warhol's films to be shown at the New York Film Festival proved too loud for the Lincoln Center authorities. Young withdrew his music rather than turn down the volume: a good illustration of the commercial opportunities lost through his refusal to compromise. The following February, encountering his solo performance of *Map of 49's Dream* (see below) at the Barbizon Plaza Theater was described by one reviewer as 'like being hit in the face with a blast of hot wind or like walking into a room full of brine and discovering that surprisingly enough it was still possible to breathe'.[81] While such high dynamics have proved crucial, 'creat[ing] a world of feelings which can't be achieved in any other way',[82] Young's severe loss of hearing in recent years may well be due to such extended exposure to loud sounds; he himself, though, argues that this may be hereditary, at least in part.

While theorising has been crucial to his practice, Young was also keen to pursue his musical endeavours with the help of other experimental aids. The connections his thinking had to the taking of hallucinogenic drugs must be mentioned here, since it seems unlikely that Young's – and, as we shall see later, also Riley's – musical development in the 1960s and beyond would have taken the form it did without these experiences. Though he has previously said little in public concerning the matter, drugs had played an important part in Young's life from the mid-1950s onwards. He says that 'everybody I knew and worked with . . . – especially because of my background as a jazz musician – was very much into drugs as a creative tool as well as a consciousness-expanding tool'. He was introduced to them by Jennings and Billy Higgins in about 1954; in the late 1950s, Young himself seems to have been responsible for Riley's first experiences of LSD, marijuana and peyote. As a listener, Young used drugs from early on: 'it was under the influence of cannabis', he says, 'that I first heard certain structural relationships in Stockhausen's *Gruppen für drei Orchester*'. While alcohol was central to the social milieu of Cage and his circle in the 1950s and 1960s, as it was to that of the Abstract Expressionists and Post-Expressionists with whom they mixed, different drugs helped define the artistic, as well as the social, experiences of many of Young's minimalist generation.

Understandably, the composer is concerned to emphasise the creative potential of drugs: chiefly, for musical purposes, cannabis. 'These tools can be used to your advantage if you're a master of [them]. . . . If used wisely – the correct tool for the correct job – they can play an important role'. He considers that 'there was something in the cannabis experience that probably helped open me up to where I went with *Trio for Strings*'. With the later, improvised and modal music, cannabis sometimes proved a disadvantage when performing anything which required keeping track of, or actually counting, the number of elapsed bars; smoking it, in particular, also apparently restricts the voice, so Young has seldom used it either in his own vocal improvisation or when singing Indian music. On the other hand, both his sopranino saxophone improvisations and the whole work with The Theatre of Eternal Music benefited from drugs: with the latter, he says, 'we got high for every concert: the whole group'. And Young has never performed *The Well-Tuned Piano* without being high on cannabis, though he often practised the piece without it.

When asked directly whether his music would have developed in the same way without the influence of drugs, Young says that he 'would have done, probably, everything I did had I never taken a drug'. He adds that 'many people have taken drugs, but I was the only one to compose the *Trio for Strings*'. In general, however, his comments make it clear that, at least in the past, he has valued their potential as both creative and listening 'tools'. The more 'experimental', extra-personal aspects of the Pythagorean aesthetic are certainly encouraged by this: 'I try to present the music as it flows through me from this higher source of inspiration', Young says, 'and to make a concrete physical manifestation of the information that's going through me that is as true as possible to the information itself. And to make it available, and not to try to temper it for this audience or that audience . . . just to let it be'. He also argues the case for the drug experience as a stimulus to listening to his music: 'It allows you to go within yourself and focus on certain frequency relationships and memory relationships in a very, very interesting way', he states. 'Things happen that allow you to hear frequency structures over time in a different way'. Young is mindful, though, of the disastrous effects that drug dependency, and dealing, can have. MacLise died a possibly drug-related death, in 1979; in 1981, Jennings was murdered, apparently on the wrong side of a bad deal. These days, Young says, he confines himself primarily to alcohol – or abstinence – but also says that he will never lose his appreciation for cannabis.

The Theatre of Eternal Music and the expansion of Young's reputation

Though not called The Theatre of Eternal Music until February 1965, and then disbanded the following year, some of the musicians involved had worked closely together from the summer of 1962 – initially with Young playing sopranino saxophone. The group embodied, in a more focused and particular way than had been possible before, the ideas about 'universal structure', harmony and the effect of sound on both mind and body which have already been discussed. The Theatre of Eternal Music's activities, too, had repercussions reaching well beyond the establishment of

Young's position as a composer and improviser in the mid-1960s, being crucial to the development of the Dream House concept as well as much of his later work besides his solo playing, some of it involving the same musicians with whom he had collaborated in the period 1963–6.

In 1963 and early 1964, Conrad, MacLise, Young and Zazeela, joined shortly by Cale, formed the group's core. While continuing to play modal and blues-derived improvisations with Young on saxophone, its next major project was a realisation of part of *The Four Dreams of China*. This was *The Second Dream of the High-Tension Line Stepdown Transformer from The Four Dreams of China*, listed as being 'for any instruments that can sustain four-note groups in just intonation'; in this 'Harmonic Version', though, each performer plays only a single pitch. The work's title relates to the power-plant transformer that had so attracted the composer as a child. According to Young's worklist, the composition was written in 1962, but its essentially improvised nature means that *The Second Dream* did not really exist as such until the group began rehearsing it in May 1963. Eight musicians were involved, the core members playing instruments different to their usual ones: Conrad on viola, MacLise on violin, Zazeela on violin, and Young on bowed mandolin. The other four performers all had associations with the New York avant-garde: Poons played viola; and the other three – Byrd (guitar), Dottie Moskowitz (lute) and the film-maker Jack Smith (mandola) – like Young, bowed the guitar-related instruments in which Conrad subsequently specialised. An outdoor performance at George Segal's farm in North Brunswick, New Jersey, on 19 May contributed to George Brecht and Robert Watts' YAM Festival, which seems to have been a day of avant-garde mayhem. As Alan Licht argues, it was here that 'the concept of eternal music was born'.[83] This 'Harmonic Version' of *The Second Dream* was subsequently performed by musicians besides those of Young's ensemble; and since 1984, The Theatre of Eternal Music Brass Ensemble, led by the trumpeter Ben Neill, and The Theatre of Eternal Music String Ensemble, led by the cellist Charles Curtis, have presented the already mentioned 'Melodic Version' in which all four pitches of each chord may be played, according to strict rules, by each performer.

The original Theatre of Eternal Music then set about attempting to give more concerts, though many of the group's activities were confined to the Youngs' new loft. Improvisations involving sopranino saxophone continued to occupy much of the group's time in its early stages. Surviving tapes, made between 1962 and 1964, each have a title prefaced by date (sometimes also the time) and place, and also by the names of the days MacLise used in his 'calendar poem', *Year*: for example, '12 I 64 AM NYC the first twelve *Sunday Morning Blues*' is a twenty-nine-minute tape in three sections which features some particularly subtle drumming from MacLise. This performance also gives an idea of the typical instrumental line-up: Young played sopranino saxophone, MacLise played hand drums, and the drone was provided by Cale (viola), Conrad (bowed guitar and plucked mandola) and Zazeela (voice). But performances naturally varied: sometimes, for instance, a set would begin with Young on saxophone over string and vocal drones, followed by a gong duet (Young and Zazeela); then Young would play piano, followed by another gong duet and then a return of the opening saxophone-and-drones line-up to complete the symmetrical, arch-form structure.

Harmonically, these tapes almost invariably apply the 'combination/permutation technique,' referred to above to a single chord, or to a very few closely related chords, throughout. The aforementioned *Sunday Morning Blues*, for instance, is typical in being rooted in an E♭^{7} chord. Because of the sopranino saxophone's structure, Young favoured the Dorian mode on B♭; as a consequence, he tends to refer to the E♭^{7} chord of *Sunday Morning Blues* as IV^7 of B♭ Dorian. Similarly, on the tape '24 XII 63 NYC third day of yule *Early Tuesday Morning Blues*', a single E♭^{7} chord forms the basis for a whole improvisation. In dramatic contrast, '19 X 63 NYC fifth day of the hammer *B♭ Dorian Blues*' applies the 'Young's-Blues'-style chord-expansion technique to drone tones outlining the chord changes of a typical twelve-bar blues in B♭ (Dorian): B♭^{7} E♭^{7} B♭^{7} F^7 E♭^{7} B♭^{7}. Eventually, the music comes to rest on an E♭^{9} chord (E♭ B♭ D♭ F) and develops a familiar 'combination/permutation' sequence on this alone. As a result, this *B♭ Dorian Blues* is less static than the others; Young likens its structure to that of an Indian classical improvisation. Though the context is entirely different from that of *Trio for Strings*, the tendency to create something potentially dramatic out of the apparently static is similar.

In *Studies in The Bowed Disc*, first worked on during the autumn of 1963, Young and Zazeela improvised as a duo on a five-foot steel gong, painted in black and white like a target and suspended on a wooden frame. Specially constructed by Morris, this was played, not with sticks as used on a gong in many realisations of *2 Sounds*, but with double-bass bows. This permitted much greater control and continuity in the production of its rich range of overtones. As with practically all Young's projects from this time on, *Studies in The Bowed Disc* was the subject of much experiment and many improvisations over a period of several years. Its performances also took on a characteristically spiritual and ritualistic quality. Wakoski describes a private performance in which Young and Zazeela, their large white gloves contrasting with their black uniforms, 'appeared to be priests of an esoteric order performing a sacred ritual'.[84] At first, the slow bowing of the gong's rim created the effect of 'a train . . . passing a room with a cello in it, and the strings were beginning to vibrate without hands touching them'. Once the space was filled with the sound of the gong, 'the room was like glass'. A section of the work, entitled *The Volga Delta*, was recorded in 1964; sounding, as Smith puts it, 'a bit like distant aeroplane engines with certain pitches booming through above the rest',[85] it formed one side of the composer's first commercial disc, the so-called 'Black LP', issued in 1970.[86]

With the departure of MacLise in February 1964, the group abandoned the rhythmic aspect altogether in the absence of drumming. The drone-based dimensions of its work were now developed more single-mindedly. Melody was forsaken in favour of a continuous stream of sound; Young started holding longer notes on the saxophone. From late 1964, Cale and Conrad began using contact microphones; Conrad played a variety of instruments – guitar, mandolin and mandola (usually bowed, occasionally plucked) – in addition to the violin. The need to balance the volume of the string drones with that of the saxophone encouraged the group to use amplification, and a high volume level soon became an important component of the total sound. But by the summer of 1964, Young had finally given up the saxophone altogether in favour of the voice: singing, as did Zazeela, in a 'nasal' style which uses the nose and throat to control the production of harmonics. Young's vocal improvisations slide from note to note of the drone frequencies, elaborating complex, rhythmically free patterns around them. While this 'nasal' style is familiar from its use by Indian vocalists – which helped make the Youngs' serious study of Indian music from 1970 a natural progression – Smith also suggests connections between the composer's use of it in conjunction with a consistent emphasis on the fourth and fifth above a tonic, and both Greek Byzantine chant and the Temiar Dream music of Malaysia.[87] The increased importance of voices allowed the group's involvement with just intonation to proceed to a new level.

These developments led to Young's *magnum opus* for the Theatre of Eternal Music: *The Tortoise, His Dreams and Journeys*, begun in 1964 and officially still, like *The Well-Tuned Piano*, a work in progress. As a symbol of static evolution and longevity, the tortoise could hardly be bettered. Young and Zazeela kept pet turtles at this time; by 26 March 1966, the drone from the motor that powered their aquarium was amplified and now provided the fundamental pitch to which the group tuned, and which sounded continuously throughout a set. (The group had used a sixty-cycle hum as a frequency reference as early as 6 June 1965.) This was to become one of several electronic drones in actual performances. The basic frequency ratios of the first *Tortoise* music were written down on 29 February 1964, and represented Young's first efforts at notating frequency ratios in just intonation. As with *The Four Dreams of China*, however, *The Tortoise* only exists in performance in the form of a variety of realisations based on a central harmonic idea. What Young calls 'a characteristic melodic pattern' was, though, also played by him on the saxophone, while the other members of the group sustained pitches from this melody as drones.

While these ideas were still coming into focus, the group improvised several proto-*Tortoise* performances. The earliest of these to survive on tape is a private performance given on 2–3 April 1964 for Harry Kraut of the Tanglewood Festival, in the hope of an engagement there. Later known as *Pre-Tortoise Dream Music*, this now included Young and Jennings (sopranino and soprano saxophone, respectively), Zazeela (voice) and the string drones of Cale and Conrad. This was a realisation based on Young's original frequency ratios. Only on 9 October that year were amplified string drones introduced, in a concert performance given the title *Prelude to the Tortoise*, at the Philadelphia College of Art.

The first mature realisations of *The Tortoise* took the form of one- to two-hour 'sections' in 1964, at which the musicians would begin playing before the audience was allowed to enter, thus enhancing the impression of continuity. The first realisation of *The Tortoise* proper was given on the weekends of 30 October–1 November and 20–22 November (either side, as it happens, of the première of Riley's *In C* on the opposite side of the continent), in two groups of three performances each at the Pocket Theater on New York's Third Avenue (the scene in the previous year of Cage's performance of Satie's *Vexations*). By this time, Cale had devised a highly individual approach to his new instrument. He had flattened the bridge in order to be able to bow several strings simultaneously, and used electric-guitar strings on the viola, which helped to create 'a drone like a jet engine!'[88] when fed through the high amplification; he also occasionally played drones on the sarinda, an Indian classical string instrument.

The title given these performances – *The Tortoise Droning Selected Pitches from The Holy Numbers for The Two Black Tigers, The Green Tiger and The Hermit* – alludes to the composer's poem later published in *Selected Writings*;[89] this refers, respectively, to Young and Zazeela (who had begun dressing in all-black denims soon after they first met), and to the string duo of Conrad and Cale. Young and Zazeela sang in front of the Morris gong, which they also bowed; all the musicians were amplified. On 12–13 December, at the same venue, there were two further performances, this time called *The Tortoise Recalling The Drone of The Holy Numbers as They were Revealed in The Dreams of The Whirlwind and The Obsidian*

Gong and Illuminated by The Sawmill, The Green Sawtooth Ocelot and The High-Tension Line Stepdown Transformer. As the music of *The Tortoise* evolved, so did the length and obscurity of each section's title, assembled collectively by the group along stream-of-consciousness lines.

Subsequent realisations of *The Tortoise* became the vehicle for much more detailed explorations of the harmonic series and its musical potential. *Map of 49's Dream The Two Systems of Eleven Sets of Galactic Intervals Ornamental Lightyears Tracery* – its major 'section', on which work was begun in 1966 – had developed to between three and four hours by the time of the 1975 concert performances. (*49* was a pet turtle.) Though the *Tortoise* project remains officially unfinished to this day, these performances – with a Theatre of Eternal Music ensemble by now rather different from that of the original – represent one culmination, at least, of the years spent exploring the potential of the original frequency ratios to sustain long spans of musical time.

Zazeela's lighting designs, on which work had begun in 1964, were first used to full effect at a performance of *The Tortoise* on 4 and 5 December 1965 at the Filmmakers' Cinematheque Festival of Expanded Cinema in the old Wurlitzer building on 41st Street, for which she devised a series of slides that were projected on to the players' silken robes. Kostelanetz's assessment of *The Tortoise*, as early as 1968, as 'among the most admired works in the new theatre'[90] suggests the importance of Zazeela's achievements to the Theatre of Eternal Music's performances. Subsequent developments in her work with light – which continues to provide the visual context for all the composer's performances and installations to this day – included an early predilection for green and, in particular, magenta theatrical gels, used to colour both slides and, later, the shadows cast on ceilings and walls by the elegant, Minimalist, white aluminium mobiles that have become a regular feature of Zazeela's highly imaginative, sculptural use of light.

The Filmmakers' Cinematheque concert marked the beginning of The Theatre of Eternal Music's demise in its original form. During 1965, Cale had already divided his time between Young's ensemble and the group that eventually became The Velvet Underground; Conrad and MacLise were other members of its chief predecessor, The Primitives. After the Cinematheque concert – feeling increasingly dissatisfied with what he regarded as the esoteric and extremist atmosphere surrounding The Theatre of Eternal Music – Cale left to devote all his attention to the other group. His place was taken by Riley, newly arrived in New York, who sang with Young until August 1966. Though Riley performed in public only twice during his involvement, his contribution was telling: with three voices in the group, the 1966 performances of *The Tortoise* relied less on the wall of sound produced by string drones and more on a vocal counterpoint in which Riley, Young and Zazeela 'soared past one another like stars shooting through space'.[91]

Despite these hopeful developments, this incarnation of The Theatre of Eternal Music came to a swift end. Riley's departure to concentrate on solo performances left only Conrad, Young and Zazeela as core members. It was at this point that existing differences between Conrad and Young over the issue of who made the musical decisions erupted into open dispute. Conrad considered that the contributions he and Cale had made to the group's improvisations 'were just much, much more central than I think La Monte would like to admit, or has'.[92] 'There was no composer, but group consensus. La Monte worked out some things that he wanted to do, but this was tangential to the main enterprise'.[93] He says that Young 'has always secreted the material that best shows the contributions of anyone other than himself' and even that he manipulated recordings 'to make him dominate'.

Young, unsurprisingly, views the matter differently, stressing his role as both the originator of the basic aesthetic and as the composer of the music which The Theatre of Eternal Music performed. The essence of *The Tortoise*, most notably, may be argued to have been the notion of 'eternal music' itself, rather than any collection of musical material as such. 'I really like to improvise', he has said, 'and I only like to write down broad, powerful, theoretical constructs'. He responded, indeed, to the demise of The Theatre of Eternal Music by concentrating for some while on his theoretical treatise *The Two Systems of Eleven Categories*, begun in August 1966. Yet Young states that he was largely or entirely responsible both for the codification of pitches in ratio form and for the musical structures involved in their elaboration. The issue of whether the music in the many surviving recordings of the group constitutes compositions by Young or improvisations in which all the performers made important creative contributions beyond the embellishment normal to musical performances remains unsettled to this day. As a consequence, the release of these recordings – something all concerned would basically welcome – is, as of this writing, still prevented by legal wrangling over the rights to the material they contain. Conrad has gone so far as to picket Young's concerts during the last few years. It may simply be that, as Young puts it, Conrad was 'more of a free spirit', while Young himself was interested in a more controlled and limited tonal palette, obsessively devoted to his chosen prime number ratios. But the dispute carries aesthetic as well as practical significance, as we have already seen.

Day of The Antler

What precisely did Young notate for these works, and to what extent can they reasonably be considered his own compositions in addition to – or even rather than – group improvisations? As an illustration of what Young has written down and how notation might be used to analyse the music after the event, let us take the single page of 'score' for the improvisation entitled *Day of The Antler 15 VIII 65 The Obsidian Ocelot, The Sawmill and The Blue Sawtooth High-Tension Line Stepdown Transformer Refracting The Legend of The Dream of The Tortoise Traversing The 189/98 Lost Ancestral Lake Region Illuminating Scenes from The Black Tiger Tapestries of The Drone of The Holy Numbers from 'The Tortoise, His Dreams and Journeys'* (see Ex. 1.9). This was actually transcribed not for performance but in order to apply for a Guggenheim Fellowship, a condition of which was that scores must be submitted.

As the title suggests, this tape was made on 15 August 1965, when the core group of performers improvising as a quartet consisted of Young and Zazeela (voices), Cale (voice and five-string viola) and Conrad (violin). These are indicated by name in the left-hand margin, and by initial in the first column, 'Articulating Instrument(s) or Voices'. As the heading of the sixth column indicates, the improvisation used a range of three octaves (represented by the ratio 512:64). For those unused to notation in frequency terms, the final column offers the easiest way in. This gives the pitches in equal-tempered *solfège* notation. One can read these *solfège* symbols off against the cent tables of the sixth column (where the pitches to be used have been precisely calculated) and the seventh column (presented as a guiding grid) with reference to the semitones and tones of the major scale. The fundamental turns out to be E at 80 cycles per second; thus the dominant is 60 or 120 cycles per second.

In the second column, these pitches are given in the form of cycles per second, presented as a single big chord. This shows, not surprisingly, that the pitches based on the fundamental E constitute not the equally tempered scale perhaps suggested by the *solfège*, but an unclassifiable mode in just intonation including flattened fourths and sevenths, very flat sixths, plus very sharp fourths and sevenths – as written in against the more precise cents of the sixth column, tuned in just intonation. While the fundamental E could be considered the tonic, B can also be heard as the basis of this mode. In the third column, each partial is given in its lowest common terms, making clear, for example, which intervals are septimally related. In the fourth column, their factorised equivalents are given for calculation purposes; this reveals that all the pitches in *Day of The Antler*

Example 1.9 *... the day of the antler...*, complete score

LaMonte Young

System of Frequencies Used on the day of the antler · 15 VIII 65 Tape of

"The Obsidian Ocelot, The Sawmill And The Blue Sawtooth High-Tension Line Stepdown Transformer Refracting The Legend of The Dream of The Tortoise Traversing The 189/98 Lost Ancestral Lake Region Illuminating Quotients from The Black Tiger Tapestries of The Drone of The Holy Numbers" from "The Tortoise, His Dreams And Journeys"

3800 F# TC
3700 F
576 F# 3803.91
$3^2 \times 2^6$
9
720
* TC Addenda

* Articulating Instrument(s) or Voice(s)	Cycles per Second	Lowest Binary Form of Partials	Factors of The Partials Within The Three Octaves 512/64	Partials Within The Three Octaves 512/64 (frequencies in ratio)	Cents of The Partials Within The Three Octaves 512/64	Cents		Major Scale in Equal Temperament ($\sqrt[12]{2}$)
TC TC	640 630	1 63	2^9 $7 \times 3^2 \times 2^5$	512 504	E 3600 D## 3572.74	3600	E	do
						3500	D#	ti
						3400	D	
TC	560	7	7×2^6	448	D↓ 3368.83			
						3300	C#	la
						3200	C	
TC TC TC	490 480 472.5	49 3 189	$7^2 \times 2^3$ 3×2^7 $7 \times 3^3 \times 2$	392 384 378	C↓↓ 3137.66 B 3101.96 A## 3074.70	3100	B	so
						3000	A#	
						2900	A	fa
TC	420	21	$7 \times 3 \times 2^4$	336	A↓ 2870.88			
						2800	G#	mi
						2700	G	
						2600	F#	re
						2500	F	
MZ/TC	320	1	2^8	256	E 2400	2400	E	do
						2300	D#	ti
						2200	D	
MZ/JC(35d)	280	7	7×2^5	224	D↓ 2168.83			
						2100	C#	la
						2000	C	
						1900	B	so
JC	236.25	189	7×3^3	189	A## 1874.70			
						1800	A#	
						1700	A	fa
						1600	G#	mi
						1500	G	
						1400	F#	re
						1300	F	
LY/JC(35d) LY	160 157.5	1 63	2^7 $7 \times 3^2 \times 2$	128 126	E 1200 D## 1172.74	1200	E	do
						1100	D#	ti
						1000	D	
LY	140	7	7×2^4	112	D↓ 968.83			
						900	C#	la
						800	C	
LY JC(35d)	122.5 120	49 3	$7^2 \times 2$ 3×2^5	98 96	C↓↓ 737.66 B 701.96	700	B	so
						600	A#	
						500	A	fa
						400	G#	mi
						300	G	
						200	F#	re
						100	F	
	80	1	2^6	64	E 0	0	E	do

Code:
LY = LaMonte Young voice
MZ = Marian Zazeela Voice
TC = Tony Conrad Violin
JC(35d) = John Cale 3-string drone
JC = John Cale voice

are factors of 2, 3 or 7. The fifth column presents all the partials laid out within the same octave range in the form of frequency ratios, which is to say in their proper ratios to each other in the improvisation itself.

This algorithmic score thus confines itself purely to pitch and instrumentation. Clearly, the detailed structure of the performance – including all matters of duration and proportion – as well as its style were established by a combination of reference to previous practice, rehearsal and the inspiration of the improvised moment. The musical results depend on the way in which intuition and imagination go to work on given material. It may be asserted that Young provided the material; but others may also have had an input into this, especially at the earlier stages of such music's conceptualisation. The group clearly provided the elaboration of it, each performer being ultimately responsible for his own part. But the interaction not only included Young as one of the protagonists but was also, on the available evidence, driven by someone who acknowledges that he is 'very authoritarian' and – in an oddly characteristic moment of self-deprecation – 'not fit to be collaborated with'. While such an approach may be said to contradict the spirit of the Pythagorean aesthetic that lies behind The Theatre of Eternal Music, it led to music of an unusually individual creative certainty.

Dream Houses and Indian classical music

Young disbanded The Theatre of Eternal Music in its original form following a performance at the Sundance Festival in Pennsylvania on 20 August 1966; after turning for a while to theoretical work, he began to perform again alone or with Zazeela. While Young's uncompromising conditions for the dissemination of his art have frequently hindered its commercial exposure, Young and Zazeela made annual tours throughout the USA and Europe between 1969 and 1975. It was during this period, in fact, that Young's music received its widest exposure. The creation of Dream Houses and other installations in art galleries and museums was now complemented by solo performances by Young, duo performances with Zazeela and, from the late 1960s, the revival of The Theatre of Eternal Music as an ensemble along lines similar to that of the mid-1960s. Some members of the original group, including Conrad, returned; musicians who now performed with the composer for the first time included Alex Dea, Jon Gibson, Jon Hassell, Lee Konitz, Garrett List and David Rosenboom.

Some of the Theatre of Eternal Music's performances, both in Europe and the USA, took place in Dream House installations. Notable among these are the ones for the Maeght Foundation in the south of France in the summer of 1970, at the invitation of Daniel Caux, and the run of performances at major international cultural exhibitions: Documenta 5 in Kassel and the Munich Olympics (1972) and Contemporanea in Rome (1973). American performances included a Dream House installation with concerts at the University of Illinois in 1973 and a week-long series of events at The Kitchen in New York, beginning on 28 April 1974, the latter announced with a Sunday feature in the *New York Times* by Tom Johnson[94] which, Zazeela says, 'drew crowds that circled the block waiting to get in'.[95]

The exposure of Young's music, particularly in Europe during the first half of the 1970s, was assisted by the composer's first commercial recordings. A 1969 realisation of a 'section' of *Map of 49's Dream* appeared on the West German Edition X label in 1970 – on the already mentioned 'Black LP', with *The Volga Delta* from 1964 on the other side – with Young and Zazeela singing over a sine wave drone. Another – in which sine wave drones accompanied Hassell's trumpet and List's trombone as well as the voices of Young and Zazeela once again – was released on the French label Shandar in 1974, together with a version of *Drift Studies*; both sides of this LP were recorded in the previous year. Though these recordings were issued on small, independent labels, they were quite widely disseminated, expanding the reputation of a composer whose work had already become known in France, West Germany, Italy and elsewhere in Europe (though very little in Britain) in the late 1960s.

The more obvious manifestations of 'eternal music' are most immediately appreciated in the Dream House projects and 'Sound and Light Environments', one of which – on the floor above the Youngs' loft, begun in 1993 – was scheduled to run for seven years, their longest to date. Young and Zazeela characterise what they call these 'extended exhibitions',[96] in which visitors may move about freely, as 'time installation[s] measured by a setting of continuous frequencies in sound and light'. Frequencies tuned to the harmonic series, generated by electronically produced sine waves creating continuous chordal drones of periodic composite waveforms, constitute the entire aural material of these installations; yet, by moving around the space, the listener is able to experience not only different relationships among the frequencies emphasised by the audible standing wave patterns, but also the combination tones brought about by the interaction of the harmonically related sine wave frequencies themselves, including the phenomenon known as 'acoustical beats'. Change may thus be experienced in the extended contemplation of apparently unchanging, or only slowly changing, acoustic situations. Zazeela's contributions – both 'environmental' (pure light) and sculptural mobiles and wall sculptures – share the concern with symmetry which has increasingly characterised Young's work with frequencies. More importantly, they are crucial to the Dream Houses' aim of encouraging their visitors 'towards self-reflection and a meditative state'.

The frequencies selected for these sound environments have sometimes been taken from Young's concert works; thus *The Tortoise*, for instance, provided chords for *Intervals and Triads from Map of 49's, etc.* (1967). The original idea of the Dream House incorporated live musicians, but this proved far too expensive. (In recent years, the exploration of new frequency relationships in sound environments has fed into the concert output.) The investigation of psycho-acoustical effects without performers was taken up as an independent 'work' in *Drift Studies* for two or more sine wave drones, precisely tuned on oscillators which must be highly stable. Like *The Tortoise* and *The Well-Tuned Piano*, this dates from 1964. The version that appeared on the already mentioned Shandar disc ten years later is typical of the sets of frequencies devised for the Dream Houses, which are also to be found in *The Two Systems of Eleven Categories*. Here, Young exploits the consequences of the instability inherent in combining waveforms generated by older 1960s and 1970s model analogue sine wave oscillators and their relationship to the 'universal truths of harmonic structure'. As the phase relationship between the sine waves alters, due to the change of air pressure within a space, both pitch and volume vary according to one's location in the room; this 'allows the listener to actually experience sound structures in the natural course of exploring the space'.[97] When 'the composite waveform of the combination tones of the two sine waves gradually, internally and organically, shifts', explains the composer, '. . . [t]he body intuitively recognizes that information having to do with basic universal structure is coming in as sound'. At high volume levels, one also 'begins to have a sensation that parts of the body are somehow locked in sync with the sine waves and slowly drifting with them in space and time'.

The idea 'that a piece could be forever, if you let the concept happen'[98] emerged in 1962, inspired by *The Four Dreams of China*. But the first of these sound installations was not established until September 1966, in the Youngs' own loft, where it continued almost without interruption until January 1970. Though not all its successors have used extremely high volumes, this early example, with which the couple lived almost continuously, was often amplified to the high levels required to 'get inside of the sound', and to hear all the components of the envelope generated by the harmonically related sine waves. The first public Dream House was opened at Friedrich's Munich art gallery in July 1969. Several others have since been set up, both in the USA and Europe, including an important one at Rice University, Houston early in 1970. A more prominent one at New York's Metropolitan Museum of Art, in the autumn of the following year, included performances in which the composer's regular musicians were joined by Konitz, who was then studying, like Young and Zazeela, with Pandit Pran Nath (of which more below). Tapes from the latter, plus 1964 recordings of *The Well-Tuned Piano* and *Sunday Morning Blues*, were broadcast on the radio in France and Germany; this led, in 1992, to the release of a two-disc bootleg recording.

The most ambitious Dream House occupied the enormous church-like space of the old Mercantile Exchange Building at 6 Harrison Street, not far from the Youngs' loft. Here, between 1979 and 1985, Young and Zazeela established themselves in splendour, financed by the Dia Foundation with the intention of providing a permanent research centre and public outlet for their activities. This came the nearest among such projects to Young's utopian vision of continuous sound which would 'last forever in Dream Houses where many musicians and students will live and execute a musical work. Dream Houses will allow music which, after a year, ten years, a hundred years or more of constant sound, would not only be a real living organism with a life and tradition of its own but one with a capacity to propel itself by its own momentum'.[99] Though funded – with oil money from the Schlumberger heirs – with a magnificence almost unparalleled in late-twentieth-century sponsorship of the arts, this project came to an abrupt end after six years when the oil market collapsed.

In the evolution of Young's work after the mid-1960s, one other biographical aspect is paramount. In 1970 Young and Zazeela both became disciples of the North Indian master singer Pandit Pran Nath. Young had already come under his influence in 1967, when Shyam Bhatnagar, already a disciple, played some tapes for him, which impressed Young with the profundity of their expression. In January 1970, the Youngs helped Bhatnagar bring Pran Nath to the USA. In the manner of the students of such spiritual as well as musical mentors, they devoted all their time and energies to him for certain periods over twenty-five years; for fifteen years their guru spent half his time in the Youngs' loft. Pran Nath died on 13 June 1996. The Youngs had maintained a close spiritual relationship with him, and continue to regard him as their musical and spiritual master. Such an involvement is scarcely surprising in the context of Young's previous concern with the connections Indian classical music had with his own: his listening to recordings by major masters, which were an important formative influence on the early development of the composer's 'static' approach; and his development of a style of saxophone playing owing something to the characteristics of the Indian shenai with which the sopranino instrument, in particular, has something in common. Closest of all, of course, is the adoption, by both Young and Zazeela in the mid-1960s, of a style of singing already owing much to the timbre and general approach of Indian singers, even though they had not yet made a systematic study of any Indian vocal style.

The influence of Pran Nath has, inevitably, been at least as much spiritual as musical. Indian theory and practice foster close connections between the two, which emerge in Pran Nath's teaching, for instance, in the form of analogies between tuning one's voice and drawing closer to the deity. 'When the voice becomes perfectly in tune with the drone, with the tambura', Young says, 'it's like leaving the body and meeting God'. The composer has said that 'while there are many profound relationships and differences between my work and Indian music', he has tried 'to keep the two forms as distinct and pure as possible'. One significant influence of Pran Nath on Young's own music, however, has been the organically evolving form of improvisation to be found in the Kirana style of which his guru was a leading practitioner. This has influenced all Young's work since the early 1970s, but in particular *The Well-Tuned Piano.*

The most important aspect of Young's activities in the period 1974–5 was his return to work on *The Well-Tuned Piano*, which now became his main project of the 1970s and 1980s, and the chief focus of his solo performances during that time. The story of his compositional development, as well as performing career, in this period is largely the story of the evolution of *The Well-Tuned Piano*, which correspondingly forms the final section of this chapter.

The Well-Tuned Piano

Though *The Tortoise, His Dreams and Journeys* may in several respects be accounted Young's *magnum opus*, it is *The Well-Tuned Piano* which has occupied the lion's share of his attention for significant periods of time since the 1970s. The work is, however, significant not only in the context of his output as a whole but more widely: in the contexts of musical minimalism, of musics working at the interface between composition and improvisation, and of twentieth-century music for solo piano. It does not seem too far-fetched to say, as Gann does in the opening sentence of the most important article so far published on the piece, that '*The Well-Tuned Piano* may well be the most important American piano work since Charles Ives's *Concord* Sonata – in size, in influence, and in revolutionary innovation'.[100] Since even its most recent performances relate intimately to the basic principles and methods conceived for the work in 1964, it seemed appropriate to extend the discussion of it beyond the cut-off date established for this book as a whole.

Work on *The Well-Tuned Piano* began in 1964, though it was not until ten years later that any version of it was performed live. Being an improvised 'composition' – though in ways somewhat different from those of the ensemble music – *The Well-Tuned Piano* is flexible both in content and structure, indeed seemingly infinitely expandable. The 1974 Rome world première realisation paved the way for all subsequent endeavours on what Young has called 'the work which has since completely captivated me and has become the source and inspiration for some of my most creative developments'.[101] *The Well-Tuned Piano* has been performed in public over sixty times. In addition to the important performances in New York in 1975, following fairly closely on the four in Rome, two series of performances – both also made in New York – are culminating, if not yet 'definitive'. Those made in 1981 include the five-hour performance on 25 October, the recording of which, issued by Gramavision in 1987, is the only realisation of *The Well-Tuned Piano* to have become widely available; the booklet notes for this are commendably informative and include a detailed structural breakdown of the performance itself. In 1987, Young performed a further series, adding much new material and extending the average length to around six hours. The last two performances in this series, and in particular the final one, represent, at least for Young himself, the present state of the work. While, as usual, every performance was recorded, the last three 1987 realisations were also videotaped; among the advantages of releasing a version of one of these would be to make Zazeela's lighting design for *The Well-Tuned Piano* more widely appreciated. Since 1987, *The Well-Tuned Piano* has never been performed. Young now wonders if it ever will be again.

The chief reason for this is the demands Young makes, on himself and others, when proposals are made to perform the work. He considers that it takes 'at least a week or two' to tune the piano properly; meanwhile, the instrument must remain *in situ*: thus, he considers, making the space, as well as the piano itself, largely unusable for other performances. In fact, he asks for three months 'on location', in the first month of which, ideally, a whole Dream-House-style environment is constructed around the constantly tended piano, allowing Young unlimited preparation and the audience the best possible conditions in which to appreciate a continuous performance of some five or six hours. Even the size and position of the audience can change the acoustic sufficiently, for instance, to affect whether specific psycho-acoustic effects discovered earlier while working in the space would actually sound in the concert itself. What he most wants, with each engagement to play *The Well-Tuned Piano*, is the opportunity to add more to it, to experiment, to compose, as well as to rehearse: the improvisational nature of the work clearly blurs the distinctions between these activities anyway. 'I get no satisfaction unless the piece grows', he says. He will only practise *The Well-Tuned Piano* during intensive periods of preparation for concert performances, free of day-to-day concerns.

Two other matters have for years prevented even a single one of the performances Young has given of *The Well-Tuned Piano* – each one meticulously taped – from being analysed with the thoroughness the work deserves. The first is the system of just intonation it uses, which for years Young kept a secret, until Gann reconstructed much of it, thus persuading the composer 'to release the tuning into public discourse'.[102] There is, considers Gann, 'virtually no way to analyze the piece without it'. The second is the nature of the musical material upon which Young constructs his improvisations, which for years Young also kept secret, though some of it was written down in the form of themes, chord structures and scales, and what Gann calls 'ornamental patterns'.[103] Though still not published, a copy of this 'score' has been obtained by the present author – who, like all those not part of the composer's own immediate circle, has in the past had to rely purely on the evidence of his own ears, plus a few tantalising glimpses of tiny portions of the material in notated form. Young says that he developed his tendency to be secretive about his ideas before they were actually published because he found that other composers liked his ideas 'so much that they felt the need to avail themselves of them'.

It is not my intention here to provide a comprehensive analysis of *The Well-Tuned Piano*, least of all with detailed regard to the issue of tuning; Gann, in any case, has already accomplished this task quite brilliantly. What follows attempts merely to establish the nature and estimate the significance of the work, in terms of Young's evolution of minimalism, by charting a little of its history, and giving some examples both of its basic material and of the structural context into which the improvisational elaborations of this material are fitted. This discussion draws not only on the 'score', but also on hearings of a number of recordings of *The Well-Tuned Piano*, going back to the 1964 tapes – not only the commercial recording of 1981, on which Gann's article is largely based. And though the booklet notes to the Gramavision release of the 1981 recording give an account of the evolution of the work to that date, they do not include the advances made in 1987.

In the spring and summer of 1964, when Young made the first tapes of *The Well-Tuned Piano*, he only had a small spinet-type piano that he had recently been given by Zazeela's parents; though almost thirty years old, the composer had never had regular access to a piano of his own before. On 23 March, he began to retune this instrument in just intonation, and soon began to play short improvisations on it. The justly tuned modality which is central to *The Well-Tuned Piano* establishes a natural link with Young's sopranino saxophone improvisations of 1962–4, on concluding which, work on this composition began. *The Well-Tuned Piano* takes as its fundamental, its 'tonic', the E♭ on the seventh chord of which he had built so many saxophone improvisations. The choice has already been explained in terms of the sopranino saxophone's structure itself; in applying this to the keyboard, Young was also following an established trend in blues playing developed over many decades. Using this E♭ as his fundamental, he devised a tuning of twelve frequencies evolved from the six used in *Pre-Tortoise Dream Music* which, earlier in 1964, had been the basis of the first sopranino saxophone improvisations to attempt just intonation. This tuning is also based on the same ratios factorable by 2, 3 and 7 used in such improvisations with the Theatre of Eternal Music as the already discussed *The Day of the Antler.*

A further connection with the saxophone improvisations is made via the 'fast combination/permutation' techniques Young now again employs on the piano, based on those he used in the work with saxophone. In *The Well-Tuned Piano*, these were to become what the composer calls 'clouds'. On the 1964 tapes, these 'clouds' are already present, if in vestigial form, as fast permutations on a single handful, sometimes two handfuls, of notes. Only later, though, does Young introduce a dimension crucial to the impact of these 'clouds': the *sostenuto* pedal lacking on the original spinet piano.

In other respects, too, the first attempts at *The Well-Tuned Piano* are, not surprisingly, more in the nature of experiments than fully formed structures. While three main 'chordal areas' – which Young calls 'The Opening Chord', 'The Tamiar Dream Chord' and 'The Early Romantic Chord' – were established in 1964, their articulation was achieved mainly by means of the fast permutation technique with fairly primitive results. By the time Fabio Sargentini arranged the first public performances of *The Well-Tuned Piano*, in Rome ten years later, Young had modified the tuning and, more importantly, obtained a Bösendorfer piano, which Sargentini purchased for his exclusive use. In 1976, the Dia Art Foundation purchased for Young a large Imperial Bösendorfer which, after custom work done under the composer's direction, was flown to New York, and between 1979 and 1985, housed permanently at Harrison Street.

Young had also begun to develop a much wider range of material. Though in 1974/5 this was still essentially in the form of 'chordal areas', the following years – culminating in the performances of 1981, which took place in Harrison Street – saw the invention of fully fledged themes, as well as greater and greater elaborations of the basic chords, proliferating into sets and subsets with exotic names such as 'The Deep in the Rainforest Chord' and 'The Ethers Churn (The Dinosaurs Dance)'. Already in 1981, Young had assembled themes with a surprising, and post-modernist, range of references to other musics, as their titles also hint at: 'The Homage to Brahms Variation of The Theme of The Dawn of Eternal Time', 'Young's Böse Brontosaurus Boogie', 'Scheherazade'. By the time of the 1987 performances, a further category of themes – 'Orpheus and Eurydice in The Elysian Fields' – had been added. Some of the material of *The Well-Tuned Piano* dates back as far as the improvisations Young used to perform in his late teens on his maternal grandmother's piano. One category of material, in particular – what the composer calls 'the more classic-sounding themes' – derives, at least in part, from this source. Example 1.10 illustrates something of the range of the material, both chordal and thematic, on which *The Well-Tuned Piano* is based.

The ideal conditions in which the piano was eventually housed permitted the further development of one of the most important discoveries that work on *The Well-Tuned Piano* had thrown up. The combination of increasingly precise tuning and the fast combination/permutation finger techniques Young had by now perfected allowed some of the composite waveforms to become audible. 'Extraordinary periodic acoustical beats became suspended in the air like a cloud over the piano', writes the composer, 'sometimes even filling the entire space during the energy accumulations of the longest passages'.[104] One development which significantly enhanced the range and impact of the 'clouds' was Young's discovery – in 1975, during a three-month-long Dream Festival at Dia's Wooster Street space – that he could synchronise the rhythms of the piano mechanism's hammers with the acoustical beats produced by his fast repeated playing. The result is 'a type of resonance system' in which the pulses of the hammer rhythms combine with those of the waveforms in a symbiotic sort of feedback; 'a controlled, audible, acoustical synchronization between rhythm and frequency in live performance (without the aid of electronics) for the first time in the history of music', Young argues.

Certainly, those who have most thoroughly investigated and exploited the connections between rhythm and frequency – Stockhausen, for example – have not only researched this with the aid of electronics but also employed tape or live electronics in realising its potential in actual compositions. Even if the claims seem a trifle hyperbolic, the effect of this synchronisation, cunningly exploited at length in the course of a slowly unfolding overall structure, is extremely powerful. The 'clouds' are central to *The Well-Tuned Piano*, leading the listener to experience a wide range of psycho-acoustic effects: French horns, saxophones and voices have all been heard on the 1987 tapes by the present author. In one of the Rome performances, Young even experimented with singing, using his own voice to provide a further dimension – acoustic this time, not psycho-acoustic – to

Example 1.10 *The Well-Tuned Piano*: (a) 'The Magic Opening Chord'; (b) 'The Romantic Chord'; (c) 'Theme for Orpheus and Eurydice in The Elysian Fields'; (d) a 'Blues Break from Young's Böse Brontesaurus Boogie'; (e) 'The Homage to Brahms Variation of the theme of the Dawn of Eternal Time'

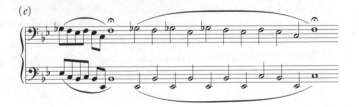

the experience. But although it was well received, he quickly found that it was very difficult, and he felt that it would be necessary to interweave the singing more systematically throughout the work to achieve a sense of timbral balance, which would have been even more difficult. Finally, he concluded that *The Well-Tuned Piano* was so complete in itself that, if anything, the addition of other timbres detracted from the achievement of the work as a piano solo. Though he tried it again in rehearsal at Harrison Street, he never repeated the experiment in a concert.

For each series of performances, Young has developed a clear notion of 'the current macro-structure', on which each individual performance will be based. Playing entirely from memory, he then improvises on a range of the material introduced above with reference to this overall scheme. With the 'piece in its present state of affairs', the structure would unfold along the following lines:

The Well-Tuned Piano: basic structural plan

'The Opening Chord'; E♭; mid-range, close position; simple statement
transition; adds notes to prepare for
'The Magic Chord'; A D; no pitches in common with 'The Opening Chord'
transition to
'The Magic Opening Chord'; E♭ B♭ and D A; mixes 'The Opening Chord' and 'The Magic Chord'; gradually unfolds in the setting of 'The Magic Harmonic Rainforest Chord' (most of the notes of the original E♭ key in a rising harmonic series, with 'The Magic Chord' added in); the longest section, with much new material added, including the major new section, 'Blues for Eurydice'
transition; unusual harmonic departures mixed with 'Baroque sequences'
'The Romantic Chord'; G-Dorian; from which 'The Magic Chord' is derived, since 'The Magic Chord' is a subset of 'The Romantic Chord'
'The Elysian Fields'; D-Aeolian
'Orpheus and Euridice in The Elysian Fields'; E♭ B♭ and D A, fused to create two new hyper-modes – one on D and one on E♭ – composed of similar-sized but not identical intervals, omitting the fourth degree
returning eventually to E♭ for
'The Ending', with a final statement, an octave lower, of the first two dyads of 'The Theme of The Dawn of Eternal Time'

Each of these main sections has many subsections within it, allowing many possibilities for varied development both of material and structure. But Young's intention is to allow the music to grow out of the opening notes 'in a way that to me sounds compositionally realistic and lifelike'. In part, this is achieved through statement, variation and restatement of the thematic material already discussed. But the structural evolution of *The Well-Tuned Piano* also owes a good deal to the key scheme which lies behind it. Beginning in E♭, this extends its way up into the harmonic series and eventually returns to the opening mode. Important in this unfolding of modal centres is the note D, which recurs throughout the work as an alternative to E♭, a procedure made more subtle and even ambiguous by the close proximity of these pitches in Young's tuning: the ratio of 64:63, or 27.26 cents. The prominence of the 'dominants' of these two pitches further complicates matters, making the mixed modality of 'The Magic Opening Chord', for example, ultimately describable only as E♭ B♭ with D A.

In addition, E♭'s seventh partial, notated as C, is used as a common pitch to link the original E♭ to the G-Dorian mode, in which this C now becomes the fourth degree. Present in 'The Opening Chord', but absent from 'The Magic Chord', C becomes crucial in the process of modulation away from and back to E♭. Its close relationship to G – which is present in 'The Magic Chord' – helps make these modulations possible, using not only common notes but those closely related to them to achieve smooth changes of mode. Modulation is generally considered problematic in just intonation. For Young, however, it is 'an exciting adventure more than a problem'. The basic difficulty he faces is the number of keys on the keyboard which, combined with the unusual nature of his chosen tuning, makes what might have appeared as closely related areas (modes a perfect fifth apart, for instance) linkable only with difficulty or compromise. Since both the D and D♭ keys were used up on other vital parts of Young's tuning, the flat minor seventh he required had to be played by the C key, already mentioned. This in turn led him to avoid using B♭ – the 'dominant' of the fundamental E♭ – as much as might have been expected, since the dominant of *its* dominant (C, a perfect fifth from F) is now already in use. This makes chord V in B♭ unavailable, and thus also its tonicisation, at least in the same way as E♭ could be tonicised. Some of the 1987 version's 'Boogie' material, which the composer describes as 'a kind of blues in B♭', is in that key, using E♭ as its IV in a typical blues manner, but using chord V sparingly and without sounding its fifth, C.

It would be foolish to deny that minimalist elements can be found even in the 1987 realisations of *The Well-Tuned Piano*. Its use of combination/permutation techniques on sets of pitch clusters, and more generally of both extended repetition and modality, represent some of the classic minimalist traits as defined both by this book and by Young himself, who employs the term with respect to *The Well-Tuned Piano* almost as cheerfully as he does with respect to *Trio for Strings*. But the work is much more besides. It confronts the challenge of building an extended musical edifice with the aid of themes and their development, which involves variation, extension and combination, not merely repetition. In particular, it employs a sophisticated large-scale formal approach that has significant evolutionary tendencies which listeners to *The Well-Tuned Piano* are encouraged to appreciate over audaciously long spans of time, and which bring to the work not only a sense of grand design but also of tension and growth, dynamism, climax and resolution. As we have seen, this is achieved through pitch structure as well as thematically. It is influenced, perhaps particularly, by Young's deeper experience of Indian classical music through his studies with Pran Nath, who taught him that modal music need not be purely static, but could change and evolve in dramatic spans of cumulative power.

In its concern for the drama of development and contrast, the overall form of *The Well-Tuned Piano* – at least in its realisations of 1981 and 1987 – is not minimalist at all but, as Daniel Wolf has said, 'maximal'.[105] In 1964, however, this structural sense was as lacking as the material was athematic. Even the available versions of 1974 and 1975, while wider in their range of material and more evolved structurally, did not aim at the sort of dramatic curve embraced by the later performances; the methods by which even such thematic material as exists is articulated and elaborated remain fundamentally minimalist. To that extent, Young's development of *The Well-Tuned Piano* to the mid-1970s runs in parallel with that of his colleagues.

In his commitment to just intonation, however, Young is unparalleled. As Gann puts it:

> This is a very original twelve-pitch tuning, quite unlike the keyboard tunings of any other composer. . . . What [Young] gains from limiting his scale steps is, not only an exotic abundance of tiny intervals, but a flexibility in harmonic modulation potential that few just intonation tunings possess. Harmonic flexibility is given precedence over filling out the melodic space. The tuning grew from the harmonic structure, and melodic considerations came afterward.[106]

In this respect, *The Well-Tuned Piano* stands as the greatest testament to its composer's belief that '[e]qual temperament reminds one of the truth; just intonation *is* the truth'.

Conclusion

Despite the distance he has travelled since *Trio for Strings* and *Composition 1960 #7*, Young's output of the late 1950s and early 1960s remains an enduring legacy to other composers. Terry Jennings was the first composer to imitate his long-note approach, and other close associates in the late 1950s – such as Dennis Johnson, whose work remains almost totally unknown, and Pauline Oliveros, whose work as composer, improviser and teacher is highly regarded, particularly in the USA – were also strongly affected by Young's early compositions. The swift loss – largely deliberate – of his position as New York's leading avant-garde figurehead, combined with his move away from conceptualism and performance art, served to reduce Young's significance for non-musicians in the New York avant-garde community after 1961. Yet many artists associated with Fluxus were influenced by his conceptual output of 1960–61, which – not least on account of its shock value and susceptibility to cheap imitation – still passes for Young's main achievement in the history of music as well as that of avant-garde art.

Young's influence on John Cage in the 1960s has already been discussed. His influence on already established composers who were themselves his student mentors is not, however, confined to Cage. Karlheinz Stockhausen's exploration of the harmonic series, notably in *Stimmung* (1968), has often been linked to Young's example. Less noted is his possible impact on *Klavierstück IX*, the piano piece by Stockhausen which is similarly dominated by a dissonant chord, repeated in sequences governed by the Fibonacci series. Cardew once described *Klavierstück IX* as a 'weak, aesthetic version'[107] of *Arabic Numeral (any integer) to H. F*, composed and first circulated in 1960. The original version of Stockhausen's piece is dated 1954, but he revised it in 1961, and surely heard, or at least heard about, Young's notoriously repetitive work in the meantime. The German composer seems to have visited Young and Zazeela when in New York, in 1964 or 1965, and listened to a rehearsal of The Theatre of Eternal Music. He requested tapes of the group's performances which, perhaps surprisingly, Young gave him. Stockhausen's own musicians visited Young and Zazeela's Dream House installation in Antwerp in 1969.

Well known from quite early on in parts of Europe, and in Japan, Young has influenced many non-American composers. Some became close colleagues: for example, the Swede Christer Hennix, who has also lent her talents in mathematics and acoustic theory to Young's investigation of intervals based on prime number ratios.[108] The list of non-Americans influenced by Young's early works and ideas includes Werner Durand, Takehisa Kosugi, Yuji Takahashi and Michael von Biel.

In Britain, which he did not visit for a public concert of his work until 1989, the composer became known chiefly through the advocacy of Cornelius Cardew, who met him in Stockhausen's Darmstadt class in 1959 and was involved in some of the early European performances of *Poem*. Cardew also subsequently visited Young in New York, and his own incorporation of improvisation into an 'experimental' approach to composition was inspired not only by the early pieces but also by the work of The Theatre of Eternal Music. Many English 'experimental' composers first learnt about Young through Cardew's correspondence and visits in the 1960s. Young first visited Britain professionally when he lectured during a Tape Concert in London's Place Theatre on 20 July 1970, organised by the Scratch Orchestra, at which a recording of The Theatre of Eternal Music was played. On 22 June 1989, an Almeida Festival programme, for which the composer came to London, was devoted entirely to his early output, including *Trio for Strings*.

Young's obsessive work since the early 1960s – and especially the conclusions from his work into tuning – has produced a creative cauldron from which many others have extracted ideas and inspiration. Though the extent of his influence has been limited by lack of access both to the music itself and to the theoretical work which helped fuel it, both musicians and non-musicians have been affected by Young's example. In this respect, the structural complexity and sophistication of *The Well-Tuned Piano* must be accounted as being of perhaps even greater significance than his work with The Theatre of Eternal Music. Drones, clusters and sheer volume are all too easily imitated. But a number of composers have seized his ideas about the potential of these things for exploring the innards of sound through the harmonic series and developed them along individual lines.

The influence of the Young of the Theatre of Eternal Music as opposed to that of the Theatre of the Singular Event can be measured partly via the group's own performers, who now cover several different generations of composers and other musicians. After the early years detailed above – involving John Cale, Tony Conrad, Terry Riley and others – The Theatre of Eternal Music's later incarnations from 1969 onwards involved musicians who went on to explore a variety of approaches: some venturing far away from Young's own style but all owing a debt to him for his approach to sustained sounds and their tuning. Jon Hassell, who first heard tapes of Young's saxophone improvisations when a composition pupil of Stockhausen, was a member of the group from 1971 to 1975; his own studies with Pran Nath encouraged him to invent a 'vocal' style for his trumpet playing. David Rosenboom, an important music theorist as well as composer, was a viola player in the group at this time. Younger generations of composer-performers involved with The Theatre of Eternal Music include another trumpet player, Ben Neill, and the cellist Charles Curtis, and many others who have more recently played in the various incarnations of The Theatre of Eternal Music Big Band and the composer's Forever Bad Blues Band.

In the USA, many composers have acknowledged Young's influence, and some have also studied as well as worked with him. These names include Glenn Branca, Jon Catler, Rhys Chatham, Alex Dea, Arnold Dreyblatt, David Hykes, Donald Miller and Raphael Mostel, several of them important members of the downtown Manhattan music scene from the 1970s onwards. Others particularly attracted by Young's concern with just intonation include Kyle Gann, Michael Harrison – the only other musician besides Young to be permitted to perform *The Well-Tuned Piano* – Michael Schumacher and Daniel Wolf.

Some of the above musicians – including Branca, Chatham and Hassell – have taken Young's ideas further than he has done himself into areas beyond the musical avant-garde, and from early on, the composer's influence has been felt in a variety of other arenas. The second half of the 1962 programme which saw the New York première of *Trio for Strings* saw an hour-long performance of *Composition 1960 #7* – the sustained B and F♯ piece – which was seemingly attended by Andy Warhol; his static films – for some of which Young was asked to provide music – were perhaps influenced by the composer's static sounds.[109] The Velvet Underground, the group popularised by Warhol, and its predecessor, The Primitives, are but two examples of the influence Young has had on 'alternative' rock and other musics related to it. Cale and MacLise, who formed The Primitives with Sterling Morrison and Lou Reed, had worked with Young; Walter de Maria and Henry Flynt, other associates of the composer, played in both groups at various times. Reed – who, according to Conrad,[110] was already tuning his guitar to a single pitch when in The Primitives – acknowledges Young as an inspiration behind his own *Metal Machine Music* in that double album's accompanying notes.[111] Musicians subsequently influenced by Young include Brian Eno – who says that *Arabic Numeral* was 'the first piece of music I ever performed publicly',[112] as early as 1967, and who once proposed that 'La Monte Young is the daddy of us all'[113] – and, more recently, the English rock group Spiritualized.[114]

It was, however, Terry Riley who responded with the greatest individuality to his student colleague's startling radicalism. And it is Riley who produced, as a direct result of Young's example and encouragement, the music which ultimately proved of greatest consequence to the furtherance of 'mainstream' musical minimalism, as we shall see in the next chapter.

2 Terry Riley

True to his hippie image, Terry Riley is a natural wanderer: happy anywhere, at home nowhere, except perhaps in the forests of the Sierra Nevada foothills where he was born. But his career can be divided geographically into three broad parts: his childhood and student years chiefly in northern California; a time spent largely away from the West Coast – mainly in France and New York, but also in Scandinavia, Morocco and Mexico; and the period of his return to the rural California of his birth, where he has lived since 1974. Though largely absent from the West Coast for about eight years – he was twenty-six when he left for Europe – Riley returned to San Francisco before moving to New York; it was during these eighteen months that the première of *In C* took place. In terms of his output as a minimalist, the story conventionally starts there, when the composer was twenty-nine; but it should really begin some three years earlier, with the innovative tape pieces that helped prepare the way for the work that represents not only Riley's personal breakthrough, but also what is perhaps the key moment in the development of musical minimalism.

Despite this early interest in the medium of tape, improvisation is as central to Riley's development as it is to Young's. His approach to improvisation also tends to be more intuitive than that of his colleague; and this lack of theoretical baggage has implications not only for the difficulties of separating 'composition' from 'improvisation' already observed with Young, but also for the continuity of Riley's career as a minimalist composer. It is, for instance, possible to argue that this career not only begins but ends with *In C* and the *Keyboard Studies* (composed and begun, respectively, in 1964), if we confine the term to notated music using modular repetition which is available for others besides the composer himself to perform. Between these pieces and the works composed for the Kronos Quartet in the 1980s, Riley concerned himself mainly with the invention of material, very little of it committed to notation, to use as the basis for solo improvisations.

It could also be argued that *Shri Camel* (1975 onwards; the commercial recording was made in 1977, though not issued until 1980) marks the end of Riley's interest in minimalism, as previously defined in this book, more clearly than the 1974 version of Young's *The Well-Tuned Piano* does for his. The consequences of its new approach to harmony and counterpoint could only be fully exploited later, in both the composed and the improvised musics of the 1980s and 1990s, which have rather different goals.

As suggested above, even Riley's output between *c.* 1962 and *c.* 1971 may be further subdivided: not only into the genres of tape compositions, notated pieces and solo improvisations – each of which to some extent have different concerns and functions – but also according to the degrees of structural freedom and stylistic variety Riley wished to encompass at this time. The handful of notated compositions after *In C* reflect this seminal work's influence more directly than do either the tape pieces or the solo improvisations. After *In C* and the *Keyboard Studies* which immediately followed it, however, Riley's music already begins to change.

Though Young and Riley come from somewhat similar backgrounds, have been friends for nearly forty years, have often worked closely together and retain a considerable admiration for each other, they are, both as musicians and as people, extremely different. Riley is ultimately interested only in what he is currently doing. He has little energy or inclination for keeping scores or tapes, a poor memory for detail and scant sympathy for anyone who regards the keeping of the historical record – even a purely musical one, let alone biography – as important and meaningful. Several tape pieces and quite a lot of notated compositions by Riley have been lost, due in part to the fact that the composer moved around a lot during the 1960s. Some years ago – significantly, he cannot remember when – he decided to turn out a lot of old tapes and scores of his work; many of these had only survived because his mother had kept them while her son and family were so much on the road. He had already packed them into his pick-up truck to take them to the dump when his wife, on discovering what he was doing, persuaded him not to destroy them. 'There are wrong dates on all my compositions', he says; 'there are always two dates on each score'.[1] Like his music, Riley lives for the moment, to an extent which is unusual for a man aged over sixty. The consequences for any attempt to provide a complete and accurate account of his development will be obvious.

Early years

Terry Mitchell Riley was born on 24 June 1935 in Colfax, California, in the Sierra Nevada foothills not far from where he still lives. As his name suggests, Riley's father was of Irish ancestry, probably American immigrants due to the potato famine of the late 1840s. His mother was from

Italian stock; both parents were born in the USA. Riley's maternal grandfather ended up in Colfax largely because it was a railroad town on the main New York to San Francisco route.

When Riley was about five, the family moved to nearby Redding, but during the Second World War became rather mobile. The composer's father was in the Marine Corps and took part in the Pacific Campaign; the young Riley was brought up by the composer's Italian immigrant maternal grandparents, speaking Italian and imbibing Italian culture. For a while, the family lived in Los Angeles. His parents were quite keen music lovers, but did not play; a maternal uncle, though, played the bass in several bands. Riley has said he was 'always doing music; almost before I could talk I could sing all the songs on the radio'.[2] His first musical experiences seem to have come via the 'standards' of Cole Porter, George Gershwin and Richard Rogers, and the 'cowboy' traditions of country and western music, as was the case with La Monte Young. But later there were the popular classics as well. Violin lessons began when he was five or six, piano lessons a little later. He first learned the piano by ear, even picking up the practice of improvising on themes from the Classical and Romantic repertoire – such as Tchaikovsky's First Piano Concerto – from an older cousin; it was not until the age of eleven or twelve that he began to learn music from scores. In 1945 he recalls Dizzie Gillespie and Charlie Parker being the subject of a cover feature in *Life* magazine; he read the article over and over again, but couldn't actually get to hear any of their music at that stage. The record store in Redding almost exclusively stocked cowboy music.

Back in Redding after the War, Riley went to high school, where his music teacher, Ralph Wadsworth, introduced him to Bartók, Stravinsky and other modern composers. Between December 1952 and June 1953 – in his final year in high school – Riley accompanied his parents to Beaufort, South Carolina, which gave him the chance to experience the American South. Then, back home between 1953 and 1955, he attended Shasta Junior College. Besides the financial advantages of staying at home, Duane Hampton, a piano teacher with an excellent reputation from his days at the prestigious Curtis Institute in Philadelphia, had come to Redding, and Riley had lessons with him for about two years. For a while, with Hampton's encouragement, he contemplated a career as a concert pianist, and took part in a performance of Poulenc's Concerto for Two Pianos.

Riley finally reached San Francisco in September 1955, enrolling at San Francisco State University for two years. He also had piano lessons at San Francisco Conservatory with Adolf Baller, Hampton's own teacher, playing Poulenc's Piano Concerto, with a second piano, for his senior recital. At university, he took up composition, merely to see if he had any talent for it. He had lessons with Wendall Otey; student colleagues included Ken Benshoof, Pauline Oliveros and Loren Rush. In his senior year, Riley decided that his late start to serious piano studies, erratic practising and nerves precluded a career as a concert pianist. Encouraged by the reactions to his composing, he started to write more music. Some time during his last months at San Francisco State, from where he graduated in June 1957, Riley wrote the earliest piece to exist on his present worklist: a *Trio* for violin, clarinet and piano. Now lost, it is described by its composer as 'neo-classic'; some songs – a couple from 1957 survive – are a little more chromatic.

Riley married Anne Smith, an elementary schoolteacher, in January 1958; they had a daughter, Colleen, the following September. (Two sons – Shahn and Gyan – were born much later, in 1973 and 1977, respectively.) He took various jobs – in a grocery store and, in particular, with an airline company – to support his new family, but managed to find some time for composing, studying privately with Robert Erickson, to whom he had been introduced by Oliveros and Rush. Riley was especially impressed by Erickson's ability to suggest new ways of developing one's material without imposing his own compositional personality on his students. Even after he went to Berkeley, he continued to go to Erickson, regarding him as 'a beacon of sanity in the midst of the Berkeley scene which I didn't like at all'.

From this period – around 1958 – we have two surviving piano pieces which Riley describes as being written 'in a free chromatic style' influenced by Schoenberg's piano pieces, opp. 11 and 19. Curiously, in view of his later development, Riley was attracted by Schoenberg's rhythmic fluidity, which contrasted sharply with the motoric rhythms of much neo-classical music. Far from being the enforced product of a repressive academic environment, this idiom was something he excitedly explored with Erickson's help at this time. Twelve-note music, on the other hand, 'didn't feel good. It was too full of anxiety, too dark; it had such a narrow range'.

Some time during 1958 or 1959, he formed an improvising trio with Oliveros and Rush, initially to record music for a film entitled *Polyester Moon*, based on polyester sculptures by Claire Falkenstein. The group performed what seem to have been free improvisations in a non-jazz style at a time when such activities were still rare. Riley played piano, Oliveros the French horn and probably the accordion, and Rush an assortment of instruments including the bassoon and the koto. This experience was important in suggesting to Riley that improvisation, which he already felt to be his natural mode of expression, could be creatively explored quite independently of any jazz idiom; though jazz, too, has been crucial to his development.

Berkeley: Young, Stockhausen and Cage; Maxfield and tape composition

In the spring of 1959, as soon as his wife was able to teach, and was therefore able to support the family, Riley enrolled at Berkeley. Despite already auditing classes, and having had some piano pieces played in class by Rush, the twenty-three-year-old composer initially failed the graduate entry examinations in harmony and counterpoint (he had never even done species counterpoint) and had to take remedial classes. First joining Seymour Shifrin's composition class, he subsequently moved on to William Denny; his other teachers included Arnold Elston. But unlike Erickson, Shifrin and the others seemed to embody a notion of academic composition which he felt to be superficial; besides, Riley has never felt at ease in any academic situation. Though he says that none of his teachers at Berkeley was themself a serialist, it appears that serial compositional projects were more acceptable to them than the work he really wanted to do. Accordingly, he submitted exercises in a kind of integral serialism for his degree – work he has not kept – while engaging privately on compositions and related activities that he mostly never showed his teachers at all.

Chief among Riley's student encounters was the close relationship he established with Young, whom he met through Shifrin's class. Young's experience as a jazz musician and knowledge of developments in contemporary art music far exceeded Riley's own at this time. Yet he needed a collaborator in his new avant-garde activities, and Riley was extremely willing, sympathetic and highly talented. A major problem Riley's teachers at Berkeley seem to have had with him was that they felt the talented composer of those earlier piano pieces influenced by Schoenberg 'was being corrupted by La Monte'.

With Young's help, Riley now quite methodically worked his way through the more progressive developments in contemporary music. He became fascinated by the rhythmic complexity that Stockhausen was generating; *Zeitmasze*, in particular, became important for him, for its simultaneous presentation of different tempi. Riley's *Spectra* for a sextet of flute, clarinet, bassoon, violin, viola and cello (dated 28 December 1959) asks for just two speeds at once, but also incorporates sustained sounds longer than those in Stockhausen's work; again, suggestive of the influence of Young, despite the fact that Riley had missed the student playthrough of *Trio for Strings* in September 1958.

His interest in sustained sounds was explored further in a single-movement String Quartet (dated 31 May 1960), lasting some ten or twelve minutes. After their marriage, the Rileys moved to Potrero Hill in Bernal Heights, then a blue-collar suburb of San Francisco; the sounds of multiple foghorns going off in the Bay were a permanent fixture of the soundscape of this community. The constant permutations of the pitches of these foghorns fascinated him; though they recurred at the same register, they seemed to have no pattern. Without the example of Young's *Trio for Strings*, however, Riley admits he would never have thought of writing a piece based on foghorn pitches; the Quartet is influenced by Young's interest in repeating and returning to a pitch at the same register. He wrote the piece on a practice-room organ at Berkeley, which allowed him to experiment with sustaining pitches for long periods, entirely intuitively, and to 'get a feeling for what the effect would be on a string quartet'. *Pace* Edward Strickland, the work is not a diatonic composition in C major, but rather an atonal one without a key signature.[3] Dynamically, though, the Quartet offers a radical approach: soft throughout, all the markings are *piano* or lower, going down to *pppp*. Within this context, the piece concentrates on single notes in constantly and unsystematically overlapping and changing pitch permutations, rather than anything resembling melody; texturally and tonally, as well as dynamically, it offers a flat landscape with minimum contrasts.

The Quartet and the later piece which is in certain respects its companion – the String Trio of 1961 – both suggest moves in the direction of the kind of minimalism already being explored by Young. Between the two works, however, come several demonstrating a less clear line of development. *Envelope*, dated July 1960, has no score, but totally independent parts for four instruments – alto saxophone, French horn, violin and piano – each of which, according to the materials, 'may be played as a solo or in any combination with the other parts'; its flexible and unsynchronised movement through the notated material points towards *In C*. For Ann Halprin's dance workshop, another collaborative venture with Young, Riley produced *Concert Piece for Two Pianists and Tape Recorder* (probably March or April 1960). As published in *An Anthology*,[4] this consists of two pages of graphic indications for two performers playing on two pianos. Some of the graphics are meaningful, though not explained in the score itself: one turns out to be an ashtray placed on the piano strings; another, a picture of Young lying inside the piano. Otherwise though, Riley says, 'it's bullshit'. The score only existed in order to qualify the performance for inclusion in a symposium concert of student compositions at Brigham Young University in Provo, Utah, on 30 April 1960, at which Young's *Poem* was also performed. In addition, Riley made five mono tapes at Halprin's studio which he describes as '*musique concrète* sounds . . . rolling steel marbles and stuff across the piano sounding board, using that as an echo device'. A surviving, and delightfully amusing, tape of the performance bears out the anarchic manner typical of such experiments in sound.

Both friends obtained a Berkeley scholarship. While Young used his to travel to New York in September 1960, Riley remained in the Bay Area to complete his M.A. Two failed attempts at a language examination, however, caused his graduation to be delayed until the summer of 1961. His remaining semesters were far less productive.

Riley's early efforts with tape technology were assisted by Richard Maxfield – yet another consequence of Young's friendship. The first of these pieces originated as music for another dance by Halprin, variously called *The Three-Legged Stool*, *The Four-Legged Stool* and *The Five-Legged Stool*. His contributions, assembled between late 1960 and the spring of 1961, included both instrumental and tape material, varying in content and assembly from performance to performance; he sometimes played piano amidst the dancers on stage. Using cheap, mono, reel-to-reel, Wollensak tape recorders, Riley now made tape loops for the first time, recording piano playing, speech, laughter and several found sounds. His Potrero Hill home gave him a 'beautiful view of the bay. It was a very romantic little spot, a very old cottage (which has since been torn down) which had a very small garden and a lot of wine bottles outside, and all the tape loops would go out the window of the studio, around the wine bottles, and back into the studio'.[5]

Late in 1961, Riley took the tapes he had made for *The Three-Legged Stool* as the basis of a tape composition called *Mescalin Mix*, or *M . . . Mix*, after the name of the psychedelic drug, discussed below. With help from Ramon Sender, he made use of an echoplex, a primitive electronic contraption allowing a sound to be repeated in an ever-accumulating counterpoint against itself. In *Mescalin Mix* – the only tape piece Riley composed before 1963 to survive – the multiple echo effect was applied to selected material from *The Three-Legged Stool* and, perhaps, some of the tapes for *Concert Piece*. While the sources of some of this material – vocal moanings, perhaps laughter, and what sounds like a popular song on a 'honky-tonk' piano – can be identified, much of it is so distorted

Example 2.1 *String Trio*, bars 1–8

that even the composer no longer recognises it. Frequencies could be altered by changing the speed of the tape, either gradually or suddenly, as well as accumulated and distorted by the echo device. Riley himself says that the results 'sounded just like an acid trip';[6] a lurid climax involving echo effects shortly before the end of this thirteen-and-a-half-minute piece helps bear this out. The repetition of short fragments of sound made possible by this technology suggested that repetition itself, rather than Young's concept of sustained sounds, could be made the chief means of musical organisation; repetition seemed, to Riley, endemic to working with tape.

Riley soon began to realise the potential that tape loops and echo devices held for his work without tape as well. The other work from this period is a String Trio which seems to have been the composer's belated final submission for graduation; the score is dated 2 May 1961. It is here that Riley first explores the modal pitch domain and regular rhythmic repetition which were to become central to his mature output. This single movement piece, lasting around fifteen minutes, is bounded by a kind of A-major tonality suggested at the outset by a constantly reiterated A C♯ quaver pulse on the viola (see Ex. 2.1). This modality is immediately challenged by the more chromatic and fragmented material which surrounds it, in music which is both rhythmically and texturally more varied than that of the earlier Quartet. But the pitches of the A-major triad, and to a certain extent a modality based on A – with some emphasis on the dominant E and a prominent place for C♮ as well as C♯ – retain their significance throughout: returning in a clearer form when the opening material is recapitulated, and maintaining a hold right to the ambiguous ending. Though less significant than Young's *Trio for Strings* of three years earlier, Riley's work, charting out a more diatonic territory in the context of repetition, is a tentative move towards *In C* of three years later.

Example 2.2 *Ear Piece*, complete text

THE PERFORMER TAKES ANY OBJECT(S) SUCH AS A PIECE OF PAPER CARDBOARD PLASTIC ETC AND PLACES IT ON HIS EAR(S) HE THEN PRODUCES THE SOUND BY RUBBING SCRATCHING TAPPING OR TEARING IT OR SIMPLY DRAGGING IT ACROSS HIS EAR HE ALSO MAY JUST HOLD IT THERE IT MAY BE PLAYED IN COUNTERPOINT WITH ANY OTHER PIECE OR SOUND SOURCE IF THE PERFORMER WEARS A HEARING AID IT WOULD BE BEST TO MAKE THE SOUNDS CLOSE TO THE MICROPHONE (OF THE HEARING AID) THE DURATION OF THE PERFORMANCE IS UP TO THE PERFORMER CHILDREN PERFORMING EARPIECE SHOULD BE WARNED NOT TO STICK THEIR FINGERS TOO FAR INTO THEIR EARS AS THEY MAY SERIOUSLY DAMAGE THE INNER EAR

Though tentative and far from all-pervading, this exploration of repetition in a modal context was to prove prescient. The discovery of a new approach to repetition in the electronic studio now combined with his earlier experiences to provide the true beginnings of his own style. The way now seemed clear for Riley to develop his own minimalist approach: based not on the sustained sounds which formed the starting point for Young's music, but on the creation of short patterns and their elaboration through constant repetition.

The two pieces he produced between graduating from Berkeley in the summer of 1961 and going to Europe in February 1962 reflect, however, like *Concert Piece*, Riley's involvement with performance art. *Ear Piece*, a text composition (reproduced as Ex. 2.2), arose from the correspondence Riley had begun with the artists with whom Young was working in New York; it also appeared in *An Anthology*. *Grab Bag* is a 'hanging sculpture' for 'a little theatre piece': underneath a poster board, with drawings on it and holes in it, hangs a bag containing a large number of verbal instructions for performers. Each player takes it in turn to reach into the bag for an instruction and perform such activities as playing without the mouthpiece and putting one's instrument back in its case and taking it out again. Riley eventually gave it to Young. 'I went through the history of Western music pretty much', the composer says, 'and Fluxus was the last stop on the road. . . . After that, I decided I had to do something. I'd gone through this whole thing, and I didn't know who I was'. The String Trio and his work with tape, however, were to provide the chief clues to Riley's subsequent development.

Europe: the search for the mystical experience

Feeling more than usually restless, Riley now determined to go to Europe: 'for reasons of health', states his biography in the programme note for the concert in which *In C* was premièred nearly three years later. On their way there in early 1962, he and his family stopped briefly in New York to see Young, leaving for France some time in February 1962. In the next two years, the Rileys spent a good deal of time there, particularly in Paris; at first, in the spring of 1962, they lived for several months in Algeciras in Spain. But they also travelled extensively, including more than one trip to Morocco, and a visit to what was then Leningrad, during which Riley worked with the Leningrad Jazz Quartet. During this period, Riley was to soak himself in cultures very different from those fully available to him as a Berkeley student.

Some of his activities in Europe continued avant-garde involvements already established back home. Riley took the opportunities offered by the sudden eruption of Fluxus activities at that time – in West Germany, in particular – to explore further the work of such artists as Erik Andersen, Jed Curtis, George Maciunas, Nam June Paik and Emmett Williams. Riley's *Concert Piece* was performed in Wiesbaden on 1 September 1962 in the opening concert of the large-scale Fluxus festival that year.[7] On the same programme was a performance of Philip Corner's *Piano Activities* by Maciunas, Williams and others, in the course of which a piano was destroyed; as a result of this experience, Riley decided that he wanted no more to do with the Fluxus movement. His *Ear Piece* was performed in the same festival on 14 September.

As dismaying to Riley was a visit to the Darmstadt Summer School the following year. The only soul-mates he could find were the Dutch composer Louis Andriessen and, despite his earlier resolve, several people – including Andersen and Curtis – involved with Fluxus. Another of this group was the Danish composer Henning Christiansen. As a result of meeting him, Riley participated soon afterwards in a happening on Christiansen's farm outside Copenhagen. On the same trip, he also visited Stockholm and worked in Finland on *Street Piece Helsinki*, an outdoor theatrical extravaganza conceived by the American writer and director Ken Dewey in collaboration with the Finnish composer and jazz and pop musician Otto Donner. In France shortly before this, Riley became involved in another alternative theatre project with Dewey, described below.

Three experiences conclusively turned Riley away from the models Darmstadt and Fluxus offered him. The first was a much greater immersion in ragtime, jazz and other so-called 'popular' Western musical forms. While at Berkeley, Riley had begun to study ragtime piano with Wally Rose. Being unsuccessful in his applications for grants and prizes, including the Prix de Rome, he had already put his skills to good use by playing ragtime piano in the Gold Street Saloon, on San Francisco's Barbary Coast, earning sufficient money during his final year in college and after to allow him and his family to travel to France. Now, he spent much of his time as pianist for a variety of club and cabaret work, including a spell at Fred Payne's Artists' Bar on the Place Pigalle in Paris. Elsewhere, he played for floor shows with circus acts (also driving the variety show agent's bus), and for dances in the officers' clubs of NATO bases in France. The circus acts proved especially entertaining, since they required Riley to provide musical accompaniment for everything from men shooting cigars out of women's mouths with a bow-and-arrow to contortionists. Almost thirty years later, one of these experiences provided the basis for 'Rubberlady's Theme Music', the foxtrot that forms the third movement of *The Sands*, a work for string quartet and orchestra in four movements composed in 1991. The officers' clubs proved especially lucrative, since they paid at American rates. Among others, Riley worked with a saxophonist named Sonny Lewis, who was to become a frequent collaborator.

Unlike Young, Riley enjoyed the social atmosphere which comes with such musical experiences, finding it more suited to his personality and outlook. Playing ragtime, blues and improvising on jazz 'standards', he began to see the potential tonality held both expressively and structurally, and to consider how he might best develop his own approach outwards from this, rather than from his university training. As Young had taught him, the reason one never tires of listening to the blues, which makes extensive use of the Dorian mode, is that its pitches 'are in perfect agreement with the overtone series of the fundamental pitch. You can keep singing the blues for ever because it's one of the few scales that are built absolutely on a chord of nature'.[8] To this day, he feels that his own music 'abstract[s] this love that I have for "standards" into another form'.

The second important aspect of Riley's European experiences arose from finding himself close to sources of non-Western musics largely new to him. In the 1950s, he had scarcely been aware of the existence of non-Western musics, even after he moved to San Francisco and despite his experiences with Rush and Young. Riley recalls that he failed to get to Ravi Shankar's first concert in San Francisco some time in the late 1950s. The first non-Western musics which seriously influenced him were the Moroccan and other North African musics he heard on the radio while living in Algeciras, only some twenty miles from the Straits of Gibraltar. Riley became obsessed by the way in which this music subjected small amounts of material to extensive repetition, including the use of cyclic techniques, and its ability to sustain interest over long periods through melodic improvisation over static harmony. One of the only two records he carried with him on his travels was a French BAM disc of Moroccan music. The other – *Cookin' With The Miles Davis Quintet* (1961), with its explorations of the different ways in which repetition and modality could refocus the relationship between a melody and the rhythmic basis familiar from earlier jazz – invited Riley to explore the links between Moroccan music and jazz, and to see more clearly the potential of both for his own work. He was helped to these conclusions by the discoveries made around this time by John Coltrane, to whose music Young had introduced him in Berkeley. Coltrane's modal and free-jazz innovations of the early 1960s – from the popularity of 'My Favorite Things' (various recorded versions from 1961 onwards) to the more esoteric *Impressions* and *Ascension* albums (1961–3 and 1965, respectively) – were much influenced by non-Western musics, not least by Moroccan Maqamat. The combination of modality and repetition was crucial to both, and the similarities were enhanced by the extent to which Coltrane's reedy soprano saxophone sounded like the double-reed instruments of the Middle East – and also of India, which was subsequently to be important for both men too. A further loop is thus created in a cycle of influences that all seemed to point in the same direction. Riley was later inspired by Coltrane's playing to take up the soprano saxophone. Jazz, Moroccan music and the example of Young all helped point the way to Riley at this time, not least through what they all had most importantly in common: 'a daily process of learning to improvise, and what all that meant', as the composer has said.

But the main reason for Riley's move towards modal improvisation, he has said, 'was that my own spirit felt happy with it. I could do it for a long time and still feel good, still feel balanced and centered'.[9] Although his knowledge of Moroccan music was derived largely from radio and recordings, the composer also visited Morocco on several occasions. While he was fascinated musically both by the lively street music he encountered and by the Islamic calls to prayer to be heard issuing from the minarets, a major reason for his visits was the search for the hallucinogenic drugs readily available there. Like Young, Riley now finds it difficult to talk about this aspect of his life. Like Young, too, he is concerned both to stress the spiritual and creative possibilities it opens up, and to make clear that, despite the much wider availability of various drugs today, he no longer takes anything besides alcohol. It is evident, however, that Riley's hallucinogenic experiences were as crucial to both his spiritual and musical development as Young's were for him.

In the late 1950s, indeed, Young seems to have been responsible for Riley's first experiences of marijuana; they also had peyote together for the first time. 'When I took peyote', Riley relates, 'then I really saw the sacredness of music'. In the late 1950s and early 1960s, various mind-opening drugs were important to the Beat poets, many of whom settled in the North Beach area of San Francisco. It was via this flourishing counter-culture that Riley had his first experiences of mescaline, one of the earliest 'psychedelic' drugs to achieve wide distribution in the 1960s. When passing through New York in 1962 on his way to Europe, Riley had been given his first psilocybin mushrooms by Maxfield, whom he had already met through Young in Berkeley. In the 1960s, LSD was, he felt, 'the element of the consciousness-raising movement . . . and marijuana as a sister drug. . . . It had a lot to do with those times, you know. There was something emerging then that people were hungry for: almost as a public at large, especially young people. I know we weren't interested in making money; we were really only interested in having these mystical experiences'.

While it is possible to overplay these drug experiences *per se*, it is probably impossible to overemphasise the changes they helped to bring about in Riley's spiritual as well as musical development in the early 1960s. 'Besides just the ordinary music that was going on', the composer has said, 'music was also able to transport us suddenly out of one reality into another. Transport us so that we would almost be having visions as we were playing. So that's what I was thinking about before I wrote *In C*. I believe music, shamanism, and magic are all connected, and when it's used that way it creates the most beautiful use of music'.[10] He has also spoken of using drugs 'to remove certain filters that we have in our brain to make our lives more ordinary. These filters filter out the extra perceptions of angels and all the other things that would make our lives a little bit wild . . . .'[11] It was during this period that Riley firmly established for himself a real purpose and direction for his music, which was, in essence, to lend his work to the search for what the mystics would call enlightenment.

In this search, the taking of drugs was intimately linked to Riley's decision to explore a modal, rather than a chromatic, music. 'It wasn't just tied up with getting high', he recalls, 'it was tied up with trying to find this deeply spiritual quality of music, which modal music had'. Smoking marijuana, in particular, 'was probably the most influential thing that happened in my life. . . . And if the music had too much angularity in it, it would pull me out of this mood which it induces'. Such experiences were also connected to the ways in which repetition led to changing perceptions of what was being repeated. 'I think I was noticing', the composer has said, 'that things didn't sound the same when you heard them more than once. And the more you heard them, the more different they did sound. Even though something was staying the same, it was changing. I became fascinated with that'. It also had more specifically technical consequences, notably for the development of his keyboard playing, discussed below. These discoveries were eventually to lead Riley to find the musical 'real me' for whom he had been searching since the mid-1950s.

While in Europe, Riley says, 'the idea of the [tape] loops, the repetition and the different cycles all came together, staying in my mind'. Through the intervention of Dewey, Riley gained access to the ORTF radio studios in Paris. Here, he explained the looping technique with the echoplex he had used in San Francisco to a French technician, who proceeded to set up a tape-delay arrangement with two Ampex tape recorders to create what the composer calls 'the first time-lag accumulator'. This offered a more sophisticated application of delay devices than were possible with the echoplex used in *Mescalin Mix*, permitting a much cleaner and more vibrant-sounding build-up of layers of the same material repeated against itself. During 1962–3, however, this new opportunity was not pursued in compositions for live performance, but in a pair of pieces – one including live material for theatrical use, one for tape alone.

She Moves She *and* Music for 'The Gift'

The tape piece is entitled *She Moves She*, composed some time during the first half of 1963. The words 'she moves she', spoken by the actor John Graham, are accompanied by a percussive sound like that of a bolt being shot. The time-lag accumulator swiftly piles speech and sound up against each other to produce an increasingly blurred textural wash. While the words 'she moves she' always remain discernible amidst their multiple reiterations, the sonic impact of individual fragments soon seems more important than any conventional semantic hold they may retain: the 'sh' of the word 'she', for instance, quickly becomes detached to form a purely percussive counterpart to the original percussive sound – a 'resulting pattern', to use Steve Reich's terminology. Though *She Moves She* was originally conceived as a separate piece, it is also a part of the music Riley composed for a theatrical extravaganza called *The Gift*.

The mastermind behind this was Ken Dewey, who both wrote the play and directed its production, under the auspices of a festival in Paris, in which members of Living Theater and Halprin's company took part. Dewey had first presented *The Gift* in San Francisco in 1962. Described by Richard Kostelanetz as 'his first public quasi-mixed-means performance',[12] this involved the reinterpretation – the playwright/director's own word is 'resurfacing'[13] – of Dewey's original text in terms of movement and 'movement-dialogue with the environment' by John Graham and Lynn Palmer. The production was mounted in some half-dozen venues, including a church, the deck of a boat Halprin owned and the streets of San Francisco. The following year, Dewey rented an old chateau outside Paris, where a more lavish version of *The Gift* was devised in the summer of 1963. Jerry Walters, a sculptor, constructed a huge mobile, which looked like a kind of aeroplane. The actors had to swing on this, a rather dangerous activity which included the need to avoid hitting the jazz musicians playing beneath. As a text, *The Gift* was what Riley describes as 'very minimal', with very few lines. The show itself changed quite substantially every night, and was sufficiently outrageous to provoke fights among the audience so boisterous that the musicians had to play very loudly to drown out the noise.

Chet Baker – the previously very popular jazz trumpeter who had recently been released from jail in Lucca, where he spent some time on a heroin charge – and his band supplied the main musical forces for *The Gift*, and acted as well as played; one night, Baker didn't show up and Riley had to take his place. Riley added tape material, including *She Moves She* as well as what came to be known as *Music for 'The Gift'*. On the last evening, an actor who had the line 'This is an incredible experience', followed this by destroying the tape recorder, as a result of which some tapes were also lost. *She Moves She* turns out to be based on a line from Dewey's play – 'She moves, she follows' – from which Riley cut the final word.

Most of the half-dozen sections of the surviving twenty-three-minute tape now called *Music for 'The Gift'* seem merely fragments. They are mainly based on a recording of Baker's band playing Miles Davis's 'So What', from his 1959 album *Kind of Blue*; Riley recorded all the instruments individually, which then allowed him to cut up and reassemble the lines as he chose. Davis's abandonment of traditional chord changes in favour of a modal approach involving a much smaller number of harmonic shifts – an approach made famous by 'So What' – was in itself a gift to someone exploring the possibilities of using the time-lag accumulator on such instrumental material for the first time. While allowing Riley to obtain rich cumulative effects, it avoided the sort of clashes inevitable when subjecting to such processes any music with a faster rate of harmonic change. The distinctive bass riff of the original was piled on top of itself to produce 'six layers of bass',[14] which were then subjected to further looping and other modifications. The result was a complex counterpoint, involving multiples of various instruments, in which Davis's original is for the most part undetectable. *She Moves She* itself also makes appearances from time to time.

While the constantly repeated 'answer' to the bass riff of Davis's 'So What' can still be perceived, contrapuntal detail is largely inaudible, since once the time-lag accumulator has really begun to do its work, the interaction of long loops in multiple pile-ups produces an essentially textural effect. Though some passages – especially those built from double bass riffs – exhibit a regular rhythm, the repetitive figures of *Music for 'The Gift'* are not played out against any pulsing grid; Riley has said that the work 'didn't have anything to do with pulse. It was much more dreamlike'.[15]

Music for 'The Gift' is, however, far from devoid of musical subtlety or significance. According to Riley, the decision – apparently Baker's – to use Davis's 'So What' was 'a masterstroke', since the bridge of the original is a semitone higher than the main section: sixteen bars of Dorian on D, followed by eight bars of Dorian on E♭. When what the composer calls the 'fields of loops' based on the Dorian mode on E♭ were mixed with those on the Dorian on D, 'it would be like a wash of colour. And then I'd gradually take away the D, and you'd have this modulation that was half a tone apart. . . . It's one of the most beautiful tonal effects I've ever heard, because it's just a half step taking over from another – a whole mode taking over from another'.

Music for 'The Gift' is the most significant work of Riley's before *In C*, marking the point when he 'really started understanding what repetition could do for musical form'.[16] It proved that it was possible to apply the principles of delay and accumulation to pitched material, as well as to speech and other 'non-musical' sounds, to make a sophisticated composition. *Music for 'The Gift'* paved the way for the more important instrumental works from *In C* itself onwards.

On 23 November 1963, President John Kennedy was assassinated, and the clubs in which the composer earned his living were closed for a lengthy period as a mark of respect. With no savings to support his wife and daughter, and already owed a considerable sum of money by his agent, Riley decided they must return to America. Before that, though, they paid a further visit to Morocco during the Ramadan celebrations of that year.

Return to San Francisco

Riley and his family returned to San Francisco, probably in early 1964, and he resumed piano playing in bars and cabaret. At first, they lodged at his mother's house; later they eked out a bohemian existence in their own apartment on Boccana Street, at the top of Potrero Hill, near where they had lived when the composer was at Berkeley. It was in one of these two places – he cannot recall which – that Riley wrote *In C* some time during that spring. The piece, he has said, came to him one night on a bus, after months of failed attempts to follow up the ideas used in *Music for 'The Gift,'* when he 'started hearing the whole first line of *In C*. It just sort of came into my ear and I wrote it down and then started working it out from there, using the techniques I'd developed in Paris'.[17] The work lay around for several months, until either Sender or Morton Subotnick invited him to share a programme with James Tenney at the San Francisco Tape Music Center the following January. Plans were subsequently changed, and Riley presented a one-man show – called 'oneyoungamerican' – at the Center two months earlier, on 4 and 6 November 1964. In addition to the première performances of *In C* (the composition of which the programme erroneously dated October 1964), these concerts included five other works: *Music for 'The Gift'*, *Coule* (a version of the first *Keyboard Study*), and three tape compositions, *Shoeshine*, *I* and *In A♭ or is it B♭?*

Between the composition and the première of *In C*, Riley met Steve Reich. That May Reich had mounted four evenings including his own works at the San Francisco Mime Troupe Theater on Boccana Street at one of which, the story goes, Riley (who by then was living in the same street) had been present but left at the interval. The following day, Reich, who also lived close by, sought him out; with his natural impetuosity, he demanded to know why Riley had walked out of his concert. Despite this unpromising beginning, and the considerable differences of temperament between them, the two discovered they had a lot in common and became, for a while, close friends. On learning that Riley had an ensemble piece ready but no ensemble to perform it, Reich offered to help get some players together.

The thirteen-piece ensemble which finally premièred *In C* consisted largely of players Riley brought in: Werner Jepson (Wurlitzer electric piano), Sonny Lewis (the tenor saxophonist who had played with Riley in Europe), James Lowe (electric piano), who in turn was introduced by Lewis, Pauline Oliveros (accordion), Ramon Sender (who played a Chamberlain organ relayed from an upstairs studio), Stan Shaff (trumpet), Morton Subotnick (clarinet), Mel Weitsman (recorder), and Phil Windsor (trumpet), plus the composer himself on electric piano. With Reich, who also played electric piano, came two other performers: Jon Gibson (soprano saxophone) and Jeannie Brechan (electric piano), Reich's girlfriend at the time. In addition, an artist called Anthony Martin, also onstage, projected 'a rhythmic/melodic light composition' of various shapes and colours simultaneously with the music.

The composition of the group varied from rehearsal to rehearsal, with a hard core provided by Riley and Reich, Brechan and Gibson: 'whoever I could get to come and play for nothing', says the composer. Some of those who played at the première had never played the piece before. With such a radical work, allowing much room for improvisation, *In C* was assembled with a high degree of collective input. 'The room was full of composers', says Riley, 'and there were always people making suggestions'. Reich is correct, Riley thinks, in claiming that the pulse was his idea, but he has no clear memory of when this was introduced. The original intention had been to perform the work without a time-keeper of any kind, but this proved impossible. Reich, himself a percussionist, may have at first suggested a drum pulse; finally, though, *In C* was co-ordinated by the constant reiteration of two high Cs on the piano, played by Brechan.

In C

The score of *In C* consists of a single page containing fifty-three modules, presented in its entirety as Example 2.3. Reproduced on the sleeve of the LP disc issued by Columbia in 1968,[18] included in several published anthologies, widely photocopied and even, in former times, hand-copied, *In C* has been more readily available via these means than from its original source.[19] Though Riley produced a list of performance instructions to accompany the score some years after the première, these have never been widely disseminated. The initial San Francisco performances evolved 'by consensus, almost', without any written instructions, and the composer has himself done much over the ensuing years to encourage performances of *In C* to be conceived more as contributions to an ongoing exploration of its potential than as merely a faithful reproduction of the score. Performance practice has consequently evolved quite freely with respect to the written source, making *In C* begin to resemble a kind of urban folk music rather than a 'composition' in a more conventional sense. Some of the salient features of this evolution are described below. Several mistakes have also crept into some of the available versions.

Example 2.3 *In C*, complete score

In C is scored for '[a]ny number of any kind of instruments'. Its 'ensemble can be aided', according to Riley's instructions, by the already mentioned pulse, which can be performed 'on the high c's of the piano or on a mallet instrument'. This has become accepted as a practical necessity, though a few performances under the composer's own direction have managed to dispense with it. Instrumentation is unspecified. The pitch range is basically the octave above middle C, with occasional excursions outside this. Since transposition at the octave is permitted, the potential line-up is almost limitless, though Riley discourages anything which would draw attention to itself. Even the modules themselves have developed variants which have Riley's own approval. For example, any module may be subject to any augmentation or diminution, though in practice few performances, even those under the composer's direction, take much advantage of this. (The interpretation of modules 22–6 at double speed on the commercial recording of a performance in celebration of *In C*'s twenty-fifth anniversary is thus not, as some might think, a mistake.) This proves especially useful in making fast modules available to bass-register instruments in forms which allow clear articulation; they can even, as the composer says, 'become almost like little drones'.

Besides, not all performers need to play all the modules; in their original forms, many of the faster patterns are best suited to keyboard instruments and tuned percussion, while others – notably the major part of no. 35, the only real melody in the entire piece – will sound particularly well on wind instruments. While most performances have followed the première in using only instruments, Riley's subsequent and deep involvement with Indian vocal traditions has encouraged the inclusion of singing as well; the twenty-fifth-anniversary New Albion recording includes three male voices, one the composer's own, and one female voice. The instructions allow vocalists to 'use any vowel and consonant sounds they like'. They also permit 'improvised percussion in strict rhythm (drum set, cymbals, bells etc.)'.

These instructions suggest that '[a] group of about 35 is desired if possible but smaller or larger groups will work'. While a half-dozen performers could produce a very interesting realisation, emphasising contrapuntal clarity, most successful performances known to the present author have used between ten and twenty musicians. Anything much larger risks degenerating into a free-for-all, discouraging the performers from attempting the kinds of close counterpoint characterising the most successful versions. (The twenty-fifth-anniversary performance, however – supervised by Riley – has thirty-one musicians. A revelatory twentieth-anniversary performance in Hartford, Connecticut, in 1984 –

also supervised by the composer, and heard by the present author – used twenty-eight top American new-music performers, including six singers. Additionally, and unusually, this performance abandoned the pulse, achieving a more lyrical interpretation in which slower modules became more tuneful: the triadic overlappings of module 29, for instance, sounded uncommonly like Bruckner.) Dynamics and articulation, too, are unspecified, offering scope for improvisation modified only by prevailing tendencies in any ensemble not subject to the sort of authoritarian direction which seems inappropriate to the spirit of such a piece.

After the pulse has commenced, each performer may enter with module 1 in his or her own time, repeating it as often as wished before moving on to the next one. While performers may move freely from module to module, omitting any along the way, it has become accepted that they should not leap ahead of the majority of the ensemble. While the musicians in many performances pause only between modules, not between repetitions of the same module, Riley permits the latter. In these cases, though, he encourages what he calls 'periodic' repetition: for example, eight repetitions of a module plus another eight, separated by a pause equivalent to four repetitions (especially useful for wind players). The composer's instructions suggest that no more than three or four modules should be in play at any one time; this avoids the joint pitfalls of excessive spareness (risking insufficient musical interest) and of an aural jamboree (in which musicianship is abandoned). They also suggest that '[t]he group should aim to merge into a unison at least once or twice during the performance'; in addition, once a performer reaches the final module, he or she should continue to repeat it until all the others have reached it too, during which Riley encourages crescendi and diminuendi to signal the work's close, the musicians eventually fading out one by one.

The notion, all too frequent, of *In C* as a kind of glorious, hippie free-for-all – the more the merrier, appreciated all the better if you're on certain substances – has tended to encourage performers to 'do their own thing', to use the terminology of the period, and not to attempt to relate much to what other musicians were doing. Yet as the Hartford performance demonstrated, the simultaneous deployment of a maximum of three or four modules encourages performers to work closely together, even to the point of exploiting the potential of playing or singing the same module in unison. The result, in the hands of sensitive musicians, is a rather different sort of *In C*: more focused, more interestingly contrapuntal, encouraging close listening on the part of its audience as well as its performers. While Riley gives his musicians a degree of leeway many would consider unusual, even in such a piece, he is adamant about the need for the development of a true ensemble style in which no performer draws attention to his own part at the expense of others; this would, in his view, 'collapse the structure of the piece'.

According to the composer's instructions, 'performances normally average between 45 minutes and an hour and a half'. Length of performance is clearly determined by the decisions of individual musicians, but also, to a degree, by the size of the ensemble. A large group will usually take longer to get through the modules than a small one, due partly to the former's capacity to sustain interest for longer with its wider range of combinations, both of timbres and modular patterns. Most good performances last over half an hour, some a good deal longer than this; the twenty-fifth-anniversary realisation – not perfect, but among the most varied and exciting – runs to 76′20″.

As will already be clear, the impact of *In C* inevitably varies a good deal, due to the extent to which an essentially improvisational ethos governs even a composition in which all the notes are written down. Yet only in realisations which deploy a large number of modules at once to effect a merely generalised exhilaration will Riley's carefully devised tonal scheme fail to register on its listeners. For *In C* is not really 'in C' at all, even if one accepts a loosely 'modal' rather than strictly tonal understanding of the term. One might even suggest that Riley's concern for modulation – inspired though it was by the example of Davis and first explored in an overtly jazz context – now takes on a more 'classical profile': the sort of description evoked by several commentators to denote the clearer cast of the rhythms and phrasing employed in the individual modules themselves.[20]

The introduction, first of F♯ (module 14), then B♭ (module 35 and, more consistently, from module 49) contributes important modifications to the C-major modality. In tandem with these alterations of accidental come more subtle changes of emphasis. While the opening modules duly stress C as the central pitch, module 8 introduces a sequence of patterns in which G is emphasised by constant reference to the pitches of the dominant-seventh chord. After F♯ replaces F♮ in module 14, introducing a somewhat Indonesian flavour to the proceedings, modules 14 and 15, in particular (the latter consisting solely of an emphatic G), suggest that we have moved into the dominant key. Interpretations retaining the primacy of C are, however, also available here and after the subsequent introduction of B♭ in module 35. Modules 14–17 suggest the Lydian mode on C; the integration of F♯ into a C-based modality is, after all, recognised theoretically both in musics of the 'cultivated' tradition (in Olivier Messiaen, for instance)[21] and in jazz (notably in the Lydian-based theories of George Russell).[22] Module 18, however, begins a long passage in which E minor can be felt as the real focus: the constantly repeated ascents up the first five notes of this key's scale occupy a significant proportion of the work's central portion, before a dramatic change of rhythmic pattern signals a return to C major (module 29) and, with the restoration of F♮, C major's dominant seventh (module 31). (It should be noted that the scalic ascents in quavers of modules 22–6 were originally conceived largely as dotted crotchets: an alternative more difficult to perform than the subdivision into repeated quavers common in versions subsequently disseminated.)

Module 35 alternates a semiquaver passage on the dominant seventh of C with the work's most extended lyrical utterance: a melody which manages to incorporate not only B♭ and F♯, but also B♮ and F♮. The former pair suggests what jazz musicians know as the 'Lydian dominant'. The presence of the natural as well as the flattened seventh, and the natural as well as the sharpened fourth, however, creates the most ambiguous modal moment in the entire work. It comes as no surprise to realise that *In C*'s single real melody comes not only at the point of maximum modal conflict, but also at almost the exact point of the Golden Section (module 35 being as close to two-thirds of the way through the work's fifty-three modules as it is possible to come).

After this, the way seems clear for the return of an Ionian C major via, once again, its dominant seventh. The pitches of the G^7 chord duly arrive (module 36 onwards). But C itself is approached more ambiguously: suggested, briefly, in module 39 and then, much more firmly, in module 42 (though, with the only A♮s in the whole piece outside the E-minor central sequences plus module 35, this could also be the relative minor); apparently confirmed in modules 43–4, but then shifted back on to a dominant focus (modules 45–8). At the point at which one might have expected a gloriously unambiguous return to C major, however, B♭ is reintroduced (module 49), leaving *In C* hanging deliciously in the air: not even on a C^7 chord, consistent with the B♭s, but on a G^7 chord in which the third has now been flattened; though when combined with the C, D or E which the immediately preceding modules 43–7 variously incorporate, the three pitches of the closing modules also suggest a Mixolydian modality on C.

Even the more carefully contrived and conscientiously contrapuntal performances of *In C* will, of course, blur the moves between these modal centres, which are thus more likely in practice to contribute to a polymodality as suggestive of jazz traditions as of any more 'exotic' ones. Like the modulation from the Dorian mode on D to that on E♭ in *Music for 'The Gift'*, *In C*'s shifts of tonal emphasis are accomplished gradually, in effect a moving and merging 'sweep of colour' rather than creating the dramatic shift of perspective characteristic of a conventional 'classical' modulation. The work's 'fields of loops' are subjected to a process at once more controlled and more comprehensive than that found in Riley's earlier use of Davis's 'So What'. While 'on C' might be a better description of the work's tonality than 'in C', even this scarcely does justice to the work's subtle changes of tonal emphasis, cunningly deployed to make structurally satisfying sense, whether a performance lasts fifteen minutes or several hours.

Mexico and New York

While feeling 'very satisfied that that message [of *In C*] had come through',[23] Riley was curiously disinclined to follow where it may have led in any clear, certainly in any careerist, terms. 'I responded', he says, 'by dropping out and going to Mexico for three months'. Riley did not, in fact, travel down to Mexico immediately, but stayed in San Francisco until the spring of 1965. His most notable musical activities during that time were with a jazz group, several members of which had played in *In C*, and for which he wrote two further works, discussed below. The performers included the already mentioned Gibson, Lewis and Weitsman, the trombonist Al Bent, the drummer Pete Magadini and Riley himself on piano. Though the group rehearsed every week for a period, it gave just one fully public concert – probably in April that year, at the San Francisco Tape Music Center – of Coltrane, Ornette Coleman, and *Tread on the Trail*, the work Riley had written specially for the occasion.

After the première of *In C*, its composer had really wanted to go back to Morocco. He heard that it was possible to get a passage on a Polish freight ship for a hundred dollars, leaving from Mexico, and was intending to take the family's Volkswagen bus to Tangier, then live in Morocco on the bus. But when the family arrived in Vera Cruz, probably in April or May 1965, the existence of any cheap passage across the Atlantic – at least one including transporting the bus – turned out to be a misunderstanding. The Rileys accordingly spent about three months in Mexico, having sold most of their possessions in order to pay for their intended trip. They then moved on to New York City where, though at first retaining some notion of sailing to Europe, Riley found himself trading in the bus, on which they had travelled across America, for a downtown loft on Grand Street – near the Bowery and Sara Roosevelt Park – previously rented by a friend of the sculptor Walter de Maria. The temptation to stay was heightened by the fact that the city's cultural scene in general, and its musical scene in particular, were much more dynamic than those of San Francisco.

Basing himself in New York for about the next four years, Riley travelled around the USA, continuing the rootless existence that reflected the emerging 'alternative' lifestyles of the period. 'I guess in those days I was a beatnik, and then I turned into a hippie', he says.[24] 'I enjoyed being in the company of poets and storytellers and other travelers. That was the life of the times. It was very exciting. Compared to the fifties, which was so dishwater dull, I thought things were really happening. And I was hoping the world would always stay like that!' Riley's wife and small daughter accompanied him; Anne found temporary teaching jobs whenever they settled anywhere for a while. In New York, she taught in Harlem, supporting the family until the Columbia recording of *In C* started to bring in some money.

Riley quickly renewed his close friendships with two men who were now established in the downtown artists community. Dewey, though a fairly recent arrival himself, mounted *Sames*, another of his theatrical extravaganzas, at the Film-Makers' Cinémathèque in November 1965. In this work, six women in bridal dress remained immobile on stage throughout, while films were projected on the theatre's walls and ceiling. Riley's music – using both tape loops and the time-lag accumulator system – incorporated three tape pieces, two of them still in progress: *I, It's Me* and *That's Not You*, discussed below.

More important in the long term was the re-establishment of his association with Young, now a close neighbour. In the Theatre of Eternal Music, Riley began to sing for the first time, initially just sitting in on rehearsals. John Cale was still playing with the group, and gave his last concert with it in December 1965. Riley's first concert with the Theatre of Eternal Music came the following February. He sang with the group for the next year or so, carefully keeping his own instrumental improvisations quite separate from his collaborations with the strong-willed and charismatic Young. He also started to study just intonation with Young's colleague Tony Conrad, which had an important, if delayed, effect on his own work.

Tape compositions, 1964–7

Though increasingly occupied with attempting to realise the potential that tape loops and the time-lag accumulator offered in live music-making, Riley continued to compose in the medium which had drawn him to modular repetition in the first place: music for tape alone. He regarded it as his own territory, and his faith in the medium of tape as a solution to his search for a personal style received a blow when Reich produced *It's Gonna Rain.* Riley's brief, intense relationship with Reich in 1964 had been based on more than merely the preparations for the première of *In C.* The two composers had also been showing each other their recent work which, in both cases, consisted largely of tape compositions. Reich recalls hearing *She Moves She*; Riley remembers showing his new friend 'two tape-recorder pieces of mine, loops of mine that I was working with'. Riley's insecurity over his friend's adoption of modular repetition using speech material on tape was compounded when, after returning to New York, 'people would say, "Oh, you're doing the kind of stuff Reich does!" And that hurts, you know'.

Riley continued, however, to compose tape pieces for some three years after the première of *In C.* While Reich built his early aesthetic on the rigour with which his compositions are constructed, Riley was uninterested in applying such structural severities to his material. His fascination was with the found sounds themselves and the process of what we would today call sampling. Riley would tape long stretches of material and loop them live, hoping for 'strange things that would happen' which would later be edited into a piece. He would even cut up pieces of tape without knowing what they were, splice them together and observe the results. While avoiding any systematic structuring of his materials, he nevertheless wanted to produce an 'abstract experience' from them, in which initially identifiable sounds would more often be extensively transformed than retained in a form readily recognisable by the listener.

Between the spring of 1964 and late 1967, Riley produced at least nine pieces, six of which can presently be reckoned to have survived; he also made a lot of other experiments in the medium.[25] Five pieces date from his period in San Francisco around the time of the composition and première of *In C*; a further four were composed later in New York. As so often, it is difficult to date many of these with any precision.

Shoeshine – the earliest of the four San Francisco pieces, composed in June 1964 – was composed for the Dancers Workshop of Marin (County). Here, a blues solo played on the Hammond organ by Jimmy Smith – its identity now forgotten by Riley, who taped the music by chance from the radio – was cut up into loops and extensively reassembled, alternating passages in which the original material is clearly audible, if highly fragmented, with others in which it is only vaguely and intermittently discernible. The programme sheet for the première performances of *In C* suggests that this tape piece received its first performances on the same occasion, but it now seems that it had already been performed with dancers in the previous August. *Shoeshine*'s twenty-one minutes take incessant repetition to curious and, at least from time to time, effective ends. *I* (July 1964) uses the voice of John Graham again, and the time-lag system developed in Paris. This is based entirely on the single word 'I', spoken by Graham using a variety of inflections and subjected to feedback processes which accumulate quite powerfully to produce a continuous drone. In late 1965 or early 1966, in New York, two further pieces (both presently lost) using only a single voice and the time-lag accumulator were completed to make a set of three. *It's Me* uses the composer's own voice, and *That's Not You* that of his daughter. This material provided the basis for the music Riley provided for *Sames*, the theatre piece by Dewey mentioned above.

The Bird of Paradise, the third San Francisco tape piece, was probably composed in the late summer of 1964. Based entirely on a rhythm-and-blues number entitled 'Shotgun', sung by Junior Walker and his All-Stars, this was one of the pieces Riley derived by using chance in his sampling method. While some sounds had been specially chosen, others were arrived at randomly, from loops constructed arbitrarily, without knowing their contents. The latter were 'like wild cards; if I didn't like them, I wouldn't use them'. One loop of Walker's group, played backwards and with the speed manipulated by hand, had what Riley calls a regular rhythmic 'choom, chucka choom' sound that reminded him 'of a huge Pterodactyl flying. . . . That was the reason for the title'. Like many of the sounds used in the piece, this is so transformed that it can barely be identified: a typical Riley technique that allows *The Bird of Paradise* to soar majestically above its sources in an exhilarating three-minute mixture of the metaphorical and the abstract.

The fourth San Francisco tape composition is the six-minute *In A♭ or is it B♭?* (dated October 1964 in the programme for the *In C* première concert). This submitted Lewis's tenor saxophone playing to distortion through immediate processing on tape, circumventing the need to make separate loops first; the material varies from long sustained sounds to a few wild riffs. The accumulating layers of playback, as well as sometimes instant distortions of single lines, call the key of the piece itself into question: hence the title, which can also be interpreted as a (probably ironic) follow-up to that of *In C*. 'Strange things would happen', says Riley, who deliberately exploited such surprising timbral or modal moments in the final mix. Its extension of the 'wash-of-colour', modal-modulation techniques explored in *Music for 'The Gift'* and *In C* was to prove significant, as discussed below. A fifth tape piece, entitled *R & R*, is listed in the programme for a concert at Cabrillo College in 1965 (see below). The programme note describes it as '[a]n electronic piece built from sound sources based on various excerpts from rock and roll stations'; it remained incomplete at the time of the concert and is now presumed lost.

The only two other tape pieces Riley recalls from his New York years are *I Can't Stop No* and *You're Nogood.* The former, probably composed in 1967, was reckoned to have been lost until it turned up quite recently; its composer retains a particular affection for the piece. Though Riley cannot remember exactly what material he used, the source of *I Can't Stop No* is, again, taped from the radio: a voice singing the words 'I just can't stop no' in a high, rising scale. He then separated each word and scrambled them in helter-skelter combinations. Combined with an obsessively repeated strummed open fifth, the spoken words audibly retain their origins in the manic rising figure, producing some interestingly bizarre pitch distortions in the process. Lasting over an hour, it uses, the composer says, 'as much tape as I could possibly fit on a reel', the idea being that the piece itself could not stop. A Long Island club called The World seems to have been interested in using *I Can't Stop No* for dancing, but closed before the piece was finished.

You're Nogood (probably late 1967, after the composition of *Poppy Nogood and the Phantom Band*, see below) is what its composer calls 'a set of variations' on a tune of this name by a New York rhythm-and-blues group called the Harvey Arverne Dozen. Riley was attracted to this source partly because by this time he had started calling himself 'Poppy Nogood'. *You're Nogood* exposes its borrowed material much more directly, and at greater length while remaining untransformed, than do the other tape pieces. By this time, its composer had acquired a sine-wave generator from Young and also, on loan from him, a small Moog synthesizer; Riley had never had access to a synthesizer before. The result was what he calls 'a combination of a synthesizer piece and a cut-up tape-loop piece', adding synthesizer sounds and their transformations to the basic techniques of tape-splicing, etc. Additionally, he now had two decent Revox tape recorders, giving him much better sound reproduction than before; Riley wanted to give his new piece, intended for replay in a discotheque, a cleaner sound.

'My idea was to make an arrangement', he says. 'So you'd have the tune, a set of improvisations, different loops of the tune: an abstract arrangement of the tune, almost like a jazz chorus. And then at some point, this tone generator which has sweeping and pulsing sounds'. A pulsing figure, taking the rhythm of the tune as its basis, starts with a very low pitch, then sweeps right upwards, at which point the tune itself enters. At the end of the piece, there are some very fast, double-speed loops, also supported by the pulses. Commissioned by a Philadelphia discotheque, *You're Nogood* apparently made a curious impact on the dance floor. Initially, the unusual effects seemed to mesh with the strobe lights and the general atmosphere. When the loops started to get out of phase with each other, however, the dancers were forced to stop and attempt to adjust to the constantly shifting metre, with apparently entertaining results.

Riley's tape pieces have both a historical and a musical importance that has been undermined by their composer's *laissez-faire* approach to his own achievements. At the very least, they provide a missing link in the story of Riley's influence on Reich and in the prehistory of sampling.

Composition or improvisation?

Riley has said that he 'never wrote any more music after [*In C*]; I started improvising'.[26] But this is not true. In addition to the tape pieces, he continued to explore the potential of single-page, module-based scores as the basis for group improvisation in two further works. Both were composed for the already mentioned jazz group of which Riley was then a member. The first piece, *Autumn Leaves*, included a tape part as well. The work strips away the chord changes, as well as the tune, of this jazz 'standard', by Johnnie Mercer, replacing them with a series of modules, based on a Mixolydian scale in B♭ with some chromatic extensions, designed to imply the original harmony. Riley did not consider it successful, and the piece was only performed once, in a private concert at Cabrillo College, Santa Cruz, on 13 March 1965, shortly after its composition.

The second piece, *Tread on the Trail*, was written soon afterwards for performance at the previously mentioned concert the jazz group gave at the San Francisco Tape Music Center in the following month. Instrumentation is free, as are dynamics and performance duration; octave transposition is permitted. The material – jaunty, somewhat fragmented melodies, the movement through which is governed by rules similar to those of *In C* – seems best suited to wind instruments; according to the performing instructions, the forces 'can include an ad lib drum set or hand drums or other percussion'. Gibson – who performed a multi-tracked version of *Tread on the Trail* for his 1992 CD as well as playing in the 1965 première – describes the score as 'five different sets of melodies of equal length, each one constructed as a mirror image of itself'.[27] Essentially modal, the five lines use eight, five, eight, eight and seven notes respectively, encompassing all pitches except B♭ and D♭.

Example 2.4 *Olson III*, modules 1–5

Though based on characterful material and in some respects more tightly controlled, *Tread on the Trail* lacks the individuality and expressive range of *In C*.

For Riley, notation itself increasingly seemed an attempt to fix something whose essence is to float freely, intuitively, spontaneously. Improvisation has always seemed central to his approach, even when composing; he delights in the immediacy of interaction with the material and in incorporating the player's own creativity in whatever he does. It therefore seems especially surprising that Riley remains the only one of the four main subjects of the present book who has never formed his own regular ensemble. He once explained this with the suggestion that he is 'not good at telling people what to do'. The fact that the single-page, module-based score proved to have less potential as a basis for group improvisation than the enormous success of *In C* had suggested it should must have played its part in Riley's wariness of regular ensembles. Within two or three years, notation itself had become such an encumbrance for him that he abandoned it altogether for more than a decade.

In 1967, Riley was invited to spend several weeks during March and April in Stockholm and commissioned to write a work for the students in the choir and orchestra of the city's Nacka School of Music. The result, premièred on 27 April, was *Olson III*, his third attempt at a piece for these forces; 'Olson's Rough-cut' was apparently the name by which marijuana was often obliquely referred to in Sweden at that time. The text for *Olson III*, by the composer himself, reads: 'Begin to think about how we are to be'. The piece is clearly modelled on the principles of *In C*: notated on a single sheet, it consists of thirty short modules, beginning in F major and ending in F minor. (See Ex. 2.4 for the first five modules.) Unlike *In C*, *Olson III* uses only equal rhythms – notated as stemless crotchets – thus effectively doing away with the need for a separate pulse. The text is set entirely syllabically throughout. A performance, Riley says, need not start at the beginning, though a complete cycle through all the notated material should be made, probably ending with the module with which it began. While benefiting from a more subtle approach to modality than *Tread on the Trail*, lack of rhythmic variety prevents *Olson III* from achieving the same sort of expressive impact as *In C*, though the piece evidently aroused the students to petition their school to dismiss its orchestral director, who had been less than sympathetic to such radical endeavours.

From keyboards to saxophone and back again

Riley's attempts to stake out some new, independent and solo ground in the years immediately following *In C* took the form of building an individual keyboard style on the basis of his skills in blues, ragtime and jazz piano, interspersed with a temporary preoccupation with the saxophone: the scenario acted out by Young himself in the early 1960s. Both in California and immediately after his move to New York, Riley made considerable efforts to extend his style of piano improvisation. Since surviving recordings are rare, the chief evidence of this essentially improvised activity is, ironically, the two *Keyboard Studies* – out of at least some half a dozen – which Riley bothered to notate. Considerable confusion surrounds the identification and dating of these. Michael Nyman argues that *In C* is 'more developed in many respects'[28] than the *Keyboard Studies*, implying that the latter predate Riley's most famous composition. The project in fact originated around the same time; but even *Keyboard Study no. 1* was first written down, perhaps even first improvised, after *In C*, and the other studies almost certainly date from rather later. The composer gives the date 1965 to the *Studies* as a whole in his own worklist.

Since several of them remain untranscribed, *Keyboard Studies* can best be viewed as a collection of ideas – some eventually notated, some not – assembled over a period of perhaps three years or more as the basis for improvisation. While intended largely for multi-tracked performance by Riley alone, the *Studies* could also be played by a keyboard ensemble, still providing opportunities for working with others and even for musicians to play without the composer present. *Keyboard Study no. 2*, the best-known of the set, in fact originated as an ensemble piece, as discussed below. But whether elaborated by a single musician or by a group, these studies are, as their name suggests, really exercises rather than fully fledged compositions. Riley describes the *Keyboard Studies* as 'a real hard-core minimalist piece'.

Example 2.5 *Keyboard Study no. 1*: (a) modules 1–2; and (b) modules 7–10

Keyboard Study no. 1

Keyboard Study no. 1 was also called *Coule*; the title is a pun on the French word for 'flowing' or 'gliding' (or, in musical terminology, the 'slur' as a phrase marking), and Riley pronounces it, as though without its acute accent, 'Cool', a term of colloquial approbation still new when the piece was first conceived. *Coule* received its first performance in the same November 1964 concerts as the première of *In C*. The first *Study* remains unpublished and little-known; indeed, the only currently extant copies of it are of what its composer calls a 're-creation' of the piece, with some of the original patterns and some new ones added, made in about 1994 for the British pianist John Tilbury.

A series of sixteen short modules, divided into three sections played without a break, *Keyboard Study no. 1* is rooted in a Dorian mode on E♭, including the sharpened leading note D♮ as well as D♭, with octave transposition permitted. The opening module of each section is played immediately with the second, interlocking with the initial module (which is notated off the beat) to produce a continuous flow of semiquavers. (Ex. 2.5a gives these two modules.) This opening module is subsequently retained as an ostinato against which all the others in that section are fitted, all to be repeated an unspecified number of times. Underneath the constant patter of semiquavers, some contrapuntal consistencies can be detected in the apparently chaotic kaleidoscope of the contrapuntal combinations; Example 2.5b gives one illustration of this. While Riley typically fails to pursue with much rigour any of the canonic structures he sets up, their complexity evolves in tandem with an overall form controlled by the gradual expansion of patterns. The result is already more than merely the setting in motion of what Nyman calls 'tiny eddies in the onflowing continuum from which any other sort of stress, or edge, is excluded'.[29]

Keyboard Study no. 2/Untitled Organ

Over eighteen months after Riley's jazz group had begun improvising on its opening modules in early 1965, Riley recorded a solo improvisation on this material, entitled *Untitled Organ*, as the A side of his first LP, *Reed Streams.* Someone had given the composer an old harmonium with several malfunctioning keys and powered by a vacuum cleaner motor; not having any money to buy anything else, he decided to try and work with it. His mother had helped with the acquisition of two Revox tape recorders, and suddenly he had a viable system to experiment with multitracking for solo keyboard performances. *Reed Streams* was made with this equipment on 4 and 5 November 1966, at the request of Mass Art Records, a small company based on Canal Street, with an issue of just one thousand copies.

What became known as *Keyboard Study no. 2* was not notated, at least in its most widely disseminated form, until Riley wrote it out as a response to a request from Cage for a contribution to the book *Notations*, published in 1969.[30] Consultation of the source of this reveals 'NYC/Nov 29, 1966', omitted from all published versions: soon after the *Reed Streams* recording was made. As with the first study, though, *Keyboard Study no. 2* exists in variant forms. Due mainly to the fact that its score became available just as the recording of *In C* began making Riley's music well known, *Keyboard Study no. 2* has been widely performed, especially as an ensemble piece.

Keyboard Study no. 2 (reproduced in its entirety as Ex. 2.6) is notated as a series of fifteen modules, each similarly to 'be repeated in a continuous manner, for a long period of time, so that it turns into a stream of notes, moving steadily, without accent'; these fast and even rhythms provide an implied pulse as firm as that to be found in *Keyboard Study no. 1.* Notes

Example 2.6 *Keyboard Study no. 2*, complete score

are now notated as pitches without stems; once again, octave transposition of modules is permitted. A choice of two ostinato modules of four notes – one a permutation of the other – is offered, one of which 'must be present at all times'. All the other modules – notated two, occasionally three, to a line – are played against these, preserving the 'sequential order of left to right, top to bottom'. Returning to an earlier module is permissible, but jumping ahead is not. Each figure of *Keyboard Study no. 2* 'may start on any note of its group'. In addition, several pitches are required to be sustained once the piece gets under way, providing a drone accompaniment to the constant repetition of the modules themselves.

Rooted in a modal, basically Dorian, scale on F, the pitch range of *Keyboard Study no. 2* gradually expands. The opening pair of four-note modules forms the basis for all the succeeding ones, which alter the

Example 2.7 *Keyboard Study no. 2*, circular version, page 7

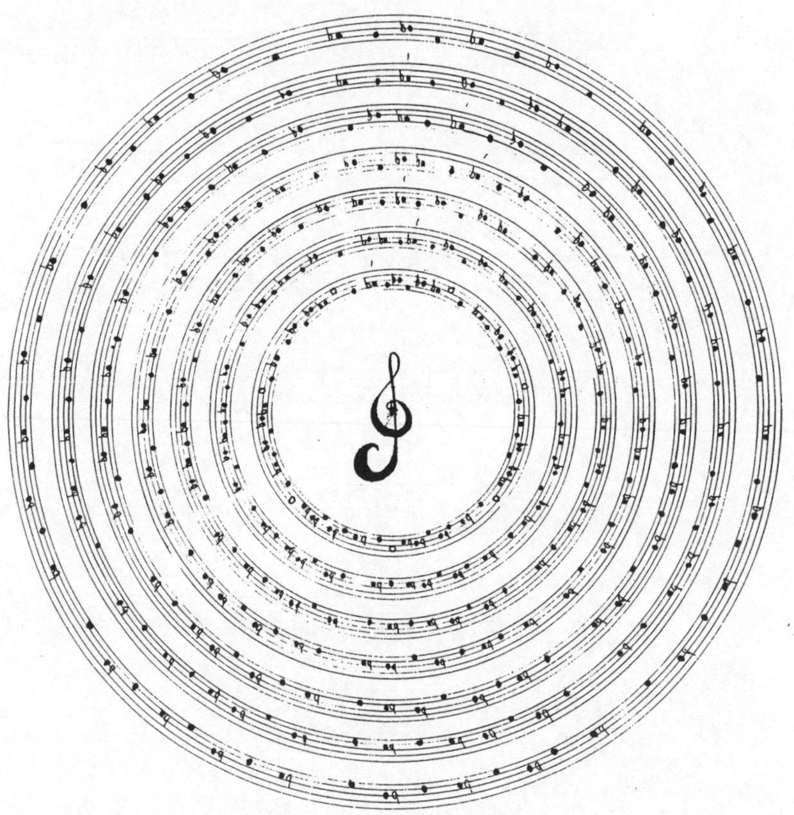

original pattern's basic shape through extension, transposition, inversion, permutation and repetition within a pattern, creating a free but often essentially canonic counterpoint with the initial modules. The fourth module additionally turns its penultimate note into a dominant drone, C: the first of five modules to create pedal points around which the music can swirl and eddy. The most commonly available version of the score adds drones on D and F; another version adds F, G and B♭.

Other notated versions of *Keyboard Study no. 2* reflect its free-wheeling, open-form aspect by transcribing the piece's pitch modules in concentric circles. A largely unpublished, eight-page manuscript – its first four pages dated 1966, the remainder 1967 – builds, respectively, four, five, six (twice), eight, seven (twice) and eight circles; mostly in the treble clef, though pages 2 and 5 are notated entirely in the bass clef, and pages 3 and 4 employ both. As Example 2.7 – page 7 of this circular version[31] – shows, Riley exerts some control on his patterns by deploying multiples of 4, 7 and 8 to give a total of fifty-six notes in each circle, since multiples of these numbers can be summed to fifty-six. But while the close connections of pitch and rhythm between the circles allows the unravelling of interesting contrapuntal combinations, no attempt is made to fill all the links in the canonic chain; the third and sixth circles (working outwards), for instance, simply duplicate each other.

Untitled Organ lasts 20′10″ and was performed live in a single take. Riley remains for long periods on a single pattern, alternating this with the polyphony of a pair of patterns. In other performances around this time, unfettered by the constraints of recording, the composer says he would stay on the same pattern for around twenty minutes. For all its limitations, this 1966 version allows the listener more opportunities than might have been expected to experience the shifting downbeats and other psycho-acoustic phenomena. Even the constant clatter of the close-miked harmonium's mechanism contributes to the effect.

Dorian Reeds *and* Poppy Nogood and the Phantom Band

To explore these new dimensions further, Riley now took up the soprano saxophone. Having taught Lewis the tenor saxophone material of *In A♭ or is it B♭?*, Riley concluded that he was perfectly capable of playing the saxophone himself. His immediate example was, of course, Young, who had been inspired to take up the sopranino by hearing Coltrane. It was Coltrane who now also provided a natural model for Riley who, like many others, had first been attracted by his playing some five years earlier. Through Young, too, Riley had come to know the work of the Indian shenai player Bismillah Khan. Gibson – himself a fine saxophonist, and a further influence on this new move – helped him buy a cheap soprano instrument and gave him a few lessons on fingering. After teaching himself to play *In A♭ or is it B♭?*, Riley was ready to deploy the saxophone in developing new improvisational methods for himself. The B side of his 1966 album *Reed Streams* was devoted to *Dorian Reeds*, the earliest surviving example of Riley's soprano saxophone playing. Shortly after this recording was made, Riley made his New York concert debut in his own loft, playing both *Untitled Organ* and *Dorian Reeds.*

Dorian Reeds, probably first worked out in 1965, was just one of Riley's many improvisations using his new equipment. Some time in 1966, he made a 'score' including diagrammatic representation of the equipment and the techniques he had devised for it, which he titled 'Solo Time-Lag Music'. The diagram demonstrates how signals coming from both the microphone (live sound) and Tape Recorder II (tape-delayed sound) can

Example 2.8 Motif used in *In A♭ or is it B♭?, Dorian Reeds, Poppy Nogood and the Phantom Band* and *Sunrise of the Planetary Dream Collector*

be controlled by separate potentiometers to produce a time-delay of about three seconds; pre-recorded, as well as live, materials can be incorporated into the system. 'Solo Time-Lag Music' offers nine scales on E, C and F♯ – including various gapped scales, such as the one identical to Messiaen's Mode 4, as well as the more familiar Dorian, Aeolian, etc. – plus some further notes regarding their elaboration. Three types of improvisation are identified. The first is slow and melodic, developing into cyclical canons over drones on the first, fourth and fifth degrees of the scale. The second is fast, consisting of chains of repeated figures of between one and nine beats' duration, assembling several alignments of what Riley's accompanying notes call 'a rotational series' both against each other and against 'sub-groups articulating the delay period or groups which may set up an opposing cylic [*sic*] period'. The third involves 'sections containing evenly spaced pulses fashioned into frequency grids which glide across one another by means of a graduall [*sic*] expansion or contraction of the gap (between pulses) over the fixed time-lag period'.

Though this composition appears in worklists under the multiple headings *Dorian Reeds/Dorian Winds/Dorian Brass*, etc., Riley has no memory of any performances by any instrument other than the saxophone. *Dorian Reeds*, meanwhile, turned out to be merely 'the first version'[32] of *Poppy Nogood and the Phantom Band*. The most important of Riley's saxophone improvisations, this uses electric organ as well as soprano saxophone, subjecting both to the multiple delays of the time-lag accumulator. He first seems to have performed this in early 1967, and has said that he 'used to play [it] in various forms at concerts for four or five years'. Riley recorded the work in 1969, when it was issued by Columbia as the B side of *A Rainbow in Curved Air*. The title is often said to be an allusion to drugs, but it actually arose from the fact that the composer was jokingly calling himself 'Poppy Nogood' at this time. His small daughter used to call him 'Poppy', and 'Poppy Nogood' when she was angry with him. Riley then developed this family joke, saying 'if you were "no good", then you could only go up! . . . So it was an attempt to start at the bottom'. The notion of the 'Phantom Band' derives from the time-lag accumulator: the composer's 'multiple, other persona that's being recycled in electronics'.

Riley's own improvised patterns for both works frequently drew on a motif which, though not written down until around 1980, can also be found in the tape piece *In A♭ or is it B♭?*, and the 1980–81 string quartet composition entitled *Sunrise of the Planetary Dream Collector* (see Ex. 2.8). In addition, *Sunrise* itself originated as a keyboard improvisation in 1976, before being reworked for the Kronos Quartet. This motif uses only the first four pitches of the D-minor scale. The sixth note is E in some versions, D in others; the group G E (D) F, marked 'x' in Example 2.8, becomes significant both melodically and as an identifiable harmonic unit. This eight-note pattern is a frequent presence on the surface of the music of the LP version of *Dorian Reeds*, also giving rise to several variants. Curiously, though, despite its apparently extensive inclusion in all the concert performances of *Poppy Nogood* which Riley now recalls, this motif is less prominent on the work's commercial recording.

The 1966 recording of *Dorian Reeds* lasts 14′55″; it was made in a single take, without editing. Moving quickly between the three musical types described in 'Solo Time-Lag Music', this improvisation is centred around the Dorian scale on D. As with *Keyboard Study no. 2*, the continuous quavers provide their own pulse. New figures and variants of old ones come thick and fast against the continuum of Example 2.8. The slower music that first occurs about four minutes in is the beginning of a sequence in which slow, fast and staccato materials alternate, and frequently overlap. B♭ and later E♭, notes foreign to the basic mode, are introduced, the former creating an uncharacteristically jarring note, reminiscent of the foghorns which inspired the String Quartet. The close canonic treatment of the original motif which appears in conjunction with the latter pitch produces a quite different texture from before, resembling an insistent buzzing around the small group of pitches involved, enhanced by sudden crescendi and diminuendi and producing, as a resulting pattern, repeated Ds. Motivic extension of the original eight-note pattern's second half, subjected to the third type of treatment described in 'Solo Time-Lag Music,' leads to contracting pulses on the dominant, A, taking the improvisation to its conclusion. In a longer performance, all these patterns would accumulate and fade more slowly, and the foreign pitches would probably insinuate themselves into the proceedings with greater subtlety. Whatever its length, however, *Dorian Reeds* effects a curious and delicate balance: neither clear enough to register every contrapuntal relationship, nor sufficiently dense and complex to cause the listener to abandon the attempt.

In *Poppy Nogood and the Phantom Band*, melodic material is immediately subjected to the dense canonic overlays made possible by more extensive applications of the time-lag accumulator. Though some of these are clearly intended to be appreciated more texturally than as audible counterpoint, what the sleeve-note to the 21′15″ LP version calls the 'spatially separated mirror images . . . adapted for studio recording by Glen Kolotkin' to 'resemble the sound Terry gets in his all-night concerts'[33] provide a stereo sound-space which permits the detailed contrapuntal unfolding of some phrases to be readily heard. The saxophone melodies of *Poppy Nogood* are also embedded from the outset in drones supplied by the electric organ, contributing significantly to the textural density and richness of this more 'orchestral' realisation of 'Solo Time-Lag Music'.

The mode is now Aeolian, once again centred on D, emphasised by the prominence of the flattened sixth falling to the fifth of the scale, and underpinned by drones including a prominent dominant, A. Short motifs are common: one based around B♭A is immediately audible at the outset. Any feeling of regular metre is essentially local. In a slow second section of greater transparency, beginning just after six minutes in, more extended melodies are counterpointed against one another by the accumulator, and the original mode is expanded, at least briefly, by the introduction of E♭, the flattened supertonic, and later by more elaborate pitch bending. The faster, skirling melodic material of the third section – suggesting comparisons with Indian music as well as a variety of world folk musics – now evolves as a series of waves, each focusing on different groups of pitches, some much more extended – both scalic and arpeggiated – than the first.

Like Young, Riley continued to play the saxophone regularly for some two or three years, for which the ideas behind *Poppy Nogood* proved sufficiently rich. With this, he exhausted what he had to say about – and what he could actually play on – the saxophone. Tied closely to the technique of the time-lag accumulator, the saxophone improvisations were governed, and shackled, by it, especially in the area of rhythm. And though he devised various ways of overcoming the restrictions – for instance, through the use of different tape-recorder channels – the kinds of counterpoint possible with such means remained limited.

A Rainbow in Curved Air

From 1967 onwards, as the keyboard gradually returned to the centre of his concerns, Riley's music developed new dimensions. Two particular influences on his keyboard improvisations from this period onwards should be noted. First, the gradual availability of more sophisticated

Example 2.9 *A Rainbow in Curved Air*, two extracts from notated version

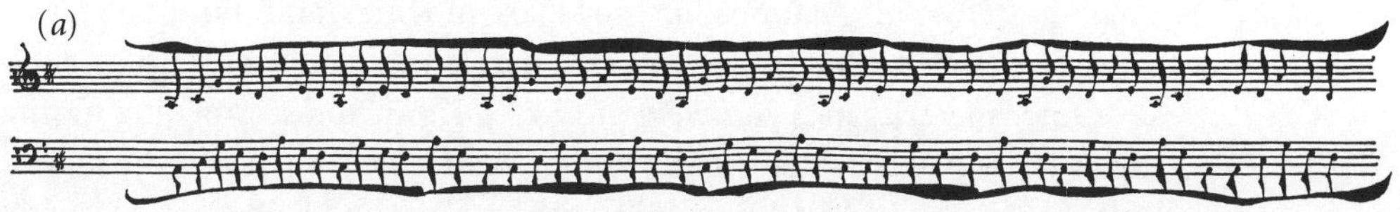

types of instrument enhanced the range of contrapuntal and structural possibilities which the continued use of tape delay permitted, as well as timbral quality and variety. Concerned to develop greater structural, and especially rhythmic, control, Riley now abandoned the time-lag accumulator. Secondly, Indian classical music soon became a major force in his life, and specifically his association with Pandit Pran Nath, discussed below.

A Rainbow in Curved Air – its title, Riley says, just an expression of 'the way the music felt', and lacking any specific allusion to drugs – marks an early stage of these developments. The electric organ, electric harpsichord and 'rocksichord', plus a dumbec (a one-sided Persian drum) and a tambourine, to be found on the Columbia recording, offer a wide timbral range. This 18′39″ improvisation mixes several contrasting musical elements in a kaleidoscope underpinned by an almost constant quaver pulse grouped into fourteen-beat cycles and a pentatonic mode centred on A: A C♯ D E G. Most idiosyncratic of the shower of ideas that erupts just after the beginning, and on which the whole improvisation is based, are the shimmering, ornamented melodic lines in quickly moving, ascending and descending shapes which are clearly modelled on the melismatic characteristics of Indian music, and in particular its employment of diminution. While the full impact of Indian classical music did not manifest itself until after he had begun studying with Pran Nath, Riley had heard a good deal both in live performance and, especially, on record by the time he began improvising *A Rainbow in Curved Air*. Its influence already plays a significant part in the work: not only in these imitative elaborations of Indian mannerisms but also in the ways in which the fourteen-beat pattern is deployed cyclically, other material manoeuvring around it in ever-changing, sometimes syncopated-sounding, patterns in relationships too fast-moving, and no doubt too unsystematic, to establish any scheme the ear can readily pick up.

Other material in *A Raiñbow in Curved Air* includes a rocking motif, with its own delay already built in, which adds new pitches to the mode, introducing C♮ and G♯ but mainly orientated around E, A, G♮ and D, with the rattle of dumbec and tambourine as accompaniment. A joyous chordal and thematic outburst around halfway through proves a natural development of the earlier material. The final one-third of the improvisation introduces a tabla-like accompaniment on the dumbec, which will underpin the whole section, and a new melody, descending from the dominant and back to the tonic, inflecting the mode with C♮ and F♮.

Several manuscript pages (dated 1968) outlining the basic material and exploring some of its cyclical and contrapuntal possibilities suggest something of the potential which Riley was trying to develop in his improvisations on *A Rainbow in Curved Air*, which are often much more extended than the one on the Columbia recording. It is characteristic that these written-out versions attempt to transcend what Riley saw as the inevitable limits of musical notation by means of some modest graphic departures from convention. Example 2.9 gives two extracts from these pages.

Example 2.9a demonstrates the basic fourteen-beat cyclic pattern in gradually unfolding canon on the five basic pitches of the mode: the right hand remaining fixed while, after beginning in unison with it, the left adds an extra quaver A to the end of each repetition; Riley's original notates the complete canonic cycle resulting from this progressive misalignment. Example 2.9b illustrates the decorative, melismatic right-hand style, unfolding three- and four-note patterns against the same fourteen-beat cycle in the left hand (starting on the second note of the original one), using decorated beams which (more or less) articulate the cycle into seven-note groupings.

Though *A Rainbow in Curved Air* demonstrates greater structural control and flexibility, as well as timbral ingenuity and the beginnings of a melodic style influenced by Indian classical music, Riley's improvisations remained confined to working with variations of the same pattern. Material from *A Rainbow in Curved Air* continued, however, to prove a potent inspiration for subsequent work: it found its way into *Jaipur Local*, a duo piece for voice and tabla for the composer and Krishna Bhatt, originally composed in 1983–4 and performed in various versions by them until 1991, when their CD *No-Man's Land* was issued.

The expansion of Riley's reputation and his changing aesthetic to 1976

Crucial in Riley's development from relatively obscure innovator to guru of late-1960s counter-culture was the much wider availability of recordings. The Columbia recording of *In C* was issued in late 1968, as a consequence of David Behrman's engagement by the company as a producer. Behrman, himself a composer, was sympathetic to new music; the twenty-five or thirty discs he put out during his brief period of influence at Columbia included three works by Reich. *In C* was released at the same time as Walter Carlos's famous *Switched-On Bach* and another, soon forgotten, album entitled *Rock and Other Four-Letter Words*; all three were designed 'to capture the imagination of the young audience', as Riley puts it.

The recording of *In C* resulted from the composer's period as a 'Creative Associate' of the Center for Creative and Performing Arts at the State University of New York at Buffalo during the early part of 1968, and a performance of the work by this group at the Carnegie Recital Hall in March that year. The forty-three-minute recording was made in the same month; it involved experienced and sympathetic musicians, including Stuart Dempster (trombone), Jon Hassell (trumpet), David Rosenboom (viola), Jan Williams (marimbaphone) and Riley himself on soprano saxophone. Though its superimposition of three complete 'takes' creates a muddy sound-perspective, this recording's wide circulation, in Europe as well as in the USA, even encouraged many to play *In C* themselves – the score being reproduced in its entirety on the record sleeve, though with some errors – and to imitate its infectious tonal and rhythmic vitality in their own compositions. Riley's second Columbia recording, issued in 1969, was devoted to *Poppy Nogood and the Phantom Band* and *A Rainbow in Curved Air*. As with *In C*, the accompanying sleeve notes – this time a poem by the composer – were very much of their time, promoting sentiments of peace, especially appropriate considering that the Vietnam War was then in progress, and utopian, and in particular ecological, concerns. In addition, Riley recorded a joint album, *Church of Anthrax*, with John Cale in 1968, at the suggestion of John McClure, now the producer at Columbia for both musicians. While this manages to integrate at least a little of the contrapuntal thinking characteristic of Riley's other output of this period with something of the energy of rock, this recording – released in 1970 – leans too far towards the blandness often characteristic of such 'fusion' projects.

Also in tune with the *Zeitgeist* were the installations, multimedia presentations, all-night concerts, experimental video projects and music for films with which Riley was involved. The first three of these categories are impossible to separate, since it seems that some events involved a variety of visual as well as aural elements, and Riley performed concerts in the installation spaces. Details of such events, too, are rather confused. All-night concerts, both solo and with *ad hoc* ensembles, became an occasional feature of Riley's career in the late 1960s and early 1970s. The first solo all-night event seems to have occurred in Philadelphia, through the agency of Jim Williams: a friend of the composer and an art teacher in the city, whose communal vision of whole families eating and drinking, then sleeping in hammocks and sleeping bags while Riley played appears to have been successfully realised.

In 1968, Riley participated in 'Intermedia '68', a series of late-night concerts in various colleges in New York State, including Albany and SUNY Buffalo (while the composer was in residence there), and ending at the Brooklyn Academy of Music. 'Environments' for these, provided by Bob Benson, consisted of a 'tiny maze of sound chambers and mirrored rooms which contained microphones to capture fragments of conversation and automatically arrange them into sound collages of repeated patterns'. A group of dancers and acrobats – recruited at each college, and known as 'The Daughters of Destruction' – also took part. Other, probably similar, installations included one in Amagansett, on Long Island, and, in the summer of 1969, an event commissioned by the Kansas City Performing Arts Foundation, which took place in the Nelson Atkins Gallery in Kansas City, as part of the Magic Theater Festival; this was repeated in New York in March 1970, at Automation House on East 68th Street.

Other notable landmarks in the development of Riley's reputation included the last two concerts, in June 1968, in the 'January through June' Festival at the Barbizon Plaza Theater (where Young had performed four months before). On 14 April 1969, he appeared at The Electric Circus: a psychedelic rock club – situated on St Mark's Place in New York's East Village, just north of SoHo – which was a crucial venue in the evolution of the late 1960s 'alternative' scene. Here, he and Rosenboom, on violin, performed both *Poppy Nogood and the Phantom Band* and *A Rainbow in Curved Air*; among the audience was Philip Glass. In the early 1970s, too, Riley began returning to Europe, performing not only *Poppy Nogood* and *Rainbow* but also the already mentioned solo keyboard improvisations entitled *Persian Surgery Dervishes* which formed their sequel. France, West Germany and Italy, in particular, were visited quite frequently, though he did not perform in Britain until 1986.

When Riley played with other musicians, the group sometimes called itself Poppy Nogood and the Persian Surgery Band; those with whom he worked at this time included several fellow Creative Associates from Buffalo, such as Edward Burnham (vibraphone), and the already mentioned Hassell and Williams. As a soloist, Riley sometimes appeared under the guise of 'Poppy Nogood's Phantom Band'. The ensemble as well as solo music for these occasions seems to have been drawn from the *Poppy Nogood*, *Rainbow in Curved Air* and, later, the *Dervish* material, elaborated into improvisations not only far more extended but also far more free-wheeling and exploratory than those to be found on the commercial recordings.

Riley was also in demand as a provider of music for experimental video projects and both experimental and more commercial films. *Music with Balls*, for instance – a half-hour video by the sculptor Arlo Acton and the producer John Coney – was made by KQED TV in San Francisco in 1969. The composer's worklist for the years 1972–6 gives the impression that he spent at least two years composing, or improvising, nothing but the film scores which came his way as a result of contacts made in the aftermath of his period of fame, though in fact most of these were done quickly and, like the music for many of his other projects of this period, based on earlier material or elaborated much more fully only later. Two examples must suffice. As released on LP by Warner Brothers in 1972, the year of its composition, *Les yeux fermés* – the English title of Joel Santini's film is 'Happy Ending' – parallels the forces, as well as developing the musical materials, of the *Rainbow in Curved Air/Poppy Nogood* album, with one side devoted to keyboard music, the other to the saxophone. *Le secret de la vie* (or 'Lifespan') – a mystery movie in French by the American director Alexander Whitelaw – was made in Holland in 1973. The two short pieces from it – released on the Stip label two years later – again feature both saxophone and organ; the second one, *G-Song*, became the second composition Riley worked up for the Kronos Quartet some five years afterwards.

Having established himself as a significant member of New York's downtown community, Riley made the decision to move back to California in 1969, at first to live once more in San Francisco. While his return to California did not mean he was entirely forgotten there – as a solo performance of 'Music from the *Persian Surgery Dervishes*' at a packed Whitney Museum on 5 April 1973 proved – he now lacked the special career base New York could have continued to provide, as it was beginning to do for Reich and Glass. The desire to return to his West-coast roots was an important part of his reason to forsake the city which he had, in any case, never originally intended to settle in at all. Strongly connected to this powerful feeling of spiritual connection to California – and to the ideals, often misleadingly labelled as 'hippie', which had their wellsprings in a West-coast culture very different from that to be found in the Eastern seaboard's mecca of commerce – was an increasing commitment to Indian classical music.

Indian classical music

Riley now found himself consumed by other matters besides his own creative work, whether composed or entirely improvised. Since 1967 or 1968, his attention had been seized by tapes which Young played him of Pandit Pran Nath, whose singing in the Kirana tradition was becoming a strong influence on Riley's old friend, himself long steeped in the musics of the East. When Young first brought Pran Nath to the USA in January 1970, he also arranged for him to travel to California, where he visited Riley. On being told by Pran Nath that he should at once become his disciple, Riley consulted Young, who advised that he should join him in this adventure. Though uncertain as to what this would involve, Riley had the confidence which came with the feeling that his 'karmic connection' with Pran Nath 'just locked in, and I realized it was meant to be'.[34] In September 1970, his family accordingly embarked on a six-month pilgrimage to the Kailash Colony in New Delhi, to be joined three months later by Young and Marian Zazeela.

Riley initially began studying tabla, on which he took lessons for about two years, learning a great deal about rhythm and the experience of time. Then, like Young, he took up singing in the Kirana style. It had been Pran Nath's particular vocal qualities that had attracted Riley from the start. 'For a while', he has said, 'you thought you were hearing everything you've ever wanted to hear out of music just out of a solo voice'. The impact of Pran Nath, and in particular the experience of attempting to sing ragas in India, caused Riley to doubt the value of his own music. He told his teacher that he wanted to give up composing and improvising in his own style, stay in India and devote his life to its music. Pran Nath, however, said he should go back, telling him it was his role to compose as well as to practise Indian music. As a result, Riley, like Young and Zazeela, continued to devote himself totally to Pran Nath for certain parts of his teacher's regular visits to the USA, as well as during further trips of his own to India; another extended visit to New Delhi was made later in 1971. He still goes regularly to India to teach. As with all relationships between an Indian disciple and his guru, this involved much more than performing with Pran Nath on a regular basis. When, in the autumn of 1971, Riley took a teaching position at Mills College – in Oakland, across the bay from San Francisco – he initiated an Indian Music programme to which Pran Nath regularly contributed. Riley taught at Mills for some ten years, taking the classes in North Indian music in each Fall semester, devoted chiefly to singing with the aid of the tamboura. Pran Nath usually came for the Spring semester.

Such close proximity to Pran Nath pulled Riley even further away from Western ways. From 1974, he and his family have lived on a remote ranch in the Sierra Nevada foothills, close to the composer's birthplace. Like Young, Riley frequently dresses in the Indian manner, adopting some Indian customs in public: for instance, in the way he acknowledges an audience's applause. More importantly, he will begin each day with the spiritual as well as musical exercise of raga singing. As with the earlier influences of jazz, Moroccan music and the example of Young, Indian music encouraged 'a daily process of learning to improvise, and what all that meant'. The discipline and context which Indian music and its intimately integrated philosophy and way of life brought could now be used to refine and focus the purpose and direction for his own spiritual development, and his own musical direction, already discovered almost a decade earlier. Riley's intimate identification with Indian musical culture played a special role in assisting his life-long quest for 'the real me'. Everything he has done since 1970 must be viewed in relation to his consuming involvement – spiritual as well as musical – with Pran Nath's teachings.

Riley's aesthetic and technical development in the 1970s

Through the first half of the 1970s, Riley moved away from 'hard-core' minimalism due to his greater concern with aspects of music which minimalism tended to avoid. Influenced by Indian music, the melodic interest in his work now increased. Lines not only themselves became more elaborate, but also combined to form new kinds of counterpoint which could only, he argues, be created through the immediacy and inspiration of improvisation. 'What could I write?' he asks. 'I could write the patterns, and I did: and got a simple-minded looking sheet of patterns, which doesn't tell the story of what was going on in the music. When I'm really on, when I'm really open, both hands seem to think independently. I can almost think two melodies at once. . . . That's really exciting, because I don't know where it's coming from'. These developments must, of course, be viewed in tandem with the continued search for ways in which repetition and modality could between them refocus the relationships between a melody, its contrapuntal elaboration and its harmonic underpinning. The more of these elements he introduced into his already established universe of repeating modules, the more Riley found that this new approach encouraged stylistic as well as technical diversity. Finally, he says, he got to the point 'where I could do anything I wanted'.

Riley's keyboard playing now also developed new dimensions as a result of his continuing experiments with drugs. Among the new kinds of counterpoint he explored were those which derived from attempting to exploit the potential for two hands on the keyboard to operate simultaneously with greater than usual independence. The practising stages of this would often evolve from a decision to explore a particular relationship: for instance, groups of seven in one hand against groups of eight in another, whether employing the same unit or, in this case, say, seven in the time of eight. But Riley was actually more interested in what could happen if such relationships were then explored freely. This was where hallucinogens could benefit his playing, opening up possibilities not available to him simply through practice and careful co-ordination. 'It had to do with not thinking technically', as he puts it, 'but conceiving something that's sort of impossible, and just watching it happen'.

As he immersed himself in his studies of singing in the Kirana style with Pran Nath, Riley found himself more and more drawn to the voice as the supreme instrument for expressing this awareness. Though it was not until 1980 – in *Remember This Oh Mind* for improvising voice and electronic keyboards – that he felt prepared to employ his own voice in his own compositions, Riley's extensive practice of Indian singing in the 1970s already took the place in his musical concerns previously occupied by the saxophone. This reinforced his increasing appreciation of the melodic potential in the more malleable context now offered not only by the more open stylistic situation in which he found himself but also by tuning systems going beyond the restrictions of equal temperament.

No dimension of Riley's work since the early 1970s illustrates better his pragmatism in balancing old and new, Eastern and Western, than his attitude to just intonation. His reasons for beginning his investigations into non-equal-tempered tuning systems are similar to those of Young, by whose example he was, once again, influenced: essentially, that he came to feel that the whole experience of music is heightened by making it more 'in tune'. Following his induction into some of the mysteries of just intonation through his association with Conrad, as well as Young, Riley began to tune his Vox electronic organ according to just intonation, with the aid of Chet Wood. From about 1972 or 1973, both Riley's new compositions and further improvisations based on older material were often explored with the aid of a variety of tuning systems. At the end of the 1970s, state-of-the-art electronic keyboards began to permit his involvement with Indian music more easily to influence the content and expressive effect, as well as the structure, of his own improvisations. In 1980 he bought the Yamaha computer-controlled piano which has been his main studio instrument for composition ever since.

The great power of just intonation arises from the resonances that build up out of simple intervallic relationships. The unequal sizes of intervals which in an equal-tempered tuning would be identical, enhance the contours of melodies played in just-tuned systems, and Riley is particularly attracted by this distinction. With equal temperament, melodic colours tend, he feels, to blandness: what he calls 'a raw, oatmeal sound'. Just intonation, on the other hand, produces 'gorgeous contours which are dependent on these unequally shaped intervals'.

Any decision in favour of such tunings, however, automatically limits what one is able to do harmonically, and thus runs counter to Riley's contemporaneous interest in more goal-directed structures driven by harmonic motion. His solutions to this contradiction are typically various and undogmatic. He has explored the possibilities of introducing chord changes into the context of improvisations for keyboards tuned to just intonation, discovering that 'you can get harmonic possibilities, they're very unusual ones'. But Riley accepts that the promotion of greater harmonic movement is essentially incompatible with the decision to get involved with just intonation, asserting that he knows of no successful pieces which combine just intonation with a high harmonic complexity. While just intonation became of major concern to him in the early 1970s, he has accordingly also been happy to explore the potential of chord changes in equal temperament. Riley has never been as consumed as Young by the notion that just intonation represents a spiritual force which must be pursued through a moral crusade. Once again, consistency is not his concern.

The Dervish improvisations

Persian Surgery Dervishes, *Rising Moonshine Dervishes* and *Descending Moonshine Dervishes*, all for solo electronic keyboard, are the only concert compositions dating from the first half of the 1970s in Riley's worklist. Falling between the still hardline-minimalist *A Rainbow in Curved Air* and the more 'post-modernist' *Shri Camel*, they form a large-scale link in the chain comparable, in certain respects at least, to Young's

The Well-Tuned Piano. Work on the series was begun in about 1970. Two public performances of *Persian Surgery Dervishes* were issued on the French label Shanti in 1972: one made on 18 April 1971 at the Californian Institute of Technology in Los Angeles, the other on 24 May 1972 at the Théâtre de la Musique in Paris. A concert performance of *Descending Moonshine Dervishes* was recorded on 29 November 1975 at the Metamusik Festival in West Berlin, but only issued, on the West German Kuckuck label, in 1982.

With these works, Riley's habit of returning to earlier material may once again be observed. *Keyboard Study no. 2* forms the basis for all three. As was by now his habit, however, Riley wrote down no material for any of the *Dervish* improvisations. No notated elaboration of this material came into being until 1994, with *Dervish in the Nursery.* This piano piece's addition of a jazz tune to the original repetitive material constitutes an apt illustration of the ultimate fate of minimalism in a post-modernist age: recycling its pattern-making into the accompanimental figures some had argued were its inevitable consequence.

Starting with the basic modules of the earlier work, Riley began to develop a much more dynamic structure, far removed from the static concerns of the original *Keyboard Study.* Continuing to use tape delay, he was able to achieve a greater flexibility with the aid of a Vox Supercontinental Combo organ. Stereo separation with a very short delay time between the two channels adds an extra dimension to the textures of *Persian Surgery Dervishes.* Three further features contributed to the more sophisticated structural approach to be found in these improvisations. Firstly, melody began to be important in its own right, rather than merely a by-product of the repeating patterns. As with *A Rainbow in Curved Air*, the influence of Indian music was becoming evident: more clearly, indeed, due to the increased role now played by melodic lines with a defined profile of their own.

With this greater concern for melodic development comes the second feature: a greater interest in quite complex contrapuntal imitation – of the kinds discussed above – as opposed to the simple, overlapping repetition of a short musical pattern against itself. Experimentation with cyclic structures, also owing an increasing amount to Riley's study of Indian music, takes a step further in the unravelling of such counterpoint. At the outset of the Paris version of *Persian Surgery Dervishes*, for instance, he immediately transforms one of the basic four-note patterns from *Keyboard Study no. 2* into a five-note pattern (see Ex. 2.10.) This allows him to unfold a cyclic structure of forty beats by multiplying the new five-note pattern by eight. While this forty-beat cycle circulates in the left

Example 2.10 Motif and drones used in *Keyboard Study no. 2* and *Persian Surgery Dervishes*

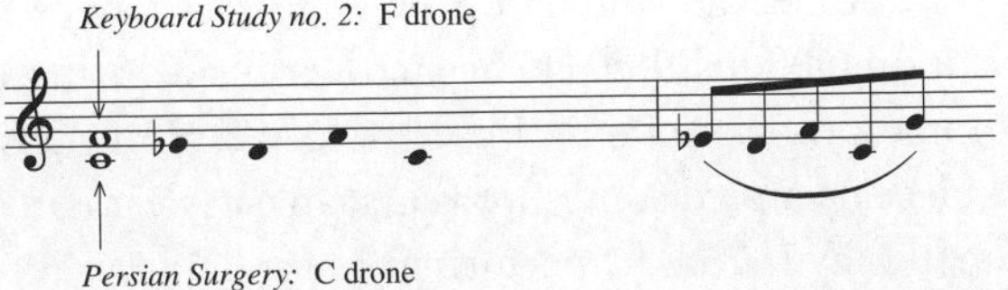

hand, the right hand evolves against it polymetrically. Due to the five-note basis of the left-hand pattern, even simple triplets played against it (three quavers in the right hand against two in the left) will quickly produce more than one layer of new alignment. Later sections see the evolution of the left-hand cyclic pattern as well. The independence of the player's hands, discussed above, can, of course, be exploited to produce many different combinations, allowing the natural expansion of extended and constantly evolving polymetric structures of a complexity difficult, or even impossible, to notate with complete accuracy.

Thirdly, a firmer sense of the evolution of an improvisation is given by the balancing and pacing of distinct sections making a contribution to a continuous whole. In particular, Riley now developed a new, slower style of playing: not so slow as to engender further stasis, but sufficiently reduced in speed to create clearer contrasts with the faster sections, and to balance with them on a more equal basis than had the slower music in, say, *A Rainbow in Curved Air.* In the *Keyboard Studies*, of course, there had been no contrast of tempo at all; even the long-held drones were only ever a background to the *perpetuum mobile* of continuous quavers at a single speed. Drone tones, too, continue to play a part in the *Dervish* improvisations. While in *Keyboard Study no. 2*, the main drone is the mode's tonic, F, *Persian Surgery Dervishes* focuses on the dominant, C (see again Ex. 2.10). Both works employ the Dorian, as well as the Aeolian, mode on F.[35]

The commercial recording of *Descending Moonshine Dervishes* uses Riley's Yamaha YC 45 D electronic organ, modified for tuning in just intonation. The whole performance – 28′18″ on Side A of the LP, 24′14″ on Side B – is, again, relayed with stereo separation of identical channels 'a fraction of a second' apart, '[permitting] a live performance in stereo and an interplay between the two parts'.[36] Once more, the contrapuntal elaboration of themes and figuration is deployed polymetrically over a fixed rhythmic cycle.

Shri Camel

Riley's first American solo album to be released since 1969, *Shri Camel,* came out on CBS in 1980. He began the music during 1975, in response to a commission from Radio Bremen, in West Germany. The main work on the piece occupied some two years; an early version was premièred in Bremen in May 1976. The performance for CBS was recorded in 1977, in the CBS Studios in San Francisco, using the already mentioned Yamaha YC 45 D organ, which offered a computerised digital delay system quite sophisticated by the standards of the day. This permitted exploration of as many as sixteen discrete contrapuntal voices, assembling textures investigating the potential of various degrees of complexity, both within a single performance and from one performance to another. Whether in concert or on the commercial recording, digital delays constitute the only electronic manipulation used; all the playing is 'live'. Different performances vary considerably in harmonic, as well as in contrapuntal, complexity. Though during the mid- and late 1970s – the most active period of engagement with the piece – he tended towards increasing elaboration of his material, Riley today still plays versions of *Shri Camel* on the piano without any delay facilities at all.

The work's title means simply 'Mr. Camel': 'shri' is an Indian title of respect. *Shri Camel* is divided into four movements: 'Anthem of the Trinity', 'Celestial Valley', 'Across the Lake of the Ancient World' and 'Desert of Ice'. The music examples used to illustrate this brief analysis (see Ex. 2.11) draw to some degree on the composer's own notation, provided for the purpose; these extracts make no attempt to reproduce the full range of contrapuntal complexities resulting from the delay systems employed, either on the CBS recording or in live performances. Riley wrote nothing down during the period in which *Shri Camel* was devised and first elaborated, and the kind of performances he plays today have, as he expresses it, put the material 'through metamorphosis'. A version of the complete score for the British group Piano Circus is currently in progress.

All four movements of *Shri Camel* are based on a C-Dorian scale subject to modification. The employment of just intonation enhances the ambiguity surrounding the leading note of the scale, extending this to the submediant which, though perfectly able to help form subdominant harmonies from time to time, is also drawn into the web of dissonances that is conjured from the upper tetrachord of the scale, rendering the harmonic focus much less certain. The combination of such a tuning with the occasional surprise of a sudden rise in dissonance level – the

Example 2.11 *Shri Camel*: (a) two bass patterns; (b) two bars from 'Anthem of the Trinity', Part One; (c) opening six bars from 'Anthem of the Trinity', Part Two; (d) two bars from 'Across the Lake of the Ancient World'; (e) two further bars from 'Across the Lake of the Ancient World'.

clash of the natural-sixth and flat-seventh degrees of the scale, for instance – allows Riley to establish a more individual harmonic idiom: one which, while still relying on a vocabulary of simple scalic and triadic elaborations around the tonic, subdominant and dominant, is crucially spiced by the fresh colours that just intonation brings. Such more adventurous chromatic advances are, however, tempered (as it were) by the incompatibility between the use of just intonation and the exploration of any real harmonic movement.

Some idea of Riley's basic harmonic approach here can be given by looking at the two bass patterns which underpin the whole of *Shri Camel* (see Ex. 2.11a (i) and (ii)). Pattern A outlines i–v–vi–♭vii, suggesting a static seventh chord, while Pattern B articulates a more active i–♭iii–iv–v–i. Neither employs any pitch outside the modified C-Dorian established as the work's basic mode, yet Pattern B lends itself more readily to harmonic motion than does Pattern A. While just intonation precludes the exploration of any real harmonic movement, not all

Example 2.11 (*cont.*)

(*c*)

Example 2.11 (*cont.*)

performances use just intonation. Riley's more recent revisitings of *Shri Camel*, on a piano lacking the delay facilities of his original Yamaha organ, have permitted a combination of the different kinds of chromatic colouring possible with equal temperament and a harmonic language that is more chordally progressive, and even modulatory, in outlook.

In *Shri Camel* Riley investigates ways of dealing with repetition somewhat different from those to be found in his previous output. The work's major innovation is the development of a changing and movable, rather than merely a strictly repeating, pattern. Riley likens the results of using such an evolving pattern to 'having a crochet stitch that you were moving from one level to another all the time'. While its identity remains essentially intact, the original pattern is thus subject not only to continuous alterations in its relationship with its context – notably with the bass line – but also to constant mutation of its own shape. The more melodic profile that emerges as a natural consequence of this malleable technique is inspired by Indian music. *Shri Camel* spins expanding lines of different lengths and complexity over a repeated bass pattern in ways which recall the cyclic principles of Indian musical structure. The schemes, in particular, by which a melodic pattern varies according to its speed – changing its relationship to its surroundings – derives from Indian practice. The bass line, too, has greater independence and flexibility than is exhibited in Riley's earlier works.

The first movement, 'Anthem of the Trinity', is in two parts, both in a slow $\frac{12}{8}$ time; the version on the CBS recording lasts around ten minutes. The first part functions in something like the manner of the ametrical *alap* of a classical Indian improvisation. The ostinato patterns which form the basis of the whole of *Shri Camel* are introduced here (see again

Ex. 2.11a (i) and (ii)). In Pattern A, used in Part One, a single-bar, rocking motif is formed from the notes i, v, vi and ♭vii over a tonic drone. This initially appears some two minutes into the piece, emerging from the more amorphous, scale-based material which provides the context out of which the main ideas and their development can proceed. After a further two minutes, the tonic drone that accompanies this is replaced by an oscillating i–iv bass line; at this point, too, the texture becomes generally thicker. More continuous melodic lines now begin to weave around each other, developing gradually into unbroken semiquavers; the first, i–v–vi–♭vii rocking pattern, meanwhile, carries on functioning as the bass over which this melody can proliferate. As the line unfolds in the right hand, its relationship to the bass pattern evolves in a constant state of flux; an extract from the early stages of this process is given as Example 2.11b.

This demonstrates the work's main innovation, to be found in all movements. While small repeated patterns remain Riley's basic building blocks, he now starts to move them around: both on different degrees of the scale, and in terms of their rhythmic relationships. Patterns can either retain their original length or be subject to augmentation or diminution. Their composer calls the result 'a kind of figuration process going on that would change the motif'. The melody of the first bar of Example 2.11b, beginning just after the initial tonic of the bass pattern, could be moved back a semiquaver on each repetition, 'phasing' right back to its opening position; it could also retain the same pitches throughout. The result – just one of many developments of this kind to be explored – is in this case groups of three semiquavers in cascading sequences occasionally enlivened by grace notes. The evolving relationships which these right-hand patterns form with the bass line are, however, by no means always as strict even as that illustrated here. Riley's improvised, entirely un-notated practice is, typically, much more flexible: not only with regard to rhythmic relationship but also in content. Thus the pattern at the beginning of Example 2.11b is soon varied and expanded, both in pitch and rhythm, in ways which appear largely unsystematic.

Part Two of 'Anthem of the Trinity' subjects Pattern B to mutation via small rhythmic changes, against which a restless, irregular figure behaves, as Riley puts it, 'like a combination of tamboura and tabla', moving quickly from a rhythmic emphasis on the tonic and dominant to expansive, almost continuous semiquaver runs involving a fairly swift expansion up the scale. (The opening six bars of Part Two in Riley's notated fragment are presented in Ex. 2.11c.) 'Celestial Valley', the second movement, turns Pattern A into a faster, two-bar ostinato in $\frac{4}{4}$, with B♮ replacing B♭. Over this, some highly lyrical intertwining melodies owing something to classical Indian practice build a counterpoint exploring new levels of complexity and a wider timbral range.

In the third movement, 'Across the Lake of the Ancient World', Pattern B is likewise speeded up, forming a new ostinato, again subject to metamorphosis. A series of variations is then constructed upon the unbroken revolutions of this pattern, forming two arcs of increased complexity to conclude with a brief, slow, chordal coda. In Example 2.11d, the continuous semiquavers in the right hand begin in groups of seven (G C D F G D F), against the grain of the beat, but quickly add new pitches and spiral away into freer pattern-making incorporating all notes of the mode. In Example 2.11e, various triplet subdivisions dominate the right hand, providing variations on the same idea against the unvarying tread of the bass part. Riley calls the results of combining such duple and triple groupings in the two hands 'a kind of ragtime'. The final movement, 'Desert of Ice', is a kind of rondo, in which Pattern B becomes the basis for an exuberant fantasy where brilliant figuration and more sustained material alternate, and sometimes collide, in a counterpoint coloured by an even brighter range of instrumental timbres. This concluding movement draws together several threads from the previous movements to provide a fitting close to the whole work.

The greater complexity of *Shri Camel* contributed to a quite new way of 'combining inner tranquillity and mental adventure', helping Riley further towards the achievement of the spiritual goals he set himself more than ten years earlier. It represents the culmination of his work with electronic keyboards in the decade after 1966. After the mid-1970s, the seeds which the work had sown for his future development were cultivated in different ground: with the aid of the new kinds of keyboard which then became available – notably the Yamaha computer-controlled piano he acquired in 1980; with the confidence to begin applying his years of training in the Kirana style of singing to his own compositions; and with the arrival of the Kronos Quartet to encourage him to re-explore the potential of notated composition.

Conclusion

Any assessment of Riley's influence must begin – some would say end – with *In C*. For those involved with its première, notably Reich, the work's impact was crucial and immediate, suggesting the potential inherent in the combination of modality and repetition. Riley himself acknowledges that, while 'it wasn't the first minimalist piece, [*In C*] was the first piece that showed people how to do it'. While Young's early exploration of sustained sounds had provided Riley, and others, with the main inspiration to develop other forms of minimalism, it was the repetition of small patterns or modules, not the drone, which was to prove capable of wide application. Young's work with sustained sounds remained little imitated, especially in the early years, due not least to its being very difficult to bring off successfully. Riley's instrumental output from 1964 onwards, on the other hand, had, as he puts it, 'an immediate effect on the audience. Steve noticed that . . . And I think it really made an impact on him: that here was a music that could be avant-garde and get an audience too'.

The rhythmic directness and essential simplicity of this approach also quickly proved captivating to audiences for many different kinds of music. These attitudes to both pitch and rhythm made the work more readily relatable to musics with which its listeners were already familiar, thus rendering it accessible to those coming from jazz or rock, in particular, as well as at least some of the audience for 'serious' music disenchanted by its more rebarbative recent developments. As William Duckworth has written, 'in the late sixties, no one could remember the last experimental composer who had used a key signature, much less written anything in C major'.[37]

In C also proved accessible because it set modality and repetition in an especially effective context in which structural evolution is controlled partly by the composer, partly by the improvisatory interaction of the performers. The notation is sufficiently precise to permit the development of real discipline among performers committed to the music's intentions, yet also sufficiently free to encourage individual expression. Crucially, however, the self-expression of each performer characteristic of all improvisation is here channelled through a collective vehicle that yields expressive results which go beyond individual tastes and intentions, 'transport[ing] us suddenly out of one reality into another', as Riley has described the experience.[38] It is here, as in all Riley's music, that the spiritual dimension of his output has also been important, challenging other composers, and particularly improvisers, to work with modal materials to achieve a contemplative music with higher purposes than mere self-expression.

For the listener, *In C* offers not merely hypnotic repetition but melodic, rhythmic and harmonic changes that not only retain moment-to-moment interest but also contribute to the evolution of the work's structure. This was immediately understood by at least a few outside the composer's own 'alternative' downtown San Francisco circle. Alfred Frankenstein, the *San Francisco Chronicle* music critic, wrote a perceptive review of one of the première performances.[39] He clearly appreciated some of the subtleties of *In C*, observing that 'climaxes of great sonority appear and are dissolved in the endlessness. At times you feel you have never done anything all your life long but listen to this music and as if that is all there is or ever will be, but it is altogether absorbing, exciting, and moving, too'. He also noted the element of ritual in the composition and its realisation, comparing it to Carlos Chavez' reworking of pre-Colombian ceremonial music.

The form in which most musicians and other listeners have experienced *In C* – an LP packaged in a style redolent of the period when the idea of a rock album with integral aspirations was still new – is of itself important. Like the *Rainbow in Curved Air* album, *In C* proclaimed itself as what came to be called a 'crossover' phenomenon. In the parlance of rock, Riley is 'a composer . . . writing pieces which had grooves and improvised around modes'.[40] For many, it is this, and the fact that the creator of such music identified closely with the emerging new technology in producing it, which is more significant than any more specific influence Riley may have had on Brian Eno or on music students.

Riley's influence on rock musicians, especially those interested in challenging the commercial status quo, has, however, perhaps been greater than that of any of the other main subjects of this book, and certainly during the period with which the book largely deals. British groups, in particular, have been affected. Pete Townshend's song 'Bob O'Riley', on The Who's *Teenage Wasteland* album of 1971, was apparently written in the composer's honour; it begins with a synthesizer sequence in a brilliant C major, evidently inspired by both *In C* itself and by the *Rainbow in Curved Air* album, as well as by the taking of psychedelic drugs. Curved Air took its own name from the latter disc; the band's keyboard player, Francis Monkman, was especially attracted to the *Keyboard Studies.*

David Allen, of The Soft Machine, became friendly with Riley. On the group's *Third* album (another product of Columbia, issued in 1970), the modular keyboard approach, coupled with Coltrane-inspired saxophone, of Mike Ratledge's 'Out-Bloody-Rageous' is clearly affected by Riley's work, which is also one of many influences on the eclecticism – as well as the sheer length (a complete LP side) – of Robert Wyatt's 'Moon in June'; the multiple repetitions of the piano riff in 'The Soft Weed Factor', on the group's *Six* album (1973), provide a further instance. The Third Ear Band made use of modal patterns in a rhythmically repetitive context that evidently owes much to his example. Riley's influence was, however, by no means confined to Britain, or to the USA. Other instances from rock music included the Berlin band Agitation Free, which even included

In C in its own concerts; and the Swedish group International Harvester, in particular the guitarist and keyboard player Bo Anders Persson, who played *In C* with its composer at Swedish Radio in 1967 and subsequently played Riley's music around Scandinavia.

Riley's output has also affected more than one generation of classically trained Western music students. As the concern to develop 'alternative' cultures and lifestyles spread out from California to make an international impact, his music found its way to musicians all over the world as an important musical emblem of the demand for new freedoms and outlooks, social and spiritual as well as musical. *In C* 'has proved to be the single most influential post-1960 composition by an American', suggested Robert Palmer in 1974, listing Glass, Reich, Frederic Rzewski, The Soft Machine, John Cale, Brian Eno and 'some contemporary jazz' among its progeny.[41] One might add composers and improvisers to such a list – the British composer Lawrence Ball is just one example – whose work has little to do with rock and much to do with the search for a new, or perhaps a very old, spirituality through the medium of musical experience. Other works by Riley – perhaps particularly *Poppy Nogood and the Phantom Band* and *A Rainbow in Curved Air* – have been influential too; and the composer's early tape pieces should find a place in history as wild and inventive early examples of sampling to rival Reich's achievement in this field. As Duckworth put it, however, it was *In C* that 'gave voice to the minimalist movement in America. In some ways, it became its anthem'.[42]

3 Steve Reich

Steve Reich's career divides geographically into three parts: his childhood and student years on the USA's East Coast; his further years of study in California; and the period that saw his full establishment as a professional composer based in New York. Reich was just short of his twenty-fifth birthday when he 'went West', almost twenty-nine when he returned to New York. In terms of his output as a minimalist, the story only begins towards the end of the second period, but is already substantial soon after the beginning of the third.

Reich is a slow, painstaking and fastidious worker; since *Music for Eighteen Musicians* (first performed in 1976), he has completed just sixteen unwithdrawn compositions (excluding arrangements of earlier pieces). As he is scarcely ever content to use the same approach, material and structure in a subsequent piece without stylistic or technical modification, almost all these can be claimed to represent an advance of some kind, some half-a-dozen of them importantly so. Yet it still makes stylistic and aesthetic sense to divide his complete output into two, with 1976 as the watershed.

Reich himself has argued that the point of maximum change did not come until around 1979. There is a close link between the instrumentation of *Eight Lines* (written in that year, and formerly known as *Octet*) – the work which its composer singles out as representing possibly *the* major point of change – and the modifications to his thinking about structure; its recuperation of melody and harmonic motion seems all of a piece with the new importance it gives to instruments of the standard Western classical orchestra and to variety of timbral resource. But it is in *Music for Eighteen Musicians* (1974–6) that we find regular instruments of the orchestra used in an ensemble context in Reich's output for the first time. In *Tehillim* (1980–81) the composer's tendencies towards more sustained and clear-cut melodic writing are set into even sharper relief by Reich's return to the task of setting a text, the first time he had done so since his student days; but the seeds of this were sown by his studies in Jewish cantillation in 1976–7.

The stylistic advances made in the immediate aftermath of *Music for Eighteen Musicians* may be seen, in part, as a response to the commissions the composer was now receiving for works for forces other than those of his own ensemble. The uniqueness of these compositions in the composer's total output can be overestimated; after all, he has continued to rely on keyboards and tuned percussion as a central force – both compositional and purely practically – in later works: both those for large forces (*The Desert Music*, 1982–4) and those for smaller ones (*Sextet*, 1984–5). *The Cave* (1989–93) and *Three Tales* (1996 onwards) demonstrate Reich's continuing rejection of aspects of the Western classical heritage (the operatic voice) and the revival of his interest in new technologies which has been a strong feature of his output since *Different Trains* (1988). For the composer himself, the latter work, with its sampling of both speech and other sounds in a live instrumental context, now marks a watershed as significant as that of *c.* 1979. But his rapprochement with the aims and intentions, as well as the forces, of Western classical music is arguably as significant for everything Reich wrote after 1976 as are the repeating structures which remain its 'structure and basis, the main dish of what I do'.[1]

Music for Eighteen Musicians offers, indeed, the best case of all for concluding the present book in that year, marking as it does the end of Reich's interest in minimalism as previously defined herein. Completed in March 1976, its increased debt to Western classical music in general, and its approach to harmony in particular, represent important new departures for its composer. The arrival of a kind of harmonic motion, in *Eighteen Musicians* and, to a lesser extent, in its predecessor, *Music for Mallet Instruments, Voices and Organ* (1973), does not, however, require the complete abandonment of the rhythmic techniques and concern for structural process that characterise Reich's music of the previous decade. *Eighteen Musicians* is crucially 'on-the-edge' aesthetically, and technically, speaking; that its composer was unable to remain in that interesting position now seems an important part of the work's achievement as well as of its historical significance. Harmonic motion – or at least the investigation of it in the surviving context of repetition – and all that came with it led both to works for symphony orchestra more 'symphonic' than we might have thought possible and to approaches to word-setting of considerable variety and imagination – even, in *The Cave* and *Three Tales*, to Reich's own brand of music-theatre.

Surprisingly, however, the achievements of *Music for Eighteen Musicians* proved troublesome for him to follow up. In fact, Reich completed nothing after this for more than two years, and only wrote himself out of what appears to have been a major crisis with a piece which, for him (though not for all his listeners), is at best problematic: *Music for a Large Ensemble* (1978). That, however, belongs to a later part of the story. In the meantime, the onset of the only hiatus of this magnitude in Reich's career creates a natural break in the narrative.

The earlier music may be further divided into two. Reich has himself advanced the notion that *Drumming* (1970–71) embodies the true transition between the phase-structured works of his early years and the more stylistically adventurous and technically varied compositions of his full maturity. The concerns which culminated in *Music for Eighteen Musicians* surfaced in *Six Pianos* and, more importantly, in *Music for Mallet Instruments, Voices and Organ* (both 1973) more clearly than they did in *Drumming*, making it possible to view all four works as a natural development away from minimalist concerns.

But while the works preceding *Drumming* constitute a viable 'early minimalist' period, the division of Reich's output between 1965 and 1976 that may first occur to his listeners is that between the handful of tape pieces composed in 1965–6 – such as *It's Gonna Rain*, with which he established the technique of phasing – and the instrumental works of 1966–7 onwards – such as *Piano Phase*, that first explored phasing in live performance and then extended its implications by incorporating a wider range both technically and stylistically. Reich's surviving interest in the possibilities of electronic technology, culminating in the phase-shifting pulse-gate pieces of 1969, forms a kind of bridge between these; this hybrid area could take in several other works of 1966–8 which combined live players with tape or other technology: notably *Violin Phase* (1967), a precursor of the later 'Counterpoint' series (which begins with *Vermont Counterpoint* of 1982). Another kind of bridge is formed by *Four Organs* (1970), a piece which succeeds in being the earliest work to transcend phasing by taking another idea generated by its composer's immersion in electronics and making live music from it. What follows here attempts an estimation of 'early' and 'mature' even within what is officially the 'early period'.

Early years

Stephen Michael Reich was born in New York City on 3 October 1936. His parents both came from wealthy, upper-middle-class Jewish families; his father was a New York lawyer, his mother born in Detroit. Reich's parents separated when the composer was only a year old and, remaining with his father, he was raised, in considerable part, by a governess, Virginia Mitchell. Until 1942, Reich frequently travelled from his father's home in New York to visit his mother, who had moved to Los Angeles, later inspiring the already mentioned *Different Trains* for string quartet and tape, in which documentary material in the form of interviews is used to contrast the young American Jewish boy's four-day rail trips across the USA with the sort of train journeys he might have been forced to take at the time if he had been a European Jew. In the 1950s, Reich's real mother became best known as the Broadway singer and lyricist June Carroll, under which name she wrote the lyrics of the song 'Love is a simple thing' (set to music by Arthur Siegel), still remembered today.

Reich was brought up Reform Jewish but received little encouragement to take the faith seriously. Leonard Reich hoped that his son would follow him into one of the established professions – law or medicine – or into industrial labour relations, for which Cornell, which the composer later attended, had a school. By opting for music, Reich junior was – from his father's point of view – reverting to his mother's sphere of influence, and father and son became estranged for many years. Only when Leonard Reich saw his son's picture in a Sunday edition of the *New York Times* in 1972 did the two re-establish contact.

Reich has frequently stressed his expansion away from the 'classical' music he heard at home towards rather more immediately exciting concerns for a teenager in the early 1950s:

> As a child I took what I would call middle-class piano lessons, and up to the age of 14 the only music that I was aware of was what I would call middle-class favourites: Beethoven's *Fifth*, Schubert's *Unfinished*, the overture to *The Mastersingers* and so on; I also heard Broadway shows and a lot of popular music. It wasn't until the age of 14 that I heard the music that would end up motivating me to become a composer and informing what I did: that was jazz, Bach and Stravinsky . . .[2]

Crucial encounters with both twentieth-century and older music new to him – including *The Rite of Spring* – thus came in about 1950–51. Jazz, in particular, was to engage him for some time and became very important to his musical development. At the age of fourteen, he took up drumming, studying with Roland Kohloff (later principal timpanist with the New York Philharmonic Orchestra). Reich was able to help form a jazz ensemble, in which he was the drummer, thereby laying the foundations for his later obsessions with rhythm and percussion instruments; his approach to pitch was also informed by his jazz experiences. Meanwhile, he began to make pocket-money by spending weekend evenings playing trap drums in dance bands: for church and synagogue dances when still in high school; and later, at university, for fraternity parties and Elks Clubs.

Reich went to Cornell University, not far up the East Coast from New York, in September 1953, just before his seventeenth birthday – unusually young even for the times. Though music was by now crucial to him, he felt he was already too old to pursue music professionally. As a student he therefore majored in philosophy. Reich developed a particular interest in

Ludwig Wittgenstein, who had himself been at Cornell until 1950, the year before he died. While Wittgenstein's ideas were of great importance to Reich at this time, any relationship with the composer's subsequent thinking is somewhat tangential and tends to be greeted with scepticism by the composer himself.[3]

While at Cornell, Reich also took some music courses. Though already mistrustful of 'musical academe', he began a friendship with his chief music professor, the musicologist William Austin, showing him some songs that are probably Reich's first efforts at composition. Austin's musical sympathies included Stravinsky, American music, jazz and non-Western musics (all unusual for an Ivy League musicologist in the 1950s).[4] Reich became increasingly interested not only in Debussy, Stravinsky and jazz but also in medieval music, especially the work of the French composer Perotin, whose use of strict structures such as cantus firmus, isorhythm and, especially, canon and augmentation has remained an influence. (*Proverb*, composed in 1995, demonstrates his continuing debt to Perotin; its setting of Wittgenstein's sentence 'How small a thought it takes to fill a whole life!'[5] also provides evidence of the philosopher's continuing influence in the form of a motto eminently suited to Reich's output as a whole.)

Reich graduated from Cornell in the summer of 1957, and went back to New York. Encouraged by Austin, he had decided to reject the option of postgraduate philosophy studies at Harvard University. Having by now a clear notion that he wanted to compose, he studied privately, from 1957–8, with Hall Overton: an apt choice, since he had both a Western classical compositional pedigree (he had studied at the Juilliard School with Vincent Persichetti) and experience in jazz (he had been a colleague of Thelonius Monk). Little of Reich's efforts at composition of this period have survived, but he says that a song he wrote for Overton in 1957 contains an example of a chord structure which would become characteristic of his mature music: a chord of 'stacked' fifths.

Then, as a student at the Juilliard School between 1958 and 1961, Reich himself studied with Persichetti. His Juilliard colleagues included Philip Glass, though Reich says they had nothing in common at that time, either musically or socially, and the two were never really friends. Arthur Murphy – who had previously studied in Oberlin, Ohio with Richard Hoffmann, Schoenberg's protégé and one-time secretary, later studied mathematics and afterwards became a member of the composer's group – was another contemporary; so were Peter Schickele (later best known as P. D. Q. Bach) and Conrad Sousa. As a whole, the school seemed conservative to Reich – 'the last stronghold of the dying Americana, the end of the Aaron Copland tradition' – and he felt little better about the contemporary music scene in New York generally.

The composer describes the style of his Juilliard output, of which several scores survive, as 'somewhere between the Third, Fourth and Fifth Quartets [of Bartók and] the Webern of Opus 5 [the Five Pieces for String Quartet]'; he has even traced the chord of 'stacked' fifths he had used in his 1957 song to the opening of the second movement of Bartók's Second Piano Concerto. Jazz, too, had a significant influence on this highly chromatic, rather than atonal, approach, with its altered and often ambiguous dominant chords. 'I never wrote a piece where I didn't feel a harmonic centre', he says. During this time, he also attempted to set some of the poetry of William Carlos Williams. Reich responded to Williams' use of American vernacular speech, but found that traditional notions of 'setting' poetry rooted in American speech rhythms to music destroyed its essence. As with his efforts to set Robert Creeley and Charles Olsen, he 'got nowhere'. A wholly original approach to 'text setting' – discovered in the tape pieces of the mid-1960s, and inspired in part by Williams' response to the vernacular – became necessary before he could turn back to poetry in English, which he did by setting Williams himself in *The Desert Music.*

Reich felt an increasing need to experience a different cultural climate. On leaving Juilliard in the summer of 1961, not long before his twenty-fifth birthday, he decided to head West. California seemed to offer not merely a different musical scene but a different social milieu, away from his father's sphere of influence. For the real reason for his move was 'the classic reason that Americans go to California: I was running away from home'.

California

Reich arrived in San Francisco in September 1961 with the intention of going to graduate school. He had recently married in New York, and his wife, Joyce Barkett, had just had a baby. Moving to California ahead of his new family in order to make arrangements for them, he took a job as a stock clerk on Fisherman's Wharf. The child, however – born with intestinal complications – died; when his wife arrived in California she brought his corpse. Stunned, and for the moment totally unclear about his own direction, the would-be composer took various jobs for a while. The couple subsequently had another child, Michael Reich; the marriage ended in divorce in 1963.

Reich had originally intended to go to Mills College in nearby Oakland to study with Leon Kirchner, but it turned out that this purveyor of 'the great Bartók tradition', as Reich thought of him, had just left. He briefly considered going to the University of California at Berkeley to work with Seymour Shifrin, as Young and Riley had done earlier. But on learning that Luciano Berio was to take Kirchner's place, he quickly enrolled at Mills after all, at the beginning of 1962; the college additionally offered the faster programme. It also offered Darius Milhaud, who was teaching alternating semesters with Berio, though by then this venerable former member of the 1920s avant-garde was old and ill. While one or two interesting students turned out to be among his contemporaries – notably Phil Lesh, later bass guitarist of The Grateful Dead – to his dismay Reich found the situation at Mills to be even more stultifying, and certainly more limiting, than that of New York.

Reich's most frequently told anecdote about Mills concerns his attempt to simplify – or subvert – serialism by composing twelve-note music which entirely avoided inversions, retrogrades and transpositions:

> I would just repeat the row over and over. By doing this you can create a kind of static harmony not entirely dissimilar to the Webern orchestral Variations, which are very static and intervallically constant and which suggest this kind of world.[6]

This approach has clear parallels with Young's compositions of 1957–8, though Reich's experience of these had been confined to joining in the general derision when some account of *Trio for Strings*, perhaps even a tape, circulated around Juilliard. The first piece in which he adopted the twelve-note procedure was *Music for String Orchestra*, dated 5/61 on the score and actually the last composition Reich wrote while in New York. His approach to a technique more commonly construed as an ideal way to avoid pitch repetition and create a constant state of flux met with a predictable response from Berio, to whom he showed the score after his enrolment at Mills. 'He liked it', says Reich, 'but he began to realise that those tones weren't going to do anything but repeat'. 'If you want to write tonal music', he apparently said, 'then write tonal music'.

The manuscript reveals a twelve-note set subjected to constant repetition. The set on which *Music for String Orchestra* is based (see Ex. 3.1) concerns itself chiefly with semitones and minor thirds, making it possible to segment it into small groups of notes along the lines Webern used, though Reich is less rigorous in his construction. The composer argues that the close-position voicing of some of the clusters formed from these segments creates 'a static and somewhat tonal situation: ambiguous, odd, but nevertheless not what was intended by the use of twelve-tone technique', and relates it to the kinds of harmonic vocabulary he still uses today; the notion of 'stacking' the same interval, or two intervals, makes a somewhat

Example 3.1 *Music for String Orchestra*, twelve-note set

tenuous connection with his subsequent practice. The set of *Music for String Orchestra* is far less triadic, or in any other sense 'tonal', than that of, say, Berg's Violin Concerto; and the music to which it gives rise is actually as secundally dissonant as most post-Webernian serial compositions, making Berio's observation a little hard to understand. Yet the interest displayed here in static harmony and repetition is the earliest indication in his pre-minimalist output of the direction Reich's mature music would take.

According to his own account, all Reich's pieces composed while he was a student at Mills College follow *Music for String Orchestra*'s approach to static harmony via row repetition. Unfortunately, on his return to New York, many of his scores (in a 'big black book') and tapes were stolen when thieves broke into his car. His description of the three semesters at Mills as 'a very unproductive time', does not, however, suggest that his investigations of twelve-note static harmony and repetition proved at all successful.

The only Mills work which survives is the last composition he wrote there, which reflects, much more directly than any of the others appear to have done, his continuing interest in jazz. Reich had already spent much of his time in New York listening, in particular, to John Coltrane; at the Jazz Workshop in San Francisco, he had even better opportunities to hear Coltrane live. As with Young and Riley during the same period, he was drawn to the startlingly innovative modal jazz that Coltrane was then evolving: a new music bringing together many of the concerns – modality, a regular pulse, influences from earlier jazz and from non-Western sources – closest to Reich's own heart. 'John Coltrane's music between 1961 and 1964 made a tremendous impression on me', the composer has said.

Four Pieces, composed in 1963 as Reich's graduation exercise, reflect a move in the direction of a clearer modality. As their instrumentation – trumpet, alto saxophone, piano, bass and drums – suggests, these are heavily indebted to the resources and idioms of jazz, which Reich attempts to combine with more 'cultivated' materials and procedures somewhat in the then currently still fashionable manner of the 'Third-Stream' jazz-fusion approach of Gunther Schuller and others. Twelve-note procedures still govern the details of their note-to-note structure, subjected to the same technique of 'repeating and repeating the row over and over again'. Here, though, the harmonic organisation owes as much to the application of an altered-dominant chordal vocabulary to a jazz context (from which this

Example 3.2 *Four Pieces*, no. 2, final two bars

vocabulary itself partly derives) as to the set itself. 'How', Reich asks, 'could I group the row into some way to make progressions that seemed to work?' One answer was to use oblique motion: keeping one or more parts at the same pitch while moving the others. (Example 3.2, concluding the second piece, is the last in a sequence in which the chord assembled in the piano is also reflected in the moving parts around it, the already characteristically 'stacked' harmony underpinned by the bass line.) Its composer describes the results as 'twelve-tone jazz licks trying to become tonal . . . somewhere between Steve Reich, Bill Evans and [Schoenberg's] Opus Eleven'. Both the altered-dominant and the oblique-motion aspects of these pieces foreshadow its composer's subsequent approach to pitch organisation. Their incorporation of improvised passages – the second piece includes improvisation on the same twelve-note set used in the written-out sections – prefigures the approach of Reich's next composition, *Pitch Charts*.

Four Pieces' only performance was given by a group of young players conversant with both jazz and fully notated musics: Einer Anderson on trumpet, Paul Breslin on bass, John Chowning (later to become famous in the field of electro-acoustic music) on drums and Jon Gibson (later to work with all four leading minimalists) who played alto saxophone. The pianist was the composer himself, who was by now coming to the conclusion that 'a healthy musical situation would only result when the functions of composer and performer were united',[7] as they so frequently are in jazz. From now on, he decided, 'despite my limitations as a performer I had to play in all my compositions'. *Four Pieces* thus in a sense mark, their composer has said, 'the birth of my ensemble'. The desire to write only what he could play must also have helped Reich towards a much simpler, reductive style.

Theatre and film; improvisation and composition; music for tape

After graduating, Reich remained in the Bay Area for the next two years. Having decided against university teaching as a career path in composition, he worked in the US Post Office for some while, did some taxi driving and taught at the Community Music School on San Francisco's Capp Street. Meanwhile, he involved himself with four main areas of musical activity: composing music for the San Francisco Mime Troupe, playing with an improvisation group and – working at his home-based studio – composing both independent tape pieces and some music for underground films and theatre.

The music Reich composed in California in the two years between leaving Mills College in the summer of 1963 and returning to New York in September 1965 may be divided into three categories: concert compositions involving live performers; music for theatre and film; and works for tape. While nothing he wrote before *It's Gonna Rain* may be much more than a historical curiosity, all the pieces involved – even *Four Pieces* and *Pitch Charts* (discussed below) – illustrate Reich's quest for a more overtly experimental approach to composition which did not deny the validity of tonality.

Before he graduated from Mills, Reich and some of his colleagues formed an improvisation group. Gibson, George Rey (a violinist), a cellist called Gwendoline Watson and others, including Reich on piano, 'met at least once a week for about six months' to play 'free, and sometimes controlled, improvisation'. Soon dissatisfied with the results, Reich concluded that the problem lay in the reliance on purely 'spur of the moment reactions', and decided to compose some material to help provide some 'musical growth'.

The result was *Pitch Charts*, the score of which is dated 11/63. Its three movements are written in open score, but including transpositions for clarinet or trumpet, alto and tenor saxophones, and double bass. The same pitches are allocated in groups, or occasionally singly, to these instruments simultaneously, though not all instruments have all pitches; rhythm remains free. While the tendency to unfold the complete chromatic gamut remains, pitches are now repeated in small units, rather than in twelve-note cycles. (Ex. 3.3 shows the opening of the first 'chart'.) The actual

Example 3.3 *Pitch Charts*, first movement, opening

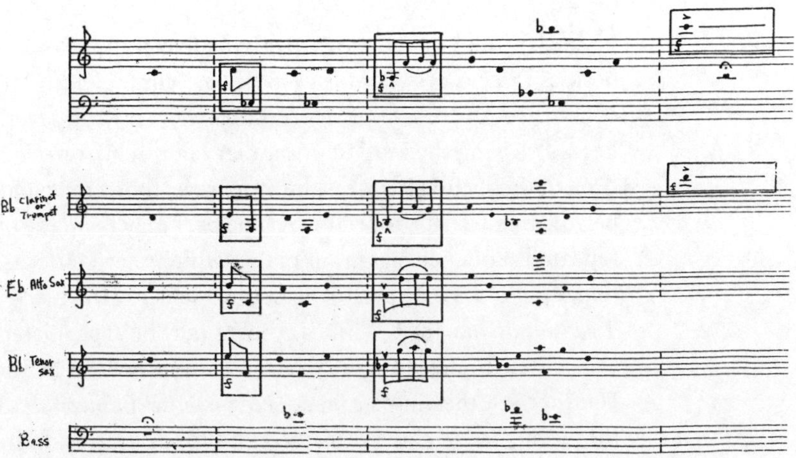

vocabulary, too, is more modal, emphasising particular centres by repetition and piling up intervals to produce chords of the type already used in *Four Pieces. Pitch Charts* was performed by students and friends at the Capp Street Community Music School. There also seem to be some other pieces from around this time which explore unconventional notations of various kinds, including two graphically notated compositions entitled *Proportional Pieces #1* and *#2*.

While still at Mills, Reich had admired the work of the San Francisco Mime Troupe, which was then mounting less overtly politicised productions than those for which the company subsequently became famous. About the time he graduated from Mills, Reich met R. G. Davis, the Mime Troupe's head, and at his suggestion wrote music for its production of Alfred Jarry's *Ubu Roi*, staged in the deconsecrated church in the Mission District used by the company on 10 December 1963 (the sixty-seventh anniversary of the play's Paris première). Billed as a '5 Act surrealist farce', its approach made it something of a *cause célèbre*. Reich describes the production as 'very broad slapstick'; the flyer advertised the performance as being 'In Cooperation with the College of Pataphysique . . . West' and promised 'Reception and Disembrainning [*sic*] Following Performance'. The artist William T. Wiley, who designed the sets and costumes, and the composer became friends. Reich's music, presently unlocatable, was apparently scored for clarinet and kazoo, playing a tune in unison, with a strummed violin accompaniment consisting of a single chord; the kazoo was amplified by means of a large Pacific Gas and Electric plastic traffic cone used as a megaphone. The musicians played this tune several times, then turned about face and left. It was, as the composer says, 'very much a thumbing-your-nose kind of thing': at his former teacher, Berio, among others.

Reich's only concert work involving live performance during this period besides *Pitch Charts* is *Music for Two or More Pianos*. Dated 2/64, the score consists simply of a sequence of nine five-, six- and seven-note chords (see Ex. 3.4). Using the kind of vocabulary familiar from *Four Pieces* and *Pitch Charts*, these chords are, as the score says, to 'be repeated as many times as performers feel appropriate'. A tape part may be made of a reading of this repeated sequence, again on piano, which may stand in for one, or more than one, of the live performers, in which case the piece is called *Music for Two Pianos and Tape*. While '[c]hords may be arpeggiated or broken in any way', performers do not have the same freedom as they do in Morton Feldman's somewhat similar *Piece for Four Pianos* (1958); Reich requires his players to 'remain with any chord for as long as desired, but as soon as any performer moves from one chord to the next, all performers should move on similarly, as soon as possible'. The result is a kind of close canonic phasing of the chord sequence. Though the composer had not heard Feldman's piece at the time, he acknowledges the influence of Stockhausen's *Refrain* (1959), a work which similarly exploits repetition of the same material by several performers, and which in turn was probably influenced by Feldman. *Music for Two or More Pianos* thus clearly anticipates the phasing technique discovered almost a year later in *It's Gonna Rain*.

While many of the composers who were members of the avant-garde community working at the San Francisco Tape Music Center on Divisidero Street favoured synthesized sounds, Reich was more interested in working with the natural sounds of *musique concrète* in undisguised form, preserving the 'added emotional layer' which comes with the recognition of familiar sounds. His first finished electronic composition was also his first tape collage: a piece, dating from early in 1964, to accompany a short film called *Plastic Haircut* by the film-maker Robert Nelson, which involved some of the Mime Troupe team. Constructions of paper and wood made by Wiley and the sculptor Robert Hudson were manipulated by Davis, the Mime Troupe's head, to make a kind of 'black-and-white animation'; these were then filmed by Nelson, who sometimes included Davis himself in the shots. Reich's tape, not synchronised with the film, used crowd noises from an LP issued by Columbia Records called *The Greatest Moments in Sports*. The result was 'rather like a surrealist rondo with all kinds of elements recurring', in which loops of individual sounds were first played alone and 'then overlaid just to make noise'. Reich considers that, in his music for *Plastic Haircut*, 'the seeds were there'; at the time, he was especially enthu-

Example 3.4 *Music for Two or More Pianos*, complete score

siastic about the ambiguous residual meanings preserved by this approach.

Like Glass after him, Reich drove a taxi cab for a living, though only in San Francisco, not following his return to New York. *Livelihood* (also 1964) is a three-minute *collage* assembled from sounds collected on these duties: conversations, 'slamming doors, meters being thrown, grunts and groans, people hitting their head . . . the noises that one hears inside of a taxi' were used, often in only tiny fragments. Reich destroyed the mastertape of this piece, along with some other material, in the mid-1980s. The present author has nevertheless heard *Livelihood*, which turns out to be a witty evocation of a taxi-driver's daily life, carefully constructed to evoke all the basic stages of a taxi ride: from stating the destination to casual conversation in the cab, ending with paying the fare and saying 'Thank you' and 'Goodnight'.

In the spring of 1964, Reich and his associates played at the San Francisco Mime Troupe Theater. Presented on no fewer than four nights – 21, 23, 29 and 30 May – 'Koncert I' began with three pieces by Reich: *Proportional Piece #1* and two improvisations on the *Pitch Charts* material ('tape and live version'), performed by a sextet including Gibson ('reeds'), Lesh (trumpet) and Reich (piano). A quintet by Lesh – and, surprisingly, Bach's Third Cello Suite, played by Watson, who also participated in all the ensemble items – closed the first half. In the second, Tom Constanten (subsequently keyboard player with The Grateful Dead) played his own *Piano Piece #3*, and the programme concluded with free improvisations performed by all six musicians, who also included the violinist Rey and the bass player Breslin once more.

It was after one of these nights that Reich first encountered Terry Riley. The story of their meeting has already been told in the previous chapter, including the participation of Reich and other members of his improvisation group in the première of *In C* on 4 November 1964. Riley's influence on his new colleague was crucial. Like so many others, Reich considers *In C* to be a seminal work, and acknowledges it as a major influence on his own development. While Reich had already used repetition to construct everything from twelve-note compositions to *collage*, the modularity of *In C* pointed the way towards a more organised and consistent kind of pattern-making with highly reductive means. Riley's method quickly proved to have greater potential than Young's static approach. It was easier to vary and develop, and it soon became apparent that it could lead to musical results which were more immediately accessible, especially when modular processes were harnessed to modal materials.

It's Gonna Rain

Though himself having had some hand in establishing *In C*'s insistent pulse, Reich did not at first employ one in his own compositions, preferring to imply this through rhythmic continuity. The modality of Riley's composition was a clearer confirmation of Reich's earlier instincts, despite his initial decision to make tape pieces manipulating speech material; speech, after all, has a melodic profile of its own, which may be exploited in the act of composition. Like *In C*, *It's Gonna Rain* begins with a pattern based on a rising major third, which becomes important to the way the work unfolds. Reich's close involvement in the première of *In C* during his preliminary work on *It's Gonna Rain* suggests more than mere coincidence, though Reich himself considers it of little significance. Later, modality of a more thorough-going kind became central to his output.

Reich's discovery of phasing in *It's Gonna Rain* was in fact influenced at least as much by the tape compositions Riley had been composing over the previous two or three years as by the more evidently seminal *In C*. Reich says he heard *She Moves She* from *The Gift*, *Shoeshine* and *I* late in 1964 or early in 1965. His new friend's manipulation of shifting patterns constructed from spoken material with the aid of the time-lag accumulator and his use of tape loops to effect the transformation of speech through repetition, overlay and slow changes of speed are clearly influences on Reich, suggesting effects to him that *In C* itself did not. Riley remembers a first attempt at what became *It's Gonna Rain* as 'more of a sound-text piece'[8] like *Livelihood* – which he had enormously enjoyed – and suggests that his tape compositions were as important to Reich's move away from *collage* as was *In C*.

Reich acknowledges a debt to his colleague's innovations, though he stresses *In C* rather than the tape compositions. At least as late as 14 January 1968 – in the notes for an Arts Now 'afternoon of live and electronic music by Steve Reich' at the Philips Exeter Academy, a preparatory school in Massachusetts – his first mature tape composition was being listed as 'It's Gonna Rain, or meet Brother Walter in Union Square after listening to Terry Riley'. 'It was Riley's work that put it all together' for him, he says, though he sees no relevance in any of his music since *In C*. But while Riley always allowed his patterns to accumulate into a psychedelic wash of sound, Reich generally stressed the audibility of his 'gradually shifting phase relations'. Riley worked by intuition; Reich attempted to bring rigour to bear in his attempt to 'find some *new* way of working with repetition as a musical technique'. With *It's Gonna Rain* and *Come Out*, Reich suggests, 'you're watching the minute hand on the watch. That's not the effect of Riley's pieces at all: there, you're taking a bath'. Reich's notes for the concert mentioned above proudly state that '[t]he use of the phase shift as a basic structure applied to a single figure against itself is, as far as I know, unique to the music on this program'.

Another, earlier, interest also helped Reich to find his own approach to the use of everyday sounds and to a method by which 'the authenticity of American speech' could be captured and turned to fresh account: the poetry of William Carlos Williams. *It's Gonna Rain* and *Come Out* were composed, Reich says, 'against the background of having failed to set text that I would have liked to have set'. Though previously unable to find a solution to the problem of setting Williams' poetry itself, Reich now learned an important lesson from this master of modern American poetry for whom he has a special admiration. He noted that Williams, refusing the blandishments of any International Style of modernism, derived his inspiration from his local roots. As a practising doctor in New Jersey, Williams had observed the speech and other sounds around him and made these the basis of his style. As a composer working in an urban environment with the new tape technology, Reich felt that the poet was 'looking over your shoulder and saying, "Go record the street! Go listen to your countrymen and get your music from the way they speak"'. Williams' example helped Reich to find a solution to the problems of writing vocal music and setting texts by turning to the tape recorder.

It's Gonna Rain is the composer's first important composition to use minimalist techniques. In the course of constructing a further *collage*-style piece, Reich failed to achieve the perfect synchronisation of tape loops which he was actually seeking. In his *Writings*, the composer states that '[i]n the process of trying to line up two identical tape loops in some particular relationship, I discovered that the most interesting music of all was made by simply lining the loops up in unison, and letting them slowly shift out of phase with each other'.[9] The two Wollensack machines, plus one borrowed Ampex, on which Reich composed *It's Gonna Rain* were the cheapest he could find, exacerbating the extent of the drift which revealed this effect to him. But as Riley had already discovered, he found that 'it was inevitable with the technology of that day that there would have been drift': a phenomenon which occurred even on the better Sony 770 and Uher portable machines he subsequently acquired, the latter pair bought on hire-purchase with Lesh. Reich now proceeded to alter the speed of one loop against the other by holding the supply reel of the tape providing the second channel with his thumb. The imperceptible slowing down of this second channel against the first produced the phasing he desired. After this, it was simply – though laboriously – a question of making a new loop of each new relationship, feeding it back into the first channel and then continually repeating the process.

The origins and purpose of *It's Gonna Rain* are at least as interesting as its significance in the evolution of musical minimalist techniques. The tale is frequently told of how, following the advice of a friend, Reich went down to San Francisco's Union Square one day in November 1964 to record a sermon by Brother Walter, a young black preacher whose occasional, very fiery, Sunday appearances there had become quite famous. The friend had expressed some intention of making a film, but this never materialised. Reich, meanwhile, had started to see the musical potential of Brother

Walter's heightened form of Black American English, and transcribed the sermon on three large manuscript pages in an attempt to analyse its material. The independent piece he eventually produced lasts 17′31″ and divides clearly into two parts, or movements, with a sizeable pause between them. Both open with untreated recordings from the sermon, from which extracts are then taken to provide the basic material for each part. (The complete text as used in *It's Gonna Rain* is reproduced as Ex. 3.5.) Part One uses only the words 'It's gonna rain'. Part Two draws on a longer passage, continuing from where the extract used in the first part left off: as Reich puts it, a 'long description of people trying to get into the Ark and finding that God had sealed the door and that they couldn't get into the Ark, and they were going to die'.

In early 1965, Brother Walter's sermon suggested something more immediate than the fire-and-brimstone message typical of its type. The Cuban missile crisis of October 1962 had created the feeling that 'nuclear disaster was a finger on the button away', and even more than two years later, this gave the story of Noah's Flood a fresh, and urgent, dimension, enhanced by the repetition characteristic of this Evangelical style of preaching. The words of *It's Gonna Rain* thus offer a metaphor for impending nuclear holocaust. While the short Part One treats its material fairly lightly, the 'controlled chaos' of Part Two is a quite different matter. When he presented *It's Gonna Rain* at the Tape Music Center in January 1965, Reich felt that Part Two was too bleak and disturbing to include at all. Part Two also reflects Reich's personal circumstances at the time, which were far from happy: 'I was not', he says, 'in a good psychic way in San Francisco'. His disinclination to 'inflict [his] neuroses on the listening public' was a further reason to stop the tape at the end of Part One. After he returned to New York, he decided the piece should henceforth be played complete.

Part Two uses complex, far less pitch-specific material than that found in Part One. In structural terms, though, this section is fairly straightforward. Firstly, the new loop is gradually phased against itself; then this two-voiced relationship is presented on channel 1, against which a duplicate is phased on channel 2. The resulting four-voiced texture is eventually further doubled, by the same process, to eight voices. The deconstruction of the original into mere noise – a development of the *Plastic Haircut*'s 'surrealist rondo' – reflects in structure and emotional effect the words selected from the sermon.

It's Gonna Rain also has a pitch dimension deriving from the tendency of the sort of declamation used here to enhance the residual pitch patterns of 'normal' speech with the more focused, and retained, melodic

Example 3.5 *It's Gonna Rain*, spoken material

STEVE REICH

It's Gonna Rain

Spoken material used in *It's Gonna Rain* (spelling according to Reich's transcription, punctuation added for ease of reference; words used for musical development presented in bold).

Part One

He be'gan to warn the people. He said: after a while, **it's gonna rain** after a while. For forty days an fo forty nites. And the people didn't believe him. And they began to laugh at him. And they begin to mock him, and they begin to say: It ain't gonna RAIN!

Part Two

They didn't believe that it was gonna rain. But - glory to God, haleluya, bless God's wonderful name dis evenin, Ah say this evenin, after a while. They didn't believe that it was gonna rain. **But, shorenuf,** it begin ta rain - haleluya.

They begin to knock upon the door. But it was too late. Whooo! The Bible tell me they knock upon a door, until the skin came off their hand. Whooo! My laud, my laud. Ah said until a skin came off der hand. They cried - Ah can just hear **der cry**, how! Ah could hear em say: ohh, Noah, would you just open the door. **But Noah couldn't open a door. It had been sealed by the hand of God!**

Example 3.6 *It's Gonna Rain*, Part One, Basic Unit

utterances of real song. Pitch most clearly becomes an issue in Part One, which uses only the single fragment of three pitches that gives *It's Gonna Rain* its title (reproduced in Ex. 3.6), suggesting the key of D major. (From here on, such a pattern will be called the Basic Unit.) In the main section of Part One, a simple phasing process takes these words from unison through a complete cycle and back to unison.

Before this, however, a rather different technique is employed. After the initial extract, the fragment 'It's gonna rain' is subjected to what Reich calls 'a kind of monophonic sampling'. The loop is stereophonically separated 'exactly 180 degrees out of phase, so that the word "it's" falls on top of "rain", more or less', he says. 'Sampling each channel in synchronisation with the voice rhythm will give you "It's gonna, it's gonna . . ." over and over again. Speed up the sampling rate, however, and the result will move from "it's gonna", inching into the "r" of "rain", then into "ain", "nnn", and finally back into "It's gonna"'. Reich achieved this by performing the process with a preamplifier switch, judging the results purely intuitively and submitting the final mix to tape. It should, in addition, be noted that the original tape of the words 'It's gonna rain' also included the sound of a pigeon flapping its wings; the composer was delighted with this extra dimension which, through constant repetition, makes a significant contribution to the overall effect.

The piece with which Reich made the technical discovery which opened the door to the whole of his mature work does not confine itself to a simple, purely mechanical operation of that technique. The monophonic sampling described above is 'phasing' of a kind, and brief at that, while the majority of Part One, like Part Two, is a 'literal embodiment' of the process of phasing itself. But the variety of procedures and the sophistication of the resulting structures make it clear from the outset that Reich is interested in note-to-note composing and in the effect of his final product, not merely in experimentation with a mechanistic process regardless of artistic result. In addition, the difficulties of identifying the musical process at work in the early stages of *It's Gonna Rain* – to which the extraneous sound of the pigeon's wings flapping adds an extra layer of confusion – make an important statement at the outset of a career sometimes interpreted as built merely on the mechanistic application of simplistic procedures to mindless material. While its composer considers that this is 'the purest process piece that I ever did', *It's Gonna Rain* already demonstrates in embryo the compositional control Reich would exert with greater force in subsequent works.

Before his departure from San Francisco, Reich completed only one other piece: *Oh dem Watermelons!*, another score for the San Francisco Mime Troupe, written for a kind of ironic, 'post-modernist' minstrel show, premièred in May 1965, which incorporated another short film by Nelson. The film uses images of watermelons as an analogy for the oppression of Black Americans. Reich's contribution combined two extracts from songs by Stephen Foster – 'Massa's in the cold, cold ground' and 'Oh dem Watermelons': both in D major, the chosen extracts stuck on an endlessly revolving II–V^7 progression on the piano that produces the effect of a dominant pedal. Around this, he constructed a kind of five-part canon for voices on the single word 'watermelon'. *Oh dem Watermelons!* extends Reich's work with tape into the territory of the more straightforward canon – of which phasing is really but a special case, as the composer has noted from the beginning.[10] Its synthesis of tonic and dominant harmonies both reflects the modal approach of Riley's *In C* and foreshadows the unresolved, elongated half cadences of the later *Four Organs* and Part Four of *Drumming*. Reich later performed 'hand-over-hand piano variations' on its material with Arthur Murphy, and sometimes Gibson, in several of his early New York concerts – and even much later on social occasions, usually under the title *Improvisations on a Watermelon*, offering 'a simple shift of accent in a repeating figure, and a gradual expansion of a two-note figure into a five-note one'.

Return to New York

In September 1965, Reich returned to New York, no longer easy with the cultural situation in California. The transformation of the Beat era into the Hippie period was showing itself in many ways, including the emergence of a heavier drug scene. While these manifestations were hardly confined to San Francisco, the city was already on the way to becoming an emblematic centre for the counter-culture of the late 1960s. 'In the group of people I seemed to form a contact with, I did not feel on solid psychic footing', Reich says; he does not, though, find the question of the influence of drugs on his music to be 'a profitable line of discussion'. He also felt that New York offered much better opportunities for the young composer. Within a few weeks, Reich had taken a loft at Duane Street, in the downtown area now known as TriBeCa, in or near which he has lived ever since. He found employment wherever he could: as a sound-man for films, as a social worker for New York University. In 1967, after he had re-established contact with Glass, Reich had a brief involvement with Chelsea Light Moving, a removals company formed by his colleague. In slowly establishing himself among the downtown arts community, Reich found he had more in common with those working in sculpture or painting, theatre or film, than with most musicians. Though he has never held a conventional, still less a full-time, teaching position, between 1969 and 1971 he was a member of the faculty of New York's radical New School for Social Research, where he taught electronic music.

Connections with Minimalist artists and Pendulum Music

When questioned in 1986 about links between his thinking and the aesthetic behind Minimalist painting and sculpture, Reich was derisive about the use of the term 'minimalist'. Interviewed in 1972 by Emily Wasserman for *Artforum*, however, he had been prepared to acknowledge that '[t]here is some relationship between my music and any Minimal art'.[11] The composer's contacts with artists have, in fact, been extensive and by no means confined to sculptors or painters conventionally labelled 'Minimalist' or 'conceptual'. He is insistent that any closeness to Minimalism they may have was of no concern to him: they have simply been artists he has admired.

Among the New York based artists with whom Reich now became acquainted was Robert Rauschenberg, whose involvement with Experiments in Art and Technology (otherwise known as EAT), a project designed to bring artists into contact with scientists and engineers, led to Reich's work with new technologies at Bell Laboratories, discussed below. Rauschenberg was also responsible for mounting a series of performances at New York's School of Visual Arts late in 1967, which included the première of *Violin Phase* (a year before Paul Zukofsky's performance listed in *Writings*) and *My Name Is* (see below).

Asked about the artists with whom he had most contact in the late 1960s and early 1970s, Reich mentions Sol Le Witt, Richard Serra and Michael Snow, the last two of whom lived very near him in the late 1960s. He acknowledges that 'there certainly was an attitude' these artists shared – 'Le Witt's work was very geometric, and *is* very geometric'; Serra's early work in lead had a consistency and objectivity – and that 'a metaphoric connection' is possible between the work of such painters or sculptors and his own. But Reich does not think Le Witt and Serra had any direct influence on him: 'we were just swimming in the same soup'. Reich and Le Witt, says the composer, 'spent a lot of time together' between 1967 and

1970. Le Witt was older and already a fairly well-established artist; in late 1970 or early 1971, he bought the original score of *Four Organs*, and some sections of *Drumming* in manuscript, so that the impecunious composer could buy glockenspiels for *Drumming*. The close contact between composer and artist during the year or so before Reich wrote the 'Music as a Gradual Process' essay in the summer of 1968 clearly has some bearing on the similarities between this and Le Witt's 'Paragraphs on Conceptual Art', as mentioned in the Introduction. Though best known from its publication in the composer's *Writings about Music* collection in 1974 (from which source all the quotations from it in the present book are taken), 'Music as a Gradual Process' first appeared in print just a year after it was written. It was included in the catalogue to 'Anti-Illusion: Procedures/Materials', an exhibition of the work of Nauman, Serra, Snow and others at the Whitney Museum of American Art in the spring of 1969.[12] While this exhibition was in progress, both Reich and Glass gave concerts at the Whitney, of which further details follow below.

Serra also acquired Reich's original score for Part One of *Piano Phase*, though in this case he exchanged it for a sculpture entitled *Candle Rack*, which the composer later sold. More importantly, it was partly through him, not Le Witt, that 'Music as a Gradual Process' came to be written. Serra, relates the composer, 'was the kind of guy who would call up and say, not "Hello" but "Now look: four by six on the wall, big plate, and then, rolled up, another, maybe six by eight, leaning up against it. You got it?" I'd say, "Yeah." He'd say, "What do you think?" I'd say, "It sounds great."' For Serra, 'the idea of matter-of-factness taken to its absolute extreme' was crucial, regardless of the metaphors that can be read into the work. Reich valued that attitude very much at the time.

But for a closer analogy with music, one must go to other time-based art forms. In this sense, the films of Michael Snow offer a much more fruitful link. The meeting between composer and film-maker arose from Reich's encounter with Snow's film *Wavelength* in 1967. Snow, whom Reich then saw regularly until the artist's move to Toronto in the mid-1970s, worked variously as a sculptor and film-maker at this period. He is also a good pianist; Reich believes that his achievements in film owe a lot to a 'musical intelligence at work organising the time'. In an article he wrote on *Wavelength* in 1968 – his only effort at art criticism – the composer comments on how Snow is '[c]ompletely taken up with the filmic variations possible on one image',[13] and how he avoids spelling out the implications of the narrative, so that 'you complete it in your head'. Snow's films, according to Reich, 'are about drastic time-lengths in the sense in which *Four Organs* is about drastic time-lengths. In one sense, *Wavelength* is a zoom in a room for an hour, but it's also a lot more than that. And what I learned from Snow, that I think probably later surfaced in *Music for Eighteen Musicians*, [is] . . . the playing back between the regular and the irregular, if you like; the purely process orientated and the various human imperfections that interrupt such a process'. While Serra stressed the mechanics of his work and the formal problems to be solved, Snow 'saw all the space in between'.

Reich also developed some connection with the Park Place Gallery, an artists' co-operative run by Paula Cooper who later set up her own, more prestigious, outlet at 542 West Broadway. Reich considers that the artists associated with the gallery, most of whom formed one of the chief clusters of hard-core Minimalists, 'were actually terrible . . . . There was only one who was important – Mark De Suvero – and he wasn't a Minimal artist'. But Park Place also showed non-members, including Le Witt, Robert Morris and Robert Smithson. The première performances of *Piano Phase*, discussed below, took place at this gallery in March 1967.

In the spring of the same year, the art patroness Audrey Sable mounted an exhibition in Philadelphia consisting of small editions of prints and reproducible sculptures, which were then offered for sale at a reasonable price. For this, Reich made a piece using cheap cartridge cassette machines. This was based on a tape of the voices of various artist contributors to the show saying 'Buy art!' or 'Buy art, buy art!'; Andy Warhol was among those whom he persuaded to record for him. He then made three identical copies of a cartridge containing an ordered version of these snippets, and let them run simultaneously. The cassette machines soon ran wildly out of synchronisation, and the result – entitled, rather inevitably, *Buy Art, Buy Art* – was an uncontrolled phasing process, producing 'a tacky overlay on the whole show'.

Also in 1967, Reich composed a somewhat similar piece entitled *My Name Is* which, unlike *Buy Art, Buy Art*, he notated as a score. In this, members of the audience are invited to speak their own first names into a microphone, preceded by the words 'My name is'; the resulting recordings are made into loops and phased against each other in a more rigorous fashion than in *Buy Art, Buy Art*. At the première, in November 1967 at the School of Visual Arts in New York, one of the obliging members of the public was Marcel Duchamp. A version of the piece, using the names of the performers in Steve Reich and Musicians instead of members of the audience, was premièred under the title *My Name Is: Ensemble Portrait* at the Whitney Museum on 6 January 1981; this demonstrates the composer's continuing search for ways of using recorded speech material in live performance situations, which led eventually to *Different Trains* and *The Cave*.

Despite his disclaimers, Reich's early mature compositions were conceived in a context in which both Minimalist art and performance art of various kinds set many aspects of the agenda for both their performance and reception. His ideas about gradual processes, their manipulation and perception received a crucial stimulus from his contacts with artists. The personal, as well as aesthetic, connections he made with the art world in the 1960s allowed Reich access to art galleries as performance spaces long before he became accepted in Western classical music circles, and audiences for his work who were often well-informed about its intentions.

Reich's enthusiasm for direct participation in the 'counter-culture' of performance art remained strong into the late 1960s. A particularly good example of this is *Pendulum Music*. According to the score (dated August 1968 but revised in May 1973), 'Three, four, or more microphones are suspended from the ceiling or from microphone boom stands by their cables so that they all hang the same distance from the floor and are all free to swing with a pendular motion'. Loudspeakers are then placed face upwards under the microphones, each connected to the microphone immediately above it. With the volume turned up, each loudspeaker will produce feedback when the microphone is directly above it. When the microphones are pulled back and released, their pendulum motion over the loudspeakers produces 'a series of feedback pulses . . . which will either be all in unison or not depending on the gradually changing phase relations of the different mike pendulums'. 'Performers', the score instructs, 'then sit down to watch and listen to this process along with the rest of the audience'. As the momentum of the microphones' swinging decreases, so the phase relation of the feedback pulses constantly changes. The piece finishes 'sometime shortly after all mikes have come to rest and are feeding back a continuous tone by performers pulling out the power cords of the amplifiers'.

Why would Reich suddenly produce such an uncharacteristically reductive, unmanipulated specimen of phasing after several much more sophisticated applications of this technique? The answer lies in the piece's context. The composer spent much of the summer of 1968 in New Mexico; he has always fled New York during the hot weather. Bill Wiley – the artist whom Reich had encountered through working on *Ubu Roi* and who had remained in the Bay Area – was teaching a summer school not very far away, at the University of Colorado at Boulder. He suggested that the two of them devise a multimedia piece, which was eventually entitled *Over Evident Falls*: a 'very hastily put-together happening in the spirit of the times'. Bruce Nauman, a former pupil of Wiley likewise based on the West Coast, had meanwhile also stopped off in Boulder. 'And while the two of them were in the room and I was sort of feeling Western', says Reich, '. . . I had [a] microphone and was . . . dangling it like a lasso'. His tape recorder happened to be on, and the passing of the microphone in front of its loudspeaker produced feedback. This accidental discovery led to the creation of *Pendulum Music*, which was immediately incorporated into *Over Evident Falls*.

The whole piece was performed in black light, then very fashionable. A big plastic sack of Ivory Snow soapflakes emptied over the performance space looked like luminescent snow under this light. The soapflakes fell on to a swing, which had two microphones attached to either side of it. The motion of the swing over the tape recorder speakers underneath it produced a 'quasi-unison version' of *Pendulum Music*. The title of the whole event, *Over Evident Falls*, arose from Wiley's somewhat surrealist and punning humour: the soapflakes evidently resembled a waterfall to him. For ease and speed, Reich had insisted on using some pre-existent music. Part of *Piano Phase* – probably just the opening section, Reich recalls – was performed by the composer himself against a tape. *My Name Is* also proved perfect for the situation; during this, Wiley threaded cards with words or syllables taken from the work's source material on a clothes-line across the stage. *Pendulum Music* itself was, both then and subsequently, often mounted using artists as the 'performers'. *Writings about Music* includes a photograph (much reproduced elsewhere) of a performance in the already mentioned Whitney Museum of American Art programme on 27 May 1969, in which the composer (controlling the amplification) and Nauman – who spent 1968–9 in New York – are joined by Serra and Snow, as well as the composer James Tenney.[14] In 1968, Wiley himself – usually described as part of the 'funk' school, not as a Minimalist – painted the watercolour design for the cover of the 1969 Columbia Records disc of *It's Gonna Rain* and *Violin Phase*.[15]

Concerned, musically speaking, purely with unmanipulated rhythm, *Pendulum Music* is the most direct fulfilment of the aesthetic creed propounded in the 'Music as a Gradual Process' essay; it is, in particular, the perfect illustration of the first of this essay's three examples of what '[p]erforming and listening to a gradual musical process resembles: pulling back a swing, releasing it, and observing it gradually come to rest'.[16] In demonstrating this, rather than merely using the idea as a metaphor, the piece remains the only work by Reich to adhere unambiguously to the slogan 'once the process is set up and loaded it runs by itself', in the overtly mechanistic sense in which this is often understood.

Among those in the art world with whom Reich has had professional and personal dealings since the early 1970s, the most important one to mention is Beryl Korot, who became the composer's second wife on 30 May 1976; they have one son, Ezra, born in 1978. From the early 1970s, Korot worked as a pioneer in multi-channel video, most famously in *Dachau 1974*, and edited *Radical Software*, the first magazine on alternative video. In the 1980s, she painted. A weaving notation – part of a five-channel video installation, text and commentary with five word pieces and five notations – adorns the cover of the 1978 ECM LP recording of *Music for Eighteen Musicians*, appropriately reflective of Reich's concerns with pattern and system. Since the late 1980s, however, when she and her husband began to assemble the footage for their large-scale 'documentary music video theatre' work *The Cave*, Korot has returned to video, adding the computer as a significant tool in her work. At the time of writing, the Reichs are working on their second video opera, *Three Tales*.

Early minimalist compositions

The fifteen works Reich composed between *It's Gonna Rain* and *Oh dem Watermelons!*, in 1964–5, and *Drumming*, in 1970–71, may be divided into four categories: the tape compositions of 1966; the instrumental works of 1966–7; a group of compositions and projects, dating from 1967–70, which continue the composer's preoccupation with electronics; and the instrumental works of 1970. Nine of these are included by their composer in the list of works given as an appendix to *Writings about Music*. The ten compositions from this total of fifteen not already discussed form the subject matter of this section.

Come Out *and* Melodica

Returning to New York shortly before his twenty-ninth birthday, Reich continued to explore the technique of phasing in two further tape pieces: *Come Out* and *Melodica*. *Come Out* was composed in March and/or April 1966; *Melodica* in a single day a month after *Come Out*'s première. The gap of a year between these works and those from San Francisco is due primarily to practical factors involving the composer's move back East; Reich had no studio space in which to work for several months after his return to New York. A follow-up to the breakthrough of *It's Gonna Rain* was now overdue.

Come Out was premièred on 17 April 1966 in New York Town Hall at a benefit concert for the retrial of the 'Harlem Six', a group of black teenagers arrested, and convicted, for the murder of a white shop-owner during the riots of 1964. Truman Nelson, a civil-rights activist, gave Reich some ten hours of taped interviews with the young men involved, and

Example 3.7

(a) *Come Out*, Basic Unit

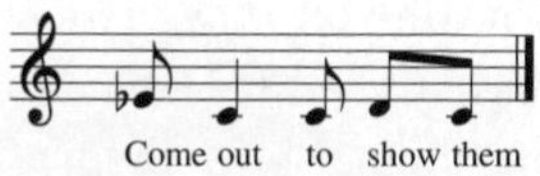

(b) *Melodica*, Basic Unit

asked him to produce a piece based on these for the benefit. As in *It's Gonna Rain*, the composer took advantage of the potential urban Black speech offers for the rich interaction of musical and semantic levels. Played as it was amidst more familiar and more popular types of 'protest music', while contributions were being collected, the piece was more or less ignored on this occasion; for the considerable impact its release on record made in the following year, see below.

Reich describes *Come Out* as 'essentially a refinement' of *It's Gonna Rain*. Once again, the piece begins with a section of unaltered text, introducing the speech material and setting its context. It was Daniel Hamm who provided the voice that Reich tape-looped to produce his basic material. Maintaining that the six boys had been beaten up when in police custody in Harlem 28th Precinct, Hamm described how he was required to prove visibly bleeding injuries in order to get transferred to hospital: 'I had to, like, open the bruise up, and let some of the bruise blood come out to show them'. By selecting, however, only five words from this as the basis for the whole of what follows – a thirteen-minute piece in a single section – Reich achieves a more purely musical focus than he had managed in *It's Gonna Rain* with the aid of a more melodic phrase demonstrating greater pitch stability: its character determined by the interval of a minor third, suggesting C minor, and enhanced by clearer vowel sounds. (Ex. 3.7a gives the Basic Unit of *Come Out*.) Phasing of the two words 'come out' itself produces identifiable motivic developments: 'co-ma-ma', 'co-ma-ma-ma', and 'co-ma-ma-ma-ma', for instance, each change in rhythm and emphasis resulting from the gradual process of canonic realignment. Even more interestingly, the 'sh' of the word 'show' contains a percussive element – many have compared it to maracas – which allows not merely timbral variety but also provides a starting point for more subtle manipulation of the material, as the 'sh' sound swoops the whole spectrum. In other words, the sounds themselves have become more divorced from their meaning, the 'sh' sound thereby producing the first example of what Reich calls 'resulting patterns'.

Additionally, the phasing process applied to *Come Out*'s Basic Unit does not simply move away from and back to unison, but from two to four to eight voices according to a pattern controlled by predetermined points of arrival. When the phasing process applied to 'Come out to show them' reaches 'Come a', come a'/show them, show them' (a more accurate transcription of the spoken words), around three minutes into the piece, the two-voice canon in quavers, previously on separate channels, splits into four voices, with two on each channel. At the point when 'Come a', come a', come a', come a'/show them, show them, show them, show them' is reached, just after eight minutes in, the four-voice canon in quavers then splits, quite dramatically, into eight voices in semiquavers. This produces a kind of shimmer or blur lasting some five minutes, in which the words have become completely inaudible. The words 'come out' now yield a kind of soft, rounded burr, while 'to show them' has been transformed into alternating pulses of machine-like ferocity. Further panning across the stereo space adds another dimension to this wall of sound before the whole thing is eventually faded out. The procedures of Part Two of *It's Gonna Rain* have thus been expanded with the aid of a much more composerly control of the work's basic material.

Come Out's combination of more purely musical quality of material and its more consistently audible manipulation has been viewed as a move towards a 'phonic' approach, governed by the musical grammar it establishes for itself, as opposed to the 'phonemic' tendencies of *It's Gonna Rain*, in which factors 'outside the music' – the emotional content of the words and their tendency to retain extra-musical meanings – impose on the way the work is perceived.[17] Part Two of *It's Gonna Rain*, as we have seen, exploits the full spectrum between verbal audibility and inaudibility by moving from clear comprehension to the chaos of sheer noise.

Come Out, it could be argued, not only focuses more firmly on the 'phonic', but does so with a mixture of systematic rigour and intuitive control which can be readily appreciated via the clarity – both textural and textual – with which the structure is articulated. One should not, however, ignore the continuing part played in the later work by the 'added emotional layer' provided by the words and their cultural resonances, which themselves help to make the musical results correspondingly richer. While still audible, the words of *Come Out*, already suggestive of social protest, achieve added weight through sheer repetition. The eventual move from 'text' to 'texture' yields, not purity of sound, but a dense complexity charged with the frustration and danger of pent-up repression, enhanced by the grim transmutation of a human outcry against injustice into the relentless machinations of a force beyond human control. And while *It's*

Gonna Rain responded to widespread concern about the escalation of the Cold War, *Come Out* not only reflected the immediate circumstances of its composition but could be interpreted as a warning against the racial strife that itself escalated in the USA shortly after its première. With both works, the acoustic, psycho-acoustic and psychological consequences of using speech sounds to make music become interestingly confused.

Melodica uses a structure almost identical to that of *Come Out*, applying to it a melodic pattern the composer dreamed. Reich 'woke up on May 22nd, 1966, and realized the piece with the melodica (a toy instrument) and tape loops, in one day'.[18] He chose this simple, basically children's, instrument because its sound approximated most closely to that which he heard in his dream. *Melodica*'s Basic Unit (see Ex. 3.7b) consists of just four pitches divided into two pairs covering an octave span – B E and B A – revolving around the central E, supported by its dominant and subdominant. The process of phasing gradually turns this into a continuous melodic line, after which, at about three minutes in, the texture expands to four voices. With this canon, the separation of the higher and lower pairs of notes seems even more pronounced than before, encouraging the listener to hear the music in terms of a lower dominant/tonic drone above which a skirling modal melody is spun; unlike *Come Out*, there is no move to an eight-voice canon. The tonal ambiguities offered by such pitch material would subsequently be explored by the composer. The fresh rhythmic perspectives thrown up by the phasing process and the complex overtone structure of each note add further dimensions. But *Melodica*'s reliance on a four-voice texture for almost eight minutes (it lasts 10′45″) ultimately offers too little to sustain musical interest. The piece has remained largely unplayed and almost entirely unknown.

The hint of the gimmick in *Melodica* may suggest that Reich was already finding the technique of phasing with tape to have its limitations. Despite the advances made in *Come Out*, he had, indeed, begun to question the potential of phasing if it could not be somehow extended beyond its use with tape. '1966 was a very depressing year', the composer has said. 'I began to feel like a mad scientist trapped in a lab'.[19] The use of musical pitches, rather than speech patterns, in *Melodica* – 'which turned out to be the last tape piece I ever made' – suggested, however, the application of phasing techniques to instrumental music. Initially, it seemed impossible to perform live a process which was, as the composer has written, 'indigenous to machines. On the other hand I could think of nothing else to do with live musicians that would be as interesting as the phasing process'.[20] 'Aching to do something instrumental', he began to search for a way to put the process of phasing into live practice. The crucial contribution made by tape technology to Reich's development in the late 1960s and beyond remains one of the most important instances in musical history of the influence of electronic music on music for instruments alone.

The early instrumental phase compositions of 1966–7

The three instrumental works composed in the year-and-a-half after *Melodica* – *Reed Phase*, *Piano Phase* and *Violin Phase* – form a natural sequence, exploring the technique of phasing in music designed either for a single player plus tape or, in the case of *Piano Phase*, for just two players. These established the model for a whole series of pieces in Reich's output in which multiples of the same instrument are chosen in order to permit audibility of structure. Despite their economy of instrumental means, the three 'Phase' pieces demonstrate increasing textural and contrapuntal elaboration.

Several principles also hold good for the larger series of phase compositions – including *Phase Patterns* and *Drumming* – of which they form part. Each is constructed from a small pattern (the Basic Unit), from which further patterns may be abstracted for independent development. The scores themselves present the different stages through which this Basic Unit goes in the process of being phased against itself. While phasing in the tape pieces had been achieved by slowing down one tape loop against the other, in the instrumental compositions one player speeds up against the other's fixed tempo, since this proved much easier. (The difference should not be overemphasised, however, since the false impression of one channel accelerating, rather than slowing down, against a fixed speed is as strong in the tape pieces for many listeners as is the true impression in the instrumental ones.) The actual phasing is notated by using dotted lines to indicate the increases in tempo that a player must make against the fixed part, each 'notch' in the sequence then being conventionally notated by showing the new alignment. (The first attempt to notate *Piano Phase* – the single-page score exchanged with Serra dated 1/67, which consists of what became Part One – can be seen in Cage's book *Notations*, published in 1969.[21]) Regularity of metre is crucial during the locked figures, but notable for its absence in what we will call the 'fuzzy transitions'. Each of these figures is to be repeated a number of times (specified but flexible), forming a seamless flow both between repetitions of each figure and between these and the 'fuzzy transitions' themselves.

While it would be perfectly possible to fix the number of repetitions of each figure in advance, in practice there is really no need, since only a

Example 3.8 *Reed Phase*, Basic Unit

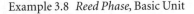

single player has to move at any one time. Dynamic markings are given but, with the exception of crescendi for the second player fading in to join the first player with the same pattern, these markings encourage a consistent, 'flat' level, at a medium volume.

Reed Phase *and* Piano Phase

At first, Reich tried the obvious transitional solution to the application of phasing techniques 'indigenous to machines' to instrumental music: a combination of live instrumental performance and accompanying tape. While *Piano Phase* and *Violin Phase* have become two of his most familiar early works, *Reed Phase*, the composer's first attempt at live phasing, has remained almost unavailable and essentially rejected, performed only by Gibson, for whom it was written. Originally intended for soprano saxophone with two pre-recorded saxophone tracks on tape, the work is dated 12/66, and given the title 'Saxophone Phase', in the programmes for its première in the art gallery of Fairleigh Dickinson University on 5 January 1967, and subsequent New York City performances in the 1967 Park Place concerts.

The programme note for the latter says that '[i]n *Saxophone Phase* a performer moves gradually ahead and out of phase with a fixed tape loop'. As published in *Source* magazine,[22] *Reed Phase* consists of three sections: a complete cycle of phasing based on a five-note, five-beat Basic Unit (see Ex. 3.8); a middle section adding a second tape voice a beat ahead of the first, against both of which the live saxophone again phases; and a repeat of the opening section. The five-beat rhythmic scheme fails, its composer himself feels, to create the sort of ambiguities essential to the success of any piece using repetition as a basic tool; the contour, probably more than the size, of its pitch content – outlining a i–v–iv–vii-v pattern on D, using just four pitch classes – similarly produces phasing which 'doesn't seem to make that much difference'. As a result, Reich finds the piece 'repetitious and boring'. Not only is it not included in his 1974 list of 'those compositions which I feel are worth keeping' in *Writings*,[23] but it is not even mentioned in passing in the main text. Gibson suggests that *Reed Phase* is not only the first piece to use live phasing, but also that it is 'probably the first formal western composition to require circular breathing . . . as a performance practice'.[24]

Early stages of work on *Piano Phase*, undertaken late in 1966, turn out to be part of the same transitional process of combining live performance and tape. 'I used tape to get away from tape', its composer says, 'because I didn't have two pianos, nor did Arthur Murphy'. Reich 'recorded a short repeating melodic pattern played on the piano, made a tape loop of that pattern, and then tried to play against the loop myself, exactly as if I were a second tape recorder'.[25] This led to the discovery not only that live phasing was possible, but also that it was highly pleasurable: 'a new and extremely satisfying way of playing that was both completely worked out beforehand . . . and yet free of actually reading notation, allowing me to become completely absorbed in listening while I played'. Reich and Murphy now rehearsed separately against tape loops, allowing each to judge his own accuracy as a performer, and thus also to estimate the potential of live phasing. Instead of simply writing a piece for piano and tape, however – which he says was never his intention – Reich took advantage of his eventual access to two pianos to press on to the next stage. When – at a try-out of *Piano Phase* in the same Fairleigh Dickinson programme that saw the première of *Reed Phase* – the two friends finally got together on two pianos, they 'found, to our delight, that we could perform this process without mechanical aid of any kind'.

Piano Phase apparently went through several versions – including one for four electric pianos with headphones, entitled 'Four Pianos', premièred in March 1967 (see below) – before Reich settled on the published three-part composition for two pianos. Four discoveries Reich made during the period of experimentation that led to this final version establish the main outlines of his future approach to such material and its manipulation. Firstly, it marked the discovery of a viable, and pliable, modal material which would give the vital extra dimension necessary to allow the composition of instrumental music based on rhythmic processes but lacking the added emotional layer of speech and everyday sounds offered by tape. The six-pitch modal fragment Reich devised for his breakthrough into instrumental music proved consistently interesting when phased against itself, as well as against altered versions, due in part to its own ambiguity and malleability. These in turn interact with the second discovery made through work on *Piano Phase*: the potential behind patterns based on units of twelve beats.

This is combined with his third discovery: the further metric ambiguities inherent in the multiple downbeats generated by the phasing process. Contrapuntal presentations of the same pattern against itself, and of related patterns with their own fresh metric emphases, proved especially fulfilling, generating a rich variety of metric resources with the simplest of

Example 3.9 *Piano Phase*: (a) Basic Unit of Part One; (b) Basic Unit of Part Two; (c) Basic Unit of Part Three.

means. Fourthly, Reich began to discover more sophisticated structural ways to complement what was still an essentially schematic deployment of rhythm and extremely limited modal vocabulary.

In *Piano Phase*, the pitch material evolves to create a three-part structure in which modulation (using the pitch centres B, E and A, respectively) plays a significant role. As its clear opposition of white notes in the left hand (E B D) and black notes in the right (F♯ C♯) suggests, the Basic Unit – a melodic pattern of twelve semiquavers, divided into two groups of six, using only five pitches – was devised at the keyboard (see Ex. 3.9a). More obvious to the ear is the division between an upper voice (B C♯ D) and a lower one (E F♯), separated by a perfect fourth. The composer exploits both voices in what is arguably a first step towards the deployment of resulting patterns using instruments rather than tape: their registral separation, for instance, is used homophonically as well as polyphonically. The richness Reich discovers in such simple material relies to a considerable extent on the ways in which white-note/black-note opposition and voice division interact.

The first of the piece's three parts performs a complete phasing operation on this twelve-semiquaver pattern. A modified version of this, eight semiquavers in length, then begins the second part (at Figure 16). Instead of being phased against itself, however, this pattern is joined by a new one, also of eight semiquavers, which in turn forms the basis for the four-semiquaver pattern on which the final part is constructed (beginning at Figure 27); see Examples 3.9b and c. The new pattern in Part Two introduces one extra pitch class (A), plus the E an octave above the already present lower tonic. After this has been pared down briefly to repeated octave Es, the central four semiquavers of the new eight-semiquaver pattern of the second part form the sole material of the third and final one. As a whole, the number of pitch classes used in *Piano Phase* moves from five up to six and finally reduces to just four.

Though its composer states that *Piano Phase* 'is as process-oriented as the tape pieces', it is already clear that Reich manipulates his material here in a quite subtle manner. All three parts perform complete cycles of phase-shifting; but while the first and third phase a pattern against itself, the middle part, as we have seen, phases one pattern against a different one. As Paul Epstein has pointed out (in an article, confined mainly to the first part of *Piano Phase*, which is among the most detailed analyses to be published of any minimalist composition), the second half of Part One's cycle of phasing 'is a retrograde of the first, with the relationship between the two players reversed'.[26] Thus Figures 3 and 13, 4 and 12, etc. present identical combinations of the Basic Unit, but with different starting points (see Ex. 3.10a and b). Figure 8 (see Ex. 3.10c) – in which the second group of six semiquavers is phased exactly against the first six, and then vice versa – marks the mid-point of the cycle, which appears only once. Any complete and strict phasing cycle of this kind will, of course, move into retrograde at the halfway stage. But this is unlikely to be noticed by the listener: an illustration of how even such a purely mechanical process hides 'secrets of structure'.

Another notable feature of Part One's phasing cycle is the alternation of patterns which form dyads of white or black notes alone, and those which combine them. Half the dyads of the patterns in the latter category, occupying the even-numbered figures (starting at Figure 3, see again Ex. 3.10a), are major or minor seconds – E F♯, B C♯, C♯ D, a pair of each – and thus emphasise dissonance; a condition that reaches its point of maximum tension in Figures 7 and 9, in which sequences of repeating seconds alternate with sequences of repeating sixths and fourths. Patterns separating white and black notes, to be found in the even-numbered figures (starting at Figure 4, see again Ex. 3.10b), alternately emphasise the perfect fifth, F♯ C♯, and a collection of unisons, minor thirds, perfect fifths and minor sevenths assembled from the pitches E, B and D, thus emphasising consonance; a condition that reaches its point of maximum repose in Figure 8 (see again Ex. 3.10c), in which white-note unisons (E B D repeated) alternate with black-note fifths (F♯ C♯).

The more consonant patterns do not necessarily lead to greater structural audibility. The relationship between the opposition of consonance and dissonance and the extent to which the 'canons' of *Piano Phase* are audible is at its richest when voice division makes a telling contribution at the same time. In Figure 4, for instance – the first consonant configuration

Example 3.10 *Piano Phase*: (a) Figures 3 and 13; (b) Figures 4 and 12; (c) Figure 8; (d) Figure 6.

following the unison (see again Ex. 3.10b) – F♯ and C♯ always occur together as a 'static' perfect fifth, and the division into two separate voices is clear because it is consistently homophonic; furthermore, the two halves of Figure 4 are identical. Yet it is the very simplicity of this texture – the syncopations of the lower voice supporting the upper voice's close-position rocking motion – which obscures both the Basic Unit and the canon upon it by establishing a clear identity of its own. In Figure 6, by contrast – the following consonant configuration (see Ex. 3.10d) – F♯ and C♯ occur in unison, and the interval between the two voices – reduced as a consequence to zero for half the time – is clear because it is consistently polyphonic (the E F♯ E semiquavers constantly alternate with the rising or falling groups based on B C♯ D). Here, the constant reduction to unison allows the Basic Unit, and perhaps even the canon itself, to be heard. In the more dissonant patterns, the repeating dyads glue the two parts together to create the effect of something texturally, even 'motivically', quite different from what surrounds it. The result is a refocusing of attention sufficient to obscure the canon itself.

This separation into consonant patterns and dissonant ones is also reflected to some degree in the treatment of metre. The absence of a clear, functional downbeat in such music leads to all kinds of interesting ambiguities. Downbeats may, for instance, be felt quite unambiguously in individual parts; when these are combined, however, the consequent multiple downbeats interact with each other to create a more complex metrical situation in which the 'acoustic' and the 'psycho-acoustic' become hard to separate. Metric ambiguities are already a feature of the tape pieces, made all the more musically interesting by the arrival of what came to be called resulting patterns in *Come Out*. But with *Piano Phase*, Reich really begins to capitalise on the metric potential of phasing. The experience of *Reed Phase* had taught him that unusual numbers of beats or notes offered less than they initially suggested. By choosing a pattern of twelve semiquavers for the first part of *Piano Phase* – in this case broken down into two clear groups of six – he began to discover the possibilities of metric reorientation which lay behind the potential subdivisions of a twelve-beat pattern; even where, as here, many (though not all) of these reorientations preserve the basic subdivision into 2×6. The metrical ambiguity between the possible sub-groupings of twelve, of which 3×4 and 4×3 are only the most obvious, is something the composer continues to explore to this day.

The 'fuzzy transitions' also create interesting metrical situations, particularly psycho-acoustically. As Epstein notes – checking his own observations with the aid of a computer realisation, as well as a live performance, of the piece to avoid any conclusions based on performer inaccuracy – several distinct stages may be perceived in the movement from one 'locked' phase structure to the next; furthermore, differences may be observed between the stages involved at different points in the phasing cycle. In the initial 'fuzzy transition' away from the unison, for example, an impression of increasing resonance precedes the effect of actual separation, followed by the replacement of any sense of a beat by what Epstein calls 'a dizzying rhythmic complexity'.[27] At the mid-point, the speed appears to double, producing a brief sensation of stability; after which the previous psycho-acoustic stage obtains until the new phase relationship is established. With the next 'fuzzy transition', on the other hand, there seem to be only three stages: gradual separation, a chaotic kind of swirling and the coalescing of the new configuration. These differences reflect the strong contrast between the dissonance of Figure 3 and the consonance of Figure 4. As Epstein wisely points out, however, such delicate psycho-acoustic situations can lead to variations between even an individual's listening experiences on different occasions.

As a whole, *Piano Phase* explores the modal territory set out by the initial five pitch classes. B, the somewhat ambiguous tonality of Part One, is established by two factors: the formation of iv–v–i in this key by the first three notes of the Basic Unit, and the rise and fall from B to D and back of the upper voice. E and F♯, constituting the lower voice, vie for a superiority probably claimed ultimately by the former: E is the first note in each group of six semiquavers as well as the lowest pitch of all, though it occurs only twice in the basic pattern, while F♯ occurs three times.

It is therefore no surprise to find E assuming an important position in Part Two, though the tonality of this is even more ambiguous than that of Part One. The new pitch, A, oscillates with B in the new pattern, contributing iv–v to the i of an E now strengthened by its representation in two registers. This A B can, however, also be interpreted as downward neighbour oscillation emphasising B: maybe the dominant rather than the tonic of Piano 2's pattern, but simultaneously the tonic of the original Basic Unit, which continues in Piano 1. With A now introduced, and *its* dominant established as the only pitch class to occur in two registers, the move to a tonal centre of A in Part Three seems the logical outcome. All the previous determinants – iv–v–i progression, neighbour-note oscillation, primacy of position as lowest note – help to establish A as tonic. While reducing the range of potential relationships and challenges to any single pitch as central, the reduction from six pitch classes to four draws attention to how much is missing – in the piece as a whole – of the framework normally supporting a more conventionally tonal composition.

Even here, then, room remains for uncertainty. Harmonic motion is more suggested than achieved in *Piano Phase*'s progression from B to E to A; any aural interpretation of its neat progression of perfect fourths in terms of ii–v–i in A is heavily qualified by modal ambiguity. Such a delicate balance – previously tipped in favour of a modal manner made more evasive by an approach to pitch which, in the tape pieces, is inherently more evanescent – is firmly established as a central feature of Reich's music from here on. The roles of rhythm and metre are also enhanced in the instrumental compositions by the precision with which they are deployed and by the extent to which the results of this precision are audible. The establishment of modal diatonicism as a norm seems to have been accepted quite naturally. 'It wasn't discussed', he says, 'it was practised'. But analysis of what were probably largely intuitive decisions on the composer's part demonstrates the role played by tonal prolongation in such music's construction. The resulting structures were to become more complex and sophisticated as time went on. The expressive focus of this music is, however, fundamentally changed by the abandonment of the necessarily less pitch-determinate sounds of speech and the substitution of equally tempered instrumental pitches. Emotionally cooler and more stable, Reich's music from *Piano Phase* onwards is more about pitches and patterns than *Come Out* could ever have been.

From now on, the considerable majority of Reich's compositions would begin with the establishment of a musical idea with a modal pitch profile. The implications of this then determine both the structure and the expressive qualities of the subsequent work. With the background and beliefs already described, the character of Reich's new modality comes as no surprise. There was at this time, indeed, he says, 'an assumption that was pretty much the case with all of us' that diatonicism of some kind would form the basis for such music.

Already very telling is the absence of the bass in Reich's output of this period: not only of a bass line but of any notes in the lower range at all. No mature work composed before *Music for Mallet Instruments, Voices and Organ* with the exception of *Four Organs* – that is, between 1965 and 1972–3 – makes any use of the bass clef. *Piano Phase* has no note lower than the E♮ above middle C; *Violin Phase* no note lower than middle C♯; *Phase Patterns* no note lower than middle C; *Drumming* has nothing lower than the G♯ below middle C; *Six Pianos* nothing below F♯. 'People used to kid me and say, your piano's all dusty on both ends, it's only used in the middle', says Reich. As he explains, 'I didn't know what to do except to have a drone bass. And I didn't want to have a drone bass; that was too boring. I didn't want to do what La Monte and Terry [were] doing with drones. . . . I didn't want any bass that would say, "this is where we are". I knew there were certain ambiguities, and I wanted to keep those ambiguities. But I didn't know how to keep them and still say what they were. So I simply shut up, I didn't say anything! Of what you can't speak, you must keep silent'.

Despite the new importance of pitch, Reich still describes rhythmic structure as 'my *sine qua non*' in 1966–7, and even beyond. 'In those early pieces', he insists, 'the focus was on rhythm, and rhythm, and then again rhythm. The pitches were chosen, and they were chosen quite carefully, believe me, but once they were chosen – *finished* with that decision. You load the machine – and it runs'. Yet the finished products of this process are never mechanistic, even in purely rhythmic or metric terms. This is due to Reich's ingenuity in the exploitation both of the metrical ambiguities inherent in a single pattern, especially in canonic counterpoint, and of the potential of employing more than one pattern.

Violin Phase

In *Violin Phase* (the score of which is dated October 1967), the exploration of live performance and tape in combination is taken up once more. The piece requires either a solo violin plus three more violins on tape or – 'preferably', the composer states in *Writings*[28] – four violins. The resulting increase in the density of texture and counterpoint marks a significant advance, though we should remember that *Piano Phase* in one of its earlier incarnations also had four lines. Reich has described *Violin Phase* as 'basically an expansion and refinement of *Piano Phase*'.

Again, the musical material Reich chooses is devised with the nature of the instrument in question in mind, here stressing the open A and E strings of the violin. The result is a Basic Unit featuring dyads as well as single pitches (see Ex. 3.11a). A and E function more as the mediant and flattened leading note of F♯ in the ambiguous modality created here. The centrality of F♯ is confirmed by its dominant: C♯ and F♯, forming the lower voice, occur as the first two notes and are repeated on beats 8 and 9, and the Basic Unit readily incorporates C♯–minor[7] as well. Since B – the seventh of this chord – as well as C♯ are emphasised as the work progresses, one could describe the modality of *Violin Phase* in terms of a tonic supported symmetrically by the perfect fourth on either side of it. Such is the ambiguity of this material, however, that one could also interpret F♯ as a modal dominant above C♯; the potential of the sort of pitch configuration Reich had first stumbled on in *Melodica* was now beginning to be understood and exploited. As in *Piano Phase*, a twelve-beat pattern forms the basis for the entire composition; here, though, a single longer note-value (in effect, a dotted crotchet) amidst the prevailing quavers introduces an extra dimension to the rhythmic/metric mix.

More important, however, is the exploitation of a new discovery. Even with only two violins playing the same pattern in such now characteristic 'staggered', close-knit counterpoint, it becomes possible to hear new groupings of pitches based, usually, on their registral proximity rather than the 'structural' separation of each line. 'As one listens to the repetition of the several violins', Reich has written, 'one may hear first the lower tones forming one or several patterns, then the higher notes are noticed forming another, then the notes in the middle may attach themselves to the lower tones to form still another'.[29] What the composer now began to call 'resulting patterns' have already been observed in embryo in the spectrum-swooping 'sh' sounds of *Come Out* and the voice divisions of *Piano Phase*. *Violin Phase* is, however, the first composition in which Reich clarifies and really begins to exploit this phenomenon.

Example 3.11 *Violin Phase*: (a) Figure 1; (b) Figure 16; (c) Figure 10; (d) Figure 20; (e) Figure 19a; (f) Figures 22f and 22g. (Ex. (c), (d), (e), and (f), Live Violin only.)

Though, as the composer points out, '[a]ll these patterns are really there',[30] listeners' response to them will differ; to some degree one can choose the patterns on which to concentrate. As a consequence, resulting patterns can be called 'psycho-acoustic by-products', a term which the composer himself uses. 'In listening' – as David Behrman, producer of the first recording of *Violin Phase*, puts it – 'one can bring out these and other combination figures by concentrating on them – a little like those puzzle drawings of geometric three-dimensional figures that can be flipped back and forth in space by an effort of will'.[31]

Reich does not, however, limit himself to allowing the listener to hear these patterns as they emerge naturally in the course of the contrapuntal elaboration. In a performance using a single live violinist and tape, the soloist phases against the static tape part until beat 5 in the process is reached at Figure 6 (about five minutes into the piece). Here, the cycle of phasing is arrested, the tape now assuming the position taken by the soloist (Figure 7). While this 'notch' in the phasing process is retained, the soloist is then required to play specific, notated resulting patterns (Figures 9–11) – some more harmonic, others more melodic – fading them in and out of the total texture. Provision is also made for the player to choose his own resulting patterns, assisted by the notation on a single staff of the complete counterpoint produced by the other parts. These possibilities add a further dimension to the process of phasing. With just two violins on tape, the introduction of a third voice already enhances textural and structural depth.

After around three more minutes, the phasing process is resumed at the point of its arrest, the soloist initially synchronising with the tape (Figure 12). This time, however, the counterpoint resulting from this 'notch' in the process is retained while further phasing takes place, taking the number of voices to three. At beat 9 (Figures 16–17), the phasing freezes again, the tape once more freeing the soloist to play further resulting patterns (Figure 18 onwards). (Ex. 3.11b shows the three voices in the fixed positions they will now occupy for the remainder of the piece.) With three voices now turning to four, the scope of both the resulting patterns themselves and the total contrapuntal fabric is greatly enriched. In addition, Reich quickly subjects the resulting patterns themselves to phasing against the already canonically presented Basic Unit (Figures 19–21). Finally, a markedly more melodic pattern is thrown up that ignores the basic metrical division (Figure 22). With the other three parts still fixed at the 'notches' in the phasing process on which they came to rest much earlier, the work ends with the soloist returning, in a single bound, to the Basic Unit in alignment with the tape, allowing the listener to hear whatever resulting patterns he likes in his head.

In addition to textural and structural depth, resulting patterns may also reinforce, and sometimes clarify, a particular tonal emphasis. While some of the composer's suggested resulting patterns hint at the prevailing F♯ modality and its dominant (Ex. 3.11c and d), others emphasise B and E, by sheer force of repetition (Ex. 3.11e), the latter being interpretable not only as the flattened leading note but also as an extension of the 'stacked'-fourths symmetry of C♯ F♯ B. These resulting patterns move from simple dyads – stressing B and E, as before – to a single repeated C♯ (the dominant of the tonic F♯ and central pitch of the dominant seventh outlined by the Basic Pattern) and a staccato pattern in continuous quavers. Part of the more melodic pattern at Figure 22 is shown in Ex. 3.11f.

Psycho-acoustic by-products and even resulting patterns have been noted in Reich's immediately preceding works, and the compositional control he exerted on these has been argued back as far as *It's Gonna Rain.* Yet the articulation, as well as identification, of resulting patterns in *Violin Phase* integrates such psycho-acoustic phenomena into the fabric of the music in a more detailed and composed-out manner than Reich had previously achieved. Arising naturally from the combinations produced by the phasing process itself, such resulting patterns allow him to transcend more easily and comprehensively the limitations of a single structural process, permitting greater flexibility in shaping the work as a whole as well as bringing an extra textural dimension. The contrapuntal and structural variety achievable through the articulation of resulting patterns already moves *Violin Phase* in the direction of Reich's mature compositions.

The discoveries and achievements of *Piano Phase* and *Violin Phase* established the path he was to pursue for the next few years. While *Violin Phase* is the more advanced musically, *Piano Phase* had already suggested the abandonment of tape altogether in favour of a live music capitalising on the musical richness to be obtained from human fallibility while supposedly attempting to imitate a machine. As it turned out, however, Reich's fascination with the potential of electronic technology was by no means yet satisfied.

The electronic projects and compositions of 1967–9

In addition to concert compositions, music composed with electronic means continued to be an important part of Reich's work at this time. Even before *Violin Phase* was completed, his interest in the compositional possibilities of the fast-developing new technologies surfaced again. This was partly due to the considerable excitement then being generated by Experiments in Art and Technology, a project designed 'to develop effective means of stimulating collaborations between artists and engineers'. A prime mover in this was the artist Robert Rauschenberg, and with him the whole circle around Cage; another important protagonist was the engineer Billy Kluver. Though already disillusioned with tape as a medium, Reich now became so impressed by the potential of technologies already beginning to offer other opportunities to composers that he set about attempting to realise two ideas, both of which emerged out of the concept of phasing.

The first of these, expressed in the form of a piece he called *Slow Motion Sound* (September 1967), was 'to take a tape loop, probably of speech, and

Example 3.12 *Pulse Music* and *Four Log Drums*, pitch material

ever so gradually slow it down to enormous length *without lowering its pitch*'.[32] It remained unrealised due to the technical limitations of the period. Though eventually able to achieve it in 1981 with the aid of the much more sophisticated, computer-based technology of IRCAM in Paris, Reich found the results musically uninteresting, and at the time took it no further. Surprisingly, however, he has returned to this 'slow motion sound' in his most recent work, *Three Tales* (1996 onwards).

The other idea was the transformation of a single pulsing chord into a series of melodic patterns by means of gradual phase shifting. Since the demands this placed on performers seemed unrealistic, Reich set about attempting to construct a device which would allow the process to be achieved mechanically, while still permitting the results to be performed live, not on tape. The EAT project enabled him to work with Larry Owens and David Flooke, technicians at Bell Laboratories in New Jersey, where the composer appears to have spent, or attempted to spend, much of his time between February 1968 and the early part of the following year. The result was the Phase Shifting Pulse Gate, which he proudly unveiled at the New School for Social Research in New York in April 1969, and subsequently in a concert at the Whitney Museum of American Art on 27 May. The score he composed for the Gate was entitled *Pulse Music* (dated 5/69). This gradually transforms an eight-note chord into melodies which finally blur into a fast pulsing chord. In the same month (that of the concert itself), he also wrote *Four Log Drums*, which uses the Gate 'as a programming device for 4 performers each playing a two-note wooden log drum'.[33] Employing the same tempo as *Pulse Music*, and immediately preceding it in the Whitney Museum programme, this changes the eight pitches of the original piece from a rhythmically spread-out version to a single chord, from which point *Pulse Music* went on to unravel it again. The basic pitch material of both pieces (see Ex. 3.12) has the same modal ambiguities – here the alternative tonics made possible by a 'stacked'-fifths structure based on A – which characterised *Melodica* and, more importantly, *Violin Phase*, and which would return later in *Four Organs*, *Phase Patterns* and *Drumming*.

While the basic idea behind these two pieces had at least been realisable – if with technology which 'could easily have ceased functioning at any time'[34] – Reich was dissatisfied with the 'stiff and un-musical' electronic realisation of the sounds and the artificiality of the performance element involved (just twisting dials). Five years later, he wrote that '[t]he Phase Shifting Pulse Gate is still in its fibre case on top of the closet in my bedroom. I haven't unpacked it yet'.[35] His efforts to harness new technologies to the principle of phasing had met only with dead ends. The single 'technology-driven' piece to survive from this period is *Pendulum Music*, itself little more than an exercise in basic physics.

Such continued reliance on electronics seems curious in the light of the course Reich's development was to take over the next twenty years; only in 1988, with *Different Trains*, was he to return with any consistency to such technology and produce a finished composition with its resources, though the *Counterpoint* series of works (starting with *Vermont Counterpoint* for flute(s) in 1982) requires multi-tracking of parts for its solo realisations. His persistence with the much more primitive electronic technology of the late 1960s is, however, certainly characteristic both of his restless concern to experiment with new ideas and of the tenacity with which he pursues them. Surprisingly, perhaps, it took him more than four years – from the beginning of 1965 to the summer of 1969 – to decide conclusively not only that he needed to move beyond music for tape alone, but also that the element of performance as conventionally understood – 'using my hands and body to actively create the music'[36] – was required to turn his technical discoveries into really interesting music.

Musical connections and the evolution of Reich's own ensemble

Reich's obsession with the Phase Shifting Pulse Gate coincides with the period when he and Glass were comparing notes on each other's attempts to discover a technique and style for themselves. While the available evidence suggests that the latter was the main beneficiary in these exchanges, it is also possible that Reich was learning, for instance, from his friend's decision to limit his involvement with electronics to amplification and the newly emerging electronic keyboards. This raises the question of the influence any of the so-called minimalist composers had on Reich, which in his case can most usefully be dealt with in conjunction with the evolution of the composer's own ensemble.

Reich acknowledges the influence of Young and, in particular, of Riley, viewing himself as, at least to a certain degree, a link in the chain of influences that passed from Young to Riley to himself and on to Glass. As we saw in Chapter 2, however, Reich's own dealings with Riley, after their brief period of friendship in 1964 which had led to the première of the latter's *In C*, were far from easy. Following their move – in Reich's case, back – to New York, where Young had by now firmly established himself, all three composers had to decide how compatible they were both personally and musically, and the extent to which their evolving careers should interact.

According to Young,[37] Reich called him some time after the latter returned to New York and asked to join the Theatre of Eternal Music. Reich denies this, and Riley – a member of Young's group at the time – considers it may have simply been a misunderstanding.[38] Whatever happened, Reich's sensibilities and mode of working are so different from those of Young and Riley that it would seem much more appropriate that he should have set up his own ensemble, just as he had in California.

Reich's New York performing group began operations in late 1966 when, as we have already seen, he began playing regularly with two other musicians, Jon Gibson and Arthur Murphy. While Murphy and Reich were mainly keyboard players, Gibson – who had already performed in Reich's improvisation group in San Francisco and was now also working with Young and Riley – used his versatility as a wind player to allow the new trio further instrumental scope. On occasion, he played other instruments too: the maracas, for example, in the early performances of *Four Organs*. Gibson and Murphy were composers as well as players; while Gibson is today better known as a saxophonist, Murphy has disappeared from the professional music scene altogether.

These three soon began to play the music of its members in SoHo galleries and other 'alternative' spaces, meshing with Reich's performance-art activities described above. Of especial significance to his own establishment as a composer were the 'Three Evenings of Music by Steve Reich', presented at the Park Place Gallery on 17, 18 and 19 March 1967; each evening offered the same programme, including, as seen earlier, the first performances of a version of *Piano Phase* for four pianos. In these, Murphy and Reich were joined by Philip Corner and James Tenney, all playing clavinetes: rudimentary electronic keyboards that were more or less state-of-the-art for the day. Three of them appear to have performed a multiple phasing process against the fixed fourth part; it isn't clear whether the tripartite structure now familiar from the final version had yet evolved.

Since the gallery was currently exhibiting sculptures by Charles Ross, described by Reich as 'plexiglass prisms filled with mineral oil', these became part of the event, as did an environmental installation called *Bi-product*. The latter was the responsibility of the sound artist Max Neuhaus who, the flyer for the concerts promised, would be 'performing and distributing' his creation nightly. Reich says that Neuhaus 'recorded people's movements and recorded them on tape loops which he gave away at the end of the evening'. The musicians played behind Ross's prisms; the audience accordingly saw not only the players, but also multiple reflections of each of them. This clearly contributed to the 'psychedelic' aspect of the occasion, which should be borne in mind when reading Carman Moore's review of the first night. 'So strong was the effect of "Four Pianos"', he writes, 'that one of the listeners, who were all sprawled on the floor, fell into a howling kind of fit from which he emerged, shaken but otherwise (I think) undamaged after the piece concluded.'[39] Curiously, *Melodica* is the only piece listed in Reich's *Writings* as having a performance at Park Place.[40] In fact, as the original programme notes confirm, three other works of his were played in addition to 'Four Pianos'. *Improvisations on a Watermelon* was performed by Murphy and the composer on clavinetes. And *Come Out*, as well as *Melodica*, represented Reich's work with tape; as did 'Saxophone Phase', the original title of *Reed Phase*.

The audiences for these three evenings consisted largely of artists and their friends, including Rauschenberg. After the second performance, a member of the audience came up to the composer and reintroduced himself as a student colleague from their Juilliard-School days. It was in this manner that Glass and Reich became reacquainted. Both attempting to establish careers in New York with a compositional approach very different from that which each had been following five years before, the two composers quickly recognised what they now had in common, and cemented a working relationship that took two symbiotic forms. Both became the prime movers in the ensemble that constituted the main outlet for their own works over the next three years or so. And as compositional associates, they naturally showed each other their pieces as they developed individual approaches along related lines. According to Glass, Reich was 'very, very pleased'[41] to see someone else working in the same territory. According to Gibson, Reich was impressed by *Strung Out*, the first piece Glass seems to have written after his re-encounter with his former Juilliard colleague; Gibson says that 'there was a lot of interaction'[42] between Glass and Reich during this period. Glass turned out to offer not only support but also a kind of legitimation of Reich's own activities: a spur to activity very different from Riley's suspicious attitude to anyone treading on ground he considered rightfully his.

On the matter of actual influence, Reich maintains the view that, just as Riley, in particular, had been important in helping him to find his own way forward, so he himself now assisted Glass in his search for a technique and a style of his own. Having discovered his basic technique of phasing more than two years before his re-encounter with Glass, Reich viewed their sharing of ideas as basically one-way traffic, the more experienced composer giving to the relative novice the benefit of his advice concerning, for instance, the need to find a systematic technical procedure to compare with his own discovery of phasing. As one piece of evidence for this, or at least as some indication of the grateful respect Glass showed him at the time, he points to the first manuscript copies of his colleague's first substantial exploration of additive process, the technical breakthrough which made Glass's later work possible. The title page of this score, dated February 1969, reveals that this piece's original title was *Two Pages for Steve Reich*; only later did it become known simply as *Two Pages.*

The trio formed by Gibson, Murphy and Reich now expanded further to include not only Glass but several other musicians brought in by one or another of the already existing members of the group, usually Reich or Glass themselves. This rather loose association of composer-performers spawned two groups – Steve Reich and Musicians, and The Philip Glass Ensemble – which exist to this day. But though Reich has dated the former from 1966, and Glass the latter from 1968, this pool of performers – meeting, sometimes, as much as two or three nights a week – had neither fixed membership nor, at first, strongly separate allegiances; as so often happens, all its members initially worked on a more equal footing than subsequently became the case. Significantly for any notion of the evolution of separate ensembles attached to Reich or Glass, no composition requiring more than three players – the early version of *Piano Phase* aside – was produced by any of its members until Glass wrote *600 Lines* in the summer of 1968.

Reich himself produced no further ensemble pieces besides *Four Log Drums* and *Pendulum Music* until *Four Organs* some eighteen months later. In the interim, Gibson had gone to Los Angeles for around eight months to work for a Brazilian musician, Marcie Santos. He says that Reich and Glass 'were close'[43] when he left New York in the summer of 1968, and were still so when he got back, probably in March 1969, one month after *Two Pages* was completed. Some time after this, however, there appears to have been something of a falling out between the two composers, leading ultimately to a complete break between them.

The group run, in the main, by Reich and Glass nevertheless jointly gave several important New York concerts in 1969–70; the two composers performed in a few of each other's pieces, but the programming of their own music was kept separate. These concerts included the two already mentioned programmes at the Whitney Museum on 20 and 27 May 1969. An important programme at the Guggenheim Museum a year later, on 7 May 1970, saw the premières of *Four Organs* and *Phase Patterns.* After the Guggenheim programme, there was an important four-night series at the

Walker Art Center, Minneapolis, a week later, with two evenings devoted to each composer. The two made no further appearances together on the platform, with the exception of the concerts on a jointly arranged tour of Germany, France and England in March 1971; playing their ensemble works in Europe for the first time, the two found it expedient to fix a combined visit.

Reich used contacts he had made with Michael Nyman in London and, through Gibson, with Chantelle D'Arcy at the record company Disques Shandar in Paris to make his first European tour. Both his concerts – at the Institute of Contemporary Arts in London on 7 March, and at the Théâtre de la Musique in Paris on 16 March – consisted of the same programme: *Four Organs*, *Piano Phase*, *Pendulum Music*, *Phase Patterns* and Part One of *Drumming*, the last described in the list for the programme as 'in progress'. The personnel for most of these was the same as before; for *Pendulum Music*, local musicians assisted the composer. The Paris concert, mounted by Shandar, led to the record company's release the following year of a disc coupling *Four Organs* and *Phase Patterns*. The London programme resulted in a closer association with Nyman: the man behind the Hayward Gallery performance of *Drumming* almost a year later and one of the composer's most receptive commentators.

Several musicians were involved specifically with Reich from early on. In addition to Gibson and Murphy, Paul Zukofsky was among the first to work with the composer, giving the first performances of *Violin Phase*, as we have seen. While Corner and Tenney were only occasional members, the keyboard player Steve Chambers joined Reich for the Guggenheim programme in May 1970 and remained until the early performances (including the first recording, made in 1976 though not issued until 1978) of *Music for Eighteen Musicians*.

It was *Drumming* (1970–71) which caused the largest single expansion in the history of the group, which now became known for the first time as Steve Reich and Musicians. The work was put together via painstaking rehearsals, allowing for 'many small compositional changes while the work is in progress and at the same time [building] a kind of ensemble solidarity that makes playing together a joy'. This included the devising of the extensive resulting patterns, in which several performers assisted the composer. With *Six Pianos*, too, in which extensive use is also made of resulting patterns, both the choice and the ordering of these were made in rehearsal.

After various 'in progress' performances, *Drumming* was finally given complete at three different venues in New York City in December 1971: the Museum of Modern Art on the 3rd, Brooklyn Academy of Music on the

11th, and New York Town Hall on the 16th. The last of these performances was issued on record in April 1972 by (a completely different) John Gibson and Multiples Inc. (an art gallery press), in a limited edition of 500 complete with full score; meanwhile, the work was also toured. In the process of its assembly, two percussionists joined the hard-core group of Chambers, Gibson, Murphy and Reich himself: Russ Hartenberger and James Preiss now became mainstays of Reich's ensemble. *Drumming* also led to the engagement of three female singers: Jay Clayton, Joan LaBarbara and Judy Sherman. With Sherman replaced by Janice Jarrett, this trio also featured in *Music for Mallet Instruments, Voices and Organ.* Bob Becker, Tim Ferchen and Glen Velez, all three of them subsequently core percussionists of Steve Reich and Musicians, did not join until 1973, by which time Murphy had left. Other members of the group stayed for shorter periods; and, since Reich could not afford to take all the performers in his newly enlarged group out of New York, the early European performances of *Drumming, Six Pianos* and *Mallet* were augmented by local musicians. After these performances, Gibson left Reich's ensemble to work only with Glass and on projects of his own.

Though the eighteen (originally twenty-one) musicians required for *Music for Eighteen Musicians* enlarged Reich's ensemble to near-orchestral proportions, this was conceived and assembled under the same intimate, intensive and exploratory conditions that had characterised all Reich's ensemble efforts. This work increases the line-up of female vocalists to four, one of whom may also take a piano part in Section IIIa; other doublings involve the vibraphonist, who plays piano in Sections II and IX, and one other percussionist, who also plays piano in Section IX. The first commercial recording of *Music for Eighteen Musicians* retains only Clayton among the composer's original singers, adding Rebecca Armstrong, Elizabeth Arnold and Pamela Fraley. The four orchestral instruments new to Reich's ensemble music were played by Shem Guibbory (violin), Ken Ishii (cello), Virgil Blackwell and Richard Cohen (clarinets doubling bass clarinets). The core team of keyboard and mallet instruments added Larry Karush, Gary Schall, Nurit Tilles and David Van Tieghem to six regulars: Becker, Chambers, Hartenberger, Preiss, Velez and the composer himself.

Rehearsals for *Music for Eighteen Musicians* were held over a long period between April or May 1974 and the work's première on 24 April 1976. Structurally, the work is so complex that no attempt was made to notate repeats or achieve synchronisation in what was written down. No complete score authenticated by the composer existed until 1996, when Marc Mellits completed what is basically a transcription of the 1978 recording.[44] *Music for Eighteen Musicians* nevertheless precipitated its creator's move into writing for larger forces not gathered together and rehearsed over long periods under the composer's own control.

The instrumental compositions of 1969–70

Four Organs

One of Reich's technology-based notions, at least, proved adaptable to more conventional instruments; he is not, after all, a composer to waste ideas. The transformation of a single pulsing chord into a series of melodic patterns could still be achieved with live musicians if the notes of the chord were simply lengthened very slowly, one by one. The result of this discovery, made in August 1969, was *Four Organs*, completed the following January. Here, four electronic organs repeat the pitches of a single chord, gradually extending them so that, while the pulse remains intact, the music gives the impression of slowing down. The piece is thus additionally a kind of realisation of *Slow Motion Sound*; it was also influenced by the augmentation techniques found in the organum of the twelfth-century composer Perotin. All that was required to keep the players together was some kind of percussive pulse. Reich decided on maracas: breaking, for the first time in more than five years, his self-imposed rule about employing only identical instruments in any single piece.

Four Organs takes as its entire pitch material a dominant-eleventh chord based on a low E (see Ex. 3.13a). It is thus Reich's first significant composition to have a real bass part; the first in which he found a solution to the problem of handling the lower register in suitably ambiguous terms. Its six pitches – E G♯ B D F♯ A – are spread over the four instruments (basically a lower and upper pair), producing a total of nine notes spanning three-and-a-half octaves. A central cluster of mainly major seconds – D E F♯ G♯ A B – gives this chord a strongly dissonant edge; yet, as its distribution among the players partly demonstrates, this can readily be interpreted as a conglomerate of 'stacked' fifths, following the example of *Four Log Drums*. At the same time, as this suggests, such a dominant-eleventh chord is a relative of the material Reich had already explored in, among other works, *Violin Phase*.

This chord occurs at first in quavers on beats 1 and 4 of a repeated figure of $^{11}_{8}$ (see again Ex. 3.13a). Constituting Reich's first use of a pulsing chord as a basic structural component, this is something he was to explore extensively in future works, often with a more regular pulse than that provided by the three + eight-beat unit to be found here. As it repeats – as a consequence establishing, of course, its own kind of regularity – single notes are progressively augmented beyond the quaver length of the chord as a

Example 3.13 *Four Organs*: (a) Figures 1–4; (b) Figure 8 (treble only).

whole: at first extending forwards, on the beats already established (G♯, Figure 2; E, Figure 3), then backwards, suggesting an anticipatory upbeat (E, Figure 4). The inevitable result of this process is the filling up of the whole figure with continuous organ sound; or, putting this another way, the substitution of notes for rests – what Reich later called 'rhythmic construction'. In temporarily abandoning phasing altogether, *Four Organs* already pointed the way towards approaches which would prove fertile in years to come.

Once the original pairs of irregularly pulsing chords have silted up into a continuous sound (at Figure 10, about 3′15″ into the work's first recording, which as a whole lasts 15′35″), the figures themselves start to lengthen (some twenty seconds later). Beginning with the basic eleven quavers, this gradually expands to an enormous 265 quavers-worth of continuous sound. *Four Organs* thus divides into two sections: the first highly rhythmic, the second focusing on the harmony that has been present all along. Both subject highly reductive material to quite systematic scrutiny. Both, however, give a powerful impression of the ground shifting uneasily and unpredictably beyond the listener's grasp, since it is only possible to follow the general trend of their unfolding, not their detailed structure.

Though transcending the technique of phasing for the first time in Reich's output since 1965, *Four Organs* is even more restrictive and reductive than *Piano Phase* or *Violin Phase.* It is the first of only three pieces in Reich's output up to 1976 that began life as an abstract idea, that 'didn't have notes right away'. (*Drumming* and *Clapping Music* are the others.) Though its two sections audibly contrast the beginning of a process with its consequences, the piece is really a single process performed, without deviation, on a single harmonic unit. Yet *Four Organs* is by no means as one-dimensional as it may at first seem. The process has several by-products: chordal subdivisions and melodic cells assembled note-by-note as the basic chord gradually unravels, for instance (some of the latter ordered in pairs of perfect fifths); and sustained notes played out of phase on two or more organs (a new purchase on phasing). Since these by-products accumulate as the work proceeds, their impact is structural, not merely incidental. Yet such contrapuntal and textural variety as exists is still overwhelmed by the relentless reductiveness. *Four Organs* is in some respects Reich's most 'difficult' score.

Tonally, however, the piece takes a significant step in line with some of the above advances. The dominant implications enhanced through the chord's constant repetition are pursued in the pitches chosen for extension into sub-chords as the work proceeds: Figure 8, for instance (see Ex. 3.13b), reveals an E^7 chord, subsequently opposed by the emergence of a triad on D. Or reinforced by it, if you take the view that this V–IV in A major (or perhaps it should be I–VII in an E modality) represents neighbour-chord oscillation prolonging E.

Reich takes advantage of the fact that the eleventh of this dominant chord is also its tonic to play some interesting games with the listener's perception of harmony. Since the dominant is the bottom note (E) and the eleventh/tonic the top (A), 'all you have to do is release the bass, and all its doublings, and pretty soon you've resolved your chord'. While on the face of it suggesting a return to the bass-less ambiguities of the immediately preceding compositions, the progressive abandonment of the bass E in *Four Organs*' closing stages implies, in context, a closure of a kind previously unknown in Reich's post-student pieces. The result is a new approach to the traditional materials of harmony: a basic V–I cadence articulated by subjecting a seemingly static object to an inspection so intense that it threatens to turn into something else. One might point out that any tonic chord takes on dominant suggestions through relentless

Example 3.14 *Phase Patterns*: (a) Figure 7; (b) Figure 8.

repetition. Reich's dominant eleventh is much more interesting, however, and his structural ingenuity in developing its potential for a kind of harmonic motion in such protracted circumstances far greater. For all its radical rigour and harmonic reductiveness, *Four Organs* marks the beginning of Reich's serious interest in harmonic motion.

Phase Patterns

Though written for the same combination of four electric organs, his next composition, *Phase Patterns* (the score of which is dated 2/70), returns, as its title tells us, to phasing. It treats these keyboard instruments as tuned drums, constructing a phasing cycle on that most elementary of percussive figures, a simple alternation of the left and right hands called the paradiddle: L–R–L–L–R–L–R–R. Players 1 and 2 phase a pitched version of this Basic Unit against itself (see top line of Ex. 3.14a), while Players 3 and 4 build resulting patterns into the mix. A complete cycle of phasing is avoided: Player 2 moves ahead of Player 1 just four times out of a possible total of eight, to beat 5 (Figure 7). This is not only exactly halfway through the sequence, but also the point at which rhythmic unison – not exact unison, but still perceptible – is reached: the right hand of the moving player synchronises with the left hand of the stationary player, and vice versa (see again Ex. 3.14a). It occurs towards the end of the piece at 11′32″ in the 16′10″-long performance on the Shandar recording. This is the cue for Players 3 and 4 to bring in, unfaded, a second pattern, at 12′20″ (Figure 8). Like the first, it is based on the paradiddle model (see Ex. 3.14b) and, again, is phased only as far as its fifth beat (Figure 12). It is not, though, accompanied by resulting patterns. Instead, in the manner of *Violin Phase*, the first two players continue with the phased version of the first pattern they had already reached as a background against which the second pattern moves forward.

The spacing and modality of Part One (see again Ex. 3.14a) recall those of the first part of *Piano Phase.* Yet its five pitch classes – with E doubled at the octave and a top G extending the span to a tenth – contain a secundal dissonance, F♯ G, all the sharper for being a minor ninth rather than a semitone. They not only reinforce the tonic E triadically, but its dominant too, combining tonic and dominant, just as *Four Organs* had, in a single chord rich in potential; a chord which makes *Phase Patterns* just the latest in the list of pieces, starting with *Melodica,* which are based on such pitch material. In the work as a whole, triadic emphasis, neighbour-note oscillation, secundal dissonance and ultimate shift to an area of more ambiguous modality all come together, however, to allow the tonality of *Phase Patterns* to condition, and underpin, its resulting patterns with an energy of its own, and to provide a 'coda' which some may indeed hear as a kind of resolution all the more effective for the surprise of its proposed new key of C major.

The trip to Africa (and his later study of Indonesian gamelan)

Reich's treatment of the organ as a percussion instrument is surprising only in the immediate context of an apparently growing interest in harmony. Pulse-dominated percussion-based music had in fact fascinated him since he was a child, as we have seen. And as a student, he had become particularly excited by African drumming, with its complex counterpoint generated with the aid of multiple downbeats in an essentially ensemble context. As a member of Berio's composition class, he had gone to a composers' conference in Ojai, California, in the summer of 1962, where he encountered the composer, conductor and musicologist Gunther Schuller, then already contemplating his authoritative history of early jazz.[45] Schuller recommended A. M. Jones's then fairly recently published, now classic, *Studies in African Music,*[46] and the following year Reich derived more of his first knowledge of African musical structures from reading this book, and its accompanying volume of transcriptions, than from actual listening. He later corresponded with Jones and had two lessons in New York from Alfred Ladzepko, a master drummer of the Ewe tribe.

Reich now determined to spend a period studying African drumming in Ghana, feeling that, as he wrote three years later, 'non-Western music is presently the single most important source of new ideas for Western composers and musicians'.[47] In the summer of 1970, he arrived in Accra, the capital of Ghana, for what was intended to be a stay of several months, supported by a travel grant from the Special Projects division of the Institute of International Education. Contracting malaria after only five weeks, his visit was cut drastically short. But this brief experience of daily

Example 3.15 Ewe tribe – Ghana, *Agbadza*

lessons with Gideon Alorworye, another Ewe master drummer, gave him just as much as he needed. Alorworye was in residence with the Ghana Dance Ensemble in the Institute of African Studies at the University of Ghana. Reich recorded each lesson with him, and later transcribed the bell, rattle and drum patterns he had learned. These experiences allowed him to find out a good deal about the structure of African ensemble music, its texture characteristically consisting of an unchanging bell (gong-gong) pattern, a related rattle pattern and the drum patterns which overlay these. It is the relationship of each drum pattern to the gong-gong that is most important, and in particular, the polyrhythmic counterpoint of patterns of different lengths and different downbeats which results.

Example 3.15, one of three transcriptions of Reich's own reproduced in the *Writings* volume,[48] demonstrates the essence of this type of musical structure. Though the other two are, he claims, the first attempts to reproduce the basic drumming of Gahu and the Hatsyiatsya patterns on which it is based, Example 3.15 is the only one of the three to have a gong-gong pattern in $\frac{12}{8}$ (top line): not only the most common in West Africa, but also the time signature which Reich had, as we have seen, come to value most for its polyrhythmic potential. Though the downstrokes of the rattle part (second line) double the gong-gong, the upper notes filling in the rests, this pattern, while of the same $\frac{12}{8}$ length, begins on the second crotchet (the third quaver beat) of the gong-gong pattern. Against these, the three drum parts illustrate different relationships. The kagan (third line) plays short, unchanging $\frac{3}{8}$ patterns with downbeats on the third, sixth, ninth and twelfth quaver beats of the gong-gong. The sogo master drummer (fifth line) begins with a four-quaver pattern dividing $\frac{12}{8}$ into three groups of four (itself subject to improvised variations); then – after continuous quavers signalling the impending change of pattern – continues with a six-quaver pattern, similarly commencing on the gong-gong's main downbeat but this time incorporating syncopations. The kidi (fourth line), meanwhile, responds to the master drummer by providing quaver beats in sogo's rests, also doubling sogo's beats with muted ones of its own, likewise in $\frac{4}{8}$

groupings but two quaver beats' distant from sogo – which means its downbeats are on the third, seventh and eleventh quavers of the gong-gong.

Wishing to penetrate beneath the 'exotic' surface of such music – thus helping to avoid the temptation, surrendered to, in his view, by earlier generations of Western composers fascinated by non-Western musics, merely to re-create its sounds – Reich was committed to learning as much as possible about its structure and essence. He was especially attracted by the polymetric ingenuities to be found in African ensemble music such as the example just described. But as a composer, rather than an ethnomusicologist, he was concerned to retain his Western individuality and not get too involved. That illness may have been a blessing in disguise.

Regarding the effect his visit to Africa had on his work, and *Drumming* in particular, Reich wrote that '[t]he answer is *confirmation.* It confirmed my intuition that acoustic instruments could be used to produce music that was genuinely richer in sound than that produced by electronic instruments, as well as confirming my natural inclination towards percussion'.[49] The trip to Accra served as a 'green light' for him to place percussion at the centre of his ensemble. It also alerted him to the potential of voices as a part of such an ensemble: not for articulating texts in any conventional Western, or for that matter African, sense – something Reich would continue to reject for another ten years – but to sing nonsense syllables tied closely to the music's rhythmic structure and to imitate the sound of instruments themselves. While this fitted in well with the expansion of timbres that was one of the main characteristics of his compositional development, African music also encouraged Reich to see new dimensions in the virtues of simplicity. The hand clapping that so often underpins an African ensemble, for instance, was surely one inspiration for his own *Clapping Music.*

Reich's aesthetic approach to non-Western music was thus governed by his already familiar constructivist attitude. Though in the course of the early 1970s he became less obsessed by the need to make the structural details of his own compositions as audible as possible, the expressive concerns behind his own work remained in marked contrast to those of Western Classical and Romantic music. Though West African music has an important improvisatory element to it, he was fascinated by the control exerted on individual expression by the limitations within which that improvisation must be conducted. 'The pleasure I get from playing', the composer wrote in 1974, 'is not the pleasure of expressing myself, but of subjugating myself to the music and experiencing the ecstasy that comes from being a part of it'.[50] That subjugation of the individual in the controlled activities of an ensemble in which each musician knows the precise nature of his contribution to the whole is, he discovered, as typical – if not more typical – of the Indonesian gamelan. In addition, Reich was attracted by the integration of dance and music in both African and Indonesian cultures. His relationship with the dancer and choreographer Laura Dean in 1970–73 led to several of his own compositions being used for dance purposes: something taken up by many other choreographers since that time.

In the summers of 1973 and 1974, Reich took advantage of Bob Brown's establishment of the American Society for Eastern Arts to travel West and take lessons, from native musicians, in Balinese gamelan. In the first year, he went to Seattle, Washington, where his main teacher was Nyo Man Sumandi; the year after to the Center for World Music in Berkeley, California, where he was taught by Pak Sinti. In both cases, he taught his own music as well. Balinese music has certain similarities to that of Ghana: its individual parts are usually simple to play, and the chief interest derives from an ensemble producing multiple downbeats. 'Not being a virtuoso', he writes, 'not being interested in improvisation, and being thoroughly committed to my own ensemble that performs music I have composed with repetitive patterns combined so that their downbeats do not always coincide, it may be natural for my interests to run strongly towards Balinese and African music'.[51] Furthermore, what Mantle Hood describes as the 'stratification'[52] of the Indonesian gamelan's complex layering of pitch as well as rhythmic material is also an apt term for Reich's music.

The gamelan, with its typical texture of fast interlocking patterns underpinned by slower, more harmonic material performed by an ensemble dominated by metallophones, seems an inevitable influence on *Music for Mallet Instruments, Voices and Organ.* Its composer, however, only undertook his formal studies in Balinese music after completing this work. The use of a percussion instrument (in Reich's case the vibraphone) as an aural cue to mark section and other changes in the later *Music for Eighteen Musicians* was inspired by the use both West African and Indonesian ensembles make of the drummer for similar purposes.

The expansion of Reich's reputation and his changing aesthetic to 1976

From his SoHo base, Reich's reputation slowly spread, fuelled in considerable part by recordings. The composer may be the first to have an important record company behind the release of every significant piece he has written. *Come Out* was issued on Columbia Records in 1967 as part of an album entitled *New Sounds in Electronic Music.* One of some two-dozen or more releases of new music produced by David Behrman at this time, including Riley's *In C*, the record received reviews and press coverage – including articles in *Time* and *New York* magazines – which 'put me on the map', says Reich. The same company's issue of *It's Gonna Rain* and *Violin Phase* (performed by Zukofsky), on the album *Steve Reich: Live/Electric Music*, furthered this process two years later. The already mentioned Whitney and Guggenheim Museum concerts in 1969 and 1970 did a good deal to further Reich's career, as did the European tour with Glass in the spring of 1971. Even before the première of the complete *Drumming* in New York at the end of that year, Reich had moved from being known largely by the downtown artistic community to national and even international attention.

Important in this development were two performances of *Four Organs* in concerts by the Boston Symphony Orchestra, mounted through the advocacy of the conductor Michael Tilson Thomas: in Boston on 8 October 1971 and New York's Carnegie Hall on 18 January 1973. Reich's first performances by musicians besides those of his own group – and his first to be given in major Western classical concerts halls – still took place, however, at his own insistence, with himself as both rehearsal supervisor and performer (and Tilson Thomas as one of the other organists). Some members of these largely very conservative audiences, including most critics, were hostile; accounts of the Carnegie Hall performance – their variations on the theme of concert as riot are a textbook case of uncorroborated, sometimes conflicting details – include the brandishing of umbrellas and a woman walking down to the front, perhaps banging her head on the platform and crying, among several alternatives, '[a]ll right – I'll confess!'[53] Despite, or just possibly because of, such notoriety, Reich could probably at this point have obtained an orchestral commission through Tilson Thomas if he had really pressed for it. Surprisingly, too, Pierre Boulez chose *Phase Patterns* for a New York Philharmonic 'Prospective Encounter' programme on 29 October 1971, just three weeks after the Boston performance of *Four Organs*; in this case, though, Reich's own musicians were the performers.

Only in the late 1970s, however – when the increasing size of Steve Reich and Musicians not only led him naturally towards the real orchestra but also posed increasing practical problems for a composer still undertaking many of the responsibilities of management – did he first attempt a work for forces other than those of his own group: *Music for a Large Ensemble*. Though a few performances by others took place in the 1970s – with the aid of manuscript copies passed on by Cornelius Cardew in Britain, for instance, and a student performance of *Drumming*, Part Two, in Seattle in the summer of 1973, in which different singers came up with new resulting patterns subsequently incorporated into performances by Steve Reich and Musicians – it was not until 1980 that any substantial number of the composer's early scores was commercially published;[54] and not until the mid-1980s, and then only slowly, that more recent scores started to become widely available.[55]

For some time, art galleries and museums, particularly those sympathetic to Minimalist art, remained the most hospitable. Following the attention his early recordings received, music critics began to write more consistently about Reich in the early 1970s. Daniel Caux's enthusiastic review of the composer's 1971 Paris concert assisted the already mentioned issue that year, by Shandar, of the LP devoted to *Four Organs* and *Phase Patterns* which helped raise his music's profile, in Europe as well as in the USA. Michael Nyman championed his cause in Britain.[56] Major exposure later that year at West German festivals in Bremen and Berlin helped consolidate Reich's position, at least on the avant-garde music scene, despite the hostility his works still sometimes created, including the psychological and social, as well as purely musical, difficulties some in Germany had with music so devoted to a regular pulse. 1973 saw the release, on the Angel label, of a second recording of *Four Organs*, involving Tilson Thomas. And in 1974, through the intervention of Rudolph Werner, the prestigious classical label Deutsche Grammophon released *Drumming* as part of a three-disc set with *Six Pianos* and *Music for Mallet Instruments, Voices and Organ.*

Back home, while critics such as Donal Henahan of the *New York Times* often continued to be scathing,[57] others more sympathetic to Reich's work were gradually emerging. As mentioned in the Introduction, Tom Johnson – himself a minimalist composer – marked the beginning of his tenure at the *Village Voice* with a review of *Drumming*'s première.[58] Soon after this, John Rockwell also began regular coverage of Reich's music, and the downtown music scene in general, for the *New York Times.*[59]

It was to be another few years, however, before the première of *Music for Eighteen Musicians*, and a further two before the commercial recording of this made Reich's music widely known internationally. Deutsche Grammophon recorded the work, but were uncertain as to whether they could successfully market it. Eventually, Roland Kommerall – in charge of the PolyGram group of which Deutsche Grammophon was part – took the unusual step of letting the recording go to Manfred Eicher's ECM label, which had a track record in the promotion of experimental jazz and other more 'difficult' musics to largely non-classical audiences. Robert Hurwitz – who worked for ECM at the time, and who later moved to the Nonesuch company, taking Reich with him in 1984 – has written that the release of *Music for Eighteen Musicians* was 'a genuine breakthrough for new music, and it proved to many of us that contemporary music could appeal to more than just a small, specialized audience'.[60]

Reich's aesthetic development in the early 1970s

It is clear that Reich's main preoccupation from 1965 to at least 1970 was with structure and, in particular, with the purity and clarity of that structure. In order to achieve structural audibility, the music had to be extremely simple, with 'all the cards . . . on the table'.[61] The rate of change, too, had to be slow: 'everyone hears what is gradually happening in a musical process'. Everything depended on how the small changes in this music were perceived. Early on, too – as we have seen – Reich had realised the joy of being free of reading notation. Yet such objective, 'experimental' absorption in pure process had, in reality, seldom been the whole story, and it had recently taken a few further knocks. As Nyman perceptively pointed out in an extended interview with the composer in 1976, the articulation of resulting patterns by instruments imposes one performer's view of them on others, and thus promotes subjectivity as much as it encourages structural clarity. Now, as Reich began to deploy resulting patterns performed by forces different from those which instigated them – as when, according to the original plan, voices produce resulting patterns from the original bongo and marimba material in, respectively, Parts One and Two of *Drumming*, and the glockenspiel material of Part Three is taken up by both vocal whistling and piccolo – the whole approach to sound is changed. '[T]he doubling', as Nyman puts it, 'separates out from what is doubled'.[62] Even before the more complex textures of Part Four are reached, *Drumming* has already accomplished the move from a quintessentially 'experimental', flat texture to something more resembling a melody-plus-accompaniment one.

In the same interview – among the most penetrating he has ever given – Reich suggests that, immediately he had written it, he found *Piano Phase* 'lacking a certain kind of musical excitement and interest that I personally am attracted to', on account of its reliance on phasing without resulting patterns. It would be naïve to suppose that a composer interested in 'a compositional process and a sounding music that are one and the same thing'[63] could ever be somehow uninterested in the actual sound his music made. Reich, however, seems constantly to have questioned whether he was over-preoccupied with structure as such, and to have increasingly felt the limitations of treating sound itself as merely the means by which structure was articulated.

Reich's move from 'structure' as such to greater concern with sound was itself a gradual process. The resulting patterns first used compositionally in *Violin Phase* may be psycho-acoustic in origin, but they arguably serve to reinforce the work's structure as much as they focus on the music's texture. Even as *Four Organs* breaks the 'mould' of phasing, it appears to enforce a new severity of structural purpose, though the process involved is, in fact, not 'pure'. These days, Reich himself views all his compositions before *Drumming* as 'very radical works that . . . have a kind of etude status. They are studies – very rigorous studies, [monomanically] exclusive studies – in a technique that I had discovered and was absolutely pursuing single-mindedly'. The extent to which *Drumming* draws on a wider range of musical techniques, as well as its significantly larger scope, makes it much more than an 'etude'. This expansion beyond phasing seems to demonstrate an impatience not only with the limitations of a technique Reich had mined assiduously for some six years, but also with being tied exclusively to any highly rigorous approach to a single technical procedure, no matter how imaginatively that technique was explored and set in new contexts. It also demonstrated the lessening importance for him of the audibility of any structural process.

Mature minimalist compositions

The year 1971 saw the completion of *Drumming*, begun the previous year and the crowning achievement of this period. *Drumming* is considerably more substantial, in terms both of length and complexity, than any of its composer's previous works, and an important breakthrough both technically and stylistically. Its rigorous reliance on rhythmic processes nevertheless still makes the work sound more like a summing up of his early music than the beginning of something new. The two pieces which followed – *Clapping Music* (1972) and *Music for Pieces of Wood* (1973) – are short, 'etude-status' pieces once again. *Six Pianos* and *Music for Mallet Instruments, Voices and Organ*, on the other hand – both completed in the first months of 1973 for their premières in the same concert on 16 May that year, at New York's John Weber Gallery – are more important statements. But it was not until March 1976 that Reich was able to complete *Music for Eighteen Musicians*, the work which capitalised on these developments and took them forward to an altogether new level.

Drumming

Drumming introduces a greater concern with sound as such: with the sheer sonic impact of timbre and texture made possible by contrasting and ultimately combining different groups of instruments as part of the evolving structure of an extended composition. Reich's ensemble was now expanded to include an extensive range of tuned percussion instruments: bongo drums, marimbas and glockenspiels. Though he chose, he writes, 'instruments that are all now commonly available in Western countries',[64] all are redolent of their various – by no means exclusively African – origins.

And not only instruments: he now also added voices to his ensemble for the first time. Though impressed by his African experiences of voices combined with drumming, it was a long-held admiration for the scat singing of Ella Fitzgerald that now inspired Reich to explore the possibilities of using voices wordlessly – 'to become part of the musical ensemble by imitating the exact sound of the instruments'. He has written that '[w]hile first playing the drums during the process of composition, I found myself sometimes singing with them, using my voice to imitate the sounds they made. I began to understand that this might also be possible with the marimbas and glockenspiels'.[65] The score suggests 'using syllables like "tak", "duk", and so forth'; all voices must be amplified. Despite his own vocal efforts, and though both male and female voices are specified at different points in the scores which have up to now been available,[66] Reich favoured the female voice from early in the work's composition and rehearsal. Men's voices were soon abandoned, though perceptive listeners may be able to detect a single male voice – the composer's – on the Deutsche Grammophon recording. Singers and/or players contribute resulting patterns at various stages of the phasing process in each movement.

The decision to use percussion, and to avoid the keyboard instruments which had dominated his instrumental output in the previous few years, suggests, perhaps surprisingly, the retention of a firm focus on rhythm at the expense of Reich's still new interest in harmony. The basic material of *Drumming* was – furthermore, and unusually for Reich – conceived initially as pure rhythm: patterns inspired, in fact, by the mundane act of strumming his fingers on a table while on the telephone. But while it was his first work to begin life in the form of a rhythmic pattern, this was later 'given a great variety of pitches'.

According to his publisher's catalogue, *Drumming* (composed between the autumn of 1970 and the autumn of 1971) may last between fifty-seven and eighty-six minutes.[67] The original 1974 LP recording takes around eighty minutes: the longest the work ever got, according to Reich himself. The 1987 Nonesuch CD version (the only one currently available, and from which the timings below are taken) takes 56′44″. Though all his works to this date from *Piano Phase* onwards permit of some variability in length, owing to the freedom allowed for the repetition of each 'figure', most performances seem to have lasted between about fifteen and twenty minutes, usually closer to the former. *Drumming* thus represents a substantial change of scope. In 1974, Reich gave the work's length as 'about one and a half hours'[68] and wrote that it had 'turned out to be the longest piece I have ever composed'.

The composer does, however, divide *Drumming* into four parts, each lasting the sort of length an earlier whole piece of his would have done. Though these are continuous in a complete performance, each part is also playable separately. The main reason for this division is the opportunity it affords to exploit, contrast and eventually bring together a timbral palette much larger than any he had previously used. Part One is scored for drums (originally plus male voices, as we have seen), Part Two for marimbas and female voices, Part Three for glockenspiels, whistling and piccolo (substitutes for the previous vocal activity, the pitches now being too high to sing); Part Four combines all the musicians required for the previous three to make a highly original kind of 'orchestra'. Transitions to each new timbre are continuous and gradual: while the previous group fades out, the new one fades in, 'the new instruments doubling the exact pattern of the instruments already playing'.[69]

The way in which these forces are deployed is designed to produce a dramatic curve: rising from Part One (17′30″) to Part Two (18′10″), then falling for the 'scherzo' of Part Three (11′12″), prior to a further rise for the climactic Part Four (9′44″). Simultaneously with this overall emotional trajectory there runs an even simpler one based on register: rising in steps from the G♯ – C♯ (a low version of composer's familiar 'low treble') of Part One through the expansion up to C♯ two octaves higher of Part Two, to the glockenspiels of Part Three, which rise to A♯ almost two octaves above that. Part Four then employs almost the full range: from the drums' low G♯ up to the glockenspiel's high A♯. In *Drumming* Reich takes on, for the first time, the challenge of sustaining the listener's attention over a long time-span, putting to good use his experiences of constructing fifteen- to twenty-minute forms of considerable structural sophistication to produce a large-scale work of cumulative complexity and power.

In *Writings*, the composer says that the work 'is the final expansion and refinement of the phasing process, as well as the first use of four new techniques'.[70] In terms of both rhythm and timbre, *Drumming* breaks important new ground. Of the new techniques, one is the already mentioned use of voices. The second is purely rhythmic: the process Reich calls 'gradually substituting beats for rests (or rests for beats) within a constantly repeating rhythmic cycle', or, respectively, 'rhythmic construction' and 'rhythmic reduction' (the former already explored in *Four Organs*). The third and fourth are, like the first, essentially timbral: 'the gradual changing of timbre while rhythm and pitch remain constant'; and 'the simultaneous combination of instruments of different timbre'.

All four parts of *Drumming* are based on a single pattern, once again of twelve quaver beats, given in Example 3.16a. The Basic Unit changes not only its phase position and timbre, but also its pitch configuration; Reich reveals the pattern's rhythmic origins when he says that 'all the performers play this pattern, or some part of it, throughout the entire piece'.[71] This typically Reichian construct gives rise to a technical *tour de force* as the potential ambiguities of different downbeats resulting from many subdivisions of twelve into twos, threes, fours and sixes are exploited. Since the crotchet, rather than the quaver, becomes the main building block both compositionally and perceptually, 'beats' will from here onwards refer to crotchets, not quavers. Part One of the work will be analysed in some detail to demonstrate how Reich combines already familiar techniques with new ones to create one of his most sophisticated structures while retaining essentially simple means. Shorter discussions of Parts Two, Three and Four will then illustrate a few more of the timbral and modal, as well as rhythmic, ingenuities to be found in the remainder of the work.

Analysis of Drumming, Part One

Part One introduces the drums in a small ensemble of eight small tuned drums, or bongos. The bongos are stand-mounted in pairs, divided into two groups (one for each pair of players), and tuned to four pitches: in ascending order, G♯, A♯, B and C♯. They are played with both hard and soft sticks. Since the two performers in each pair face each other, playing the same four drums, neither pitch order nor use of left and right hands will be the same for each, and the latter is left to the musicians' choice.

The second 'new technique' mentioned above – that of 'rhythmic construction' – makes its appearance at the outset, as two drummers assemble the Basic Unit note by note. (The original score suggests 'two, three or four drummers', but the revised score adopts the simple pair of players long since used by the composer's own ensemble.) This process, which takes just over a minute, is later reversed; after Figure 15 (9′36″), the Basic Unit is progressively reduced to a single note, played just once. Within this framework, a series of 'fuzzy transitions' carries the phasing process forward; each of these transitions occupies between about twenty and thirty seconds. There are four such transitions, in which the Basic Unit is twice moved out of phase on a simple crotchet-by-crotchet basis, then subjected to a more complex procedure described below. On three of these stages, resulting patterns are constructed, the patterns entering and leaving in the now familiar crescendo/diminuendo fashion. The score specifies no lengths for these sections; on the 1987 recording, each occupies between about one and three minutes. They provide the main 'meat' of the movement.

When 'rhythmic reduction' has reversed the opening process (10′54″), soft sticks are exchanged for the original hard ones, and a slightly different version of the Basic Unit is now assembled (from Figure 23). A further series of 'fuzzy transitions' of similar length then unfolds. This time, there are five of them, in which the Basic Unit is again twice moved out of phase, then subjected to more complex treatment, once again described below. In this shorter section, though, no resulting patterns are highlighted. Instead (starting at Figure 35), all four players prepare for the timbral change to Part Two by alternating between hard and soft sticks. While Players 1–3 retain the phasing positions they have reached, three marimba players, using soft rubber mallets, fade in with the same patterns (Figure 47), which the drummers now fade out (concluding at 17′30″).

Each figure gradually assembling the Basic Unit, at the opening of Part One, is repeated 'at least six or eight' times; when one drummer moves to the next figure, the other may either join him at once or continue with the same figure and join him after a few more repeats. This initial process of rhythmic construction already offers a subtle range of ambiguities both metrical (it can be heard, for instance, in both $\frac{6}{4}$ and $\frac{3}{2}$) and tonal (G♯ and B establishing positions of primacy in a pitch gamut reductive even by Reich's standards).

Players 1 and 2 then commence the sequence of 'fixed' and 'moving' patterns of the basic phasing process that follows. The other pair (Players 3 and 4) now participates in the resulting patterns against this continuing 'grid'. The score's range of resulting patterns for 'drummers 3 & 4 and/or male voices' rings the changes on a Basic Unit using only four pitches with considerable resourcefulness; both Reich's previous instrumental compositions with separately articulated resulting patterns had employed five pitch classes for their Basic Units (and, in *Phase Patterns*, a second pattern introducing a sixth one). The distribution of phasing patterns and resulting patterns is the most complex combination of the two which Reich ever devised for a single pattern without pitch extensions. Example 3.16b–d demonstrates the nature of these patterns' evolution through the

Example 3.16 *Drumming*, Part One: (a) Figure 9 (Basic Unit); (b) Figure 10; (c) Figure 11 (Drummers 1 and 2 and composite of resulting patterns only); (d) Figure 13 (Drummers 1–3 and composite of resulting patterns only); (e) Figure 28; (f) Figure 42.

Example 3.16 (*cont.*)

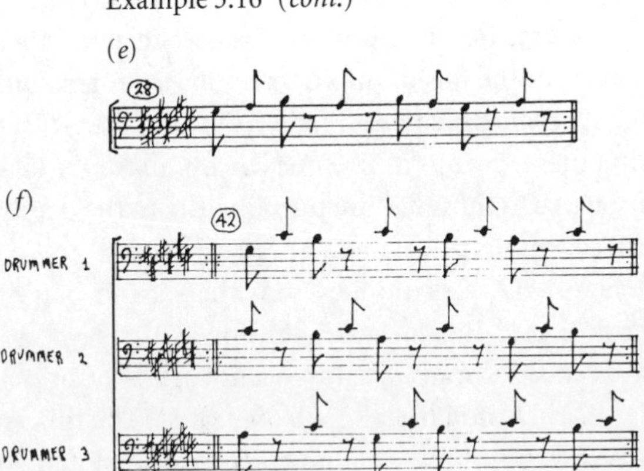

three figures involved; the following notes also make a few observations on what can be heard on the Nonesuch recording.

In Stage One (Figure 10), both resulting patterns notated in the score are four bars in length, each covering four statements of the Basic Unit, itself now written out in two-bar repeating sequences (see Ex. 3.16b). Each resulting pattern outlines a broadly descending sequence in each bar, revolving initially around C♯ and B, the upper pair of pitches; one pattern obligingly picks up all four available C♯s on the first four beats, alternating them with B. More important, however, is the fact that almost every bar articulates the lower pair of pitches, A♯ and G♯, in a kind of extended upbeat to the next bar's main downbeat, implying a ii–i reinforcing G♯ (sometimes accompanied by its mediant, B) as the central pitch. This is further emphasised by a crotchet-based pattern using all four pitches in a descending sequence from C♯ to G♯. It is this which dominates the early moments of Stage One in the 1987 recording; they can, in fact, be heard for some time in every bar, either as the effect of multiple repetitions of the two notated patterns, or as a consequence of newly invented ones. Later, the focus is on A♯G♯. The patterns here suggest $\frac{6}{4}$ rather than the previously dominant $\frac{3}{2}$.

In Stage Two (Figure 11), one notated resulting pattern is eight bars long, the other four bars (see Ex. 3.16c, which gives only the composite of this stage of the phasing process). In the composite itself, C♯ now occurs on the second, fourth and sixth beats, making it suitable for incorporation into a resulting pattern establishing a strong alternative downbeat and a marked contrast to Figure 10. Instead, the eight-bar pattern makes the C♯ on beat 4 the top of the curve of a short sequence in mid-bar that initially alternates with the other pitches' emphasis on beats 1, 3 and 5, suggesting $\frac{3}{2}$. After repeating this in bar 3, though, this pattern abandons C♯ until the second beat of its penultimate bar. The four-bar pattern offers just a single C♯, on beat 2 of its first bar, being more concerned with stressing the opening G♯B quavers of the Basic Unit in its unphased form. On the 1987 recording, the most obvious elements seem to be, first, the G♯A♯ sequences in $\frac{3}{2}$ and, following these, groups of five quavers on quavers 1–5 and 7–11, which suggest $\frac{6}{4}$. Cross-rhythms feature prominently in the deployment of the resulting patterns in this performance of Stage Two.

After this, at Figure 12, a drummer from the second pair (Player 3) enters with the unphased Basic Unit in unison with Player 1, prior to phasing one beat ahead (beat 2), thus occupying a position midway between Player 1 (beat 1) and Player 2 (still on beat 3). The third section of resulting patterns thus has three simultaneous canonic statements of the Basic Unit from which to draw its material, but only one drummer (Player 4) to perform them.

In Stage Three (Figure 13), the score offers four patterns: one of four bars, plus three each of a single bar to be repeated (see Ex. 3.16d, which gives, again, only the composite). A notable feature of the new contrapuntal composite is that B now occurs on every quaver. One of these single repeated bars is accordingly devoted solely to quaver Bs, which are also taken up by beats 5 and 6 of the four-bar pattern. Additionally, all the other bars of the longer pattern place B at their beginning, and in general they offset the potential metric anarchy of continuous quaver Bs by emphasising the main crotchet beats. On the 1987 recording, the main effect is again of descending sequences, moving quite quickly from C♯ to stress A♯ and G♯.

Following this, at Figure 14, Player 4 moves directly, without phasing, to Stage Four (beat 4). When the consequent four simultaneous statements of the Basic Unit have been held for about a minute, Players 2, 3 and 4 move ahead, without pausing on each 'notch', until all are back in unison with Player 1's 'fixed' version (Figures 15–16). The cycle of phasing has thus been completed in a telescoped manner taking '30–45 seconds', characterised by a tumble of patterns, more chaotic and exciting than usual, moving in 'fuzzy' mode from different positions at slightly different speeds. With the return of all four players to the Basic Unit in unison, 'rhythmic reduction' now proceeds (Figures 16–22) until only a single, unrepeated G♯ remains: the logical conclusion of the tonal focus that this process has itself highlighted. With the switch to soft sticks (Figure 23), the altered version of the Basic Unit, now constructed by at least two players, leaves out C♯ entirely for the moment, but preserves not only the rhythms but also the shape and tonal emphasis of the original (see Ex. 3.16e).

As before, Players 1 and 2 begin the phasing sequence, the latter moving progressively to the third 'notch'. While this combination (on beats 1 and

3) is once again frozen, Player 3 this time joins Player 2, then proceeds from this new position a further two 'notches', to beat 5. With no separately articulated resulting patterns to be performed this time, on these three phasing positions – on beats 1, 3 and 5, the combination itself suggesting $\frac{3}{2}$ – Player 4 briefly replaces each of his colleagues in turn to facilitate the change back to hard sticks. This accomplished, and Players 1–3 all remaining in position, Player 1 exchanges the A♯s on quavers 5 and 8 in the alternative Basic Unit to C♯s, a procedure progressively adopted by Players 2 and 3 (Figures 39–41). Further modification – involving exchange of another A♯ for a C♯, but also the replacement of a G♯ by A♯ itself – allows the emergence, though not the players' own reinforcement, of a resulting pattern of continuous quaver C♯s (see Ex. 3.16f). Also audible as a response to the previously reiterated Bs of Stage Three, this nicely complements the C♯ tonality of the incoming Part Two, allowing the G♯ of Part One to be interpreted as its dominant: another instance in Reich's output of accepting the 'natural forces' inherent in the repetition of a single pitch, while retaining the modal complexities that come with this. A final change back to soft sticks, again with the aid of Player 4, permits the three main drummers of Part One to blend with the emerging three main marimba players of Part Two.

Parts Two, Three *and* Four

Part Two uses only three instruments. But the choice of marimbas and number of performers involved here are crucial: with nine players altogether, the sound is newly rich and strange. To this marimba mini-orchestra are added two female singers ('two, three, or more female singers' in the original score), vocalising wordlessly. These supply a further dimension to the woody percussive timbre, exploiting and enhancing the marimbas' natural tendency to produce a halo of upper partials. Marimbas and voices together provide not only a much fuller texture than any its composer had previously used, but also one in which tonal emphasis can play a particularly well-defined and subtle part in the uncovering of resulting patterns. In the sections for marimbas alone, on the other hand, the nature of these instruments contributes almost as much to the difficulties of hearing the structural details of the basic phasing process as does the increased contrapuntal complexity of that phasing process itself.

Once the marimbas have phase-shifted the drumming pattern of Part One back to unison, they begin to add a sequence of patterns – all derived from the Basic Unit – expanding the register upwards via the gradual addition of new players: first to G♯ (Figure 51), then to F♯ (Figure 58) and finally to high C♯ (Figure 63), adding the pitches on which the glockenspiels of

Part Three can enter, after the marimbas' lower patterns have gradually been faded out. Example 3.17a gives the combined patterns of Part Two, demonstrating their differing responses to the shape of the opening one, and the now expanded modality incorporating all seven pitch classes in the six-sharp key signature. With C♯ occupying a stronger, partly because more regular, position in the pattern than it had in the majority of Part One, Reich is now able to exploit much further the kind of dominant/tonic ambiguities which he favoured earlier. Player 1's left-hand lower voice, for instance – all pitches other than C♯ – simultaneously forms a iii–ii–i cadence emphasising G♯ as a tonal centre.

The progressive expansion is based on the now familiar 'stacked' fourths/fifths scheme, allowing different pitches to emerge as it proceeds. The first new pattern to be added, for instance – starting on D♯, in parallel fifths with the opening one – reinforces G♯, implying an initial modulation from C♯ to G♯. Ambiguities are compounded by the stacking up of patterns itself, eventually producing a complex interaction of multiple tonal centres forming the common pentatonic scale, with G♯, C♯ and F♯ emerging as the strongest pitches. As the patterns fade out at the end, however, D♯, F♯ and finally A♯ emerge in turn in a kind of modulatory process which Reich was to explore again in later works.

Meanwhile, the resulting patterns arising from Part Two's cycle of phasing provide further modifications to the modal mix. These resulting patterns are now performed by a separate group, the singers; the score gives them a much wider range of patterns and offers them considerable flexibility in their use, as well as the option of creating new ones. Released from any responsibility to supply resulting patterns, all nine marimba players are free to pile versions of their proliferating phase patterns on top of each other. Like Part One, Part Two evolves in a two-part sequence. Firstly, a two-stage process offers repeating patterns on the first two, and then the first three beats (Figures 49–55, based on the expansion to G♯). Secondly, after a return to unison, a three-stage process yields repeating patterns up to a combination of beats 1, 2 and 3 (Figures 56–63). With the arrival of top C♯, Player 7's new pattern is immediately supplied, by Players 8 and 9, with 'notches' of its own phasing cycle on beats 2 and 3 without any intervening 'fuzzy transitions'. After the fade-out process described above, it is these three players who are left holding their patterns while three of the erstwhile marimba players transfer to glockenspiels, and Part Three begins.

Part Three, at 11′12″, is much shorter. Its move to the high register of three glockenspiels played by four musicians – plus the amplified whistling of resulting patterns by a single performer or a pair of performers, moving

Example 3.17 *Drumming*: (a) Part Two, Figure 63 (Marimbas and composite of resulting patterns only); (b) Part Three, Figure 71; (c) Part Four, Figure 109.

to the piccolo when the register becomes too high to whistle – forms a natural conclusion to the upward registral expansion charted by Parts One and Two. Though it functions as *Drumming*'s scherzo, it is structurally the most complex movement yet encountered.

Part Three preserves the broad outlines and tonal approach of Part Two, while modifying the relationship between the cycle of phasing, articulation of resulting patterns and registral expansion. After a phase-shifting of the final marimba pattern of Part Two back to unison, following the practice adopted earlier, phasing of its own version of the Basic Unit (see Ex. 3.17b) is carried forward two 'notches', involving all four players (Figures 70–77). Registral expansion to its upper limit, E♯, has, though, already occurred with the arrival of Player 2 at Figure 72. And before the expected resulting patterns can occur – on the patterns now formed on the expected beats 1, 2 and 3 of the phasing process – Player 4 modifies his pattern: clarifying the combination then available at Figure 78 for the resulting patterns' Stage One. One dimension of this clarification is the reintroduction of pitches below E♯: in particular, A♯, which now, providing its mediant, underpins a clear tonal focus on F♯. Player 4's modified version is then adopted in turn by Players 1 and 3, Player 2 retaining his original pattern with the high E♯s. Stage Two of the resulting patterns, in which the piccolo takes over from the whistling, now takes place (Figure 80).

Stage Three is formed on a further modification of the pattern, which is assembled and phased by three players – to produce patterns on beats 1, 2 and 3 once more – around the previous version, which Player 1 continues alone (Figures 80–87). Lowering the top pitch to D♯, this modification also includes B♯s for the first time in *Drumming* (Figures 83–90), suggesting a modulation to C♯ major; the resulting patterns themselves, though, tend to emphasise the high D♯ itself. One interpretation of the tonal scheme of Part Three – emboldened partly, it would seem, by the appearance of B♯s – argues for a symmetrical progression from F♯ through C♯ and A♯ to D♯, and back again. The final minutes (Figures 88–101) – in which yet another version of the pattern, revolving around F♯ itself, takes over – certainly emphasise the return to F♯. This is eventually subjected to the substitution of notes by rests, its reduction to a single F♯ mirroring the close of Part One.

While Part Three's F♯ tonality fits nicely into what appears to be an evolving scheme of central pitches – G♯ (Part One), C♯ (Part Two), F♯ – itself derived from Reich's favoured 'stacked' fourths/fifths, it should be noted that the high register of the glockenspiels, and their accompanying whistling, makes the detailed pitch content of Part Three quite difficult to discern; the higher glockenspiel patterns, in particular, are heard more as rhythmic articulations, or even as merely a jumble of overlapping pulses, than as pitch sequences, though the resulting patterns suggest pitch content and direction more readily. In Part Four, however, the previous movement's focus on F♯ contributes to a combination of tonal emphases as rich and complex as are the finale's bringing together of the textural and rhythmic characteristics of all three earlier movements. Part Four represents *Drumming*'s natural, indeed inevitable, culmination, combining the three groups of performers previously deployed separately into a celebratory final ten minutes (9′44″ on the 1987 recording). Its relative brevity can be accounted for not only by the psychological requirements of a composition that has already held its audience for nearly three-quarters of an hour before the movement arrives, but also by the amount of information it packs into its contrapuntal space.

At its start, pairs of glockenspiels, marimbas and drums each assemble their own further new version of the Basic Unit by 'rhythmic construction' (Figures 102–9; Ex. 3.17c gives the completed pattern). This starts with, and centres on, the glockenspiels' F♯. The more prominent first three pitches of the marimba – D♯ C♯ G♯ – give its beginning a temporary focus on C♯, though: simultaneously suggesting the tonalities of Parts One and Two and anticipating Part Four's subsequent tonal development (see below). Phase shifting is then performed on all three patterns, the forward motion of each against its fixed timbral partner being staggered. The marimba is the first to move, followed by drum and glockenspiel (Figures 110–12). This sequence is then repeated, moving each player to beat 3 against his partner (Figures 113–15). At this point, each pair is turned into a trio by the addition of a new player on beat 3, and phasing moves ahead once more, to beat 4 (Figures 116–19) and beat 5 (Figures 120–22). With phasing now established on beats 1, 3 and 5 of each timbral group's independent pattern, a final riot of resulting patterns – which can occupy more than a third of this movement's length – brings the work to its conclusion.

Reich points out that the complexities of both the phase shifting itself and the resulting patterns here are saved from sheer confusion by timbral contrast.[72] The interdependence of the processes involved and their ultimate derivation from a single rhythmic pattern also give Part Four a cohesion amidst its undoubted variety; a cohesion further enhanced by the feeling one gains of the movement as an essentially unitary process, a single unravelling sweep of phasing leading straight into the consequences of its own momentum. That variety is tonal as well as timbral, and again it demonstrates a certain unity. On the one hand, each group's pattern demonstrates the wealth of ambiguities typical of such material, even when, as we saw earlier, one tonal centre may be interpreted as of greater significance than the rest. On the other hand, the progression from G♯ via C♯ to F♯ may now be said to culminate in a gigantic half cadence, implying closure on B♮ (now restored, after the B♯s of Part Three, and the next logical pitch in that 'stacked' sequence), but actually coming to rest on its dominant, F♯ (see Ex. 3.18). As in *Four Organs*, tonic and dominant, tension and

Example 3.18 *Drumming*, Part Four, Figure 122

resolution, are combined, fused into an entity different from that of conventional Western tonality, yet supplying something of that tonality's strength of purpose to modal certainties that are as old as the hills.

In *Drumming*, Reich extends his practice of using groups of identical instruments to develop a fresh approach to his instrumental forces; the blending, as well as the variety, of timbres found here is new in his output.

His abandonment, for the moment, both of any of the usual instruments of the Western 'classical' orchestra in their conventional groupings and of the keyboards which had been central to his music since 1966, suggested that the emerging Steve Reich and Musicians would focus on the tuned percussion inspired by Reich's trip to Africa. With this new array of timbral possibilities, he proved the continuing viability of a music based ultimately on rhythm, even if the details of that music's structures were now less audible than before. Yet *Drumming* also demonstrates an already quite sophisticated concern with harmony and tonality that would increasingly characterise Reich's output during the decade it helped set in motion.

1972–3

Clapping Music *and* Music for Pieces of Wood

In the immediate aftermath of *Drumming*, however, Reich bided his time over its pitch concerns, and wrote a small-scale piece devoted purely to his continuing fascination with rhythm. *Clapping Music* (its score dated April 1972) was written merely for the pairs of hands of two performers. Inspired by experiencing the rhythmic hand-clapping of a Brussels flamenco troupe, this was also a response to the practical complications which accompanied the touring of a work for a van-load of percussion instruments. Since the gradual sliding of phasing's 'fuzzy transitions' would be too difficult in this case, Reich simply subjected a typical twelve-beat Basic Unit (see Ex. 3.19) to a process of jumping directly from 'notch' to 'notch' of an otherwise typical cycle of phasing.

Each 'notch' in the second player's movement away from the fixed position of his partner gives the impression of creating a new pattern: another example of Reich's sleight-of-hand approach to the ambiguities of $\frac{12}{8}$ metre. The Basic Unit of *Clapping Music* throws not only placement within the metre but metre itself into doubt, by including notes on the fifth, eighth and tenth quavers. The listener can thus hear the complete pattern in a variety of ways; when performed in canon, the choice of downbeats is naturally increased. In addition, it can be difficult to hear that both performers are clapping the same pattern, despite the elementary character of the timbre involved. Even in a simple piece such as this, audibility of process is relegated in favour of its broader rhythmic consequences. Reich's fascination with $\frac{12}{8}$, and indeed with this particular pattern, was to be explored further when it became the Basic Unit of many of his later works, including *Music for Eighteen Musicians.*

Example 3.19 *Clapping Music*, Basic Unit

The composer's only other piece since *Drumming* to give primacy to rhythm over pitch is *Music for Pieces of Wood*, which followed *Clapping Music* over a year later, in November 1973. Its five pairs of claves deploy patterns built on the process of rhythmic construction found in *Drumming* as extended by the already composed *Six Pianos* and *Music for Mallet Instruments, Voices and Organ*, for which see below. Though rhythm remains crucial in an elementary percussive situation that rivals *Clapping Music* for audacious simplicity, the claves of *Music for Pieces of Wood* are tuned in seconds, except for the high pulse, thus allowing the contrapuntal consequences of the process to be heard as melodies as well as interlocking rhythmic sequences.

Six Pianos

Drumming's expansion of timbral resources continued to be put on hold while Reich returned to keyboard instruments alone to explore further his passion for using only a group of identical instruments. His initial idea had been to compose a piece for all the pianos in a piano shop: hence its working title, 'Piano Store'. Jack Romann made it possible for Reich and his colleagues to spend many evenings during the autumn and winter of 1972–3 at the Baldwin Piano and Organ Company's New York premises, trying out ideas. The eventual choice of a half-dozen upright 'spinet' pianos for *Six Pianos* (undated on the published score, but completed in March 1973) permitted the rapid articulation of complicated counterpoint without too much resonance, as well as the players' close proximity and the assistance this gave to ensemble precision for such a seemingly unwieldy combination. (*Six Marimbas*, the alternative scoring the composer made in 1986, represents a more practical version.) *Six Pianos*' application of 'drumming on the keyboard' is more sophisticated than that of *Phase Patterns*, but scarcely a new departure. The harmonic potential of half-a-dozen keyboard instruments, on the other hand, was just what Reich needed to renew his exploration of tonality.

Six Pianos presents a more developed form of 'rhythmic construction': the gradual assembly of a rhythmic pattern does not emerge out of silence, as at the beginning of *Drumming*, but unfolds in canon against a fully formed statement of the same rhythmic pattern using the same pitches. At the opening, for instance (see Ex. 3.20), Pianos 1 and 6 present the eight-quaver rhythmic Basic Unit in unison, doubled an octave lower by Piano 3

Example 3.20 *Six Pianos*, Figures 1–8

and a perfect fifth lower by Piano 2. Against this, Pianos 4 and 5, playing in unison, then assemble a further version of the first pattern in canon, at Piano 3's lower octave.

Beginning with the dyad to be found on the fifth quaver beat of the other parts (the half-bar, in other words; the time signature is $\frac{4}{4}$ throughout), the Basic Unit is gradually built up. The complete statement, though, turns out not to be in unison with the original, but starts two quaver beats later, on the third crotchet beat of the $\frac{4}{4}$ bar. Discounting the octave doubling of Piano 3, this means that three pitch patterns are presented simultaneously, all based on the rhythms of the Basic Unit, and all in parallel, though not exactly similar, motion. The resulting patterns accruing from this contrapuntal combination are then themselves doubled by players whose contribution to the basic three-voice texture can be spared. This process of rhythmic construction followed by doubling the resulting patterns is presented a second time, again with three different pitch patterns. After this, a third section performs rhythmic construction on a further three pitch patterns, concluding the work without further resulting patterns. The deployment of resulting patterns in a work not itself based on phasing is typical of Reich in bringing a fresh perspective to an apparently well-worn technique. Again, however, the detailed working out of these patterns is made more difficult to hear by his adherence to the use of identical instruments.

Six Pianos' deployment of three separate modal areas – D major, E-Dorian and B minor, respectively – corresponds to the three-part rhythmic scheme described above, making the overall progression of the work easier to follow. The three patterns in each of the three modal areas may, like those of earlier works, be analysed for their ambiguities both within themselves and via their effect on each other. In Section One, for instance, Example 3.20 contributes to the prime modality of D major, but breaks down into three levels prolonging, in descending order, D, B and F♯. This suggests B minor rather than D major, though it encompasses not only the characteristic relationship of a perfect fourth met earlier, but also the minor third of two keys linked as relative major/minor, and thus incorporates both these. This, too, will become important in Reich's subsequent development of tonality.

The three modal areas of *Six Pianos* share a key signature of two sharps and could even be said, for example, to articulate III–IV–I in B minor. Yet precisely because all three keys use the same seven pitch classes, there is less modulation in *Six Pianos* than there is in *Drumming*, despite the fact that all nine patterns, in the three sections together, prolong at least two different pitch centres in the manner described above; and though *Six Pianos* is admittedly a good deal shorter, and thus changes modal focus at greater speed.

Music for Mallet Instruments, Voices and Organ

The dense textures of *Six Pianos* rival those of *Drumming* while resorting to Reich's tried-and-tested use of a single group of identical instruments. His other composition completed in the early part of 1973 has a sumptuousness – textural, timbral and also harmonic – based on percussion and voices that is new in its composer's output. Reich asked himself 'what if you really have an orchestra of your own, and mix the timbres right from the very beginning?' He began to experiment with wind instruments – a pair each of clarinets and bass clarinets, later a brass group – doubled by voices, male as well as female. Finding these combinations difficult to keep in tune, as well as too heavy, his eventual answer was an ensemble consisting of four marimbas, two glockenspiels, vibraphone without motor, three

Example 3.21 *Music for Mallet Instruments, Voices and Organ*, Figures 1–2

female voices and electric organ: a grouping guaranteed to seduce the ear, while retaining something of the woody crispness of *Drumming*. Important in the composer's approach to what he calls 'the prototype of what was going to become my orchestra' is the doubling of female voices and electric organ. This 'new timbre which is both instrumental and vocal at the same time'[73] articulates identical pitches and rhythms along lines long familiar in Western orchestral music. In Reich's mature output, however, such doubling is new. It makes manifest an extended process of augmentation and diminution of sustained notes which not only forms one of the two rhythmic devices used in the work, but also helps to focus attention on the harmony.

This technique, the first of what the composer calls 'two simultaneous, interrelated rhythmic processes,'[74] derives from *Four Organs*. In *Music for Mallet Instruments, Voices and Organ*, two chords are used (performed on the electric organ, doubled by two female voices), their choice suggesting an ambiguous 'cadential progression',[75] initially in a Dorian F minor (see Ex. 3.21). The ambiguity of this 'progression' is strengthened by its refusal to behave in a 'proper' cadential manner: all four parts move downwards; there is no traditionally functional movement in the bass line; the upper two parts prolong B♭ rather than F; and a ninth chord followed by a seventh chord scarcely constitutes a standard cadence. But the oscillation between its two components is in itself sufficient to give a greater sense of motion than anything in Reich's previous output. Cs in the right hand of the vibraphone – first in sustained notes, then in semiquavers – meanwhile follow the same process of augmentation and diminution, adding a dominant to the prevailing F, while the left-hand prolongs B♭. The two glockenspiels play a continuous pattern, in two canonic positions, that further emphasises F.

The functioning of this new feature is triggered by the second of the 'two simultaneous, interrelated rhythmic processes': the rhythmic construction of a pattern against an already existing version of itself, already familiar from *Six Pianos.* In the first of the work's four sections, for instance, three marimbas, doubled by the third female voice, play parallel pitch patterns on the rhythmic Basic Unit, while a fourth assembles the middle one of these against the others in a different canonic position, in the manner of the earlier work. Again, as with *Six Pianos*, a range of central pitches is shared and prolonged, here underpinned by the main tonal centre of the lowest pattern to produce an overall F-Dorian modality. Once the rhythmic construction is under way, the two voices and organ begin augmentation of the 'cadential progression' (see again Ex. 3.21); this naturally also prolongs the F-Dorian modality, though with suggestions of B♭, adding yet another fourths relationship to the list in Reich's output. The lengthening and shortening of this process create what the composer describes as 'a certain richness and a certain power'; this also allows the pair of chords to register in a proto-cadential manner. Set against the rhythmic construction, the potential of these constantly rocking oscillations to create a feeling of tonal motion, however limited, begins to achieve something quite unprecedented in his work. Also essentially new in the composer's acknowledged output is the use of an arch form: inspired, Reich says, by the model of Bartók's Fourth and Fifth String Quartets.

The overall structure of *Music for Mallet Instruments, Voices and Organ* consists of four sections, based on this linked pair of processes and creating four arch forms. The putative tonal motion of the chords within each section is now enhanced by something more akin to real modulation. These sections themselves form two pairs, each articulating a modulation to a different modality centred on A♭. The already mentioned Dorian F of Section One gives way to the Dorian A♭ of Section Two. Though their pitch centres have a relative minor/major relationship, the minor (Dorian), rather than major, version of the scale on A♭ brings about the modulation, making three changes to the key signature, which moves from three to six flats. In $\frac{2}{4}$, Section Two is the only one of the four to employ a duple metre; all the others are in $\frac{3}{4}$. The B♭ minor of Section Three shifts the tonic a tone higher, creating just a single pitch change, the return of C♮. The modulation to the Mixolydian A♭ major/A♭ dominant of the concluding Section Four moves the tonic back again, retaining the five flats.

Music for Eighteen Musicians

It is with *Music for Eighteen Musicians* that we reach the culmination of Reich's achievements in the works composed between 1965 and 1976. A summation of a decade's efforts, this composition also introduces several innovations. The new expressivity of *Music for Eighteen Musicians* is certainly discovered with the aid of procedures which his previous music had neglected. Yet its innovatory aspects should not prevent us from observing the close connections which exist between the techniques and structural processes of the new work and both those of Reich's earlier output in general and those of the compositions immediately preceding it in particular.

Lasting almost an hour, *Music for Eighteen Musicians* is longer than any of its composer's earlier works except *Drumming*. This offers scope not only for structural and other kinds of technical variety, but also for a significant expressive extension of the composer's musical language. The most obvious advance the work makes is in its instrumentation. As a 'Work in Progress for 21 musicians and singers', as it was billed for some try-out performances at The Kitchen in May 1975, it required ten more performers than had *Music for Mallet Instruments, Voices and Organ*, seven more than the maximum forces its composer has deployed in *Drumming*. Though this number had been reduced through some judicious doubling by the time of *Music for Eighteen Musicians*' full première, the group was still significantly larger than Reich had ever employed before. Of especial importance is his use, for the first time in an ensemble context since the early sixties, of regular orchestral instruments – a violin, a cello, and two clarinets doubling bass clarinets – in addition to the now familiar tuned percussion (three marimbas, two xylophones and vibraphone without motor), keyboards (four pianos) and (four) women's voices. While some of these are amplified, the absence of electric organs – an original intention behind *Music for Mallet Instruments, Voices and Organ* – is notable; with the emphasis firmly on acoustic instruments from all sections of the standard orchestra except brass, Reich has here taken a significant step towards working with the conventional, as well as larger, forces of the Western classical tradition. It should be noted, though, that he originally intended the string bass role to be taken by a viola da gamba: a decision influenced by the composer's ongoing interest in 'early music'. The textures produced by this highly individual 'orchestra' have all the allure of those in his previous mixed-ensemble works, plus much greater variety.

One of the work's new techniques is a consequence of Reich's wish to avoid using a conductor for such a large ensemble. Instead, the vibraphone plays aural cues at the end of each section, and at moments of structural change within sections as well. These short melodic patterns in octaves signal transitions not only to the players, of course, but also to listeners, making a long and complex composition easier to follow.

Music for Eighteen Musicians' developments in the fields of harmony and tonality are even more significant. Structures unconnected to the work's basic rhythmic processes play an even more important role than did the augmentation of two-chord 'cadential progressions' in *Music for Mallet Instruments, Voices and Organ.* The basic technique of these 'cadential progressions' is now borrowed in the course of devising a more evolved role for harmony. The work begins and ends with a cycle of eleven chords, each performed twice by the whole ensemble. As a result, in 1978 Reich made the often-quoted remark that '[t]here is more harmonic movement in the first 5 minutes of "Music for 18 Musicians" than in any other complete work of mine to date'.[76] On the two commercial recordings available in 1998, each chord is held for between fifteen and thirty seconds. In between, the bulk of the composition consists essentially of each of these chords held in turn – for between four and six minutes each – while what the composer calls 'a small piece' is constructed on them in turn; two 'pieces' – marked 'IIIa' and 'IIIb' in the score – are constructed on chord iii. Most sections chart an arch form in a clear tripartite structure, another feature borrowed from *Music for Mallet Instruments, Voices and Organ.*

The sense of progression this brings gives harmony a structural force new in Reich's output. The composer himself has, though, pointed out the connection with twelfth-century organum – with its initial statement of a complete cantus firmus followed by a sequence of organum sections taking each note in turn as a harmonic centre – to which he had so long been attracted. Typical, too, is the fast and unvarying quaver pulse (at ♩= 204); the constant presence of this pulse on the music's surface provides a textural, as well as rhythmic, patina against which the panoply of patterns can unfold. These patterns, in turn, borrow the process of rhythmic construction from a single beat (introduced in *Drumming*) applied to an already existing version of itself (as in *Six Pianos* and, again, *Music for Mallet Instruments, Voices and Organ*).

Other new techniques also affect the way in which tonal grammar operates in *Music for Eighteen Musicians.* Most immediately evident is the use of pulsing notes played or sung for the length of a breath. While mallet instruments and pianos maintain the kind of regular pulse familiar from *Drumming* and its successors, voices and clarinets (expanded, sometimes to dramatic effect, by strings, and other mallet instruments and pianos) offer a different approach: what Reich calls 'the rhythm of the human breath'.[77] Here, the notes of a chord are repeated as an insistent pulse, their duration controlled only by the length for which each performer's breath may comfortably be sustained. These pulsing figures rise and fall in dynamic, from silence to *forte* and back to silence; each swell is slightly staggered between instruments, again following a natural breathing rhythm. The effect is striking: '[t]he combination of one breath after another gradually washing up like waves against the constant rhythm of the pianos and mallet instruments', as the composer himself describes it. They occur throughout the introductory and concluding chord cycles, and at some point – usually the central panel of the characteristic arch-form shape Reich chiefly deploys – during each of the work's main sections.

A new freedom and depth to the articulation of the harmony is thereby also achieved, as the flexibility and naturalness of this ebb and flow contrast with the grid of the fixed tempo. By permitting his performers an expressive input previously denied them even via the articulation of resulting patterns, Reich – thinking once more of Snow's film *Wavelength*, as already noted – brought a new kind of irregularity into productive conflict with the apparently prevailing regularity. Different kinds of periodicity could be combined; stasis was confronted with new possibilities of motion. Previously in Reich's work, too, any departure from a single dynamic level sustained for the length of a whole section, or even a whole work, had been due purely to the mechanics of the rhythmic processes involved and their accompanying resulting patterns. Now, dynamic markings have an expressive, as well as structural, role.

Another technique first explored in *Music for Eighteen Musicians* is that of underpinning a repeated melodic pattern by rhythmically shifting chord changes. While owing something to the link between rhythmic construction and the expansions of the cadential figure in *Music for Mallet Instruments, Voices and Organ*, in *Music for Eighteen Musicians* a two- or four-chord sequence may begin on different beats of a melodic pattern. Though these patterns remain constant against the shifting harmonic rhythm, 'a sense of changing accent in the melody will be heard',[78] as Reich puts it, allowing a new kind of relationship between melody and harmony. As with the combination of regularity and irregularity, '[i]ts effect, the clear distinction between foreground and background that this affords, sets the stage for all the harmonic, thematic and developmental explorations' for which this work is so important.

The cycle of chords

The cycle of eleven chords on which *Music for Eighteen Musicians* is based (see Ex. 3.22) is built on a mode of seven pitches in three sharps. Individual

Example 3.22 *Music for Eighteen Musicians*, cycle of chords

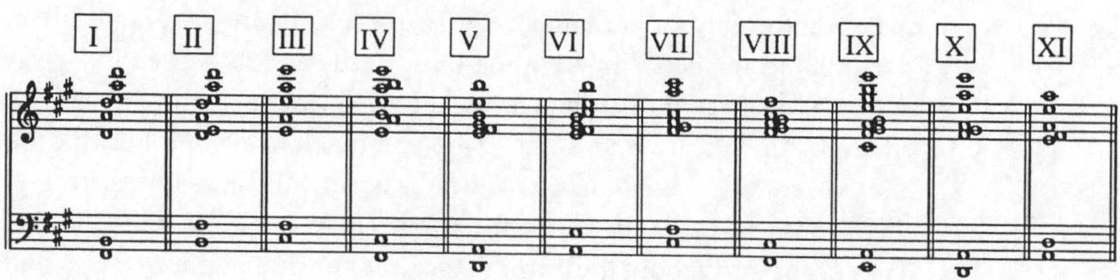

chords are constructed on the now familiar principle of 'stacked' fourths and fifths. All chords are divided into clearly separate treble and bass levels, often with an octave or more between them. Even as first tried out in performances of what the composer calls 'the opening chorale',[79] these chords originally lacked a bass level entirely, recalling the 'treble-dominated' approach of everything he composed before *Music for Mallet Instruments, Voices and Organ*, with the exception of *Four Organs*. Despite his experiments with lower pitches in the former work, Reich was still wary of spelling out the bass, fearing this would over-define and limit the function of each chord.

When he came to add lower pitches to the 'chorale' – inspired by the suggestion from a member of his group that he bring a bass clarinet to the next rehearsal – these notes were accordingly kept separate from the upper ones. The independence of treble and bass, and the greater importance of the former over the latter, is maintained throughout. It is immediately to be noticed in the Introduction, where each treble crescendo (women's voices and violin) is audible before the bass one (bass clarinets, pianos and cellos) that accompanies it. In the main sections of *Music for Eighteen Musicians*, the pitches of the chord sequence's treble as well as bass register are in fact subject to change; omission and, in particular, addition of pitches can be found in both registers, as can occasional pitches foreign to the basic mode. Reich acknowledges that he treated this cycle of chords very freely in the main body of the work. The appearance of the treble level with different bass notes, or no bass notes at all, is nevertheless a fundamental clue to understanding the work. Though its composer says that 'it was clear to me that what was important in *Music for Eighteen Musicians* was the introduction of some kind of functional harmony',[80] it is by continuing to be evasive about the role of the bass, in particular, that the work pointedly avoids any clear fulfilment of such 'functional' expectations as it sets up.

As a consequence of this, the actual bass line of the chord sequence has been described as 'no more than decorative'.[81] Some chords in the cycle are simply inversions or revoicings of the preceding one, further implying a colouristic approach. Yet it is helpful to regard the pitches of the bass register as offering another level of tonal interpretation to the pitches of the treble: in other words, as another example of the dualities and other ambiguities which pervade Reich's approach to tonality. Even though the bass line proper may indeed be elusive, the dyads of the bass register, with their consistent suggestions either of root position or of second inversion, do have some role to play in activating tonal motion. In keeping with this, the total aggregates themselves can have a true harmonic, as well as a colouristic, function.

Taken as a whole, indeed, the bass register of Example 3.22 would seem to offer potential for functionality. It outlines (with an interpretation of the dyads given in brackets) a i–iv–v–i (iv–iv–i–i) progression in F♯ minor (the minor key with three sharps), followed by a iv–i–iii–vi–v–iv–i (iv–i–vi–vi–i–iv–iv) progression in A major (its relative major). It is hard not to experience something of these progressions in the Introduction and Epilogue, especially when the two interpretations coincide or suggestively collude: an initial iv–v–i in F♯ minor, say, followed by vi–iv–i–vi–vi–v–iv–i in A major. As we shall discover, however, Reich is prepared to depart from his original chord sequence sufficiently to challenge such conclusions based on listening to the Introduction and Epilogue alone. Sometimes, only complete separation of its treble and bass registers can make sense of the music based on them.

Other progressions may also be noted in Example 3.22: three sequences, each charting a move to the greater consonance of chords containing only four pitch classes (chords iii, vii and xi); the fact that, from chord vii onwards, triadic elements in the treble reinforce, rather than undermine, the tonality suggested by the bass; the gradual reduction in secundal clusters in the concluding sequence of chords viii–xi. The division into two types of chord change – smooth (between inversions of the same chord, as in chords i and ii) and abrupt (between chords of more differing content, as in chords vi and vii) – is employed in the transitions from section to section in the main body of *Music for Eighteen Musicians* to make quite dramatic contrasts between evolution and juxtaposition.

With a single harmonic aggregate as the basis for each arch-form structure, all the composer's imaginative powers are required to avoid monotony in constructing this sequence of eleven 'small pieces'. Reich's strategies for ensuring momentum as well as variety may be illustrated by analysing Section I in detail, and then looking, more briefly, at the other ten.

Section I

In Section I, which lasts just four minutes, articulations of the basic chord frame a series of 'length-of-a-breath' pulsings in the typical arch-form structure. Its material and layout are illustrated in Example 3.23. After the A-major close of the introduction, the return to the first chord (Ex. 3.23a) makes it sound even more like D major; E is a now easily assimilable added second or ninth; B is readily accommodated as an added sixth, with the bass F♯, when it is audible, providing a first inversion. To the constant chatter of two marimbas and two pianos familiar from the opening, an additional marimba and piano supply single-bar patterns, built on the Basic Unit of *Clapping Music* and already flavouring the original treble harmony of chord i with C♯s (Ex. 3.23b). (Such single-bar patterns – naturally related to the more prominent ones similarly derived from the Basic Unit, and present throughout the section in which they occur – are also a feature of some of the work's later sections.) As mentioned earlier, the pattern already used in *Clapping Music* constitutes the chief rhythmic material of *Music for Eighteen Musicians*; Reich was attracted to the metric flexibilities offered by its now familiar twelve beats in a bar. Like the various versions of this pattern to be found in subsequent sections, some identical to the first, the one used in Section I is subsumed into the accompaniment to what follows.

Then the main business begins: to an oscillating accompaniment of voice, violin and cello, two clarinets introduce a variant of the third marimba's continuing counterpoint (without the C♯) that becomes the basic melodic material of the whole section. This turns out to be the preliminary stage in assembling the old friend mentioned earlier, and already present in the accompaniment: the Basic Unit of *Clapping Music*, now supplied with the beginnings of a melody. While based on the familiar process of rhythmic construction, this is expanded in a more subtle manner, involving not only the substitution of beats for rests, but also length, changes of doubling, accompaniment and texture, and the shifting of register. Also found frequently in the ensuing sections, this method of generation naturally varies in detail, each version characterised by its particular balance of elements and the way this affects the overall design.

Example 3.23 *Music for Eighteen Musicians*, Section I: (a) basic chord; (b) Figure 97 (versions of *Clapping Music* pattern); (c) Figures 103–04 (melody based on *Clapping Music* pattern); (d) Figures 108–12 (melody and chords only); (e) Figures 124–28 (melody and chords only).

Cued by the vibraphone, the Basic Unit of *Clapping Music* soon develops into its familiar form with an expansion to two bars, now doubled by the second clarinet and two voices, in parallel fourths (see Ex. 3.23c). Increasing to four bars, by adding repetitions of the *Clapping Music* Basic Unit, it proceeds to alter its accompanying line (from parallel fourths to fifths, then thirds; each repeated several times), and to rise in pitch. As it develops, the figure takes exploration of the ambiguities of $\frac{12}{8}$ a stage further. The extension of chord i via augmentation of a two-chord 'cadential progression' results in a two-chord structure of alternating B minor and F♯7 chords, subjected to expansion and contraction. Expanding to a total of twenty-two beats, the different lengths of the chords – 3 + 3, 4 + 2, 3 + 3 and 2 + 2 – shift the harmonic rhythm while the melodic pattern remains the same (see Ex. 3.23d). These subtle manoeuvres contribute to the 'sense of changing accent in the melody' referred to above, and feature throughout the work.

The thirds-based version of the clarinet pattern brings harmonic as well as rhythmic changes, replacing B by the extraneous pitch C♯ in the melodic pattern itself, and altering the 'cadential progression' to G^7 and D^7 (both with sharpened sevenths), now presented in progressive diminution as 6 + 6, 3 + 3 and 2 + 2, to make the same total of twenty-two beats as before (see Ex. 3.23e). Including G♮ – a pitch foreign to the mode of the chord sequence itself, reinforcing D major – this progression underpins everything through the middle panel to the following return of the thirds-based pattern. As the clarinets fade out, the two voices continue the basic pattern over the same shifting accompaniment.

It is at this point that the pulsing figures of the central panel begin, on the two clarinets. Confined to the dyad of D A – first low, then high, each repeated – they emphasise D major against the same ambiguously shifting harmony beneath. The pair of voices continues with the same material throughout this middle section, as do the original chord and its first offshoots in the marimbas and pianos. After this, the material of the first panel returns, reducing back to its opening by presenting the elements described above in reverse order. Thus the overall shape of Section I – as of most other sections of *Music for Eighteen Musicians* – is A B C D C B A, with D representing the pulsing figures at its centre. It is interesting that foreign as well as extra pitches are added so early in the work. No pitches foreign to the basic mode now feature until Section V.

Sections II to XI

Example 3.24 offers some of the material of Sections II–V. Since the pitch content of chords i and ii is identical, Section II might be expected to operate with the same basic tonal centres as its predecessor. The restricted compass of the new melody rhythmically constructed on the Basic Unit of *Clapping Music* (see Ex. 3.24a) suggests F♯ minor. While this continues in the voices, a xylophone-and-piano pair simultaneously assembles two further patterns, both related to the first, in rhythmic unison on the Basic Unit of *Clapping Music* (see Ex. 3.24b). After this is completed, a further xylophone-and-piano pair constructs the same patterns in canon in the manner of *Six Pianos*. This requires the addition of a fifth pianist, made possible by the already mentioned 'doubling'. Length-of-a-breath pulsings arrive just one minute into the section. When the contrapuntal structure has been assembled, these pulsings expand registrally and texturally: adding a pair of xylophones, and subsequently a single piano, to the clarinet and strings. They dissolve barely half a minute before the whole section's close, having taken over a larger proportion of it than is generally the case elsewhere. These pulsings include pitches in the bass register.

The F♯-minor^7 of chord iii – the first, more consonant, four-pitch aggregate – has two contrasting 'small pieces' built on it: Sections IIIa and IIIb. Section IIIa builds its xylophone and marimba patterns on E A alone, but these are filled out – in the treble as well as the bass – not only by C♯ (once again) and F♯ but also by B and (again) G♯, pitches additional to chord iii; the melodic patterns on clarinets and strings are similar to those of Section II. The alternating F♯-minor/C♯^{7} of the outer 'cadential progression' is soon pulsed by two pianos in the lower register, their repeated quavers articulating a fairly slow harmonic rhythm. When the parallel-sixth stage is reached in the unfolding of melodic patterns, the alternating I–V of the pianos' root-position chords gives an unusually dramatic feel to the F♯-minor tonality. The cello's sustained dyads of D A and E A and the vibraphone cues subsequently suggest a move to A major, but the repeated upward curve to C♯ of the expanded melodic patterns seems more ambiguous. This key finds a clearer tonal focus in Section IIIb, which acts as a sweeter, almost placid foil to the energies of IIIa, though the bass of the 'cadential progressions', descending to F♯, reminds us of the key signature's alternative.

A less secure, more evasive A major seems to be the basis of Section IV, with D♮ returning for the first time since Section II to complete the chord sequence's basic mode. The marimba and piano's single-bar pattern is especially prominent here, its dalliances with top A already implying the centrality of that pitch. Clarinets and a single voice take the melodic patterns, all in parallel fourths, circling around C♯ and G♯. The other three voices join the strings in 'cadential progressions' in which C♯ features as a

Example 3.24 *Music for Eighteen Musicians*, Sections II to V: (a) Section II, Figure 175 (first version of *Clapping Music* pattern); (b) Section II, Figure 180/ii (second version of *Clapping Music* pattern); (c) Section IV, Figures 326–30 (melody, chords and drone only); (d) Section V, Figures 372–4 (final canonic position and first resulting pattern only).

drone. The relationship between melody and accompaniment here – based on the latter's expansion to crotchet beats of 3+3+4+2+3+3+2+2, plus 2 beats rest, against which the four-bar melody creates its own ambiguously shifting metre – is one of the work's most compelling (see Ex. 3.24c). The length-of-a-breath pulsings on the bass clarinets recall F♯ minor again. But the next three pairs of pulsings expand the E A dyads which had alternated with the bass clarinets' F♯ C♯ into rich five-voiced chords emphasising A major. The bass of the first chord then descends to D, and that of the second chord to C♯, to create the C♯-minor^{11} chord on which Section V begins.

Section V establishes its place at the work's centre by three new departures. Firstly, the key signature now changes to four sharps, the new pitch, D♯, being incorporated into a C♯-minor tonality. As described above, the bass register of chord v (the source of this section) proposed D major as the IV of a progression leading to the final A major: an interpretation completely undermined, of course, by the new pitch. When the bass register arrives for the length-of-a-breath pulsings, on bass clarinets, two voices and strings, an A^{9}–E^{7}–C♯-minor^{7}–C♯-minor^{11}, then alternately A^{7} and E^{7}, progression is outlined with typical 'stacked' fourths and fifths, suggesting the possibility of a move to A major.

Before this, however, we find the second of this section's new departures: the first, and only, use in *Music for Eighteen Musicians* of a pattern unrelated to the *Clapping Music* Basic Unit. This is, however, nothing other than the one already used in *Violin Phase*, transposed down a perfect fourth and now deployed in a double exposition of rhythmic construction with canon similar to that of Section II. It is first presented complete on two pianos, taking the place of any less closely related single-bar pattern common as a supplement to the pulsing quavers. A canon on quaver 9 of the twelve beats is then assembled by the two other pianos; this begins with what will turn out to be the second of its two D♯s, on quaver 7 of the original pattern. (In *Violin Phase*, the Basic Unit had also been phased to the ninth quaver, but only after the 'notch' on beat 5 had been held.) Then, while this canonic position is maintained by one pair of pianos, a third one is assembled, by the other pair, on quaver 3 of the original; after which first just a single piano then also two marimbas and two voices perform resulting patterns on the three-stage canonic position (Ex. 3.24d gives the latter, plus the first resulting pattern).

Underpinned at the very beginning by the already mentioned C♯-minor^{11} chord and, much more extensively, by the pulsing chords which follow the arrival of the resulting patterns, the C♯-minor tonality of this process reflects the higher dissonance level of chord v's treble register, which itself already included G♯. In its early stages, however, it does so in ways more reminiscent than almost anything else in *Music for Eighteen Musicians* of the structural clarity of Reich's treble-dominated earlier compositions. In doing so, it reinforces its refusal to succumb to any tonal interpretation involving harmonic motion propelled by a bass line.

Example 3.25 offers some of the material of Sections VI–XI. The continuous rattle of maracas decorates Sections VI–VIII, giving them – as did the glockenspiels of *Drumming*, Part Three – something of the feel of a scherzo before the more complex machinations of the finale; they also include an appropriately recapitulatory element. Despite its basis on chord vi (the first chord with A as its root), and the previous section's oscillating chords prolonging E as potential dominant, Section VI uses the return to a three-sharp key signature to revisit the root-position, F♯-minor certainties of Section IIIa. That section's pulsings on the more ambiguous sustained dyads of D A and E A are again included, bringing back D♮ after the aberrant D♯. The elaborations of the melodic pattern themselves, though – a relative of the Basic Unit of *Clapping Music* – are now articulated by pairs of clarinets, marimbas, pianos and voices, plus violin and, occasionally, cello: a texturally more complex combination than before (see Ex. 3.25a).

Sections VI and VII share not only the complete modal gamut of seven pitches – Section VII adding B and E, as well as D, to its official basic chord – but also narrow-range, predominantly thirds-based melodic patterns. Section VII returns, however, to the *Clapping Music* Basic Unit proper. The measured tread of dyads in the bass – related to those of the previous section, though now not only more foursquare but also extending its bass progression to make a clear I–VI–VII–I – helps retain the focus on F♯ minor (see Ex. 3.25b). With the shorter Section VIII, the sun finally comes out on a bright A major; though the single-bar introductory pattern and the process of rhythmic construction built on a further version of the Basic Unit of *Clapping Music* are rather uncertain about their tonality, both are firmly underpinned by tonic and dominant harmonies in A, backed up by dominant-based pulsings and vibraphone cues. The absence of D in this case seems to assist the dominant focus.

In Section IX, D♯ returns in a four-sharp key signature that once again ignores the absence of D in the section's official chordal basis to effect a return to C♯ minor. Built, like Sections II and V (the latter sharing the same key with the present section), on the process of rhythmic construction overlaid with canons, it is clearly designed to function as the final climax of *Music for Eighteen Musicians*, and it is too complex to detail all its delights

Example 3.25 *Music for Eighteen Musicians*, Sections VI, VII and IX: (a) Section VI, Figures 408–11 (melodic pattern only); (b) Section VII, Figures 487–9 (melodic pattern and chords only).

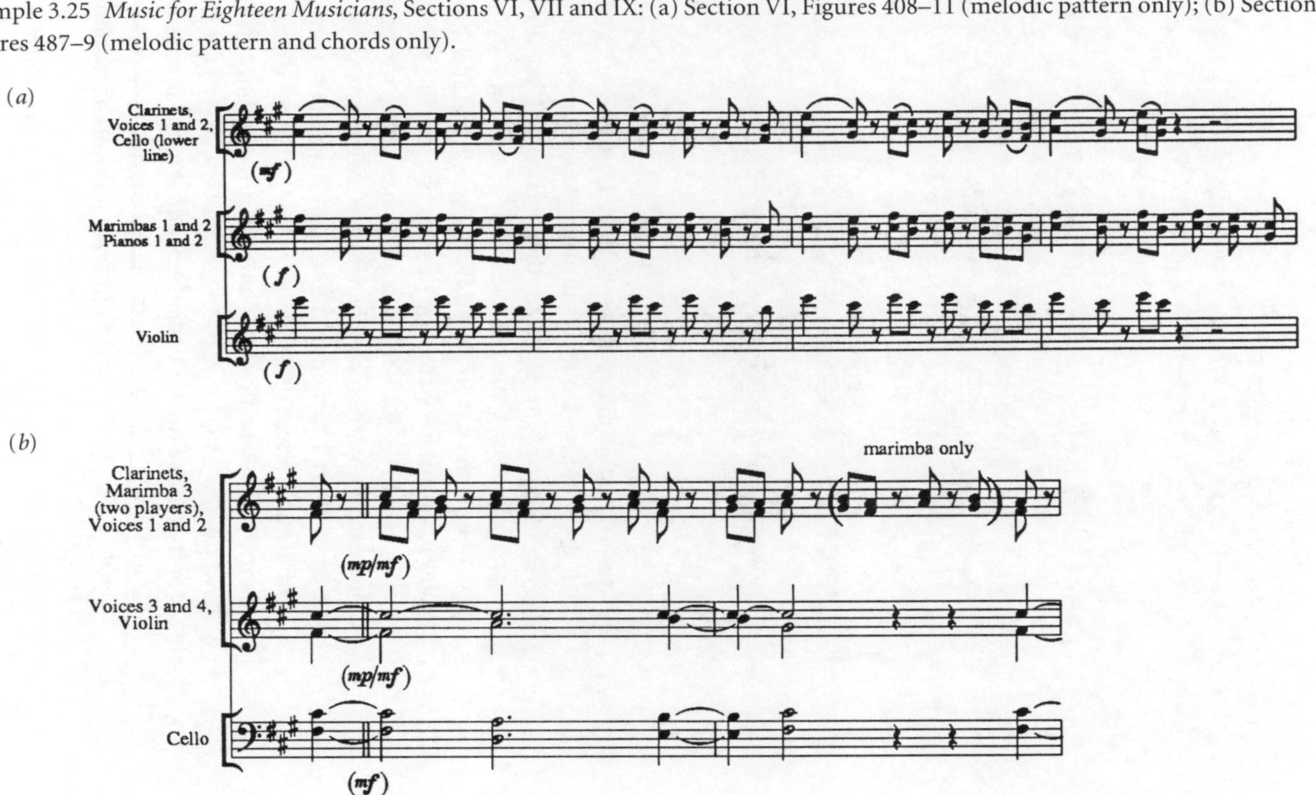

Example 3.25 (*cont.*)

(c) Section IX: (i) Figure 617 (newly completed melodic pattern only); (ii) Figure 622 (newly completed melodic pattern only); (iii) Figure 627 (newly completed melodic pattern only).

here. The basic material is given in Example 3.25c. After a single-bar melodic pattern of more than usual prominence on the piano, another thirds-based version of yet another variant of *Clapping Music*'s Basic Unit is assembled on pairs of clarinets, voices and strings (Ex. 3.25 *c*i). Xylophone and piano then fill this out in parallel motion in the same canonic position, assembling their notes according to a different constructive scheme (Ex. 3.25 *c*ii). The third process of rhythmic construction is then carried out canonically, another xylophone-and-piano pair assembling an altered version in canon on quaver 9 (Ex. 3.25 *c*iii). Overlapping with this, an unusually, and increasingly, rich collection of pulsing chords – joined by two pianos in its latter stages – outlines an extended sequence in C♯ minor.

Section X is little more than a pendant to the preceding activities. Using the first dyad, D A, of the bass register of chord x in oscillation with F♯ C♯, it simply alternates D^{13} and F♯-minor^{11} pulsing chords above these in a stack of pitches ascending high into the treble, with two xylophones joining those which had concluded Section IX. This reminder of earlier bass lines which moved from D to E while themselves only tentatively suggesting F♯ (Sections IIIa and VI) is accompanied by the piano's single-bar melodic pattern from Section IX, now an octave higher. Including all pitches of the basic mode, it adds only B to chord x.

Section XI adds G♮, and further extends chord xi with B and C♯. This makes what is in several respects a return to familiar territory – a simple arch-form structure with 'cadential progression', plus length-of-a-breath pulsings – less conclusive than it might have been, leaving the final say to the chord sequence itself in the Epilogue. The pulsings of the central panel, though – now without pianos – outline E-minor^{7} and A^{11}, giving the latter at least some suggestion of a closure on A.

The above analysis demonstrates that the 'tonal motion' of the main sections themselves has a rather different agenda from that of the chord sequence on which they are based. This is surely as it should be, since not only is such a sequence – even one as rich in ambiguous harmonic potential as this is – literally stretched to its limits as the basis for an hour's music, but there is much to be gained from supplying further layers of ambiguity by such 'departures from the text'.

The possibility of a double progression – one in F♯ minor, followed by one in A major – suggested by the chord sequence itself has been replaced by a more complex progression of tonalities. These have incorporated a four-sharp key signature, with strong suggestions of C♯ minor, at what seem critical moments (Sections V and IX) when the arsenal of rhythmic techniques is also replenished. Three sharps have sometimes indicated an F♯ minor which is surprisingly clear, elsewhere a more unstable implication of that key, and A major less than one might have expected, even at the end. D♮ has sometimes been removed altogether, while G♮ – the only pitch foreign to the mode besides D♯ – has been brought in at either end of the work's main body, pushing the modal territory towards two sharps as well. All this has been achieved with the aid of a wealth of rhythmic, melodic, contrapuntal and, by no means least, timbral and textural elaboration, drawing on all Reich's experience during the preceding decade, and on more than one piece of borrowed material from those years too. The result has such an inevitable momentum about it that it comes as no surprise to learn from its composer that the work 'virtually wrote itself, especially the second half'. *Music for Eighteen Musicians* is surely one of the masterpieces of late twentieth-century music.

If the consolidation of sonic impact and putative harmonic motion already redefines the minimalism of *Music for Mallet Instruments, Voices and Organ*, its successor's extensions of these render *Music for Eighteen Musicians* more clearly 'post-minimalist'. Conducted in the context of such a rich display of melodic, rhythmic and timbral techniques – some old, some new – these tonal discoveries were eventually to show its composer the path to fresh and fertile territory. Composing it demonstrated, he says, 'a way of working, which enabled me to continue the kind of work that I've been doing'. Such increased preoccupation with texture and timbre – with what the composer calls 'beautiful music' – as well as with harmony and tonality led inevitably to a further decrease in concern for the old minimalist virtues of 'filling the structure' and audibility of process.

Reich at first, however, found it impossible to capitalise on the advances of *Music for Eighteen Musicians.* The reasons for this seem complex, and their full examination, in any case, beyond the scope of this book. Crucial among them is the composer's absorption in Hebrew cantillation. This already began when the work was on tour; after its British première, in January 1977, he went on a trip to Jerusalem particularly for this purpose. Over the next year or so, Reich became so involved with exploring his Jewish roots that he seriously considered giving up composition to become a rabbi. More purely musical explanations for his difficulties must begin with his realisation that, as he puts it, he 'couldn't stay put in one key as long as I had'. It became clear that the 'on the edge' qualities which make *Music for Eighteen Musicians* what it is could not be sustained: something which the work's imitators have also discovered.

For more than two years, from March 1976 onwards, Reich composed almost nothing. Several tours of *Music for Eighteen Musicians*, for which he was effectively business manager as well as artistic director, left him no time. Besides, as he puts it, 'the faucet was dry'; when he began to find time to write again, he had lost all compositional momentum and, as usual, was determined not to repeat himself. The only piece dating from this period is an aborted one based, surprisingly, purely on pulsing rhythms. Reich describes it as 'all colour and harmony, all skin and no bones'. It was apparently loosely scored for 'whoever was around', and a sizeable group of musicians – between eighteen and twenty-five, the composer remembers – even tried it out in rehearsal before it was abandoned. Determined to honour the commission that he had by now received from the Holland Festival for the Netherlands Wind Ensemble, he borrowed the basic techniques of *Music for Mallet Instruments, Voices and Organ* and *Music for Eighteen Musicians* to assemble *Music for a Large Ensemble*, completed in December 1978: the first work Reich had written for forces besides those of his own group.

Octet – finished in April 1979, on his second commission, from Hessischer Rundfunk in Frankfurt – has become one of his best-loved and most-played pieces, not least for the way it begins to integrate ideas from Hebrew cantillation into a new emphasis on melody. But Reich's first really successful composition for anything more fully resembling Western orchestral forces is *Variations for Winds, Strings, and Keyboards*, completed in December 1979 for the San Francisco Symphony Orchestra. Also the first work after *Music for Eighteen Musicians* in which a harmonic cycle was the clear starting point, this 'mega-chaconne' takes functional, and faster, harmonic motion beyond the stage it had reached in anything he had composed before, thus truly paving the way for Reich's development in the 1980s.

Conclusion

While the tape recorders via which Reich discovered the technique of phasing may have soon been set aside by him in the pursuit of instrumental music, the transferral of phasing from tape to live performance must count among the major influences which electronic music has had on the development of music for players of conventional Western instruments. The composer's use of the sounds of American vernacular speech as a basis for composition has inspired a host of others, whether they wished to explore this territory in similarly experimental ways (Scott Johnson is just one of many examples) or in the more conventional Western contexts of opera and song (for instance, John Adams). The advent of what we now call 'sampling' in the mid-1980s not only gave a new lease of life to the use of tape (and later entirely computer-controlled) sounds (and, also subsequently, visual images too) in the composer's own more recent output (spearheaded by *Different Trains* of 1988), but has also led to the re-evaluation of *It's Gonna Rain* and *Come Out* as pioneering examples of a technique central to late twentieth-century composition.

Since Reich has been uninterested in following Young and Riley into singing and playing non-Western music regularly – including their adoption of a version of Indian lifestyle – his own, more purely technical, example of how to integrate ideas from non-Western musics into Western composition has probably been more widely appreciated, and his influence correspondingly greater. The composer's ensemble, in which he himself continues to perform, has long demonstrated the advantages to composers of direct involvement in playing their own music, whether inspired by non-Western models or not. The Western influences on his work – medieval music, Debussy, Stravinsky, Bartók, Coltrane and the drummer Kenny Clarke – remain potent to him, and no doubt to others too, partly because not one of them is itself purely 'Western classical'.

Of the five 'Optimistic Predictions . . . about the Future of Music' which

Reich offered in 1970, the most significant is the one suggesting that '[t]he pulse and the concept of clear tonal center will re-emerge as basic sources of new music'.[82] Rhythmic repetition underpins everything the composer has done since *It's Gonna Rain*, even those works, or parts of works – such as the first movement of *The Four Sections*, his orchestral composition of 1987 – in which his typically fast audible pulsing all but disappears. The contrapuntal potential of polyrhythmic composition has been explored by Reich with the kind of rigour which brings greater approval from Western classical composers and theorists than does any other so-called minimalist music. Such structural strictness is in itself generally less attractive to improvisers and others outside the Western classical tradition. But its results still possess sufficient 'vernacular' energy to stimulate a wide range of musicians and their listeners in more 'popular' fields too.

Radicalisation of harmony lies at the heart of Reich's present endeavours. While it would be wrong to inflect his present stance on his past output, one does not have to view what Ronald Woodley has called the composer's 'gradual realignment with certain branches of "mainstream" European music'[83] as antithetical to his previous concerns. Reich's interrogation of the Western classical tradition, as Woodley would put it, had to begin with the purging power of rhythm on pitch materials so reduced that little remained of their traditional force. Yet an important part of Reich's achievement has been a specifically harmonic interrogation of that 'tradition' which quickly supplies energies brought in from outside 'the post-Renaissance inheritance of harmony'. This process began in earnest as early as *Piano Phase*, and allowed its composer to question, from then on, the notion of a modal melodic and harmonic language as simply conservative. That Reich soon found himself doing this with the aid of the same engine – harmonic motion – that drove that post-Renaissance inheritance itself is one of the most interesting conundrums of late twentieth-century composition. Though harmonic motion also became a compelling concern to Glass, and even to Young and Riley, no one has impelled it with more vigour, and rigour, than Reich himself.

The development of Reich's reputation outside the downtown Manhattan artistic community can be pinpointed in three quite different musical areas. Firstly, Reich had a particular effect on the development of English 'experimental music', largely through his early friendship with Michael Nyman. There are, as we saw in the Introduction, several aesthetic parallels between minimalism and this sort of 'experimental music'; and for a while, in the early and mid-1970s, Reich's rigorous approach was a strong influence on what composers such as Chris Hobbs, Dave Smith and

John White called 'systems music', despite the wider range of musical references that this kind of composition brought with it.

Secondly, there is the composer's subsequent, and still increasing, impact on the Western classical music scene itself. Though he only really became at all widely known, and appreciated, by the audiences for such music after the period to which this book is primarily devoted, Reich has not only become an important member of its worldwide community, but also an influence on a considerable number of composers brought up in that tradition, including its avant-garde wing. The 'post-minimalism' he represents has more points of contact with the Western tradition than does the music of Young or Riley, and he was at crucial periods an influence on figures such as his compatriot John Adams and the English composers Simon Bainbridge and Colin Matthews.

Lastly, there is the arena of Western popular music. Significant parts of Reich's reputation from the mid-1970s onwards have been made in the world of pop music; a world in which electric guitars and keyboards had arguably already fulfilled the first of Reich's predictions, concerning the integration of electronic and instrumental music, by the early 1970s. A performance of *Music for Eighteen Musicians* sold out the New York nightclub The Bottom Line in the autumn of 1978; the ECM recording of the same work – which sold over 10,000 copies – prompted articles and reviews in *Rolling Stone* and *Billboard* magazines. In Britain, Brian Eno attended the Steve Reich and Musicians concert at London's Queen Elizabeth Hall on 4 February 1974, which included the then recent *Six Pianos* and *Music for Mallet Instruments, Voices and Organ.* Eleven years later, he said that he considered Reich's abandonment of his earlier, more rigorous and minimalist approach 'rather fortunate because that meant I could carry on with it';[84] he describes his own *Music for Airports* as 'one of the products of that'. Eno's one-time associate, David Bowie, once called the composer 'a tonetrack into the future'.[85] And even today, some listeners are introduced to musical minimalism via Mike Oldfield's *Tubular Bells* album, originally issued in 1973, which seems to owe at least as much to Reich as to Riley.

At the end of the 1970s, a younger generation of composers with roots in all three of these musical arenas – English 'experimental music', Western classical music and rock – found *Music for Eighteen Musicians* a particular influence; the English composers Jeremy Peyton Jones and Andrew Poppy are two of them. This is but one illustration of Reich's significance above and beyond the categories listed here. Two generations on, the English group The Orb acknowledged Reich's seminal role in the development of music which thrives on the sampling of musical cultures still thought incompatible by some, when 'Little Fluffy Clouds', the first track on the group's 1991 double album, *The Orb's Adventures Beyond the Ultraworld*, sampled the composer's *Electric Counterpoint* of 1987. The ultimate acts, so far, of sampling the work of this pioneer of the technique himself are the English artist Chris Hughes' *Shift* (1994) – a whole album of reworkings of Reich's early compositions from *Piano Phase* to *Drumming* – and, in particular, *Reich: Remixed* (1999), on which several leading 1990s 'techno' artists (including Coldcut, Ken Ishii and DJ Spooky) remix a whole panoply of the composer's music from the last thirty-five years.

4 Philip Glass

Philip Glass's career divides geographically into three parts: his childhood, student and, briefly, professional years in the USA; his time as student once again in Paris; and the period that saw his full establishment as a professional composer based in New York. Glass was twenty-seven when he went to Paris; just thirty when he moved back to New York. In terms of his output as a minimalist, the story only begins during the second period, and becomes of substance only in the third.

Glass must be among the most prolific of contemporary composers, and the years since the première of *Einstein on the Beach* in 1976 have seen a considerable rise in his rate of production. Yet it still makes stylistic and aesthetic sense to divide his complete output into two, with 1975–6 as the watershed. Some commentators have argued that the album *Glassworks* (1982) marks a significant trend towards the greater commercialism which so often troubles listeners, and critics, from the Western classical music world; but *North Star*, dating from 1977, attempted a similar 'accessibility' and is only infrequently mentioned because it failed to circulate as widely as was intended; Glass's involvement with whatever trends were current in rock music grew much deeper from about 1977, too. Operatically, Glass's first work for the resources of the conventional opera house is *Satyagraha*, premièred in 1980; but this was conceived and composed well before that, and the urge to move from the performance-art approach of *Einstein* towards the conventions of 'proper opera' came as early as 1976.[1]

Most importantly, *Einstein* (composed in 1975) marks the end of Glass's interest in minimalism as previously defined in this book as clearly as *Music for Eighteen Musicians* (1974–6) does for Reich. The arrival of harmonic motion, in *Einstein* and the compositions immediately preceding it, does not yet require the abandonment of the rhythmic techniques and concern for structural process that characterise Glass's music of the previous decade. *Einstein* in particular, dealing with all the concerns of drama as well as music, is crucially 'on the edge' aesthetically, and technically, speaking: that Glass was unable to remain in that interesting position now seems an important part of its achievement as well as of its historical significance. Harmonic motion – or at least the investigation of it in the surviving context of repetition – and all that came with it led both to opera as we more normally understand it and to the composer's more rock-orientated and commercial endeavours. The music he wrote before that had rather different goals.

That earlier music may be further divided into two. The concerns which culminated in *Einstein* first surfaced in 1970, causing everything from *Music with Changing Parts* onwards to be seen as part of a natural development away from previous minimalist concerns. Even Glass's output between 1965 and 1969 may be further subdivided: most sensibly, perhaps, according to the adoption of a rigorous, as opposed to more 'intuitive', approach to Glass's most basic minimalist technique, additive process. Since the works from *1 + 1* (1968), and more particularly *Two Pages* (1969), which use rigorous additive techniques are so much more successful than those which precede them, this also allows a division into 'early' and 'mature' even within what is officially the 'early period'.

Early American years

Philip Glass was born in Baltimore on 31 January 1937; he is thus scarcely four months younger than Reich. His father's parents were Lithuanian Jews, his mother's were Jews from Belorussia; both his own parents were born in the USA. His father owned a small record shop, his mother was a teacher and librarian.[2] Glass grew up surrounded by music: of the vernacular traditions of what was then called 'hillbilly' music from West Virginia and the Appalachians (both nearby), the commercially popular songs of the 1930s and 1940s, a certain amount of jazz; but also music of the European classical tradition – eighteenth- and nineteenth-century chamber music and even the 'modern music' of Bartók, Hindemith and others – via the 78 rpm records that his father brought home from the shop when they didn't sell. He began playing the violin at the age of six, the flute at eight; he attended, part-time, the Peabody Conservatory in Baltimore from 1945 to 1952. From early on, too, he seems to have had composition lessons, paid for by working in his father's shop. Glass also played in school orchestras, marching and theatre bands, and even for some amateur television, while attending Baltimore City College, a selective and competitive boys' high school. There was something of a family tradition in vaudeville and other kinds of popular theatre: Al Jolson was an uncle of Glass's father, and another uncle had played drums for the Marx Brothers. But his parents – 'working-class aspiring to be middle-class people'[3] – discouraged him from entering the music profession.

Glass must have been a precocious youngster, since he gained entrance to the University of Chicago by the age of fifteen. It was at this age, he has said, that he attempted his first composition: a string trio written 'in a strict twelve-tone manner'.[4] He graduated in 1956, aged nineteen, having studied philosophy and maths, as well as music, and obtaining an A.B. liberal arts degree. During the summer of 1955, he had, in addition, studied harmony with Louis Cheslock. In 1957 Glass went to the Juilliard School in New York City, initially as a non-matriculating student in 1957–8. Wishing to specialise in composition, he submitted about a dozen pieces for the entrance examination and began regular composition studies at Juilliard in September 1958. His teachers included William Bergsma and Vincent Persichetti; student colleagues at Juilliard included Peter Schickele and, more importantly to Glass's future development, Steve Reich. Glass obtained a School diploma in 1960 and an M.S. in 1962. Meanwhile, he also attended the Aspen Music Festival summer school in 1960, where he worked with Darius Milhaud. Interviewers are sometimes told that he became fascinated at this time by the new jazz of Ornette Coleman and John Coltrane; though Glass, unlike Reich, hardly ever elaborates on any style of jazz as an influence.

In 1962, on leaving Juilliard at the age of twenty-five, Glass obtained one of the earliest school-based composer-in-residence jobs to be offered in the USA, and for the next two years was based in Pittsburgh, working in the public school system there on a $10,000 Ford Foundation Young Composer's Award. The demands of this job no doubt influenced his output, which may at least partly account for the style of works such as *The Haddock and the Mermaid* (1962 or 1963). This is a choral setting, with piano accompaniment, of words by Gertrude Norman in a modal E♭ major, with occasional chromatic sidesteps; perhaps interestingly, the bass line is confined throughout to an accompanying twenty-bar ground to the word 'doo-doo', which is just beginning its fourth revolution when the upper parts bring the piece to a conventional end (see Ex. 4.1). Joan LaBarbara discovers – in another a cappella choral work, *Haze Gold* (1962) – 'an early indication of Glass's attraction to steady rhythmic foundation: a slow eighth-note ostinato figure, first in the alto and later in the tenor voices, forms the base over which a melody is floated'.[5] But though some accounts suggest the use of twelve-note or even more radical techniques, Glass describes all his output from these six years as 'straight, middle-of-the-road Americana'.[6] All the pieces the present author has seen are rhythmically quite unadventurous, even if some explore a 'wrong-note tonal' manner. Few precise dates of composition can be established.

From the beginning of this period, if not earlier, Glass was prolific and, in circumstances which encouraged immediate performance, in the fortunate position of hearing most of his music played almost as soon as he had written it, as well as winning several awards. By the end of the Pittsburgh

Example 4.1 *The Haddock and the Mermaid*, bars 1–9

period, he had apparently composed over seventy pieces, some twenty of which had been published. 'I was getting things into print as soon as I wrote them. That's what happens when you play the game',[7] he suggested, when his reputation had still to achieve its peak. As editor of Theodore Presser, his teacher Persichetti had been instrumental in getting Glass's music published; other companies, though, including Novello in London, also took pieces at this time.

Europe and the East

At this point – he was now twenty-seven – Glass might have been expected to settle into a university or conservatory post and continue a perhaps unexceptional academic compositional career. Instead, he decided on further study: in Paris with Nadia Boulanger, with whom he worked from the autumn of 1964 to the summer of 1966. Here, Glass was following an already well-trodden path. American composers since Aaron Copland in 1921 had been making the pilgrimage to Paris; and though by the 1960s Boulanger was accustomed to teaching American students with more money than talent, Glass was playing his part in a tradition that also had its honourable, and musically very significant, side. The one-year Fulbright award must have been an incentive, too. He used it to help him stay for a second year, during which he took odd jobs and received lessons on credit, though Boulanger – who had encouraged him to stay on – died before her former pupil was earning sufficient to be able to pay her back.

Glass says that his main motivation for going to Boulanger was his need to return to basic musical principles. He felt that his Juilliard lessons, though extremely practical, had not laid sufficient emphasis on the theoretical aspects of music. Boulanger taught harmony and counterpoint according to strict classical procedures. In addition, he was able to spend two years in Paris free to pursue his own interests. Increasing impatience with current musical modernism led him to dismiss the musical avant-garde he encountered there, centred around Pierre Boulez, whose Domaine Musical concerts he attended. Two other encounters, however, were to become formative in the development of the minimalist style that had at least some of its roots in Glass's Paris period.

Theatre (i)

Glass's interest in experimental theatre was motivated in part by a personal concern. His developing relationship with JoAnne Akalaitis – a theatre director and actress whom he had met in New York while still working in Pittsburgh – had led him to invite her to join him in Paris. The couple married in July 1965, going over to Gibraltar for the ceremony because Gibraltarian law made it easier to wed quickly and cheaply there than in France. Jean-Louis Barrault's Paris company regularly presented new plays by Samuel Beckett and Jean Genet at the Théâtre Odéon which particularly impressed these young Americans. Glass and Akalaitis met Beckett in Paris some time in 1964 or 1965, through the actor David Warrilow. The Irish-born writer's output was to become central to the work of Akalaitis and her fellow actors for some years afterwards. The couple also developed an especial interest in the types of non-narrative performance art that were beginning to evolve around this time. In the summer of 1964, they saw the Living Theater's première production of *Frankenstein* in a small festival outside Marseilles; Glass had already gained some knowledge of the collective's work while at Juilliard. *Frankenstein* particularly impressed him in its extension of theatrical time: the performance lasted some seven hours. He was later to experience a similar scale not only in the work of Robert Wilson but in Khatikali theatre of South India. The following winter, Glass and Akalaitis met Julian Beck and Judith Malina, the prime movers behind the Living Theater, in Berlin; they also saw the Berliner Ensemble in the city's Eastern sector.

The experimental theatre collective with which Glass became involved in Paris at this time consisted largely of American *émigrés.* Of its original four members – Akalaitis, Lee Breuer, Ruth Maleczech and Warrilow – all except the last-named had been involved with the San Francisco-based Actors' Workshop and the San Francisco Tape Music Center. This Parisian group subsequently survived removal to New York to become the nucleus for the theatre company Mabou Mines.

While still in Paris, the collective presented English-language versions of two classics of European modernist theatre, both directed by Breuer. Mabou Mines' archives state that Bertolt Brecht's *Mother Courage*, with Glass as musical director (the original Paul Dessau score was used), was performed at Gordon Heath's Studio Theatre. The performances were probably in the spring of 1966; Jack Kripl – the saxophonist who later recorded the musical material for *Play* (see below) and subsequently became a member of the Philip Glass Ensemble – says that they took place at the American Church.[8]

Mother Courage was preceded by the group's first Beckett production, *Play*. Beckett has been central to Mabou Mines' work throughout its existence; Glass himself, though, had little direct contact with the playwright, who, he says, preferred to work though a 'designated person', in this case Warrilow. *Play*, directed by Breuer, had been mounted at the American Cultural Center on the Rue du Dragon, possibly in late 1965, though it has been impossible to establish precisely when. The three characters in Beckett's *Play* – a man (performed by Warrilow), his wife (played by Akalaitis) and his mistress (performed by Maleczech), all encased in funeral urns – speak in interrupted monologues, each spotlit only when talking and apparently unaware of the other two. The complete text takes some twelve minutes, after which there is a total blackout and the whole thing is repeated. A second repeat, following a further blackout, is abruptly curtailed.

The music Glass provided for this production was his first original theatre score for the company. It was also, as he assesses it, 'the first of the highly reductive and repetitive pieces that occupied me for years afterward'.[9] The music for *Play* was written – somewhat eccentrically but partly, no doubt, with practical considerations in mind – for a soprano saxophone overdubbed on tape. The performer was Kripl, then a Fulbright Scholar also studying with Boulanger. The score, as Glass recalls it, was 'a series of five or six short pieces separated by equal lengths of silence'. It is described by its composer as

> a piece of music based on two lines, each played by soprano saxophone, having only two notes so that each line represented an alternating, pulsing interval. When combined, these two intervals (they were written in two different repeating rhythms) formed a shifting pattern of sounds that stayed within the four pitches of the two intervals. The result was a very static piece that was still full of rhythmic variety.[10]

No score or recording of *Play* seems to survive. The absence of a score is hardly surprising, since this consisted simply of the four pitches Glass wrote down for Kripl to record – which he did separately for each pair of notes – and the tape consisted of loops which could be played, either separately or together, in a variety of ways each night. Kripl remembers the upper saxophone line as a descending major third, but cannot recall the lower one. He says that, as with the stage action itself, there was a lot of silence in the resulting music, which was in any case 'almost inaudible . . . very ghostly'. Kripl felt that Glass's response to Beckett demonstrated 'a great sense of theatre'. It also suggests that the composer's interest in reductive repetition was first awakened by realising the powerful impact repetitive elements were contributing to Beckett's *Play* itself.

Like other new European theatre of the time, Beckett's plays go a lot further than the drama of earlier periods in requiring their audiences to devise interpretative strategies of their own. What Glass calls 'the assumption that the audience itself completed the work'[11] leads to quite different experiences by the same viewer at different performances: including, as the composer himself found, that 'the emotional quickening (or epiphany) of the work seemed to occur in a different place in each performance'. This desire to transcend 'a theatrical mechanism with an interior mechanism designed to evoke a specific response' can readily be connected with the aesthetic behind *Einstein on the Beach*: Glass's first major collaboration, with Wilson, on a theatrical project in which his music becomes manifestly integral, rather than 'incidental'. The composer, however, seems to suggest that its underlying aesthetic also affected his approach to concert works as well, as also discussed below. A developing association with Beckett, meanwhile, subsequently allowed Mabou Mines to continue performing his plays, in adapted as well as original versions, with music (something the writer's estate normally forbade), thus giving Glass several more opportunities to explore these ideas inside, as well as outside, the theatre.

Soon after the Paris production of *Mother Courage*, however, the group temporarily disbanded. Neither of its productions had been a great success in the French capital, due not least to being staged in a foreign language. Besides, Glass and Akalaitis had developed a strong desire to travel and to explore some non-Western, non-narrative theatre traditions at first hand.

Indian classical music

For Glass, an interest in Indian theatre traditions had recently been augmented by his first experience of North Indian classical music, in the winter or spring of 1965–6. A friend of the composer was engaged as a photographer on a film called *Chappaqua*, directed by Conrad Rook, then being made in Paris. Glass himself describes the film as 'a psychedelic fantasy involving such heavies from the New York literary scene as Allen Ginsberg, Peter Orlovsky and William Burroughs';[12] John Rockwell calls *Chappaqua* 'an archetypically sixties hippie film'.[13] The composer was originally hired by Rook to edit soundtrack material already provided by Ornette Coleman, but discouraged the director from meddling with a perfectly acceptable tape by such a major figure.

In the end, the music for this film was composed by Ravi Shankar, already well established as a sitar player in the West as well as in India. Shankar, though, needed an assistant to transcribe his work into Western notation for the French musicians recording the soundtrack, as well as to do a little conducting and translating. Additionally, it turned out, some sections of the score needed what he called 'modern music' – for 'the scary parts of the film . . . psychedelic trips' – and Glass wrote this as well. Kripl, who was a member of the standard jazz quartet line-up of tenor saxophone, bass, drums and piano which performed the 'Western' part of the musical contribution, says that the players spent a wasted jam session attempting to improvise freely to repeating loops of images taken from the film. Since this did not work at all, he himself suggested a melody to use as a basis; Glass then simply wrote this down, and the four musicians improvised on it.

It appears that Glass's understanding of the technicalities of Indian rhythmic practice – and even more those of Indian theory – were somewhat shaky. But the important thing for the composer's future development was that working for at least two months with Shankar – and also with Shankar's tabla player, Alla Rakha – provided his first full exposure to the very different technical methods, as well as style, which lie behind this music. In particular, Glass noted that it is based on the accretion of small units to make larger ones, rather than on the Western method of taking 'a length of time and [slicing] it the way you slice a loaf of bread'.[14] In other words, while Western music worked on the principle of division, Indian music – and, as he soon discovered, many other non-Western musics – worked on the principle of addition. The basic, but crucial, distinction between additive rhythm and 'divisive' rhythm was the epiphany Glass was seeking. The principle of additive rhythm was to revolutionise the way he thought about composition, and it seems that the initial inspiration for this was Shankar. 'That was the closest I'll ever get to a moment when the creative light suddenly kicks on',[15] Glass subsequently said. Yet the rhythmic techniques, discussed below, to which this experience introduced him would not be properly investigated for almost another two years.

Glass and Akalaitis spent the winter of 1966–7 travelling in North

Africa, Central Asia and India. Hitchhiking first from France to Morocco, they finally found their way to India, with various stops in Central Asia; the composer spent his thirtieth birthday – 31 January 1967 – in Darjeeling. '[S]oaking up Eastern music and analyzing its processes'[16] was, of course, important for Glass. But both he and Akalaitis were also concerned to discover the cultures of which these musics formed part. Both developed what amounted to an obsession with India, in particular, later returning in alternate years for trips lasting anything from three weeks to two months. Glass has travelled the whole subcontinent, 'from the Himalayas in the North to Tamil Nadu in the South. I witnessed theater in the South, ashrams (spiritual communities) in the North, dancers and musicians everywhere'.[17] The integration of dance, theatre and music with religious traditions soon began to take on a particular fascination. Glass himself has said that the thing which especially interests him in Khatikali theatre 'is that it's a theatre that joins together music and dance and acting. . . . [T]hat's why I keep coming back and seeing it'. He also points out that Indian theatre is both popular and sophisticated: 'it has no trouble being communicative'. For both his immediate development as a composer of music for the theatre and his longer-term emergence as a composer of opera, these experiences were crucial, both aesthetically and practically.

Soon after his return to New York, Glass learned more about the basic rhythmic principles of Indian classical music. In the winter of 1967–8, Shankar and Rakha came to teach at City College, and Glass took the opportunity to have private tabla lessons with Rakha. A great deal of the inspiration he found in Indian music for his own compositions derived from this experience; his subsequent study of South Indian music taught him yet more about the different ways in which melody can combine with a rhythmic cycle. It was as a consequence of these later experiences that he really began to come to grips with the possibilities of cyclic processes.

While the techniques of Indian classical music became important to Glass in the late 1960s, their significance later faded for him. His interest in Indian culture – and in the cultures of other countries of the Orient, particularly Tibet – has, on the other hand, continued and developed. Glass remains to this day a practising Buddhist; first encountering Tibetan refugees on his first trip to India, he later became associated with several New York groups involved in bringing them and their culture to the USA. Ideas about the transformation of society by non-violent means and 'the power of an idea' permeate the operatic trilogy of which *Einstein on the Beach* forms the first part. (*Satyagraha* – based on the early South African years of Mahatma Gandhi – is the second; *Akhnaten* – premièred in 1984 – the third.) Glass has, however, never adopted the more overt Indian lifestyle embraced by La Monte Young or Terry Riley, and Indian music has affected him in very different ways from them. In 1990 he collaborated again with Shankar on a compact disc entitled *Passages.*[18]

Return to New York

Probably in late February 1967, Glass returned briefly to Paris before embarking for home. He was back in New York by mid-March, certain that this was the best place to set about re-establishing himself as a composer with an approach very different from the one with which he had made his previous reputation. For the next ten years, rejected by those who had formerly championed him, he was to work entirely outside the domain of Western classical music and its support systems: a situation very different to the one he had experienced while at Juilliard and later in Pittsburgh. To earn a living, he took any job offering sufficient flexibility to allow him at least some opportunity for composition. Later, Glass's publicists were able to capitalise on his other 'professions'. His employment as a taxi driver has been turned into the stuff of legend; so, too, via a story involving the art critic Robert Hughes, has his work as a plumber.[19] One of the significant aspects of such occupations is that they were still necessary as late as the beginning of 1978. Glass drove a taxi, on and off, for a living for five years from 1973: the period that saw the completion and complete première of *Music in Twelve Parts* and the creation, first performances and immediate aftermath of *Einstein.* Though the latter was an enormous artistic success, he returned to cab driving after its performances at New York's Metropolitan Opera House in November 1976, partly to help pay the considerable debts the production incurred. In the spring of 1978, soon after his forty-first birthday, he received both the Netherlands Opera commission for *Satyagraha* and a $15,000 Rockefeller Foundation grant, renewable for several years. These sources of income marked the beginning of Glass's wider recognition, and the end of his need to earn money from non-musical employment.

Less well known are some of the earlier occupations he had: from being a crane operator in a steelmill to running a removal business with his cousin, the sculptor Jene Highstein. Chelsea Light Moving provided Glass with his first main employment for at least eighteen months after his return to the city; the company was quite successful once it acquired its more *chic* title, abandoning its original name, Prime Movers. 'No-one got the joke, and we didn't get the work', the composer observes ruefully. Employment was flexible, allowing time for music. According to Glass, he was joined in this job for one weekend only by Reich, though the latter suggests he had a longer-term involvement. Plumbing, also with Highstein, overlapped with the furniture removing, and continued until some time in 1971; it was better paid but too hard on a musician's hands.

At first Glass and Akalaitis lived in a loft on Sixth Avenue, near 25th Street, but soon moved to 23rd Street near Ninth Avenue. Here the couple rented the upper two floors of a house, Highstein occupying the remainder. At 23rd Street, the singer and songwriter Moondog had a room for about a year, during 1969–70, having been invited by Glass to stay when he had nowhere else to live. Private tapes, made on Reich's Revox machine, of some of Moondog's songs were made at the house by Jon Gibson, Glass, Reich and Moondog himself. In late 1970 or early 1971, the family – about to add a son, Wolfe-Zachary, to a two-year-old daughter, Juliet – moved to Second Avenue on 4th Street, in the East Village, retaining the 23rd-Street apartment until 1997.

Developing his contacts in the downtown Manhattan arts scene, Glass continued to find experimental theatre and other newly nascent forms of performance art especially invigorating and open to the possibilities of musical collaboration. Contacts with the sculptors and painters of Minimalist art also offered not only further ground to fertilise his own compositional ideas, but one significant further employment opportunity. Glass gladly gave up plumbing when, some time in late 1971 or early 1972, he secured a position as full-time assistant to Richard Serra. He had first met the sculptor in Paris when the artist and his then partner Nancy Graves, a sculptor and painter, were in Europe on travelling fellowships; Serra settled in New York in late 1966, and after Glass's return the following spring, the two became collaborators, in addition to friends, in the late 1960s as well as the early 1970s. The composer's association with Serra will be discussed below.

Musical connections

Glass considers that the suggestion of any linear development from Young to Riley to Reich and on to himself fails to represent the real situation, stressing instead the 'supportive environment' which he found on his return to New York. In this 'more spontaneous' set of circumstances, a variety of other musicians – those fairly well known today and some less familiar, at least outside what now survives of this community; and both those widely associated with minimalism and others less often contextualised in that way – all operated within the larger orbit of a downtown Manhattan art scene characterised, for Glass, by its concern for 'the reform of language' in a range of sometimes conflicting ways. Any notion of a 'torch' being passed between the members of an elite group now seems a nonsense to him.

The actual question of the influence on Glass of any of these other three composers, however, remains to be addressed. Like Reich, he may have heard about, if not seen a score of, Young's *Trio for Strings* while still at Juilliard; as with Reich, though, this seems to have made little impression on him at the time and he says he has never heard the work. In 1961, Glass saw Young's performance of *Composition 1960 #7* (Draw a straight line and follow it) at Yoko Ono's loft. 'He had a pendulum hung to the ceiling', he says, 'and he would swing the pendulum and wait until it came to a halt. And when it came to a halt, he would draw a long white line. And he did that for about three hours. And I stayed for three hours; it was just a fabulous performance'. But for Glass, this – like the performances by Robert Morris, Claes Oldenburg and others which he saw around that time – was Dada or performance art; 'there was no music content to any of that work'. The first actual music by Young he heard seems to have been one of the performances at the Barbizon Plaza in 1968. Though he knew little of his music, he says that 'La Monte was a part of our life' for downtown artists like himself.

Glass can recall hearing nothing by Riley – whom, like Young, he says he never met until much later – until the Columbia recording of *In C*, which came out in 1968. David Behrman – the producer for *In C* and the Columbia disc of Reich's music released the previous year – apparently told Glass that he would be next, but Behrman then lost his job with the record company and no LP materialised. Glass may have even heard the Columbia recording on tape before its release. In addition, Reich has said he had earlier played Glass a tape of the San Francisco première of *In C*. Glass now agrees he may have heard it, and seen the score, prior to writing *Two Pages* (his first piece to use rigorous additive process with fully composed-out modular patterns) in February 1969. Gibson, who was already working with Glass as well as Reich by this time, says he is sure that Glass heard it.[20] 'Steve', Glass observes, though, 'was very quiet about Terry'. Glass also heard Riley perform at The Electric Circus in April that year. Riley's essentially improvised music is 'too unstructured for me', says Glass, who cannot recall ever hearing a live performance of *In C* itself.

It is unlikely that Glass even knew about the existence of Reich's early tape pieces before his return to the USA in 1967. In 1978, in the course of a probably unique live discussion between the two composers on radio, Glass said that he and Reich 'had been developing our own music in our own distinctive ways'[21] since their Juilliard days. This remark was presumably intended to assert an already existing interest in reductive repetition developed before 1967, entirely independent of Reich. Glass's first experience of his erstwhile student colleague's post-Juilliard output came, as already related in Chapter 3, when he attended one of Reich's Park Place Gallery concerts in March that year. Attending at Serra's suggestion, Glass recalls the occasion as 'a beautiful concert, a very striking concert'. The association the two composers went on to form has already been discussed. On the matter of specific advice being traded by Glass and Reich while works were in progress, Glass says that little went in either direction. 'The pieces were usually done so fast that there wasn't much time to do that. We had rehearsals with finished pieces, basically'. He emphasises that the general sympathy and support – of Gibson and others besides Reich – were the most important things. Agreeing with this view, Gibson nevertheless acknowledges not only that 'Reich was very giving to Glass' at this time, but also that Reich and Glass were both 'much more driven' than their other colleagues in the search for compositional solutions. And Glass today acknowledges that, among the composers working in this community, Reich 'probably had the most commitment and the greatest clarity of vision, the most intelligence and energy'; he was also 'one of the most inspiring'.

It is clear that, as stated in the previous chapter, 'there was a lot of interaction'[22] between Reich and Glass for at least two years. But it is also evident that a mixture of influences was making itself felt on Glass at this time. Such disputes concerning intellectual property can never be fully resolved; it is easier to conclude, as Robert T. Jones does, that '[n]o one composer invented this new music. It was an eruption of the times, an inevitability. It *happened*'.[23] Yet an understanding of the role played in Glass's search for new ideas by compositional developments close to his own need not damage his significance in the emerging story of musical minimalism. Further discussion of the relationship between Glass and Reich may be found below.

Theatre (ii)

For some while, Glass's theatrical involvements in New York helped sustain his compositional efforts. While scarcely providing him with much income, they gave him an outlet for his work and a sympathetic context for it. His closest and most regular theatrical collaborations continued to be made with the company that, from 1970, became known as Mabou Mines, following the regrouping in New York of most of the actors involved in the earlier Paris-based ensemble. The following details attempt to supplement, and where necessary to correct, the information given in the composer's own book.

This group was active soon after Glass and Akalaitis's return to New York. Resuming its connections with Beckett, the company began to make a speciality of devising 'theatre pieces based on texts which Beckett never originally intended to be staged'. It has also operated on the principle that theatre is essentially a collaborative act, working closely with visual artists as well as with Glass, and comfortable with material generated by the group itself, including adaptations of non-theatrical writing by other authors. Beckett's *Play* was eventually revived at La Mama Experimental Theater Club (E.T.C.), on East 4th Street, in June 1971 with a tape of the music made for it in Paris. Several further USA performances of this production helped Mabou Mines survive during the next few years, though not all included Glass's music.

The first major new work to involve Glass was Breuer's *The Red Horse Animation* for three actors: probably composed in the spring or early summer of 1970, though only two years later the composer gave its date as 1969.[24] A two-page extract from the score for *Red Horse Animation*, published in the company's own *A Comic of The Red Horse Animation*, is copyrighted 1971.[25] The summer of 1970 was the first spent completely at the vacation home the Glasses had acquired the previous year, a thousand miles up the coast from New York City, in Nova Scotia; the abandoned summer camp they bought, together with the writer Rudolph Wurlitzer, was near the town of Mabou Mines, which is how the theatre group finally got its name. It was here that the piece was extensively rehearsed.

Devised and directed by Breuer, *Red Horse Animation* is especially significant – both in the development of 'alternative' theatre in general and in Glass's evolution as a composer – for the integration of its different components. The three actors jointly represented the Red Horse which embodied, as Breuer explained it, 'psyches as actual animals, in the sense that you can be in the human world and the animal world – or the world of ghosts – at the same time. [The animations are] sort of choral monologues, each one dealing with a different psychological personality'.[26] Seeing the action from above, at a 45° angle to the stage, the audience could follow the images both vertically and horizontally.

Movement and sound were closely allied by the simple process of deriving both from a single, essentially rhythmic, source. For the piece, a special floor was constructed (with the aid of the painter and sculptor Power Boothe) which, when amplified by contact microphones, became 'the instrument on which the actors performed the music – stamping, tapping, using all manner of percussive effects'.[27] Ruth Maleczech recalls that the piece was divided into three sections, devoted respectively to 'singing, singing and tapping, and tapping'.[28] Such 'text' as exists for the work was not only collectively evolved in close integration with the theatre piece's other elements but also published – as a 'comic book', with drawings by Ann Elizabeth Horton – in a form which makes clear its inseparability from its visual imagery.

Money to pay for the floor, New York rehearsal space and even a basic salary for the five members of the company, including Glass, was provided by Ellen Stewart of La Mama. The completed *Red Horse Animation* was finally mounted at the Guggenheim Museum on 18–21 November 1970; a partial version had earlier been seen at the Paula Cooper Gallery. A surviving videotape formed the basis for a revival of the piece in 1996, in which several children of the original actors took part; here, clapping took the place of the floor-tapping which had been such a feature of the original version.

Another theatre piece from this period with music by Glass – *Music for Voices*, apparently devised in the winter of 1970–71, though possibly later; in 1972 its composer described it as 'a new piece'[29] – also exploited links between sound and gesture. In this work, 'six or eight people, whoever was around' sat in a circle facing inwards, filmed in extreme close-up by cameras whose operators lay on the floor in the circle's centre. While the mouths of individual singers appeared on monitor screens visible to the audience, vocal sounds would be passed across the circle. Its composer actually calls *Music for Voices* a 'concert piece', and as a work of only eight or ten minutes' duration for a theatre group, it was usually performed as a prelude to the main theatrical event of the evening. A 'work-in-progress' performance was given at the Paula Cooper Gallery in June 1972, together with *Arc Welding Piece*, in which performers reacted to the cutting of a seven-foot steel cylinder by Highstein, the composer's former colleague in his removing and plumbing activities. The official première performances of *Music for Voices* took place at The Kitchen on 19 and 20 February 1973. More information on the scores of both *The Red Horse Animation* and *Music for Voices* can be found below. Glass continued his association with Mabou Mines up to the mid-1980s, estimating that he has written 'at least a dozen scores for the company'.[30]

Connections with Minimalist artists

In contrast to his enthusiasm for discussing theatrical connections, Glass has often proved unwilling, in published interviews, to talk about the nature and extent of his relationships with the Minimalist artists. In 1972, he said that

> I don't make a direct connection between my work and visual work. Obviously I'm close to a number of artists that we know, and some I've worked with, but I never consciously make references to their work in a direct way. . . . I know the relations are there, but it bothers me to make those kinds of assertions directly, because it sounds as if I'm trying to define something which I'd rather leave undefined. I feel more comfortable relating to people's work subjectively and indirectly, rather than think of myself as . . . let's say music as a form of sculpture or sculpture as a form of music. . . . I think those ideas can best be developed by other people.[31]

In his own book, there is much more about theatre than about the fine arts, though this can be explained by its operatic focus.

Yet some connections with fine art are not hard to find. As we have seen, Glass had already met the sculptor Richard Serra and the sculptor and painter Nancy Graves in Paris. There, too, he became reacquainted with the art critic Barbara Rose, whom he first came to know when the two were students on a summer school in Paris in 1957. Rose's influential article, 'ABC Art', was published in 1965,[32] around the time of the renewal of her friendship with the composer. Immediately on his return to New York, Glass began to make gallery connections. 'I was basically working in the art world', he says, 'and I knew all those people'. He quickly realised the potential offered by the considerable interest shown in minimal music by sculptors and painters who appreciated the kinship with what they themselves were doing. Various artists helped Glass with money and assisted in setting up contacts with the galleries, museums and arts festivals that proved to be much more interested in his music than were the main concert halls. Among these were Graves and Sol Le Witt; Graves, as already noted, was also involved with Mabou Mines. Glass and his colleagues were also invited to play in the SoHo lofts of artists such as Donald Judd. Graves and Le Witt were among the many artists who designed posters for Glass's concerts; others included Barry Le Va, Brice Marden, James Rosenquist, Joel Shapiro and Keith Sonnier. Chuck Close made the famous Photo-Realist painting of the composer, *Phil*, in 1969. In 1977, several of these artists contributed work for sale when Joe Helman, of the Blum-Helman Gallery, organised an art auction to help pay off the debts incurred in mounting *Einstein on the Beach*.

Notable among Glass's links with such artists is an early association with the Canadian film-maker, and occasional musician, Michael Snow and, in particular, the impact of his already discussed film *Wavelength*, which also made such an impression on Reich. The theatre director Richard Foreman wrote an article about Glass and Snow in 1970,[33] in which he drew attention to the way in which both composer and film-maker were confronting 'the consciousness mechanism of the spectator' – 'encrusted with a web of associational conditioning' – with 'minimal, systemic, primary structure space objects'. 'The light, color and textural variations of the image [of *Wavelength*'s 'single, slow, forty-five minute zoom down the length of Snow's studio']' he observes, 'briefly punctuate, at five- or ten-minute intervals, the unceasing zoom'; such variations are 'filmic events on an equal basis with several events involving people'. Neither creative artist sought 'to re-create the image of an intuited or sensed reality that is normally unavailable to consciousness; rather [they took] the material ([in Snow's case] the view of the room, in Glass's case the musical phrase) and [subjected] it to a series of reiterated manipulations in which its elements are held in unchanging relation.... The changes that are slowly introduced respect the integrity of the found image or structure and are specifically designed to show how they sustain themselves under the impact of *time*. Going back and forth over the image or the musical [phrase], time is a heavy truck knocking them a little this way, a little that way . . . repeatedly impressing a bit of dirt from the road'.

The result is an art in which the listener or spectator, wrote Foreman, 'in order simply to *notice* the work itself, *must* replace himself so that he is no longer confronting an object, but putting "himself-as-self" elsewhere, so that naked presence is the mode and matter of the artistic experience'. Not surprisingly, such an analysis fits Glass's output of the late 1960s better than it does his subsequent music. It is, though, tempting to suggest a comparison between the 'textural' approach of Snow's film and Glass's attitude to the psycho-acoustic by-products of his music, of which more later. Foreman's suggestion that his own work – and that of film-makers such as Hollis Frampton and choreographers such as Yvonne Rainer, as well as the music of all four composers featured in the present volume – teaches those who experience it 'to be more attuned to the ontological truths and categories' does, however, add a further dimension to our perspective on the extent to which such downtown creative artists of this period shared aesthetic goals, as well as resources and outlets. Snow, also an occasional improvising pianist, issued a double LP of his group's improvisations on Glass's Chatham Square label in 1971.

But the closest personal relationship Glass established in the late 1960s with any of the Minimalist artists was probably with Serra, some two years his junior. Though Serra says that when he arrived in New York, just a few months ahead of Glass, 'the critic-gallery-museum system was completely closed to me',[34] he became the most helpful of all the composer's Manhattan colleagues in offering financial aid, gallery contacts and so on. Both the artist's support and the composer's manual labour on behalf of his colleague began before their friendship led to Glass's full-time assistantship. Deploying gravity as an essential forming agent, Serra's sculptures often consist of slabs or sheets of metal balanced precariously against each other, gaining an important part of their impact through their threat of imminent collapse. In 1969, Close, Glass, the performance artist Spaulding Gray, Dicky Landry (a member of the composer's ensemble) and others helped the sculptor mount his 'second lead series' of pieces – entitled *1–1–1, 2–1–1, 2–1–2,* somewhat reminiscent of Glass's own recent *1+1* (see below) – at the Castelli Warehouse: in itself a 'choreographed' exercise (to use Serra's own word)[35] demanding considerable skill. At least one of Serra's sculptures – *Slow Roll: For Philip Glass* (1968) – is dedicated to the composer.

In March 1969, Glass's first solo tour to Europe was put together by Serra, chiefly to persuade the composer to travel with him to help install a series of his own exhibitions. Fascinated by film at this stage of his career, and himself a film-maker, Serra also showed Snow's *Wavelength* several times on this trip, being as enamoured of it as were Reich and Glass. Playing either electric organ or piano, Glass performed *Two Pages* at the Stedtelijke Museum in Amsterdam on 10 March and at the Galerie Ricke on 14 March, and *How Now* at the Kunsthalle in Bern on 22 March; *Wavelength* was screened on each occasion, and a tape of Reich's *Reed Phase* was played. Audiences became extremely exasperated. At the Amsterdam performance, someone joined in on the keyboard; Glass (who had done some wrestling while a student in Chicago) punched him, knocking him off the stage, and continued playing. In the same venue, Serra says, the audience for *Wavelength* toppled over the projector.[36]

Like *Wavelength* and *Back and Forth,* also by Snow, three of Serra's own films were included two months later as part of the 'Extended Time' works in the Whitney Museum's 'Anti-Illusion: Procedures/Materials' show, mentioned in Chapter 3. Made in early 1969, these 'hand films', as Serra calls them, consist of *Hand Catching Lead,* a three-minute study of the artist's own hand in the repeated attempt to grab constantly falling strips of lead; a seemingly untitled film, in which the same single hand is eventually forced, through sheer exhaustion, to drop the roll of cloth it is holding; and *Hands Scraping,* in which two pairs of hands (those of the sculptor and Glass) attempt to untie the rope which binds them by the wrists and then gather it up.

In addition, Glass and Serra collaborated on several other occasions, both on what the composer calls 'art/music pieces'[37] and on at least one other project without music at all. In June 1969, immediately after the Whitney show, the composer made tape music for an installation at Loveladies, in the New Jersey marshes, by Serra called *Long Beach Island, Word Location.* In this, fifteen-minute tape loops consisting entirely of the word 'is' were relayed on thirty-two loudspeakers positioned around a thirty-acre site so that, wherever a listener stood, he or she could only hear one of them. 'Our inability', states a text jointly credited to Glass and Serra, 'to form a meaningful relationship between the coinciding occurrences, i.e., the word system and the experience of the place, points to the failure of language to comprehend experience'.[38]

For around three years, ending some time in 1974 – a period which largely overlaps with the composition of *Music in Twelve Parts* – Glass then became the artist's regular studio assistant. Serra liked having technical help from a knowledgeable non-professional, since other sculptors in this role had a tendency to claim some rights in the authorship of the finished artworks. The two friends spent even more time together during these years, cementing their personal attachment and also bringing them close as colleagues, even though they were working in different media. Whilst he was as wary as Serra of anything resembling 'one-to-one' connections between different art forms, Glass now acknowledges Serra's influence on his own development as comparable to that of Snow, and today includes Bruce Nauman in this list as well. Serra denies any 'shared stylistic premises',[39] but argues that the two were part of a group 'investigating the logic of material and its potential for personal extension – be it sound, lead, film, body, whatever'.

While the concern of all these artists with process and the unity of form and content affected the composer profoundly, the period of his closest contact with Serra interestingly coincides with the sculptor's further development of 'post-minimalist' processes and his movement towards what has been characterised as the 'expanded field' of post-modernist art. Here, the boundaries between 'sculpture' and 'architecture' were challenged in new ways by continuing to employ sculptural means. Already working in non-sculptural media, and moving towards this position by the time of the important 1969 Whitney show, Serra took these concerns much further in his more public, situation-specific work of the early 1970s onwards. From 1970, Glass began his move away from a hard-line structuralist approach to one involving a more malleable attitude to sound and an increased concern with the sensuous effect of his music on the listener.

Once again, 'one-to-one' comparisons risk misrepresenting both their creators' intentions and their achievements. It can, however, be suggested that Glass's change of approach during this period was affected by his unusually intimate knowledge of Serra's work and the ideas which lay behind it. Both developments, indeed, may be described as critiques of the more evidently constructivist concerns which had triggered these men's first individual creative efforts. It is interesting, however, to discover that when composer and artist conducted the already quoted dialogue in 1986 for publication in a catalogue for a forthcoming collaborative installation in Columbus, Ohio, Glass argued a larger role for what he called 'subjective aesthetics' in the sculptor's choice and manipulation of materials than Serra himself would acknowledge.[40] To understand the trajectory of Glass's move towards post-modernism, however, we must return to its process-orientated origins.

1 + 1: *Additive and cyclic processes*

The first composition to be mentioned in many accounts of Glass's development is *1 + 1*, the piece for amplified tabletop and a single player.[41] Dated 11/68 on the score, it is the obvious work to introduce any technical discussion of his minimalist output, since it pares its material down just about as far as one could go. Despite the improvised looseness of its appearance, it is the earliest example of the composer's rigorous use of additive process. An understanding of how *1 + 1* works will – for all the piece's simplicity, even *naïveté* – be valuable as a key to all Glass's minimalist output. The score is reproduced complete as Example 4.2.

1 + 1 is concerned purely with rhythm, emphasising immediately that Glass's starting point, like Reich's, was rhythm not pitch. The player taps on a tabletop amplified by means of a contact microphone; though Michael Nyman's account suggests that other surfaces are also permitted, the score itself fails to indicate this. Glass does not give a fully composed score; instead, he offers just two basic 'rythmic units' (*sic*; like many musicians, Glass seemingly cannot spell 'rhythm'), plus examples of the ways in which these may be used as 'building blocks' to construct a performance. While 'length is determined by the player', the score does not indicate whether the music should be improvised – which it conceivably could be – or realised in advance. It is interesting that its improvised character has led the US Copyright Office to refuse to register *1 + 1*, regarding it as a 'theoretical model' rather than a real composition.

In addition, the score of *1 + 1* specifies only that the two given rhythms should be combined 'in continuous, regular arithmetic progressions'. The music is so simple that it only takes a moment to realise that the composer is referring to 'additive process': numbering the two 'units' as 1 and 2, for instance, the first of Glass's three examples comes out as 1 + 2; 1 + 2 + 2;

Example 4.2 *1+1*, complete score

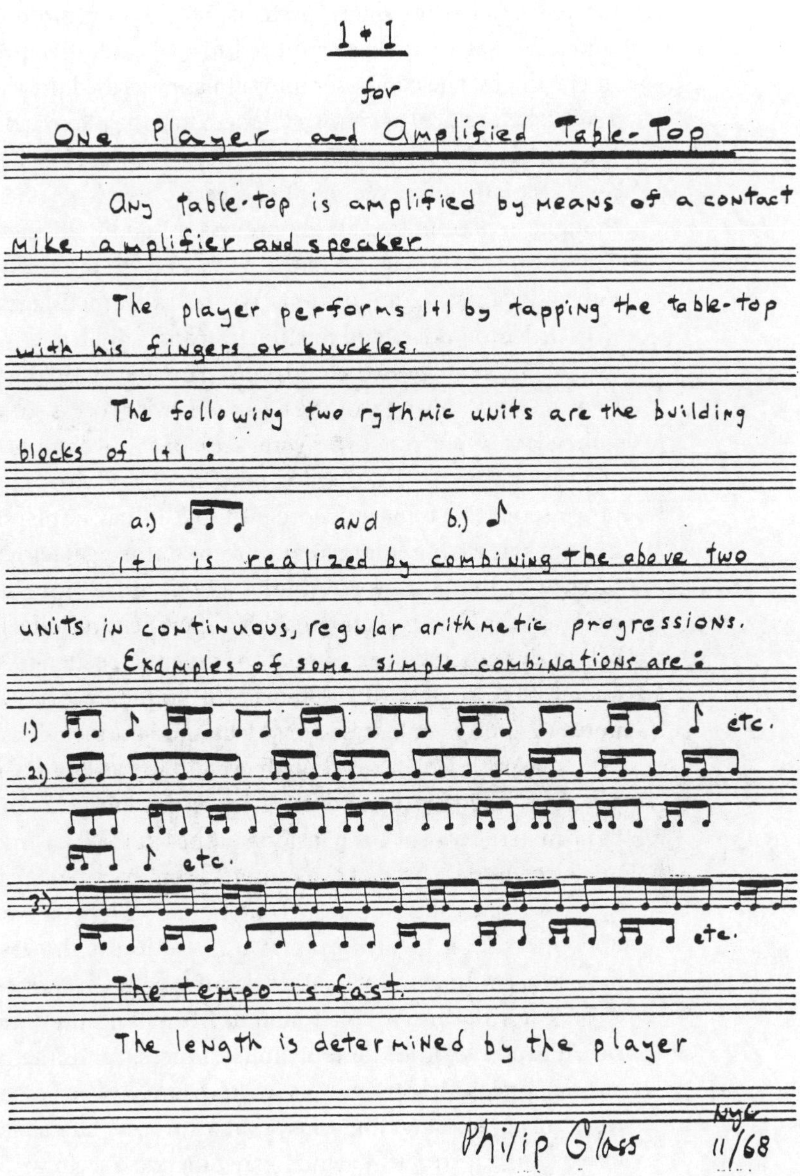

1+2+2+2; 1+2+2; 1+2 etc. That is, while the first unit is represented only once in each alternation, the second unit expands and contracts, consistently, so that the last combination is the same as the first.

This rigorous, though not fully composed-out, approach to additive process is the equivalent – conceptually, perceptually, and in terms of style and compositional development as well – to Reich's notion of phasing, and it served Glass well as his main structural technique for the better part of ten years. Yet surprisingly, perhaps, it took him more than two years to conclude that rigour was required to make additive process work really interestingly. The composer himself has described the works composed in 1967–8 before *1 + 1* as coming 'before I had the idea of additive process. It's funny, it's such a simple idea, but believe it or not I just hadn't thought of it then. Actually it was the result of a year or two's work: I looked back and thought of simplifying all the processes I had used into that one idea'.[42] This means that even within the years 1965–9, the period of Glass's most radically minimal compositions, two fairly distinct stages are involved.

In order to understand the function and significance of this, it is necessary to disentangle two confusions. The first is the distinction between rigorous and non-rigorous uses of additive process. In the above quotation, Glass is referring to a *rigorous* use of this technique. Works immediately pre-dating *1 + 1*, such as *Strung Out*, clearly also use a kind of additive process, but this is looser, more intuitive. It may not be sufficiently free to prevent at least one commentator from confusing it with the kind of structures to be found in works from *1 + 1* onwards.[43] Any intelligent listener, however, can readily distinguish this approach from the later, stricter uses of additive process on account of the different challenges these offer to following the progress of the music. In both categories of compositions, notes or groups of notes are added, and subtracted, on the alternating principle outlined above; though even in works employing strict additive processes, the identity and integrity of the sub-units that constitute the basic material for such expansion may be left for the work's structure itself to clarify, not exposed at the outset. (From here on, such initial material will usually be called the Basic Unit, in line with the use of this term in the previous chapter.) Only works from *1 + 1* onwards, however, elaborate this process according to systematic rules of expansion and contraction.

This has the important function of making the unfolding structure clearly audible; the compositional process and the sounding music become one, as it were, just as we have already seen is the case in Reich's works using phasing. Rigorous additive process offers, like phasing, a way into a musical structure which may otherwise seem merely aimless. One does not *have* to concentrate on its machinations, at least *all* the time – free-wheeling, sensuous experience is always available for those who want it. But additive process offers the listener the possibility of combining a thrilling aural experience based on rhythmic and textural immediacy with the opportunity of appreciating the note-to-note details of the music's structure as it unfolds.

The second confusion is between additive process and cyclic structures.

Glass's cornerstone technique of additive process was, as we have seen, inspired by his initial contact with Shankar in Paris and nurtured by his lessons with Rakha two years later in New York. The kind of additive processes which Glass made the basis of his own music are not, however, to be found in Indian practice; even the rigorous application of these is not a direct borrowing but an extrapolation of the composer's own from the Indian approach to rhythm. Cyclic rhythmic structures, on the other hand, are to be found in Indian practice. Cyclic process, as the composer later described it, involves 'something that lasts maybe thirty-five beats and then begins the cycle again. Then you join cycles of different beats, like wheels inside wheels, everything going at the same time and always changing'.[44] The full significance of this in Indian practice can only be understood in relation to the melodic improvisation based on the chosen *raga*: as the composer put it, '[t]he interaction of melodic invention – or improvisation – with the rhythmic cycle (the *Thal*) provides the tension in Indian music, much as that between melody and harmony (rhythm is the poor relation here) provides it in Western music'.[45]

Glass's attempts to incorporate cyclic techniques into his early minimalist approach in fact predate his rigorous use of additive rhythms and even his espousal of the modal approach to pitch organisation which characterises his output after his return to New York. The 1966 String Quartet is an early example, and *In Again Out Again* – a piece for two pianos composed in March 1968 – is of particular importance in this development; both works are discussed below. Such attempts proved problematic, however, when the material was otherwise shaped only by literal repetition or with the casualness of 'intuitive' additive process. Glass's slowness in finding fruitful ways of incorporating cyclic techniques in his own work may also be related to his initial determination to purge his music of genuinely melodic, as well as harmonic, constructs altogether, thus depriving himself of such interaction between dimensions. Yet the stimulus to make rhythm, rather than pitch, the basis for a new kind of Western music itself derived ultimately from Indian practice, suggesting the rich potential offered by the reintegration of melody and harmony. This reintegration could, however, only be explored after rhythmic techniques had been pared down, subjected to rigorous manipulation and turned to new account.

Early minimalist compositions

The twelve works composed in the three or four years before *1 + 1* (that is, before November 1968) may themselves be divided into four categories: three works written in Paris in *c.* 1965–7, all now lost; a string quartet (its score dated August 1966) that is the only surviving Paris piece, and thus also Glass's earliest extant minimal composition; a group of seven works written in 1967–8 for single instruments, duos or trio, before the composer's group had taken on a more permanent form; and *600 Lines*, the single work he wrote, some time during the summer of 1968, for a larger line-up that was clearly the first manifestation of what later became the Philip Glass Ensemble. Following *1+1* come the five works of 1969–70 written for that ensemble, which apply additive process in the rigorous and vigorous manner which was to characterise Glass's mature output. Together with *Music with Changing Parts* (which, though also dating from 1970, must be considered separately) and *Music in Twelve Parts* (1971–4), these five compositions are the works by which Glass first became known outside his immediate SoHo circle. They are, though, very much the product of that downtown ethos, and did not become known at all widely until about 1973 or 1974. In addition, the already discussed music for theatrical use also helped to establish Glass's reputation in the early 1970s; *The Red Horse Animation* and *Music for Voices* will be discussed further below. Only one out of all these compositions, *Strung Out*, has been conventionally published; and only one, *Music in Similar Motion*, remains in the regular repertoire of the Philip Glass Ensemble to this day.

The Paris compositions

Most of the pieces Glass composed before *1+1* are largely unknown today and differ technically from *1+1* and the compositions of 1969. Though perhaps little more than historical curiosities, they illuminate an interesting stage in the development of musical minimalism. Three works surround, probably all actually predate, the Quartet: all, according to Glass's own book,[46] were composed in 1965–6 (though precise dates and even ordering are not clear); all are seemingly lost.

What was possibly the earliest of them – *Play*, the music for the Paris production of Beckett's play of the same name – has already been discussed. In 1974, Joan LaBarbara wrote that all four works written in Paris used cyclic structures,[47] which suggests that Glass may have already been attempting to use some kind of cyclic technique *before* his encounter with Shankar in the winter or spring of 1965–6. *Play* was probably written late in 1965; the other three pieces could all have been composed after this.

The other two lost works from this Paris period are *Music for Woodwind Quartet and Two Actresses* and *Music for Small Ensemble*. Both are part of what Glass calls 'a whole series I wrote at this time'[48] built, it seems, on the basic principles of *Play*. *Music for Woodwind Quartet and Two Actresses* is described by its composer as 'a concert work for JoAnne Akalaitis and Ruth

Maleczech (in which they declaimed a soufflé recipe over my music)'. LaBarbara wrote that the work 'had two movements of serial writing and two movements based on repetitive structures and steady pulse with abrupt starts and stops and no dynamic changes',[49] suggesting a more hybrid, even confused, approach. In 1997, Glass remembered it as 'a one-movement ensemble piece based on tonal modular repetition'. Kripl recalls the composition as 'more traditional', along the lines of the works which Glass wrote during his Juilliard days. What must be *Music for Small Ensemble*, the second piece in question, is described by LaBarbara as 'for winds', having 'parts dropping out and re-entering with new material so that the cycle kept changing'.[50] Its composer's failure to find sympathetic performers for this work in Paris was a factor in his decision to return to New York.

The First String Quartet

The string quartet written in Paris in August 1966 is now known as the First String Quartet, since there are, to date, four more; Glass no longer counts a 1963 quartet from his Pittsburgh period, despite its publication soon after completion. LaBarbara, writing only eight years after the 1966 quartet's composition, stated that 'Glass considers [it] . . . to be the most successful'[51] of the four Paris pieces, which is no doubt why the work – written shortly before he and his wife left Paris for the East – has survived. Its composer says that 'I was 29 and for the first time my music didn't sound like anybody else's'.[52]

The First String Quartet consists of two 'parts', divided into twenty and sixteen sections, respectively. Between the two parts, which the score estimates should take a total of about sixteen minutes, a 'pause of about 2 minutes' is specified. All sections are very short, each containing between seven and ten bars; a 'pause of 1½ to 2 seconds' is indicated between these. Speed relationships between sections are based on a strict system of metronome markings: all seven-bar sections are to be played at ♩= 80, and those of eight, nine and ten bars at ♩= 88, 92 and 100, respectively. This schematic arrangement, linking speed change incrementally to the number of bars, results in the actual length of each section being exactly the same.

There are, in fact, only eight different sections of material in the quartet as a whole: a pair of sections for each of the four categories listed above. The sustained level of secundal dissonance, both melodic and harmonic, is surprising, in view of the essentially modal approach of everything Glass has written since 1967, though this also seems a characteristic of at least parts of the lost Paris scores.

Example 4.3 First String Quartet, Part One, bars 1–8

The opening eight-bar section – shown in Example 4.3 – should make clear the quartet's approach to a kind of atonality; note that the first violin does not play here. Within a section, each instrument usually has only two or three notes, which rock to and fro and are repeated exactly several times; occasionally an instrument is confined to a single repeated pitch. While other sections employ *pizzicato* as well as *arco*, and occasional hairpin dynamics for some repeated patterns, the surface of the whole work is, like that of Example 4.3, essentially static, with no changes of speed or dynamic within any section.

This extract also serves to illustrate something more typical of the quartet's composer: experimentation with a rather basic cyclic structuring in which the patterns underpinning the 'main' part are simply cut off in mid-stream when the 'main' part finishes. Here, the two-bar (basically eight-crotchet) repeating pattern (rocking F♯s and G♯s) of the second violin has two further patterns cycling underneath it. A six-crotchet-plus-one-crotchet-rest cycle in the viola (C and E) starts one quaver later than the violin and, being one crotchet beat shorter, has begun its fifth statement by the eighth bar. A ten-crotchet pattern (two minims plus a crotchet rest, then the same again, articulated by three octave Fs) in the cello meanwhile completes one full cycle against the violin in five bars, begins again at bar 6, but manages only one note of the second statement of this second cycle before it too is curtailed. While probably akin to the rhythmic structuring Glass had employed in his other Paris compositions, such a cyclic process would not be taken up again with such enthusiasm, and even with this degree of strictness, until *In Again Out Again* a year-and-a-half later.

Glass's subsequent concern with structural rigour is, in addition, foreshadowed by the Quartet's extended deployment of structural repetition, animating such apparently static music into a fairly readily perceptible shape. The material discussed above is assembled to form two alternating sequences characterised by almost completely strict palindromic repetition.

The early New York compositions

Glass composed at least nine works between the summer of 1967 and the end of 1968, including *1+1*. These are clearly designed to experiment more fully with his new-found minimalist approach. As near a definitive list of these as possible runs as follows: *Strung Out* for solo amplified violin (dated July/August 1967); *Head-On* for violin, cello and piano (October 1967); *for Jon Gibson*, also known as *Gradus*, for soprano saxophone (dated February 1968, though Gibson thinks it was begun, if not finished, rather earlier); *Two Down* for two saxophones (composed after *Gradus*, say both Glass and Gibson; there is no date on the only score I have been able to obtain); *In Again Out Again* for two pianos (March 1968); *Piece in the Shape of a Square* for two flutes (May 1968); *How Now* for solo piano or, alternatively, ensemble (undated in the score, but probably written in April or early May 1968); and *600 Lines*, officially the first of Glass's 'open' scores (again undated in the score, but seemingly composed in the summer of 1968); as well as *1+1* (November 1968).

All eight works prior to *1+1* apply 'intuitive' additive procedures to basically modal pitch materials. *Strung Out*, *Gradus* and *Piece in the Shape of a Square* also reflect Glass's continuing concern to build a theatrical dimension into his 'concert' pieces. LaBarbara calls this '[t]rying to alter the traditional staid concert situation . . . scores which made shapes and had performers move around a space to follow a score'.[53] But he was also responding to the conditions in which these works had their first performances: not in conventional concert halls, for the most part, but in art galleries, lofts and other 'alternative' venues. Space permits detailed

Example 4.4 *Strung Out*, first three lines

discussion of *Strung Out* (which, though the earliest, is the only one to have been published), with brief references to the other seven pieces.

Strung Out

Strung Out for solo amplified violin gets its name from the way the original manuscript score of some twenty pages was bound. It unfolded in such a way that it could be 'strung out' around the performing space on music stands, or even pasted on the walls. The violinist's manoeuvres round the space thus became part of the event; a contact microphone was used in order to amplify the sound while giving the player complete freedom of movement. With the exception of two short sections, the work consists of a continuous string of fast quavers, marked 'mechanically'. The published score estimates a playing time of '*c.* 21 minutes';[54] Paul Zukofsky's 1976 LP recording lasts twenty-three minutes.[55] Glass himself says that the title of *Strung Out* related both to the idea of stringing a violin and to the colloquial expression meaning 'at the end of one's tether';[56] it also has drug-related implications, but the composer does not seem to have ever mentioned these.

The opening lines of *Strung Out* may serve as an illustration of the intuitive, non-systematic approach to additive process mentioned above (see Ex. 4.4). The absence of bar lines in this score, the earliest to profit from Glass's studies with Rakha, demonstrates that Glass had already found his own way of conveying his tabla teacher's insistence that '[a]ll the notes are equal'.[57] The initial division of a five-note Basic Unit (E G, E D C) into 2 + 3 notes forms the basis for an additive expansion of these two sub-units independently of one another, as in *1 + 1*. The sub-units are continually grouped and regrouped, in a constant quaver motion, to form repetitive sequences which look at a glance as though they might be rigorously additive. The opening E G immediately returns, played twice, as one might expect. Yet on its next appearance, it not only fails to increase this to the expected three, but also gets tangled up – at what is obviously still so early a stage that the musical building blocks have scarcely had time to register – with a note (C) which the listener has probably already registered as part of the *other* group of pitches. Not until the next line is E G offered three times uninterruptedly; but in the first three lines we hear these two notes as part of a phrase with C almost as many times as we hear them separately. (Clearly, a certain amount depends on phrasing, too, since there is no actual gap between any of the notes.) The original five-note Basic Unit returns quite frequently in the piece's early stages. But no rigorously consistent pattern of additive expansion can be observed.

Yet if it predates Glass's realisation that it is the rigour of additive process that makes it musically interesting, *Strung Out* already demonstrates a certain structural sophistication. The descending group of pitches, E D C, emphasising a C-major modality, proves to be the basis for a downward expansion: first to B (page 2, line 2), then to A (page 2, line 5); and later to G (page 4, line 4), F (page 4, line 10), E (page 5, line 4) and finally D (page 5, line 11). And as this expansion is revealed, the first group of pitches, E G, is progressively abandoned in favour of scalic patterns, using E D C as a point of departure, retaining E as the highest pitch and incorporating each downward expansion as it is introduced, or shortly thereafter, as the departure point for patterns which ascend, especially once A is reached, as well as descend. After A is firmly established, the even patter of quavers is broken by discontinuous fragments stressing A and B (from page 3, line 5). The expanding scalic patterns are then resumed.

When the downward expansion reaches E, the E G sub-unit is reintroduced (from page 5, line 6), but it soon gives way to conjunct movement once more. After D is reached, discontinuous fragments reoccur, this time based on D and E (from page 6, line 1). E is re-established as both top and bottom note (page 7, line 1), suggesting a retrograde of the whole process, but this is soon followed by an unsystematic series of contractions and expansions – involving G, E, D and A as lower notes, and E, D, C and B as the upper pitches – now emphasising ascending scalic patterns.

After the range finally contracts more decisively in favour of the upper notes, high Fs and Gs briefly burst the E–E octave frame (from page 8, line 10), after which the original complete five-note Basic Unit returns and almost the whole piece is repeated. The *Da Capo*'s omission of the last three lines leads to the eventual prominence of the pattern B C D E: as conclusive a resolution as can perhaps be achieved in a work which delights in several kinds of repetition but almost entirely excludes one of the most obvious: repetition of a single note.

For the listener, *Strung Out* is disconcerting. It is hard to get much out of such simple music, and in particular to concentrate on its progress, when what *appears* logical on a note-to-note level cannot be 'read' on a note-to-note level as it unfolds, when rigour is implied but not offered. The sorts of structural properties outlined above – which can be readily followed by any intelligent listener – show that, even at this early stage, Glass is composing with a clear overall and audible design. But analysis in greater detail here risks merely providing evidence to frustrate the listener more than to assist the listening process.

Other compositions of 1967–8

In his next composition, Glass addressed the problem of applying additive processes to music for more than one instrument. *Head-On* (omitted from the worklist in the composer's own book) is scored for violin, cello and piano. According to Glass, the title refers to a basic progression from a sparse texture to a dense one, with 'a collision of music at the end', though the contrast is in practice more a matter of tessitura than of instrumental voices in play. The piece develops rhythmically independent parts for violin, cello and piano at a steady tempo in a rather brittle G major, their unwinding co-ordinated by reverting to bar lines. The piano's initially high-lying interlocking patterns of continuous quavers gradually descend over the course of the piece, loosening and re-establishing their connections and continuity as the 'grid' they provide is notated in bars of slowly decreasing length, from twenty-eight quavers to the bar to just five. But overall, the details of this work's rhythmic processes are even harder to follow than the additive elaborations of *Strung Out.*

Glass assesses *for Jon Gibson*, also known as *Gradus*, for soprano saxophone as 'a better version of *Strung Out*'. Apparently searching for a more systematic approach, he applied a strict scheme of thirty-two-beat lines to the unfolding of his material. The piece is based on a five-pitch Basic Unit, its two sub-units – a 2 + 3 structure like that of the violin piece – almost immediately losing any clear identity. An extended sequence of registral contractions and expansions, beginning with an octave's span, A–A, and concluding with the note at its top, transforms an initially pentatonic gamut into a Mixolydian one. While playing it, Gibson moved along two intersecting lines of music stands which reflected the two-part structure of the piece.

Two Down for two saxophones – described by its composer as 'an elaboration of *Gradus*' – is the second of three pieces from this period written with Gibson in mind; the other player was probably Landry. Both were permitted to choose which type of saxophone to use. Its two lines demonstrate a high degree of similarity, being contrapuntal elaborations of an initial four-note Basic Unit – A B D F – which at first expands upwards, fragmenting unsystematically, then contracts. A thirty-two-beat line scheme is again deployed to bring some further control to this, but, curiously, in a more casual fashion than was the case in *Gradus*. Imitation between the two saxophones remains the broad principle, and for short passages this can be rigorously canonic in terms of pitch and at least consistent in terms of rhythmic relationship. Glass describes the piece's rhythmic scheme, with its tendency towards fragmentation, as a 'count down'; the title of *Two Down* derives from the combination of progressive reduction and its articulation by two musicians.

With *In Again Out Again* for two pianos – intended for its composer and Reich to play – Glass hit on the idea of single figures subjected to unwritten-out repetition. He also attempted to develop the kind of counterpoint first explored in *Head-On* in the context of a more practicable framework, in particular by returning to a more rigorous investigation of cyclic processes in combination with additive structures. The combination of related repeated figures, in an F-minor modality, in close and constantly shifting counterpoint on two pianos suggests the influence of Reich's *Piano Phase*, completed exactly a year before. The relationship between the two players – one continuous, the other moving against it, the latter constantly alternating between entering into a relationship (motivic, contrapuntal and cyclic) with the former and then abandoning it – gives *In Again Out Again* its title. Halfway through the piece, the pianos exchange functions, and their material is presented in retrograde. This whole ingenious structure fits neatly on to just two pages.

Some of the advances of *In Again Out Again* were then pursued in the context of another thirty-two-quavers-per-line structure. *Piece in the Shape of a Square*, the third of these seven compositions to involve Gibson, is for two flutes; its title is a pun on Erik Satie's 1903 *Trois morceaux en forme de poire* for piano duet. Like *Strung Out*, the piece has a theatrical dimension: for it, he said in 1975, the composer constructed 'a big square about twelve feet by twelve feet and pinned up the music around it. There was music on the inside of the square and on the outside, and Jon Gibson and I played it, walking round in opposite directions and coming back to the beginning'.[58] In his own book – where the alternative titles 'Music in the Shape of a Square' and 'Music in the Form of a Square' may be found, and in which he reports the side of the square as being about ten feet – Glass writes that Gibson played inside the square, with himself on the outside; as in *Strung Out*, use was made of the contact microphone.[59]

Each of the piece's 160 lines unravels a disjunct modal melody constantly doubling back on itself, which is subjected to additive rhythmic expansions becoming more scalic as the centre of the piece is reached. The application of additive process to this scheme is somewhat stricter than that to be found in *Strung Out*. The second flute part is basically a line-by-line retrograde of that of the first, with some significant modifications, mirroring the scheme of perambulation described above. *Piece in the Shape of a Square* moves from a pentatonic mode with G as tonic to one on E mixing Phrygian and Lydian tendencies, and back again.

The title of *How Now* is apparently a reference, made by a somewhat self-conscious as well as assertive young composer, to the up-to-date nature of the procedures which he was using. Originally conceived as a piece for solo piano, it was turned into an ensemble work for saxophones (played by Gibson and Landry, using both soprano and alto) and electric organs (played by Murphy, Reich and the composer) as Glass began to employ a more regular group of musicians. Returning to the short figures subjected to unwritten-out repetition that had brought such notational economy to *In Again Out Again*, he constructed a similar series of related patterns to articulate a simple retrograde structure. Beginning in an ambiguous D♭ major, subsequently expanding to a black-note pentatonic modality, *How Now* has a middle section outlining a move from A minor to D minor before returning whence it came.

Eleven figures based on quavers in a steady tempo should each, according to the score, 'be repeated for twenty to thirty seconds before changing to the next figure. A good average length for "How Now" is twenty-five to thirty minutes'. The eleven figures of *How Now* are not, however, played in exactly this order, but according to a fixed sequence given in the score. This advances according to a scheme which is itself essentially additive, allowing the original Basic Unit to be accompanied, additively altered and transposed before the player advances towards and then away from the central figure, no. 8, using the last untransposed figure, no. 4, as a reference point before completing the retrograde sequence to return the piece to the opening right-hand pattern on its own. While lacking the additive sophistication or, necessarily, the contrapuntal ingenuity of *In Again Out Again* or *Piece in the Shape of a Square*, this solo piano piece assembles as many of the ingredients that were to prove fruitful to Glass in the ensuing few years as do any of his other early compositions.

The only work from this period originally intended for more than three performers is *600 Lines*. Omitted from the worklist in Glass's book, it seems unlikely to be successful in performance. Like all his compositions after *1+1* and before *Einstein on the Beach*, the score does not actually specify instrumentation; *600 Lines* is in fact the 'training piece' for the ensemble of assorted electric keyboards and wind instruments that Glass was shortly to make his own.

The piece consists, as might be expected, of 600 single lines of music, presumably to be played, as with the composer's later works, by the whole ensemble throughout, players dropping out to rest as necessary. Employing again a 'grid' of thirty-two quavers, the composer fits into this framework – a much more extended one than any he had previously constructed – a varied sequence of additive and subtractive processes using a mere five notes – C, D, E, G and high C – in a clear modal C major reminiscent of the opening material of *Strung Out.* Several schemes – simple repetition, a retrograde which is not literal but reverses the order of patterns, additive process, altering the placing of rests as expansions and contractions occur – operate on this basic material, extending and transforming it in ways familiar from its predecessors. Processes such as these tend to undermine any establishment of Basic Unit and sub-units which such simple five-note material inevitably sets up. Neither 'internal' additive process nor line repetition (whether of prime or retrograde) is consistently adhered to as the work unfolds. And though the 'grid' of thirty-two quavers per line conditions and confines these elaborations, there seems to be no particularly systematic exploration of the interaction between the additive processes themselves and the cyclic framework within which they are contained.

The effect appears likely to offset any musical interest created by such unpredictability by confounding the listener's chances of following the work's development with any consistency. Any overall tendencies observable in the deployment of the five pitches – for instance, that individual notes are abandoned, sometimes for short periods, occasionally for long ones – are similarly loose in nature. There is, however, a certain logic to the work's conclusion on the bare fifth C G: though less obvious than the frequent octave Cs that have preceded it, this still represents a reduction of modality to its primal, 'perfect' essence, as it were.

The combination of Glass's rather casual use of additive process and the time estimated to play all 600 lines – some two hours – would in all probability render the work impossible to listen to. Reich has said that it was through his guidance that his friend abandoned *600 Lines* and began to concentrate exclusively on a rigorous application of additive process late in 1968.[60] The work also presented, in an extreme form, a practical problem raised by some of Glass's other pieces of this period. Music based on such repetitive structures apparently necessitated many pages to notate, and some of his scores had attempted solutions to this encumbrance. Now that these compositions were venturing into ensemble territory, though, the burden was exacerbated. For *600 Lines*, Glass devised a system involving slide projections of the score changed by a foot pedal, but this proved unreliable. Though endlessly rehearsed, *600 Lines* was in fact never performed in concert.

Glass describes all eight of these scores, including *String Out*, as 'rather awkward pieces' and says that he felt he 'had practically reached an impasse' by the time of the sprawling impracticalities of *600 Lines*. He now solved the problem by taking the matter of how a score could be notated to the opposite extreme. The result was the single-page, improvised 'model of a piece', *1+1*. 'In order to solve the notational problem, I had to define the structural essence of the idea', says its composer. Rethinking his notation led directly to the realisation that a rigorous, rather than more intuitive, use of additive process offered much greater potential. As we have seen, *1+1* 'was the first real additive piece'.

The evolution of the composer's own ensemble

The group that from some time in 1968 was referred to as the Philip Glass Ensemble had its beginnings in the same loose association of composer-performers which produced Steve Reich and Musicians, as we have seen in Chapter 3. *600 Lines* was the first unrevised composition any member of this circle produced to require more than three players.

Several musicians were involved specifically with Glass from early on. The violinist Dorothy Pixley-Rothschild, another ex-Juilliard colleague, gave the première of *Strung Out*, but did not stay long. Gibson, by contrast, now quickly became a permanent member of the ensemble, despite the fact that he went to work in Los Angeles for around eight months at a crucial period for both Glass and Reich. Glass pleaded with him by letter to return, sending him not only a copy of *600 Lines*, but also, on 10 February 1969, the score of a little piece for him entitled *Come Back*: a play on the words of the title in the manner of *1+1*.[61]

As Glass's need for wind players, especially saxophonists, grew, both Landry and Richard Peck became regular members, helping to form the nucleus of the Philip Glass Ensemble after the break with Reich in 1971; Anthony Braxton, too, was an occasional member. Kripl, an ally from the time when both were Boulanger pupils in Paris, joined later, in 1979. Kurt Munkacsi, the Ensemble's sound designer and mixer, joined in the autumn of 1970, having been introduced by Gibson, who met him when both were working for Young in France that summer. His contribution became increasingly significant in the early and mid-1970s, as we shall see; he also later became Glass's regular record producer.

Keyboard parts, the other central feature of the group, were initially provided by Glass, Murphy and Reich, as well as several visitors, some quite well known. Frederic Rzewski, Richard Teitelbaum and James Tenney, all important composers as well as players in the emerging downtown scene, were among them. Among the regular performers, Gibson, another composer, played electric keyboard as well as saxophone and, occasionally, flute. Steve Chambers and Robert Telson, the former subsequently more associated with Reich, were other early keyboard players; Michael Riesman – a central figure in the Ensemble and for several years now its music director – only joined in 1974. Like Reich, Glass began to incorporate voices into his group from 1970. As we shall see, this arose more or less accidentally, and at first – notably in *Music with Changing Parts* – vocal sounds were provided by the (predominantly male) instrumentalists. The arrival of a female singer as a formal member of the group dates from 1971, when Glass was approached by Joan LaBarbara. Despite her current involvement with Reich – something of a problem, given the two composers' increasing estrangement – LaBarbara remained a member of the Philip Glass Ensemble until the early performances of *Einstein on the Beach* in Avignon in the summer of 1976; she was unique in managing to perform with both composers in the mid-1970s. The soprano Iris Hiskey, who replaced her, also arrived quite early in the group's history. Further occasional members of the ensemble at this time included David Behrman (viola), Barbara Benary (electric violin and voice) and Beverley Lauridsen (cello). Rusty Gilder and Robert Prado, two unusually versatile musicians from Louisiana with backgrounds largely in more vernacular traditions, joined for a while in 1971–2. Both played trumpet, though Gilder had originally been an electric bass player. Prado performed mainly on keyboard with the group, and occasionally added flute and voice as well; he died in an oil-field accident not long after the ensemble's West Coast and European tours of 1972.

When Glass wanted to organise a concert, he says, he 'went to the Film-Makers' Cinémathèque or the Public Theater. I would never go to a concert hall; they wouldn't have had me anyway'. Early New York performances included one at Queen's College on 13 April 1968 (including *Strung Out, for Jon Gibson* and *In Again Out Again*) and at the New School for Social Research on 9 May (including *Strung Out*). Several of Glass's early compositions – including *Strung Out, for Jon Gibson, In Again Out Again, Piece in the Shape of a Square* and *How Now* – were performed (the last two of these their premières; *How Now* in its original solo piano form, played by the composer) at his first major New York concert: on 19 May 1968 at the Cinémathèque, on 80 Wooster Street. Through Tenney, who was an occasional member of the circle, Glass had met the film-maker and critic

Jonas Mekas, who made the Cinémathèque available to him. Though the space could only hold about 120 people, the event was clearly significant in the development of the composer's reputation: Gibson calls it 'Philip's first NY coming out concert for sure'.[62]

Following Glass's solo European tour with Serra, the ensemble's next important New York concert came on 20 May 1969. The earlier of the pair of concerts that Glass, Reich and their colleagues gave at the Whitney Museum, this included films by Serra, framed by *How Now* and *Two Pages* performed by soprano saxophones and electric keyboards. In January 1970, there were two consecutive nights (the 16th and 17th) at the Guggenheim Museum with a programme that included the first major performances of *Music in Fifths, Music in Eight Parts* and *Music in Similar Motion.* Glass's first important American engagement outside New York City was a two-night stand at the Walker Art Center, Minneapolis, on 13 and 14 May 1970, following the two programmes of Reich's compositions. The concert at Fifth Avenue Church on 10 November 1970 that included the première of *Music with Changing Parts* was the last in which Reich performed with Glass, with the exception of the programmes on their European tour in February and March 1971. Glass's concerts in the latter, all of which included *Music with Changing Parts,* included one in Düsseldorf on 3 March, and two rather low-profile events in London, following Reich's programme at the Institute of Contemporary Arts, already mentioned in Chapter 3. The first of these took place at Wimbledon College of Art on 8 March, the second two days later at the Royal College of Art. The latter was held in the entrance hall; in the audience were David Bowie and Brian Eno, both by then former RCA students.

The compositions of 1969

The ensemble works written immediately after *1+1* took swift advantage of the potential offered by its combination of additive process and notational economy. Now able to 'collapse twenty minutes of music into two pages', Glass composed a continuous single line (the 'unison' of Nyman's reference to the piece as '*Music in Unison*'),[63] in which additive expansions and contractions of an initial five-note Basic Unit (see Ex. 4.5a, below), presented complete at the outset, provide the only material and sole process. The fully composed-out modular patterns in open scoring are reminiscent of Riley's *In C,* and *Two Pages* became the first piece in the repertoire of the composer's emerging group. Reich says that Glass originally headed the score '*Two Pages for Steve Reich*' but, when the recording came out in 1974, dropped the homage to his erstwhile friend: in the continuing aftermath of their break-up a few years earlier, Reich felt this to be a further act of denial of his significance for Glass's development.[64] Glass says that Reich liked *Two Pages* so much in rehearsal that he appended the words 'for Steve Reich' to a score and presented it to him, never intending this as anything more than the spontaneous gift of a copy.

The economy of Glass's new notational solution seems in turn to have helped suggest the use of rigorous, as opposed to intuitive, additive process. The composer then embarked on a logical sequence of works in which quite strict application of additive and subtractive processes is explored via increasing textural and contrapuntal elaboration. The titles of these compositions – *Music in Fifths, Music in Contrary Motion, Music in Similar Motion, Music in Eight Parts* – suggest the basis in each case.

Several principles also hold good for the whole series, which may be described as a rationalisation of the explorations and discoveries Glass had made during the previous few years. Each work is constructed from a Basic Unit, which may vary in length from piece to piece and is usually easily divisible into two or more sub-units, which may be worked on independently. The scores simply notate the expansions and contractions of the Basic Unit that form the structure of each work. They do this, though, by grouping sub-units and their expansions and contractions into figures of varying lengths; there is, importantly, no regular metre. Furthermore – and crucially – each of these figures is to be repeated an unspecified number of times, forming a seamless flow both between repetitions of each figure and between each figure and the next.

Instrumentation is never specified in these scores, and register can be flexible; while the earliest of them may – stamina permitting – be attempted by solo performers, Glass's own ensemble soon turned them into quartets, quintets, sextets or beyond, using electric keyboards of various kinds as a basis plus, most often, amplified wind instruments – usually soprano saxophones and flutes. The number of repetitions of each figure may be fixed in advance; whether the latter is the case or not, the composer indicates transfer to the next figure by a necessarily rather exaggerated movement of the head. Also missing from the scores are dynamic markings or any other interpretative indications, though several are headed simply 'fast, steady'. While Glass himself has usually played all these works at a high intensity – loud as well as fast – there is no reason why performances should not explore quieter dynamics, if not slower speeds, thus altering, most notably, the listener's perception of structure and, in particular, the nature and extent of its tensions, their accumulation and any potential they may have for resolution. It would, however, seem to run counter both to the music's natural logic and to the 'experimental' aesthetic to which they subscribe to subject dynamics to frequent change, especially via 'expressive' crescendi or diminuendi.

Two Pages

Two Pages (February 1969) represents Glass's first use of rigorous additive process in a composed-out score. Though octave doubling of a single line – played on the commercial recording by piano (Riesman) and electric organ (the composer) – does little to colour its deliberately barren soundscape, the work's technical procedures quickly proved their potential for deploying a variety of ways of balancing moment-to-moment unfolding of material, holding attention through the rigour of its operations upon it, and the need to provide a satisfying overall formal structure. They were soon taken up in works which were more lasting contributions to the repertoire of the composer's full ensemble.

As Wes York has pointed out (in an article on the piece which is among the most detailed analyses to be published of any minimalist composition),[65] the procedures in operation here are already quite sophisticated. York's transcription of the 1974 Shandar recording, made for his own analysis, is the only currently available published version. The following analysis makes use of surviving copies of the composer's manuscript score (which York was unable to see); the figure numbers employed here follow this definitive version and are accordingly sometimes different from York's. When the latter's 'measure numbers' differ from the manuscript's figure numbers, they are given in square brackets. Since York's interpretation of where a new part begins sometimes contradicts the original manuscript, his measure numbers have been adjusted to fit.

Example 4.5 gives the Basic Unit – G C D E♭ F – and some illustrations of the operations performed upon it in the five parts of *Two Pages*. The contrast between the opening interval of a perfect fourth and the ensuing conjunct motion helps suggest the possibility of two sub-units, while simultaneously permitting the usual sorts of ambiguity: notably that between the 'common-sense' division into G C and D E♭ F (2 + 3) and the 'psycho-acoustic' isolation of G suggested by the larger interval separating it from the other four notes. The five additive (and in two cases also subtractive) processes performed using these five pitches explore these and other sorts of subdivision. York identifies four processes at work: expansion and contraction of whole figures, expansion and contraction of parts of them, and what York terms 'external' and 'internal' repetition (the number of repetitions of each figure actually played, again applied to whole figures ['external'] and to parts of them ['internal']). These pro-

Example 4.5 *Two Pages*: (a) Figures 1–7; (b) Figure 15; (c) Figure 44; (d) Figure 61; (e) Figure 78.

cesses of expansion/contraction and repetition interact in various ways throughout the work, with 'external' repetition, one section excepted, a constant feature.

Part One (Figures 1–7, lasting about three minutes on the commercial recording; see Ex. 4.5a) treats these five notes as a single unit. To complete statements of G C D E♭ F, the first four, three and two notes (what York terms a 'subtractive process') are each added in turn, to give a fourteen-note figure; at this point (Figure 4), the process is reversed. Part Two (Figures 8–41 [mm. 8–39 in York's transcription], lasting some six minutes) again takes off from the original five-note pattern. While a single G C sub-unit begins each figure, the sub-unit D E♭ F is expanded in additively rigorous fashion: adding a note each time, until (at Figure 15) three complete statements of this three-note pattern, plus a 'tail' consisting of the notes D and E♭ alone, have been assembled (see Ex. 4.5b). From Figure 16, the number of repetitions of the whole sub-unit D E♭ F is then gradually enlarged to thirty statements. Following this, contraction occurs, using the same repetitions in reverse order and returning to a single statement of the whole five-note unit, plus the two-note 'tail', at Figure 41 [m. 39].

Part Three (Figures 42–59 [mm. 39–55a], which also takes around six minutes) builds a still more complex additive structure around this seven-note figure by adding a second one to it. The 'new' figure placed in front of it – another seven-note grouping, at first eliding with the previous one (Figure 43 [m. 40]) before achieving full separation (Figure 44 [m. 41]) – has built-in subtraction (1234 123, or G C D E♭, G C D) of the kind first encountered in Figure 3 (see Ex. 4.5c). Figure 45 [m. 42] begins this seven-note pattern's additive expansion, but also treats D E♭ F D E♭ as a further semi-detached five-note pattern, with its own built-in subtractive tendencies, by repeating this as a sub-unit. These two figures now both proceed by additive expansion to twenty statements each.

Part Four (Figures 60–78 [mm. 55b–71], lasting some two-and-a-half minutes) begins by abandoning G and C altogether; Figure 60 [m. 55b] squeezes a final additive expansion from the five-note pattern of Part Three. Figure 61 [m. 56] then adds C D E♭ F in front of this, and it is this four-note pattern which is now additively expanded; the pitch G remains entirely absent from this section (see Ex. 4.5d). Twenty repetitions are assembled in the manner of the previous scheme until, in Figure 78 [m. 71], the five notes with which this section had begun – now themselves assuming the function of a 'tail' – are abandoned altogether, and C D E♭ F becomes the kernel for the expansion of Part Five (Figures 78–81 [mm. 72–4], which takes less than two minutes). This begins by placing the original five-note unit in front of C D E♭ F, returning G to the mode (see Ex. 4.5e). Finally, two more patterns – D E♭ F and E♭ F – are added to give a sequence mirroring Part One's 'subtractive' accumulation of 5 + 4 + 3 + 2 quaver patterns to produce the fourteen-note bar with which the work concludes.

York's analysis demonstrates how the simple arch shape of Part One is first contradicted, then subsumed by the unfolding of *Two Pages* as a whole. While Part One employs whole-figure development and purely 'external' repetition, Part Two dissects its figure and involves 'internal' as well as 'external' repetition. Both, however, involve contraction as well as expansion. The basic shape of Part Three, on the other hand – a rise not followed by a corresponding fall – is a kind of contradiction responding to the essentially expanding characteristic of the additive structure itself. So is its division into two parts: the first (Figures 42–4 [mm. 39–41]) a logical continuation of Part Two; the much longer second part (Figures 45–59 [mm. 42–55a]) superimposing internal repetitions equally logically on to an additively expanding version of what has preceded it. Part Three's pivotal status is further established by its simultaneous use of all four processes deployed on the basic material of *Two Pages.*

Throughout Part One, G appears to function as the dominant of a clear-cut C-minor mode. Due to amplification and repetition, however, G C starts to be heard as a kind of drone, while G maintains a degree of independence by rhythmic means. In Part Two, Figure 8's initial expansion of the basic five-note pattern to six quavers suggests a clarification of the v–i relationship between G and C; it is quite easy to hear the new four-note pattern D E♭ F D and the immediately following G as outlining G^7, which then resolves on to C. The expansion of the sub-unit D E♭ F, however, gradually refocuses attention on these three pitches as an independent entity contrasting with the dominance of Part One's C D E♭, and on the potential of both F and D as a 'tonic'. The impossibility of mentally ordering these D E♭ F repetitions into predictable shapes is highly subversive, their almost inordinate prolongations sending Part Two into a spiral of tension only resolved as these D E♭ F repetitions gradually return to an uneasy equilibrium with those of G C.

The return of C D E♭ enables Part Three to offer a more tonally stable answer to the previously hesitant modality. Here, syncopation reinforcing C as tonic – a characteristic of all patterns in which C, D and E♭ are interrupted by G – is now fully exploited, the constant returns of the seven-note pattern of which all these pitches form part acting as a strong foil to the five-note alternative exclusively derived from D E♭ F. While the single G C isolated by the additive process in operation here forms a pivot point, the reassembling of the opening five-note unit allows G C to be readily subsumed: a constant reminder of the original unit's possible return.

Part Four destroys this equilibrium by abandoning both G and C and reducing matters to a whirling, climactic celebration of the second sub-unit, D E♭ F. C then returns (Figure 61 [m. 56]), as part of an additively expanding C D E♭ F pattern, prising apart the first sub-unit for the first time and suggesting the centrality of C without the help, or hindrance, of any dominant associations at all. Though now assisted by the psycho-acoustic energy associated with the lowest note in any incessantly repeating sequence, underlined by the only example in *Two Pages* of four-note modular repetition, the centrality of C here lacks the dominant dimension which gave to Part Three's syncopated tonic assertions a suggestion of tonal depth. While the D E♭ F D E♭ pattern is confined to single statements amidst the developing, and eventually enveloping, C D E♭ F, its presence remains rhythmically disruptive, allowing the listener to supply a down-beat anywhere, or nowhere. All this continues to feature in what York identifies as the second section of Part Four (Figures 65–78 [mm. 60–71]):

a seamless continuation of the additive process of the first section, but distinguishable from it through its absence, unique in *Two Pages*, of 'external' repetition, as performed on the commercial recording.

With its rhythmic and tonal processes now in gear to drive the work to a critical point in a context which does not imply the existence of convenient and clear resolution, *Two Pages* could have concluded here. The more conventionally conclusive Part Five, however, brings about a different kind of resolution. The reincorporation of G now brings with it the return of many of the characteristics of Part One: the original five-note unit (not heard since Part Three), and a 'wedge'-shaped 'subtractive' accumulation involving patterns of rigorously decreasing size to produce a fourteen-note pattern. The unencumbered recapitulation of these initial components of the work's surprisingly varied scheme brings a strong sense of finality to the last moments of *Two Pages*, despite the absence of a return to the arch-shape structure which had characterised Parts One and Two and then been abandoned. The structural openness of Part Five is mirrored by a degree of tonal ambiguity; its tendency to conclusiveness is, however, enhanced by the focus on purely 'external' repetitions.

Music in Fifths *and* Music in Contrary Motion

For *Music in Fifths* (June 1969), Glass took the same pitch array as he had used in *Two Pages* and simply moved the dominant up an octave, so that it now became part of the stepwise movement of what Nyman calls a 'five-finger exercise'[66] (see Ex. 4.6b). One further pitch decision remained – one that was to become important in subsequent compositions. To create a second line, consistently doubling the other a perfect fifth below, he transposed the C minor of the first into F minor; in Glass's own recording, both lines are doubled an octave below. The combination creates a modal ambiguity in which two lines a fifth apart maintain a certain, rather rigid, independence resolutely focused on the lower five pitches of their respective scales – or even circling around A♭ and E♭, the relative major tonics of the two keys involved – yet are simultaneously yoked together to form a composite readily describable as in the F-Dorian mode. While the fast repetition of patterns based entirely on these two parallel sequences of pitches produces an uncertain euphony by creating the suggestion of thirds and sevenths in the resulting 'harmony', the continuous parallel fifths make for a raw and uningratiating sound. The perpetrator of this rough ride in such a relentless machine encourages the notion that its rigorous adherence to the consecutive fifths banned in the conventional training a Western music student receives is 'a sort of teasing homage' to his former teacher Boulanger. Reich apparently once said that *Music in Fifths* was 'like a freight train'.[67]

Example 4.6 *Music in Fifths*: (a) Figure 1; (b) Figure 13.

(*a*)

(*b*)

Rigorous operation of additive process, using two immediately identifiable sub-units, only begins at Figure 13. Figures 1–12 offer an irregular, already deconstructed version of Figure 13's 4 + 4 unit of eight quavers, divided into two sub-units of 6 + 7 (see Example 4.6a). The first, six-quaver sub-unit serves, in unaltered form, to introduce each figure. The second, seven-quaver sub-unit leads, in Figure 2, to a statement of what will prove to be the 'proper' eight-quaver Basic Unit of Figure 13. The latter then gradually takes over, accumulating repetitions in the course of alternately following single statements of the seven-quaver sub-unit and replacing it altogether (in the odd-numbered figures up to 7).

The eight-note 'five-finger' pattern of Example 4.6b is now revealed as the essential kernel of *Music in Fifths.* It is subjected to a purely additive process, expanding the eight-note pattern to a total of 210 quavers in the course of twenty-three figures (Figures 13–35). Changes first occur alternately in the ascending first sub-unit or the descending second one; from Figure 19, they appear in both sub-units at once, consistently turning the expansions of the second sub-unit into inversions of the first. As figures become longer, notes are added in groups of six and seven, recapitulating in the process the patterns of the introduction.

While the additive procedures of *Music in Fifths* obviously modify any rhythmic regularity, its basis in a unit of eight quavers dividing easily into 4 + 4 offers more sense of real metre than does the 2 + 3 unit of *Two Pages.* The advantages of establishing a regular metre – against which other possibilities can then be measured and compared – first seem evident here. The sheer relentlessness of *Music in Fifths,* on the other hand, draws attention to its lack of both structural and harmonic sophistication.

Only a month later, in July 1969, came *Music in Contrary Motion.* This

Example 4.7 *Music in Contrary Motion*, Figure 1

proved tricky as a group piece, and the only commercial recording is of a solo version played on electric organ by the composer himself. Glass's train of thought at this period may also be gathered from the following response to a question about the evolution of his early minimalist methods:

> My reasons for writing pieces were often very strange . . . *Two Pages*, you remember, is in unison. Someone asked me if I was attempting to trace the progress of musical history and if, therefore, my next piece would follow on logically and be fifths. So I wrote *Music in Fifths.* That was all in parallel motion, so I obviously had to do one in contrary motion next. And after *Music in Contrary Motion* came its opposite again, *Music in Similar Motion.* It was a very easy going thing. In 1969 nobody knew me or cared much what I wrote, so I could make any jokes I liked.[68]

Whatever this idea – of building a compositional development in ironic homage to Western musical history's expansion from plainchant to organum and so on to more elaborate contrapuntal forms – tells us about his attitude, it helped to provide Glass with a sense of continuity about his compositional development for the first time.

Music in Contrary Motion is devoted entirely to two-part contrary motion, the lower part being a 'tonal' inversion of the upper one; the five pitch classes used (A B C D E) produce a modal A minor uninflected either by the contrapuntal layout or by any additional pitches (see Ex. 4.7). There are, in fact, really only two sub-units at work in this piece – the four-note scale and the five-note third-based pattern – plus their inversions, giving rise to a notable degree of economy, a highly symbiotic relationship between the parts, and an exact mirror relationship between the first and second half of each figure. Glass's own recorded performance crucially adds a pair of pedal points – one on the tonic, the other on the dominant – to signal each half figure, though these are not indicated in the score.

Once more, additive process governs the structure, here supplemented at the close by a hint that a subtractive process could eventually eat away what the additive one had built. The fluctuating fortunes of scale- and third-based sub-units become the main feature of the structural design. Sudden, subsequently drastic, expansion of third-based sub-units and slower expansion of scalic sub-units give rise to the basic structure of

Music in Contrary Motion. With Figure 20, however, the two kinds of sub-unit offshoots, so far kept pretty much intact, now start to alternate with greater speed, and the third-based sub-unit decreases for the first time as the work reaches its last stages. The additive and (more briefly) subtractive processes of *Music in Contrary Motion* are harder to follow than those of *Two Pages* and *Music in Fifths*, despite the articulation, and suggestion of tonal motion, provided by the pedal points on the commercial recording. The effect, as the composer's description 'open form' suggests, is of music spun out endlessly with no reason for concluding even when it does: like *Music in Fifths*, a more typical model of musical minimalism as often understood.

Music in Similar Motion *and* Music in Eight Parts

In *Music in Similar Motion* (November 1969), Glass returned to the parallel motion explored in *Music in Fifths*, changing and expanding both the number and the consistency of the parallel intervals involved and thus creating a situation in which the ambiguous approach to modality found in the earlier work could be turned to more complex and satisfying account. The work readily divides into four parts according to the progressive accumulation of its lines. Part One (Figures 1–5) consists of a single line doubled at the octave; Part Two (Figures 6–11) supplies a new treble line, basically a perfect fourth higher. Part Three (Figures 12–23) adds a bass line notably less strictly parallel than the new upper line; Part Four (Figures 24–33) completes the textural expansion with a further top line, partly a perfect fourth above the previous treble.

The work begins with an eight-note figure (see Ex. 4.8a), the Basic Unit for the now familiar expansion and contraction across a total of thirty-three figures. On the page, these eight quavers form a rhythmically irregular 2 + 3 + 3, suggesting three sub-units for the additive process to work on. Yet initial hearings, without access to a score, of the commercial recording suggested that the opening module was 4 + 4. While this could be due as much as anything to our conditioning as listeners, the ambiguity here is telling. Like Reich, Glass found the potential of twelve beats in a bar especially fruitful. The pairs of figures which provide the transitions between Parts One and Two (Figures 5 and 6) and between Parts Three and Four (Figures 23 and 24; see Ex. 4.8c for the latter) all have twelve quavers subdividable by the ear in ways different from the notated 3 + 2 + 3 + 4; the same rhythmic structure provides the fixed element in the evolving additive patterns of Part Two and – since the first figure of its successor (Figure 12; see Ex. 4.8b) is also the same as the last figure of Part Two (Figure 11) – the beginning of Part Three as well.

Example 4.8 *Music in Similar Motion*: (a) Figures 1–6; (b) Figure 12; (c) Figure 24.

The additive structure of *Music in Similar Motion* is shown as a whole in Example 4.9, some further details of it in Example 4.8. As Example 4.8a demonstrates, the division into three sub-units is brought into operation straight away. Figure 2 repeats the second sub-unit, suggesting merely a simple additive process involving the expansion of each sub-unit in turn. Figure 3, however, adds on a 'new' pattern which, partly due to its incorporation of the first sub-unit, to which it supplies a small extension, has a strong cadential feel. From here on, every figure will conclude with

Example 4.9 *Music in Similar Motion*, additive structure

Figure No.	
1	12 123 432
2	12 123 123 432
3	12 123 123 432 12 52
4	123 123 43 432 12 52
5	123 43 432 12 52
6*	123 43 432 12 52
7	123 432 123 43 432 12 52
8	123 432 123 43 123 43 432 12 52
9	123 432 123 43 1234 123 43 432 12 52
10	123 432 123 43 1234 123 123 43 432 12 52
11	123 432 123 43 1234 123 12 123 43 432 12 52
12**	123 432 123 43 1234 123 12 123 43 432 12 52
13	123 432 123 43 1234 123 12 123 43 432 432 12 52
14	123 432 123 43 1234 123 12 123 43 432 43 23 432 12 52
15	123 432 123 43 1234 123 12 123 43 432 43 23 43 432 12 52
16	123 43 1234 123 12 123 43 432 43 23 43 432 12 52
17	1234 123 12 123 43 432 43 23 43 432 12 52
18	123 12 123 43 432 43 23 43 432 12 52
19	12 123 43 432 43 23 43 432 12 52
20	123 43 432 43 23 43 432 12 52
21	123 43 432 43 432 12 52
22	123 43 43 432 12 52
23	123 43 432 12 52
24***	123 43 432 12 52
25	123 43 432 12 52 12 52
26	123 43 432 12 52 12 52 12 52 12 52
27	123 43 432 12 52 12 52 12 52 12 52 12 52 12 52 12 52 12 52
28	123 43 432 12 52 12 52 12 52 12 52 12 52 12 52 12 52 12 52
29	12 52
30	12 12 52
31	12 12 52 52
32	12 52 12 12 52 52
33	12 12 52 12 52 52
34	12 12 12 52 12 12 52 52 12 52 52 52 12 12 52 52

	G = 1
* + 4ths	B♭ = 2
	C = 3
** + bass	D = 4
*** = 7ths, etc.	F = 5

this four-note 'tag'. Figure 4 drops the first sub-unit, adds two notes to the third sub-unit and repeats the new pattern, making three changes to the previous figure but preserving its fifteen-quaver length. Figure 5 then subtracts the repetition of the second sub-unit introduced in Figure 2.

While it would be tedious to proceed with such a blow-by-blow account, Example 4.9 demonstrates several further ingenuities which help to mould *Music in Similar Motion* into a more complex and, in its way, evolutionary structure than *Music in Fifths* or *Music in Contrary Motion*: the most sophisticated instance yet of Glass's exploration of additive process. Beginning with the twelve-beat pattern established in Figure 5 (the end of Part One; see again Ex. 4.8a), Part Two expands to thirty-two quavers, progressively prefacing this undeviating pattern with additive expansions of sub-units two and three until, in the last bar (Figure 11), the first sub-unit also appears as a natural outcome of this process itself (another product of 'redundant overlapping').

Beginning with the thirty-two-quaver pattern of Figure 12 (see Ex. 4.8b), Part Three initially takes the expansion to forty-one quavers (at Figure 15) by breaking open the now well-established concluding twelve-beat pattern with logical extensions of the third sub-unit. The bulk of this part is, however, concerned with subtraction. Figures 16–20 drop the first six, five, four, three and two quavers respectively of the six-note pattern that had begun Figures 7–15, until only the twenty-one-quaver concluding pattern of Figure 15 remains. This is the pattern formed by extending the 'transitional' twelve-beat grouping, and Figures 20–23 now progressively subtract the extra notes (43 23 43 432) by four, three and two quavers respectively until only this twelve-beat pattern itself remains again to take matters forward to the final part.

Here, in Part Four, there is a double process of expansion and contraction to match the single one of the previous part. Up to this point, the four-note 'cadential' pattern introduced in Figure 3 has been notable for its occurrence, unrepeated, at the end of each figure. Now this 'tag' itself becomes the focal point, subjected for the first time to additive expansion. Beginning with Figure 24 (see Ex. 4.8c), it grows exponentially, from two statements up to sixteen. After this (from Figure 29) it takes over entirely, the twelve-beat pattern itself finally being jettisoned in favour of repetitions of the four-note 'cadential' pattern, now broken down for the first time into two two-note sub-units. Having swallowed the rest of the work's material, this deconstructed form of what started life as a mere 'tag' accumulates repetitions as it goes along, its two components locked in rivalry in a fairly rigorous additive pattern.

Modally, too, *Music in Similar Motion* extends the territory mapped out by its immediate predecessors. The single line of Part One (Ex. 4.8a) establishes a pentatonic modality which the opposition of conjunct and non-conjunct movement within the G–D frame suggests is centred on G; the absence of As reinforces the centrality of G, since the gap between G and B♭ renders the repetitions of G more prominent. Figures 1 and 2 use only four pitches (G, B♭, C and D), the fifth, F – expanding the original perfect-fifth frame – being added only at Figure 3. B♭, the relative major, had initially suggested itself as an ambiguous alternative to G minor, but the arrival of F seems more to confirm G by providing its flattened leading note than to offer a dominant to B♭.

The new treble line of Part Two (last figure of Ex. 4.8a) reproduces the pattern of the continuing G-minor line a perfect fourth higher, except for the penultimate note of each figure, which falls not to B♭ but to G, thus spanning an octave. Introducing C, the only further new pitch of the work, this line seems to be in C minor. Once again, the two lines taken together create a more ambiguous modal mix, which the G seems to inflect significantly, suggesting E♭ major as much as C minor by allowing the B♭ E♭ dyads on either side of it to be heard as first inversions of the tonic chord in this key, and consequently the preceding G F E♭ descents as 321 in E♭ rather than 543 in C minor. The major second produced by this G with the F of the lower line blurs the harmonic outline, though, creating a fleeting tension amidst the chain of parallel fourths.

The arrival of the bass line at the beginning of Part Three (Ex. 4.8b) provides the most dramatic moment in *Music in Similar Motion*, due partly to the new weight and depth it brings to the texture. But the modality of this line, with the potential it offers to operate as a functional bass for the emerging harmony of the now three-part structure, is also significant. Its emphasis on G, C and D, employing an upper as well as lower tonic, supplies an underlying i–iv–v in G minor which supports and to some extent refocuses the movement above it, reconfirming G minor as the true tonic key.

Part Four (see Ex. 4.8c) blurs the tonal issues once again by adding a further top line centred on F, operating partly in parallel sevenths with the original part and offering another dominant, C, in place of the strictly parallel flattened leading note, E♭. This further transformation of the original material unfolding exultantly over everything that has come before can, of course, be read in the modalities already established, G minor and C minor, as well as filling out the harmony to supply extra weight, for instance, to the C-minor^7 chords. These latter recur with increasing frequency during the protracted second section of Part Four, in which the former 'cadential' tag takes over from the other, predominantly stepwise, material. C minor is, meanwhile, given a further final boost by becoming the insistently reiterated i in alternation with its own v and iv.

Music in Similar Motion's piling up of lines produces the effect of a much richer, more complex modality than may be found in any of Glass's earlier works. The particular delight in thwarting any expectation of rhythmic regularity is surprising in a work that consists entirely of continuous quavers. As a result of this carefully proportioned and integratedly progressive approach to texture, additive process and modality, *Music in Similar Motion* possesses a subtlety, richness and depth foreign to its predecessors: the main reason why it is the composer's only work before *Einstein on the Beach* both to remain in the repertoire of the Philip Glass Ensemble and to have been frequently performed by others.

Music in Eight Parts is described by Glass as 'an abandoned piece', and for years he thought no manuscript had survived: in itself, some indication of his estimate of its worth. Though a copy recently surfaced, the composer has not released it for inspection. Probably completed at the end of 1969, possibly early 1970, it continues Glass's lighthearted gloss on 'attempting to trace the progress of musical history'. The title of the culminating work in this series, *Music in Twelve Parts*, indicates that this work is in twelve sections; since that work is much better known, it may be thought that the 'parts' of its predecessors also refer to sections or movements. In fact, both *Music in Eight Parts* and *Music with Changing Parts* are single-movement compositions, the titles of which refer to the number or nature of instrumental lines involved. Glass describes *Music in Eight Parts* as

> actually for eight contrapuntal parts. The piece begins in unison and with each successive note the number of parts increases. As it goes on, you get eventually to a twelve-note figure and the piece comes to sound like an accordion: it keeps opening up and closing. That's what I meant by 'parts' there.[69]

Though clearly an advance texturally speaking on its predecessors, and likely to produce an opulence of sound rivalling that of its immediate successors, it seems logical to regard *Music in Eight Parts* as the final work of Glass's 'early minimal' period. Its transitional nature is one reason its composer adduces for its status as a problem piece. 'I think it was a fumbling attempt at something which I did much better when I got to *Music in Twelve Parts*', he says.

The Red Horse Animation *and* Music for Voices

With *1+1* and its immediate progeny now examined, it is possible to understand the scores Glass composed at around the same time for the two theatre pieces mentioned earlier. Since the actors of *The Red Horse Animation* (the piece using the specially constructed floor) could not read music, its composer taught them their parts by rote; he agrees that the more rigorous the rhythmic systems used, the easier the music would have been to learn in such circumstances. In his book, Glass recalls that the music was 'organized into a highly logical arithmetic system I later began to call "additive process", a cornerstone technique that has served me well ever since.'[70] In what is evidently a homage to the father figure behind so much of the downtown Manhattan artistic aesthetic, the surviving extracts (two pages, the first headed with the Roman numeral V) reveal that Glass used the pitch sequence C A G E to construct a sequence of short figures for additive expansions to be devised in rehearsal. (Example 4.10 gives the first of these pages).[71] Though employing a five-line staff, the score is a series of simple 'grid' systems in proportional rather than conventional rhythmic notation, assembling figures ranging between four and fourteen beats in length, often in symmetrical patterns. The first stages of each additive process are sometimes shown, in the manner previously employed in the score of *1+1*; 'percussion' is both indicated on the staves and added separately.

The repeating patterns of *Music for Voices* were assembled into an informal score which divided the performers into pairs; each singer's part rose and fell in volume in a regular pattern, and the entry of each voice coincided with the dynamic peak of its partner. The unaccompanied vocal parts used only *solfège* as text; its composer describes it as 'a piece for nine voices in which I define a rhythmic phrase by the use of repeated syllables, building up a continuous rhythmic structure out of this material'. Once again, he conveyed his music to the members of Mabou Mines without recourse to conventional notation, and whatever he used seems not to have survived. Though it apparently explored the psycho-acoustic possibilities of overtone production to which he was concurrently directing his attention in his instrumental works, the piece employed no amplification.

The fact that both these theatre pieces are contemporary with the composer's discovery of the potential that voices had in his instrumental ensemble suggests that the earlier of them, *Red Horse Animation*, was probably an influence on Glass's development of vocal sounds in his concert music. With its use of *solfège* syllables, *Music for Voices* was in turn to be the inspiration for their deployment in *Music in Twelve Parts* and *Einstein on the Beach.*

The *Comic of The Red Horse Animation* also includes a page of graphics consisting of two parts.[72] The first is a representation of the additive process technique of *1=1* – 'in which I . . . in which I demonstrate my sound' – less specific than the original score. The other is a cartoon sequence entitled 'That's My Sound Now', in which a character (presumably the composer) muses, in an alternating sequence vaguely mimicking the *1+1* technique, as follows: 'I don't think/I used to sound like much of anything./I think/I'm making things up as I go along./I've come along/. . . I'm in a different place./I/guess that means/this isn't the beginning./If this were/the end/And I were still here making things up/I'd be crazy./I don't think/I'm crazy'. An apt summary of his situation and state of mind in 1970, this suggests that

Example 4.10 *The Red Horse Animation*, V, page 1

having rejected his earlier manner in favour of a 'back-to-basics' approach, Glass now realised he was on the brink of capitalising on these new discoveries. The compositions of the previous year or so were certainly not 'the end', but they may be regarded as 'the end of the beginning'.

The expansion of Glass's reputation and his changing aesthetic to 1976

From its SoHo base, Glass's reputation now slowly spread. From about 1971 to 1974, the composer mounted unadvertised Sunday afternoon concerts in his loft on Bleecker Street. An important stage in his move from local to national, and international, fame was the first complete performance of *Music in Twelve Parts* at the New York Town Hall on 1 June 1974. Even though it had to be organised and promoted by the composer himself, this was Glass's first major mid- or uptown concert. At this time, John Rockwell suggested that 'Glass still plays his music with his own ensemble because he can't get performances – or at least adequate performances – elsewhere'.[73] This may have been true; but the composer's attitude at that time to proposals from performers outside his own immediate circle should also be noted. As Dave Smith wrote in the following year, 'Glass is not interested in publishing his compositions. . . . To make scores easily available would result in a good number of mediocre performances which, apart from anything else, would be detrimental to the music'.[74] Smith tactfully fails to mention that this approach also generated more work for Glass's own ensemble, which effectively retained exclusive rights to his music. This situation was to change at the end of the 1970s, when Glass started writing operas for the forces of the conventional opera house. Even now, however, few of the composer's early scores, in particular, are available to performers, or to others.

Beyond New York, meanwhile, Glass's reputation grew. His first important American engagement outside the city was at the Walker Art Center, Minneapolis, in January 1970, already detailed; in the same year, the composer's first tours were backed by the art departments of American universities, as well as by art schools and museums in Europe. Though already viewed by some of his downtown colleagues as increasingly a businessman rather than an artist – a taunt that has stuck ever since – in the early 1970s Glass was still operating on a very small and independent scale, avoiding commercial distributors. In 1971, he started his own record company, Chatham Square Productions, in collaboration with Klaus Kertess, owner of the Bykert Gallery on East 77th Street, who had previously helped the composer with funds and bookings. Only two recordings of his own music were issued by Chatham Square Productions: a double album of his then latest work, *Music with Changing Parts*, released that year; followed by a single album of *Music in Fifths* and *Music in Similar Motion*, issued in 1973. Munkacsi used his contacts with John Lennon to gain access to a mobile recording studio for a weekend in May 1971 to record *Music with Changing Parts*; this was used again for *Music in Similar Motion*, recorded the following month, and *Music in Fifths* exactly two years later. In 1975, the French label Shandar released an LP devoted to *Two Pages* and *Music in Contrary Motion*. The whole of *Music in Twelve Parts* was also recorded at this time, though only the first two parts were released immediately: on the Caroline label, a subsidiary of Virgin Records. These discs significantly raised the profile of Glass's music, in Europe as well as in the USA.

As was the case with Reich, European interest in Glass not only made his work more widely available, but also promoted a helpful sense of legitimacy back home. The composer became particularly popular in France at this period. In 1973, Michel Guy, director of the Festival d'Automne in Paris, invited the Philip Glass Ensemble to play; by the following year, Guy had been appointed Secretary of State for Culture, and he soon commissioned the work which enhanced Glass's reputation more than any other: *Einstein on the Beach*. Premièred at the Avignon Theatre Festival on 25 July 1976, this immediately toured Europe with great success. Two performances at New York's Metropolitan Opera House later that year – on 21 and 28 November – brought even greater attention. While this collaboration with the American director and designer Robert Wilson triggered its composer's eventual move into opera – and his return to patronage and promotion by the support systems underwriting Western classical music – interest in Glass's music elsewhere was to take his work into the even bigger arena of rock music. The composer's early involvements with such music had as much to do with the British and German rock scenes as with downtown Manhattan developments in popular musics; further reference to this will be found in the conclusion to this chapter.

Glass's aesthetic development in the early 1970s

The common ground between Glass and the Minimalist artists has, as we have seen, been described as 'formalist' or even 'structuralist'. It is clear that the composer's main preoccupation from 1965 to 1969 was with structure and, in particular, with the purity and clarity of that structure. In order to achieve purity and clarity – and especially the audibility which was its most particular manifestation – the resulting music had to exhibit a strong surface simplicity. Everything depended on how that music was perceived. Yet Glass's note-to-note processes arose directly from the basic ideas of additive rhythm and cyclical structuring which – though derived, at least in part, from Indian practice allied to an improvising tradition – were turned into composed-out structures pursued with the aid of notation which limited the expressive input of both composer and performer in a conceptually highly formalist fashion.

Glass himself hints at this in an already quoted 1972 interview which is among the most penetrating that he has ever given. He had, he says, 'to get over my preoccupation with formalism before I began noticing what I was doing'.[75] What he was doing was dealing ultimately with sound, and he started to feel that this had begun to get lost amidst the concern for process which had so crucially defined his development during the previous few years. Foreman has argued that the noticing of process could itself become exhilarating in Glass's music.[76] And this had been borne out by the resilience which that music had already shown in sustaining musical interest with such highly reductive material. The trouble was, however, that by 1970 its creator was already questioning the validity of an approach which ultimately seemed to him to be divorced from aural realities.

Glass came to feel that he had been over-preoccupied with structure as such; the limitations of treating sound itself as merely the means by which structure was to be articulated increasingly concerned him. To some extent, he was responding to what he understood his audiences were actually doing when they listened to his music. They were, he found, despite his efforts to encourage structural listening, less preoccupied than he with such matters. '[W]hen I was still superconscious of structure and purity of form', he said, 'my audiences were already picking up on the sound'.[77] Glass also notes a parallel with the ways in which those involved in other art forms were thinking at the same period. 'In the last two years', he said in that same 1972 interview, 'there's been a real change of sensibility, in the content of the experiences we're interested in'.

One stage in the move to greater concern with sound can be dated unusually precisely in Glass's case, since it was precipitated by an actual experience of *Music in Similar Motion* in rehearsal, in May 1970. As the composer explains,

> We were playing in a theatre-in-the-round made of wood in Minneapolis. It was like playing inside a Stradivarius. It was the most beautiful sound I ever dreamed of.... [W]hen we go [*sic*] into the end of the piece, I thought I heard someone singing. I *did* hear someone singing, in fact, and I stopped, thinking Arthur [Murphy], one of the guys who likes to horse around, was improvising and I said, come on, who's singing, and we looked around because we thought someone was there. It was that real an experience. It

> wasn't us playing. But there was no-one in the room; as I said, it was a rehearsal. So we started playing again and the sound came back, and of course then we realized that the sound happened because of the acoustical properties of that room and because of the texture of the music . . . I thought that was the most interesting thing that I had seen in my music up to that point: it was a spontaneous thing, an acoustical phenomenon but it sounded like a human voice. So the next piece I did that summer, *Music with Changing Parts*, had a lot of singing in it.[78]

This experience led the composer to investigate the possibilities of using the female voice wordlessly: instrumentally, one might say. *Red Horse Animation*, the composer's first theatre piece using voices, also dates from around this time, possibly earlier, concurrently with Reich's development of his own approach to the 'instrumental' use of voices. Glass says that his colleague was present at the Minneapolis rehearsal. Reich performed in the première of *Music with Changing Parts* the following December; he actually hated the work and, as we have seen, quit his involvement with Glass's music shortly afterwards. At the time of the Minneapolis incident, Reich's work on *Drumming* had probably not proceeded very far. Though, once again, it is impossible to establish with any security a sequence of events which is open to different interpretations, Glass may have preceded Reich here.

Glass now allowed the instrumentalists of *Music with Changing Parts* to contribute unspecified sustained notes, either played or sung, in certain sections, introducing an element of individual improvisation into his ensemble works. While the number of repetitions of each figure was left unspecified in the original scores, decisions about this were, though, necessarily controlled. And although performers are permitted to drop out from time to time, this is purely to allow them some respite.

But it was, of course, more than simply a question of writing music which 'had a lot of singing in it'. More important was the encouragement that this event gave Glass to take account of the 'psycho-acoustic by-products' of his compositions. These included not only the illusion of voices singing (which continued to function, ambiguously, in conjunction with the use of *real* voices), but also such related phenomena as the hearing of lines in the music which were not in fact composed. That is, the combination of instrumental parts which Glass actually had written, and which were present acoustically in a performance, sometimes turned out to produce other, illusory effects, even of actual counterpoint. These were usually the result of overtones or undertones formed by the combined notated pitches as actually performed.

The reason for the, apparently sudden, occurrence of such phenomena was the increasingly heavy amplification which the composer was beginning to use for his ensemble as his music became more popular and he started to perform in larger halls. Crucial to the changing sound of the Philip Glass Ensemble was the arrival of Munkacsi as sound designer and mixer in the autumn following the Minneapolis incident. His creation of an amplification system for the group to deploy at dynamic levels common in rock music had its own effect on the composer's increasing interest in texture and timbre.

Mature minimalist compositions

1970 saw the completion of just one concert composition, *Music with Changing Parts. Music in Twelve Parts*, Glass's crowning achievement of this period, then occupied its composer for some three years, between the spring of 1971 and April 1974. These two works are considerably more substantial, in terms of both length and complexity, than any of Glass's previous compositions. The harmonic and textural advances of *Music with Changing Parts* resulted in a composition which is essentially experimental and transitional. It was only with *Music in Twelve Parts* that Glass was able fully to capitalise on these developments and take them forward to an altogether new level.

Music in Twelve Parts in many respects takes on the function in its composer's output which in Reich's is fulfilled by *Music for Eighteen Musicians.* During the period in which Reich was composing the latter piece, Glass proceeded to explore his own discoveries further in the context of a stage work, *Einstein on the Beach*, completed in 1975. It was with the new language he had forged in a purely concert context that he was then in a position to approach the writing of this ambitious 'opera', much longer and more complex even than *Music in Twelve Parts.*

Music with Changing Parts

Rhythmically, *Music with Changing Parts* breaks no new ground; the first of its two large parts confines itself to units and sub-units of only two or four notes. In pitch and, particularly, timbral terms, however, the work is more adventurous. The deployment of sustained notes allows the emergence, for the first time in Glass's mature music, of harmony as more than merely an accidental by-product of the rhythmic and melodic repetition, their articulation improvised by using a range of timbres unusual in the composer's ensemble. Changes of section are too few to suggest a real ambiguity of meaning in the work's title: though never clarified by the composer, this would seem to be a further case of 'parts' as 'lines' – though possibly too as specifically 'instrumental lines', implying a greater interest in colour and texture, a suggestion borne out by the recorded performance. Even the lean, treble-dominated character of the early Philip Glass Ensemble's sound presents an appropriate background against which the sustained pitches can generate powerful contrasts. Vocal drones are, for example, complemented by others on the trumpet. Deciding whether these sustained sounds act as background or foreground is, in fact, one of the fascinations of listening to the work. So, too, is deciding whether these notes provide a secure harmonic, even structural, focus or, as the pitch-bending on the recording might suggest, that they are more 'experimental', more Young-like.

The indications for the entry point of improvisation in general and the employment of sustained pitches in particular represent the only additions to the sort of modular material by now familiar from Glass's previous scores. The set of eleven 'changing figures' (marked 'C.F. #1', etc.) that help to give *Music with Changing Parts* its title is also to be found on a tabular reduction of the score (similarly dated August 1970, with the added inscription 'Cape Breton, N.S.') that charts its additive schemes. Glass explains that these 'C.F.' signs indicate that 'individual players were permitted to play one note for the length of a breath . . . a note they heard emerging from the pattern of the music'. The employment of purely sustained pitches suggests a comparison with Reich's use of resulting patterns. This is strengthened by the fact that, on the recording of the work, shorter note values are also incorporated. The 1973 performance in fact offers an interpretation which is much more varied than a literal reading of the score might suggest; this is, after all, a work designed to thrive on the improvising skills of the composer's now maturing ensemble.

A simple two-part texture forms the basis of the first four minutes, during which the two sub-units on which the music is built gradually become clarified. (Ex. 4.11 gives the Basic Unit of *Music with Changing Parts.*) Almost immediately, though (Figure 1, C.F. #1), first dominant and then tonic drones, in the key of C minor, are introduced. From Figure 6 (C.F. #2) it is increasingly hard to account for everything one hears in terms of the notated score, or to distinguish between the 'acoustic' and the 'psycho-acoustic'. The psycho-acoustic effect which results in greater emphasis on E♭ and D in what is still the top line in the ensuing section, for instance, is seemingly turned into a resulting pattern on these two pitches played on what sounds like the electric piano (first emerging at 4′40″ on the recording), drawing attention to the first two ten-quaver, five-beat figures (Figures 8 and 9) by emphasising each figure's anacrusis and down-

Example 4.11 *Music with Changing Parts*, Figure 1

beat. This seems to be the first example in Glass's music of an actually articulated resulting pattern which is not simply a sustained pitch.

Sustained pitches soon also return, though, heralding the arrival of Figure 11 (C.F. #3). With voices now more prominent, a fresh expansion occurs, involving high Cs which protrude above the texture with considerable force – piccolo and soprano saxophone supplying further treble energy. These arise as part of an extra beat added to the two sub-units in Figure 12. A more familiar additive and subtractive sequence based on this three-beat pattern takes us into a sequence tumbling deliciously through ambiguous metrical territory – each high C sounding more like a downbeat than do the B♭s the notation itself offers – which is further enhanced by resulting patterns. At Figure 19 (C.F. #4), the full six parts enter in the recorded version for the first time, with an additive process having a transitional function, suggested by its emphasis on a further variety of treble textures (including piccolo, flute and saxophones), rather than any dramatic emphasis on bass lines or sustained notes.

It is Figure 23/C.F. #5 which ushers in a more decisive change. Here, electric keyboards lay down a more evenly balanced version of the six-part texture; the bass, so long delayed, outlines F C F E♭ which, while scarcely complemented in any clear fashion by the harmony above it, offers sufficient sense of root movement in the already half-established E♭ major to provide a further, crucial stage in the move from C minor to its relative major. A veritable textural orgy now ensues, unsanctioned by the tabular score, in which the performers are given their head to improvise sustained pitches in profusion around an unravelling sequence of additive schemes. During the second of these (Figures 28–33, with C.F. #6 occurring at Figure 28 and C.F. #7 at Figure 34), this full, rich texture is further developed via pitch expansion upwards and a more concerted, especially telling approach to the dynamic unfolding of sustained pitches. The result of these co-ordinated crescendi and diminuendi is a wave-like rise and fall of fixed pitches against the familiar constant rhythmic repetition akin to that achieved some four or five years later by Reich in *Music for Eighteen Musicians.*

In the main, however, the effect of these sections is less disciplined, not only because such extemporised collaboration encourages spontaneity, but also due to the fact that Glass permits a surprising degree of pitch bending in the improvised sustained notes. In addition, some rather bumpy new resulting patterns break up the flow, increasing the variety of musical energy involved, but disturbing the evolution of any longer-range drama. The third and final additive scheme of Part One (Figures 36–49) underpins a continuation of this development, allowing improvisation to unfold for some time against a low series of readily assimilable six-beat figures before contracting to the two-beat pattern that ushers in Part Two.

After Figure 50/C.F. #10, metre and, later, modality move to new territory. The first ten figures of Part Two (Figures 50–59), which served as an introduction to the main section, have been largely cut on the recording and in the only available manuscript score. From Figure 51, the metre changes to $\frac{6}{8}$: a fairly seismic shift, considering that more than half an hour has just been devoted to music built largely on crotchet beats. In pitch terms, matters initially remain much the same, though the greater conjunct melodic movement leads to faster harmonic motion. Previous certainties are further undermined by the score's leaner, basically three-part counterpoint in contrary motion. $\frac{6}{8}$ provides the basis for the ensuing additive expansions. On the recording, sustained notes return at Figure 61, the starting point of these.

Following a further small excision in both score and recording (Figures 71–2), Figure 73 returns to the basic six-quaver figure. The two unsegmented sub-units of this are performed in reverse order in Figure 75, following the juxtaposition of the two versions in Figure 74. Figure 76 rotates all parts to begin, respectively, on the second and fourth notes of the original pattern, juxtaposing this with its own reverse statement. From Figure 77, these altered versions then form the second part of each figure, alternating with the originals. Expanding to fifty-four quavers at Figure 79, these then reduce to forty-two quavers at the close (Figure 81).

After the return to a regular $\frac{6}{8}$ at Figure 73, the recorded performance elaborates on the above description by making an unscored upward shift during the same figure at 49′23″: maintaining the mode, of course, but heightening the tension by drawing more attention to the dissonances of the contrapuntal lines as well as by registral expansion. The sense of denouement is quickly strengthened by the arrival of sustained E♭s at 50′11″. The final expansion of Figures 76–9 returns the voices to prominence, saxophones and flutes also playing a significant role. The apparently intended final riot of sustained pitches is, admittedly, somewhat spoilt in the recording by a falling away in the texture and some poor co-ordination. The final additive manoeuvres do, however, suggest a flatter landscape after the earlier peaks. The performance retains, moreover, an unpredictable wild streak which seems in character with the work's spirit.

While rhythmically relying mainly on the techniques its composer had already established in his compositions of 1969, *Music with Changing Parts* is much more forward-looking in harmonic and textural terms. For the first time in Glass's output, the rate of textural change rivals that of rhythmic change; as a consequence, the emphasis seems more firmly placed on the shifting sound-world than on the structure beneath it. The sustained notes allow the emergence of harmony as a real issue. Resulting patterns of other kinds, too, bring another new dimension to his output. And the range of timbral combinations available from the composer's newly expanded ensemble suggests a new depth to what is still essentially undeveloped modal harmony. The exploration of drones and improvisation, and the delight in the discovery and exploitation of psycho-acoustic aspects, may seem to categorise *Music with Changing Parts* as an experimental *cul-de-sac*. It is true that Glass never followed up this work's more obviously adventurous aspects; the composer himself has suggested that, even at the time of its composition, the work 'was a little too spacey for my tastes'.[79] On the other hand, *Music with Changing Parts* offers a foretaste of the textural variety, the dramatic flair, and even an interest in creating attention through harmonic emphasis and elaboration, which only came to full fruition later.

Music in Twelve Parts

With *Music in Twelve Parts*, we reach the culmination of Glass's achievements in the works written for his own ensemble between 1968 and 1974. The twelve parts, or movements, of this composition each last between fifteen and twenty minutes, making a total performance time of more than four hours with suitable intervals. A work of such length offers considerable scope not only for structural and other kinds of technical variety but also for a significant, and progressive, extension of Glass's musical language and expression.

The composer's own programme notes of the period record that the function of *Music in Twelve Parts* was to 'describe a vocabulary of techniques which have [appeared] and are appearing in my music'.[80] '[I]ndividual parts', Glass wrote, 'feature one or several aspects of a common musical language, presenting and developing them in somewhat unusual ways'. But he also points out that 'the individual parts of *Music in Twelve Parts* tend to be highly divergent from each other, exhibiting a range as wide as I could conceive of at the time of writing'. Additive process continues to be a mainstay, now explored in a variety of new structural as well as harmonic contexts, and pointed up via the use of *solfège* syllables in the female vocal parts.

Building on the ways in which chordal oscillations and hints of root movement in the bass line, already features of his own earlier music, had been developed in the more experimental context of *Music with Changing Parts*, Glass abandoned that work's sustained sounds and other more psycho-acoustically adventurous aspects to focus on his own approach to what, in Reich's music, has already been called the 'cadential progression'. By the time *Music in Twelve Parts* was complete – in April 1974, just a month before Reich began the first sketches for *Music for Eighteen Musicians* – Glass had extended the oscillation of two-chord 'cadential progressions' to the deployment of a whole chord sequence with real root movement in the bass line: a different approach to harmonic motion from that of his former colleague.

The work began as a single-movement piece, itself entitled *Music in Twelve Parts*, completed in April 1971 and first performed at Yale University on 16 April that year. Following the composer's recent practice, the 'parts' of this title referred to the individual instrumental lines. As he related in 1975:

> We played it at a concert in 1971, and afterwards someone in the audience asked me when I was going to write the other 'parts'. I realised that they meant 'parts' in the sense of sections. And that's where I got the idea for the whole piece. At first I tried to keep the idea of twelve contrapuntal parts throughout, but it broke down right away. It seemed like a useless encumberance [*sic*].[81]

In 1994, Glass said that the composer Eliane Radigue had given him the idea after hearing a recording of the piece.

The original twenty-minute composition now became Part One, and the other eleven 'parts', or movements, followed over the next three years. Composed mostly in the order in which they were finally presented, the sequence was supplemented by at least two new movements every year. Each would be tried out in informal concerts at 10 Bleeker Street or in a gallery. At first, the new addition would be performed with all its predecessors, but once the work became too long for a single programme, only the preceding two movements would be heard before the new one. Concerts usually consisted of three movements; if four were performed, there was an interval between the two pairs. The completed work was premièred on 1 June 1974 at New York Town Hall.

As Example 4.12 indicates, *Music in Twelve Parts* is constructed to make a complex but coherent tonal statement, in which the key of each individual part finds its place in a cumulative sweep of the whole that is new in Glass's output. Continued advantage is taken of the fact that apparent modal stasis activated by rhythmic repetition readily leads to ambiguity between any key and its relative major or minor, and this is exploited from the outset: hence the alternatives offered in Example 4.12 for the tonalities of Parts One and Two. But until he had discovered a flexible but more consistent way of exploring the vertical dimension of his music, and a means to control its horizontal unravelling with more moment-to-moment precision, Glass could not fully explore the sort of richness and variety which allow the full perspective of 'development' to unfold. *Music with Changing Parts* had shown how particular pitches, and even whole chords, could be enhanced by the use of improvised long notes. The short-range source of such flexible consistency, however, lay, as Reich had already discovered, in what both composers called 'cadential progressions'. The long-range source of such consistency was to be found in modulation between one part and its successor, and in the overall tonal planning this necessitated.

As his work was slowly assembled, transitions between movements – at first seen merely as juxtapositions; the composer called them 'joining-places' – were soon considered by Glass in terms of their modulatory potential; at one stage, the work was entitled 'Music with Modulations'. As Example 4.12 shows, key connections between movements are not usually as conventional as the tonic/dominant relationship between Parts One and Two. The tonal centres of Parts Two and Three, for instance, are separated by a tritone: the most distant relationship possible. The dominant/tonic connection between Parts Three and Four is compromised by the latter part's unusually high level of secundal dissonance. Links can, on the other hand, be as simple as the drone of a single pitch. At the end of Part Four, for instance, B♮ – one of only two pitches which this part has in common with its successor – clashes insistently, and consistently, with the rest of Part Four's pitch gamut, and in particular with C, the movement's notional tonal centre. This paves the way for the B-major tonality of Part Five, the modal clarity of which comes as a dramatic release after the tensions of Part Four.

Example 4.12 *Music in Twelve Parts*, tonal structure

Part *Date of composition*	*Tonality*	*Pitches used*	*Number of pitches*	*Chord/scale type*
1 (April 1971)	F-sharp minor (A major)	F# A B C# D E	6	13th/Aeolian (without 3rd)
2 (March-May 1973)	D-flat major (B-flat mino)	D♭ E♭ F A♭ B♭	5	pentatonic
3 (July 1971)	G major (D minor)	G A C D	4	stacked fourths
4 (August 1971)	C major	C D E F G A B	7	major
5 (August 1971)	B major/Mixolydian	B C# D# E F# G#	6	13th/major or Mixolydian (without 7th)
6 (February-March 1972)	D-flat major (F minor)	D♭ E♭ F A♭ B♭ C	6	major scale/stacked fifths
7 (September 1972)	C minor	C D E♭ E F G A♭ B♭ B		harmonic minor plus E and B
8 (July 1973)	F Mixolydian	F G A B♭ C D E♭	7	13th/Mixolydian
9 (winter 1973-4)	A major	A B C# D E F# G# E♭ G B♭	7 8, 9, 10	major scale plus "tritonic triad"
10 (ditto)	F-sharp minor>A major	A B C# E F#	5	pentatonic
11 (ditto)	A major/E major/F#-minor A-flat major C major	A B C# D# E F# G# A♭ B♭ C D♭ E♭ F C D E F G A B	7 6 7	Lydian/stacked fifths major scale/stacked fifths major scale
12 (April 1974)	A major/ C minor modulating >>>	A C# E F# C E♭ F G >>> +	4	A^6 C-minor^4 modulating

Composed in quick succession, the first large-scale statement of climax and resolution formed by these two movements shows its composer getting into his stride, and even beginning to see tonal, rather than rhythmic, processes as the most fruitful constructional tool to deploy in conjunction with his new concern for texture. While the tonal centres of *Music in Twelve Parts* adopt no simple schematic pattern, A and C, each in several tonal guises, become the two focal points of the work's progress towards its conclusion. C major forms one of the three ingredients in the new, more developmental kind of tonality to be found in Part Eleven. The F♯/A 'relative' relationship can now be seen as an important cog in the wheel of the overall tonal scheme. Another of the three ingredients in the developing tonality of Part Eleven is an A major/F♯ minor which develops by acquiring D♯s, taking on a strong E-major aspect as it progresses. This, too, will play a role in the final denouement of Part Twelve which, with that of Part Eleven, is detailed below.

Within this scheme, *Music in Twelve Parts* unfolds a sequence of movements demonstrating considerable stylistic, as well as technical, variety. Part One is Glass's first slow minimalist piece, its impression of sustained F♯ C♯s achieved as a resulting pattern derived from the interaction of its shifting counterpoint. Parts Three, Four and Seven also explore resulting patterns, while Parts Two, Five, Six and Eight unfold a process of augmentation and diminution within a fixed rhythmic cycle, extending Glass's early efforts at cyclic process to new levels of sophistication. While most earlier movements operate 'monothematically' with a single process, Parts Seven to Nine are more sectional and complex; Part Two, written at around the same time as these, also falls into this category. While Parts Ten to Twelve are essentially single processes once again, they chart a rising curve, the highly chromatic Part Ten leading to the harmonic motion of the concluding two movements to bring *Music in Twelve Parts* to a dramatic conclusion.

Part Five

The B major of Part Five is clarified by bass movement emphasising iv, iv and i and, more audibly, by the repeated i–ii and v–vi–v–iii in the upper parts and the held D♯ (iii) near the top of the texture. But the already mentioned feeling of release after the tensions of Part Four is celebrated more by rhythmic than by harmonic ingenuity. The most significant aspect of Part Five is its delineation of a process of augmentation and diminution within a fixed rhythmic cycle.

Example 4.13a gives the opening two figures of Part Five, while Example 4.13b outlines the rhythmic elements involved. A bar-length of six quavers is maintained throughout; characteristically, though, Glass rings the changes on its equal potential for $\frac{6}{8}$ and $\frac{3}{4}$ from the outset. Continuity is provided by the repeated quaver patterns: in both treble and bass, but most clearly in the left hand of Organ 4, its unchanging pitch patterns being notated, like those of the treble, in whichever metre best suits the tendency of those other parts which change. As one would expect, the listener may choose to hear the metre at almost any point as either $\frac{6}{8}$ or $\frac{3}{4}$. The opening texture (Example 4.13a) demonstrates the variety of both metric

Example 4.13 *Music in Twelve Parts*: (a) Part Five, Figures 1–2.

Example 4.13 (cont.) *Music in Twelve Parts*: (b) Part Five, rhythmic structure.

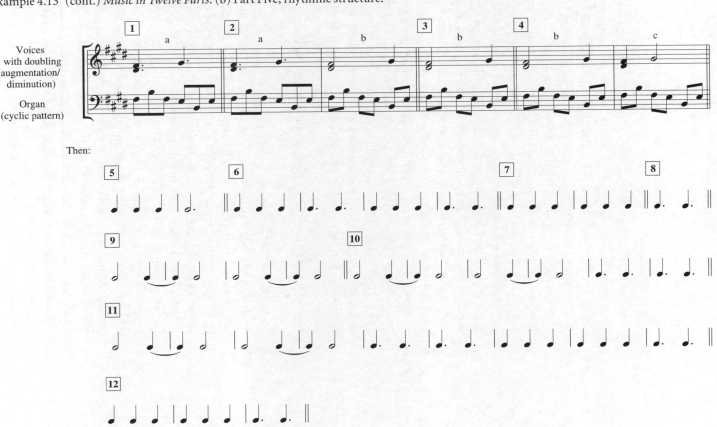

1 a 2 a 3 b 4 b b c

Voices with doubling augmentation/ diminution)

Organ (cyclic pattern)

Then:

5 6 7 8

9 10

11

12

emphases and contrapuntal elaboration. The various doublings of the bass include one (Organ 2) which reproduces part of the basic pattern exactly, but also introduces a cross-rhythm. Another bass line (Organ 1) picks up this cross-rhythm in a resulting pattern formed from the E F♯ of the bass and the D♯ drone.

While the clearly audible top instrumental line helps provide the already mentioned v–vi–v–iii, it is the rocking iii/v–vi of the voice parts singing *solfège* syllables, aided by some instrumental doubling, which unfolds the process of augmentation and diminution, oscillating a dyad and a single note over the repeating cycles of six quavers beneath. Example 4.13b shows how this clearly audible augmentation/diminution process unravels against the cyclic underlay. The composer's ensemble would seem to have experimented with different versions of this scheme at different periods; the one given here is that to be found in the only manuscript score which the present author has been able to see. In Figures 1–4, the rhythmic progress of these oscillations unfolds in a strict scheme alternating a single bar with a pair adding a new configuration to the first. As the figures increase in length, they establish four-bar minim groupings (forming cross-rhythms with the six-quaver cycle below) which first alternate with, and are eventually succeeded by, differently ordered sequences of crotchets and dotted crotchets. The effect is of an endlessly shifting metre, always grounded, however, by the underlying cyclic 'grid'. Amidst its greater focus on sheer sonority and harmonic sophistication, *Music in Twelve Parts* still finds room for the rigours of rhythmic process.

Parts Eleven and Twelve

With Parts Eleven and Twelve, Glass infuses harmonic motion with an additive process of its own to create a suitably charged and fulfilling climax to a composition of such length and complexity. Part Eleven consists of twelve basic chords (see Ex. 4.14) defining three tonal areas. In Area A, chords i, iv and vi are constructed on the bass notes A, B and F♯, being built on the principle of 'stacked' fifths (from A upwards) to produce: firstly, five-pitch aggregates of increasing density on A (chords ia, ib and ic); then, with the bass note B, a chord containing all seven pitches of the A-Lydian mode, adding G♯ and D♯ to the previous 'stack' of fifths (chord iv); then, with the bass note moving to F♯, a four-pitch aggregate built on an inner segment (E B F♯C♯) of the 'stacked'-fifths gamut (chord vi).

Area B – to be found in chords ii, v, ix and xii – is constructed on the bass notes A♭, C and B♭, being built, again, on the principle of 'stacked' fifths (from A♭ upwards) to produce: firstly, a five-pitch aggregate on A♭ (chord ii); then, with the bass note C, a chord adding D♭ to chord ii (in 'stacked'-

Example 4.14 *Music in Twelve Parts*, Part Eleven, twelve basic chords

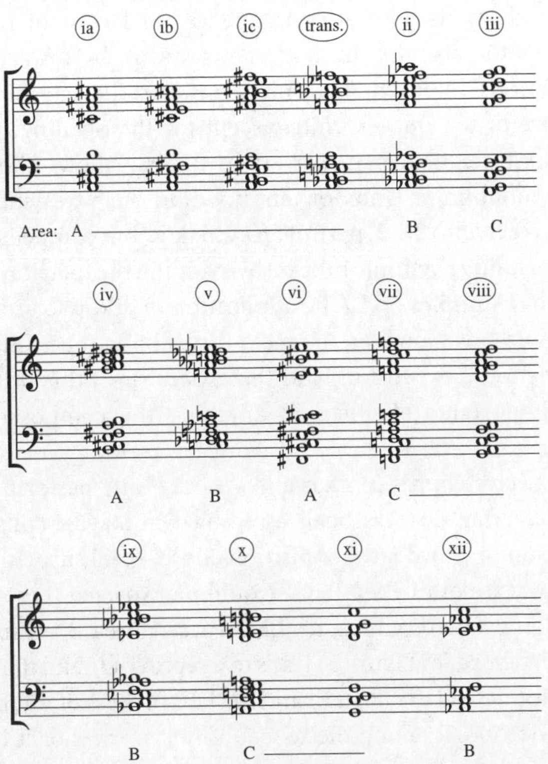

fifths terms, theoretically below A♭) to produce all pitches of the A♭ major scale except G (chord v); then a pentatonic aggregate with the bass note B♭ (chord ix); and finally, returning to a bass note of A♭, two pairs segmented from the original 'stack' of fifths on A♭ (chord xii). A single transitional, thirteenth chord (marked 'trans' in Ex. 4.14) mediates between Areas A and B, transposing all pitches but one of chord ic down a semitone to produce the pitch content of the 'stacked' fifths above A♭ characteristic of Area B, but retaining the bass note A♮ as the fifth pitch.

Area C – to be found in chords iii, vii, viii, x and xi – is constructed on the sequence of bass notes F F G A G, and is also built on 'stacked' fifths (from F upwards) to produce 'white-note' aggregates revealing their 'stacked'-fifths origins to the listener more clearly than do the chords of Areas A and B. The first, four-pitch aggregate on F (chord iii) returns in a different form on G (chord xi) to conclude this group. Chords vii and viii add A to the 'stack' of fifths, the former assembled on the bass note F, the latter on G. Chord x, on the bass note A, adds E and B, expanding the 'stack' of fifths to produce all seven 'white' notes.

Glass cleverly juxtaposes these three tonal areas, leading the listener to perceive a logic to the progression of his chords, yet periodically doubling back to delay its natural consequences in favour of repeating a whole sequence to raise the dramatic temperature by thwarting the listener's expectations. In purely rhythmic terms, Part Eleven is simply an extended sequence of ten-quaver units; except for the opening, whose expansion from six to eight to ten quavers in the bar allows chord i to assemble further doublings. Units of ten, dividing their two subdivisions of five quavers each into 2 + 3, permit an even flow, but compensate for the lack of any expanding rhythmic process by avoiding the metric predictability produced by multiples of 4. The application of additive process to harmonic motion itself is, however, the main thrust behind Part Eleven's unfolding, allowing tonal expansion, and the expectations this brings, to take on a more important role than in anything the composer had previously written.

The twelve chords of Example 4.14 are only performed as a complete sequence after this has been assembled in stages. Following the initial exposition of chord i, the transition chord – still surprising even after the chromatic scales of Part Ten – would be expected to move the harmony from the A♮-based Area A to the A♭-based Area B. At first, however, the return of chord ic (Figure 5) leads to a repeat of ic and the transition chord before the arrival of chords ii and iii. This process of doubling back is then used twice more, taking the sequence first from chords ic to viii (Figures 9–17), and finally to the complete twelve-chord progression (Figures 18–30).

The function of the two female voices in this process is crucial, their oscillating dyads doing as much, sometimes more, to point the path of harmonic movement as do the bass line, the periodic scale passages or any other structural devices to be found in the instrumental parts. For instance, the descending C B♭ in the voice parts of Figure 6 (transition chord) is followed very naturally by the A♭C of Figure 7 (chord ii), which leads equally smoothly to the G C of Figure 8 (chord iii). The voices thus suggest – more than does the bass line's shifts from A♮ to A♭ to F, though the latter is followed by G in the actual arpeggiation – that the goal of this progression really lies in the C major of Area C, potentially extending the feeling of suspension generated by chord iii to some more permanent resolution. Yet the first time we heard the descending C B♭ in the transition chord (Figure 4), it was followed, in the doubling-back process, by the abruptly juxtaposed A C♯ of Area A's chord ic. In addition, any hints of impending resolution offered by chord iii are in turn thwarted by avoidance of the 'white-note' Area C in the choice of modality all this chord's successors are permitted: the Area A of chord ic again in Figure 9, of chord iv in Figure 13 and, after repetitions of this whole sequence, the Area B of chords ix (Figure 27) and xii (Figure 30).

Though Part Eleven concludes in Area B, both other tonal areas are notable for their expansion during its course. This expansion takes different forms. Area A's addition of D♯s (Figures 13 and 22) pushes its A-major modality towards its dominant, while chord vi – with its bass note F♯ and, again, in particular the voice parts, which oscillate F♯ B – suggests a suspension on the dominant of B major. The chords of Area C also fluctuate in the number of pitches they employ; more significant, though, is the progressive importance of its 'white-note' modality as the complete chord sequence unravels.

Such still ambiguously shifting tonal areas were now to be superseded by chordal progressions articulating harmonic motion with greater direction and consistency, and integrating this more thoroughly with additive process. In Part Twelve, Glass replaces the three areas of Part Eleven with just two. The first, the new Area A – an added-sixth chord on the major triad of A, the key which had already dominated the previous three movements – could not be simpler, and its arpeggiations retain a firm hold on the root position of this chord throughout the whole twenty minutes of the concluding movement. The second, Area B – a chromatic sequence beginning with an added-fourth chord on C minor, the key of Parts Four and Seven, and a strong candidate for the goal of Part Eleven – is quite complex; its ramifications become the determining factor in the work's denouement, despite the fact that A major has the final say.

Example 4.15 gives a harmonic outline of Part Twelve. During the opening three-and-a-half minutes, A^6 and C-minor^4 chords alternate in the kind of expanding then contracting rhythmic process long the stock-in-trade of the composer's output. For a further two minutes, C-minor^4 is joined by what Glass himself seems to regard as an added-fourth chord on B♭, though it is also interpretable as an added-second chord on E♭; this pair of tonally related aggregates now contrasts with the single aggregate of Area A. As Area B continues to expand, however, its starting point on C and tonal focus on a key signature of three flats are dissolved in a sequence of triads juxtaposed with surprising abandon. B major and A♭ major arrive as a linked pair; the other four – major triads on E♭, D♭, D♮ and E♮ – are similarly linked, joining the sequence at about nine-and-a-half minutes into the movement. This constitutes what the performance materials for the work term Part Twelve A.

The sustained tonal expansion of Area B, at first forming such a contrast with that of Area A, makes it seem likely that it will devour the latter and conclude the work in the ambiguous chromatic space which Area B has surprisingly opened up. Part Twelve B initially confirms that suspicion,

Example 4.15 *Music in Twelve Parts*, Part Twelve, harmonic outline

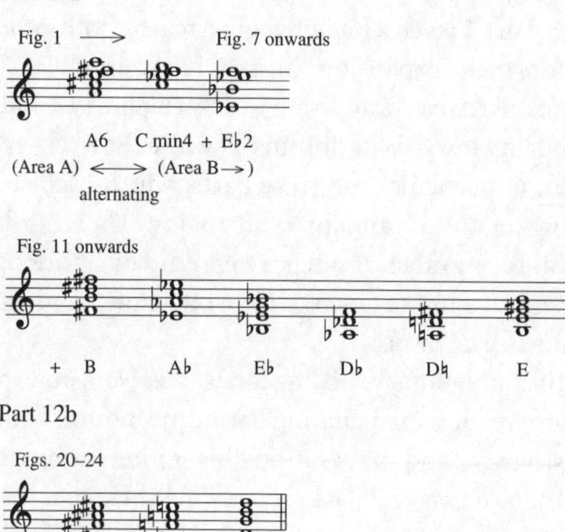

adding, some three minutes further on, three more major triads – on F♯, F♮ and G – to complete the formation of triads on all twelve pitch classes. These chromatic sequences have, however, three rather different functions. Firstly, they describe a swift and bumpy ride through the chromatic gamut which, in Part Twelve A, has already included chords on all three pitches – D, E♭ and E♮ – which failed to find a place either as the main key of an individual movement or of one of its separate tonal areas. Secondly, Glass's choice of triads in Part Twelve A has a more specific, and audible, tonal function. Initially moving freely between flat and sharp keys, its final four chords not only include all the above-mentioned roots, D, E♭ and E♮ (plus D♭), but also conclude with E major, the dominant of the A^6 of Area A to which the completed sequence of Area B now leads. This link between the two alternating Areas A and B brings them together as ultimately a single process of 'preparation' (a chromatic sequence moving from distant tonal terrain to the dominant) and 'resolution' (the tonic A of Part Twelve, and indeed of *Music in Twelve Parts* as a whole). Thirdly, with the aid of such renewed confirmation in the potential of harmonic motion, the cumulatively unfolding procession of chords in Parts 12 A and B taken together creates a powerful sense of dramatic tension and resolution as a fitting climax to a composition several hours long.

Music in Twelve Parts has been viewed as 'a musical lexicon of Seventies minimalism';[82] in 1992, the composer still hoped that it would 'keep his purist fans happy'. But if the consolidation of sonic impact, and the concomitant concern with texture and psycho-acoustics, already redefines the minimalism of *Music with Changing Parts*, its successor's extension and clarification of these render *Music in Twelve Parts* more clearly 'post-minimalist'. Conducted in the context of such a rich display of rhythmic techniques – some old, some new – these tonal discoveries were soon to show their composer the path to a stage work in which even more extended structures would be impelled by the harmonic motion already explored in what is one of Glass's most captivating compositions.

Einstein on the Beach

In the early 1970s, Glass says, he and Robert Wilson 'shared the same community of support'[83] in and around SoHo, and that they 'were bound to meet'. Not for the first time, though, the composer was fortunate in encountering the right person to help him at the right time of his career.

Glass first saw Wilson's work at the Brooklyn Academy of Music in 1973, and met this 'rapidly emerging . . . formidable theater [talent]' at the cast party afterwards. The work he saw, *The Life and Times of Joseph Stalin* (1972), lasts – like its predecessor, *The Life and Times of Sigmund Freud* (1969) – around twelve hours. *Stalin* is a seven-act play which, like other works of his before *Einstein*, Wilson himself called an 'opera'; it ran from 7pm to 7am and had a cast of 144. Expansiveness in one direction is, though, offset by a positively minimalist reduction in another. In Wilson's predominantly visual theatre, the action is sparse and glacially slow; the importance of such texts as exist is minimised rather than emphasised through repetition. When words are used, Wilson was already frequently employing the unusual talents of Christopher Knowles, an autistic boy whose alienation from 'normal' approaches to language clearly struck Wilson as having both practical and metaphorical parallels with his own; outside the theatre, he was also working extensively with handicapped children at this time.

Sheer length forms the most obvious connection between *Music in Twelve Parts* and the theatrical concerns with which Glass was now to become heavily re-engaged in the collaboration on *Einstein*. On the one hand, such drastic extension of theatrical time could be said to aid the creation of an experimental artistic space, a kind of theatre which sought to avoid all the connotations of 'narrative' and even characterisation in a quest for new kinds of experience which were image-based and tended to distort not only 'real time' but also previous kinds of 'theatrical time'. On the other, the construction of such a large edifice clearly necessitated decisions about the ordering, as well as the content, of its building blocks, and decisions about what sort of effect those building blocks would have. Was any cumulative effect to be entirely avoided? And could dramatic notions of the sort already countenanced by Glass in the 'pure' music of *Music in Twelve Parts* play some role?

The drama

Dramatic considerations were, of course, primarily Wilson's concern, and the main artistic thrust of *Einstein on the Beach* has often been interpreted as coming from the theatrical rather than the musical side. (The question of who the real creator of *Einstein* was subsequently contributed to the break-up of the collaboration between Glass and Wilson. Glass was, though, one of several composers involved with Wilson's massive *the CIVIL warS* project in 1984. More recently, the two have worked together again: for instance, on *Monsters of Grace* and *The White Raven*, both premièred in 1998.) The composer's experience of experimental drama, and his understanding of Khatikali theatre, with its (by Western standards) unusual sense of time, gave him both knowledge of, and ideas of his own about, the potential of what Wilson came to call a 'theatre of images'. Besides, *Einstein* is probably unique – even by the standards of experimental theatre of the 1960s and 1970s – for its integration of music, image, dance and speech into what previous terminology can only label a theatrical *Gesamtkunstwerk*.

Glass and Wilson decided at that 1973 party to investigate the possibility of working together, and from the spring of 1974 they met, sometimes weekly, for the next year or so. The work's subject was decided after the composer had rejected his new colleague's earlier suggestions of Hitler and Chaplin as their central focus. Later, Glass was to argue that *Einstein* was the first in a trilogy of operas; this first 'panel' represented not only Einstein himself but also 'science: technology and ecology'.[84] Yet this is probably commercially conceived as well as retrospective; it also implies more common ground between the performance-art-orientated *Einstein* and the more 'regular' operas, *Satyagraha* and *Akhnaten*, which followed. As is clear, the choice of Albert Einstein – the physicist whose discoveries made possible the creation of, among other things, the atom bomb – was to a degree extraneous to Wilson and Glass's main concerns. Wilson, though, saw the work as 'a poetic exploration of Einstein',[85] who is treated as essentially a mythic character. Since the historical Einstein was an amateur fiddle player, a solo violinist occupied a prominent place, visually as well as musically, dressed to look like the scientist as an old man. (In the forty-odd performances of the original 1976 production, this role was taken by Robert Brown; for the first recording – made in the spring of 1977, at the former Big Apple Recording Studios on Greene Street – Paul Zukofsky, the still young but already well-known professional soloist, took over.) While he plays a crucial musical role, this Einstein does not participate in the stage action; occupying a raised dais in the orchestra pit, he is, rather, a witness to the events on stage, and arguably not 'really' the character, imagined or otherwise, at all.

Einstein on the Beach on Wall Street – as it was originally called (for no clear reason) – was conceived from a series of drawings made by Wilson following some general agreement between him and Glass on themes, length and the work's division into four acts, with a total of nine scenes and five connecting sections. The latter Wilson termed 'Knee Plays', explaining that this clarified their 'joining function'.[86] In its first performances, the resulting work lasted almost exactly five-and-a-half hours without intermission. The following description is of the 1976 production, for which, given *Einstein*'s nature, Wilson was naturally designer as well as director.

In *Einstein*, theme and structure are ordered not by narrative, either spoken or even merely mimed, but by a kind of loose association built around three recurring visual images: a train, a trial and something called Field with Spaceship. Act I deals with the train and the trial; Act II with the spaceship and a reworking of the train image, which has now become Night Train. Act III combines the trial with a prison, and follows this with a second Field with Spaceship scene. Act IV is concerned with the radical transmutation of all these images into new ones: the train becomes a building, the trial a bed, and the field now simply a spaceship. These transmutations have been interpreted in terms of Einstein's theory of relativity. It is easy to see how a train, the most commonly used illustration of relativity theory, might form part of such a reading; and it is not hard to read the Act IV Spaceship scene – the work's final 'main' scene, with its wildly flashing lights and belching smoke, its collapsing astronauts and, just to make the point more than merely relatively clear, the equation $E=Mc^2$ on the curtain which then descends – as a vision of nuclear holocaust. On the other hand, the process by which a trial becomes a bed, which itself resembles a beam of light, is more elusive.

While all this can be taken as the main action (however resistant parts of it are to interpretation), the five Knee Plays which form the prologue, interludes and epilogue to the four acts seem of equal significance in both length and dramatic content, even though Knee Play 1 is already in progress as the audience is admitted to the auditorium. The subject matter of these Knee Plays is, though, related only obliquely to that of the 'main' acts; as a result, they are even more difficult to decode. In the Knee Plays, two women (Lucinda Childs and Sheryl Sutton in the first performances) sit at tables placed at the front of the stage to the right; in Knee Play 4 they lie on glass tables, and for the fifth they become Two Lovers sitting on a park bench. Other images counterpoint their action (or inaction): all, like their own movements and words (which here take on greater importance than elsewhere), potentially related to Einstein's achievements, or even to the figure of Einstein himself, in some way.

While image- rather than text-driven, *Einstein* contains important spoken material. This consists of several texts by Knowles, and one each by Samuel M. Johnson (an elderly amateur who auditioned for an acting role and turned out to have a curious creative talent) and Childs (primarily a dancer and choreographer – she was, as we have seen, one of the two women in the Knee Plays – whose work in these areas also contributed much to the original production). These eleven texts are simply read: some are poetic in form, some prose, some a combination of the two. Nothing in their imagery relates in any obvious way to the simultaneous stage action; their respect for grammar, and even straightforward meaning, is sometimes only intermittent. The only text (the one by Childs) even to refer to either Einstein or the beach (only the latter, in fact) concerns *avoidance* of the beach. Yet narrative as well as grammatical sense of some sort is by no means entirely avoided in these spoken texts. Sung material, on the other hand, is confined to numbers and *solfège* syllables. The action covers a wide variety of stylised motion and dance, in which some of the singers themselves took part. For the 1976 performances, Andrew de Groat, who had worked previously with Wilson, choreographed the dance ensembles, while Childs composed her own dance solos. The two remaining original solo roles were taken by Paul Mann (who played a young boy) and the already mentioned Johnson (who played an old man).

The music

Musically, *Einstein on the Beach* is a natural development from *Music in Twelve Parts*. But whereas that work applies a vocabulary of techniques to structures which are still essentially based on rhythmic devices, Glass now turned, as he puts it, 'to problems of harmonic structure or, more accurately, structural harmony – new solutions to problems of harmonic usage, where the evolution of material can become the basis of an overall formal structure intrinsic to the music itself'.[87]

Einstein in fact draws on an intervening work for the Philip Glass Ensemble called *Another Look at Harmony*, a large-scale piece in four sections, begun in the spring of 1975. Parts One and Two of this became the basis of the opening scenes of the opera's first two acts, 'the starting points from which additional material and devices were developed'. Though this other work was not completed until 1977, the year after *Einstein*'s première performances, the overlap between the two compositions is considerable, rendering any detailed comment on *Another Look at Harmony* superfluous. The significance of harmony, already established as a newly expressive as well as structural element in *Music in Twelve Parts*, is now accompanied, in *Einstein*, by a tonal plan even more extended and complex than that of the earlier work. This is given as Example 4.16.

The shift of focus towards tonal motion did not, of course, mean that Glass's previous rhythmic and other related technical apparatus had now been abandoned. The continuing use of additive and cyclic processes is often clarified by the extensive use of sung numbers and *solfège*; the solo violin part is also audibly based on such structures. The use of voices in *Music with Changing Parts* and *Music in Twelve Parts* is now extended and formalised, with the sung *solfège* syllables already found in the latter work supplemented with numbers. Both solo and choral singers act more independently of the instrumental ensemble, their roles considerably enhanced from those of the vocalists in the earlier works. This greater conventionality, relatively speaking, is even more noticeable in Glass's reduced interest in psycho-acoustic effects. The larger forces might have suggested new possibilities in this territory; but in fact they encouraged a more familiar separation into vocal and instrumental, melody and accompaniment, foreground and background, than before.

The opera is bounded by a clear cadential progression in C major: a vi–v–i repeating bass line in that key provides the sole material for the Prologue and the chaconne bass above which the framing Knee Plays 1 and 5 unfold their elaborations. While *Einstein* is scarcely 'in C major', individual sections use different tonalities to articulate a totality which, especially when experienced in the theatre, exhibits a surprisingly conventional approach to such matters as proportion and climax. Though C major itself is confined to the Knee Plays, the structural ambiguity of these sections (are they 'main action' or merely 'interludes'?) if anything enhances the importance of this key in the opera as a whole.

Besides, other tonalities in *Einstein* are related to C major. A minor first occurs in Trial (Act I, scene ii) and the immediately following Knee Play 2. In Dance 1 (Act II, scene i), this gives way to a rather unstable D minor that allows A to emerge as its dominant in terms of long-range tonal development. This A/D relationship is replicated later on: in Trial 2/Prison (Act III, scene i), a Phrygian-A tonality acts as a preface to the fairly chromatic

Example 4.16 *Einstein on the Beach*, tonal structure

Prologue	A, G, C repeating bass
Knee Play 1	C major
Act I	
Scene 1: Train	a) Pentatonic 'A flat major' (the key signature is three flats, but no D flats, or Gs, occur, and E flat is clearly the dominant, not the tonic) b) Pentatonic 'E flat major' (instrumental) c) F minor modulating constantly to E major
Scene 2: Trial	A minor 'rootless' four-chord sequence ('All Men Are Equal') plus two-chord link to
Knee Play 2	A minor alternating with F minor>E major five-chord progression
Act II	
Scene 1: Dance 1	D minor (unstable)
Scene 2: Night Train	Pentatonic A flat major
Knee Play 3	F minor modulating to E major (both keys and the modulation more ambiguous than in Train 1, but the relationship is clear) alternating with C major (a stepwise contrary-motion version of the original chaconne)

Example 4.16 (*cont.*)

Act III

Scene 1: Trial 2/Prison	Phrygian mode on A
Scene 2: Dance 2	D minor (chromatically inflected)
Knee Play 4	F minor/E major alternating with C major

(Knee 4 as a whole is a further variation of Train/Knee 3)

Act IV

Scene 1: Building/Train	Pentatonic 'A flat major'
Scene 2: Bed/Trial	A minor (including organ cadenza), 'rootless' four-chord sequence
Scene 3: Spaceship	F minor/E major (more akin again to Train 1) alternating and combining with A minor (but scale patterns only, quickly becoming highly chromatic and soon discernible as a further variation on the F minor/E major sequence rather than on A)
Knee Play 5	C major (as Knee 1)

D minor of the ensuing Dance 2 (Act III, scene ii). The tonality of the Dance scenes – uneasily dissonant though both dances are, in ways untypical of the opera as a whole – suggests that C major, A minor and D minor, together with their modal and chromatic extensions, can be understood as a single group of keys central to *Einstein*'s progress: a view reinforced by the return of A minor in the crucial Bed/Trial (Act IV, scene ii).

Another group of tonalities, however, proves to have greater significance than this. In Train (Act I, scene i), a pentatonic scale (A♭ B♭ D♭ E♭ G♭) is inflected by the emphasis which the bass line gives, first to A♭, then to E♭; this is succeeded by an F-minor arpeggio. A pentatonic/F-minor 'hinge' is used in the lead-back to the entry of the voices in the alternating vocal-plus-instrumental and purely instrumental sections of this scene. It is clear that *Einstein* deploys a group of keys centring around A♭ major/F minor: Night Train (Act II, scene ii) has the same pentatonic character as Train; so has the much later Building/Train (Act IV, scene i). In Train itself, however, the F-minor arpeggio acquires a bass line, B♭ C, and moves, not into F minor, but to an arpeggiated and repeated F-minor/E-major modulation. Despite its initial air of being a mere offshoot of the already established A♭ territory, it is this F-minor/E-major 'cadential pattern' which occupies a central position in the opera's overall structure, integrating local harmonic motion and long-range tonal planning.

Glass calls this five-chord cadential pattern '[t]he most prominent "theme" of the opera';[88] this is given as Example 4.17c. Following its appearance in Train, it occurs in Knee Plays 2, 3 and 4, and furnishes almost the entire basis of Spaceship (Act IV, scene iii). As the composer himself points out, '[w]hat makes the formula distinctive and even useful is . . . the way in which the IV♭ (B𝄫) becomes IV (A) of the new key, thereby making the phrase resolve a half-step lower. This, in turn, provides the leading tone for the original i (F minor). As it is a formula which invites repetition, it is particularly suited to my kind of musical thinking'. This progression's strong character cunningly avoids the potential monotony of having long stretches of music in one key; it derives much of its impact in *Einstein*, indeed, from its sharp contrast with other, more harmonically static, sections.

The F-minor/E-major pattern is limited by its property of looping back on itself, the final arpeggio of E major leading – with an inevitability admittedly enforced more by familiarity through extended repetition than by conformity to the grammatical conventions of tonal music – directly to the return of F minor, thus locking the progression into itself. And in the short term, its function may seem more colouristic than structural: Train (Act I, scene i) returns after about two minutes to its previous alternations.

At the end of this scene, however, the F-minor/E-major 'theme' returns, bringing a finality which the other material could not have done. More importantly, the concluding E major now provides a link, not back to F minor – or, thinking in longer-range terms, to A♭ – as the repetition has by this time taught us to expect, but to the modal A minor of the next scene, Trial. In other words, the F-minor/E-major cadential pattern offers the crucial connection between the two main tonal groups of *Einstein* (C major/A minor/D minor and A♭ major/F minor). The incessant repetitions of this pattern cause E major to take on the role of the dominant, thereby making the arrival of the unambiguous A minor of the Trial scene a natural step. As in the closing stages of *Music in Twelve Parts*, Glass is putting the discoveries of his earlier compositions to good use in the contexts of harmonic progression and tonal resolution, musical drama and long-range structural planning.

This cadential pattern is in fact the last of what the composer calls the three 'themes' which form the basis of the opening Train scene and are developed elsewhere; their deployment offers a good illustration of Glass's basic working methods in *Einstein.* Example 4.17a, based on the combination of two patterns of different lengths, shows, on a simple level, the continued working of cyclic processes in the opera. Example 4.17b, a reworking of this idea, is itself developed further in Building/Train (Act IV, scene i); it demonstrates how Glass continues to construct repeated figures into sequences by means of additive process. Example 4.17c, the F-minor/E-major pattern itself, also functions as the first of five elements which the composer describes as the 'musical material of the opera . . . 5 chords, 4 chords, 3 chords, 2 chords and 1 chord'.[89] The opening F-minor harmony of Example 4.17c provides the starting point for the four-chord pattern, which ends on D major (see Ex. 4.18a). First heard at the end of Trial (Act I, scene ii), it also occurs in Trial 2/Prison (Act III, scene i) and Bed/Trial (Act IV, scene ii). Example 4.18b demonstrates how this is subjected to rhythmic expansion in the first of these three scenes. The three-chord theme (Ex. 4.19a) is reserved for the two Dance scenes (Act II, scene i, and Act III, scene ii) and revolves around D minor. Examples 4.19b and 4.19c show the two-chord and one-chord material: the former oscillating between A-minor^7 and G-minor^7 in Trial 2/Prison (Act III, scene i); the latter outlining A-minor^7 (plus D♮) in the arpeggiated figures to be found in Trial (Act I, scene ii), Trial 2/Prison (Act III, scene i) and Bed/Trial (Act IV, scene ii).

As a further illustration of Glass's structural inventiveness within an individual scene, Knee Play 3's spare, much altered version, for unaccompanied chorus, of the five-chord F-minor/E-major progression is typical

Example 4.17 *Einstein on the Beach*, Train: (a) Figure 2 (First theme); (b) Figure 20 (Second theme); (c) Figure 59 (Third theme; five-chord cadential pattern).

(*a*)

(*b*)

Example 4.17 (*cont.*)

(*c*)

Example 4.18 *Einstein on the Beach*, Trial: (a) Figure 53; (b) Figure 54.

(*a*)

(*b*)

Example 4.19 *Einstein on the Beach*: (a) Dance 1, Figures 1–2; (b) Trial 2/Prison, Figures 11–13; (c) Trial, Figures 20–3.

(*a*)

(*b*)

Example 4.19 (*cont.*)

(*c*)

(see Ex. 4.20). What started as a ceaseless round of arpeggiations has now become a rarefied, angular reinterpretation of the plain triads of the original progression strung in an additive process on sung numbers. In between two presentations of an 8+8+8+10 repetitive scheme, with pauses between each group, comes the variation, again *a cappella*, on the opening chaconne; a reduced version of this also forms a coda. The second presentation of the main section makes further substitutions – the opening F-minor chord, for instance, is reduced simply to a unison C♮ – and is structurally reduced to repetitions of 6+6.

In Dance 2 (Act III, scene ii), just two scenes later, the spaceship already seen in the earlier Dance scene (Act II, scene i) draws nearer. The positioning of this scene around *Einstein*'s point of Golden Section underlines its pivotal status; the two Dance scenes are, for Glass, 'two pillars equidistant from either end of the opera'. It is here that the three-chord 'theme' (Ex. 4.19a) makes its second and final appearance. By its end, we are almost exactly three-quarters of the way through *Einstein*, according to the performance timings of the 1993 recording. After Knee Play 4, Building/Train (Act IV, scene i) takes up the challenge to find a way forward to a conclusion in such dramatically and musically ambiguous circumstances by displaying the greatest contrast the opera offers between static and developmental harmony. The latter is rendered almost ironic by occupying only the scene's concluding seconds. Before this, for some ten minutes, a single harmony – the pentatonic chord familiar from Train and Night Train – is subjected to an additive rhythmic process on two chords; meanwhile, chords built from these notes swell and die away periodically in the chorus (these are in theory improvised), and woodwind – chiefly a tenor saxophone – improvise around the chord, unconfined to the prevailing pentatony. Surprisingly static by the new harmonic standards *Einstein* has set, in context this scene offers a palpable feeling of expectation. Suddenly, all this ceases, and out of nowhere comes the F-minor/E-major five-chord

Example 4.20 *Einstein on the Beach*, Knee Play 3, Figure 1

progression, played four times – impatiently, urgently – in familiar arpeggiated form by winds and organs.

Bed/Trial (Act IV, scene ii) opens with an organ cadenza that, in the score, consists simply of a few modal scalic passages around A; on the 1993 recording, Riesman plays a two-minute solo that seems deliberately reminiscent of Bach, and even Monteverdi, in its elaborations (an example of stylistic allusion more familiar from recent Glass and Adams). Bed proper then continues with the laid-back, modal A minor of Trial and Knee Play 2, plus the four-chord progression of Example 4.18a, seeming to thwart the denouement Building/Train promised.

A Prelude and Aria now further interrupt the progress of the action: the former a much-reduced version of the A-minor material of Trial for solo organ; the latter an eight-minute vocalise for soprano and organ (see Ex. 4.21), the ethereal, triadically harmonised melody of which – spun over the Trial scene's four-chord progression (Exs. 4.18a and b) – offers something quite new in Glass's music. Then, with Spaceship (Act IV, scene iii), we finally reach the climax for which the previous scenes have prepared us, all the greater in impact for having been so long delayed. The preceding scene has given the wind players the break they needed to make their ascent to the high stage gantry where, amidst the flashing lights and general mayhem of Wilson's representation not merely of space flight but also of nuclear holocaust, they too become part of the action. Musically, Spaceship offers the only possible *dénouement*: a wild fantasy at first based entirely on the five-chord F-minor/E-major progression, now subjected to an extended additive process. The expanding bass line of this underpins the revolving arpeggios of the upper instrumental lines (unbroken except by brief recourse to repeated notes), the chanted numbers of the chorus and the more sustained *solfège* of the solo soprano with an ever more emphatic insistence that this repeated modulation is somehow the key to the whole work. In the later stages of this first section, the chorus abandons its number-chanting for *solfège*.

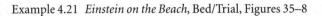

Example 4.21 *Einstein on the Beach*, Bed/Trial, Figures 35–8

Then, prepared only by the extent to which the concluding E major of this progression retains any shreds of its dominant propensities, instruments alone launch into the fast and furious modal A-minor scales from Trial. Subject first to additive and subtractive process, they then turn more chromatic and plunge back into the F-minor/E-major progression. Chromaticism soon infects the bass line of this as well, eventually causing the loss of the final E-major chord. The repetitions of this version sound at once more regular (four- rather than five-bar sequences) and more awkward (the jump from B^7 to the F-minor triad takes some getting used to). Instrumental chromatic scales in parallel fifths lead to a concluding burst of the full five-chord progression, which takes us to the C major of the final Knee Play 5 and the music with which *Einstein on the Beach* began.

The music of *Einstein* still avoids the full implications of narrative and of thematic structuring, just as it avoids a firm commitment to the directed motion of classical tonality. The capability musical minimalism possesses to move flexibly between different grammars for what remains a reassuringly familiar vocabulary is perhaps demonstrated more completely and more successfully in *Einstein on the Beach* than in any other work by Glass. On the one hand, the larger formal units, as well as the timbres Glass chooses, have an experimental 'rough edge' to them. The opera's large scale, too, still allows it to operate in what its composer calls 'non-colloquial time'. On the other hand, the awakening of interest in harmonic progression and directed motion leads him to notate this music using barred metres and rounded phrasing: for the first time, Glass's music 'hugs' the bar line. Sections are much more clearly demarcated; while this might be considered inevitable with such a long work, it is true of sub-sections within the larger units as well.

A sense of motion, of development, is, moreover, indulgently celebrated in *Einstein*'s overall shaping. Glass – reliant to some degree, of course, on Wilson here, as elsewhere – is almost manipulative in the way he deals with the opera's dramatic unfolding so that, as he says, it 'works towards a finale; you can't miss it. A real finale; a real razzle-dazzle finale', he calls it: 'a piece that left the audience standing'. This is borne out by experience of the opera in the theatre; the last Spaceship scene has, indeed, a terrific feeling of release about it, which is all the greater coming, as it does, after about four hours strung on the tensions of Wilson's static stage pictures and Glass's repetitive patterns. Encountering the work in the theatrical space for which it was conceived – rather than experiencing it on record alone – confirms the impression that *Einstein on the Beach* is another masterpiece of late twentieth-century music.

The composer's increasing interest in tonally directed motion forms the crucial link between his music of the early 1970s, especially the final stages of *Music in Twelve Parts*, and the whole of his later, 'post-minimalist' development. It was this exploration of harmonic motion, however limited at this stage, which was to allow Glass to move into more conventional operatic territory after 1976. For all his previous interest in finding a complementary approach to 'non-narrative' theatre, the composer seems to have come to the conclusion that music-theatre is only sustainable if the stage action is complemented by something resembling familiar tonal motion, no matter how vague, or intermittent. In *Satyagraha* (1980), his first 'proper opera', each scene is constructed on a 'chaconne' bass with harmonic elaborations above it. In the arrival of the chord progression, Glass had forced some rapprochement with functional harmony. In this first really thorough exploration of a vocal line quarried from the chords of a simple tonal progression, he had now discovered a new meaning and purpose for melody: another essential ingredient of opera. In *Satyagraha*, opera singers are required to sing words with quite clear meanings for both character development and plot, even if the text is in Sanskrit – and the plot unchronological. Such expansion, both technically and stylistically, also gave Glass the opportunity to explore further the links with more popular musical forms already established via the sound-world and energy of his ensemble.

Conclusion

Much of Glass's activity since the late 1970s, and a great deal of his influence, can in fact be charted in the arena of rock music and the achievements of a wide popularity for music with a clear beat which also has a tune. The composer's willingness to get involved with the rock world on several levels – to promote his own work on a highly commercial basis, and even as a record producer for other musicians (for instance, Polyrock and The Raybeats in the late 1970s) – has made him much the best known of the four subjects of this book.

Glass was, though, involved with rock from early on. While this initially related to his downtown Manhattan roots, his early European performances, as well as the Chatham Square recordings, gained him a reputation in Britain, West Germany and elsewhere as a seminal influence on the art-rock of the 1970s. The composer's impact on German groups was probably the earliest and in some respects the most significant; among these were Cluster, Kraftwerk, Neu! and the bands involved with what became known as the German wave of 'metronomic' keyboard music. In Germany, too, Glass met Tangerine Dream; the group helped him obtain the contract for Virgin Records which resulted not only in the release of Parts 1 and 2 of *Music in Twelve Parts* in 1975, but also, two years later, of *North Star*.

David Bowie and Brian Eno – who both heard the composer's music in London in 1971 – have been particularly influenced by Glass. Eno's first album with Robert Fripp – *No Pussyfooting* (1973) – is an early example, evidently indebted to the sustained pitches of *Music with Changing Parts*, which was performed in Glass's first London concerts. Eno's 'ambient music' is but one example of the influence of minimalism on his later work. With Bowie, the debt is clearest on the *Low* and *Heroes* albums of 1977, on which Eno was a collaborator. In the 1990s, Glass has written 'symphonic commentaries' on both these. More clearly commercial developments in rock music have also been affected by Glass's early music: for instance, the disco and syntho-pop of the late 1970s, of which Giorgio Moroder's Donna Summer seventeen-minute disco record, 'Love to Love You' of 1975 is probably the most notorious example.

It was only after the tour of *Einstein on the Beach* in 1976 that Glass became seriously involved with Manhattan rock clubs and the then current punk and post-punk movements. From the late 1970s, his ensemble began to play in more 'mainstream' rock venues such as New York's Peppermint Lounge and the Roxy in Los Angeles. Art-rock developments in downtown Manhattan which were influenced by Glass's example, in the 1970s and beyond, include everything from the more obviously rock-orientated band Theoretical Girls to the more experimental work of such composer-performers as Glenn Branca (who early on worked with Theoretical Girls) and Rhys Chatham. Following *Songs from Liquid Days* – his 1986 album of songs with lyrics and vocals provided by a range of major rock and 'alternative' rock singers – Glass's more recent collaborators have included the British artist Richard James, more familiarly known as Aphex Twin.

While Glass has never commanded the respect and attention given to Reich in the Western classical arena, his influence has been felt both there and in developments which, like the composer's own, have sought to cross the boundaries between such categories of music-making. His later operas, in particular, have been staged worldwide, making a particularly strong impression in Germany, where the complete *Einstein–Satyagraha–Akhnaten* trilogy was assembled in Stuttgart in the 1980s. While Michael Nyman has been personally closer to Reich, his root-based chord techniques and vigorous rhythmic style have more in common with Glass. And where Glass and Nyman have led, a whole host of younger composers of all nationalities has followed.

Perhaps the most interesting aspect of Glass's subsequent development has been his ability to work in several musical fields at once, crossing and recrossing the borders normally erected between, for instance, 'concert music' and opera on the one hand, and popular songs, music for films and even television advertising on the other. Practically speaking, the composer has achieved this by taking on more obviously commercial work in order to subsidise his more experimental projects: especially the challenging theatrical and film works such as *1,000 Airplanes on the Roof* (1988) and the operatic setting of the Jean Cocteau film *La Belle et la Bête* (1994). Musically speaking, while it would be foolish to suggest that there is complete uniformity of style between the outputs in each of these territories, the connections between them are more evident than their differences. If the true musical minimalism of the 1960s and early 1970s emerged as a consequence of a realignment of avant-garde, 'cultivated' and 'vernacular' elements which he helped to bring about, then the international, and post-modernist, 'post-minimalism' that has further eroded such previously significant boundaries in the 1980s and 1990s likewise owes much to the example of Philip Glass.

Notes

Introduction

1 From the author's interviews with the composers. Observations of this kind, including direct quotations, which remain unreferenced in this volume are for the most part taken from these sources.
2 Sol Le Witt, 'Paragraphs on Conceptual Art', *Artforum*, 8/5 (June 1967), p. 80.
3 Lawrence Alloway, 'Serial Forms', originally published in the catalogue for the exhibition 'American Sculpture of the 60s' (arranged by Maurice Tuchman at the Los Angeles County Museum, 1967); reprinted in *Topics in American Art Since 1945* (New York: Norton, 1975), p. 95.
4 Tom Johnson, 'The Minimal Slow-Motion Approach: Alvin Lucier and Others', originally published in the *Village Voice*, 30 March 1972; reprinted in *The Voice of New Music: New York City 1972–1982* (Eindhoven: Het Apollohuis, 1989), pp. 31–3.
5 Johnson, *The Voice of New Music*, p. 27.
6 Johnson, 'Philip Glass's New Parts', originally published in the *Village Voice*, 6 April 1972; reprinted in *The Voice of New Music*, pp. 33–5.
7 Johnson, 'LaMonte Young, Steve Reich, Terry Riley, Philip Glass', originally published in the *Village Voice*, 7 September 1972; reprinted in *The Voice of New Music*, pp. 43–5.
8 Originally published in the *Village Voice*, 13 June 1977; reprinted in Johnson, *The Voice of New Music*, pp. 296–8.
9 Michael Nyman, 'Minimal music', *The Spectator*, 221/7320 (Friday 11 October, 1968), pp. 518–19.
10 John Cage, 'COMPOSITION: To Describe the Process of Composition Used in *Music of Changes* and *Imaginary Landscape No. 4*', originally published as part of 'Four Musicians at Work', *trans/formation*, 1/3 (1952); reprinted in *Silence* (Middletown, Conn.: Wesleyan University Press, 1962), p. 59.
11 Michael Nyman (with Hugh Davies and Richard Orton), 'Steve Reich: An Interview with Michael Nyman', *The Musical Times*, 112/1537 (March 1971), p. 229–31.
12 Michael Nyman, 'Believe it or not, melody rides again', *Music and Musicians*, 20/2 (October 1971), p. 28.
13 Michael Nyman, 'SR – mysteries of the phase', *Music and Musicians*, 20/6 (February 1972), pp. 20–1.
14 Michael Nyman, *Experimental Music: Cage and Beyond* (London: Studio Vista/NewYork: Schirmer, 1974).
15 Reported in, for instance, John Rockwell's entry on Glenn Branca in H. Wiley Hitchcock and Stanley Sadie, eds., *The New Grove Dictionary of American*

Music (London: Macmillan/New York: Grove's Dictionaries of Music, 1986), I, p. 285.

16 John Cage, quoted in Daniel Wheeler, *Art Since Mid-Century: 1945 to the Present* (New York: Vendome Press/London:Thames and Hudson, 1991), p. 129.

17 Jonathan W. Bernard, 'The Minimalist Aesthetic in the Plastic Arts and in Music', *Perspectives of New Music*, 31/1 (Winter 1993), p. 126, n. 6.

18 *Ibid.*, p. 105.

19 Morton Feldman, quoted in the composer's promotional leaflet published by Universal Edition, *c.* 1971.

20 Irving Sandler, *American Art of the 1960s* (New York: Harper and Row, 1988), p. 60.

21 Frank Stella, quoted in Bruce Glaser, ed. Lucy R. Lippard, 'Questions to Stella and Judd', *Art News*, 65/5 (September 1966), republished in Gregory Battcock, ed., *Minimal Art: A Critical Anthology* (New York: Dutton, 1968/London: Studio Vista, 1969), p. 158.

22 Kenneth Baker, *Minimalism: Art of Circumstance* (New York: Abbeville Press, 1988), p. 34.

23 Sandler, *American Art of the 1960s*, p. 60.

24 Jasper Johns, quoted in Wheeler, *Art Since Mid-Century*, p. 136.

25 Christin J. Mamiya, *Pop Art and Consumer Culture: American Super Market* (Austin: University of Texas Press, 1992), p. 160.

26 See, for example, 'Avant-Garde and Kitsch', *Partisan Review*, 6/5 (Fall 1939), pp. 34–49.

27 Originally published as one of a number of statements by artists in Barbara Rose and Irving Sandler, eds., 'Sensibility of the Sixties', *Art in America* (January–February 1967), p. 48; reprinted in Sandler, *American Art of the 1960s*, p. 60.

28 Steve Reich, 'Music as a Gradual Process', in Reich, ed. Kaspar Koenig, *Writings about Music* (Halifax, Canada: Nova Scotia College of Art and Design/New York: New York University Press/London: Universal Edition, 1974), pp. 9–11.

29 Michael Nyman, 'Steve Reich: Interview', *Studio International*, 192/984 (November–December 1976), p. 304.

30 Baker, *Minimalism*, p. 43.

31 Barbara Rose, referring to the 'object sculptures' of Judd and Morris, 'ABC Art', *Art in America*, 53/6 (October–November 1965), p. 66. One of the seminal early statements on Minimalism in the fine arts, this article is reprinted in Battcock, ed., *Minimal Art*, pp. 274–97.

32 Frances Colpitt, *Minimal Art: The Critical Perspective* (Ann Arbor: UMI Research Press, 1990), p. 3.

33 In Tim Page, 'Steve Reich, a Former Young Turk, Approaches 50', *New York Times*, 1 June 1986, section 2, p. 23.

34 Philip Glass, quoted in Sheryl Garratt, 'Fun With Monotony', *The Face*, 75 (July 1986), p. 37.

35 Samuel Lipman, 'From Avant-Garde to Pop', in his collection of articles entitled *The House of Music: Art in an Era of Institutions* (Boston: David R. Godine, 1984), p. 48.

36 Richard Toop, 'On Complexity', *Perspectives of New Music*, 31/1 (Winter 1993), p. 44.

37 *Ibid.*, p. 98, n. 6.

38 See William Brooks, 'The Americas, 1945–70', in Robert Morgan, ed., *Modern Times: From World War I to the Present* (Basingstoke: Macmillan, 1993/Englewood Cliffs, N.J: Prentice Hall, 1994), pp. 342–4.

39 This and the following two quotations are taken from Michael Parsons, 'Systems in Art and Music', *The Musical Times*, 127/1604 (October 1976), p. 816.

40 This and the following quotation are taken from Reich, *Writings about Music*, p. 10.

41 Bernard, 'The Minimalist Aesthetic in the Plastic Arts and in Music', p. 97.

42 Reich, *Writings about Music*, p. 10.

43 In interview in Richard Kostelanetz, *The Theatre of Mixed Means: An Introduction to Happenings, Kinetic Environments and Other Mixed-Means Presentations* (New York: Dial Press, 1968/RK Editions, 1980), p. 187.

44 See Robert Carl, 'The Politics of Definition in New Music', *College Music Symposium*, 29 (1989), pp. 101–14.

45 See Kyle Gann, 'Let X=X: Minimalism v. Serialism', *Village Voice*, 24 February 1987, p. 76.

46 Björk, in the course of a Channel 4 TV programme on the arts in the 1990s, August 1998.

47 Quoted in David Lodge, 'Modernism, Antimodernism and Postmodernism', *Working with Structuralism: Essays and Reviews on Nineteenth- and Twentieth-Century Literature* (London: Routledge and Kegan Paul, 1981), p. 9.

48 See, for example, Roland Barthes, 'The Death of the Author', in Barthes, trans. Richard Howard, *The Rustle of Language* (Oxford: Basil Blackwell, 1986), pp. 49–55.

49 Toop, 'On Complexity', p. 97, n. 1.

50 Brian Ferneyhough, in conversation with David Osmond-Smith during the interval of a recording, for BBC Radio Three, of Ferneyhough's *Carceri d'Invenzione* cycle, first broadcast on 18 July 1993.

51 Wim Mertens, trans. J. Hautekiet, *American Minimal Music: La Monte Young, Terry Riley, Steve Reich, Philip Glass* (London: Kahn and Averill/New York: Alexander Broude, 1983), p. 88.

52 Elaine Broad, 'A New X? An Examination of the Aesthetic Foundations of Early Minimalism', *Music Research Forum*, 5 (1990), pp. 51–2; the italics are Broad's.

53 Bernard, 'The Minimalist Aesthetic in the Plastic Arts and in Music', p. 106.

54 This and the following quotations in this paragraph are taken from Timothy

A. Johnson, 'Minimalism: Aesthetic, Style, or Technique?' *The Musical Quarterly*, 78/4 (Winter 1994), pp. 742–3, esp. pp. 742 and 751.

55 See Jonathan Kramer, *The Time of Music: New Meanings, New Temporalities, New Listening Strategies* (New York: Schirmer Books/London: Collier Macmillan, 1988), especially the analysis of Frederic Rzewski's *Les moutons de Panurge*, pp. 388–94.

56 This and the following quotation are taken from John Rockwell, *All American Music: Composition in the Late Twentieth Century* (New York: Alfred A. Knopf, 1983/London: Kahn & Averill, 1985; rev. edn., New York: Da Capo Press, 1997), pp. 3–4.

57 See Russell Jacoby, *The Last Intellectuals: American Culture in the Age of Academe* (New York: Basic Books, 1987).

58 Sally Banes, *Greenwich Village 1963: Avant-Garde Performance and the Effervescent Body* (Durham and London: Duke University Press, 1993), p. 7.

59 *Ibid.*, p. 6. Banes' list occurs on pp. 5–6.

60 Rockwell, *All American Music*, p. 4.

61 For a collection of this author's writings on this subject, see Theodor Adorno, *The Culture Industry: Selected Essays on Mass Culture*, ed. Jay Bernstein (London: Routledge, 1991).

62 See Foster's own introductory essay in Foster, ed. *Postmodern Culture* (London and Sydney: Pluto Press), pp. i–xii.

63 See Keith Potter, 'The Pursuit of the Unimaginable by the Unnarratable, or Some Potentially Telling Developments in Non-Developmental Music', *Contemporary Music Review*, 15/3–4 (1996), pp. 3–11.

64 Lang, in interview with the present author, November 1993.

1 La Monte Young

1 Wim Mertens, trans. J. Hautekiet, *American Minimal Music: La Monte Young, Terry Riley, Steve Reich, Philip Glass* (London: Kahn and Averill/New York: Alexander Broude, 1983), p. 24.

2 The term is used by the composer himself; it is also employed, for instance, by Edward Strickland in *Minimalism: Origins* (Bloomington and Indianapolis: Indiana University Press, 1993).

3 For details of all commercial recordings of Young's music covered in this book, see the Discography.

4 This and all following quotations not individually acknowledged are taken from the author's interviews with the composer.

5 Interview in Richard Kostelanetz, *The Theatre of Mixed Means: An Introduction to Happenings, Kinetic Environments and Other Mixed-Means Presentations* (New York: Dial Press, 1968/RK Editions, 1980), p. 186.

6 Mark Swed, 'La Monte Young Tunes the Piano His Way', *Los Angeles Herald Examiner*, 1 November 1985, p. 36.

7 In Kostelanetz, *The Theatre of Mixed Means*, p. 185.
8 This and the other quotations in this paragraph are taken from correspondence with Young.
9 In Kostelanetz, *The Theatre of Mixed Means*, p. 187.
10 This and the following quotations in this paragraph are taken from unpublished material in the composer's archive.
11 In Kostelanetz, *The Theatre of Mixed Means*, p. 190.
12 *Ibid.*, p. 189.
13 *Ibid.*, p. 188.
14 *Ibid.*, p. 189.
15 This and the quotations in the next two paragraphs are taken from unpublished material and programme notes in the composer's archive.
16 In Kostelanetz, *The Theatre of Mixed Means*, p. 190.
17 This and the following quotations in this paragraph are taken from unpublished material and programme notes in the composer's archive.
18 Taken from the author's correspondence with the composer.
19 This and the quotation in the next paragraph are taken from a programme note in the composer's archive.
20 From a version of the composer's own programme note for *Trio for Strings.*
21 See Dave Smith, 'Following a Straight Line: La Monte Young', *Contact*, 18 (Winter 1977–8), p. 5. Example 1.5 is borrowed, with the permission of its author, from the Corrigenda to this article in *Contact*, 19 (Summer 1978), p. 2.
22 From a version of the composer's own programme note for *Trio for Strings.*
23 Smith, 'Following a Straight Line', p. 4.
24 Strickland, *Minimalism*, p. 124.
25 This and the following quotation, *ibid.*, p. 125.
26 This and all the other quotations in the present paragraph except the last one are taken from Kostelanetz, *The Theatre of Mixed Means*, p. 190.
27 Taken from unpublished material in the composer's archive.
28 This and the other quotations in this and the following paragraph are taken from Kostelanetz, *The Theatre of Mixed Means*, p. 190.
29 Quoted in Robert Palmer, 'A Father Figure for the Avant-Garde', *The Atlantic Monthly*, 247/5 (May 1981), p. 51.
30 From the transcript of an interview with Terry Riley by Neil Strauss, broadcast on WKCR-FM, New York, October 1991, p. 1.
31 This and the following quotations in the present paragraph are taken from the composer's own programme note for *Study I.*
32 This and the following quotation are taken from the composer's own programme note for *Study III.*
33 In Kostelanetz, *The Theatre of Mixed Means*, p. 191.
34 In interview in Cole Gagne, *Soundpieces 2: Interviews with American Composers* (Metuchen, N.J., and London: The Scarecrow Press, 1993), p. 491.
35 In Kostelanetz, *The Theatre of Mixed Means*, p. 191.

36 This and the following two quotations are taken from Kostelanetz, *The Theatre of Mixed Means*, p. 194.
37 From the unpublished notes which constitute the work's score.
38 Taken from unpublished material in the composer's archive.
39 Cornelius Cardew, 'One Sound: La Monte Young', *The Musical Times*, 107/1485 (November 1966), p. 959.
40 Taken from unpublished material in the composer's archive.
41 From a programme note for *Poem* by Michael Parsons, Fluxus retrospective concert, AIR Gallery, London, 23 May 1977.
42 Michael Nyman, *Experimental Music: Cage and Beyond* (London: Studio Vista/New York: Schirmer, 1974), p. 69.
43 Cardew, 'One Sound', p. 959.
44 This and the quotation at the beginning of the next paragraph are taken from unpublished material in the composer's archive.
45 Cardew, 'One Sound', p. 960.
46 This and the following quotation are taken from unpublished material in the composer's archive.
47 Strauss and Riley interview transcript, p. 2.
48 This and the following quotation are taken from Cardew, 'On the Role of the Instructions in the Interpretation of Indeterminate Music', in *Treatise Handbook* (London: Peters Edition, 1971), p. xiv.
49 In Kostelanetz, *The Theatre of Mixed Means*, p. 195.
50 'Lecture 1960', published in Young and Marian Zazeela, *Selected Writings* (Munich: Heiner Friedrich, 1969), no pagination.
51 Henry A. Flynt, Jr., 'Mutations of the Vanguard', in Gino Di Maggio, ed., *Ubi Fluxus Ibi Motus: 1990–1962* (Milan: Nuove Edizione Gabriele Mazzotta, 1990), p. 101.
52 Flynt's 'Mutations of the Vanguard', p. 110, documents these and other gallery-based performances mentioned below.
53 In Kostelanetz, *The Theatre of Mixed Means*, p. 192.
54 Cardew, 'One Sound', p. 959.
55 Transcribed by Young and Zazeela from a telephone conversation with Diane Wakoski, 23 August 1996.
56 From the composer's own programme note for *Piano Pieces for David Tudor #s 1, 2 and 3.*
57 Smith, 'Following a Straight Line', p. 4.
58 Nyman, *Experimental Music*, p. 69.
59 This and the following quotation, *ibid.*, p. 71.
60 Flynt, 'Mutations of the Vanguard', p. 110, and also personal communications with the present author.
61 'John Cage and Roger Reynolds: a Conversation', in R. Dunn, ed., *John Cage* (New York: Henmar Press, 1962), p. 81.
62 This and the following quotation are taken from Flynt, 'Mutations of the Vanguard', pp.101, 103 and 105.
63 In Kostelanetz, *The Theatre of Mixed Means*, pp. 194–5.

64 This and the following quotation are taken from Douglas Kahn, 'Cage and Fluxus', in Louwrien Wijers, *Fluxus Today and Yesterday* (New York: Dutton, 1993), p. 105.
65 Quoted in *ibid.*, p. 8.
66 For full details of the rather complicated situation surrounding these publications, see Jon Hendricks, *Fluxus Codex* (New York: The Gilbert and Lila Silverman Fluxus Collection/Harry N. Abrams, 1988), pp. 582–6.
67 Quoted in Kahn, 'Cage and Fluxus', p. 101.
68 Flynt, 'Mutations of the Vanguard', p. 99.
69 *Ibid.*, p. 101.
70 *Ibid.*
71 Flynt, 'Essay: Concept Art', in La Monte Young, ed., *An Anthology* (New York: Young and Jackson MacLow, 1963; 2nd edn., Munich: Heiner Friedrich, 1970), unpaginated.
72 Flynt, 'Mutations of the Vanguard', p. 105.
73 La Monte Young and Marian Zazeela, eds., *Selected Writings* (Munich: Heiner Friedrich, 1969).
74 David Farneth, entry on Young in H. Wiley Hitchcock and Stanley Sadie, eds., *The New Grove Dictionary of American Music* (London: Macmillan/New York: Grove's Dictionaries of Music, 1986), IV, p. 579.
75 This and the following two quotations are taken from unpublished material in the composer's archive.
76 Cole Gagne, in interview with Young and Zazeela in *Soundpieces 2: Interviews with American Composers*, p. 493.
77 In Kostelanetz, *The Theatre of Mixed Means*, p. 187.
78 This and the following quotation are taken from the composer's accompanying notes to the recording of *90 XII 9 c. 9.35 – 10.52 PM NYC, The Melodic Version of the Second Dream of The High-Tension Line Stepdown Transformer from The Four Dreams of China*, Gramavision 79467 (1991), unpaginated.
79 From unpublished material in the composer's archive.
80 This and the other quotation in this paragraph, *ibid.*
81 John Perreault, 'La Monte Young's Tracery: The Voice of the Tortoise', *Village Voice*, 22 February 1968, p. 27.
82 From unpublished material in the composer's archive.
83 Alan Licht, 'The History of La Monte Young's Theatre of Eternal Music', *Forced Exposure*, 16 (1990), p. 62.
84 This and the following two quotations are taken from *ibid.*, p. 66.
85 Smith, 'Following a Straight Line', p. 6.
86 Two versions of *Drift Study* – different from the one released on Shandar in 1974 – had been privately released in 1968 and 1969: see the Discography.
87 Smith, 'Following a Straight Line', p. 6.
88 An uncredited quotation in Licht, 'The History of La Monte Young's Theatre of Eternal Music', p. 66.

89 Young and Zazeela, eds., *Selected Writings*, p. 5.
90 Kostelanetz, *The Theatre of Mixed Means*, p. 183.
91 Licht, 'The History of La Monte Young's Theatre of Eternal Music', p. 66.
92 This and the last quotation in this paragraph are taken from the present author's interview with Conrad in February 1995.
93 This and the following quotation are taken from John Corbett, 'Minimal Compact', *The Wire*, 132 (February 1995), p. 35.
94 Tom Johnson, 'In Their "Dream House", Music Becomes a Means of Meditation', *New York Times*, 28 April 1974, section ii, p. 13.
95 Taken from the author's correspondence with Zazeela.
96 All quotations in this paragraph are taken from unpublished material in the composer's archive, some of which has been used as publicity material for the 1990s 'Sound and Light Environment'.
97 This and the following quotations in this paragraph are taken from unpublished material in the composer's archive.
98 Young's accompanying notes to *The Melodic Version of the Second Dream*.
99 This and the following quotations in this paragraph are taken from unpublished material in the composer's archive.
100 Kyle Gann, 'La Monte Young's *The Well-Tuned Piano*', *Perspectives of New Music*, 31/1 (Winter 1993), p. 134.
101 The composer's own 'Notes on *The Well-Tuned Piano*', in the accompanying booklet for the work's recording, Gramavision 18-8701-1 (LP, 1987)/79452 (CD, 1992), p. 7.
102 This and the following quotation are taken from Gann, 'La Monte Young's *The Well-Tuned Piano*', p. 135.
103 *Ibid.*, p. 134.
104 This and all the other quotations in this paragraph are taken from Young, 'Notes on *The Well-Tuned Piano*', p. 8.
105 Daniel Wolf, 'What is *The Well-Tuned Piano*?', accompanying notes to the Gramavision recording, p. 3.
106 Gann, 'La Monte Young's *The Well-Tuned Piano*', pp. 137–8.
107 Cardew, 'One Sound', p. 959.
108 See, for example, her unpublished 'An Axiomatization of Some Minimal Admissible Sets of Concurrent Frequencies Determined by La Monte Young's "Two Systems of Eleven Categories Revised from Vertical Hearing or Hearing in The Present Tense 1967"'.
109 See Uwe Husslein, *Pop Goes Art*, exhibition catalogue (Uppertal: Institut für Pop Kultur, 1990), p. 8, where a 1990 interview with Jonas Mekas is cited in confirmation of this suggestion.
110 In Licht, 'The History of La Monte Young's Theatre of Eternal Music', p. 68.
111 Lou Reed, *Metal Machine Music*, CPL2-1101 (1975); La Monte Young's name is, though, misspelled.
112 Quoted in Jim Aitkin, 'Brian Eno', *Keyboard*, 7 (July 1981), p. 60.
113 Quoted in Palmer, 'A Father Figure for the Avant-Garde', p. 49.

114 For a discussion of the relationship between the minimalism of all four subjects of the present book and the more recent developments of Techno, see Daniel Caux, 'Des jeux avec les sons: techno et minimalisme', *Artpress*, 9 (1998), pp. 105–11.

2 Terry Riley

1 This and all following quotations not individually acknowledged are taken from the author's interviews with the composer.
2 From Robert Palmer, 'Terry Riley: Doctor of Improvised Surgery', *Downbeat*, 42/19 (20 November 1975), p. 17.
3 See Edward Strickland, *Minimalism: Origins* (Bloomington and Indianapolis: Indiana University Press, 1993), pp. 124 and 143.
4 La Monte Young, ed., *An Anthology* (New York: Young and Jackson MacLow, 1963; 2nd edn., Munich: Heiner Friedrich, 1970), unpaginated.
5 Cole Gagne, *Soundpieces 2: Interviews with American Composers* (Metuchen, N.J., and London: The Scarecrow Press, 1993), p. 238.
6 Interview in Edward Strickland, *American Composers: Dialogues on Contemporary Music* (Bloomington and Indianapolis: Indiana University Press, 1991), p. 112.
7 See, for example, 'Tentative Programme for the Festival of Very New Music', reprinted in H. Sohm, ed., *Happening & Fluxus: Materialen*, catalogue for exhibition in the Koelnischer Kunstverein, 6 February 1970 – 6 January 1971, unpaginated.
8 This and the following quotation are used, without crediting any source, in Keith and Rita Knox, 'Relax and Fully Concentrate: The Time of Terry Riley', *Friends* magazine, 20 February 1970, unpaginated.
9 Quoted in Palmer, 'Terry Riley', p. 17.
10 Interview in William Duckworth, *Talking Music* (New York: Schirmer Books, 1995), p. 269.
11 *Ibid.*, p. 270.
12 Richard Kostelanetz, *The Theatre of Mixed Means: An Introduction to Happenings, Kinetic Environments and Other Mixed-Means Presentations* (New York: Dial Press, 1968/RK Editions, 1980), p. 164.
13 This and the following quotation, *ibid.*, p. 168.
14 In Palmer, 'Terry Riley', p. 17.
15 In Duckworth, *Talking Music*, p. 276.
16 In Strickland, *American Composers*, p. 113.
17 In Palmer, 'Terry Riley', pp. 17–18.
18 For details of all commercial recordings of Riley's music covered in this book, see the Discography.
19 *In C* is published by the composer.
20 See, for example, Robert P. Morgan, *Twentieth-Century Music: A History of Musical Style in Modern Europe and America* (New York and London: W. W. Norton, 1991), p. 426.

21 See, notably, Olivier Messiaen, *Le technique de mon langage musicale* (Paris: Alphonse Leduc, 1944); translated into English by John Satterfield as *The Technique of My Musical Language* (Paris: Alphonse Leduc, 1956).
22 See George Russell, *The Lydian Chromatic Concept of Tonal Organization for Improvisation* (Cambridge, Mass.: Concept, 1959).
23 This and the following quotation are taken from Duckworth, *Talking Music*, p. 272.
24 This and the following quotation are taken from *ibid.*, p. 275.
25 Gary Todd has done much to reclaim these tape compositions, and other early performances of Riley's music; these are in the process of being issued on CD by the Cortical Foundation.
26 In Palmer, 'Terry Riley', p. 18.
27 Jon Gibson, accompanying notes to 'Jon Gibson: In Good Company', Point Music 434 873-2 (1992).
28 Michael Nyman, *Experimental Music: Cage and Beyond* (London: Studio Vista/New York: Schirmer, 1974), p. 126.
29 *Ibid.*, p. 124.
30 John Cage, with Alison Knowles, *Notations* (New York: Something Else Press, 1969), p. 204. Though labelled 'Page two', the undated manuscript reproduced here is otherwise identical to the one subsequently published in, for example, the books by Mertens and Nyman.
31 Wim Mertens reproduces the same page in *American Minimal Music* (p. 40), but erroneously entitles it 'Keyboard Studies No. 7'.
32 Riley, in Duckworth, *Talking Music*, p. 275.
33 Uncredited accompanying note to the original recording, Columbia MS 7315 (1969).
34 This and the following quotation are taken from Gagne, *Soundpieces 2*, p. 248.
35 Daniel Caux's accompanying notes to the Shanti recording of *Persian Surgery Dervishes*, Shandar/Shanti 83.501-2 (1972) suggest that only the latter is used.
36 Uncredited accompanying note to the recording of *Descending Moonshine Dervishes*, Kuckuck 047 (1982).
37 Duckworth, *Talking Music*, p. 268.
38 *Ibid.*, p. 269.
39 Alfred Frankenstein, 'Music Like None Other On Earth', *San Francisco Chronicle*, 8 November 1964, p. 28. Part of this was subsequently reprinted on the sleeve of the Columbia recording of *In C*, CBS MK 64565 (1968). The following quotation is taken from this review.
40 David Toop, 'Altered Statesman', *The Wire*, 135 (May 1995), p. 22.
41 Palmer, 'Terry Riley', p. 17.
42 Duckworth, *Talking Music*, p. 266.

3 Steve Reich

1 This and all following quotations not individually acknowledged are taken from the author's interviews with the composer.

2 In Geoff Smith and Nicola Walker Smith, *American Originals: 25 Interviews with Contemporary Composers* (London and Boston: Faber and Faber, 1994), p. 212.

3 For an example of an attempt to investigate this relationship, see Robert Cowan, 'Reich and Wittgenstein: Notes Towards a Synthesis', *Tempo*, 157 (June 1986), pp. 2–7.

4 See, for example, his book, *Music in the Twentieth Century* (New York: Norton, 1966).

5 See, for example, Ludwig Wittgenstein, ed. G. H. von Wright, trans. Peter Winch, *Culture and Value.* (Oxford: Basil Blackwell, 1980), pp. 50 and 50e. The text in question dates from 1946.

6 In Andrew Ford, *Composer to Composer: Conversations about Contemporary Music* (London: Quartet Books, 1993), p. 63.

7 This and the following quotation are taken from Steve Reich, 'Notes on the Ensemble' in *Writings about Music*, ed. Kaspar Koenig (Halifax, Canada: Nova Scotia College of Art and Design/New York: New York University Press/London: Universal Edition, 1974), p. 45.

8 From one of the author's own interviews with Riley.

9 'Notes on Compositions', in Reich, *Writings about Music*, p. 50.

10 See, for example, *ibid.*, p. 50.

11 Emily Wasserman, 'An Interview with Composer Steve Reich', *Artforum*, 10/9 (May 1972), p. 44.

12 'Music as a Gradual Process' may be found in Reich, *Writings about Music*, pp. 9–11. In addition to its initial publication in *Anti-Illusion: Procedures/Materials* (New York: Whitney Museum of American Art, 1969), pp. 56–7, it also appeared in *Source*, 10 (1972), p. 30 (along with *Pendulum Music* and other material also republished in the *Writings*), and in the accompanying notes to the Deutsche Grammophon recording of *Drumming, Six Pianos* and *Music for Mallet Instruments, Voices and Organ* (DG 2740-106, 1974). Le Witt's 'Paragraphs on Conceptual Art' may be found in *Artforum*, 8/5 (June 1967), pp. 79–83.

13 This and the following quotation are taken from Steve Reich, '*Wavelength* by Michael Snow', unpublished.

14 Reich, *Writings about Music*, pp. 12–13.

15 For details of all commercial recordings of Reich's music covered in this book, see the Discography.

16 This and the following quotation are taken from Reich, *Writings about Music*, p. 9.

17 Mark Cromar advances this argument in 'Minimal Music: Proposals for a Redefinition', unpublished B.A. dissertation, Oxford University (1986).

18 'Notes on Compositions', in Reich, *Writings about Music*, p. 51.

19 'Steve Reich: An Interview with Michael Nyman', *The Musical Times*, 112/1537 (March 1971), p. 230.

20 'Notes on Compositions', in Reich, *Writings about Music*, p. 51.

21 John Cage, with Alison Knowles, *Notations* (New York: Something Else Press, 1969), p. 178.
22 *Source: The Magazine of the Avant-Garde*, 3 (1968), pp. 69–71.
23 'Appendix: List of Works', in Reich, *Writings about Music*, p. 73.
24 Jon Gibson, accompanying notes to 'Jon Gibson: In Good Company', Point Music 434 873-2 (1992).
25 This and the following quotations in this paragraph are taken from 'Notes on Compositions', in Reich, *Writings about Music*, pp. 51–2.
26 Paul Epstein, 'Pattern Structure and Process in Steve Reich's *Piano Phase*', *The Musical Quarterly*, 72/4 (1986), p. 495.
27 *Ibid.*, p. 498.
28 This and the following quotation are taken from 'Notes on Compositions', in Reich, *Writings about Music*, p. 53.
29 *Ibid.*
30 This and the following quotation are taken from *ibid.*
31 David Behrman, accompanying notes to 'Live/Electric', Columbia MS-7265 (1969).
32 'Slow Motion Sound', in Reich, *Writings about Music*, p. 15.
33 'The Phase Shifting Pulse Gate [etc.]', in *ibid.*, p. 23.
34 This and the following quotation are taken from *ibid.*, p. 25.
35 *Ibid.*, p. 27.
36 *Ibid.*, p. 25.
37 From one of the author's own interviews with Young.
38 From one of the author's own interviews with Riley.
39 Carman Moore, 'Music: Park Place Pianos', *Village Voice*, 23 March 1967, p. 15.
40 See 'Appendix: List of Works', in Reich, *Writings about Music*, p. 73.
41 From one of the author's own interviews with Glass.
42 From one of the author's own interviews with Gibson.
43 *Ibid.*
44 Published, by Boosey and Hawkes, in 1998.
45 Gunther Schuller, *Early Jazz: Its Roots and Musical Development* (New York: Dutton, 1968).
46 A. M. Jones, *Studies in African Music*, 2 vols. (London: Oxford University Press, 1959).
47 'Postscript to a Brief Study of Balinese and African Music', in Reich, *Writings about Music*, p. 38.
48 'Gahu: A Dance of the Ewe Tribe in Ghana', in *ibid.*, p. 35.
49 'Notes on Compositions', in *ibid.*, p. 58.
50 'From Program Notes', in *ibid.*, p. 44.
51 'Postscript to a Brief Study of Balinese and African Music', in *ibid.*, p. 39.
52 Mantle Hood and Jose Maceda, *Music* (Leiden: Brill, 1972), p. 8.
53 See, for example, K. Robert Schwarz, *Minimalism* (London: Phaidon Press, 1996), p. 204.
54 Seven scores – *Piano Phase, Violin Phase, Pendulum Music, Four Organs, Phase*

Patterns, *Clapping Music* and *Music for Pieces of Wood* – were published by Universal Edition London in that year.

55 In 1983, the composer began an association with Boosey and Hawkes in New York that led first to the availability of several scores in manuscript form and, slowly, to the publication of properly printed scores by that company, especially from the early 1990s.

56 See, for example, in addition to several reviews – and the promotion of the British première of *Drumming* – 'Steve Reich: An Interview with Michael Nyman', and *Experimental Music: Cage and Beyond* (London: Studio Vista/New York: Schirmer, 1974).

57 Though Henahan also wrote one of the earliest sympathetic profiles of Reich to be published in a major newspaper: 'Reich? Philharmonic? Paradiddling?', *New York Times*, 24 October 1971, Section ii, pp. 13 and 26 – a preview article for the 'Prospective Encounter' performance of *Phase Patterns* mentioned above.

58 Johnson's frequent reviews of the composer are collected in *The Voice of New Music: New York City 1972–1982* (Eindhoven: Het Apollohuis, 1989).

59 The first of many reviews of Reich's output by Rockwell is that of the premières of *Six Pianos* and *Music for Mallet Instruments, Voices and Organ*: 'Music: Reich Meditations', *New York Times*, 19 May 1973, Section ii, p. 28.

60 In the accompanying notes to 'Steve Reich: Works: 1965 – 1995', ten-CD boxed set, Nonesuch Records, 7559-79451-2 (1997), p. 24.

61 This and the following quotation are taken from 'Music as a Gradual Process', in Reich, *Writings about Music*, p. 10.

62 This and the quotation from Reich at the beginning of the next paragraph are taken from Michael Nyman, 'Steve Reich: Interview', *Studio International*, 192/6 (November–December 1976), p. 301.

63 'Music as a Gradual Process', in Reich, *Writings about Music*, p. 10.

64 This and the first quotation in the next paragraph are taken from 'Notes on Compositions', in *ibid.*, p. 58.

65 *Ibid.*, p. 61.

66 A revised score is due for publication by Boosey and Hawkes shortly.

67 'Steve Reich' (New York: Boosey and Hawkes, n.d.).

68 This and the following quotation are taken from 'Notes on Compositions', in Reich, *Writings about Music*, p. 58.

69 *Ibid.*, p. 60.

70 This and all the other quotations in this paragraph, *ibid.*, p. 58.

71 Steve Reich, various published programme notes for *Drumming.*

72 *Ibid.*

73 'Notes on Compositions', in Reich, *Writings about Music*, p. 70.

74 *Ibid.*, p. 69.

75 This term seems to have originated not with the composer but in K. Robert Schwarz, 'Steve Reich: Music as a Gradual Process', Part Two, *Perspectives of New Music*, 20 (Fall–Winter 1981/Spring–Summer 1982) pp. 225–86; it is

adopted here as a convenient shorthand with connotations of harmonic motion which seem basically appropriate.

76 This and the following quotation are taken from Steve Reich, accompanying notes to the work's first recording, ECM Records, ECM-1-1129 (1978), unpaginated.

77 This and the following quotation, *ibid.*

78 This and the following quotation, *ibid.*

79 *Ibid.*

80 *Ibid.*

81 Schwarz, 'Steve Reich: Music as a Gradual Process', Part Two, p. 249.

82 Reich, *Writings about Music*, p. 28.

83 This and the following quotation are taken from Ronald Woodley, entry on Reich in Brian Morton and Pamela Collins, eds., *Contemporary Composers* (London: St James Press, 1992), p. 768.

84 This and the following quotation are to be found in Rob Tannenbaum, 'A Meeting of Sound Minds: John Cage and Brian Eno', *Musician*, 83 (September 1985), p. 68.

85 Quoted in Robert Christgau, *Christgau's Guide to Rock Albums of the Seventies* (New Haven, Conn.: Ticknor and Fields, 1981/London: Vermilion, 1982), p. 82.

4 Philip Glass

1 For an account of this, see Philip Glass, *The Music of Philip Glass*, ed. with supplementary material by Robert T. Jones (New York: Harper and Row, 1987)/*Opera on the Beach* (London and Boston: Faber and Faber, 1988), pp. 87–9.

2 For more detailed accounts of the composer's early life, see, in particular, Eve Grimes, 'Interview: Education' (1989) in *Writings on Glass: Essays, Interviews, Criticism*, ed. Richard Kostelanetz (New York: Schirmer Books/London: Prentice Hall International, 1997), pp. 12–36.

3 The composer, quoted in Sheryl Garratt, 'Fun with Monotony', *The Face*, 75 (July 1986), p. 39.

4 The composer, quoted in Robert Matthew-Walker, 'Glass Roots', *CD Review*, 61 (February 1992), p. 18.

5 Joan LaBarbara, 'Philip Glass e Steve Reich: Two from the Steady State School', dual language Italian/English, *Data: pratica e teoria delle arti*, 4/13 (Autumn 1974), pp. 36–9. This unusually detailed article is probably only the second attempt in print to discuss Glass's music from anything resembling a scholarly point of view, the first being Nyman's book, *Experimental Music*. The former is reprinted in Kostelanetz, ed., *Writings on Glass*, pp. 39–45.

6 This and all following quotations not individually acknowledged are taken from the present author's interviews with the composer.

7 Quoted in Robert T. Jones, 'Philip Glass [Musician of the Month]', *High Fidelity/Musical America*, 29/4 (April 1979), p. MA-4.

8 This and the comments attributed to him elsewhere in this chapter are taken from a telephone interview with Kripl in August 1998.
9 This and the following quotation are taken from Glass, ed. Jones, *The Music of Philip Glass/Opera on the Beach*, p. 35.
10 *Ibid.*, p. 19.
11 This and the following two quotations are taken from Glass, ed. Jones, *The Music of Philip Glass/Opera on the Beach*, pp. 35–6.
12 *Ibid.*, p. 16.
13 John Rockwell, 'Philip Glass: The Orient, the Visual Arts and the Evolution of Minimalism', in *All American Music: Composition in the Late Twentieth Century* (New York: Alfred A. Knopf, 1983/London: Kahn and Averill, 1985; rev. edn.: New York: Da Capo Press, 1997), p. 111.
14 Glass, ed. Jones, *The Music of Philip Glass/Opera on the Beach*, p. 17.
15 Quoted in Michael Walsh, 'Making a Joyful Noise', *Time*, 125/26 (1 July 1985), p. 47.
16 Jones, *High Fidelity/Musical America*, p. MA-5.
17 Glass, ed. Jones, *The Music of Philip Glass/Opera on the Beach*, p. 90.
18 Philip Glass and Ravi Shankar, *Passages*, Private Music/BMG 2074-2 P (1990).
19 See Glass, ed. Jones, *The Music of Philip Glass/Opera on the Beach*, pp. 53–4.
20 This and other observations by him below are taken from various conversations with Gibson from August 1986 onwards.
21 In Tim Page, 'A Conversation with Philip Glass and Steve Reich', *Music from the Road: Views and Reviews 1978–1992* (New York and Oxford: Oxford University Press, 1992), p. 67.
22 Gibson, in interview with the present author.
23 Glass, ed. Jones, *The Music of Philip Glass/Opera on the Beach*, p. xiii.
24 In Willoughby Sharp and Liza Bear, 'Phil Glass: An Interview in Two Parts', *Avalanche*, 5 (Summer 1972), p. 33.
25 Lee Breuer and Ann Elizabeth Horton, *A Comic of The Red Horse Animation* (New York, 1976), unpaginated.
26 *Ibid.*
27 Glass, ed. Jones, *The Music of Philip Glass/Opera on the Beach*, p. 8.
28 From a telephone interview with Maleczech in August 1997.
29 In Sharp and Bear, 'Phil Glass', p. 33.
30 Glass, ed. Jones, *The Music of Philip Glass/Opera on the Beach*, p. 7.
31 In Sharp and Bear, 'Phil Glass', p. 28.
32 Barbara Rose, 'ABC Art', *Art in America*, 53/6 (October/November 1965), pp. 57–69; reprinted in Gregory Battcock, ed., *Minimal Art: A Critical Anthology* (New York: Dutton, 1968/London: Studio Vista, 1969), pp. 102–14.
33 Richard Foreman, 'Glass and Snow', *Arts Magazine* (February 1970); reprinted in Kostelanetz, ed., *Writings on Glass*, pp. 80–6. It provides the source for all the quotations in this and the following paragraph.
34 Quoted in Peter Eisenman, 'Interview' (1983), reprinted in Richard Serra,

Writings, Interviews (Chicago and London: University of Chicago Press, 1994), p. 142.

35 Serra, 'Rigging' (1980), reprinted in an edited version in Serra, *Writings, Interviews*, p. 97.

36 Annette Michelson, Richard Serra and Clara Weyergraf, 'The Films of Richard Serra: An Interview' (1979), reprinted in Serra, *Writings, Interviews*, p. 63.

37 Glass, ed. Jones, *The Music of Philip Glass/Opera on the Beach*, p. 23.

38 'Long Beach Island, Word Location', June 1969, Loveladies, New Jersey, reprinted in Serra, *Writings, Interviews*, p. 7.

39 This and the following quotation are taken from Michelson, etc., 'The Films of Serra: An Interview', p. 64.

40 Serra, 'Dialogue with Philip Glass' (1986), reprinted in Kostelanetz, ed., *Writings on Glass*, p. 298.

41 See, for example, Michael Nyman, 'Minimal Music, Determinacy and the New Tonality', *Experimental Music: Cage and Beyond* (London: Studio Vista/New York: Schirmer, 1974), p. 127, and Dave Smith, 'The Music of Phil Glass', *Contact*, 11 (Summer 1975), p. 27.

42 In Keith Potter and Dave Smith, 'Interview with Philip Glass', *Contact*, 13 (Spring 1976), p. 25.

43 See Wim Mertens, trans. J. Hautekiet, *American Minimal Music: La Monte Young, Terry Riley, Steve Reich, Philip Glass* (London: Kahn and Averill/New York: Alexander Broude, 1983), pp. 68–9.

44 Potter and Smith, 'Interview with Philip Glass', p. 28.

45 Glass, ed. Jones, *The Music of Philip Glass/Opera on the Beach*, p. 18.

46 'Music Catalog', in *ibid.*, p. 211.

47 LaBarbara, 'Philip Glass e Steve Reich', p. 36.

48 This and the following quotation are taken from Glass, ed. Jones, *The Music of Philip Glass/Opera on the Beach*, p. 19.

49 LaBarbara, 'Philip Glass e Steve Reich', p. 37.

50 *Ibid.*, p. 37.

51 *Ibid.*, pp. 37 and 39.

52 Quoted in Matthew-Walker, 'Glass Roots', p. 19.

53 LaBarbara, 'Philip Glass e Steve Reich', p. 39.

54 Published by Dunvagen Music in 1984.

55 For details of all commercial recordings of Glass's music covered in this book, see the Discography.

56 Glass, ed. Jones, *The Music of Philip Glass/Opera on the Beach*, p. 20.

57 *Ibid.*, p. 18.

58 In Potter and Smith, 'Interview with Philip Glass', p. 25.

59 Glass, ed. Jones, *The Music of Philip Glass/Opera on the Beach*, pp. 20–1.

60 Reich, in interview with the present author.

61 Gibson, in interview with the present author.

62 Gibson, comment attached to 'PGE Tours and Shows', unpublished

documentation of performances by the Philip Glass Ensemble, compiled by Dan Mather.

63 Nyman, *Experimental Music*, p. 128.
64 Reich, in interview with the present author.
65 Wesley York, 'Form and Process in *Two Pages* of Philip Glass', *Sonus*, 1/2 (Spring 1982), pp. 28–50; reprinted in Thomas DeLio, ed., *Contiguous Lines: Issues and Ideas in the Music of the '60s and '70s* (Lanham, London etc: University Press of America, 1985), pp. 81–106; also reprinted in Kostelanetz, ed. *Writings on Glass*, pp. 60–79.
66 Nyman, *Experimental Music*, p. 128.
67 The precise origin of this quotation is unknown. The present author first saw it in publicity material, produced by the New York company Artservices, for Glass's British tour of *Music in Twelve Parts* in 1975.
68 In Potter and Smith, 'Interview with Philip Glass', p. 26.
69 *Ibid.*, p. 25.
70 Glass, ed. Jones, *The Music of Philip Glass/Opera on the Beach*, p. 8.
71 Taken from Breuer and Horton, *A Comic of The Red Horse Animation.*
72 *Ibid.*
73 John Rockwell, 'There's Nothing Quite Like the Sound of Glass', *New York Times*, 26 May 1974, Section ii, p.11.
74 Smith, 'The Music of Phil Glass', p. 32.
75 In Sharp and Bear, 'Phil Glass', p. 28.
76 Foreman, 'Glass and Snow', pp. 80ff.
77 This and the following quotation are taken from Sharp and Bear, 'Phil Glass', p. 28.
78 *Ibid.*
79 Quoted in Tim Page's accompanying notes to the CD reissue of *Music with Changing Parts*, Elektra/Nonesuch 7559-79325-2 (1994), unpaginated.
80 This and the other quotations in this paragraph are taken from Glass's unpaginated typescript notes for *Music in Twelve Parts.* Probably written in 1974, they form the basis of several programme notes on the work published in 1974–5 and subsequently, including the accompanying notes to the various commercial recordings (see the Discography).
81 In Potter and Smith, 'Interview with Philip Glass', p. 25.
82 This and the following quotation are taken from Mark Pappenheim, 'Shards of Glass', *The Independent*, 11 April 1992, Section ii, p. 28.
83 This and the following two quotations, including the one in the next paragraph, are taken from Glass, ed. Jones, *The Music of Philip Glass/ Opera on the Beach*, p. 27.
84 See, for example, *ibid.*, pp. 136ff. It seems that the idea of linking *Einstein on the Beach* with *Satyagraha* (1980) and *Akhnaten* (1984) was motivated primarily by the opportunity this afforded to mount all three works in Stuttgart as a 'trilogy'.
85 Quoted in *ibid.*, p. 32.

86 See, for example, *ibid.*, p. 30. Here the proffered explanation is that 'the "knee" refer[s] to the joining function that humans' anatomical knees perform'.

87 Philip Glass, accompanying notes to the original LP and subsequent CD recordings of *Einstein on the Beach* (1978 and 1993 respectively).

88 This and the quotation in the next paragraph are taken from Glass's accompanying notes, *ibid.*

89 *Ibid.*

Discography

N.B.This discography lists only the works which form the main subject of this book. While it distinguishes between LPs and CDs, particularly since many LPs have subsequently been reissued in CD format, no attempt is made, for the most part, to indicate the subsequent availability in cassette form of any already existing recordings.

La Monte Young

Excerpt from *Drift Study 5 VIII 68 4:37:40 – 5:09:50 PM* (Theatre of Eternal Music): S.M.S. magazine, no. 4 (5′ reel-to-reel audio tape, 1968; reissued on cassette, 1988)

Excerpt from *Drift Study 31 I 69 12:17:33 – 12:49:58 PM* (Theatre of Eternal Music): Aspen magazine, no. 8 (LP, 1969)

Map of 49's Dream The Two Systems of Eleven Sets of Galactic Intervals Ornamental Lightyears Tracery 31 VII 69 10:26 – 10:49 PM Munich, the Volga Delta from *Studies In The Bowed Disc 23 VIII 64 2:50:45 – 3:11 AM* (La Monte Young and Marian Zazeela): [Galerie Heiner Friedrich] Edition X (known as 'The Black LP', 1969)

Drift Study 13 I 73 5:35 – 6:14:03 PM NYC, Map of 49's Dream The Two Systems of Eleven Sets of Galactic Intervals Ornamental Lightyears Tracery 14 VII 73 9:27:27 – 10:15:33 PM NYC (Theatre of Eternal Music): 'Dream House', Disques Shandar 83.510 (LP, 1974)

The Well-Tuned Piano 81 X 25 6:17:50 – 11:18:59 PM NYC (La Monte Young): Gramavision 79452, etc. (5 LPs, CDs and cassette tapes, 1987)

Poem for Chairs, Tables, Benches, etc. 89 VI 8 c. 1:45 – 1:52 AM Paris, the 'Paris Encore' (Theatre of Eternal Music): 'FluxTellus', Tellus, no. 24, Harvestworks (cassette, 1990)

The Melodic Version of The Second Dream of The High-Tension Line Stepdown Transformer from *The Four Dreams of China 90 XII 9 c. 9:35 – 10:52 PM NYC* (Theatre of Eternal Music): Gramavision 79467 (CD, 1991)

Sunday AM [Morning] Blues [1964, edited], *B♭ Dorian Blues* [1963, ed.], *The Well-Tuned Piano* [1964, ed.], *Map of 49's Dream* [1971, ed.] (La Monte Young): RIP, unauthorised bootleg edition, source unknown (2 LPs, *c.* 1992)

Excerpt from *The Well-Tuned Piano 81 X 25 NYC* (La Monte Young): 'Numbers Racket', Just Intonation Network compilation, vol. II, JIN-002 (cassette, 1992)

Five Small Pieces for String Quartet, On Remembering a Naiad [plus works by other composers], (Arditti String Quartet): 'U.S.A.', Disques Montaigne 782010 (CD, 1993)

Young's Dorian Blues in G (La Monte Young and The Forever Bad Blues Band): 'Just Stompin': Live at the Kitchen', Gramavision R279487 (2 CDs, 1993)

Sarabande [plus works by other composers] (John Schneider, guitar; Amy Schulman, harp): 'Just West Coast: microtonal music for guitar and harp', Bridge Records BCD 9041 (CD, 1993)

Terry Riley

Untitled Organ (= *Keyboard Study no. 2*), *Dorian Reeds* (Terry Riley): 'Reed Streams', Mass Art M-131 (LP, 1966)

In C (Center of the Creative and Performing Arts in the State University of New York at Buffalo/Terry Riley): CBS MK 64565/MS 7178/CBS Classics 61237 (LP, 1968 and later; reissued on CD, 1988)

A Rainbow in Curved Air, Poppy Nogood and the Phantom Band (Terry Riley): CBS MK 64564/ MS 7315 (LP, 1969; reissued on CD, 1988)

with John Cale, *Church of Anthrax* (John Cale and Terry Riley): CBS 30131/64259 (LP, 1971)

Les Yeux Fermés (Happy Ending) (Terry Riley): [Warner Brothers,] WEA Filipacchi Music 46 125 U (LP, 1972)

Persian Surgery Dervishes (Terry Riley): Shandar/Shanti 83.501–2 (2 LPs, 1972); reissued on Robi Droli, New Tone nt 6715 (2 CDs, 1993)

Keyboard Study no. 2, [Pierre Mariétan, *Systemes*] (Groupe Germ): Actuel BYG 529 327 (LP, n.d.)

Le Secret de la Vie (Lifespan) (Terry Riley): Stip 1011 (LP, 1975)

A Rainbow in Curved Air, [Samuel Barber, *Sonata*, Katrina Krimsky, *Specs*, Woody Shaw, *Katrina Ballerina*, Shaw/Krimsky, *Epilogue*] (Katrina Krimsky): Transonic 3008 (LP, *c.* 1976)

Shri Camel (Terry Riley): CBS 73 929 (LP, 1980); reissued on CBS 35164 (CD, 1988)

Descending Moonshine Dervishes (Terry Riley): Kuckuck 047 (LP, 1982); reissued on Celestial Harmonies 12047-2 (CD, 1991)

In C, [David Mingyue Liang, *Music of a Thousand Springs, Zen (Ch'an) of Water*] (Shanghai Film Orchestra/Wang Yongji, [Wang Zhaoxiang]): Celestial Harmonies 7689 (CD, 1990)

In C, [Reich, *Six Pianos*] (Piano Circus): Decca, Argo 430 380–2 (CD, 1990)

Tread on the Trail, [Jon Gibson, *Waltz*, John Adams, *Pat's Aria*, Steve Reich, *Reed Phase*, Terry Jennings, *Terry's G Dorian Blues*, Philip Glass, *Bed*, Gibson, *Song 3*, Glass, *Gradus (For Jon Gibson)* [*sic*], Gibson, *Extensions II*] (Jon Gibson, plus La Monte Young [Jennings only]): 'Jon Gibson: In Good Company', Point Music 434 873–2 (CD, 1992)

A 'Terry Riley Archive Series' of recordings is promised by Gary Todd's Cortical Foundation. Details available from the Cortical Foundation, 23715 West Malibu Road, #419, Malibu, CA 90265, USA.

Steve Reich

Come Out [plus works by other composers]: 'New Sounds in Electronic Music', CBS Odyssey, 32-16-0160 (LP, 1967)

It's Gonna Rain, Violin Phase (Paul Zukofsky, violin): 'Live/Electric', Columbia MS-7265 (LP, 1969)

Four Organs, Phase Patterns (Steve Reich and Musicians): Disques Shandar, SR 10005 (LP, 1971); reissued on Robi Droli, RDC 5018 (CD, 1994)

Drumming (Steve Reich and Musicians): John Gibson and Multiples, Inc. (2 LPs, 1972). This signed and numbered limited edition of 500, complete with a full score, was recorded at the New York Town Hall première performance of the work.

Four Organs, [Cage, *Three Dances*] (Ralph Gierson, Roger Kellaway, Tom Raney, Steve Reich and Michael Tilson Thomas): Angel, S-36059 (LP, 1973)

Drumming, Music for Mallet Instruments, Voices and Organ, Six Pianos (Steve Reich and Musicians): Deutsche Grammophon Gesellschaft, 2740-106 (3 LPs, 1974)

Music for Eighteen Musicians (Steve Reich and Musicians): ECM Records, ECM-1-1129 (LP, 1978; reissued on CD, 1988)

Violin Phase, [*Music for a Large Ensemble, Octet*] (Shem Guibbory, violin, [Steve Reich and Musicians]): ECM Records, ECM 1168 (LP, 1980; reissued on CD, 1989)

Music for Pieces of Wood ('Zene fadarabokra'), [Tibor Szemzö, *Vizicsoda* ('Water-Wonder'), László Melis, *Etüd három tükörre* ('Etude for Three Mirrors'), Frederic Rzewski, *Coming Together*] (Group 180): Hungaroton SLPX 12545 (LP, 1983); reissued on Hungaroton Classic HCD 12545 (CD, 1995)

Piano Phase, [*Octet*, Béla Faragó, *A pók halála + Sírfelirat* ('Death of the Spider + Epitaph'), András Soós, *Duett* ('A Duet')] (Group 180): Hungaroton SLPX 12799 (LP, 1985)

Melodica, [plus music by twenty-one other composers and improvisers, performed by various musicians]: 'Music from Mills: in celebration of the Centennial of the Chartering of Mills College 1885–1985', Mills College MC 001 (3 LPs, 1986)

Six Marimbas, [*Sextet*] (Steve Reich and Musicians): Elektra Nonesuch 7559-79138 (LP & CD, 1987)

Come Out, Piano Phase, Clapping Music, It's Gonna Rain (Double Edge, Russ Hartenberger & Steve Reich): Elektra Nonesuch 7559-79169 (LP & CD, 1987)

Drumming (Steve Reich and Musicians): Elektra Nonesuch 7559-79170 (2 LPs & CD, 1987)

[*The Four Sections*], *Music for Mallet Instruments, Voices and Organ*, ([London Symphony Orchestra/Michael Tilson Thomas], Steve Reich and Musicians): Elektra Nonesuch 7559-79220 (CD, 1990)

Six Pianos, [Riley, *In C*] (Piano Circus): Decca, Argo 430 380-2 (CD, 1990)

Reed Phase, [plus works by Gibson, Adams, Jennings, Glass and Riley: see Riley,

Tread on the Trail, above] (Jon Gibson, etc.): 'Jon Gibson: In Good Company', Point Music 434 873–2 (CD, 1992)

Music for Mallet Instruments, Voices and Organ, Piano Phase, [*Octet, Sextet*] (Amadinda Percussion Group and Group 180): 'Steve Reich: Another Look at Counterpoint', Amiata Records, ARNR 0393 (CD, 1993)

Four Organs, [Kevin Volans, *Kneeling Dance*; David Lang, *Face So Pale*; Robert Moran, *Three Dances*] (Piano Circus): Decca, Argo 440 294-2 (CD, 1993)

Piano Phase [in version for two marimbas], [István Márta, *Doll's House Story*, László Sáry, *Pebble Playing in a Pot*, John Cage, *Second Construction in Metal*, Traditional African Music, George Hamilton Green, *Log Cabin Blues*, *Charleston Capers*, *Jovial Jasper*] (Amadinda Percussion Group): Hungaroton Classic HCD 12855, (CD, 1994)

It's Gonna Rain, Come Out, Piano Phase, Four Organs, Drumming, Clapping Music, Music for Eighteen Musicians, [Eight Lines, Tehillim, The Desert Music, New York Counterpoint, Three Movements, The Four Sections, Electric Counterpoint, Different Trains, The Cave (excerpts), *City Life, Proverb*] 'Steve Reich: 1965–1995', 10-CD boxed set: Elektra Nonesuch 7559-79451-2 (1997). This sixtieth-birthday compilation includes a valuable interview with the composer by Jonathan Cott and much other useful commentary.

Music for Eighteen Musicians (same recording as above), issued separately: Elektra Nonesuch (CD, 1998)

Philip Glass

Music with Changing Parts (Philip Glass Ensemble): Chatham Square 1001/2 (2 LPs, 1971); reissued on Elektra/Nonesuch 7559-79325-2 (CD, 1994)

Music in Fifths; *Music in Similar Motion* (Philip Glass Ensemble): Chatham Square 1003 (LP, 1973); reissued (with *Two Pages* & *[Music in] Contrary Motion*, see below) on Elektra/Nonesuch 7559-79326-2 (CD, 1994)

Two Pages [plus works by other composers] (Philip Glass and Michael Riesman): Folkways FTS 33902 (LP, 1975)

[Music in] Contrary Motion, Two Pages (same performance as above) (Philip Glass and electric organ): 'Solo Music', Shandar 83.515 (LP, 1975); reissued (with *Music in Fifths* & *Music in Similar Motion*, see above) on Elektra/Nonesuch 7559-79326-2 (CD, 1994)

Music in Twelve Parts, Parts 1 & 2 (Philip Glass Ensemble): Caroline/Virgin CA 2010 (LP, 1975)

Strung Out, [Giacinto Scelsi, *Anahit*, Iannis Xenakis, *Mikka* and *Mikka 'S'*] (Paul Zukofsky, [unnamed ensemble/Kenneth Moore]): CP^2 108 (LP, 1976)

Einstein on the Beach, excerpts (Philip Glass Ensemble, etc.): Tomato TOM-101 (LP, 1978)

Einstein on the Beach (Philip Glass Ensemble, etc.): Tomato TOM-4-2901 (4 LPs, 1979); reissued on 4 LPs & 3 CDs, Sony Masterworks M4K 38875 (1984). Includes extensive notes by Robert Palmer and Philip Glass.

Einstein on the Beach (solo violin music), [Aaron Copland, *Duo for Violin and Piano*, Leo Ornstein, *Sonata for Violin and Piano*, Richard Wernick, *Cadenzas and Variations*] (Gregory Fulkerson, [Robert Shannon and Alan Feinberg]): New World Records NW 313 (LP, 1981)

Music in Twelve Parts (Philip Glass Ensemble): Venture/Virgin 802768995 (6 LPs & 3 CDs, 1988, UK); reissued on Virgin 91311-2 (6 LPs & 3 CDs, 1989, USA)

Einstein on the Beach, extracts (Philip Glass Ensemble), [with music from *Satyagraha* & *Akhnaten*]: 'Songs from the Trilogy', Sony Masterworks MK 45580 (CD, 1987)

Bed (from *Einstein on the Beach*), *Gradus (For Jon Gibson)* [*sic*], [plus works by Gibson, Adams, Reich, Jennings, Glass and Riley: see Riley, *Tread on the Trail*, above] (Jon Gibson, etc.): 'Jon Gibson: In Good Company', Point Music 434 873–2 (CD, 1992)

[Music in] Contrary Motion [with *Dance IV for Organ, Mad Rush, Dance II for Organ* & *Satyagraha*, Act III conclusion, arr. Michael Riesman] (Donald Joyce, organ): 'Glass Organ Works', BMG Catalyst 09026-61825-2 (CD, 1993)

Einstein on the Beach, 'Bed' (Act IV, scene 2) (Philip Glass Ensemble) [with twelve extracts from later works]: 'The Essential Philip Glass', Sony Masterworks SK 64133 (CD, 1993)

Einstein on the Beach (Philip Glass Ensemble, etc.): Elektra/Nonesuch 7559-79323-2 (3 CDs, 1993)

Music in Twelve Parts (Philip Glass Ensemble): Elektra/Nonesuch 7559-79324-2 (3 CDs, 1996)

Einstein on the Beach 'Spaceship' (Act IV, scene 3), 'Building/Train' (Act IV, scene 1) 'Knee Plays 3 & 5' (Philip Glass Ensemble) [with sixteen extracts from later works]: 'Glassmasters', Sony Masterworks SM3K 62960 (3 CDs, 1997)

Bibliography

This bibliography mainly lists the published material on which this book has drawn directly. No attempt has been made to list the extensive unpublished sources consulted. Reviews and more journalistic articles, of which there are many, have been included only when they seem of especial significance or historical interest from the perspective of the present volume. Like the extensive unpublished sources consulted, these have been detailed in endnotes when quoted in the main text. Accompanying booklet notes to recordings have not been included in this bibliography, though, again, some references to these may be found in endnotes; see also the Discography. Documentary videos and radio programmes have not been included. Studies of musical theory and the more standard textbooks and reference books on twentieth-century music are not included, though some individual dictionary and encyclopaedia entries on the four subjects of this volume are listed. The listed literature on the many other subjects having a more background or peripheral function in the present context – Minimalist art, for instance – is confined to those books and articles, including some of the seminal texts, which this author has found particularly useful for present purposes; for convenience, some are included in their anthologised form.

Adams, John, 'Steve Reich', in *The New Grove Dictionary of American Music*, eds. H. Wiley Hitchcock, H. and Stanley Sadie (London: Macmillan/New York: Grove's Dictionaries of Music, 1986), IX, pp. 23–6

Adorno, Theodor, *The Culture Industry: Selected Essays on Mass Culture*, ed. Jay Bernstein (London: Routledge, 1991)

Ahlgren, C., 'Terry Riley: Music is Path to Heaven', *San Francisco Chronicle*, 17 April 1983

Aikin, J. and Rothstein, J., 'Terry Riley: The Composer of *In C* Explores Indian Sources and Synthesizer Soloing', *Keyboard*, 8/4 (1982), pp. 11–14

Alloway, Lawrence, *Topics in American Art Since 1945* (New York: Norton, 1975)

Amirkhanian, Charles, 'Steve Reich', *Ear [West]*, 7 (March–April 1979), Section I, pp. 4–5

Baker, Kenneth, *Minimalism: Art of Circumstance* (New York: Abbeville Press, 1988)

Banes, Sally, *Greenwich Village 1963: Avant-Garde Performance and the Effervescent Body* (Durham, N.C., and London: Duke University Press, 1993)

Battcock, Gregory, ed., *Minimal Art: A Critical Anthology* (New York: Dutton, 1968/London: Studio Vista, 1969)

Breaking the Sound Barrier: A Critical Anthology of the New Music (New York: Dutton, 1981)

Beard, Rick, and Berlowitz, Leslie Cohen, eds., *Greenwich Village: Culture and Counterculture* (New Brunswick, N.J.: Rutgers University Press/The Museum of the City of New York, 1993)

Berger, Maurice, *Labyrinths: Robert Morris, Minimalism, and the 1960s* (New York: Harper and Row, 1989)

Bernard, Jonathan W., 'The Minimalist Aesthetic in the Plastic Arts and in Music', *Perspectives of New Music*, 31/1 (Winter 1993), pp. 86–132

Borden, Lizzie, 'The New Dialectic', *Artforum*, 12/7 (1974), pp. 44–8

Brecht, Stefan, *The Theatre of Visions: Robert Wilson* (Frankfurt: Suhrkamp Verlag, 1979)

Breuer, Lee, and Horton, Ann Elizabeth, *A Comic of the Red Horse Animation* (New York: [Mabou Mines], 1976)

Brinkman, R., ed., *Avant-garde Jazz Pop: Tendenzen zwischen Tonalität und Atonalität* (Mainz and London, 1978)

Broad, Elaine, 'A New X? An Examination of the Aesthetic Foundations of Early Minimalism', *Music Research Forum*, 5 (1990), pp. 51–62

Cage, John, *Silence* (Middletown: Wesleyan University Press, 1961)

Cage, John, and Knowles, Alison, *Notations* (New York: Something Else Press, 1969)

Calas, Nicolas, and Elena, *Icons and Images of the Sixties* (New York: Dutton, 1971)

Cardew, Cornelius, 'One Sound: La Monte Young', *The Musical Times*, 107/1485 (November 1966), pp. 959–60

Treatise Handbook (London: Peters Edition, 1971)

Carl, Robert, 'The Politics of Definition in New Music', *College Music Symposium*, 29 (1989), pp. 101–14

Caux, Daniel, 'Des jeux avec les sons: techno of minimalisme', *Artpress*, 9 (1998), pp. 105–11.

Chave, Anna C., 'Minimalism and the Rhetoric of Power', *The Arts Magazine*, 64/5 (January 1990), pp. 44–63

Christgau, Robert, *Christgau's Guide to Rock Albums of the Seventies* (New Haven, Conn.: Ticknor and Fields, 1981/London: Vermilion, 1982)

Clarke, Garry E., 'Music', in *The Postmodern Movement: A Handbook of Contemporary Innovation in the Arts,* ed. Stanley Trachtenberg (Westport, Conn., and London: Greenwood Press, 1985), pp. 157–76

Cohn, Richard, 'Transpositional Combination of Beat-Class Sets in Steve Reich's Phase-Shifting Music', *Perspectives of New Music*, 30/1 (1992), pp. 146–77

Colpitt, Frances, *Minimal Art: The Critical Perspective* (Ann Arbor: UMI Research Press, 1990)

Corbett, John, 'Minimal Compact', *The Wire*, 132 (February 1995), pp. 34–5

Cowan, Robert, 'Reich and Wittgenstein: Notes Towards a Synthesis', *Tempo*, 157 (June 1986), pp. 2–7

Crane, Diana, *The Transformation of the Avant-Garde: The New York Art World, 1940–1985* (Chicago and London: University of Chicago Press, 1987)

Danninger, H., 'Destruktion und Heimweh: Anmerkungen zur Neuen Musik Amerikas', *Musica*, 32/1 (1978), pp. 20–5

de la Falaise, Maxime, 'Creating *Einstein on the Beach*: Philip Glass and Robert

Wilson Speak to Maxime de la Falaise', *On the Next Wave: The Audience Magazine of BAM's Next Wave Festival*, 2/4 (1984), pp. 5–9

Dennis, Brian, 'Repetitive and Systemic Music', *The Musical Times*, 115/1582 (December 1974), pp. 1036–8

Di Maggio, Gino, ed., *Ubi Fluxus Ibi Motus: 1990–1962* (Milan: Nuove Edizione Gabriele Mazzotta, 1990)

Dreier, Ruth, 'Minimalism', in *The New Grove Dictionary of American Music*, eds. H. Wiley Hitchcock and Stanley Sadie (London: Macmillan/New York: Grove's Dictionaries of Music, 1986), III, pp. 240–2

Duckworth, William, *Talking Music* (New York: Schirmer Books, 1995)

Duckworth, William, and Fleming, Richard, eds., *Sound and Light: La Monte Young, Marian Zazeela* (Lewisburg, Penn.: Bucknell University Press, 1996)

Dunn, R., ed., *John Cage* (New York: Henmar Press, 1962)

Epstein, Paul, 'Pattern Structure and Process in Steve Reich's *Piano Phase*', *The Musical Quarterly*, 72/4 (1986), pp. 146–77

Farneth, David, 'La Monte Young', in *The New Grove Dictionary of American Music*, eds. H. Wiley Hitchcock and Stanley Sadie (London: Macmillan/New York: Grove's Dictionaries of Music, 1986), IX, pp. 579–81

Ford, Andrew, *Composer to Composer: Conversations about Contemporary Music* (London: Quartet Books, 1993)

Foster, Hal, ed., *Postmodern Culture* (London and Sydney: Pluto Press, 1985)

Frascina, Francis, ed., *Pollock and After: The Critical Debate* (New York: Harper and Row, 1985)

Fried, Michael, 'Art and Objecthood', *Artforum*, 8/5 (June 1967), pp. 12–23

Gagne, Cole, *Sonic Transports: New Frontiers In Our Music* (New York: de Falco Books, 1990)

Soundpieces 2: Interviews With American Composers (Metuchen, N.J., and London: The Scarecrow Press, 1993)

Gagne, Cole, and Caras, Tracy, *Soundpieces: Interviews With American Composers* (Metuchen, N.J., and London: The Scarecrow Press, 1982)

Gann, Kyle, 'Let X = X: Minimalism v. Serialism', *Village Voice*, 24 February 1987, p. 76

'La Monte Young's *The Well-Tuned Piano*', *Perspectives of New Music*, 31/1 (Winter 1993), pp. 134–62

Garratt, Sheryl, 'Fun With Monotony' [Interview with Philip Glass], *The Face*, 75 (July 1986), pp. 36–41

Gena, Peter, 'Freedom in Experimental Music: The New York Revolution', *Tri-Quarterly*, 52 (1981), pp. 236–8

Geysen, F., 'Eigen kompositorische bevindingen in vergelijking met het werk van de jonge amerikaanse school', *Adem*, 10/1 (1974), pp. 24–6

Glass, Philip, 'Notes: *Einstein on the Beach*', *Performing Arts Journal*, 2/3 (1978), pp. 63–70

Glass, Philip, ed. with supplementary material by Robert T. Jones, *The Music of Philip Glass* (New York: Harper and Row, 1987)/ *Opera on the Beach* (London and Boston: Faber and Faber, 1988)

Goldberg, Rose Lee, *Performance Art: From Futurism to the Present* (New York:

Harry N. Abrams, 1988; originally published as *Performance: Live Art 1909 to the Present*, 1979)

Gordon, Peter, 'Philip Glass: Music of the Moment', *Painted Bride Quarterly*, 4/2 (1977), pp. 56–63

Gottwald, Clytus, 'Signale zwischen Exotik und Industrie: Steve Reich auf der Suche nach einer neuen Identität von Klang und Struktur', *Melos/Neue Zeitschrift für Musik*, o (January-February 1975), pp. 3–6

'Tendenzen der neuen Musik in den USA: György Ligeti im Gesprach mit Clytus Gottwald', *Musik und Bildung*, 8 (February 1976), pp. 57–61

Greenberg, Clement, *Art and Culture* (Boston: Beacon Press, 1961); this collection of the author's articles includes 'Avant-Garde and Kitsch', *Partisan Review*, 6/5 (Fall 1939), pp. 34–49

Henahan, Donal, 'Reich? Philharmonic? Paradiddling?', *New York Times*, 24 October 1971, Section ii, pp. 13 and 26

Hendricks, Jon, *Fluxus Codex* (New York: The Gilbert and Lila Silverman Fluxus Collection/Harry N. Abrams, 1988)

Hitchcock, H. Wiley, 'Minimalism in Art and Music: Origins and Aesthetics', *College Art Journal*, 27 (Summer 1994), pp. 12–18

Jacoby, Russell, *The Last Intellectuals: American Culture in the Age of Academe* (New York: Basic Books, 1987)

Jencks, Charles, *What Is Post-Modernism?* (London: Academy Editions/New York: St Martin's Press, 1986; 2nd edn., 1987)

Johnson, Jill, 'Music: La Monte Young', *Village Voice*, 19 November 1964, pp. 14 and 20

Johnson, Timothy A., 'Minimalism: Aesthetic, Style, or Technique?', *The Musical Quarterly*, 78/4 (Winter 1994), pp. 742–73

Johnson, Tom, *The Voice of New Music: New York City 1972–1982* (Eindhoven: Het Apollohuis, 1989)

Jones, Robert T., 'Philip Glass [Musician of the Month]', *High Fidelity/Musical America*, 29/4 (April 1979), pp. MA-4-6

'*Einstein on the Beach*: Return of a Legend', *On the Next Wave: the Audience Magazine of BAM's Next Wave Festival*, 2/4 (1984), pp. 1–4

Judd, Donald, *Complete Writings 1959–1975* (New York: New York University Press, 1975)

Kaye, Nick, *Postmodernism and Performance* (New York: St Martin's Press, 1994)

King, Bruce, ed., *Contemporary American Theatre* (Basingstoke: Macmillan, 1991). Includes a chapter on 'Lee Breuer and Mabou Mines' by S. E. Gontarski, pp. 135–48, and discussion of Robert Wilson and Philip Glass in 'Beyond the Broadway Musical: Crossovers, Confusions and Crisis', pp. 151–76.

Knox, Kenneth, 'The Parametric Music of Terry Riley', *Jazz Monthly*, 13/5 (1967), pp. 9–12

Knox, Kenneth, and Knox, R., 'Relax and Fully Concentrate: The Time of Terry Riley', *Friends Magazine*, 20 February 1970, unpaginated

Kostek, M. C., *The Velvet Underground Handbook* (London: Black Spring Press, 1992)

Kostelanetz, Richard, *The Theatre of Mixed Means: An Introduction to Happenings, Kinetic Environments and Other Mixed-Means Presentations* (New York: Dial Press, 1968/RK Editions, 1980)

Metamorphosis in the Arts: A Critical History of the 1960s (Brooklyn: Assembling Press, 1980)

Kostelanetz, Richard, ed., *Writings on Glass: Essays, Interviews, Criticism* (New York: Schirmer Books/London: Prentice Hall International, 1997). Includes previously published material by Charles Merrell Berg, Thomas Rain Crowe, Peter G. Davis, Paul John Frandsen, Kyle Gann, John Howell, Tom Johnson, John Koopman, Richard Kostelanetz, Allan Kozinn, Art Lange, Robert C. Morgan, Tim Page, Joseph Roddy, Aaron M. Shatzman, Edward Strickland, Mark Swed, Helen Tworkov/Robert Coe, David Walters, in addition to those entries detailed in chapter 4.

Kozinn, Allan, 'Philip Glass', *Ovation*, 5/1 (1984), pp. 12–14

Kramer, Jonathan D., *The Time of Music: New Meanings, New Temporalities, New Listening Strategies* (New York: Schirmer/London: Collier Macmillan, 1988)

La Barbara, Joan, 'Philip Glass e Steve Reich: Two from the Steady State School', dual language Italian/English, *Data: pratica e teoria delle arti*, 4/13 (Autumn 1974), pp. 36–9; reprinted in Kostelanetz 1997 (see above)

'New Music', *High Fidelity/Musical America*, 27/11 (November 1977), pp. MA 14–15

Lasch, Christopher, *The Minimal Self: Psychic Survival in Troubled Times* (New York and London: W. W. Norton, 1984)

Le Witt, Sol, 'Paragraphs on Conceptual Art', *Artforum*, 8/5 (June 1967), pp. 79–83

Licht, Alan, 'The History of La Monte Young's Theatre of Eternal Music', *Forced Exposure*, 16 (1990), pp. 60–9

Lipman, Samuel, *The House of Music: Art in an Era of Institutions* (Boston: David R. Godine, 1984)

Lippard, Lucy R., ed., *Pop Art* (London: Thames and Hudson, 1966, rev. edns. 1967 and 1970)

Lodge, David, *Working with Structuralism: Essays and Reviews on Nineteenth- and Twentieth-Century Literature* (London: Routledge and Kegan Paul, 1981)

MacDonald, Ian, 'What is the Use of Minimalism?', *The Face*, 83 (March 1987), pp. 102–09

Mamiya, Christin J., *Pop Art and Consumer Culture: American Super Market* (Austin: University of Texas Press, 1992)

Marranca, Bonnie, *The Theatre of Images* (New York: Drama Books, 1977)

Matthew-Walker, Robert, 'Glass Roots', *CD Review*, 61 (February 1992), pp. 17–21

Mellers, Wilfrid, 'A Minimalist Definition', *The Musical Times*, 125/1696 (June 1984), p. 328

Mertens, Wim, trans. J. Hautekiet, *American Minimal Music: La Monte Young, Terry Riley, Steve Reich, Philip Glass* (London: Kahn and Averill/New York: Alexander Broude, 1983)

Moore, Carman, 'Music: Park Place Electronics', *Village Voice*, 9 June 1966, p. 17
'Music: Park Place Pianos', *Village Voice*, 23 March 1967, p. 15
'Fragments', *Village Voice*, 18 January 1968, pp. 25 and 28
'Music: Zukofsky', *Village Voice*, 1 May 1969, p. 28
Morgan, Robert P., ed., *Modern Times: From World War I to the Present* (Basingstoke: Macmillan, 1993/Englewood Cliffs, N.J: Prentice Hall, 1994). Commentary on minimalism may be found in William Brooks's chapter, 'The Americas, 1945–70', pp. 309–48, the present author's own 'The Current Musical Scene', pp. 349–87, and Michael Tenzer's 'Western Music in the Context of World Music', pp. 388–410.
Morrissey, Lee, ed., *The Kitchen Turns Twenty: A Retrospective Anthology* (New York: The Kitchen/Haleakala, 1992)
Neilson, John, 'La Monte Young', *Creem* (November 1987), p. 44–7.
Nelson, C., ed., *Robert Wilson: The Theatre of Images* (New York: Harper and Row, 1984)
Nicholls, David, *American Experimental Music: 1890–1940* (Cambridge: Cambridge University Press, 1990)
'Transethnicism and the American Experimental Tradition', *The Musical Quarterly*, 80/4 (Winter 1996), pp. 569–94
Norris, Christopher, ed., *Music and the Politics of Culture* (London: Lawrence and Wishart, 1989). Includes Claire Polin's essay, 'Why Minimalism Now?' pp. 226–39.
Nyman, Michael, with Hugh Davies and Richard Orton, 'Steve Reich: An Interview with Michael Nyman', *The Musical Times*, 112/1537 (March 1971), pp. 229–31
'Steve Reich, Phil Glass', *The Musical Times*, 112/1539 (May 1971), pp. 463–4
'SR-mysteries of the phase', *Music and Musicians*, 20/6 (February 1972), pp. 20–1
Experimental Music: Cage and Beyond (London: Studio Vista/New York: Schirmer, 1974; rev. edn., Cambridge: Cambridge University Press 1999)
'Steve Reich: Interview', *Studio International*, 192/6 (November–December 1976), pp. 300–07
'Steve Reich', *Music and Musicians*, 25/5 (January 1977), pp. 18–19
'Against Intellectual Complexity in Music', *October*, 13 (1980), pp. 81–9
O'Grady, Terence J., 'Aesthetic Value in Indeterminate Music', *Musical Quarterly*, 67 (July 1981), pp. 366–81
Oesterreich, Norbert, 'Music with Roots in the Aether', *Perspectives of New Music*, 16 (Fall–Winter 1977), pp. 214–28
Page, Tim, 'Framing the River: A Minimalist Primer', *High Fidelity/Musical America*, 31/11 (November 1981), pp. 64–8 and 117
'The New Romance with Tonality', *New York Times Magazine*, 29 May 1983, pp. 22–5 and 28
'Steve Reich, a Former Young Turk, Approaches 50', *New York Times*, 1 June 1986, Section ii, pp. 23–4
Music from the Road: Views and Reviews 1978–1992 (New York and Oxford: Oxford University Press, 1992)

Palmer, Robert, 'La Monte Young: Lost in the Drone Zone', *Rolling Stone*, 13 February 1975, p. 24

'A Father Figure for the Avant-garde', *The Atlantic*, 247/5 (May 1981), pp. 48–56

'Get Ready for the Music of Harmonics', *New York Times*, 17 July 1983, Section C, p. 17

Parsons, Michael, 'Systems in Art and Music', *The Musical Times*, 117/1604 (October 1976), pp. 815–18

Pincus-Witten, Robert, *Postminimalism into Maximalism: American Art, 1966–1986* (New York: Dutton, 1989)

Porter, Andrew, *Music of Three Seasons: 1974–1977* (New York: Farrar, Straus and Giroux, 1978). A collection of reviews originally published during this period in *The New Yorker* magazine, including 'Many-Colored Glass', a review of one of the Metropolitan Opera House performances of Glass's *Einstein on the Beach*, pp. 459–63.

Potter, Keith, 'Terry Riley Encountered', *Classical Music*, 11 August 1984, p. 17

'The Recent Phases of Steve Reich', *Contact*, 29 (Spring 1985), pp. 28–34

'Steve Reich: Thoughts for his 50th-Birthday Year', *The Musical Times*, 127/1715 (January 1986), pp. 13–17

'Philip Glass', in *The Viking Opera Guide*, ed. Amanda Holden (London: Penguin, 1993), pp. 360–5; reprinted in Holden, ed., *The Penguin Opera Guide* (London: Penguin, 1995), pp. 142–7

'The Pursuit of the Unimaginable by the Unnarratable, or Some Potentially Telling Developments in Non-Developmental Music', *Contemporary Music Review*, 15/ 3–4 (1996), pp. 3–11

Potter, Keith, and Smith, Dave, 'Interview with Philip Glass', *Contact*, 13 (Spring 1976), pp. 25–30

Reich, Steve, *Writings about Music*, ed. Kaspar Koenig (Halifax, Canada: Nova Scotia College of Art and Design/New York: New York University Press/London: Universal Edition, 1974)

'Texture-Space-Survival', *Perspectives of New Music*, 26/2 (Summer 1988), pp. 272–80

Autori Vari: Reich, ed. Enzo Restagno (Turin: Edizioni di Torino, 1994). A much expanded version, in Italian, of *Writings about Music*

Reinhard, J., 'A Conversation with La Monte Young and Marian Zazeela', *Ear*, 7/5 (1982–3), pp. 4–6

Reynolds, Roger, *Mind Models: New Forms of Musical Experience* (New York: Praeger, 1975)

Rockwell, John, 'Boulez and Young: Enormous Gulf or Unwitting Allies?' *Los Angeles Times*, 13 February 1972, p. 38

'Music: Reich Meditations', *New York Times*, 19 May 1973, Section ii, p. 28

'What's New?' *High Fidelity/Musical America*, 23/8 (August 1973), pp. MA 31–2

'There's Nothing Quite Like the Sound of Glass', *New York Times*, 26 May 1974, Section ii, pp. 11 and 21

'The Evolution of Steve Reich', *New York Times*, 14 March 1982, Section ii, pp. 23–4

All American Music: Composition in the Late Twentieth Century (New York: Alfred A. Knopf, 1983/London: Kahn and Averill, 1985; rev. edn., New York: Da Capo Press, 1997)

'"Einstein" Returns Briefly', *New York Times*, 17 December 1984, Section ii

'The Life and Death of Minimalism', *New York Times*, 21 December 1986, Section ii, pp. 1 and 29

'Feldman's Minimalism in Maximal Doses', *New York Times*, 12 January 1992, Section ii, p. 28

Rosenbaum, R., 'Eternal Music in a Dreamhouse Barn', *Village Voice*, 12 February 1970, pp. 5–6 and 63–6

Rothstein, J., 'Terry Riley', *Down Beat*, 48/5 (1981), pp. 26–8

Ruppenthal, Stephen, 'Terry Riley', in *The New Grove Dictionary of American Music*, eds. H. Wiley Hitchcock and Stanley Sadie (London: Macmillan/New York: Grove's Dictionaries of Music, 1986), IX, pp. 48–9

Salzman, Eric, 'The *New York Times* Was Supposed to Print This But Didn't', *Ear Magazine East*, 5 (November–December 1979), pp. 6–7

Sandford, Mariellen R., *Happenings and Other Acts* (London and New York: Routledge, 1995)

Sandler, Irving, *American Art of the 1960s* (New York: Harper and Row, 1988)

Sandow, Gregory, 'Philip Glass', in *The New Grove Dictionary of American Music*, eds. H. Wiley Hitchcock and Stanley Sadie (London: Macmillan/New York: Grove's Dictionaries of Music, 1986), II, pp. 228–30

Sayres, Sohnya, Stephanson, Anders, Aronowitz, Stanley, and Jameson, Fredric, eds. *The 60s Without Apology* (Minneapolis: University of Minnesota Press, in co-operation with *Social Text* 3/3 and 4/1, 1984)

Schaefer, John, *New Sounds: A Listener's Guide to New Music* (New York: Harper and Row, 1987)

Schwarz, David, 'Listening Subjects: Semiotics, Psychoanalysis, and the Music of John Adams and Steve Reich', *Perspectives of New Music*, 31/2 (Summer 1993), pp. 24–56

Schwarz, K. Robert, 'Steve Reich: Music as a Gradual Process', *Perspectives of New Music*, 19 (Fall–Winter 1980/Spring–Summer 1981), pp. 373–92, and 20 (Fall–Winter 1981/Spring–Summer 1982), pp. 225–86

Mininalism (London: Phaidon Press, 1996)

Scott, Derek, 'Postmodernism and Music', in *The Icon Critical Dictionary of Postmodern Thought*, ed. Stuart Sim (Duxford: Icon Books, 1998), pp. 134–46

Serra, Richard, *Writings, Interviews* (Chicago and London: University of Chicago Press, 1994)

Sharp, Willoughby, 'The Phil Glass Ensemble . . . Music in Twelve Parts', *Avalanche*, December 1974 (unnumbered), pp. 39–43

Sharp, Willoughby, and Bear, Liza, 'Phil Glass: An Interview in Two Parts', *Avalanche*, 5 (Summer 1972), pp. 26–35

Shyer, Laurence, *Robert Wilson and His Collaborators* (New York: Theatre Communications Group, 1989)

Smith, Dave, 'The Music of Phil Glass', *Contact*, 11 (Summer 1975), pp. 27–33
'Following a Straight Line: La Monte Young', *Contact*, 18 (Winter 1977–8), pp. 4–9
Smith, Geoff, and Smith, Nicola Walker, *American Originals: Interviews with 25 Contemporary Composers* (London and Boston: Faber and Faber, 1994)
Sontag, Susan, ed., *A Barthes Reader* (New York: Hill and Wang, 1982)
Sterritt, David, 'Tradition Reseen: Composer Steve Reich', *Christian Science Monitor*, 23 October 1980, p. 20
Strickland, Edward, *American Composers: Dialogues on Contemporary Music* (Bloomington and Indianapolis: Indiana University Press, 1991)
Minimalism: Origins (Bloomington and Indianapolis: Indiana University Press, 1993)
Swed, Mark, 'La Monte Young Tunes the Piano His Way', *Los Angeles Herald Examiner*, 1 November 1985, p. 36
Tamm, Eric, *Brian Eno: His Music and the Vertical Color of Sound* (Boston and London: Faber and Faber, 1989)
Taylor, Sean, '*Einstein* on the Stage', Brooklyn Academy of Music programme book (December 1984), p. 3
Terry, Ken, 'La Monte Young – Avant-Garde Visionary Composer and Pianist', *Contemporary Keyboard*, August 1980, p. 16
Toop, David, *Oceans of Sound: Aether Talk, Ambient Sound and Imaginary Worlds* (London: Serpent's Tail, 1995); with two CDs (Virgin Records)
Walsh, Michael, 'Making a Joyful Noise', *Time*, 125/26 (1 July 1985), pp. 47–8
Warburton, Dan, 'A Working Terminology for Minimal Music', *Integral*, 2 (1988), pp. 135–59
Wasserman, Emily, 'An Interview With Composer Steve Reich', *Artforum*, 10/9 (May 1972), pp. 44–8
Wetzler, Peter, 'Minimal Music', *Ear Magazine East*, 6 (June–July–August 1981), p. 6
Wheeler, Daniel, *Art Since Mid-Century: 1945 to the Present* (New York: Vendome Press/London: Thames and Hudson, 1991)
Wijers, Louwrien, *Fluxus Today and Yesterday* (New York: Dutton, 1993)
Williams, Emmett, and Noel, Ann, eds., *Mr. Fluxus: A Collective Portrait of George Maciunas, 1931–1978* (London: Thames and Hudson, 1997/New York: Thames and Hudson, 1998)
Wilson, Robert, et al., *Einstein on the Beach* (New York: EDS Enterprises, 1976)
Wolf, Daniel J., 'Living and Listening in Real Time', *Interval*, Winter 1982–3, pp.14–26 and Spring 1983, pp. 27–37
Woodley, Ronald, 'Steve Reich', in *Contemporary Composers*, eds. Brian Morton and Pamela Collins (London: St. James Press, 1992), pp. 767–9
Yalkut, Jud, 'Philip Glass and Jon Gibson', *Ear [West]*, 19 (Summer 1981), pp. 4–5
Vidic, Ljerka, 'La Monte Young and Marian Zazeela', *Ear*, 13 (May 1987), pp. 24–6
York, Wesley, 'Form and Process in *Two Pages* of Philip Glass', *Sonus*, 1/2 (Spring 1982), pp. 28–50; reprinted in *Contiguous Lines: Issues and Ideas in the Music of the '60s and '70s*, ed. Thomas, DeLio (Lanham, London, etc.: University Press of America, 1985), pp. 81–106; also reprinted in Kostelanetz 1997 (see above)

Young, La Monte, ed., *An Anthology* (New York: Young and Jackson MacLow, 1963; 2nd edn., Munich: Heiner Friedrich, 1970)
Young, La Monte, and Zazeela, Marian, *Selected Writings* (Munich: Heiner Friedrich, 1969)
Zak, Albin, ed., *The Velvet Underground: Four Decades of Commentary* (London, New York and Sydney: Omnibus Press [Schirmer], 1997)
Zimmermann, Walter, *Desert Plants: Conversations with 23 American Musicians* (Vancouver: Walter Zimmermann and A.R.C. Publications, 1976)
Zimmermann, Walter, ed., *Morton Feldman Essays* (Korpen: Beginner Press, 1985)
Zwerzin, M., 'The Moveable Feast: Philip Glass', *Jazz Forum*, 88 (1984), p. 28

Catalogues

Introduction to *Systemic Painting*, catalogue for the New York Guggenheim Museum exhibition, 1966
Anti-Illusion: Procedures/Materials, catalogue for New York Whitney Museum exhibition (New York: Whitney Museum of American Art, 1969)
'Art and Experimental Music' issue of *Studio International*, 192/984 (November–December 1976)
Haskell, Barbara, *Blam! The Explosion of Pop, Minimalism, and Performance 1958–1964*, catalogue for the New York Whitney Museum exhibition (New York: Norton/Whitney Museum, 1984)
Husslein, Uwe, catalogue for *Pop Goes Art* exhibition, (Uppertal: Institut für Pop Kultur, 1990)
McShine, Kynaston, catalogue for *Primary Structures* exhibition, Jewish Museum, New York, 1966
Phillpot, Clive, and Hendricks, Jon, *Fluxus: Selections from the Gilbert and Lila Silverman Collection*, catalogue for the Museum of Modern Art Library exhibition, New York, 17 November 1988 – 10 March 1989
Rose, Barbara, catalogue article for *A New Aesthetic* exhibition, Washington Gallery of Modern Art, 1967
Rubin, William S., *Frank Stella* (New York: The Museum of Modern Art, 1970)
Sohm, H., ed., *Happening & Fluxus: Materialen*, catalogue for the Koelnischer Kunstverein exhibition, 6 February 1970 – 6 January 1971
New York – Downtown Manhattan: SoHo, catalogue for the Akademie der Kunste/Berliner Festwochen exhibition, 5 September – 17 October 1976. Includes a chapter on music by Joan La Barbara, pp. 142–66.
Serra, Richard, *Interviews, etc. 1970–1980* (Yonkers: Hudson River Museum, 1980)
Sol Le Witt: Prints, 1970–86, catalogue for Tate Gallery exhibition, London, 17 September – 30 November 1986

Index